FOUNDATION PRESS

MODEL RULES
OF PROFESSIONAL CONDUCT
and
OTHER SELECTED STANDARDS

Including California and New York Rules

on

PROFESSIONAL
RESPONSIBILITY

By

THOMAS D. MORGAN
Oppenheim Professor of Law,
George Washington University

RONALD D. ROTUNDA
G.M.U. Foundation Professor of Law,
George Mason University School of Law

D1530292

FOUNDATION PRESS
New York, New York
2003

COPYRIGHT © 1976, 1978–1981, 1983–2002 FOUNDATION PRESS

COPYRIGHT © 2003

By

FOUNDATION PRESS
All Rights Reserved

ISBN 1–58778–389–4

 TEXT IS PRINTED ON 10% POST
CONSUMER RECYCLED PAPER

PREFACE

This 2003 Supplement reflects changes in the included ethics standards through August 2002. The ABA Model Rules, for example, reflect the many changes that the ABA House of Delegates approved in February and August 2002.

For the last several years, the ABA Commission on Evaluation of Professional Standards, popularly know at the Ethics 2000 Commission, has been reevaluating the ABA Model Rules. In August 2001 and February 2002, the ABA House of Delegates approved most of the proposals that Ethics 2000 Commission tendered. In August 2002, the ABA House of Delegates also approved amendments proposed by the ABA Commission on Multijuridictional Practice.

So that teachers and students can see what changes the ABA House approved, the Supplement reprints the ABA Model Rules in what is called a "legislative format." New additions to the Model Rules are indicated by <u>underlining,</u> and deletions are indicated by ~~strike-outs.~~ No jurisdiction has adopted this new version of the ABA Rules yet, because they are so new, but we should expect that to change in the near future. And, even before their adoption by the states, the new rules will be the subject of intensive debate and may influence the way the courts apply existing law.

In addition, we include a "clean" version of the Model Rules before the 2002 changes. This is the version most like the Rules currently applicable in a majority of jurisdictions. It is also the version to be tested on 2003 administrations of the Multistate Professional Responsibility Exam.

The American Law Institute's Restatement Third, The Law Governing Lawyers, was completed in 2000 and its final black letter provisions are included in this Supplement. This final version reflects stylistic changes from the Proposed Official Drafts cited in the 7th edition of our casebook. More important, the final version has been renumbered. A table showing both the old and new numbering is included in this Supplement as well.

Finally, Appendices to the Model Rules, giving a state-by-state analysis of ethics rules on client confidences, imputed disqualification, and when a written fee agreement is required have all been updated as well.

We thank all those who have helped in the preparation of this Supplement, particularly James N. Markel.

T.D.M.
R.D.R.

November 2002

*

TABLE OF CONTENTS

TABLE OF CONTENTS

2003 SELECTED STANDARDS

on

PROFESSIONAL
RESPONSIBILITY

*

THE AMERICAN BAR ASSOCIATION
MODEL RULES OF PROFESSIONAL CONDUCT
Legislative Format (August, 2002)

The Model Rules of Professional Conduct were adopted by the House of Delegates of the American Bar Association on August 2, 1983. They were amended through the years, and were subject to substantial amendments in August, 2001 and February and August, 2002.

In August 2001 and February and August of 2002, the ABA House of Delegates approved substantial changes to the ABA Model Rules of Professional Conduct. The House of Delegates responded to changes recommended by the ABA Commission on Evaluation of the Rules of Professional Conduct, popularly called, "Ethics 2000," and the ABA Commission on Multijurisdictional Practice.

What follows is what the ABA House of Delegates has now approved. It is in "legislative" format. That is, new additions to the Model Rules are indicated by <u>underlining</u>, and deletions are indicated by ~~strike-outs~~.

While no jurisdiction has adopted this latest version of the ABA Model Rules yet, that may change in the near future. In addition, these new rules will be the subject of intensive debate and may influence the way the courts apply existing law.

Contents

PREAMBLE: A LAWYER'S RESPONSIBILITIES

[1] A lawyer, as a member of the legal profession, is a representative of clients, an officer of the legal system and a public citizen having special responsibility for the quality of justice.

[2] As a representative of clients, a lawyer performs various functions. As advisor, a lawyer provides a client with an informed understanding of the client's legal rights and obligations and explains their practical implications. As advocate, a lawyer zealously asserts the client's position under the rules of the adversary system. As negotiator, a lawyer seeks a result advantageous to the client but consistent with requirements of honest dealings with others. ~~As intermediary between clients, a lawyer seeks to reconcile their divergent interests as an advisor and, to a limited extent, as a spokesperson for each client. A~~ As an evaluator, a lawyer acts ~~as evaluator~~ by examining a client's legal affairs and reporting about them to the client or to others.

[3] In addition to these representational functions, a lawyer may serve as a third-party neutral, a nonrepresentational role helping the parties to resolve a dispute or other matter. Some of these Rules apply directly to lawyers who are or have served as third-party neutrals. See, e.g., Rules 1.12 and 2.4. In addition, there are Rules that apply to lawyers who are not active in the practice of law or to practicing lawyers even when they are acting in a nonprofessional capacity. For example, a lawyer who commits fraud in the conduct of a business is subject to discipline for engaging in conduct involving dishonesty, fraud, deceit or misrepresentation. See Rule 8.4.

~~[3]~~ [4] In all professional functions a lawyer should be competent, prompt and diligent. A lawyer should maintain communication with a client concerning the representation. A lawyer should keep in confidence information relating to representation of a client except so far as disclosure is required or permitted by the Rules of Professional Conduct or other law.

~~[4]~~ [5] A lawyer's conduct should conform to the requirements of the law, both in professional service to clients and in the lawyer's business and personal affairs. A lawyer should use the law's procedures only for legitimate purposes and not to harass or intimidate others. A lawyer should demonstrate respect for the legal system and for those who serve it, including judges, other lawyers and public officials. While it is a lawyer's duty, when necessary, to challenge the rectitude of official action, it is also a lawyer's duty to uphold legal process.

~~[5]~~ [6] As a public citizen, a lawyer should seek improvement of the law, access to the legal system, the administration of justice and the quality of service rendered by the legal profession. As a member of a learned profession, a lawyer should cultivate knowledge of the law beyond its use for clients, employ that knowledge in reform of the law and work to strengthen legal education. In addition, a lawyer should further the public's understanding of and confidence in the rule of law and the justice system because legal institutions in a constitutional democracy depend on popular participation and support to maintain their authority. A lawyer should be mindful of deficiencies in the administration of justice and of the fact that the poor, and sometimes persons who are not poor, cannot afford adequate legal assistance, and. Therefore, all lawyers should ~~therefore~~ devote professional time, resources and civic influence ~~in their behalf~~ to ensure equal access to our system of justice for all those who because of economic or social barriers cannot afford or secure adequate legal counsel. A lawyer should aid the legal profession in pursuing these objectives and should help the bar regulate itself in the public interest.

[6] [7] Many of a lawyer's professional responsibilities are prescribed in the Rules of Professional Conduct, as well as substantive and procedural law. However, a lawyer is also guided by personal conscience and the approbation of professional peers. A lawyer should strive to attain the highest level of skill, to improve the law and the legal profession and to exemplify the legal profession's ideals of public service.

[7] [8] A lawyer's responsibilities as a representative of clients, an officer of the legal system and a public citizen are usually harmonious. Thus, when ~~an opposing party~~ is well represented, a lawyer can be a zealous advocate on behalf of a client and at the same time assume that justice is being done. So also, a lawyer can be sure that preserving client confidences ordinarily serves the public interest because people are more likely to seek legal advice, and thereby heed their legal obligations, when they know their communications will be private.

[8] [9] In the nature of law practice, however, conflicting responsibilities are encountered. Virtually all difficult ethical problems arise from conflict between a lawyer's responsibilities to clients, to the legal system and to the lawyer's own interest in remaining an ~~upright~~ ethical person while earning a satisfactory living. The Rules of Professional Conduct often prescribe terms for resolving such conflicts. Within the framework of these Rules, however, many difficult issues of professional discretion can arise. Such issues must be resolved through the exercise of sensitive professional and moral judgment guided by the basic principles underlying the Rules. These principles include the lawyer's obligation zealously to protect and pursue a client's legitimate interests, within the bounds of the law, while maintaining a professional, courteous and civil attitude toward all persons involved in the legal system.

[9] [10] The legal profession is largely self-governing. Although other professions also have been granted powers of self-government, the legal profession is unique in this respect because of the close relationship between the profession and the processes of government and law enforcement. This connection is manifested in the fact that ultimate authority over the legal profession is vested largely in the courts.

[10] [11] To the extent that lawyers meet the obligations of their professional calling, the occasion for government regulation is obviated. Self-regulation also helps maintain the legal profession's independence from

government domination. An independent legal profession is an important force in preserving government under law, for abuse of legal authority is more readily challenged by a profession whose members are not dependent on government for the right to practice.

[11] [12] The legal profession's relative autonomy carries with it special responsibilities of self-government. The profession has a responsibility to assure that its regulations are conceived in the public interest and not in furtherance of parochial or self-interested concerns of the bar. Every lawyer is responsible for observance of the Rules of Professional Conduct. A lawyer should also aid in securing their observance by other lawyers. Neglect of these responsibilities compromises the independence of the profession and the public interest which it serves.

[12] [13] Lawyers play a vital role in the preservation of society. The fulfillment of this role requires an understanding by lawyers of their relationship to our legal system. The Rules of Professional Conduct, when properly applied, serve to define that relationship.

SCOPE

[13] [14] The Rules of Professional Conduct are rules of reason. They should be interpreted with reference to the purposes of legal representation and of the law itself. Some of the Rules are imperatives, cast in the terms "shall" or "shall not." These define proper conduct for purposes of professional discipline. Others, generally cast in the term "may," are permissive and define areas under the Rules in which the lawyer has professional discretion to exercise professional judgment. No disciplinary action should be taken when the lawyer chooses not to act or acts within the bounds of such discretion. Other Rules define the nature of relationships between the lawyer and others. The Rules are thus partly obligatory and disciplinary and partly constitutive and descriptive in that they define a lawyer's professional role. Many of the Comments use the term "should." Comments do not add obligations to the Rules but provide guidance for practicing in compliance with the Rules.

[14] [15] The Rules presuppose a larger legal context shaping the lawyer's role. That context includes court rules and statutes relating to matters of licensure, laws defining specific obligations of lawyers and substantive and procedural law in general. The Comments are sometimes used to alert lawyers to their responsibilities under such other law.

[16] Compliance with the Rules, as with all law in an open society, depends primarily upon understanding and voluntary compliance, secondarily upon reinforcement by peer and public opinion and finally, when necessary, upon enforcement through disciplinary proceedings. The Rules do not, however, exhaust the moral and ethical considerations that should inform a lawyer, for no worthwhile human activity can be completely defined by legal rules. The Rules simply provide a framework for the ethical practice of law.

6

[15] [17] Furthermore, for purposes of determining the lawyer's authority and responsibility, principles of substantive law external to these Rules determine whether a client-lawyer relationship exists. Most of the duties flowing from the client-lawyer relationship attach only after the client has requested the lawyer to render legal services and the lawyer has agreed to do so. But there are some duties, such as that of confidentiality under Rule 1.6, that ~~may~~ attach when the lawyer agrees to consider whether a client-lawyer relationship shall be established. See Rule 1.18. Whether a client-lawyer relationship exists for any specific purpose can depend on the circumstances and may be a question of fact.

[16] [18] Under various legal provisions, including constitutional, statutory and common law, the responsibilities of government lawyers may include authority concerning legal matters that ordinarily reposes in the client in private client-lawyer relationships. For example, a lawyer for a government agency may have authority on behalf of the government to decide upon settlement or whether to appeal from an adverse judgment. Such authority in various respects is generally vested in the attorney general and the state's attorney in state government, and their federal counterparts, and the same may be true of other government law officers. Also, lawyers under the supervision of these officers may be authorized to represent several government agencies in intragovernmental legal controversies in circumstances where a private lawyer could not represent multiple private clients. ~~They also may have authority to represent the "public interest" in circumstances where a private lawyer would not be authorized to do so.~~ These Rules do not abrogate any such authority.

[17] [19] Failure to comply with an obligation or prohibition imposed by a Rule is a basis for invoking the disciplinary process. The Rules presuppose that disciplinary assessment of a lawyer's conduct will be made on the basis of the facts and circumstances as they existed at the time of the conduct in question and in recognition of the fact that a lawyer often has to act upon uncertain or incomplete evidence of the situation. Moreover, the Rules presuppose that whether or not discipline should be imposed for a violation, and the severity of a sanction, depend on all the circumstances, such as the willfulness and seriousness of the violation, extenuating factors and whether there have been previous violations.

[18] [20] Violation of a Rule should not itself give rise to a cause of action against a lawyer nor should it create any presumption in such a case that a legal duty has been breached. In addition, violation of a Rule does not necessarily warrant any other nondisciplinary remedy, such as disqualification of a lawyer in pending litigation. The Rules are designed to provide guidance to lawyers and to provide a structure for regulating conduct through disciplinary agencies. They are not designed to be a basis for civil liability. Furthermore, the purpose of the Rules can be subverted when they are invoked by opposing parties as procedural weapons. The fact that a Rule is a just basis for a lawyer's self-assessment, or for sanctioning a lawyer under the administration of a disciplinary authority, does not imply that an antagonist in a

collateral proceeding or transaction has standing to seek enforcement of the Rule. ~~Accordingly, nothing in the Rules should be deemed to augment any substantive legal duty of lawyers or the extra-disciplinary consequences of violating such a duty.~~ Nevertheless, since the Rules do establish standards of conduct by lawyers, a lawyer's violation of a Rule may be evidence of breach of the applicable standard of conduct.

[19] ~~Moreover, these Rules are not intended to govern or affect judicial application of either the attorney-client or work product privilege. Those privileges were developed to promote compliance with law and fairness in litigation. In reliance on the attorney-client privilege, clients are entitled to expect that communications within the scope of the privilege will be protected against compelled disclosure. The attorney-client privilege is that of the client and not of the lawyer. The fact that in exceptional situations the lawyer under the rules has a limited discretion to disclose a client confidence does not vitiate the proposition that, as a general matter, the client has a reasonable expectation that information relating to the client will not be voluntarily disclosed and that disclosure of such information may be judicially compelled only in accordance with recognized exceptions to the attorney-client and work product privileges.~~

[20] ~~The lawyer's exercise of discretion not to disclose information under Rule 1.6 should not be subject to reexamination. Permitting such reexamination would be incompatible with the general policy of promoting compliance with law through assurances that communications will be protected against disclosure.~~

[21] The Comment accompanying each Rule explains and illustrates the meaning and purpose of the Rule. The Preamble and this note on Scope provide general orientation. The Comments are intended as guides to interpretation, but the text of each Rule is authoritative. ~~Research notes were prepared to compare counterparts in the ABA Model Code of Professional Responsibility (adopted 1969, as amended) and to provide selected references to other authorities. The notes have not been adopted, do not constitute part of the Model Rules, and are not intended to affect the application or interpretation of the Rules and Comments.~~

RULE 1.0: TERMINOLOGY

(a) "Belief" or "believes" denotes that the person involved actually supposed the fact in question to be true. A person's belief may be inferred from circumstances.

~~"Consult" or "consultation" denotes communication of information reasonably sufficient to permit the client to appreciate the significance of the matter in question.~~

(b) "Confirmed in writing," when used in reference to the informed consent of a person, denotes informed consent that is given in writing by the person or a writing that a lawyer promptly transmits to the person confirming an oral informed consent. See paragraph (e) for the definition of "informed consent."

(c) "Firm" or "law firm" denotes a lawyer or lawyers in a ~~private firm,~~ law partnership, professional corporation, sole proprietorship or other association, or in a legal services organization; or lawyers employed in the legal department of a corporation or other organization ~~and lawyers employed in a legal services organization. See Comment, Rule 1.10.~~

(d) "Fraud" or "fraudulent" denotes conduct ~~having~~ that is fraudulent under the substantive or procedural law of the applicable jurisdiction and has a purpose to deceive ~~and not merely negligent misrepresentation or failure to apprise another of relevant information.~~

(e) "Informed consent" denotes the agreement to a proposed course of conduct after the lawyer has communicated adequate information and explanation about the material risks of and reasonably available alternatives to the proposed course of conduct.

(f) "Knowingly," "known," or "knows" denotes actual knowledge of the fact in question. A person's knowledge may be inferred from circumstances.

(g) "Partner" denotes a member of a partnership and a shareholder in a law firm organized as a professional corporation.

(h) "Reasonable" or "reasonably" when used in relation to conduct by a lawyer denotes the conduct of a reasonably prudent and competent lawyer.

(i) "Reasonable belief" or "reasonably believes" when used in reference to a lawyer denotes that the lawyer believes the matter in question and that the circumstances are such that the belief is reasonable.

(j) "Reasonably should know" when used in reference to a lawyer denotes that a lawyer of reasonable prudence and competence would ascertain the matter in question.

(k) "Screened" denotes the isolation of a lawyer from any participation in a matter through the timely imposition of procedures within a firm that are reasonably adequate under the circumstances to protect information that the isolated lawyer is obligated to protect under these Rules or other law.

(l) "Substantial" when used in reference to degree or extent denotes a material matter of clear and weighty importance.

(m) "Tribunal" denotes a court, an arbitrator in a binding arbitration proceeding or a legislative body, administrative agency or other body acting in an adjudicative capacity. A legislative body, administrative agency or other body acts in an adjudicative capacity when a neutral official, after the presentation of evidence or legal argument by a party or parties, will render a binding legal judgment directly affecting a party's interests in a particular matter.

(n) "Writing" or "written" denotes a tangible or electronic record of a communication or representation, including handwriting, typewriting, printing, photostating, photography, audio or videorecording and e-mail. A "signed" writing includes an electronic sound, symbol or process attached to or logically associated with a writing and executed or adopted by a person with the intent to sign the writing.

Comment
Confirmed in Writing

[1]   If it is not feasible to obtain or transmit a written confirmation at the time the client gives informed consent, then the lawyer must obtain or transmit it within a reasonable time thereafter. If a lawyer has obtained a client's informed consent, the lawyer may act in reliance on that consent so long as it is confirmed in writing within a reasonable time thereafter.

Firm

[2]   Whether two or more lawyers constitute a firm within paragraph (c) can depend on the specific facts. For example, two practitioners who share office space and occasionally consult or assist each other ordinarily would not be regarded as constituting a firm. However, if they present themselves to the public in a way that suggests that they are a firm or conduct themselves as a firm, they should be regarded as a firm for purposes of the Rules. The terms of any formal agreement between associated lawyers are relevant in determining whether they are a firm, as is the fact that they have mutual access to information concerning the clients they serve. Furthermore, it is relevant in doubtful cases to consider the underlying purpose of the Rule that is involved. A group of lawyers could be regarded as a firm for purposes of the Rule that the same lawyer should not represent opposing parties in litigation, while it might not be so regarded for purposes of the Rule that information acquired by one lawyer is attributed to another.

[3]   With respect to the law department of an organization, including the government, there is ordinarily no question that the members of the department constitute a firm within the meaning of the Rules of Professional Conduct. However, there can be uncertainty as to the identity of the client. For example, it may not be clear whether the law department of a corporation represents a subsidiary or an affiliated corporation, as well as the corporation by which the members of the department are directly employed. A similar question can arise concerning an unincorporated association and its local affiliates.

[4]   Similar questions can also arise with respect to lawyers in legal aid. Lawyers employed in the same unit of a legal service organization constitute a

firm but not necessarily those employed in separate units. As in the case of independent practitioners, whether the lawyers should be treated as associated with each other can depend on the particular Rule that is involved and on the specific facts of the situation.

Fraud

[5] When used in these Rules, the terms "fraud" or "fraudulent" refer to conduct that is characterized as such under the substantive or procedural law of the applicable jurisdiction and has a purpose to deceive. This does not include merely negligent misrepresentation or negligent failure to apprise another of relevant information. For purposes of these Rules, it is not necessary that anyone has suffered damages or relied on the misrepresentation or failure to inform.

Informed Consent

[6] Many of the Rules of Professional Conduct require the lawyer to obtain the informed consent of a client or other person (e.g., a former client or, under certain circumstances, a prospective client) before accepting or continuing representation or pursuing a course of conduct. See, e.g., Rules 1.2(c), 1.6(a) and 1.7(b). The communication necessary to obtain such consent will vary according to the Rule involved and the circumstances giving rise to the need to obtain informed consent. The lawyer must make reasonable efforts to ensure that the client or other person possesses information reasonably adequate to make an informed decision. Ordinarily, this will require communication that includes a disclosure of the facts and circumstances giving rise to the situation, any explanation reasonably necessary to inform the client or other person of the material advantages and disadvantages of the proposed course of conduct and a discussion of the client's or other person's options and alternatives. In some circumstances it may be appropriate for a lawyer to advise a client or other person to seek the advice of other counsel. A lawyer need not inform a client or other person of facts or implications already known to the client or other person; nevertheless, a lawyer who does not personally inform the client or other person assumes the risk that the client or other person is inadequately informed and the consent is invalid. In determining whether the information and explanation provided are reasonably adequate, relevant factors include whether the client or other person is experienced in legal matters generally and in making decisions of the type involved, and whether independently represented by other counsel in giving the consent. Normally, such persons need less information and explanation than others, and generally a client or other person who is independently represented by other counsel in giving the consent should be presumed to have given informed consent.

[7] Obtaining informed consent will usually require an affirmative response by the client or other person. In general, a lawyer may not assume consent from a client's or other person's silence. Consent may be inferred, however, from the conduct of a client or other person who has reasonably

11

adequate information about the matter. A number of Rules require that a person's consent be confirmed in writing. See Rules 1.7(b) and 1.9(a). For a definition of "writing" and "confirmed in writing," see paragraphs (n) and (b). Other Rules require that a client's consent be obtained in a writing signed by the client. See, e.g., Rules 1.8(a) and (g). For a definition of "signed," see paragraph (n).

Screened

[8]   This definition applies to situations where screening of a personally disqualified lawyer is permitted to remove imputation of a conflict of interest under Rules 1.10, 1.11, 1.12 or 1.18.

[9]   The specific screening measures that are appropriate for any particular matter will depend on the circumstances but should provide reasonable assurance that there will be no significant risk to any information that the disqualified lawyer is obligated to protect. Where appropriate, such procedures could include a written undertaking by the screened lawyer to avoid any communication with other firm personnel and any contact with any firm files or other materials relating to the matter, written notice and instructions to all other firm personnel forbidding any communication with the screened lawyer relating to the matter, denial of access by the screened lawyer to firm files or other materials relating to the matter and periodic reminders of the screen to the screened lawyer and all other firm personnel.

[10]   In order to be effective, screening measures must be implemented as soon as practical after a lawyer or law firm knows or reasonably should know that there is a need for screening.

CLIENT–LAWYER RELATIONSHIP

RULE 1.1: COMPETENCE

A lawyer shall provide competent representation to a client. Competent representation requires the legal knowledge, skill, thoroughness and preparation reasonably necessary for the representation.

Comment
Legal Knowledge and Skill

[1]   In determining whether a lawyer employs the requisite knowledge and skill in a particular matter, relevant factors include the relative complexity and specialized nature of the matter, the lawyer's general experience, the lawyer's training and experience in the field in question, the preparation and study the lawyer is able to give the matter and whether it is feasible to refer the matter to, or associate or consult with, a lawyer of established competence in the field in question. In many instances, the required proficiency is that of a general practitioner. Expertise in a particular field of law may be required in some circumstances.

[2]   A lawyer need not necessarily have special training or prior experience to handle legal problems of a type with which the lawyer is unfamiliar. A newly admitted lawyer can be as competent as a practitioner with long experience. Some important legal skills, such as the analysis of precedent, the evaluation of evidence and legal drafting, are required in all legal problems. Perhaps the most fundamental legal skill consists of determining what kind of legal problems a situation may involve, a skill that necessarily transcends any particular specialized knowledge. A lawyer can provide adequate representation in a wholly novel field through necessary study. Competent representation can also be provided through the association of a lawyer of established competence in the field in question.

[3]   In an emergency a lawyer may give advice or assistance in a matter in which the lawyer does not have the skill ordinarily required where referral to or consultation or association with another lawyer would be impractical. Even in an emergency, however, assistance should be limited to that reasonably necessary in the circumstances, for ill-considered action under emergency conditions can jeopardize the client's interest.

[4]   A lawyer may accept representation where the requisite level of competence can be achieved by reasonable preparation. This applies as well to a lawyer who is appointed as counsel for an unrepresented person. See also Rule 6.2.

Thoroughness and Preparation

[5]   Competent handling of a particular matter includes inquiry into and analysis of the factual and legal elements of the problem, and use of methods and procedures meeting the standards of competent practitioners. It also includes adequate preparation. The required attention and preparation are determined in part by what is at stake; major litigation and complex transactions ordinarily require more ~~elaborate~~ extensive treatment than matters of lesser complexity and consequence. An agreement between the lawyer and the client regarding the scope of the representation may limit the matters for which the lawyer is responsible. See Rule 1.2(c).

Maintaining Competence

[6]   To maintain the requisite knowledge and skill, a lawyer should keep abreast of changes in the law and its practice, engage in continuing study and education and comply with all continuing legal education requirements to which the lawyer is subject. ~~If a system of peer review has been established, the lawyer should consider making use of it in appropriate circumstances.~~

RULE 1.2: SCOPE OF REPRESENTATION AND ALLOCATION OF AUTHORITY BETWEEN CLIENT AND LAWYER

(a) A Subject to paragraphs (c) and (d), a lawyer shall abide by a client's decisions concerning the objectives of representation, ~~subject to paragraphs (c), (d) and (e),~~ and, as required by Rule 1.4, shall consult with the client as to the means by which they are to be pursued. A lawyer may take such action on behalf of the client as is impliedly authorized to carry out the representation. A lawyer shall abide by a client's decision whether to ~~accept an offer of settlement of~~ settle a matter. In a criminal case, the lawyer shall abide by the client's decision, after consultation with the lawyer, as to a plea to be entered, whether to waive jury trial and whether the client will testify.

(b) A lawyer's representation of a client, including representation by appointment, does not constitute an endorsement of the client's political, economic, social or moral views or activities.

(c) A lawyer may limit the ~~objectives~~ scope of the representation if the limitation is reasonable under the circumstances and the client ~~consents after consultation~~ gives informed consent.

(d) A lawyer shall not counsel a client to engage, or assist a client, in conduct that the lawyer knows is criminal or fraudulent, but a lawyer may discuss the legal consequences of any proposed course of conduct with a client and may counsel or assist a client to make a good faith effort to determine the validity, scope, meaning or application of the law.

~~(e) When a lawyer knows that a client expects assistance not permitted by the rules of professional conduct or other law, the lawyer shall consult with the client regarding the relevant limitations on the lawyer's conduct.~~

Comment

~~Scope of Representation~~ Allocation of Authority between Client and Lawyer

[1] ~~Both lawyer and client have authority and responsibility in the objectives and means of representation. The~~ Paragraph (a) confers upon the client ~~has~~ the ultimate authority to determine the purposes to be served by legal representation, within the limits imposed by law and the lawyer's professional obligations. ~~Within those limits, a client also has a right to consult with the lawyer about the means to be used in pursuing those objectives. At the same time, a lawyer is not required to pursue objectives or employ means simply because a client may wish that the lawyer do so. A clear distinction between objectives and means sometimes cannot be drawn, and in many cases the client-lawyer relationship partakes of a joint undertaking. In questions of means the lawyer should assume responsibility for technical and legal tactical issues, but should defer to the client regarding such questions as the expense to be incurred and concern for third persons who might be adversely affected. Law defining the lawyer's scope of authority in litigation varies among jurisdictions.~~ The decisions specified in paragraph (a), such as whether to settle a civil matter, must also be made by the client. See Rule 1.4(a)(1) for the lawyer's duty to communicate with the client about such

decisions. With respect to the means by which the client's objectives are to be pursued, the lawyer shall consult with the client as required by Rule 1.4(a)(2) and may take such action as is impliedly authorized to carry out the representation.

[2] On occasion, however, a lawyer and a client may disagree about the means to be used to accomplish the client's objectives. Clients normally defer to the special knowledge and skill of their lawyer with respect to the means to be used to accomplish their objectives, particularly with respect to technical, legal and tactical matters. Conversely, lawyers usually defer to the client regarding such questions as the expense to be incurred and concern for third persons who might be adversely affected. Because of the varied nature of the matters about which a lawyer and client might disagree and because the actions in question may implicate the interests of a tribunal or other persons, this Rule does not prescribe how such disagreements are to be resolved. Other law, however, may be applicable and should be consulted by the lawyer. The lawyer should also consult with the client and seek a mutually acceptable resolution of the disagreement. If such efforts are unavailing and the lawyer has a fundamental disagreement with the client, the lawyer may withdraw from the representation. See Rule 1.16(b)(4). Conversely, the client may resolve the disagreement by discharging the lawyer. See Rule 1.16(a)(3).

[3] At the outset of a representation, the client may authorize the lawyer to take specific action on the client's behalf without further consultation. Absent a material change in circumstances and subject to Rule 1.4, a lawyer may rely on such an advance authorization. The client may, however, revoke such authority at any time.

[2] [4] In a case in which the client appears to be suffering ~~mental disability~~ diminished capacity, the lawyer's duty to abide by the client's decisions is to be guided by reference to Rule 1.14.

Independence from Client's Views or Activities

[3] [5] Legal representation should not be denied to people who are unable to afford legal services, or whose cause is controversial or the subject of popular disapproval. By the same token, representing a client does not constitute approval of the client's views or activities.

~~Services Limited in Objectives or Means~~ Agreements Limiting Scope of Representation

[4] [6] The ~~objectives or~~ scope of services to be provided by a lawyer may be limited by agreement with the client or by the terms under which the lawyer's services are made available to the client. ~~For example, a retainer may be for a specifically defined purpose. Representation provided through a legal aid agency may be subject to limitations on the types of cases the agency handles.~~ When a lawyer has been retained by an insurer to represent an insured, for example, the representation may be limited to matters related to the insurance coverage. ~~The~~ A limited representation may be appropriate because the client has limited objectives for the representation. In addition,

the terms upon which representation is undertaken may exclude specific ~~objectives or~~ means that might otherwise be used to accomplish the client's objectives. Such limitations may exclude ~~objectives or means~~ actions that the client thinks are too costly or that the lawyer regards as repugnant or imprudent.

[7]   Although this Rule affords the lawyer and client substantial latitude to limit the representation, the limitation must be reasonable under the circumstances. If, for example, a client's objective is limited to securing general information about the law the client needs in order to handle a common and typically uncomplicated legal problem, the lawyer and client may agree that the lawyer's services will be limited to a brief telephone consultation. Such a limitation, however, would not be reasonable if the time allotted was not sufficient to yield advice upon which the client could rely. Although an agreement for a limited representation does not exempt a lawyer from the duty to provide competent representation, the limitation is a factor to be considered when determining the legal knowledge, skill, thoroughness and preparation reasonably necessary for the representation. See Rule 1.1.

~~[5]~~ [8] ~~An agreement~~ All agreements concerning ~~the scope of~~ a lawyer's representation of a client must accord with the Rules of Professional Conduct and other law. ~~Thus, the client may not be asked to agree to representation so limited in scope as to violate Rule 1.1, or to surrender the right to terminate the lawyer's services or the right to settle litigation that the lawyer might wish to continue.~~ See, e.g., Rules 1.1, 1.8 and 5.6.

Criminal, Fraudulent and Prohibited Transactions

~~[6]~~ [9] ~~A~~ Paragraph (d) prohibits a lawyer from knowingly counseling or assisting a client to commit a crime or fraud. This prohibition, however, does not preclude the lawyer ~~is required to give~~ from giving an honest opinion about the actual consequences that appear likely to result from a client's conduct. ~~The~~ Nor does the fact that a client uses advice in a course of action that is criminal or fraudulent ~~does not,~~ of itself, make a lawyer a party to the course of action. ~~However, a lawyer may not knowingly assist a client in criminal or fraudulent conduct.~~ There is a critical distinction between presenting an analysis of legal aspects of questionable conduct and recommending the means by which a crime or fraud might be committed with impunity.

~~[7]~~ [10] When the client's course of action has already begun and is continuing, the lawyer's responsibility is especially delicate. ~~The lawyer is not permitted to reveal the client's wrongdoing, except where permitted by Rule 1.6. However, the~~ The lawyer is required to avoid ~~furthering the purpose~~ assisting the client, for example, by drafting or delivering documents that the lawyer knows are fraudulent or by suggesting how ~~it~~ the wrongdoing might be concealed. A lawyer may not continue assisting a client in conduct that the lawyer originally ~~supposes is~~ supposed was legally proper but then discovers is criminal or fraudulent. ~~Withdrawal~~ The lawyer must, therefore, withdraw from the representation~~, therefore, may be required~~ of the client in the matter. See Rule 1.16(a). In some cases, withdrawal alone might be insufficlient. It may be necessary for the lawyer to give notice of the fact of withdrawal and to disaffirm any opinion, document, affirmation or the like. In extreme cases, substantive law may require a lawyer to disclose information relating to the representation to avoid being deemed to have assisted the client's crime or fraud. See Rule 4.1.

[8] [11] Where the client is a fiduciary, the lawyer may be charged with special obligations in dealings with a beneficiary.

[9] [12] Paragraph (d) applies whether or not the defrauded party is a party to the transaction. Hence, a lawyer should must not participate in a sham transaction; for example, a transaction to effectuate criminal or fraudulent escape of tax liability. Paragraph (d) does not preclude undertaking a criminal defense incident to a general retainer for legal services to a lawful enterprise. The last clause of paragraph (d) recognizes that determining the validity or interpretation of a statute or regulation may require a course of action involving disobedience of the statute or regulation or of the interpretation placed upon it by governmental authorities.

[13] If a lawyer comes to know or reasonably should know that a client expects assistance not permitted by the Rules of Professional Conduct or other law or if the lawyer intends to act contrary to the client's instructions, the lawyer must consult with the client regarding the limitations on the lawyer's conduct. See Rule 1.4(a)(5).

RULE 1.3: DILIGENCE

A lawyer shall act with reasonable diligence and promptness in representing a client.

Comment

[1] A lawyer should pursue a matter on behalf of a client despite opposition, obstruction or personal inconvenience to the lawyer, and may take whatever lawful and ethical measures are required to vindicate a client's cause or endeavor. A lawyer should must also act with commitment and dedication to the interests of the client and with zeal in advocacy upon the client's behalf. However, a A lawyer is not bound, however, to press for every advantage that might be realized for a client. A For example, a lawyer has may have authority to exercise professional discretion in determining the means by which a matter should be pursued. See Rule 1.2. A lawyer's work load should be controlled so that each matter can be handled adequately. The lawyer's duty to act with reasonable diligence does not require the use of offensive tactics or preclude the treating of all persons involved in the legal process with courtesy and respect.

[2] A lawyer's work load must be controlled so that each matter can be handled competently.

[2] [3] Perhaps no professional shortcoming is more widely resented than procrastination. A client's interests often can be adversely affected by the

passage of time or the change of conditions; in extreme instances, as when a lawyer overlooks a statute of limitations, the client's legal position may be destroyed. Even when the client's interests are not affected in substance, however, unreasonable delay can cause a client needless anxiety and undermine confidence in the lawyer's trustworthiness. A lawyer's duty to act with reasonable promptness, however, does not preclude the lawyer from agreeing to a reasonable request for a postponement that will not prejudice the lawyer's client.

[3] [4] Unless the relationship is terminated as provided in Rule 1.16, a lawyer should carry through to conclusion all matters undertaken for a client. If a lawyer's employment is limited to a specific matter, the relationship terminates when the matter has been resolved. If a lawyer has served a client over a substantial period in a variety of matters, the client sometimes may assume that the lawyer will continue to serve on a continuing basis unless the lawyer gives notice of withdrawal. Doubt about whether a client-lawyer relationship still exists should be clarified by the lawyer, preferably in writing, so that the client will not mistakenly suppose the lawyer is looking after the client's affairs when the lawyer has ceased to do so. For example, if a lawyer has handled a judicial or administrative proceeding that produced a result adverse to the client but has not been specifically instructed concerning pursuit of an and the lawyer and the client have not agreed that the lawyer will handle the matter on appeal, the lawyer should advise must consult with the client of about the possibility of appeal before relinquishing responsibility for the matter. See Rule 1.4(a)(2). Whether the lawyer is obligated to prosecute the appeal for the client depends on the scope of the representation the lawyer has agreed to provide to the client. See Rule 1.2.

[5] To prevent neglect of client matters in the event of a sole practitioner's death or disability, the duty of diligence may require that each sole practitioner prepare a plan, in conformity with applicable rules, that designates another competent lawyer to review client files, notify each client of the lawyer's death or disability, and determine whether there is need for immediate protective action. Cf. Rule 28 of the American Bar Association Model Rules for Lawyer Disciplinary Enforcement (providing for court appointment of a lawyer to inventory files and take other protective action in absence of a plan providing for another lawyer to protect the interest of the clients of a deceased or disabled lawyer).

RULE 1.4: COMMUNICATION

(a) A lawyer shall keep a client reasonably informed about the status of a matter and promptly comply with reasonable requests for information.:

(1) promptly inform the client of any decision or circumstance with respect to which the client's informed consent, as defined in Rule 1.0(e), is required by these Rules;

(2) reasonably consult with the client about the means by which the client's objectives are to be accomplished;

(3) keep the client reasonably informed about the status of the matter;

(4) promptly comply with reasonable requests for information; and

(5) consult with the client about any relevant limitation on the lawyer's conduct when the lawyer knows that the client expects assistance not permitted by the Rules of Professional Conduct or other law.

(b) A lawyer shall explain a matter to the extent reasonably necessary to permit the client to make informed decisions regarding the representation.

Comment

[1] Reasonable communication between the lawyer and the client is necessary for the client effectively to participate in the representation.

Communicating with Client

[2] If these Rules require that a particular decision about the representation be made by the client, paragraph (a)(1) requires that the lawyer promptly consult with and secure the client's consent prior to taking action unless prior discussions with the client have resolved what action the client wants the lawyer to take. For example, a lawyer who receives from opposing counsel an offer of settlement in a civil controversy or a proffered plea bargain in a criminal case must promptly inform the client of its substance unless the client has previously indicated that the proposal will be acceptable or unacceptable or has authorized the lawyer to accept or to reject the offer. See Rule 1.2(a).

[3] Paragraph (a)(2) requires the lawyer to reasonably consult with the client about the means to be used to accomplish the client's objectives. In some situations—depending on both the importance of the action under consideration and the feasibility of consulting with the client—this duty will require consultation prior to taking action. In other circumstances, such as during a trial when an immediate decision must be made, the exigency of the situation may require the lawyer to act without prior consultation. In such cases the lawyer must nonetheless act reasonably to inform the client of actions the lawyer has taken on the client's behalf. Additionally, paragraph (a)(3) requires that the lawyer keep the client reasonably informed about the status of the matter, such as significant developments affecting the timing or the substance of the representation.

[4] A lawyer's regular communication with clients will minimize the occasions on which a client will need to request information concerning the representation. When a client makes a reasonable request for information, however, paragraph (a)(4) requires prompt compliance with the request, or if a prompt response is not feasible, that the lawyer, or a member of the lawyer's staff, acknowledge receipt of the request and advise the client when a

response may be expected. Client telephone calls should be promptly returned or acknowledged.

Explaining Matters

[1] [5] The client should have sufficient information to participate intelligently in decisions concerning the objectives of the representation and the means by which they are to be pursued, to the extent the client is willing and able to do so. ~~For example, a lawyer negotiating on behalf of a client should provide the client with facts relevant to the matter, inform the client of communications from another party and take other reasonable steps that permit the client to make a decision regarding a serious offer from another party. A lawyer who receives from opposing counsel an offer of settlement in a civil controversy or a proffered plea bargain in a criminal case should promptly inform the client of its substance unless prior discussions with the client have left it clear that the proposal will be unacceptable. See Rule 1.2(a). Even when a client delegates authority to the lawyer, the client should be kept advised of the status of the matter.~~ [2] Adequacy of communication depends in part on the kind of advice or assistance that is involved. For example, ~~in negotiations where~~ when there is time to explain a proposal made in a negotiation, the lawyer should review all important provisions with the client before proceeding to an agreement. In litigation a lawyer should explain the general strategy and prospects of success and ordinarily should consult the client on tactics that ~~might~~ are likely to result in significant expense or to injure or coerce others. On the other hand, a lawyer ordinarily ~~cannot~~ will not be expected to describe trial or negotiation strategy in detail. The guiding principle is that the lawyer should fulfill reasonable client expectations for information consistent with the duty to act in the client's best interests, and the client's overall requirements as to the character of representation. In certain circumstances, such as when a lawyer asks a client to consent to a representation affected by a conflict of interest, the client must give informed consent, as defined in Rule 1.0(e).

[3] [6] Ordinarily, the information to be provided is that appropriate for a client who is a comprehending and responsible adult. However, fully informing the client according to this standard may be impracticable, for example, where the client is a child or suffers from mental disability. See Rule 1.14. When the client is an organization or group, it is often impossible or inappropriate to inform every one of its members about its legal affairs; ordinarily, the lawyer should address communications to the appropriate officials of the organization. See Rule 1.13. Where many routine matters are involved, a system of limited or occasional reporting may be arranged with the client. ~~Practical exigency may also require a lawyer to act for a client without prior consultation.~~

Withholding Information

[4] [7] In some circumstances, a lawyer may be justified in delaying transmission of information when the client would be likely to react impru-

dently to an immediate communication. Thus, a lawyer might withhold a psychiatric diagnosis of a client when the examining psychiatrist indicates that disclosure would harm the client. A lawyer may not withhold information to serve the lawyer's own interest or convenience or the interests or convenience of another person. Rules or court orders governing litigation may provide that information supplied to a lawyer may not be disclosed to the client. Rule 3.4(c) directs compliance with such rules or orders.

RULE 1.5: FEES

(a) A ~~lawyer's fee~~ lawyer shall ~~be reasonable~~ **not make an agreement for, charge, or collect an unreasonable fee or an unreasonable amount for expenses.** The factors to be considered in determining the reasonableness of a fee include the following:

(1) the time and labor required, the novelty and difficulty of the questions involved, and the skill requisite to perform the legal service properly;

(2) the likelihood, if apparent to the client, that the acceptance of the particular employment will preclude other employment by the lawyer;

(3) the fee customarily charged in the locality for similar legal services;

(4) the amount involved and the results obtained;

(5) the time limitations imposed by the client or by the circumstances;

(6) the nature and length of the professional relationship with the client;

(7) the experience, reputation, and ability of the lawyer or lawyers performing the services; and

(8) whether the fee is fixed or contingent.

(b) ~~When the lawyer has not regularly represented the client~~ The scope of the representation and the basis or rate of the fee and expenses for which the client will be responsible shall be communicated to the client, preferably in writing, before or within a reasonable time after commencing the representation, except when the lawyer will charge a regularly represented client on the same basis or rate. Any changes in the basis or rate of the fee or expenses shall be communicated to the client.*

---

* Editors' Note: As proposed by the Ethics 2000 Commission to the ABA House of Delegates in August, 2001, Rule 1.5(b) would have read as follows:

"(b) The scope of the representation and the basis or rate of the fee and expenses for which the client will be responsible shall be communicated to the client, in writing, before or within a reasonable time after commencing the representation, except when the lawyer will charge a regularly represented client on the same basis or rate. Any changes in the basis or rate of the fee or expenses shall also be communicated in writing. This paragraph does not apply in any matter in which it is reasonably foreseeable that total cost to a client, including attorney fees, will be [$500] or less."

(c) **A fee may be contingent on the outcome of the matter for which the service is rendered, except in a matter in which a contingent fee is prohibited by paragraph (d) or other law. A contingent fee agreement shall be in a writing signed by the client and shall state the method by which the fee is to be determined, including the percentage or percentages that shall accrue to the lawyer in the event of settlement, trial or appeal, litigation and other expenses to be deducted from the recovery, and whether such expenses are to be deducted before or after the contingent fee is calculated. The agreement must clearly notify the client of any expenses for which the client will be liable whether or not the client is the prevailing party. Upon conclusion of a contingent fee matter, the lawyer shall provide the client with a written statement stating the outcome of the matter and, if there is a recovery, showing the remittance to the client and the method of its determination.**

(d) **A lawyer shall not enter into an arrangement for, charge, or collect:**

(1) **any fee in a domestic relations matter, the payment or amount of which is contingent upon the securing of a divorce or upon the amount of alimony or support, or property settlement in lieu thereof; or**

(2) **a contingent fee for representing a defendant in a criminal case.**

(e) **A division of a fee between lawyers who are not in the same firm may be made only if:**

(1) **the division is in proportion to the services performed by each lawyer or, by written agreement with the client, each lawyer assumes joint responsibility for the representation;**

(2) **the client is advised of and does not object to the participation of all the lawyers involved agrees to the arrangement, including the share each lawyer will receive, and the agreement is confirmed in writing; and**

(3) **the total fee is reasonable.**

Comment

Reasonableness of Fee and Expenses

[1]   Paragraph (a) requires that lawyers charge fees that are reasonable under the circumstances. The factors specified in (1) through (8) are not exclusive. Nor will each factor be relevant in each instance. Paragraph (a) also requires that expenses for which the client will be charged must be reasonable. A lawyer may seek reimbursement for the cost of services performed in-

house, such as copying, or for other expenses incurred in-house, such as telephone charges, either by charging a reasonable amount to which the client has agreed in advance or by charging an amount that reasonably reflects the cost incurred by the lawyer.

Basis or Rate of Fee

~~[1]~~ [2] When the lawyer has regularly represented a client, they ordinarily will have evolved an understanding concerning the basis or rate of the fee and the expenses for which the client will be responsible. In a new client-lawyer relationship, however, an understanding as to ~~the fee~~ fees and expenses ~~should~~ must be promptly established. ~~It is not necessary to recite all the factors that underlie the basis of the fee, but only those that are directly involved in its computation. It is sufficient, for example, to state that the basic rate is an hourly charge or a fixed amount or an estimated amount, or to identify the factors that may be taken into account in finally fixing the fee. When developments occur during the representation that render an earlier estimate substantially inaccurate, a revised estimate should be provided to the client.~~ Generally, it is desirable to furnish the client with at least a simple memorandum or copy of the lawyer's customary fee arrangements that states the general nature of the legal services to be provided, the basis, rate or total amount of the fee and whether and to what extent the client will be responsible for any costs, expenses or disbursements in the course of the representation. A written statement concerning the ~~fee~~ terms of the engagement reduces the possibility of misunderstanding. ~~Furnishing the client with a simple memorandum or a copy of the lawyer's customary fee schedule is sufficient if the basis or rate of the fee is set forth.~~

[3] Contingent fees, like any other fees, are subject to the reasonableness standard of paragraph (a) of this Rule, including consideration of the degree of risk assumed by the lawyer at the outset of the representation. In determining whether a particular contingent fee is reasonable, or whether it is reasonable to charge any form of contingent fee, a lawyer must consider all of the factors that are relevant under the circumstances. Applicable law may impose limitations on contingent fees, such as a ceiling on the percentage allowable, or may require a lawyer to offer clients an alternative basis for the fee. Applicable law also may apply to situations other than a contingent fee, for example, government regulations regarding fees in certain tax matters.

Terms of Payment

~~[2]~~ [4] A lawyer may require advance payment of a fee, but is obliged to return any unearned portion. See Rule 1.16(d). A lawyer may accept property in payment for services, such as an ownership interest in an enterprise, providing this does not involve acquisition of a proprietary interest in the cause of action or subject matter of the litigation contrary to Rule 1.8~~(j)~~(i). However, a fee paid in property instead of money may be subject to ~~special scrutiny because it involves questions concerning both the value of the services and the lawyer's special knowledge of the value of the property~~ the requirements of Rule 1.8(a) because such fees often have the essential qualities of a business transaction with the client.

[3] [5] An agreement may not be made whose terms might induce the lawyer improperly to curtail services for the client or perform them in a way contrary to the client's interest. For example, a lawyer should not enter into an agreement whereby services are to be provided only up to a stated amount when it is foreseeable that more extensive services probably will be required, unless the situation is adequately explained to the client. Otherwise, the client might have to bargain for further assistance in the midst of a proceeding or transaction. However, it is proper to define the extent of services in light of the client's ability to pay. A lawyer should not exploit a fee arrangement based primarily on hourly charges by using wasteful procedures. ~~When there is doubt whether a contingent fee is consistent with the client's best interest, the lawyer should offer the client alternative bases for the fee and explain their implications. Applicable law may impose limitations on contingent fees, such as a ceiling on the percentage.~~

Prohibited Contingent Fees

[6]   Paragraph (d) prohibits a lawyer from charging a contingent fee in a domestic relations matter when payment is contingent upon the securing of a divorce or upon the amount of alimony or support or property settlement to be obtained. This provision does not preclude a contract for a contingent fee for legal representation in connection with the recovery of post-judgment balances due under support, alimony or other financial orders because such contracts do not implicate the same policy concerns.

Division of Fee

[4] [7] A division of fee is a single billing to a client covering the fee of two or more lawyers who are not in the same firm. A division of fee facilitates association of more than one lawyer in a matter in which neither alone could serve the client as well, and most often is used when the fee is contingent and the division is between a referring lawyer and a trial specialist. Paragraph (e) permits the lawyers to divide a fee ~~on~~ either on the basis of the proportion of services they render or ~~by agreement between the participating lawyers~~ if ~~all assume~~ each lawyer assumes responsibility for the representation as a whole. ~~and~~ In addition, the client ~~is advised and does not object. It does not require disclosure to the client of~~ must agree to the arrangement, including the share that each lawyer is to receive, and the agreement must be confirmed in writing. Contingent fee agreements must be in writing signed by the client and must otherwise comply with paragraph (c) of this Rule. Joint responsibility for the representation entails ~~the obligations stated in Rule 5.1 for purposes of the matter involved~~ financial and ethical responsibility for the representation as if the lawyers were associated in a partnership. A lawyer should only refer a matter to a lawyer whom the referring lawyer reasonably believes is competent to handle the matter. See Rule 1.1.

[8]   Paragraph (e) does not prohibit or regulate division of fees to be received in the future for work done when lawyers were previously associated in a law firm.

Disputes over Fees

[5] [9] If a procedure has been established for resolution of fee disputes, such as an arbitration or mediation procedure established by the bar, the lawyer must comply with the procedure when it is mandatory, and, even when it is voluntary, the lawyer should conscientiously consider submitting to it. Law may prescribe a procedure for determining a lawyer's fee, for example, in representation of an executor or administrator, a class or a person entitled to a reasonable fee as part of the measure of damages. The lawyer entitled to such a fee and a lawyer representing another party concerned with the fee should comply with the prescribed procedure.

RULE 1.6: CONFIDENTIALITY OF INFORMATION*

(a) A lawyer shall not reveal information relating to the representation of a client unless the client ~~consents after consultation, except for disclosures that are~~ **gives informed consent, the disclosure**

* Editors' Note: As previously proposed by the Kutak Commission, Rule 1.6 (Revised Final Draft, June 30, 1982) read as follows:

RULE 1.6 Confidentiality of Information

(a) A lawyer shall not reveal information relating to the representation of a client unless the client consents after consultation, except for disclosures that are impliedly authorized in order to carry out the representation, and except as stated in paragraph (b).

(b) A lawyer may reveal such information to the extent the lawyer reasonably believes necessary:

(1) to prevent the client from committing a criminal act or fraudulent act that the lawyer reasonably believes is likely to result in death or substantial bodily harm, or substantial injury to the financial interests or property of another;

(2) to rectify the consequences of a client's criminal or fraudulent act in the furtherance of which the lawyer's services had been used;

(3) to establish a claim or defense on behalf of the lawyer in a controversy between the lawyer and the client, or to establish a defense to a criminal charge, civil claim or disciplinary complaint against the lawyer based upon conduct in which the client was involved; or

(4) to comply with other law.

In 1991, the ABA House of Delegates again rejected a proposal from its ethics committee to amend Rule 1.6(b) to add the rectification language found in subsection(b)(2) of the 1982 Revised Final Draft.

As proposed by the Ethics 2000 Commission to the ABA House of Delegates in August 2001, Rule 1.6 (b) would have had two additional subsections that would have read as follows:

"(b) A lawyer may reveal information relating to the representation of a client to the extent the lawyer reasonably believes necessary: ***

(2) to prevent the client from committing a crime or fraud that is reasonably certain to result in substantial injury to the financial interests or property of another and in furtherance of which the client has used or is using the lawyer's services;

(3) to prevent, mitigate or rectify substantial injury to the financial interests or property of another that is reasonably certain to result or has resulted from client's commission of a crime or fraud in furtherance of which the client has used the lawyer's services.

The House of Delegates voted to delete proposed subsection (2) from the new Rule, and thereafter, the Ethics 2000 Commission withdrew proposed subsection (3) from consideration.

For current information about how Model Rule 1.6 has been adopted in the states, see *Appendix A – Ethics Rules on Client Confidences*, reprinted after these Model Rules.

25

is impliedly authorized in order to carry out the representation, ~~and except as stated in~~ or the disclosure is permitted by paragraph (b).

(b) A lawyer may reveal ~~such~~ information relating to the representation of a client to the extent the lawyer reasonably believes necessary:

(1) to prevent ~~the client from committing a criminal act that the lawyer believes is likely to result in imminent~~ reasonably certain death or substantial bodily harm; ~~or~~

(2) to secure legal advice about the lawyer's compliance with these Rules;

~~(2)~~ (3) to establish a claim or defense on behalf of the lawyer in a controversy between the lawyer and the client, to establish a defense to a criminal charge or civil claim against the lawyer based upon conduct in which the client was involved, or to respond to allegations in any proceeding concerning the lawyer's representation of the client; or

(4) to comply with other law or a court order.

Comment

~~[1] The lawyer is part of a judicial system charged with upholding the law. One of the lawyer's functions is to advise clients so that they avoid any violation of the law in the proper exercise of their rights.~~

~~[2] The observance of the ethical obligation of a lawyer to hold inviolate confidential information of the client not only facilitates the full development of facts essential to proper representation of the client but also encourages people to seek early legal assistance.~~

~~[3] Almost without exception, clients come to lawyers in order to determine what their rights are and what is, in the maze of laws and regulations, deemed to be legal and correct. The common law recognizes that the client's confidences must be protected from disclosure. Based upon experience, lawyers know that almost all clients follow the advice given, and the law is upheld.~~

[1] This Rule governs the disclosure by a lawyer of information relating to the representation of a client during the lawyer's representation of the client. See Rule 1.18 for the lawyer's duties with respect to information provided to the lawyer by a prospective client, Rule 1.9(c)(2) for the lawyer's duty not to reveal information relating to the lawyer's prior representation of a former client and Rules 1.8(b) and 1.9(c)(1) for the lawyer's duties with respect to the use of such information to the disadvantage of clients and former clients.

~~[4]~~ [2] A fundamental principle in the client-lawyer relationship is that, in the absence of the client's informed consent, the lawyer ~~maintain confidentiality of~~ must not reveal information relating to the representation. See Rule 1.0(e) for the definition of informed consent. This contributes to the trust that is the hallmark of the client-lawyer relationship. The client is thereby encouraged to seek legal assistance and to communicate fully and frankly with the lawyer even as to embarrassing or legally damaging subject matter. The lawyer needs this information to represent the client effectively and, if necessary, to advise the client to refrain from wrongful conduct. Almost without exception, clients come to lawyers in order to determine their rights and what is, in the complex of laws and regulations, deemed to be legal and correct. Based upon experience, lawyers know that almost all clients follow the advice given, and the law is upheld.

[5] [3] The principle of client-lawyer confidentiality is given effect in two by related bodies of law,: the attorney-client privilege, (which includes the work product doctrine) in the law of evidence and the rule of confidentiality established in professional ethics. The attorney-client privilege applies and work-product doctrine apply in judicial and other proceedings in which a lawyer may be called as a witness or otherwise required to produce evidence concerning a client. The rule of client-lawyer confidentiality applies in situations other than those where evidence is sought from the lawyer through compulsion of law. The confidentiality rule, for example, applies not merely only to matters communicated in confidence by the client but also to all information relating to the representation, whatever its source. A lawyer may not disclose such information except as authorized or required by the Rules of Professional Conduct or other law. See also Scope.

[6] The requirement of maintaining confidentiality of information relating to representation applies to government lawyers who may disagree with the policy goals that their representation is designed to advance.

[4] Paragraph (a) prohibits a lawyer from revealing information relating to the representation of a client. This prohibition also applies to disclosures by a lawyer that do not in themselves reveal protected information but could reasonably lead to the discovery of such information by a third person. A lawyer's use of a hypothetical to discuss issues relating to the representation is permissible so long as there is no reasonable likelihood that the listener will be able to ascertain the identity of the client or the situation involved.

Authorized Disclosure

[7] [5] A Except to the extent that the client's instructions or special circumstances limit that authority, a lawyer is impliedly authorized to make disclosures about a client when appropriate in carrying out the representation, except to the extent that the client's instructions or special circumstances limit that authority. In litigation some situations, for example, a lawyer may disclose information by admitting be impliedly authorized to admit a fact that cannot properly be disputed or, in negotiation by making to make a disclosure that facilitates a satisfactory conclusion to a matter. [8] Lawyers in a firm may, in the course of the firm's practice, disclose to each other information relating to a client of the firm, unless the client has instructed that particular information be confined to specified lawyers.

27

Disclosure Adverse to Client

[9] [6] ~~The~~ Although the public interest is usually best served by a strict rule requiring lawyers to preserve the confidentiality of information relating to the representation of their clients, the confidentiality rule is subject to limited exceptions. ~~In becoming privy to information about a client, a lawyer may foresee that the client intends serious harm to another person. However, to the extent a lawyer is required or permitted to disclose a client's purposes, the client will be inhibited from revealing facts which would enable the lawyer to counsel against a wrongful course of action. The public is better protected if full and open communication by the client is encouraged than if it is inhibited.~~ Paragraph (b)(1) recognizes the overriding value of life and physical integrity and permits disclosure reasonably necessary to prevent reasonably certain death or substantial bodily harm. Such harm is reasonably certain to occur if it will be suffered imminently or if there is a present and substantial threat that a person will suffer such harm at a later date if the lawyer fails to take action necessary to eliminate the threat. Thus, a lawyer who knows that a client has accidentally discharged toxic waste into a town's water supply may reveal this information to the authorities if there is a present and substantial risk that a person who drinks the water will contract a life-threatening or debilitating disease and the lawyer's disclosure is necessary to eliminate the threat or reduce the number of victims.

[10] ~~Several situations must be distinguished.~~

[11] ~~First, the lawyer may not counsel or assist a client in conduct that is criminal or fraudulent. See Rule 1.2(d). Similarly, a lawyer has a duty under Rule 3.3(a)(4) not to use false evidence. This duty is essentially a special instance of the duty prescribed in Rule 1.2(d) to avoid assisting a client in criminal or fraudulent conduct.~~

[12] ~~Second, the lawyer may have been innocently involved in past conduct by the client that was criminal or fraudulent. In such a situation the lawyer has not violated Rule 1.2(d), because to "counsel or assist" criminal or fraudulent conduct requires knowing that the conduct is of that character.~~

[13] ~~Third, the lawyer may learn that a client intends prospective conduct that is criminal and likely to result in imminent death or substantial bodily harm. As stated in paragraph (b)(1), the lawyer has professional discretion to reveal information in order to prevent such consequences. The lawyer may make a disclosure in order to prevent homicide or serious bodily injury which the lawyer reasonably believes is intended by a client. It is very difficult for a lawyer to "know" when such a heinous purpose will actually be carried out, for the client may have a change of mind.~~

[14] ~~The lawyer's exercise of discretion requires consideration of such factors as the nature of the lawyer's relationship with the client and with those who might be injured by the client, the lawyer's own involvement in the transaction and factors that may extenuate the conduct in question. Where practical, the lawyer should seek to persuade the client to take suitable action. In any case, a disclosure adverse to the client's interest should be no greater~~

than the lawyer reasonably believes necessary to the purpose. A lawyer's decision not to take preventive action permitted by paragraph (b)(1) does not violate this Rule.

[7]   A lawyer's confidentiality obligations do not preclude a lawyer from securing confidential legal advice about the lawyer's personal responsibility to comply with these Rules. In most situations, disclosing information to secure such advice will be impliedly authorized for the lawyer to carry out the representation. Even when the disclosure is not impliedly authorized, paragraph (b)(2) permits such disclosure because of the importance of a lawyer's compliance with the Rules of Professional Conduct.

Dispute Concerning a Lawyer's Conduct

[18] [8] Where a legal claim or disciplinary charge alleges complicity of the lawyer in a client's conduct or other misconduct of the lawyer involving representation of the client, the lawyer may respond to the extent the lawyer reasonably believes necessary to establish a defense. The same is true with respect to a claim involving the conduct or representation of a former client. Such a charge can arise in a civil, criminal, disciplinary or other proceeding and can be based on a wrong allegedly committed by the lawyer against the client or on a wrong alleged by a third person, for example, a person claiming to have been defrauded by the lawyer and client acting together. The lawyer's right to respond arises when an assertion of such complicity has been made. Paragraph (b)(2)(3) does not require the lawyer to await the commencement of an action or proceeding that charges such complicity, so that the defense may be established by responding directly to a third party who has made such an assertion. The right to defend also applies, of course, applies where a proceeding has been commenced. Where practicable and not prejudicial to the lawyer's ability to establish the defense, the lawyer should advise the client of the third party's assertion and request that the client respond appropriately. In any event, disclosure should be no greater than the lawyer reasonably believes is necessary to vindicate innocence, the disclosure should be made in a manner which limits access to the information to the tribunal or other persons having a need to know it, and appropriate protective orders or other arrangements should be sought by the lawyer to the fullest extent practicable.

[19] [9] If the lawyer is charged with wrongdoing in which the client's conduct is implicated, the rule of confidentiality should not prevent the lawyer from defending against the charge. Such a charge can arise in a civil, criminal or professional disciplinary proceeding, and can be based on a wrong allegedly committed by the lawyer against the client, or on a wrong alleged by a third person; for example, a person claiming to have been defrauded by the lawyer and client acting together. A lawyer entitled to a fee is permitted by paragraph (b)(2)(3) to prove the services rendered in an action to collect it. This aspect of the rule expresses the principle that the beneficiary of a fiduciary relationship may not exploit it to the detriment of the fiduciary. As stated above, the lawyer must make every effort practicable to avoid unnecessary disclosure of information relating to a representation, to limit disclosure to

~~those having the need to know it, and to obtain protective orders or make other arrangements minimizing the risk of disclosure.~~

[10]   Other law may require that a lawyer disclose information about a client. Whether such a law supersedes Rule 1.6 is a question of law beyond the scope of these Rules. When disclosure of information relating to the representation appears to be required by other law, the lawyer must discuss the matter with the client to the extent required by Rule 1.4. If, however, the other law supersedes this Rule and requires disclosure, paragraph (b)(4) permits the lawyer to make such disclosures as are necessary to comply with the law.

[11]   A lawyer may be ordered to reveal information relating to the representation of a client by a court or by another tribunal or governmental entity claiming authority pursuant to other law to compel the disclosure. Absent informed consent of the client to do otherwise, the lawyer should assert on behalf of the client all nonfrivolous claims that the order is not authorized by other law or that the information sought is protected against disclosure by the attorney-client privilege or other applicable law. In the event of an adverse ruling, the lawyer must consult with the client about the possibility of appeal to the extent required by Rule 1.4. Unless review is sought, however, paragraph (b)(4) permits the lawyer to comply with the court's order.

[12]   Paragraph (b) permits disclosure only to the extent the lawyer reasonably believes the disclosure is necessary to accomplish one of the purposes specified. Where practicable, the lawyer should first seek to persuade the client to take suitable action to obviate the need for disclosure. In any case, a disclosure adverse to the client's interest should be no greater than the lawyer reasonably believes necessary to accomplish the purpose. If the disclosure will be made in connection with a judicial proceeding, the disclosure should be made in a manner that limits access to the information to the tribunal or other persons having a need to know it and appropriate protective orders or other arrangements should be sought by the lawyer to the fullest extent practicable.

[13]   Paragraph (b) permits but does not require the disclosure of information relating to a client's representation to accomplish the purposes specified in paragraphs (b)(1) through (b)(4). In exercising the discretion conferred by this Rule, the lawyer may consider such factors as the nature of the lawyer's relationship with the client and with those who might be injured by the client, the lawyer's own involvement in the transaction and factors that may extenuate the conduct in question. A lawyer's decision not to disclose as permitted by paragraph (b) does not violate this Rule. Disclosure may be required, however, by other Rules. Some Rules require disclosure only if such disclosure would be permitted by paragraph (b). See Rules 1.2(d), 4.1(b), 8.1 and 8.3. Rule 3.3, on the other hand, requires disclosure in some circumstances regardless of whether such disclosure is permitted by this Rule. See Rule 3.3(c).

Withdrawal

[~~15~~] [14] If the lawyer's services will be used by the client in materially furthering a course of criminal or fraudulent conduct, the lawyer must withdraw, as stated in Rule 1.16(a)(1). [~~16~~] After withdrawal the lawyer is required to refrain from making disclosure of the client's confidences, except as otherwise provided in Rule 1.6. Neither this rule nor Rule 1.8(b) nor Rule 1.16(d) prevents the lawyer from giving notice of the fact of withdrawal, and the lawyer may also withdraw or disaffirm any opinion, document, affirmation, or the like. [~~17~~] Where the client is an organization, the lawyer may be in doubt whether contemplated conduct will actually be carried out by the organization. Where necessary to guide conduct in connection with this Rule, the lawyer may make inquiry within the organization as indicated in Rule 1.13(b).

~~Disclosures Otherwise Required or Authorized~~

[~~20~~] ~~The attorney-client privilege is differently defined in various jurisdictions. If a lawyer is called as a witness to give testimony concerning a client, absent waiver by the client, paragraph (a) requires the lawyer to invoke the privilege when it is applicable. The lawyer must comply with the final orders of a court or other tribunal of competent jurisdiction requiring the lawyer to give information about the client.~~

[~~21~~] ~~The Rules of Professional Conduct in various circumstances permit or require a lawyer to disclose information relating to the representation. See Rules 2.2, 2.3, 3.3 and 4.1. In addition to these provisions, a lawyer may be obligated or permitted by other provisions of law to give information about a client. Whether another provision of law supercedes Rule 1.6 is a matter of interpretation beyond the scope of these Rules, but a presumption should exist against such a supersession.~~

Acting Competently to Preserve Confidentiality

[15] A lawyer must act competently to safeguard information relating to the representation of a client against inadvertent or unauthorized disclosure by the lawyer or other persons who are participating in the representation of the client or who are subject to the lawyer's supervision. See Rules 1.1, 5.1 and 5.3.

[16] When transmitting a communication that includes information relating to the representation of a client, the lawyer must take reasonable precautions to prevent the information from coming into the hands of unintended recipients. This duty, however, does not require that the lawyer use special security measures if the method of communication affords a reasonable expectation of privacy. Special circumstances, however, may warrant special precautions. Factors to be considered in determining the reasonableness of the lawyer's expectation of confidentiality include the sensitivity of the information and the extent to which the privacy of the communication is protected by law or by a confidentiality agreement. A client may require the lawyer to implement special security measures not required by this Rule or

may give informed consent to the use of a means of communication that would otherwise be prohibited by this Rule.

Former Client

[22] [17] The duty of confidentiality continues after the client-lawyer relationship has terminated. See Rule 1.9(c)(2). See Rule 1.9(c)(1) for the prohibition against using such information to the disadvantage of the former client.

RULE 1.7: CONFLICT OF INTEREST: ~~GENERAL RULE~~ CURRENT CLIENTS

~~(a) A lawyer shall not represent a client if the representation of that client will be directly adverse to another client, unless:~~

~~(1) the lawyer reasonably believes the representation will not adversely affect the relationship with the other client; and~~

~~(2) each client consents after consultation.~~

~~(b) A lawyer shall not represent a client if the representation of that client may be materially limited by the lawyer's responsibilities to another client or to a third person, or by the lawyer's own interests, unless:~~

~~(1) the lawyer reasonably believes the representation will not be adversely affected; and~~

~~(2) the client consents after consultation. When representation of multiple clients in a single matter is undertaken, the consultation shall include explanation of the implications of the common representation and the advantages and risks involved.~~

(a) Except as provided in paragraph (b), a lawyer shall not represent a client if the representation involves a concurrent conflict of interest. A concurrent conflict of interest exists if:

(1) the representation of one client will be directly adverse to another client; or

(2) there is a significant risk that the representation of one or more clients will be materially limited by the lawyer's responsibilities to another client, a former client or a third person or by a personal interest of the lawyer.

(b) Notwithstanding the existence of a concurrent conflict of interest under paragraph (a), a lawyer may represent a client if:

(1) the lawyer reasonably believes that the lawyer will be able to provide competent and diligent representation to each affected client;

(2) the representation is not prohibited by law;

(3) the representation does not involve the assertion of a claim by one client against another client represented by the lawyer in the same litigation or other proceeding before a tribunal; and

(4) each affected client gives informed consent, confirmed in writing.

Comment

~~Loyalty to a Client~~ General Principles

[1]   Loyalty ~~is an~~ and independent judgment are essential ~~element~~ elements in the lawyer's relationship to a client. Concurrent conflicts of interest can arise from the lawyer's responsibilities to another client, a former client or a third person or from the lawyer's own interests. For specific Rules regarding certain concurrent conflicts of interest, see Rule 1.8. For former client conflicts of interest, see Rule 1.9. For conflicts of interest involving prospective clients, see Rule 1.18. For definitions of "informed consent" and "confirmed in writing," see Rule 1.0(e) and (b).

[2]   Resolution of a conflict of interest problem under this Rule requires the lawyer to: 1) clearly identify the client or clients; 2) determine whether a conflict of interest exists; 3) decide whether the representation may be undertaken despite the existence of a conflict, i.e., whether the conflict is consentable; and 4) if so, consult with the clients affected under paragraph (a) and obtain their informed consent, confirmed in writing. The clients affected under paragraph (a) include both of the clients referred to in paragraph (a)(1) and the one or more clients whose representation might be materially limited under paragraph (a)(2).

[3]   ~~An impermissible~~ A conflict of interest may exist before representation is undertaken, in which event the representation ~~should~~ must be declined, unless the lawyer obtains the informed consent of each client under the conditions of paragraph (b). ~~The~~ To determine whether a conflict of interest exists, a lawyer should adopt reasonable procedures, appropriate for the size and type of firm and practice, to determine in both litigation and non-litigation matters the ~~parties~~ persons and issues involved ~~and to determine whether there are actual or potential conflicts of interest~~. See also Comment to Rule 5.1. Ignorance caused by a failure to institute such procedures will not excuse a lawyer's violation of this Rule. As to whether a client-lawyer relationship exists or, having once been established, is continuing, see Comment to Rule 1.3 and Scope.

~~[2]~~ [4] If ~~such~~ a conflict arises after representation has been undertaken, the lawyer ~~should~~ ordinarily must withdraw from the representation, unless the lawyer has obtained the informed consent of the client under the conditions of paragraph (b). See Rule 1.16. Where more than one client is involved and the lawyer withdraws ~~because a conflict arises after representation~~, whether the lawyer may continue to represent any of the clients is determined both by the lawyer's ability to comply with duties owed to the former client and by the lawyer's ability to represent adequately the remaining client or clients, given the lawyer's duties to the former client. See Rule 1.9. See also ~~Rule 2.2(e)~~ Comments [5] and [29]. ~~As to whether a client-lawyer relationship exists or, having once been established, is continuing, see Comment to Rule 1.3 and Scope.~~

[5] Unforeseeable developments, such as changes in corporate and other organizational affiliations or the addition or realignment of parties in litigation, might create conflicts in the midst of a representation, as when a company sued by the lawyer on behalf of one client is bought by another client represented by the lawyer in an unrelated matter. In these circumstances, the lawyer may withdraw from one of the representations in order to avoid the conflict. The lawyer must seek court approval where necessary and take steps to minimize harm to the clients. See Rule 1.16. The lawyer must continue to protect the confidences of the client from whose representation the lawyer has withdrawn. See Rule 1.9(c).

Identifying Conflicts of Interest: Directly Adverse

~~[3]~~ [6] ~~As a general proposition, loyalty~~ Loyalty to a current client prohibits undertaking representation directly adverse to that client without that client's informed consent. ~~Paragraph (a) expresses that general rule.~~ Thus, absent consent, a lawyer ~~ordinarily~~ may not act as an advocate in one matter against a person the lawyer represents in some other matter, even ~~if it is~~ when the matters are wholly unrelated. The client as to whom the representation is directly adverse is likely to feel betrayed, and the resulting damage to the client-lawyer relationship is likely to impair the lawyer's ability to represent the client effectively. In addition, the client on whose behalf the adverse representation is undertaken reasonably may fear that the lawyer will pursue that client's case less effectively out of deference to the other client, i.e., that the representation may be materially limited by the lawyer's interest in retaining the current client. Similarly, a directly adverse conflict may arise when a lawyer is required to cross-examine a client who appears as a witness in a lawsuit involving another client, as when the testimony will be damaging to the client who is represented in the lawsuit. On the other hand, simultaneous representation in unrelated matters of clients whose interests are only ~~generally~~ economically adverse, such as representation of competing economic enterprises in unrelated litigation, does not ordinarily constitute a conflict of interest and thus may not require consent of the respective clients. ~~Paragraph (a) applies only when the representation of one client would be directly adverse to the other.~~

[7] Directly adverse conflicts can also arise in transactional matters. For example, if a lawyer is asked to represent a seller in negotiations with a buyer represented by the lawyer, not in the same transaction but in another, unrelated matter, the lawyer could not undertake the representation without the informed consent of each client.

Identifying Conflicts of Interest: Material Limitation

[4] [8] ~~Loyalty to a client is also impaired when~~ Even where there is no direct adverseness, a conflict of interest exists if there is a significant risk that a ~~lawyer cannot~~ lawyer's ability to consider, recommend or carry out an appropriate course of action for the client ~~because~~ will be materially limited as a result of the lawyer's other responsibilities or interests. For example, a lawyer asked to represent several individuals seeking to form a joint venture is likely to be materially limited in the lawyer's ability to recommend or advocate all possible positions that each might take because of the lawyer's duty of loyalty to the others. The conflict in effect forecloses alternatives that would otherwise be available to the client. ~~Paragraph (b) addresses such situations. A possible conflict~~ The mere possibility of subsequent harm does not itself ~~preclude the representation~~ require disclosure and consent. The critical questions are the likelihood that a ~~conflict~~ difference in interests will eventuate and, if it does, whether it will materially interfere with the lawyer's independent professional judgment in considering alternatives or foreclose courses of action that reasonably should be pursued on behalf of the client. ~~Consideration should be given to whether the client wishes to accommodate the other interest involved.~~

Lawyer's ~~Interests~~ Responsibilities to Former Clients and Other Third Persons

[9]   In addition to conflicts with other current clients, a lawyer's duties of loyalty and independence may be materially limited by responsibilities to former clients under Rule 1.9 or by the lawyer's responsibilities to other persons, such as fiduciary duties arising from a lawyer's service as a trustee, executor or corporate director.

Personal Interest Conflicts

[6] [10] The lawyer's own interests should not be permitted to have an adverse effect on representation of a client. For example, ~~a lawyer's need for income should not lead the lawyer to undertake matters that cannot be handled competently and at a reasonable fee. See Rules 1.1 and 1.5. If~~ if the probity of a lawyer's own conduct in a transaction is in serious question, it may be difficult or impossible for the lawyer to give a client detached advice. ~~A~~ Similarly, when a lawyer has discussions concerning possible employment with an opponent of the lawyer's client, or with a law firm representing the opponent, such discussions could materially limit the lawyer's representation of the client. In addition, a lawyer may not allow related business interests to affect representation, for example, by referring clients to an enterprise in which the lawyer has an undisclosed financial interest. See Rule 1.8 for specific Rules pertaining to a number of personal interest conflicts, including business transactions with clients. See also Rule 1.10 (personal interest conflicts under Rule 1.7 ordinarily are not imputed to other lawyers in a law firm).

[11] When lawyers representing different clients in the same matter or in substantially related matters are closely related by blood or marriage, there may be a significant risk that client confidences will be revealed and that the lawyer's family relationship will interfere with both loyalty and independent professional judgment. As a result, each client is entitled to know of the existence and implications of the relationship between the lawyers before the lawyer agrees to undertake the representation. Thus, a lawyer related to another lawyer, e.g., as parent, child, sibling or spouse, ordinarily may not represent a client in a matter where that lawyer is representing another party, unless each client gives informed consent. The disqualification arising from a close family relationship is personal and ordinarily is not imputed to members of firms with whom the lawyers are associated. See Rule 1.10.

[12] A lawyer is prohibited from engaging in sexual relationships with a client unless the sexual relationship predates the formation of the client-lawyer relationship. See Rule 1.8(j).

Interest of Person Paying for a Lawyer's Service

[10] [13] A lawyer may be paid from a source other than the client, including a co-client, if the client is informed of that fact and consents and the arrangement does not compromise the lawyer's duty of loyalty or independent judgment to the client. See Rule 1.8(f). ~~For example, when an insurer and its insured have conflicting interests in a matter arising from a liability insurance agreement, and the insurer is required to provide special counsel for the insured, the arrangement should assure the special counsel's professional independence. So also, when a corporation and its directors or employees are involved in a controversy in which they have conflicting interests, the corporation may provide funds for separate legal representation of the directors or employees, if the clients consent after consultation and the arrangement ensures the lawyer's professional independence.~~ If acceptance of the payment from any other source presents a significant risk that the lawyer's representation of the client will be materially limited by the lawyer's own interest in accommodating the person paying the lawyer's fee or by the lawyer's responsibilities to a payer who is also a co-client, then the lawyer must comply with the requirements of paragraph (b) before accepting the representation, including determining whether the conflict is consentable and, if so, that the client has adequate information about the material risks of the representation.

~~Consultation and Consent~~ Prohibited Representations

[5] [14] ~~A client~~ Ordinarily, clients may consent to representation notwithstanding a conflict. However, as indicated in paragraph ~~(a)(1) with respect to representation directly adverse to a client, and paragraph (b)(1) with respect to material limitations on representation of a client, when a disinterested lawyer would conclude that the client should not agree to the representation under the circumstances,~~ some conflicts are nonconsentable, meaning that the lawyer involved cannot properly ask for such agreement or provide representation on the basis of the client's consent. When the lawyer is

36

representing more than one client ~~is involved~~, the question of ~~conflict~~ consentability must be resolved as to each client. ~~Moreover, there may be circumstances where it is impossible to make the disclosure necessary to obtain consent. For example, when the lawyer represents different clients in related matters and one of the clients refuses to consent to the disclosure necessary to permit the other client to make an informed decision, the lawyer cannot properly ask the latter to consent.~~

[15]   Consentability is typically determined by considering whether the interests of the clients will be adequately protected if the clients are permitted to give their informed consent to representation burdened by a conflict of interest. Thus, under paragraph (b)(1), representation is prohibited if in the circumstances the lawyer cannot reasonably conclude that the lawyer will be able to provide competent and diligent representation. See Rule 1.1 (competence) and Rule 1.3 (diligence).

[16]   Paragraph (b)(2) describes conflicts that are nonconsentable because the representation is prohibited by applicable law. For example, in some states substantive law provides that the same lawyer may not represent more than one defendant in a capital case, even with the consent of the clients, and under federal criminal statutes certain representations by a former government lawyer are prohibited, despite the informed consent of the former client. In addition, decisional law in some states limits the ability of a governmental client, such as a municipality, to consent to a conflict of interest.

[17]   Paragraph (b)(3) describes conflicts that are nonconsentable because of the institutional interest in vigorous development of each client's position when the clients are aligned directly against each other in the same litigation or other proceeding before a tribunal. Whether clients are aligned directly against each other within the meaning of this paragraph requires examination of the context of the proceeding. Although this paragraph does not preclude a lawyer's multiple representation of adverse parties to a mediation (because mediation is not a proceeding before a "tribunal" under Rule 1.0(m)), such representation may be precluded by paragraph (b)(1).

Informed Consent

[18]   Informed consent requires that each affected client be aware of the relevant circumstances and of the material and reasonably foreseeable ways that the conflict could have adverse effects on the interests of that client. See Rule 1.0(e) (informed consent). The information required depends on the nature of the conflict and the nature of the risks involved. When representation of multiple clients in a single matter is undertaken, the information must include the implications of the common representation, including possible effects on loyalty, confidentiality and the attorney-client privilege and the advantages and risks involved. See Comments [30] and [31] (effect of common representation on confidentiality).

[19]   Under some circumstances it may be impossible to make the disclosure necessary to obtain consent. For example, when the lawyer repre-

sents different clients in related matters and one of the clients refuses to consent to the disclosure necessary to permit the other client to make an informed decision, the lawyer cannot properly ask the latter to consent. In some cases the alternative to common representation can be that each party may have to obtain separate representation with the possibility of incurring additional costs. The cost benefits of common representation may be considered by the affected client in determining whether common representation is in the client's interests.

Consent Confirmed in Writing

[20] Paragraph (b) requires the lawyer to obtain the informed consent of the client, confirmed in writing. Such a writing may consist of a document executed by the client or one that the lawyer promptly records and transmits to the client following an oral consent. See Rule 1.0(b). See also Rule 1.0(n) (writing includes electronic transmission). If it is not feasible to obtain or transmit the writing at the time the client gives informed consent, then the lawyer must obtain or transmit it within a reasonable time thereafter. See Rule 1.0(b). The requirement of a writing does not supplant the need in most cases for the lawyer to talk with the client, to explain the risks and advantages, if any, of representation burdened with a conflict of interest, as well as reasonably available alternatives, and to afford the client a reasonable opportunity to consider the risks and alternatives and to raise questions and concerns. Rather, the writing is required in order to impress upon clients the seriousness of the decision the client is being asked to make and to avoid disputes or ambiguities that might later occur in the absence of a writing.

Revoking Consent

[21] A client who has given consent to a conflict may revoke the consent and, like any other client, may terminate the lawyer's representation at any time. Whether revoking consent to the client's own representation precludes the lawyer from continuing to represent other clients depends on the circumstances, including the nature of the conflict, whether the client revoked consent because of a material change in circumstances, the reasonable expectations of the other client and whether material detriment to the other clients or the lawyer would result.

Consent to Future Conflict

[22] Whether a lawyer may properly request a client to waive conflicts that might arise in the future is subject to the test of paragraph (b). The effectiveness of such waivers is generally determined by the extent to which the client reasonably understands the material risks that the waiver entails. The more comprehensive the explanation of the types of future representations that might arise and the actual and reasonably foreseeable adverse consequences of those representations, the greater the likelihood that the client will have the requisite understanding. Thus, if the client agrees to consent to a particular type of conflict with which the client is already

familiar, then the consent ordinarily will be effective with regard to that type of conflict. If the consent is general and open-ended, then the consent ordinarily will be ineffective, because it is not reasonably likely that the client will have understood the material risks involved. On the other hand, if the client is an experienced user of the legal services involved and is reasonably informed regarding the risk that an unforeseeable conflict may arise, such consent is more likely to be effective, particularly if, e.g., the client is independently represented by other counsel in giving consent and the consent is limited to future conflicts unrelated to the subject of the representation. In any case, advance consent cannot be effective if the circumstances that materialize in the future are such as would make the conflict nonconsentable under paragraph (b).

Conflicts in Litigation

[7] [23] Paragraph (a) (b)(3) prohibits representation of opposing parties in the same litigation, regardless of the clients' consent. Simultaneous On the other hand, simultaneous representation of parties whose interests in litigation may conflict, such as coplaintiffs or codefendants, is governed by paragraph (b) (a)(2). An impermissible A conflict may exist by reason of substantial discrepancy in the parties' testimony, incompatibility in positions in relation to an opposing party or the fact that there are substantially different possibilities of settlement of the claims or liabilities in question. Such conflicts can arise in criminal cases as well as civil. The potential for conflict of interest in representing multiple defendants in a criminal case is so grave that ordinarily a lawyer should decline to represent more than one codefendant. On the other hand, common representation of persons having similar interests in civil litigation is proper if the risk of adverse effect is minimal and the requirements of paragraph (b) are met. Compare Rule 2.2 involving intermediation between clients.

[8] Ordinarily, a lawyer may not act as advocate against a client the lawyer represents in some other matter, even if the other matter is wholly unrelated. However, there are circumstances in which a lawyer may act as advocate against a client. For example, a lawyer representing an enterprise with diverse operations may accept employment as an advocate against the enterprise in an unrelated matter if doing so will not adversely affect the lawyer's relationship with the enterprise or conduct of the suit and if both clients consent upon consultation. By the same token, government lawyers in some circumstances may represent government employees in proceedings in which a government agency is the opposing party. The propriety of concurrent representation can depend on the nature of the litigation. For example, a suit charging fraud entails conflict to a degree not involved in a suit for a declaratory judgment concerning statutory interpretation.

[9] A lawyer may represent parties having antagonistic positions on a legal question that has arisen in different cases, unless representation of either client would be adversely affected. Thus, it is ordinarily not improper to

~~assert such positions in cases pending in different trial courts, but it may be improper to do so in cases pending at the same time in an appellate court.~~

[24]   Ordinarily a lawyer may take inconsistent legal positions in different tribunals at different times on behalf of different clients. The mere fact that advocating a legal position on behalf of one client might create precedent adverse to the interests of a client represented by the lawyer in an unrelated matter does not create a conflict of interest. A conflict of interest exists, however, if there is a significant risk that a lawyer's action on behalf of one client will materially limit the lawyer's effectiveness in representing another client in a different case; for example, when a decision favoring one client will create a precedent likely to seriously weaken the position taken on behalf of the other client. Factors relevant in determining whether the clients need to be advised of the risk include: where the cases are pending, whether the issue is substantive or procedural, the temporal relationship between the matters, the significance of the issue to the immediate and long-term interests of the clients involved and the clients' reasonable expectations in retaining the lawyer. If there is significant risk of material limitation, then absent informed consent of the affected clients, the lawyer must refuse one of the representations or withdraw from one or both matters.

[25]   When a lawyer represents or seeks to represent a class of plaintiffs or defendants in a class-action lawsuit, unnamed members of the class are ordinarily not considered to be clients of the lawyer for purposes of applying paragraph (a)(1) of this Rule. Thus, the lawyer does not typically need to get the consent of such a person before representing a client suing the person in an unrelated matter. Similarly, a lawyer seeking to represent an opponent in a class action does not typically need the consent of an unnamed member of the class whom the lawyer represents in an unrelated matter.

~~Other Conflict Situations~~ Nonlitigation Conflicts

~~[11]~~ [26] Conflicts of interest under paragraphs (a)(1) and (a)(2) arise in contexts other than litigation ~~sometimes may be difficult to assess~~. For a discussion of directly adverse conflicts in transactional matters, see Comment [7]. Relevant factors in determining whether there is significant potential for ~~adverse effect~~ material limitation include the duration and intimacy of the lawyer's relationship with the client or clients involved, the functions being performed by the lawyer, the likelihood that ~~actual conflict~~ disagreements will arise and the likely prejudice to the client from the conflict ~~if it does arise~~. The question is often one of proximity and degree. See Comment [8].

~~[13]~~ [27] ~~Conflict~~ For example, conflict questions may ~~also~~ arise in estate planning and estate administration. A lawyer may be called upon to prepare wills for several family members, such as husband and wife, and, depending upon the circumstances, a conflict of interest may ~~arise~~ be present. In estate administration the identity of the client may be unclear under the law of a particular jurisdiction. Under one view, the client is the fiduciary; under another view the client is the estate or trust, including its beneficiaries. ~~The~~

In order to comply with conflict of interest rules, the lawyer should make clear the lawyer's relationship to the parties involved.

[12] [28] Whether a conflict is consentable depends on the circumstances. For example, a lawyer may not represent multiple parties to a negotiation whose interests are fundamentally antagonistic to each other, but common representation is permissible where the clients are generally aligned in interest even though there is some difference in interest among them. Thus, a lawyer may seek to establish or adjust a relationship between clients on an amicable and mutually advantageous basis; for example, in helping to organize a business in which two or more clients are entrepreneurs, working out the financial reorganization of an enterprise in which two or more clients have an interest or arranging a property distribution in settlement of an estate. The lawyer seeks to resolve potentially adverse interests by developing the parties' mutual interests. Otherwise, each party might have to obtain separate representation, with the possibility of incurring additional cost, complication or even litigation. Given these and other relevant factors, the clients may prefer that the lawyer act for all of them.

Special Considerations in Common Representation

[29] In considering whether to represent multiple clients in the same matter, a lawyer should be mindful that if the common representation fails because the potentially adverse interests cannot be reconciled, the result can be additional cost, embarrassment and recrimination. Ordinarily, the lawyer will be forced to withdraw from representing all of the clients if the common representation fails. In some situations, the risk of failure is so great that multiple representation is plainly impossible. For example, a lawyer cannot undertake common representation of clients where contentious litigation or negotiations between them are imminent or contemplated. Moreover, because the lawyer is required to be impartial between commonly represented clients, representation of multiple clients is improper when it is unlikely that impartiality can be maintained. Generally, if the relationship between the parties has already assumed antagonism, the possibility that the clients' interests can be adequately served by common representation is not very good. Other relevant factors are whether the lawyer subsequently will represent both parties on a continuing basis and whether the situation involves creating or terminating a relationship between the parties.

[30] A particularly important factor in determining the appropriateness of common representation is the effect on client-lawyer confidentiality and the attorney-client privilege. With regard to the attorney-client privilege, the prevailing rule is that, as between commonly represented clients, the privilege does not attach. Hence, it must be assumed that if litigation eventuates between the clients, the privilege will not protect any such communications, and the clients should be so advised.

[31] As to the duty of confidentiality, continued common representation will almost certainly be inadequate if one client attempts to keep something in confidence between the lawyer and that client, which is not to be disclosed to

the other client. This is so because the lawyer has an equal duty of loyalty to each client, and each client has the right to be informed of anything bearing on the representation that might affect that client's interests and the right to expect that the lawyer will use that information to that client's benefit. See Rule 1.4. The lawyer should, at the outset of the common representation and as part of the process of obtaining each client's informed consent, advise each client that information will be shared and that the lawyer will have to withdraw if one client decides that some matter material to the representation should be kept from the other. In limited circumstances, it may be appropriate for the lawyer to proceed with the representation when the clients have agreed, after being properly informed, that the lawyer will keep certain information confidential. For example, the lawyer may reasonably conclude that failure to disclose one client's trade secrets to another client will not adversely affect representation involving a joint venture between the clients and agree to keep that information confidential with the informed consent of both clients.

[32] When seeking to establish or adjust a relationship between clients, the lawyer should make clear that the lawyer's role is not that of partisanship normally expected in other circumstances and, thus, that the clients may be required to assume greater responsibility for decisions than when each client is separately represented. Any limitations on the scope of the representation made necessary as a result of the common representation should be fully explained to the clients at the outset of the representation. See Rule 1.2(c).

[33] Subject to the above limitations, each client in the common representation has the right to loyal and diligent representation and the protection of Rule 1.9 concerning the obligations to a former client. The client also has the right to discharge the lawyer as stated in Rule 1.16.

Organizational Clients

[34] A lawyer who represents a corporation or other organization does not, by virtue of that representation, necessarily represent any constituent or affiliated organization, such as a parent or subsidiary. See Rule 1.13(a). Thus, the lawyer for an organization is not barred from accepting representation adverse to an affiliate in an unrelated matter, unless the circumstances are such that the affiliate should also be considered a client of the lawyer, there is an understanding between the lawyer and the organizational client that the lawyer will avoid representation adverse to the client's affiliates, or the lawyer's obligations to either the organizational client or the new client are likely to limit materially the lawyer's representation of the other client.

[14] [35] A lawyer for a corporation or other organization who is also a member of its board of directors should determine whether the responsibilities of the two roles may conflict. The lawyer may be called on to advise the corporation in matters involving actions of the directors. Consideration should be given to the frequency with which such situations may arise, the potential intensity of the conflict, the effect of the lawyer's resignation from the board and the possibility of the corporation's obtaining legal advice from another

lawyer in such situations. If there is material risk that the dual role will compromise the lawyer's independence of professional judgment, the lawyer should not serve as a director <u>or should cease to act as the corporation's lawyer when conflicts of interest arise</u>. The lawyer should advise the other <u>members of the board that in some circumstances matters discussed at board meetings while the lawyer is present in the capacity of director might not be protected by the attorney-client privilege and that conflict of interest considerations might require the lawyer's recusal as a director or might require the lawyer and the lawyer's firm to decline representation of the corporation in a matter.</u>

~~Conflict Charged by an Opposing Party~~

~~[15] Resolving questions of conflict of interest is primarily the responsibility of the lawyer undertaking the representation. In litigation, a court may raise the question when there is reason to infer that the lawyer has neglected the responsibility. In a criminal case, inquiry by the court is generally required when a lawyer represents multiple defendants. Where the conflict is such as clearly to call in question the fair or efficient administration of justice, opposing counsel may properly raise the question. Such an objection should be viewed with caution, however, for it can be misused as a technique of harassment. See Scope.~~

RULE 1.8: CONFLICT OF INTEREST: ~~PROHIBITED TRANSACTIONS~~ CURRENT CLIENTS: SPECIFIC RULES

(a) A lawyer shall not enter into a business transaction with a client or knowingly acquire an ownership, possessory, security or other pecuniary interest adverse to a client unless:

(1) the transaction and terms on which the lawyer acquires the interest are fair and reasonable to the client and are fully disclosed and transmitted in writing ~~to the client~~ in a manner ~~which~~ <u>that</u> can be reasonably understood by the client;

(2) the client is <u>advised in writing of the desirability of seeking and is</u> given a reasonable opportunity to seek the advice of independent <u>legal</u> counsel ~~in~~ <u>on</u> the transaction; and

(3) the client ~~consents~~ <u>gives informed consent, in a writing</u> ~~thereto~~ <u>signed by the client, to the essential terms of the transaction and the lawyer's role in the transaction, including whether the lawyer is representing the client in the transaction.</u>

(b) A lawyer shall not use information relating to representation of a client to the disadvantage of the client unless the client ~~consents after consultation~~ <u>gives informed consent</u>, except as permitted or required by ~~Rule 1.6 or Rule 3.3~~ <u>these Rules.</u>

(c) A lawyer shall not ~~solicit any substantial gift from a client,~~ including a testamentary gift, or prepare ~~on behalf of a client~~ an instrument giving the lawyer or a person related to the lawyer ~~as parent, child, sibling, or spouse~~ any substantial gift ~~from a client, including a testamentary~~ unless the lawyer or other recipient of the gift, ~~except where the client~~ is related to the ~~donee~~ client. For purposes of this paragraph, related persons include a spouse, child, grandchild, parent, grandparent or other relative or individual with whom the lawyer or the client maintains a close, familial relationship.

(d) Prior to the conclusion of representation of a client, a lawyer shall not make or negotiate an agreement giving the lawyer literary or media rights to a portrayal or account based in substantial part on information relating to the representation.

(e) A lawyer shall not provide financial assistance to a client in connection with pending or contemplated litigation, except that:

(1) a lawyer may advance court costs and expenses of litigation, the repayment of which may be contingent on the outcome of the matter; and

(2) a lawyer representing an indigent client may pay court costs and expenses of litigation on behalf of the client.

(f) A lawyer shall not accept compensation for representing a client from one other than the client unless:

(1) the client ~~consents after consultation~~ gives informed consent;

(2) there is no interference with the lawyer's independence of professional judgment or with the client-lawyer relationship; and

(3) information relating to representation of a client is protected as required by Rule 1.6.

(g) A lawyer who represents two or more clients shall not participate in making an aggregate settlement of the claims of or against the clients, or in a criminal case an aggregated agreement as to guilty or nolo contendere pleas, unless each client ~~consents after consultation, including~~ gives informed consent, in a writing signed by the client. The lawyer's disclosure ~~of~~ shall include the existence and nature of all the claims or pleas involved and of the participation of each person in the settlement.

(h) A lawyer shall not:

(1) make an agreement prospectively limiting the lawyer's liability to a client for malpractice unless ~~permitted by law and~~ the client is independently represented in making the agreement~~,~~; or

(2) settle a claim ~~or potential claim~~ for such liability with an unrepresented client or former client ~~without first advising~~ unless that person is advised in writing ~~that~~ of the desirability of seeking and is given a reasonable opportunity to seek the advice of independent ~~representation is appropriate~~ legal counsel in connection therewith.

~~(i) A lawyer related to another lawyer as parent, child, sibling or spouse shall not represent a client in a representation directly adverse to a person whom the lawyer knows is represented by the other lawyer except upon consent by the client after consultation regarding the relationship.~~

~~(j)~~ (i) A lawyer shall not acquire a proprietary interest in the cause of action or subject matter of litigation the lawyer is conducting for a client, except that the lawyer may:

(1) acquire a lien ~~granted~~ authorized by law to secure the lawyer's fee or expenses; and

(2) contract with a client for a reasonable contingent fee in a civil case.

(j) A lawyer shall not have sexual relations with a client unless a consensual sexual relationship existed between them when the client-lawyer relationship commenced.

(k) While lawyers are associated in a firm, a prohibition in the foregoing paragraphs (a) through (i) that applies to any one of them shall apply to all of them.

Comment

Business Transactions Between Client and Lawyer

[1] ~~As a general principle, all transactions between client and lawyer should be fair and reasonable to the client. In such transactions a review by independent counsel on behalf of the client is often advisable. Furthermore, a lawyer may not exploit information relating to the representation to the client's disadvantage. For example, a lawyer who has learned that the client is investing in specific real estate may not, without the client's consent, seek to acquire nearby property where doing so would adversely affect the client's plan for investment. Paragraph (a)~~ A lawyer's legal skill and training, together with the relationship of trust and confidence between lawyer and client, create the possibility of overreaching when the lawyer participates in a business, property or financial transaction with a client, for example, a loan or sales transaction or a lawyer investment on behalf of a client. The requirements of paragraph (a) must be met even when the transaction is not closely related to the subject matter of the representation, as when a lawyer drafting a will for a client learns that the client needs money for unrelated expenses and offers to make a loan to the client. The Rule applies to lawyers engaged in the sale of goods or services related to the practice of law, for example, the sale of title insurance or investment services to existing clients of the lawyer's

legal practice. See Rule 5.7. It also applies to lawyers purchasing property from estates they represent. It does not apply to ordinary fee arrangements between client and lawyer, which are governed by Rule 1.5, although its requirements must be met when the lawyer accepts an interest in the client's business or other nonmonetary property as payment of all or part of a fee. In addition, the Rule does not, however, apply to standard commercial transactions between the lawyer and the client for products or services that the client generally markets to others, for example, banking or brokerage services, medical services, products manufactured or distributed by the client, and utilities' services. In such transactions, the lawyer has no advantage in dealing with the client, and the restrictions in paragraph (a) are unnecessary and impracticable.

[2] Paragraph (a)(1) requires that the transaction itself be fair to the client and that its essential terms be communicated to the client, in writing, in a manner that can be reasonably understood. Paragraph (a)(2) requires that the client also be advised, in writing, of the desirability of seeking the advice of independent legal counsel. It also requires that the client be given a reasonable opportunity to obtain such advice. Paragraph (a)(3) requires that the lawyer obtain the client's informed consent, in a writing signed by the client, both to the essential terms of the transaction and to the lawyer's role. When necessary, the lawyer should discuss both the material risks of the proposed transaction, including any risk presented by the lawyer's involvement, and the existence of reasonably available alternatives and should explain why the advice of independent legal counsel is desirable. See Rule 1.0(e) (definition of informed consent).

[3] The risk to a client is greatest when the client expects the lawyer to represent the client in the transaction itself or when the lawyer's financial interest otherwise poses a significant risk that the lawyer's representation of the client will be materially limited by the lawyer's financial interest in the transaction. Here the lawyer's role requires that the lawyer must comply, not only with the requirements of paragraph (a), but also with the requirements of Rule 1.7. Under that Rule, the lawyer must disclose the risks associated with the lawyer's dual role as both legal adviser and participant in the transaction, such as the risk that the lawyer will structure the transaction or give legal advice in a way that favors the lawyer's interests at the expense of the client. Moreover, the lawyer must obtain the client's informed consent. In some cases, the lawyer's interest may be such that Rule 1.7 will preclude the lawyer from seeking the client's consent to the transaction.

[4] If the client is independently represented in the transaction, paragraph (a)(2) of this Rule is inapplicable, and the paragraph (a)(1) requirement for full disclosure is satisfied either by a written disclosure by the lawyer involved in the transaction or by the client's independent counsel. The fact that the client was independently represented in the transaction is relevant in determining whether the agreement was fair and reasonable to the client as paragraph (a)(1) further requires.

Use of Information Related to Representation

[5]   Use of information relating to the representation to the disadvantage of the client violates the lawyer's duty of loyalty. Paragraph (b) applies when the information is used to benefit either the lawyer or a third person, such as another client or business associate of the lawyer. For example, if a lawyer learns that a client intends to purchase and develop several parcels of land, the lawyer may not use that information to purchase one of the parcels in competition with the client or to recommend that another client make such a purchase. The Rule does not prohibit uses that do not disadvantage the client. For example, a lawyer who learns a government agency's interpretation of trade legislation during the representation of one client may properly use that information to benefit other clients. Paragraph (b) prohibits disadvantageous use of client information unless the client gives informed consent, except as permitted or required by these Rules. See Rules 1.2(d), 1.6, 1.9(c), 3.3, 4.1(b), 8.1 and 8.3.

Gifts to Lawyers

[2] [6] A lawyer may accept a gift from a client, if the transaction meets general standards of fairness. For example, a simple gift such as a present given at a holiday or as a token of appreciation is permitted. If a client offers the lawyer a more substantial gift, paragraph (c) does not prohibit the lawyer from accepting it, although such a gift may be voidable by the client under the doctrine of undue influence, which treats client gifts as presumptively fraudulent. In any event, due to concerns about overreaching and imposition on clients, a lawyer may not suggest that a substantial gift be made to the lawyer or for the lawyer's benefit, except where the lawyer is related to the client as set forth in paragraph (c).

[7]   If effectuation of a substantial gift requires preparing a legal instrument such as a will or conveyance, however, the client should have the detached advice that another lawyer can provide. Paragraph (c) recognizes an The sole exception to this Rule is where the client is a relative of the donee or the gift is not substantial.

[8]   This Rule does not prohibit a lawyer from seeking to have the lawyer or a partner or associate of the lawyer named as executor of the client's estate or to another potentially lucrative fiduciary position. Nevertheless, such appointments will be subject to the general conflict of interest provision in Rule 1.7 when there is a significant risk that the lawyer's interest in obtaining the appointment will materially limit the lawyer's independent professional judgment in advising the client concerning the choice of an executor or other fiduciary. In obtaining the client's informed consent to the conflict, the lawyer should advise the client concerning the nature and extent of the lawyer's financial interest in the appointment, as well as the availability of alternative candidates for the position.

Literary Rights

[3] [9] An agreement by which a lawyer acquires literary or media rights concerning the conduct of the representation creates a conflict between the interests of the client and the personal interests of the lawyer. Measures suitable in the representation of the client may detract from the publication value of an account of the representation. Paragraph (d) does not prohibit a lawyer representing a client in a transaction concerning literary property from agreeing that the lawyer's fee shall consist of a share in ownership in the property, if the arrangement conforms to Rule 1.5 and ~~paragraph (j)~~ paragraphs (a) and (i).

Financial Assistance

[10]   Lawyers may not subsidize lawsuits or administrative proceedings brought on behalf of their clients, including making or guaranteeing loans to their clients for living expenses, because to do so would encourage clients to pursue lawsuits that might not otherwise be brought and because such assistance gives lawyers too great a financial stake in the litigation. These dangers do not warrant a prohibition on a lawyer lending a client court costs and litigation expenses, including the expenses of medical examination and the costs of obtaining and presenting evidence, because these advances are virtually indistinguishable from contingent fees and help ensure access to the courts. Similarly, an exception allowing lawyers representing indigent clients to pay court costs and litigation expenses regardless of whether these funds will be repaid is warranted.

Person Paying for a Lawyer's Services

~~[4]   Paragraph (f) requires disclosure of the fact that the lawyer's services are being paid for by a third party. Such an arrangement must also conform to the requirements of Rule 1.6 concerning confidentiality and Rule 1.7 concerning conflict of interest. Where the client is a class, consent may be obtained on behalf of the class by court-supervised procedure.~~

[11]   Lawyers are frequently asked to represent a client under circumstances in which a third person will compensate the lawyer, in whole or in part. The third person might be a relative or friend, an indemnitor (such as a liability insurance company) or a co-client (such as a corporation sued along with one or more of its employees). Because third-party payers frequently have interests that differ from those of the client, including interests in minimizing the amount spent on the representation and in learning how the representation is progressing, lawyers are prohibited from accepting or continuing such representations unless the lawyer determines that there will be no interference with the lawyer's independent professional judgment and there is informed consent from the client. See also Rule 5.4(c) (prohibiting interference with a lawyer's professional judgment by one who recommends, employs or pays the lawyer to render legal services for another).

[12]   Sometimes, it will be sufficient for the lawyer to obtain the client's informed consent regarding the fact of the payment and the identity of the

third-party payer. If, however, the fee arrangement creates a conflict of interest for the lawyer, then the lawyer must comply with Rule. 1.7. The lawyer must also conform to the requirements of Rule 1.6 concerning confidentiality. Under Rule 1.7(a), a conflict of interest exists if there is significant risk that the lawyer's representation of the client will be materially limited by the lawyer's own interest in the fee arrangement or by the lawyer's responsibilities to the third-party payer (for example, when the third-party payer is a co-client). Under Rule 1.7(b), the lawyer may accept or continue the representation with the informed consent of each affected client, unless the conflict is nonconsentable under that paragraph. Under Rule 1.7(b), the informed consent must be confirmed in writing.

Aggregate Settlements

[13]   Differences in willingness to make or accept an offer of settlement are among the risks of common representation of multiple clients by a single lawyer. Under Rule 1.7, this is one of the risks that should be discussed before undertaking the representation, as part of the process of obtaining the clients' informed consent. In addition, Rule 1.2(a) protects each client's right to have the final say in deciding whether to accept or reject an offer of settlement and in deciding whether to enter a guilty or nolo contendere plea in a criminal case. The rule stated in this paragraph is a corollary of both these Rules and provides that, before any settlement offer or plea bargain is made or accepted on behalf of multiple clients, the lawyer must inform each of them about all the material terms of the settlement, including what the other clients will receive or pay if the settlement or plea offer is accepted. See also Rule 1.0(e) (definition of informed consent). Lawyers representing a class of plaintiffs or defendants, or those proceeding derivatively, may not have a full client-lawyer relationship with each member of the class; nevertheless, such lawyers must comply with applicable rules regulating notification of class members and other procedural requirements designed to ensure adequate protection of the entire class.

Limiting Liability and Settling Malpractice Claims

[5]   Paragraph (h) is not intended to apply to customary qualifications and limitations in legal opinions and memoranda.

[14]   Agreements prospectively limiting a lawyer's liability for malpractice are prohibited unless the client is independently represented in making the agreement because they are likely to undermine competent and diligent representation. Also, many clients are unable to evaluate the desirability of making such an agreement before a dispute has arisen, particularly if they are then represented by the lawyer seeking the agreement. This paragraph does not, however, prohibit a lawyer from entering into an agreement with the client to arbitrate legal malpractice claims, provided such agreements are enforceable and the client is fully informed of the scope and effect of the agreement. Nor does this paragraph limit the ability of lawyers to practice in the form of a limited-liability entity, where permitted by law, provided that

each lawyer remains personally liable to the client for his or her own conduct and the firm complies with any conditions required by law, such as provisions requiring client notification or maintenance of adequate liability insurance. Nor does it prohibit an agreement in accordance with Rule 1.2 that defines the scope of the representation, although a definition of scope that makes the obligations of representation illusory will amount to an attempt to limit liability.

[15] Agreements settling a claim or a potential claim for malpractice are not prohibited by this Rule. Nevertheless, in view of the danger that a lawyer will take unfair advantage of an unrepresented client or former client, the lawyer must first advise such a person in writing of the appropriateness of independent representation in connection with such a settlement. In addition, the lawyer must give the client or former client a reasonable opportunity to find and consult independent counsel.

~~Family Relationships Between Lawyers~~

~~[6] Paragraph (i) applies to related lawyers who are in different firms. Related lawyers in the same firm are governed by Rules 1.7, 1.9, and 1.10. The disqualification stated in paragraph (i) is personal and is not imputed to members of firms with whom the lawyers are associated.~~

~~Acquisition of~~ Acquiring Proprietary Interest in Litigation

~~[7]~~ [16] Paragraph ~~(j)~~ (i) states the traditional general rule that lawyers are prohibited from acquiring a proprietary interest in litigation. ~~This~~ Like paragraph (e), the general rule~~, which~~ has its basis in common law champerty and maintenance~~,~~ and is designed to avoid giving the lawyer too great an interest in the representation. In addition, when the lawyer acquires an ownership interest in the subject of the representation, it will be more difficult for a client to discharge the lawyer if the client so desires. The Rule is subject to specific exceptions developed in decisional law and continued in these Rules~~, such as the exception for reasonable contingent fees set forth in Rule 1.5 and the exception for certain advances of the costs of litigation set forth in paragraph (e)~~. The exception for certain advances of the costs of litigation is set forth in paragraph (e). In addition, paragraph (i) sets forth exceptions for liens authorized by law to secure the lawyer's fees or expenses and contracts for reasonable contingent fees. The law of each jurisdiction determines which liens are authorized by law. These may include liens granted by statute, liens originating in common law and liens acquired by contract with the client. When a lawyer acquires by contract a security interest in property other than that recovered through the lawyer's efforts in the litigation, such an acquisition is a business or financial transaction with a client and is governed by the requirements of paragraph (a). Contracts for contingent fees in civil cases are governed by Rule 1.5.

Client-Lawyer Sexual Relationships

[17] The relationship between lawyer and client is a fiduciary one in which the lawyer occupies the highest position of trust and confidence. The

relationship is almost always unequal; thus, a sexual relationship between lawyer and client can involve unfair exploitation of the lawyer's fiduciary role, in violation of the lawyer's basic ethical obligation not to use the trust of the client to the client's disadvantage. In addition, such a relationship presents a significant danger that, because of the lawyer's emotional involvement, the lawyer will be unable to represent the client without impairment of the exercise of independent professional judgment. Moreover, a blurred line between the professional and personal relationships may make it difficult to predict to what extent client confidences will be protected by the attorney-client evidentiary privilege, since client confidences are protected by privilege only when they are imparted in the context of the client-lawyer relationship. Because of the significant danger of harm to client interests and because the client's own emotional involvement renders it unlikely that the client could give adequate informed consent, this Rule prohibits the lawyer from having sexual relations with a client regardless of whether the relationship is consensual and regardless of the absence of prejudice to the client.

[18]   Sexual relationships that predate the client-lawyer relationship are not prohibited. Issues relating to the exploitation of the fiduciary relationship and client dependency are diminished when the sexual relationship existed prior to the commencement of the client-lawyer relationship. However, before proceeding with the representation in these circumstances, the lawyer should consider whether the lawyer's ability to represent the client will be materially limited by the relationship. See Rule 1.7(a)(2).

[19]   When the client is an organization, paragraph (j) of this Rule prohibits a lawyer for the organization (whether inside counsel or outside counsel) from having a sexual relationship with a constituent of the organization who supervises, directs or regularly consults with that lawyer concerning the organization's legal matters.

Imputation of Prohibitions

[20]   Under paragraph (k), a prohibition on conduct by an individual lawyer in paragraphs (a) through (i) also applies to all lawyers associated in a firm with the personally prohibited lawyer. For example, one lawyer in a firm may not enter into a business transaction with a client of another member of the firm without complying with paragraph (a), even if the first lawyer is not personally involved in the representation of the client. The prohibition set forth in paragraph (j) is personal and is not applied to associated lawyers.

RULE 1.9: ~~CONFLICT OF INTEREST:~~ DUTIES TO FORMER ~~CLIENT~~ CLIENTS

(a) A lawyer who has formerly represented a client in a matter shall not thereafter represent another person in the same or a substantially related matter in which that person's interests are materially adverse to the interests of the former client unless the former client ~~consents after consultation~~ gives informed consent, confirmed in writing.

51

(b) A lawyer shall not knowingly represent a person in the same or a substantially related matter in which a firm with which the lawyer formerly was associated had previously represented a client

(1) whose interests are materially adverse to that person; and

(2) about whom the lawyer had acquired information protected by Rules 1.6 and 1.9(c) that is material to the matter;

unless the former client ~~consents after consultation~~ gives informed consent, confirmed in writing.

(c) A lawyer who has formerly represented a client in a matter or whose present or former firm has formerly represented a client in a matter shall not thereafter:

(1) use information relating to the representation to the disadvantage of the former client except as ~~Rule 1.6 or Rule 3.3~~ these Rules would permit or require with respect to a client, or when the information has become generally known; or

(2) reveal information relating to the representation except as ~~Rule 1.6 or Rule 3.3~~ these Rules would permit or require with respect to a client.

Comment

[1]   After termination of a client-lawyer relationship, a lawyer has certain continuing duties with respect to confidentiality and conflicts of interest and thus may not represent another client except in conformity with this Rule. ~~The principles in Rule 1.7 determine whether the interests of the present and former client are adverse. Thus~~ Under this Rule, for example, a lawyer could not properly seek to rescind on behalf of a new client a contract drafted on behalf of the former client. So also a lawyer who has prosecuted an accused person could not properly represent the accused in a subsequent civil action against the government concerning the same transaction. Nor could a lawyer who has represented multiple clients in a matter represent one of the clients against the others in the same or a substantially related matter after a dispute arose among the clients, unless all affected clients give informed consent. See Comment [9]. Current and former government lawyers must comply with this Rule to the extent required by Rule 1.11.

[2]   The scope of a "matter" for purposes of this Rule may depend on the facts of a particular situation or transaction. The lawyer's involvement in a matter can also be a question of degree. When a lawyer has been directly involved in a specific transaction, subsequent representation of other clients with materially adverse interests clearly is prohibited. On the other hand, a lawyer who recurrently handled a type of problem for a former client is not precluded from later representing another client in a wholly distinct problem of that type even though the subsequent representation involves a position adverse to the prior client. Similar considerations can apply to the reassign-

ment of military lawyers between defense and prosecution functions within the same military jurisdictions. The underlying question is whether the lawyer was so involved in the matter that the subsequent representation can be justly regarded as a changing of sides in the matter in question.

[3] Matters are "substantially related" for purposes of this Rule if they involve the same subject matter or if there otherwise is a substantial risk that confidential information as would normally have been obtained in the prior representation would materially advance the client's position in the subsequent matter. For example, a lawyer who has represented a businessperson and learned extensive private financial information about that person may not then represent that person's spouse in seeking a divorce. Similarly, a lawyer who has previously represented a client in securing environmental permits to build a shopping center would be precluded from representing neighbors seeking to oppose rezoning of the property but would not be precluded, on the grounds of substantial relationship, from defending a tenant of the completed shopping center in resisting eviction for nonpayment of rent. Information that has been disclosed to the public or to other parties adverse to the former client ordinarily will not be disqualifying. Information acquired in a prior representation may have been rendered obsolete by the passage of time, a circumstance that may be relevant in determining whether two representations are substantially related. In the case of an organizational client, general knowledge of the client's policies and practices ordinarily will not preclude a subsequent representation; on the other hand, knowledge of specific facts gained in a prior representation that are relevant to the matter in question ordinarily will preclude such representation. A former client is not required to reveal the confidential information learned by the lawyer in order to establish a substantial risk that the lawyer has confidential information to use in the subsequent matter. A conclusion about the possession of such information may be based on the general nature of the services the lawyer provided the former client and information that would in ordinary practice be learned by a lawyer providing such services.

Lawyers Moving Between Firms

[3] [4] When lawyers have been associated within a firm but then end their association, the question of whether a lawyer should undertake representation is more complicated. There are several competing considerations. First, the client previously represented by the former firm must be reasonably assured that the principle of loyalty to the client is not compromised. Second, the rule should not be so broadly cast as to preclude other persons from having reasonable choice of legal counsel. Third, the rule should not unreasonably hamper lawyers from forming new associations and taking on new clients after having left a previous association. In this connection, it should be recognized that today many lawyers practice in firms, that many lawyers to some degree limit their practice to one field or another, and that many move from one association to another several times in their careers. If the concept of imputation were applied with unqualified rigor, the result would be radical

curtailment of the opportunity of lawyers to move from one practice setting to another and of the opportunity of clients to change counsel.

[4] ~~Reconciliation of these competing principles in the past has been attempted under two rubrics. One approach has been to seek per se rules of disqualification. For example, it has been held that a partner in a law firm is conclusively presumed to have access to all confidences concerning all clients of the firm. Under this analysis, if a lawyer has been a partner in one law firm and then becomes a partner in another law firm, there may be a presumption that all confidences known by the partner in the first firm are known to all partners in the second firm. This presumption might properly be applied in some circumstances, especially where the client has been extensively represented, but may be unrealistic where the client was represented only for limited purposes. Furthermore, such a rigid rule exaggerates the difference between a partner and an associate in modern law firms.~~

[5] ~~The other rubric formerly used for dealing with disqualification is the appearance of impropriety proscribed in Canon 9 of the ABA Model Code of Professional Responsibility. This rubric has a two-fold problem. First, the appearance of impropriety can be taken to include any new client-lawyer relationship that might make a former client feel anxious. If that meaning were adopted, disqualification would become little more than a question of subjective judgment by the former client. Second, since "impropriety" is undefined, the term "appearance of impropriety" is question-begging. It therefore has to be recognized that the problem of disqualification cannot be properly resolved either by simple analogy to a lawyer practicing alone or by the very general concept of appearance of impropriety.~~

~~Confidentiality~~

[~~8~~] [5] Paragraph (b) operates to disqualify the lawyer only when the lawyer involved has actual knowledge of information protected by Rules 1.6 and 1.9~~(b)~~(c). Thus, if a lawyer while with one firm acquired no knowledge or information relating to a particular client of the firm, and that lawyer later joined another firm, neither the lawyer individually nor the second firm is disqualified from representing another client in the same or a related matter even though the interests of the two clients conflict. See Rule 1.10(b) for the restrictions on a firm once a lawyer has terminated association with the firm.

[6] ~~Preserving confidentiality is a question of access to information. Access to information, in turn, is essentially a question of fact in~~ Application of paragraph (b) depends on a situation's particular ~~circumstances~~ facts, aided by inferences, deductions or working presumptions that reasonably may be made about the way in which lawyers work together. A lawyer may have general access to files of all clients of a law firm and may regularly participate in discussions of their affairs; it should be inferred that such a lawyer in fact is privy to all information about all the firm's clients. In contrast, another lawyer may have access to the files of only a limited number of clients and participate in discussions of the affairs of no other clients; in the absence of information to the contrary, it should be inferred that such a lawyer in fact is

privy to information about the clients actually served but not those of other clients. In such an inquiry, the burden of proof should rest upon the firm whose disqualification is sought.

[7] Application of paragraph (b) depends on a situation's particular facts. In such an inquiry, the burden of proof should rest upon the firm whose disqualification is sought.

[9] [7] Independent of the question of disqualification of a firm, a lawyer changing professional association has a continuing duty to preserve confidentiality of information about a client formerly represented. See Rules 1.6 and 1.9(c).

Adverse Positions

[10] The second aspect of loyalty to a client is the lawyer's obligation to decline subsequent representations involving positions adverse to a former client arising in substantially related matters. This obligation requires abstention from adverse representation by the individual lawyer involved, but does not properly entail abstention of other lawyers through imputed disqualification. Hence, this aspect of the problem is governed by Rule 1.9(a). Thus, if a lawyer left one firm for another, the new affiliation would not preclude the firms involved from continuing to represent clients with adverse interests in the same or related matters, so long as the conditions of paragraphs (b) and (c) concerning confidentiality have been met.

[11] [8] Information Paragraph (c) provides that information acquired by the lawyer in the course of representing a client may not subsequently be used or revealed by the lawyer to the disadvantage of the client. However, the fact that a lawyer has once served a client does not preclude the lawyer from using generally known information about that client when later representing another client.

[12] [9] Disqualification from subsequent representation is The provisions of this Rule are for the protection of former clients and can be waived by them. A waiver is effective only if there is disclosure of the circumstances, including the lawyer's intended role in behalf of the new client if the client gives informed consent, which consent must be confirmed in writing under paragraphs (a) and (b). See Rule 1.0(e). [13] With regard to an opposing party's raising a question of conflict of interest the effectiveness of an advance waiver, see Comment [22] to Rule 1.7. With regard to disqualification of a firm with which a lawyer is or was formerly associated, see Rule 1.10.

RULE 1.10: IMPUTED DISQUALIFICATION IMPUTATION OF CONFLICTS OF INTEREST: GENERAL RULE*

(a) While lawyers are associated in a firm, none of them shall knowingly represent a client when any one of them practicing alone

---

* Editors' note: As proposed by the Ethics 2000 Commission to the ABA House of Delegates in August 2001, Rule 1.10 had an additional subsection that read as follows:

would be prohibited from doing so by Rules 1.7, ~~1.8(c),~~ or 1.9 ~~or 2.2,~~ unless the prohibition is based on a personal interest of the prohibited lawyer and does not present a significant risk of materially limiting the representation of the client by the remaining lawyers in the firm.

(b) When a lawyer has terminated an association with a firm, the firm is not prohibited from thereafter representing a person with interests materially adverse to those of a client represented by the formerly associated lawyer and not currently represented by the firm, unless:

(1) the matter is the same or substantially related to that in which the formerly associated lawyer represented the client; and

(2) any lawyer remaining in the firm has information protected by Rules 1.6 and 1.9(c) that is material to the matter.

(c) A disqualification prescribed by this rule may be waived by the affected client under the conditions stated in Rule 1.7.

(d) The disqualification of lawyers associated in a firm with former or current government lawyers is governed by Rule 1.11.

Comment
Definition of "Firm"

[1] For purposes of the Rules of Professional Conduct, the term "firm" ~~includes~~ denotes lawyers in a ~~private firm, and~~ law partnership, professional corporation, sole proprietorship or other association, or in a legal services organization; or lawyers in the legal department of a corporation or other organization~~, or in a legal services organization~~. See Rule 1.0(c). Whether two or more lawyers constitute a firm within this definition can depend on the specific facts. ~~For example, two practitioners who share office space and~~

(c) When a lawyer becomes associated with a firm, no lawyer associated in the firm shall knowingly represent a person in a matter in which that lawyer is disqualified under Rule 1.9 unless:

(1) the personally disqualified lawyer is timely screened from any participation in the matter and is apportioned no part of the fee therefrom; and

(2) written notice is promptly given to any affected former client to enable it to ascertain compliance with the provisions of this Rule.

In addition, three comments that explained this provision read:

[6] Where the conditions of paragraph (c) are met, imputation is removed, and consent to the new representation is not required. Lawyers should be aware, however, that courts may impose more stringent obligations in ruling upon motions to disqualify a lawyer from pending litigation.

[7] Requirements for screening procedures are stated in Rule 1.0(k). Paragraph (c)(2) does not prohibit the screened lawyer from receiving a salary or partnership share established by prior independent agreement, but that lawyer may not receive compensation directly related to the matter in which the lawyer is disqualified.

[8] Notice, including a description of the screened lawyer's prior representation and of the screening procedures employed, generally should be given as soon as practicable after the need for screening becomes apparent.

The ABA House of Delegates, deleted this possibility of screening from Rule 1.10 before adopting the remaining provisions of the proposed Rule.

occasionally consult or assist each other ordinarily would not be regarded as constituting a firm. However, if they present themselves to the public in a way suggesting that they are a firm or conduct themselves as a firm, they should be regarded as a firm for purposes of the Rules. The terms of any formal agreement between associated lawyers are relevant in determining whether they are a firm, as is the fact that they have mutual access to information concerning the clients they serve. Furthermore, it is relevant in doubtful cases to consider the underlying purpose of the Rule that is involved. A group of lawyers could be regarded as a firm for purposes of the rule that the same lawyer should not represent opposing parties in litigation, while it might not be so regarded for purposes of the rule that information acquired by one lawyer is attributed to another. See Rule 1.0, Comments [2]–[4].

[2] With respect to the law department of an organization, there is ordinarily no question that the members of the department constitute a firm within the meaning of the Rules of Professional Conduct. However, there can be uncertainty as to the identity of the client. For example, it may not be clear whether the law department of a corporation represents a subsidiary or an affiliated corporation, as well as the corporation by which the members of the department are directly employed. A similar question can arise concerning an unincorporated association and its local affiliates.

[3] Similar questions can also arise with respect to lawyers in legal aid. Lawyers employed in the same unit of a legal service organization constitute a firm, but not necessarily those employed in separate units. As in the case of independent practitioners, whether the lawyers should be treated as associated with each other can depend on the particular rule that is involved, and on the specific facts of the situation.

[5] Different provisions are thus made for movement of a lawyer from one private firm to another and for movement of a lawyer between a private firm and the government. The government is entitled to protection of its client confidences and, therefore, to the protections provided in Rules 1.6, 1.9 and 1.11. However, if the more extensive disqualification in Rule 1.10 were applied to former government lawyers, the potential effect on the government would be unduly burdensome. The government deals with all private citizens and organizations and, thus, has a much wider circle of adverse legal interests than does any private law firm. In these circumstances, the government's recruitment of lawyers would be seriously impaired if Rule 1.10 were applied to the government. On balance, therefore, the government is better served in the long run by the protections stated in Rule 1.11.

Principles of Imputed Disqualification

[6] [2] The rule of imputed disqualification stated in paragraph (a) gives effect to the principle of loyalty to the client as it applies to lawyers who practice in a law firm. Such situations can be considered from the premise that a firm of lawyers is essentially one lawyer for purposes of the rules governing loyalty to the client, or from the premise that each lawyer is vicariously bound by the obligation of loyalty owed by each lawyer with whom

the lawyer is associated. Paragraph (a) operates only among the lawyers currently associated in a firm. When a lawyer moves from one firm to another, the situation is governed by Rules 1.9(b) and 1.10(b).

[3]   The rule in paragraph (a) does not prohibit representation where neither questions of client loyalty nor protection of confidential information are presented. Where one lawyer in a firm could not effectively represent a given client because of strong political beliefs, for example, but that lawyer will do no work on the case, the firm should not be disqualified. On the other hand, if an opposing party in a case were owned by a lawyer in the law firm, and others in the firm would be materially limited in pursuing the matter because of loyalty to that lawyer, the personal disqualification of the lawyer would be imputed to all others in the firm.

[4]   The rule in paragraph (a) also does not prohibit representation by others in the law firm where the person prohibited from involvement in a matter is a nonlawyer, such as a paralegal or legal secretary. Nor does paragraph (a) prohibit representation if the lawyer is prohibited from acting because of events before the person became a lawyer, for example, work that the person did while a law student. Such persons, however, ordinarily must be screened from any personal participation in the matter to avoid communication to others in the firm of confidential information that both the nonlawyers and the firm have a legal duty to protect. See Rules 1.0(k) and 5.3.

[7] [5] Rule 1.10(b) operates to permit a law firm, under certain circumstances, to represent a person with interests directly adverse to those of a client represented by a lawyer who formerly was associated with the firm. The Rule applies regardless of when the formerly associated lawyer represented the client. However, the law firm may not represent a person with interests adverse to those of a present client of the firm, which would violate Rule 1.7. Moreover, the firm may not represent the person where the matter is the same or substantially related to that in which the formerly associated lawyer represented the client and any other lawyer currently in the firm has material information protected by Rules 1.6 and 1.9(c).

[9] [6] Rule 1.10(c) removes imputation with the informed consent of the affected client or former client under the conditions stated in Rule 1.7. The conditions stated in Rule 1.7 require the lawyer to determine that the representation is not prohibited by Rule 1.7(b) and that each affected client or former client has given informed consent to the representation, confirmed in writing. In some cases, the risk may be so severe that the conflict may not be cured by client consent. For a discussion of the effectiveness of client waivers of conflicts that might arise in the future, see Rule 1.7, Comment [22]. For a definition of informed consent, see Rule 1.0(e).

[4] [7] Where a lawyer has joined a private firm after having represented the government, the situation imputation is governed by Rule 1.11(a) and (b) and (c);, not this Rule. Under Rule 1.11(d), where a lawyer represents the government after having served private clients, the situation is governed by Rule 1.11(c)(1). The individual lawyer involved is bound by the Rules general-

ly, including Rules 1.6, 1.7 and 1.9 in private practice, nongovernmental employment or in another government agency, former-client conflicts are not imputed to government lawyers associated with the individually disqualified lawyer.

[8] Where a lawyer is prohibited from engaging in certain transactions under Rule 1.8, paragraph (k) of that Rule, and not this Rule, determines whether that prohibition also applies to other lawyers associated in a firm with the personally prohibited lawyer.

RULE 1.11: ~~SUCCESSIVE~~ SPECIAL CONFLICTS OF INTEREST FOR FORMER AND CURRENT GOVERNMENT OFFICERS AND ~~PRIVATE EMPLOYMENT~~ EMPLOYEES

(a) Except as law may otherwise expressly permit, a lawyer who has formerly served as a public officer or employee of the government:

(1) is subject to Rule 1.9(c); and

(2) shall not otherwise represent a ~~private~~ client in connection with a matter in which the lawyer participated personally and substantially as a public officer or employee, unless the appropriate government agency ~~consents after consultation~~ gives its informed consent, confirmed in writing, to the representation.

(b) ~~No~~ When a lawyer is disqualified from representation under paragraph (a), no lawyer in a firm with which that lawyer is associated may knowingly undertake or continue representation in such a matter unless:

(1) the disqualified lawyer is timely screened from any participation in the matter and is apportioned no part of the fee therefrom; and

(2) written notice is promptly given to the appropriate government agency to enable it to ascertain compliance with the provisions of this rule.

~~(b)~~ (c) Except as law may otherwise expressly permit, a lawyer having information that the lawyer knows is confidential government information about a person acquired when the lawyer was a public officer or employee, may not represent a private client whose interests are adverse to that person in a matter in which the information could be used to the material disadvantage of that person. As used in this Rule, the term "confidential government information" means information that has been obtained under governmental authority and which, at the time this Rule is applied, the government is prohibited by law from disclosing to the public or has a legal privilege not to disclose and which is not otherwise available to the public. A firm with which that lawyer is associated may undertake or continue representation in the matter only if the disqualified lawyer is <u>timely</u> screened from any participation in the matter and is apportioned no part of the fee therefrom.

~~(c)~~ <u>(d)</u> Except as law may otherwise expressly permit, a lawyer <u>currently</u> serving as a public officer or employee:

> (1) is subject to Rules 1.7 and 1.9; and

> (2) shall not:

>> ~~(1)~~ <u>(i)</u> participate in a matter in which the lawyer participated personally and substantially while in private practice or nongovernmental employment, unless ~~under applicable law no one is, or by lawful delegation may be, authorized to act in the lawyer's stead in the matter~~ the appropriate government agency gives its informed consent, confirmed in writing; or

>> ~~(2)~~ <u>(ii)</u> negotiate for private employment with any person who is involved as a party or as lawyer for a party in a matter in which the lawyer is participating personally and substantially, except that a lawyer serving as a law clerk to a judge, other adjudicative officer or arbitrator may negotiate for private employment as permitted by Rule 1.12(b) and subject to the conditions stated in Rule 1.12(b).

~~(d)~~ <u>(e)</u> As used in this Rule, the term "matter" includes:

> (1) any judicial or other proceeding, application, request for a ruling or other determination, contract, claim, controversy, investigation, charge, accusation, arrest or other particular matter involving a specific party or parties, and

> (2) any other matter covered by the conflict of interest rules of the appropriate government agency.

~~(e) As used in this Rule, the term "confidential government information" means information which has been obtained under governmental authority and which, at the time this rule is applied, the government is prohibited by law from disclosing to the public or has a legal privilege not to disclose, and which is not otherwise available to the public.~~

Comment

~~[1] This Rule prevents a lawyer from exploiting public office for the advantage of a private client. It is a counterpart of Rule 1.10(b), which applies to lawyers moving from one firm to another.~~

~~[2]~~ [1] A lawyer ~~representing a government agency, whether employed or specially retained by the government,~~ who has served or is currently serving as a public officer or employee is personally subject to the Rules of Professional Conduct, including the prohibition against ~~representing adverse interests~~

concurrent conflicts of interest stated in Rule 1.7 ~~and the protections afforded former clients in Rule 1.9~~. In addition, such a lawyer ~~is~~ may be subject to ~~Rule 1.11 and to~~ statutes and government regulations regarding conflict of interest. Such statutes and regulations may circumscribe the extent to which the government agency may give consent under this Rule. See Rule 1.0(e) for the definition of informed consent.

[2]   Paragraphs (a)(1), (a)(2) and (d)(1) restate the obligations of an individual lawyer who has served or is currently serving as an officer or employee of the government toward a former government or private client under Rule 1.9. Rule 1.10, however, is not applicable to the conflicts of interest addressed by this Rule. Rather, paragraph (b) sets forth a special imputation rule for former government lawyers that provides for screening and notice. Because of the special problems raised by imputation within a government agency, paragraph (d) does not impute the conflicts of a lawyer currently serving as an officer or employee of the government to other associated government officers or employees, although ordinarily it will be prudent to screen such lawyers.

[3]   Paragraphs (a)(3) and (d)(2), apply regardless of whether a lawyer is adverse to a former client and thus are designed not only to protect the former client, but also to prevent a lawyer from exploiting public office for the advantage of another client. For example, a lawyer who has pursued a claim on behalf of the government may not pursue the same claim on behalf of a later private client after the lawyer has left government service, except when authorized to do so by the government agency under paragraph (a). Similarly, a lawyer who has pursued a claim on behalf of a private client may not pursue the claim on behalf of the government, except when authorized to do so by paragraph (d). As with paragraphs (a)(1), (a)(2) and (d)(1), Rule 1.10 is not applicable to the conflicts of interest addressed by these paragraphs.

~~[3]~~ [4] ~~Where~~ This Rule represents a balancing of interests. On the one hand, where the successive clients are a public agency and ~~a private~~ another client, public or private, the risk exists that power or discretion vested in public authority might be used for the special benefit of ~~a private~~ the other client. A lawyer should not be in a position where benefit to ~~a private~~ the other client might affect performance of the lawyer's professional functions on behalf of public authority. Also, unfair advantage could accrue to the ~~private~~ other client by reason of access to confidential government information about the client's adversary obtainable only through the lawyer's government service. ~~However~~ On the other hand, the rules governing lawyers presently or formerly employed by a government agency should not be so restrictive as to inhibit transfer of employment to and from the government. The government has a legitimate need to attract qualified lawyers as well as to maintain high ethical standards. Thus, a former government lawyer is disqualified only from particular matters in which the lawyer participated personally and substantially. The provisions for screening and waiver in paragraph (b) are necessary to prevent the disqualification rule from imposing too severe a deterrent against entering public service. The limitation of disqualification in paragraphs (a)(2) and (d)(2) to matters involving a specific party or parties, rather than extending disqualification to all substantive issues on which the lawyer worked, serves a similar function.

[4] [5] When ~~the client is an agency of~~ a lawyer has been employed by one government agency and then moves to a second government agency, it may be appropriate to treat that second agency ~~should be treated~~ as ~~a private~~ another client for purposes of this Rule ~~if the lawyer thereafter represents an agency of another government~~, as when a lawyer ~~represents~~ is employed by a city and subsequently is employed by a federal agency. However, because the conflict of interest is governed by paragraph (d), the latter agency is not required to screen the lawyer as paragraph (b) requires a law firm to do. The question of whether two government agencies should be regarded as the same or different clients for conflict of interest purposes is beyond the scope of these Rules. See Rule 1.13, Comment [6].

[5] [6] Paragraphs ~~(a)(1) and~~ (b) and (c) contemplate a screening arrangement. See Rule 1.0(k) (requirements for screening procedures). These paragraphs do not prohibit a lawyer from receiving a salary or partnership share established by prior independent agreement. ~~They prohibit,~~ but that lawyer may not receive compensation directly relating the lawyer's compensation to the fee in the matter in which the lawyer is disqualified.

[7] Notice, including a description of the screened lawyer's prior representation and of the screening procedures employed, generally should be given as soon as practicable after the need for screening becomes apparent.

~~[6] Paragraph (a)(2) does not require that a lawyer give notice to the government agency at a time when premature disclosure would injure the client; a requirement for premature disclosure might preclude engagement of the lawyer. Such notice is, however, required to be given as soon as practicable in order that the government agency will have a reasonable opportunity to ascertain that the lawyer is complying with Rule 1.11 and to take appropriate action if it believes the lawyer is not complying.~~

[7] [8] Paragraph ~~(b)~~ (c) operates only when the lawyer in question has knowledge of the information, which means actual knowledge; it does not operate with respect to information that merely could be imputed to the lawyer.

[8] [9] Paragraphs (a) and ~~(c)~~ (d) do not prohibit a lawyer from jointly representing a private party and a government agency when doing so is permitted by Rule 1.7 and is not otherwise prohibited by law.

~~[9] Paragraph (c) does not disqualify other lawyers in the agency with which the lawyer in question has become associated.~~

[10] For purposes of paragraph (e) of this Rule, a "matter" may continue in another form. In determining whether two particular matters are the same, the lawyer should consider the extent to which the matters involve the same basic facts, the same or related parties, and the time elapsed.

RULE 1.12: FORMER JUDGE ~~OR~~, ARBITRATOR, MEDIATOR OR OTHER THIRD–PARTY NEUTRAL

(a) Except as stated in paragraph (d), a lawyer shall not represent anyone in connection with a matter in which the lawyer participated personally and substantially as a judge or other adjudicative officer, ~~arbitrator~~ or law clerk to such a person or as an arbitrator, mediator or other third-party neutral, unless all parties to the proceeding give informed consent ~~after consultation~~, confirmed in writing.

(b) A lawyer shall not negotiate for employment with any person who is involved as a party or as lawyer for a party in a matter in which the lawyer is participating personally and substantially as a judge or other adjudicative officer or as an arbitrator, mediator or other third-party neutral. A lawyer serving as a law clerk to a judge, or other adjudicative officer ~~or arbitrator~~ may negotiate for employment with a party or lawyer involved in a matter in which the clerk is participating personally and substantially, but only after the lawyer has notified the judge, or other adjudicative officer ~~or arbitrator~~.

(c) If a lawyer is disqualified by paragraph (a), no lawyer in a firm with which that lawyer is associated may knowingly undertake or continue representation in the matter unless:

(1) the disqualified lawyer is timely screened from any participation in the matter and is apportioned no part of the fee therefrom; and

(2) written notice is promptly given to the parties and any appropriate tribunal to enable ~~it~~ them to ascertain compliance with the provisions of this rule.

(d) An arbitrator selected as a partisan of a party in a multimember arbitration panel is not prohibited from subsequently representing that party.

Comment

[1] This Rule generally parallels Rule 1.11. The term "personally and substantially" signifies that a judge who was a member of a multimember court, and thereafter left judicial office to practice law, is not prohibited from representing a client in a matter pending in the court, but in which the former judge did not participate. So also the fact that a former judge exercised administrative responsibility in a court does not prevent the former judge from acting as a lawyer in a matter where the judge had previously exercised remote or incidental administrative responsibility that did not affect the merits. Compare the Comment to Rule 1.11. The term "adjudicative officer" includes such officials as judges pro tempore, referees, special masters, hearing officers and other parajudicial officers, and also lawyers who serve as part-

time judges. Compliance Canons A(2), B(2) and C of the Model Code of Judicial Conduct provide that a part-time judge, judge pro tempore or retired judge recalled to active service, may not "act as a lawyer in any proceeding in which he served as a judge or in any other proceeding related thereto." Although phrased differently from this Rule, those Rules correspond in meaning.

[2]   Like former judges, lawyers who have served as arbitrators, mediators or other third-party neutrals may be asked to represent a client in a matter in which the lawyer participated personally and substantially. This Rule forbids such representation unless all of the parties to the proceedings give their informed consent, confirmed in writing. See Rule 1.0(e) and (b). Other law or codes of ethics governing third-party neutrals may impose more stringent standards of personal or imputed disqualification. See Rule 2.4.

[3]   Although lawyers who serve as third-party neutrals do not have information concerning the parties that is protected under Rule 1.6, they typically owe the parties an obligation of confidentiality under law or codes of ethics governing third-party neutrals. Thus, paragraph (c) provides that conflicts of the personally disqualified lawyer will be imputed to other lawyers in a law firm unless the conditions of this paragraph are met.

[4]   Requirements for screening procedures are stated in Rule 1.0(k). Paragraph (c)(1) does not prohibit the screened lawyer from receiving a salary or partnership share established by prior independent agreement, but that lawyer may not receive compensation directly related to the matter in which the lawyer is disqualified.

[5]   Notice, including a description of the screened lawyer's prior representation and of the screening procedures employed, generally should be given as soon as practicable after the need for screening becomes apparent.

RULE 1.13: ORGANIZATION AS CLIENT

(a) **A lawyer employed or retained by an organization represents the organization acting through its duly authorized constituents.**

(b) **If a lawyer for an organization knows that an officer, employee or other person associated with the organization is engaged in action, intends to act or refuses to act in a matter related to the representation that is a violation of a legal obligation to the organization, or a violation of law which reasonably might be imputed to the organization, and is likely to result in substantial injury to the organization, the lawyer shall proceed as is reasonably necessary in the best interest of the organization. In determining how to proceed, the lawyer shall give due consideration to the seriousness of the violation and its consequences, the scope and nature of the lawyer's representation, the responsibility in the organization and the apparent motivation of the person involved, the policies of the organization concerning such matters and any other relevant considerations.**

Any measures taken shall be designed to minimize disruption of the organization and the risk of revealing information relating to the representation to persons outside the organization. Such measures may include among others:

(1) asking for reconsideration of the matter;

(2) advising that a separate legal opinion on the matter be sought for presentation to appropriate authority in the organization; and

(3) referring the matter to higher authority in the organization, including, if warranted by the seriousness of the matter, referral to the highest authority that can act in on behalf of the organization as determined by applicable law.

(c) If, despite the lawyer's efforts in accordance with paragraph (b), the highest authority that can act on behalf of the organization insists upon action, or a refusal to act, that is clearly a violation of law and is likely to result in substantial injury to the organization, the lawyer may resign in accordance with Rule 1.16.*

(d) In dealing with an organization's directors, officers, employees, members, shareholders or other constituents, a lawyer shall explain the identity of the client when it is apparent the lawyer knows or reasonably should know that the organization's interests are adverse to those of the constituents with whom the lawyer is dealing.

(e) A lawyer representing an organization may also represent any of its directors, officers, employees, members, shareholders or other constituents, subject to the provisions of Rule 1.7. If the organization's consent to the dual representation is required by Rule 1.7, the consent shall be given by an appropriate official of the organization other than the individual who is to be represented, or by the shareholders.

Comment

The Entity as the Client

[1] An organizational client is a legal entity, but it cannot act except through its officers, directors, employees, shareholders and other constituents.

* Editors' Note: As previously proposed by the Kutak Commission, Rule 1.13(c)(Revised Final Draft, June 30, 1982) read as follows:

(c) When the organization's highest authorities insist upon action, or refuses to take action, that is clearly a violation of a legal obligation to the organization, or a violation of law which reasonably might be imputed to the organization, and is likely to result in substantial injury to the organization, the lawyer may take further remedial action that the lawyer reasonably believes to be in the best interest of the organization. Such action may include reveal-

ing information otherwise protected by Rule 1.6 only if the lawyer reasonably believes that:

(1) the highest authority in the organization has acted to further the personal or financial interests of members of that authority which are in conflict with the interest of the organization; and

(2) revealing the information is necessary in the best interest of the organization.

The report of the Ethics 2000 Commission did not propose adoption of this language.

Officers, directors, employees and shareholders are the constituents of the corporate organizational client. The duties defined in this Comment apply equally to unincorporated associations. "Other constituents" as used in this Comment means the positions equivalent to officers, directors, employees and shareholders held by persons acting for organizational clients that are not corporations.

[2] When one of the constituents of an organizational client communicates with the organization's lawyer in that person's organizational capacity, the communication is protected by Rule 1.6. Thus, by way of example, if an organizational client requests its lawyer to investigate allegations of wrongdoing, interviews made in the course of that investigation between the lawyer and the client's employees or other constituents are covered by Rule 1.6. This does not mean, however, that constituents of an organizational client are the clients of the lawyer. The lawyer may not disclose to such constituents information relating to the representation except for disclosures explicitly or impliedly authorized by the organizational client in order to carry out the representation or as otherwise permitted by Rule 1.6.

[3] When constituents of the organization make decisions for it, the decisions ordinarily must be accepted by the lawyer even if their utility or prudence is doubtful. Decisions concerning policy and operations, including ones entailing serious risk, are not as such in the lawyer's province. However, different considerations arise when the lawyer knows that the organization may be substantially injured by action of a constituent that is in violation of law. In such a circumstance, it may be reasonably necessary for the lawyer to ask the constituent to reconsider the matter. If that fails, or if the matter is of sufficient seriousness and importance to the organization, it may be reasonably necessary for the lawyer to take steps to have the matter reviewed by a higher authority in the organization. Clear justification should exist for seeking review over the head of the constituent normally responsible for it. The stated policy of the organization may define circumstances and prescribe channels for such review, and a lawyer should encourage the formulation of such a policy. Even in the absence of organization policy, however, the lawyer may have an obligation to refer a matter to higher authority, depending on the seriousness of the matter and whether the constituent in question has apparent motives to act at variance with the organization's interest. Review by the chief executive officer or by the board of directors may be required when the matter is of importance commensurate with their authority. At some point it may be useful or essential to obtain an independent legal opinion.

[4] ~~In an extreme case, it may be reasonably necessary for the lawyer to refer the matter to the~~ The organization's highest authority. ~~Ordinarily, that is~~ to whom a matter may be referred ordinarily will be the board of directors or similar governing body. However, applicable law may prescribe that under certain conditions the highest authority reposes elsewhere, for example, in the independent directors of a corporation.

66

Relation to Other Rules

[5]   The authority and responsibility provided in ~~paragraph (b)~~ this Rule are concurrent with the authority and responsibility provided in other Rules. In particular, this Rule does not limit or expand the lawyer's responsibility under Rule 1.6, 1.8, 1.16, 3.3 or 4.1. If the lawyer's services are being used by an organization to further a crime or fraud by the organization, Rule 1.2(d) can be applicable.

Government Agency

[6]   The duty defined in this Rule applies to governmental organizations. ~~However, when the client is a governmental organization, a different balance may be appropriate between maintaining confidentiality and assuring that the wrongful official act is prevented or rectified, for public business is involved. In addition, duties of lawyers employed by the government or lawyers in military service may be defined by statutes and regulation. Therefore, defining~~ Defining precisely the identity of the client and prescribing the resulting obligations of such lawyers may be more difficult in the government context and is a matter beyond the scope of these Rules. See Scope [18]. Although in some circumstances the client may be a specific agency, it ~~is generally~~ may also be a branch of government, such as the executive branch, or the government as a whole. For example, if the action or failure to act involves the head of a bureau, either the department of which the bureau is a part or the relevant branch of government ~~as a whole~~ may be the client for ~~purpose~~ purposes of this Rule. Moreover, in a matter involving the conduct of government officials, a government lawyer may have authority under applicable law to question such conduct more extensively than that of a lawyer for a private organization in similar circumstances. Thus, when the client is a governmental organization, a different balance may be appropriate between maintaining confidentiality and assuring that the wrongful act is prevented or rectified, for public business is involved. In addition, duties of lawyers employed by the government or lawyers in military service may be defined by statutes and regulations. This rule does not limit that authority. See ~~note on~~ Scope.

Clarifying the Lawyer's Role

[7]   There are times when the organization's interest may be or become adverse to those of one or more of its constituents. In such circumstances the lawyer should advise any constituent, whose interest the lawyer finds adverse to that of the organization of the conflict or potential conflict of interest, that the lawyer cannot represent such constituent, and that such person may wish to obtain independent representation. Care must be taken to assure that the individual understands that, when there is such adversity of interest, the lawyer for the organization cannot provide legal representation for that constituent individual, and that discussions between the lawyer for the organization and the individual may not be privileged.

[8]   Whether such a warning should be given by the lawyer for the organization to any constituent individual may turn on the facts of each case.

Dual Representation

[9]   Paragraph (e) recognizes that a lawyer for an organization may also represent a principal officer or major shareholder.

Derivative Actions

[10]   Under generally prevailing law, the shareholders or members of a corporation may bring suit to compel the directors to perform their legal obligations in the supervision of the organization. Members of unincorporated associations have essentially the same right. Such an action may be brought nominally by the organization, but usually is, in fact, a legal controversy over management of the organization.

[11]   The question can arise whether counsel for the organization may defend such an action. The proposition that the organization is the lawyer's client does not alone resolve the issue. Most derivative actions are a normal incident of an organization's affairs, to be defended by the organization's lawyer like any other suit. However, if the claim involves serious charges of wrongdoing by those in control of the organization, a conflict may arise between the lawyer's duty to the organization and the lawyer's relationship with the board. In those circumstances, Rule 1.7 governs who should represent the directors and the organization.

RULE 1.14: CLIENT ~~UNDER A DISABILITY~~ WITH DIMINISHED CAPACITY

(a) When a client's ~~ability~~ capacity to make adequately considered decisions in connection with ~~the~~ a representation is ~~impaired~~ diminished, whether because of minority, mental ~~disability~~ impairment or for some other reason, the lawyer shall, as far as reasonably possible, maintain a normal client-lawyer relationship with the client.

(b) ~~A lawyer may seek the appointment of a guardian or take other protective action with respect to a client only when~~ When the lawyer reasonably believes that the client has diminished capacity, is at risk of substantial physical, financial or other harm unless action is taken and cannot adequately act in the client's own interest, the lawyer may take reasonably necessary protective action, including consulting with individuals or entities that have the ability to take action to protect the client and, in appropriate cases, seeking the appointment of a guardian ad litem, conservator or guardian.

(c) Information relating to the representation of a client with diminished capacity is protected by Rule 1.6. When taking protective action pursuant to paragraph (b), the lawyer is impliedly authorized

under Rule 1.6(a) to reveal information about the client, but only to the extent reasonably necessary to protect the client's interests.

Comment

[1] The normal client-lawyer relationship is based on the assumption that the client, when properly advised and assisted, is capable of making decisions about important matters. When the client is a minor or suffers from a diminished mental capacity ~~disorder or disability~~, however, maintaining the ordinary client-lawyer relationship may not be possible in all respects. In particular, ~~an~~ a severely incapacitated person may have no power to make legally binding decisions. Nevertheless, a client ~~lacking legal competence~~ with diminished capacity often has the ability to understand, deliberate upon, and reach conclusions about matters affecting the client's own well-being. ~~Furthermore, to an increasing extent the law recognizes intermediate degrees of competence.~~ For example, children as young as five or six years of age, and certainly those of ten or twelve, are regarded as having opinions that are entitled to weight in legal proceedings concerning their custody. So also, it is recognized that some persons of advanced age can be quite capable of handling routine financial matters while needing special legal protection concerning major transactions.

[2] The fact that a client suffers a disability does not diminish the lawyer's obligation to treat the client with attention and respect. ~~If the person has no guardian or legal representative, the lawyer often must act as de facto guardian.~~ Even if the person ~~does have~~ has a legal representative, the lawyer should as far as possible accord the represented person the status of client, particularly in maintaining communication.

[3] The client may wish to have family members or other persons participate in discussions with the lawyer. When necessary to assist in the representation, the presence of such persons generally does not affect the applicability of the attorney-client evidentiary privilege. Nevertheless, the lawyer must keep the client's interests foremost and, except for protective action authorized under paragraph (b), must to look to the client, and not family members, to make decisions on the client's behalf.

~~[3]~~ [4] If a legal representative has already been appointed for the client, the lawyer should ordinarily look to the representative for decisions on behalf of the client. ~~If a legal representative has not been appointed, the lawyer should see to such an appointment where it would serve the client's best interests. Thus, if a disabled client has substantial property that should be sold for the client's benefit, effective completion of the transaction ordinarily requires appointment of a legal representative. In many circumstances, however, appointment of a legal representative may be expensive or traumatic for the client. Evaluation of these considerations is a matter of professional judgment on the lawyer's part.~~ In matters involving a minor, whether the lawyer should look to the parents as natural guardians may depend on the type of proceeding or matter in which the lawyer is representing the minor. ~~[4]~~ If the lawyer represents the guardian as distinct from the ward, and is aware that the guardian is acting adversely to the ward's interest, the lawyer may have an obligation to prevent or rectify the guardian's misconduct. See Rule 1.2(d).

Taking Protective Action

[5]   If a lawyer reasonably believes that a client is at risk of substantial physical, financial or other harm unless action is taken, and that a normal client-lawyer relationship cannot be maintained as provided in paragraph (a) because the client lacks sufficient capacity to communicate or to make adequately considered decisions in connection with the representation, then paragraph (b) permits the lawyer to take protective measures deemed necessary. Such measures could include: consulting with family members, using a reconsideration period to permit clarification or improvement of circumstances, using voluntary surrogate decisionmaking tools such as durable powers of attorney or consulting with support groups, professional services, adult-protective agencies or other individuals or entities that have the ability to protect the client. In taking any protective action, the lawyer should be guided by such factors as the wishes and values of the client to the extent known, the client's best interests and the goals of intruding into the client's decisionmaking autonomy to the least extent feasible, maximizing client capacities and respecting the client's family and social connections.

[6]   In determining the extent of the client's diminished capacity, the lawyer should consider and balance such factors as: the client's ability to articulate reasoning leading to a decision, variability of state of mind and ability to appreciate consequences of a decision; the substantive fairness of a decision; and the consistency of a decision with the known long-term commitments and values of the client. In appropriate circumstances, the lawyer may seek guidance from an appropriate diagnostician.

[7]   If a legal representative has not been appointed, the lawyer should consider whether appointment of a guardian ad litem, conservator or guardian is necessary to protect the client's interests. Thus, if a client with diminished capacity has substantial property that should be sold for the client's benefit, effective completion of the transaction may require appointment of a legal representative. In addition, rules of procedure in litigation sometimes provide that minors or persons with diminished capacity must be represented by a guardian or next friend if they do not have a general guardian. In many circumstances, however, appointment of a legal representative may be more expensive or traumatic for the client than circumstances in fact require. Evaluation of such circumstances is a matter entrusted to the professional judgment of the lawyer. In considering alternatives, however, the lawyer should be aware of any law that requires the lawyer to advocate the least restrictive action on behalf of the client.

Disclosure of the Client's Condition

[5] [8]   ~~Rules of procedure in litigation generally provide that minors or persons suffering mental disability shall be represented by a guardian or next~~

~~friend if they do not have a general guardian. However, disclosure~~ Disclosure of the client's ~~disability can~~ diminished capacity could adversely affect the client's interests. For example, raising the question of ~~disability~~ diminished capacity could, in some circumstances, lead to proceedings for involuntary commitment. Information relating to the representation is protected by Rule 1.6. Therefore, unless authorized to do so, the lawyer may not disclose such information. When taking protective action pursuant to paragraph (b), the lawyer is impliedly authorized to make the necessary disclosures, even when the client directs the lawyer to the contrary. Nevertheless, given the risks of disclosure, paragraph (c) limits what the lawyer may disclose in consulting with other individuals or entities or seeking the appointment of a legal representative. At the very least, the lawyer should determine whether it is likely that the person or entity consulted with will act adversely to the client's interests before discussing matters related to the client. The lawyer's position in such cases is an unavoidably difficult one. ~~The lawyer may seek guidance from an appropriate diagnostician.~~

Emergency Legal Assistance

~~[6]~~ [9] In an emergency where the health, safety or a financial interest of a person ~~under a disability~~ with seriously diminished capacity is threatened with imminent and irreparable harm, a lawyer may take legal action on behalf of such a person even though the person is unable to establish a client-lawyer relationship or to make or express considered judgments about the matter, when the ~~disabled~~ person or another acting in good faith on that person's behalf has consulted with the lawyer. Even in such an emergency, however, the lawyer should not act unless the lawyer reasonably believes that the person has no other lawyer, agent or other representative available. The lawyer should take legal action on behalf of the ~~disabled~~ person only to the extent reasonably necessary to maintain the status quo or otherwise avoid imminent and irreparable harm. A lawyer who undertakes to represent a person in such an exigent situation has the same duties under these Rules as the lawyer would with respect to a client.

~~[7]~~ [10] A lawyer who acts on behalf of a ~~disabled~~ person with seriously diminished capacity in an emergency should keep the confidences of the ~~disabled~~ person as if dealing with a client, disclosing them only to the extent necessary to accomplish the intended protective action. The lawyer should disclose to any tribunal involved and to any other counsel involved the nature of his or her relationship with the ~~disabled~~ person. The lawyer should take steps to regularize the relationship or implement other protective solutions as soon as possible. Normally, a lawyer would not seek compensation for such emergency actions taken ~~on behalf of a disabled person~~.

RULE 1.15: SAFEKEEPING PROPERTY

(a) A lawyer shall hold property of clients or third persons that is in a lawyer's possession in connection with a representation sepa-

rate from the lawyer's own property. Funds shall be kept in a separate account maintained in the state where the lawyer's office is situated, or elsewhere with the consent of the client or third person. Other property shall be identified as such and appropriately safeguarded. Complete records of such account funds and other property shall be kept by the lawyer and shall be preserved for a period of [five years] after termination of the representation.

(b) A lawyer may deposit the lawyer's own funds in a client trust account for the sole purpose of paying bank service charges on that account, but only in an amount necessary for that purpose.

(c) A lawyer shall deposit into a client trust account legal fees and expenses that have been paid in advance, to be withdrawn by the lawyer only as fees are earned or expenses incurred.

(b) (d) Upon receiving funds or other property in which a client or third person has an interest, a lawyer shall promptly notify the client or third person. Except as stated in this rule or otherwise permitted by law or by agreement with the client, a lawyer shall promptly deliver to the client or third person any funds or other property that the client or third person is entitled to receive and, upon request by the client or third person, shall promptly render a full accounting regarding such property.

(e) (e) When in the course of representation a lawyer is in possession of property in which both two or more persons (one of whom may be the lawyer and another person) claim interests, the property shall be kept separate by the lawyer until there is an accounting and severance of their interests. If a dispute arises concerning their respective interests, the portion in dispute shall be kept separate by the lawyer until the dispute is resolved. The lawyer shall promptly distribute all portions of the property as to which the interests are not in dispute.

Comment

[1] A lawyer should hold property of others with the care required of a professional fiduciary. Securities should be kept in a safe deposit box, except when some other form of safekeeping is warranted by special circumstances. All property which is the property of clients or third persons should, including prospective clients, must be kept separate from the lawyer's business and personal property and, if monies, in one or more trust accounts. Separate trust accounts may be warranted when administering estate monies or acting in similar fiduciary capacities. A lawyer should maintain on a current basis books and records in accordance with generally accepted accounting practice and comply with any recordkeeping rules established by law or court order. See, e.g., ABA Model Financial Recordkeeping Rule.

[2] While normally it is impermissible to commingle the lawyer's own funds with client funds, paragraph (b) provides that it is permissible when

necessary to pay bank service charges on that account. Accurate records must be kept regarding which part of the funds are the lawyer's.

[2] [3] Lawyers often receive funds from ~~third parties from~~ which the lawyer's fee will be paid. ~~If there is risk that the client may divert the funds without paying the fee, the~~ The lawyer is not required to remit ~~the portion from which the fee is to be paid~~ to the client funds that the lawyer reasonably believes represent fees owed. However, a lawyer may not hold funds to coerce a client into accepting the lawyer's contention. The disputed portion of the funds ~~should~~ must be kept in a trust account and the lawyer should suggest means for prompt resolution of the dispute, such as arbitration. The undisputed portion of the funds shall be promptly distributed.

[3] [4] ~~Third~~ Paragraph (e) also recognizes that third parties, ~~such as a client's creditors,~~ may have ~~just~~ lawful claims against specific funds or other property in a lawyer's custody, such as a client's creditor who has a lien on funds recovered in a personal-injury action. A lawyer may have a duty under applicable law to protect such third-party claims against wrongful interference by the client, ~~and accordingly may~~. In such cases, when the third-party claim is not frivolous under applicable law, the lawyer must refuse to surrender the property to the client until the claims are resolved. ~~However, a~~ A lawyer should not unilaterally assume to arbitrate a dispute between the client and the third party, but, when there are substantial grounds for dispute as to the person entitled to the funds, the lawyer may file an action to have a court resolve the dispute.

[4] [5] The obligations of a lawyer under this Rule are independent of those arising from activity other than rendering legal services. For example, a lawyer who serves only as an escrow agent is governed by the applicable law relating to fiduciaries even though the lawyer does not render legal services in the transaction and is not governed by this Rule.

[5] [6] A "~~clients' security~~ lawyers' fund" for client protection provides a means through the collective efforts of the bar to reimburse persons who have lost money or property as a result of dishonest conduct of a lawyer. Where such a fund has been established, a lawyer must participate where it is mandatory, and, even when it is voluntary, the lawyer should participate.

RULE 1.16: DECLINING OR TERMINATING REPRESENTATION

(a) Except as stated in paragraph (c), a lawyer shall not represent a client or, where representation has commenced, shall withdraw from the representation of a client if:

> **(1) the representation will result in violation of the rules of professional conduct or other law;**

> **(2) the lawyer's physical or mental condition materially impairs the lawyer's ability to represent the client; or**

> **(3) the lawyer is discharged.**

73

(b) Except as stated in paragraph (c), a lawyer may withdraw from representing a client if:

(1) **withdrawal can be accomplished without material adverse effect on the interests of the client,** ~~or if:~~;

~~(1)~~ (2) **the client persists in a course of action involving the lawyer's services that the lawyer reasonably believes is criminal or fraudulent;**

~~(2)~~ (3) **the client has used the lawyer's services to perpetrate a crime or fraud;**

~~(3)~~ (4) **a the client insists upon** ~~pursuing an objective~~ **taking action that the lawyer considers repugnant or** ~~imprudent~~ **with which the lawyer has a fundamental disagreement;**

~~(4)~~ (5) **the client fails substantially to fulfill an obligation to the lawyer regarding the lawyer's services and has been given reasonable warning that the lawyer will withdraw unless the obligation is fulfilled;**

~~(5)~~ (6) **the representation will result in an unreasonable financial burden on the lawyer or has been rendered unreasonably difficult by the client; or**

~~(6)~~ (7) **other good cause for withdrawal exists.**

(c) A lawyer must comply with applicable law requiring notice to or permission of a tribunal when terminating a representation. When ordered to do so by a tribunal, a lawyer shall continue representation notwithstanding good cause for terminating the representation.

(d) Upon termination of representation, a lawyer shall take steps to the extent reasonably practicable to protect a client's interests, such as giving reasonable notice to the client, allowing time for employment of other counsel, surrendering papers and property to which the client is entitled and refunding any advance payment of fee or expense that has not been earned or incurred. The lawyer may retain papers relating to the client to the extent permitted by other law.

Comment

[1]   A lawyer should not accept representation in a matter unless it can be performed competently, promptly, without improper conflict of interest and to completion. Ordinarily, a representation in a matter is completed when the agreed-upon assistance has been concluded. See Rules 1.2(c) and 6.5. See also Rule 1.3, Comment [4].

Mandatory Withdrawal

[2]   A lawyer ordinarily must decline or withdraw from representation if the client demands that the lawyer engage in conduct that is illegal or violates the Rules of Professional Conduct or other law. The lawyer is not obliged to

decline or withdraw simply because the client suggests such a course of conduct; a client may make such a suggestion in the hope that a lawyer will not be constrained by a professional obligation.

[3] When a lawyer has been appointed to represent a client, withdrawal ordinarily requires approval of the appointing authority. See also Rule 6.2. Similarly, court approval or notice to the court is often required by applicable law before a lawyer withdraws from pending litigation. Difficulty may be encountered if withdrawal is based on the client's demand that the lawyer engage in unprofessional conduct. The court may ~~wish~~ request an explanation for the withdrawal, while the lawyer may be bound to keep confidential the facts that would constitute such an explanation. The lawyer's statement that professional considerations require termination of the representation ordinarily should be accepted as sufficient. Lawyers should be mindful of their obligations to both clients and the court under Rules 1.6 and 3.3.

Discharge

[4] A client has a right to discharge a lawyer at any time, with or without cause, subject to liability for payment for the lawyer's services. Where future dispute about the withdrawal may be anticipated, it may be advisable to prepare a written statement reciting the circumstances.

[5] Whether a client can discharge appointed counsel may depend on applicable law. A client seeking to do so should be given a full explanation of the consequences. These consequences may include a decision by the appointing authority that appointment of successor counsel is unjustified, thus requiring self-representation by the client.

[6] If the client ~~is mentally incompetent~~ has severely diminished capacity, the client may lack the legal capacity to discharge the lawyer, and in any event the discharge may be seriously adverse to the client's interests. The lawyer should make special effort to help the client consider the consequences and~~, in an extreme case,~~ may ~~initiate proceedings for a conservatorship or similar protection of the client. See~~ take reasonably necessary protective action as provided in Rule 1.14.

Optional Withdrawal

[7] A lawyer may withdraw from representation in some circumstances. The lawyer has the option to withdraw if it can be accomplished without material adverse effect on the client's interests. Withdrawal is also justified if the client persists in a course of action that the lawyer reasonably believes is criminal or fraudulent, for a lawyer is not required to be associated with such conduct even if the lawyer does not further it. Withdrawal is also permitted if the lawyer's services were misused in the past even if that would materially prejudice the client. The lawyer may also withdraw where the client insists on ~~a~~ taking action that the lawyer considers repugnant or ~~imprudent objective~~ with which the lawyer has a fundamental disagreement.

[8]   A lawyer may withdraw if the client refuses to abide by the terms of an agreement relating to the representation, such as an agreement concerning fees or court costs or an agreement limiting the objectives of the representation.

Assisting the Client upon Withdrawal

[9]   Even if the lawyer has been unfairly discharged by the client, a lawyer must take all reasonable steps to mitigate the consequences to the client. The lawyer may retain papers as security for a fee only to the extent permitted by law. ~~Whether or not a lawyer for an organization may under certain unusual circumstances have a legal obligation to the organization after withdrawing or being discharged by the organization's highest authority is beyond the scope of these Rules.~~ See Rule 1.15.

RULE 1.17: SALE OF LAW PRACTICE

A lawyer or a law firm may sell or purchase a law practice, <u>or an area of law practice</u>, including good will, if the following conditions are satisfied:

(a) The seller ceases to engage in the private practice of law, <u>or in the area of practice that has been sold,</u> [in the geographic area] [in the jurisdiction] (a jurisdiction may elect either version) in which the practice has been conducted;

(b) The <u>entire</u> practice, <u>or the entire area of practice,</u> is sold ~~as an entirety~~ to ~~another lawyer~~ <u>one or more lawyers</u> or law ~~firm~~ <u>firms</u>;

(c) ~~Actual~~ <u>The seller gives</u> written notice ~~is given~~ to each of the seller's clients regarding:

(1) the proposed sale;

~~(2) the terms of any proposed change in the fee arrangement authorized by paragraph (d);~~

~~(3)~~ <u>(2)</u> the client's right to retain other counsel or to take possession of the file; and

~~(4)~~ <u>(3)</u> the fact that the client's consent to the ~~sale~~ <u>transfer of the client's files</u> will be presumed if the client does not take any action or does not otherwise object within ninety (90) days of receipt of the notice.

If a client cannot be given notice, the representation of that client may be transferred to the purchaser only upon entry of an order so authorizing by a court having jurisdiction. The seller may disclose to the court in camera information relating to the representation only to the extent necessary to obtain an order authorizing the transfer of a file.

(d) The fees charged clients shall not be increased by reason of the sale. ~~The purchaser may, however, refuse to undertake the repre-~~

~~sentation unless the client consents to pay the purchaser fees at a rate not exceeding the fees charged by the purchaser for rendering substantially similar services prior to the initiation of the purchase negotiations.~~

Comment

[1]   The practice of law is a profession, not merely a business. Clients are not commodities that can be purchased and sold at will. Pursuant to this Rule, when a lawyer or an entire firm ceases to practice, or ceases to practice in an area of law, and ~~another lawyer~~ other lawyers or ~~firm takes~~ firms take over the representation, the selling lawyer or firm may obtain compensation for the reasonable value of the practice as may withdrawing partners of law firms. See Rules 5.4 and 5.6.

Termination of Practice by the Seller

[2]   The requirement that all of the private practice, or all of an area of practice, be sold is satisfied if the seller in good faith makes the entire practice, or the area of practice, available for sale to the ~~purchaser~~ purchasers. The fact that a number of the seller's clients decide not to be represented by the ~~purchaser~~ purchasers but take their matters elsewhere, therefore, does not result in a violation. ~~Neither does a return~~ Return to private practice as a result of an unanticipated change in circumstances does not necessarily result in a violation. For example, a lawyer who has sold the practice to accept an appointment to judicial office does not violate the requirement that the sale be attendant to cessation of practice if the lawyer later resumes private practice upon being defeated in a contested or a retention election for the office or resigns from a judiciary position.

[3]   The requirement that the seller cease to engage in the private practice of law does not prohibit employment as a lawyer on the staff of a public agency or a legal services entity which provides legal services to the poor, or as in-house counsel to a business.

[4]   The Rule permits a sale of an entire practice attendant upon retirement from the private practice of law within the jurisdiction. Its provisions, therefore, accommodate the lawyer who sells the practice upon the occasion of moving to another state. Some states are so large that a move from one locale therein to another is tantamount to leaving the jurisdiction in which the lawyer has engaged in the practice of law. To also accommodate lawyers so situated, states may permit the sale of the practice when the lawyer leaves the geographic area rather than the jurisdiction. The alternative desired should be indicated by selecting one of the two provided for in Rule 1.17(a).

[5]   This Rule also permits a lawyer or law firm to sell an area of practice.If an area of practice is sold and the lawyer remains in the active practice of law, the lawyer must cease accepting any matter in the area of practice that has been sold, either as counsel or co-counsel or by assuming joint responsibility for a matter in connection with the division of a fee with

another lawyer as would otherwise be permitted by Rule 1.5(e). For example, a lawyer with a substantial number of estate planning matters and a substantial number of probate administration cases may sell the estate planning portion of the practice but remain in the practice of law by concentrating on probate administration; however, that practitioner may not thereafter accept any estate planning matters. Although a lawyer who leaves a jurisdiction or geographical area typically would sell the entire practice, this Rule permits the lawyer to limit the sale to one or more areas of the practice, thereby preserving the lawyer's right to continue in the areas of the practice that were not sold.

~~Single Purchaser~~ Sale of Entire Practice or Entire Area of Practice

[5] [6] The Rule requires ~~a single purchaser~~ that the seller's entire practice, or an entire area of practice, be sold. The prohibition against ~~piecemeal~~ sale of a less than an entire practice area protects those clients whose matters are less lucrative and who might find it difficult to secure other counsel if a sale could be limited to substantial fee-generating matters. The ~~purchaser is~~ purchasers are required to undertake all client matters in the practice, or practice area, subject to client consent. ~~If~~ This requirement is satisfied, however, ~~the~~ even if a purchaser is unable to undertake ~~all~~ a particular client ~~matters~~ matter because of a conflict of interest ~~in a specific matter respecting which the purchaser is not permitted by Rule 1.7 or another rule to represent the client, the requirement that there be a single purchaser is nevertheless satisfied.~~

Client Confidences, Consent and Notice

[6] [7] Negotiations between seller and prospective purchaser prior to disclosure of information relating to a specific representation of an identifiable client no more violate the confidentiality provisions of Model Rule 1.6 than do preliminary discussions concerning the possible association of another lawyer or mergers between firms, with respect to which client consent is not required. Providing the purchaser access to client-specific information relating to the representation and to the file, however, requires client consent. The Rule provides that before such information can be disclosed by the seller to the purchaser the client must be given actual written notice of the contemplated sale, including the identity of the purchaser ~~and any proposed change in the terms of future representation~~, and must be told that the decision to consent or make other arrangements must be made within 90 days. If nothing is heard from the client within that time, consent to the sale is presumed.

[7] [8] A lawyer or law firm ceasing to practice cannot be required to remain in practice because some clients cannot be given actual notice of the proposed purchase. Since these clients cannot themselves consent to the purchase or direct any other disposition of their files, the Rule requires an order from a court having jurisdiction authorizing their transfer or other disposition. The Court can be expected to determine whether reasonable efforts to locate the client have been exhausted, and whether the absent

client's legitimate interests will be served by authorizing the transfer of the file so that the purchaser may continue the representation. Preservation of client confidences requires that the petition for a court order be considered in camera. (A procedure by which such an order can be obtained needs to be established in jurisdictions in which it presently does not exist.)

[8] [9] All the elements of client autonomy, including the client's absolute right to discharge a lawyer and transfer the representation to another, survive the sale of the practice or area of practice.

Fee Arrangements Between Client and Purchaser

[9] [10] The sale may not be financed by increases in fees charged the clients of the practice. Existing agreements between the seller and the client as to fees and the scope of the work must be honored by the purchaser, unless the client consents after consultation. The purchaser may, however, advise the client that the purchaser will not undertake the representation unless the client consents to pay the higher fees the purchaser usually charges. To prevent client financing of the sale, the higher fee the purchaser may charge must not exceed the fees charged by the purchaser for substantially similar service rendered prior to the initiation of the purchase negotiations.

[10] The purchaser may not intentionally fragment the practice which is the subject of the sale by charging significantly different fees in substantially similar matters. Doing so would make it possible for the purchaser to avoid the obligation to take over the entire practice by charging arbitrarily higher fees for less lucrative matters, thereby increasing the likelihood that those clients would not consent to the new representation.

Other Applicable Ethical Standards

[11] Lawyers participating in the sale of a law practice, or a practice area are subject to the ethical standards applicable to involving another lawyer in the representation of a client. These include, for example, the seller's obligation to exercise competence in identifying a purchaser qualified to assume the practice and the purchaser's obligation to undertake the representation competently (see Rule 1.1); the obligation to avoid disqualifying conflicts, and to secure client the client's informed consent after consultation for those conflicts which can be agreed to (see Rule 1.7 regarding conflicts and Rule 1.0(e) for the definition of informed consent); and the obligation to protect information relating to the representation (see Rules 1.6 and 1.9).

[12] If approval of the substitution of the purchasing lawyer for the selling lawyer is required by the rules of any tribunal in which a matter is pending, such approval must be obtained before the matter can be included in the sale (see Rule 1.16).

Applicability of the Rule

[13] This Rule applies to the sale of a law practice by representatives of a deceased, disabled or disappeared lawyer. Thus, the seller may be represent-

ed by a non-lawyer representative not subject to these Rules. Since, however, no lawyer may participate in a sale of a law practice which does not conform to the requirements of this Rule, the representatives of the seller as well as the purchasing lawyer can be expected to see to it that they are met.

[14]   Admission to or retirement from a law partnership or professional association, retirement plans and similar arrangements, and a sale of tangible assets of a law practice, do not constitute a sale or purchase governed by this Rule.

[15]   This Rule does not apply to the transfers of legal representation between lawyers when such transfers are unrelated to the sale of a practice or an area of practice.

RULE 1.18: DUTIES TO PROSPECTIVE CLIENT

(a) A person who discusses with a lawyer the possibility of forming a client-lawyer relationship with respect to a matter is a prospective client.

(b) Even when no client-lawyer relationship ensues, a lawyer who has had discussions with a prospective client shall not use or reveal information learned in the consultation, except as Rule 1.9 would permit with respect to information of a former client.

(c) A lawyer subject to paragraph (b) shall not represent a client with interests materially adverse to those of a prospective client in the same or a substantially related matter if the lawyer received information from the prospective client that could be significantly harmful to that person in the matter, except as provided in paragraph (d). If a lawyer is disqualified from representation under this paragraph, no lawyer in a firm with which that lawyer is associated may knowingly undertake or continue representation in such a matter, except as provided in paragraph (d).

(d) When the lawyer has received disqualifying information as defined in paragraph (c), representation is permissible if:

(1) both the affected client and the prospective client have given informed consent, confirmed in writing, or:

(2) the lawyer who received the information took reasonable measures to avoid exposure to more disqualifying information than was reasonably necessary to determine whether to represent the prospective client; and

(i) the disqualified lawyer is timely screened from any participation in the matter and is apportioned no part of the fee therefrom; and

(ii) written notice is promptly given to the prospective client.

Comment

[1]　Prospective clients, like clients, may disclose information to a lawyer, place documents or other property in the lawyer's custody, or rely on the lawyer's advice. A lawyer's discussions with a prospective client usually are limited in time and depth and leave both the prospective client and the lawyer free (and sometimes required) to proceed no further. Hence, prospective clients should receive some but not all of the protection afforded clients.

[2]　Not all persons who communicate information to a lawyer are entitled to protection under this Rule. A person who communicates information unilaterally to a lawyer, without any reasonable expectation that the lawyer is willing to discuss the possibility of forming a client-lawyer relationship, is not a "prospective client" within the meaning of paragraph (a).

[3]　It is often necessary for a prospective client to reveal information to the lawyer during an initial consultation prior to the decision about formation of a client-lawyer relationship. The lawyer often must learn such information to determine whether there is a conflict of interest with an existing client and whether the matter is one that the lawyer is willing to undertake. Paragraph (b) prohibits the lawyer from using or revealing that information, except as permitted by Rule 1.9, even if the client or lawyer decides not to proceed with the representation. The duty exists regardless of how brief the initial conference may be.

[4]　In order to avoid acquiring disqualifying information from a prospective client, a lawyer considering whether or not to undertake a new matter should limit the initial interview to only such information as reasonably appears necessary for that purpose. Where the information indicates that a conflict of interest or other reason for non-representation exists, the lawyer should so inform the prospective client or decline the representation. If the prospective client wishes to retain the lawyer, and if consent is possible under Rule 1.7, then consent from all affected present or former clients must be obtained before accepting the representation.

[5]　A lawyer may condition conversations with a prospective client on the person's informed consent that no information disclosed during the consultation will prohibit the lawyer from representing a different client in the matter. See Rule 1.0(e) for the definition of informed consent. If the agreement expressly so provides, the prospective client may also consent to the lawyer's subsequent use of information received from the prospective client.

[6]　Even in the absence of an agreement, under paragraph (c), the lawyer is not prohibited from representing a client with interests adverse to those of the prospective client in the same or a substantially related matter unless the lawyer has received from the prospective client information that could be significantly harmful if used against the prospective client in the matter.

[7]　Under paragraph (c), the prohibition in this Rule is imputed to other lawyers as provided in Rule 1.10, but, under paragraph (d)(1) imputation may

be avoided if the lawyer obtains the informed consent, confirmed in writing, of both the prospective and affected clients. In the alternative, imputation may be avoided if the conditions of paragraph (d)(2) are met and all disqualified lawyers are timely screened and written notice is promptly given to the prospective client. See Rule 1.0(k) (requirements for screening procedures). Paragraph (d)(2)(i) does not prohibit the screened lawyer from receiving a salary or partnership share established by prior independent agreement, but that lawyer may not receive compensation directly related to the matter in which the lawyer is disqualified.

[8]   Notice, including a description of the screened lawyer's prior representation and of the screening procedures employed, generally should be given as soon as practicable after the need for screening becomes apparent.

[9]   For the duty of competence of a lawyer who gives assistance on the merits of a matter to a prospective client, see Rule 1.1. For a lawyer's duties when a prospective client entrusts valuables or papers to the lawyer's care, see Rule 1.15.

COUNSELOR

RULE 2.1: ADVISOR

In representing a client, a lawyer shall exercise independent professional judgment and render candid advice. In rendering advice, a lawyer may refer not only to law but to other considerations such as moral, economic, social and political factors, that may be relevant to the client's situation.

Comment
Scope of Advice

[1]   A client is entitled to straightforward advice expressing the lawyer's honest assessment. Legal advice often involves unpleasant facts and alternatives that a client may be disinclined to confront. In presenting advice, a lawyer endeavors to sustain the client's morale and may put advice in as acceptable a form as honesty permits. However, a lawyer should not be deterred from giving candid advice by the prospect that the advice will be unpalatable to the client.

[2]   Advice couched in narrowly legal terms may be of little value to a client, especially where practical considerations, such as cost or effects on other people, are predominant. Purely technical legal advice, therefore, can sometimes be inadequate. It is proper for a lawyer to refer to relevant moral and ethical considerations in giving advice. Although a lawyer is not a moral advisor as such, moral and ethical considerations impinge upon most legal questions and may decisively influence how the law will be applied.

[3]   A client may expressly or impliedly ask the lawyer for purely technical advice. When such a request is made by a client experienced in legal matters, the lawyer may accept it at face value. When such a request is made

by a client inexperienced in legal matters, however, the lawyer's responsibility as advisor may include indicating that more may be involved than strictly legal considerations.

[4]   Matters that go beyond strictly legal questions may also be in the domain of another profession. Family matters can involve problems within the professional competence of psychiatry, clinical psychology or social work; business matters can involve problems within the competence of the accounting profession or of financial specialists. Where consultation with a professional in another field is itself something a competent lawyer would recommend, the lawyer should make such a recommendation. At the same time, a lawyer's advice at its best often consists of recommending a course of action in the face of conflicting recommendations of experts.

Offering Advice

[5]   In general, a lawyer is not expected to give advice until asked by the client. However, when a lawyer knows that a client proposes a course of action that is likely to result in substantial adverse legal consequences to the client, the lawyer's duty to the client under Rule 1.4 may require that the lawyer act offer advice if the client's course of action is related to the representation. Similarly, when a matter is likely to involve litigation, it may be necessary under Rule 1.4 to inform the client of forms of dispute resolution that might constitute reasonable alternatives to litigation. A lawyer ordinarily has no duty to initiate investigation of a client's affairs or to give advice that the client has indicated is unwanted, but a lawyer may initiate advice to a client when doing so appears to be in the client's interest.

RULE 2.2: INTERMEDIARY

(a) A lawyer may act as intermediary between clients if:

(1) the lawyer consults with each client concerning the implications of the common representation, including the advantages and risks involved, and the effect on the attorney-client privileges, and obtains each client's consent to the common representation;

(2) the lawyer reasonably believes that the matter can be resolved on terms compatible with the clients' best interests, that each client will be able to make adequately informed decisions in the matter and that there is little risk of material prejudice to the interests of any of the clients if the contemplated resolution is unsuccessful; and

(3) the lawyer reasonably believes that the common representation can be undertaken impartially and without improper effect on other responsibilities the lawyer has to any of the clients.

83

(b) While acting as intermediary, the lawyer shall consult with each client concerning the decisions to be made and the considerations relevant in making them, so that each client can make adequately informed decisions.

(c) A lawyer shall withdraw as intermediary if any of the clients so requests, or if any of the conditions stated in paragraph (a) is no longer satisfied. Upon withdrawal, the lawyer shall not continue to represent any of the clients in the matter that was the subject of the intermediation.

Comment

[1] A lawyer acts as intermediary under this Rule when the lawyer represents two or more parties with potentially conflicting interests. A key factor in defining the relationship is whether the parties share responsibility for the lawyer's fee, but the common representation may be inferred from other circumstances. Because confusion can arise as to the lawyer's role where each party is not separately represented, it is important that the lawyer make clear the relationship.

[2] The Rule does not apply to a lawyer acting as arbitrator or mediator between or among parties who are not clients of the lawyer, even where the lawyer has been appointed with the concurrence of the parties. In performing such a role the lawyer may be subject to applicable codes of ethics, such as the Code of Ethics for Arbitration in Commercial Disputes prepared by a joint Committee of the American Bar Association and the American Arbitration Association.

[3] A lawyer acts as intermediary in seeking to establish or adjust a relationship between clients on an amicable and mutually advantageous basis; for example, in helping to organize a business in which two or more clients are entrepreneurs, working out the financial reorganization of an enterprise in which two or more clients have an interest, arranging a property distribution in settlement of an estate or mediating a dispute between clients. The lawyer seeks to resolve potentially conflicting interests by developing the parties' mutual interests. The alternative can be that each party may have to obtain separate representation, with the possibility in some situations of incurring additional cost, complication or even litigation. Given these and other relevant factors, all the clients may prefer that the lawyer act as intermediary.

[4] In considering whether to act as intermediary between clients, a lawyer should be mindful that if the intermediation fails the result can be additional cost, embarrassment and recrimination. In some situations the risk of failure is so great that intermediation is plainly impossible. For example, a lawyer cannot undertake common representation of clients between whom contentious litigation is imminent or who contemplate contentious negotiations. More generally, if the relationship between the parties has already

assumed definite antagonism, the possibility that the clients' interests can be adjusted by intermediation ordinarily is not very good.

[5] The appropriateness of intermediation can depend on its form. Forms of intermediation range from informal arbitration, where each client's case is presented by the respective client and the lawyer decides the outcome, to mediation, to common representation where the clients' interests are substantially though not entirely compatible. One form may be appropriate in circumstances where another would not. Other relevant factors are whether the lawyer subsequently will represent both parties on a continuing basis and whether the situation involves creating a relationship between the parties or terminating one.

Confidentiality and Privilege

[6] A particularly important factor in determining the appropriateness of intermediation is the effect on client-lawyer confidentiality and the attorney-client privilege. In a common representation, the lawyer is still required both to keep each client adequately informed and to maintain confidentiality of information relating to the representation. See Rules 1.4 and 1.6. Complying with both requirements while acting as intermediary requires a delicate balance. If the balance cannot be maintained, the common representation is improper. With regard to the attorney-client privilege, the prevailing rule is that as between commonly represented clients the privilege does not attach. Hence, it must be assumed that if litigation eventuates between the clients, the privilege will not protect any such communications, and the clients should be so advised.

[7] Since the lawyer is required to be impartial between commonly represented clients, intermediation is improper when that impartiality cannot be maintained. For example, a lawyer who has represented one of the clients for a long period and in a variety of matters might have difficulty being impartial between that client and one to whom the lawyer has only recently been introduced.

Consultation

[8] In acting as intermediary between clients, the lawyer is required to consult with the clients on the implications of doing so, and proceed only upon consent based on such a consultation. The consultation should make clear that the lawyer's role is not that of partisanship normally expected in other circumstances.

[9] Paragraph (b) is an application of the principle expressed in Rule 1.4. Where the lawyer is intermediary, the clients ordinarily must assume greater responsibility for decisions than when each client is independently represented.

Withdrawal

[10] Common representation does not diminish the rights of each client in the client-lawyer relationship. Each has the right to loyal and diligent

~~representation, the right to discharge the lawyer as stated in Rule 1.16, and the protection of Rule 1.9 concerning obligations to a former client.~~

RULE 2.3: EVALUATION FOR USE BY THIRD PERSONS

(a) A lawyer may ~~undertake~~ provide an evaluation of a matter affecting a client for the use of someone other than the client if: ~~(1)~~ the lawyer reasonably believes that making the evaluation is compatible with other aspects of the lawyer's relationship with the client; ~~and~~.

~~(2)~~ (b) When the lawyer knows or reasonably should know that the evaluation is likely to affect the client's interests materially and adversely, the lawyer shall not provide the evaluation unless the client ~~consents after consultation~~ gives informed consent.

~~(b)~~ (c) Except as disclosure is ~~required~~ authorized in connection with a report of an evaluation, information relating to the evaluation is otherwise protected by Rule 1.6.

Comment

Definition

[1] An evaluation may be performed at the client's direction ~~but~~ or when impliedly authorized in order to carry out the representation. See Rule 1.2. Such an evaluation may be for the primary purpose of establishing information for the benefit of third parties; for example, an opinion concerning the title of property rendered at the behest of a vendor for the information of a prospective purchaser, or at the behest of a borrower for the information of a prospective lender. In some situations, the evaluation may be required by a government agency; for example, an opinion concerning the legality of the securities registered for sale under the securities laws. In other instances, the evaluation may be required by a third person, such as a purchaser of a business.

~~[2] Lawyers for the government may be called upon to give a formal opinion on the legality of contemplated government agency action. In making such an evaluation, the government lawyer acts at the behest of the government as the client but for the purpose of establishing the limits of the agency's authorized activity. Such an opinion is to be distinguished from confidential legal advice given agency officials. The critical question is whether the opinion is to be made public.~~

~~[3]~~ [2] A legal evaluation should be distinguished from an investigation of a person with whom the lawyer does not have a client-lawyer relationship. For example, a lawyer retained by a purchaser to analyze a vendor's title to property does not have a client-lawyer relationship with the vendor. So also, an investigation into a person's affairs by a government lawyer, or by special counsel by a government lawyer, or by special counsel employed by the government, is not an evaluation as that term is used in this Rule. The question is whether the lawyer is retained by the person whose affairs are being examined. When the lawyer is retained by that person, the general rules concerning loyalty to client and preservation of confidences apply, which is not the case if the lawyer is retained by someone else. For this reason, it is essential to identify the person by whom the lawyer is retained. This should be made clear not only to the person under examination, but also to others to whom the results are to be made available.

~~Duty~~ Duties Owed to Third Person and Client

[4] [3] When the evaluation is intended for the information or use of a third person, a legal duty to that person may or may not arise. That legal question is beyond the scope of this Rule. However, since such an evaluation involves a departure from the normal client-lawyer relationship, careful analysis of the situation is required. The lawyer must be satisfied as a matter of professional judgment that making the evaluation is compatible with other functions undertaken in behalf of the client. For example, if the lawyer is acting as advocate in defending the client against charges of fraud, it would normally be incompatible with that responsibility for the lawyer to perform an evaluation for others concerning the same or a related transaction. Assuming no such impediment is apparent, however, the lawyer should advise the client of the implications of the evaluation, particularly the lawyer's responsibilities to third persons and the duty to disseminate the findings.

Access to and Disclosure of Information

[5] [4] The quality of an evaluation depends on the freedom and extent of the investigation upon which it is based. Ordinarily a lawyer should have whatever latitude of investigation seems necessary as a matter of professional judgment. Under some circumstances, however, the terms of the evaluation may be limited. For example, certain issues or sources may be categorically excluded, or the scope of search may be limited by time constraints or the noncooperation of persons having relevant information. Any such limitations which are material to the evaluation should be described in the report. If after a lawyer has commenced an evaluation, the client refuses to comply with the terms upon which it was understood the evaluation was to have been made, the lawyer's obligations are determined by law, having reference to the terms of the client's agreement and the surrounding circumstances. In no circumstances is the lawyer permitted to knowingly make a false statement of material fact or law in providing an evaluation under this Rule. See Rule 4.1.

Obtaining Client's Informed Consent

[5] Information relating to an evaluation is protected by Rule 1.6. In many situations, providing an evaluation to a third party poses no significant risk to the client; thus, the lawyer may be impliedly authorized to disclose information to carry out the representation. See Rule 1.6(a). Where, however, it is reasonably likely that providing the evaluation will affect the client's interests materially and adversely, the lawyer must first obtain the client's

consent after the client has been adequately informed concerning the important possible effects on the client's interests. See Rules 1.6(a) and 1.0(e).

Financial Auditors' Requests for Information

[6] When a question concerning the legal situation of a client arises at the instance of the client's financial auditor and the question is referred to the lawyer, the lawyer's response may be made in accordance with procedures recognized in the legal profession. Such a procedure is set forth in the American Bar Association Statement of Policy Regarding Lawyers' Responses to Auditors' Requests for Information, adopted in 1975.

RULE 2.4: LAWYER SERVING AS THIRD–PARTY NEUTRAL

(a) A lawyer serves as a third-party neutral when the lawyer assists two or more persons who are not clients of the lawyer to reach a resolution of a dispute or other matter that has arisen between them. Service as a third-party neutral may include service as an arbitrator, a mediator or in such other capacity as will enable the lawyer to assist the parties to resolve the matter.

(b) A lawyer serving as a third-party neutral shall inform unrepresented parties that the lawyer is not representing them. When the lawyer knows or reasonably should know that a party does not understand the lawyer's role in the matter, the lawyer shall explain the difference between the lawyer's role as a third-party neutral and a lawyer's role as one who represents a client.

Comment

[1] Alternative dispute resolution has become a substantial part of the civil justice system. Aside from representing clients in dispute-resolution processes, lawyers often serve as third-party neutrals. A third-party neutral is a person, such as a mediator, arbitrator, conciliator or evaluator, who assists the parties, represented or unrepresented, in the resolution of a dispute or in the arrangement of a transaction. Whether a third-party neutral serves primarily as a facilitator, evaluator or decisionmaker depends on the particular process that is either selected by the parties or mandated by a court.

[2] The role of a third-party neutral is not unique to lawyers, although, in some court-connected contexts, only lawyers are allowed to serve in this role or to handle certain types of cases. In performing this role, the lawyer may be subject to court rules or other law that apply either to third-party neutrals generally or to lawyers serving as third-party neutrals. Lawyer-neutrals may also be subject to various codes of ethics, such as the Code of Ethics for Arbitration in Commercial Disputes prepared by a joint committee of the American Bar Association and the American Arbitration Association or the Model Standards of Conduct for Mediators jointly prepared by the American Bar Association, the American Arbitration Association and the Society of Professionals in Dispute Resolution.

[3]   Unlike nonlawyers who serve as third-party neutrals, lawyers serving in this role may experience unique problems as a result of differences between the role of a third-party neutral and a lawyer's service as a client representative. The potential for confusion is significant when the parties are unrepresented in the process. Thus, paragraph (b) requires a lawyer-neutral to inform unrepresented parties that the lawyer is not representing them. For some parties, particularly parties who frequently use dispute-resolution processes, this information will be sufficient. For others, particularly those who are using the process for the first time, more information will be required. Where appropriate, the lawyer should inform unrepresented parties of the important differences between the lawyer's role as third-party neutral and a lawyer's role as a client representative, including the inapplicability of the attorney-client evidentiary privilege. The extent of disclosure required under this paragraph will depend on the particular parties involved and the subject matter of the proceeding, as well as the particular features of the dispute-resolution process selected.

[4]   A lawyer who serves as a third-party neutral subsequently may be asked to serve as a lawyer representing a client in the same matter. The conflicts of interest that arise for both the individual lawyer and the lawyer's law firm are addressed in Rule 1.12.

[5]   Lawyers who represent clients in alternative dispute-resolution processes are governed by the Rules of Professional Conduct. When the dispute-resolution process takes place before a tribunal, as in binding arbitration (see Rule 1.0(m)), the lawyer's duty of candor is governed by Rule 3.3. Otherwise, the lawyer's duty of candor toward both the third-party neutral and other parties is governed by Rule 4.1.

ADVOCATE

RULE 3.1: MERITORIOUS CLAIMS AND CONTENTIONS

A lawyer shall not bring or defend a proceeding, or assert or controvert an issue therein, unless there is a basis in law and fact for doing so that is not frivolous, which includes a good faith argument for an extension, modification or reversal of existing law. A lawyer for the defendant in a criminal proceeding, or the respondent in a proceeding that could result in incarceration, may nevertheless so defend the proceeding as to require that every element of the case be established.

Comment

[1]   The advocate has a duty to use legal procedure for the fullest benefit of the client's cause, but also a duty not to abuse legal procedure. The law, both procedural and substantive, establishes the limits within which an advocate may proceed. However, the law is not always clear and never is static. Accordingly, in determining the proper scope of advocacy, account must be taken of the law's ambiguities and potential for change.

[2]   The filing of an action or defense or similar action taken for a client is not frivolous merely because the facts have not first been fully substantiated or because the lawyer expects to develop vital evidence only by discovery. What is required of lawyers, however, is that they inform themselves about the facts of their clients' cases and the applicable law and determine that they can make good faith arguments in support of their clients' positions. Such action is not frivolous even though the lawyer believes that the client's position ultimately will not prevail. The action is frivolous, however, if the ~~client desires to have the action is taken primarily for the purpose of harassing or maliciously injuring a person, or, if the~~ lawyer is unable either to make a good faith argument on the merits of the action taken or to support the action taken by a good faith argument for an extension, modification or reversal of existing law.

[3]   The lawyer's obligations under this Rule are subordinate to federal or state constitutional law that entitles a defendant in a criminal matter to the assistance of counsel in presenting a claim or contention that otherwise would be prohibited by this Rule.

RULE 3.2: EXPEDITING LITIGATION

A lawyer shall make reasonable efforts to expedite litigation consistent with the interests of the client.

Comment

[1]   Dilatory practices bring the administration of justice into disrepute. ~~Delay should not be indulged merely for the convenience of the advocates, or~~ Although there will be occasions when a lawyer may properly seek a postponement for personal reasons, it is not proper for a lawyer to routinely fail to expedite litigation solely for the convenience of the advocates. Nor will failure to expedite be reasonable if done for the purpose of frustrating an opposing party's attempt to obtain rightful redress or repose. It is not a justification that similar conduct is often tolerated by the bench and bar. The question is whether a competent lawyer acting in good faith would regard the course of action as having some substantial purpose other than delay. Realizing financial or other benefit from otherwise improper delay in litigation is not a legitimate interest of the client.

RULE 3.3: CANDOR TOWARD THE TRIBUNAL

(a) A lawyer shall not knowingly:

(1)   make a false statement of ~~material~~ fact or law to a tribunal or fail to correct a false statement of material fact or law previously made to the tribunal by the lawyer;

(2) ~~fail to disclose a material fact to a tribunal when disclosure is necessary to avoid assisting a criminal or fraudulent act by the client;~~

(3) (2) **fail to disclose to the tribunal legal authority in the controlling jurisdiction known to the lawyer to be directly adverse to the position of the client and not disclosed by opposing counsel; or**

(4) (3) **offer evidence that the lawyer knows to be false. If a lawyer, the lawyer's client, or a witness called by the lawyer, has offered material evidence and the lawyer comes to know of its falsity, the lawyer shall take reasonable remedial measures, including, if necessary, disclosure to the tribunal. A lawyer may refuse to offer evidence, other than the testimony of a defendant in a criminal matter, that the lawyer reasonably believes is false.**

(b) **A lawyer who represents a client in an adjudicative proceeding and who knows that a person intends to engage, is engaging or has engaged in criminal or fraudulent conduct related to the proceeding shall take reasonable remedial measures, including, if necessary, disclosure to the tribunal.**

(b) (c) **The duties stated in paragraph paragraphs (a) and (b) continue to the conclusion of the proceeding, and apply even if compliance requires disclosure of information otherwise protected by Rule 1.6.**

(c) A lawyer may refuse to offer evidence that the lawyer reasonably believes is false.

(d) **In an ex parte proceeding, a lawyer shall inform the tribunal of all material facts known to the lawyer which will enable the tribunal to make an informed decision, whether or not the facts are adverse.**

Comment

[1]   This Rule governs the conduct of a lawyer who is representing a client in the proceedings of a tribunal. See Rule 1.0(m) for the definition of "tribunal." It also applies when the lawyer is representing a client in an ancillary proceeding conducted pursuant to the tribunal's adjudicative authority, such as a deposition. Thus, for example, paragraph (a)(3) requires a lawyer to take reasonable remedial measures if the lawyer comes to know that a client who is testifying in a deposition has offered evidence that is false.

[1] [2] The advocate's task is This Rule sets forth the special duties of lawyers as officers of the court to avoid conduct that undermines the integrity of the adjudicative process. A lawyer acting as an advocate in an adjudicative proceeding has an obligation to present the client's case with persuasive force. Performance of that duty while maintaining confidences of the client, however, is qualified by the advocate's duty of candor to the tribunal. However Consequently, an advocate does although a lawyer in an adversary proceeding is not required to present an impartial exposition of the law or to vouch for the evidence submitted in a cause;, the lawyer must not allow the tribunal is

~~responsible for assessing its probative value~~ to be misled by false statements of law or fact or evidence that the lawyer knows to be false.

Representations by a Lawyer

~~[2]~~ [3] An advocate is responsible for pleadings and other documents prepared for litigation, but is usually not required to have personal knowledge of matters asserted therein, for litigation documents ordinarily present assertions by the client, or by someone on the client's behalf, and not assertions by the lawyer. Compare Rule 3.1. However, an assertion purporting to be on the lawyer's own knowledge, as in an affidavit by the lawyer or in a statement in open court, may properly be made only when the lawyer knows the assertion is true or believes it to be true on the basis of a reasonably diligent inquiry. There are circumstances where failure to make a disclosure is the equivalent of an affirmative misrepresentation. The obligation prescribed in Rule 1.2(d) not to counsel a client to commit or assist the client in committing a fraud applies in litigation. Regarding compliance with Rule 1.2(d), see the Comment to that Rule. See also the Comment to Rule 8.4(b).

~~Misleading~~ Legal Argument

~~[3]~~ [4] Legal argument based on a knowingly false representation of law constitutes dishonesty toward the tribunal. A lawyer is not required to make a disinterested exposition of the law, but must recognize the existence of pertinent legal authorities. Furthermore, as stated in paragraph (a)~~(3)~~(2), an advocate has a duty to disclose directly adverse authority in the controlling jurisdiction which has not been disclosed by the opposing party. The underlying concept is that legal argument is a discussion seeking to determine the legal premises properly applicable to the case.

~~False~~ Offering Evidence

~~[4] When evidence that a lawyer knows to be false is provided by a person who is not the client, the lawyer must refuse to offer it regardless of the client's wishes.~~

~~[5] When false evidence is offered by the client, however, a conflict may arise between the lawyer's duty to keep the client's revelations confidential and the duty of candor to the court. Upon ascertaining that material evidence is false, the lawyer should seek to persuade the client that the evidence should not be offered or, if it has been offered, that its false character should immediately be disclosed. If the persuasion is ineffective, the lawyer must take reasonable remedial measures.~~

[5] Paragraph (a)(3) requires that the lawyer refuse to offer evidence that the lawyer knows to be false, regardless of the client's wishes. This duty is premised on the lawyer's obligation as an officer of the court to prevent the trier of fact from being misled by false evidence. A lawyer does not violate this Rule if the lawyer offers the evidence for the purpose of establishing its falsity.

[6]   If a lawyer knows that the client intends to testify falsely or wants the lawyer to introduce false evidence, the lawyer should seek to persuade the client that the evidence should not be offered. If the persuasion is ineffective and the lawyer continues to represent the client, the lawyer must refuse to offer the false evidence. If only a portion of a witness's testimony will be false, the lawyer may call the witness to testify but may not elicit or otherwise permit the witness to present the testimony that the lawyer knows is false.

[7]   The duties stated in paragraphs (a) and (b) apply to all lawyers, including defense counsel in criminal cases. In some jurisdictions, however, courts have required counsel to present the accused as a witness or to give a narrative statement if the accused so desires, even if counsel knows that the testimony or statement will be false. The obligation of the advocate under the Rules of Professional Conduct is subordinate to such requirements. See also Comment [9].

[8]   The prohibition against offering false evidence only applies if the lawyer knows that the evidence is false. A lawyer's reasonable belief that evidence is false does not preclude its presentation to the trier of fact. A lawyer's knowledge that evidence is false, however, can be inferred from the circumstances. See Rule 1.0(f). Thus, although a lawyer should resolve doubts about the veracity of testimony or other evidence in favor of the client, the lawyer cannot ignore an obvious falsehood.

Refusing to Offer Proof Believed to Be False

[14] [9] ~~Generally speaking,~~ Although paragraph (a)(3) only prohibits a lawyer ~~has authority~~ from offering evidence the lawyer knows to be false, it permits the lawyer to refuse to offer testimony or other proof that the lawyer reasonably believes is ~~untrustworthy~~ false. Offering such proof may reflect adversely on the lawyer's ability to discriminate in the quality of evidence and thus impair the lawyer's effectiveness as an advocate. ~~In criminal cases, however, a lawyer may, in some jurisdictions, be denied this authority by constitutional requirements governing the right to counsel.~~ Because of the special protections historically provided criminal defendants, however, this Rule does not permit a lawyer to refuse to offer the testimony of such a client where the lawyer reasonably believes but does not know that the testimony will be false. Unless the lawyer knows the testimony will be false, the lawyer must honor the client's decision to testify. See also Comment [7].

Perjury by a Criminal Defendant

~~[7] Whether an advocate for a criminally accused has the same duty of disclosure has been intensely debated. While it is agreed that the lawyer should seek to persuade the client to refrain from perjurious testimony, there has been dispute concerning the lawyer's duty when that persuasion fails. If the confrontation with the client occurs before trial, the lawyer ordinarily can withdraw. Withdrawal before trial may not be possible, however, either because trial is imminent, or because the confrontation with the client does not take place until the trial itself, or because no other counsel is available.~~

[8] ~~The most difficult situation, therefore, arises in a criminal case where the accused insists on testifying when the lawyer knows that the testimony is perjurious. The lawyer's effort to rectify the situation can increase the likelihood of the client's being convicted as well as opening the possibility of a prosecution for perjury. On the other hand, if the lawyer does not exercise control over the proof, the lawyer participates, although in a merely passive way, in deception of the court.~~

[9] ~~Three resolutions of this dilemma have been proposed. One is to permit the accused to testify by a narrative without guidance through the lawyer's questioning. This compromises both contending principles; it exempts the lawyer from the duty to disclose false evidence but subjects the client to an implicit disclosure of information imparted to counsel. Another suggested resolution, of relatively recent origin, is that the advocate be entirely excused from the duty to reveal perjury if the perjury is that of the client. This is a coherent solution but makes the advocate a knowing instrument of perjury.~~

[10] ~~The other resolution of the dilemma is that the lawyer must reveal the client's perjury if necessary to rectify the situation. A criminal accused has a right to the assistance of an advocate, a right to testify and a right of confidential communication with counsel. However, an accused should not have a right to assistance of counsel in committing perjury. Furthermore, an advocate has an obligation, not only in professional ethics but under the law as well, to avoid implication in the commission of perjury or other falsification of evidence. See Rule 1.2(d).~~

Remedial Measures

[~~11~~] [10] ~~If perjured testimony or false~~ Having offered material evidence ~~has been offered~~ in the belief that it was true, a lawyer may subsequently come to know that the evidence is false. Or, a lawyer may be surprised when the lawyer's client or another witness called by the lawyer offers testimony the lawyer knows to be false, either during the lawyer's direct examination or in response to cross-examination by the opposing lawyer. In such situations or if the lawyer knows of the falsity of testimony elicited from the client during a deposition, the lawyer must take reasonable remedial measures. In such situations, the advocate's proper course ~~ordinarily~~ is to remonstrate with the client confidentially, advise the client of the lawyer's duty of candor to the tribunal and seek the client's cooperation with respect to the withdrawal or correction of the false statements or evidence. If that fails, the advocate ~~should seek to withdraw if that will remedy the situation~~ must take further remedial action. If withdrawal from the representation is not permitted or will not ~~remedy the situation or is impossible~~ undo the effect of the false evidence, the advocate ~~should~~ must make such disclosure to the ~~court~~ tribunal as is reasonably necessary to remedy the situation, even if doing so requires the lawyer to reveal information that otherwise would be protected by Rule 1.6. It is for the ~~court~~ tribunal then to determine what should be done—making a statement about the matter to the trier of fact, ordering a mistrial or perhaps nothing. ~~If the false testimony was that of the client, the client may controvert the lawyer's version of their communication when the lawyer discloses the situation to the court. If there is an issue whether the client has committed perjury, the lawyer cannot represent the client in resolution of the issue, and a mistrial may be unavoidable. An unscrupulous client might in this way attempt to produce a series of mistrials and thus escape prosecution. However, a second such encounter could be construed as a deliberate abuse of the right to counsel and as such a waiver of the right to further representation.~~

~~[6]~~ [11] ~~Except in the defense of a criminal accused, the rule generally recognized is that, if necessary to rectify the situation, an advocate must disclose the existence of the client's deception to the court or to the other party. Such a~~ The disclosure of a client's false testimony can result in grave consequences to the client, including not only a sense of betrayal but also loss of the case and perhaps a prosecution for perjury. But the alternative is that the lawyer cooperate in deceiving the court, thereby subverting the truthfinding process which the adversary system is designed to implement. See Rule 1.2(d). Furthermore, unless it is clearly understood that the lawyer will act upon the duty to disclose the existence of false evidence, the client can simply reject the lawyer's advice to reveal the false evidence and insist that the lawyer keep silent. Thus the client could in effect coerce the lawyer into being a party to fraud on the court.

Preserving Integrity of Adjudicative Process

[12]   Lawyers have a special obligation to protect a tribunal against criminal or fraudulent conduct that undermines the integrity of the adjudicative process, such as bribing, intimidating or otherwise unlawfully communicating with a witness, juror, court official or other participant in the proceeding, unlawfully destroying or concealing documents or other evidence or failing to disclose information to the tribunal when required by law to do so. Thus, paragraph (b) requires a lawyer to take reasonable remedial measures, including disclosure if necessary, whenever the lawyer knows that a person, including the lawyer's client, intends to engage, is engaging or has engaged in criminal or fraudulent conduct related to the proceeding.

~~Constitutional Requirements~~

~~[12] The general rule—that an advocate must reveal the existence of perjury with respect to a material fact, even that of a client—applies to defense counsel in criminal cases, as well as in other instances. However, the definition of the lawyer's ethical duty in such a situation may be qualified by constitutional provisions for due process and the right to counsel in criminal cases. In some jurisdictions these provisions have been construed to require that counsel present an accused as a witness if the accused wishes to testify, even if counsel knows the testimony will be false. The obligation of the advocate under these Rules is subordinate to such a constitutional requirement.~~

Duration of Obligation

[13] A practical time limit on the obligation to rectify ~~the presentation of~~ false evidence or false statements of law and fact has to be established. The conclusion of the proceeding is a reasonably definite point for the termination of the obligation. A proceeding has concluded within the meaning of this Rule when a final judgment in the proceeding has been affirmed on appeal or the time for review has passed.

Ex Parte Proceedings

[~~15~~] [14] Ordinarily, an advocate has the limited responsibility of presenting one side of the matters that a tribunal should consider in reaching a decision; the conflicting position is expected to be presented by the opposing party. However, in any ex parte proceeding, such as an application for a temporary restraining order, there is no balance of presentation by opposing advocates. The object of an ex parte proceeding is nevertheless to yield a substantially just result. The judge has an affirmative responsibility to accord the absent party just consideration. The lawyer for the represented party has the correlative duty to make disclosures of material facts known to the lawyer and that the lawyer reasonably believes are necessary to an informed decision.

Withdrawal

[15] Normally, a lawyer's compliance with the duty of candor imposed by this Rule does not require that the lawyer withdraw from the representation of a client whose interests will be or have been adversely affected by the lawyer's disclosure. The lawyer may, however, be required by Rule 1.16(a) to seek permission of the tribunal to withdraw if the lawyer's compliance with this Rule's duty of candor results in such an extreme deterioration of the client-lawyer relationship that the lawyer can no longer competently represent the client. Also see Rule 1.16(b) for the circumstances in which a lawyer will be permitted to seek a tribunal's permission to withdraw. In connection with a request for permission to withdraw that is premised on a client's misconduct, a lawyer may reveal information relating to the representation only to the extent reasonably necessary to comply with this Rule or as otherwise permitted by Rule 1.6.

RULE 3.4: FAIRNESS TO OPPOSING PARTY AND COUNSEL

A lawyer shall not:

(a) unlawfully obstruct another party's access to evidence or unlawfully alter, destroy or conceal a document or other material having potential evidentiary value. A lawyer shall not counsel or assist another person to do any such act;

(b) falsify evidence, counsel or assist a witness to testify falsely, or offer an inducement to a witness that is prohibited by law;

(c) knowingly disobey an obligation under the rules of a tribunal, except for an open refusal based on an assertion that no valid obligation exists;

(d) in pretrial procedure, make a frivolous discovery request or fail to make reasonably diligent effort to comply with a legally proper discovery request by an opposing party;

(e) in trial, allude to any matter that the lawyer does not reasonably believe is relevant or that will not be supported by admissible evidence, assert personal knowledge of facts in issue except when testifying as a witness, or state a personal opinion as to the justness of a cause, the credibility of a witness, the culpability of a civil litigant or the guilt or innocence of an accused; or

(f) request a person other than a client to refrain from voluntarily giving relevant information to another party unless:

(1) the person is a relative or an employee or other agent of a client; and

(2) the lawyer reasonably believes that the person's interests will not be adversely affected by refraining from giving such information.

Comment

[1] The procedure of the adversary system contemplates that the evidence in a case is to be marshalled competitively by the contending parties. Fair competition in the adversary system is secured by prohibitions against destruction or concealment of evidence, improperly influencing witnesses, obstructive tactics in discovery procedure, and the like.

[2] Documents and other items of evidence are often essential to establish a claim or defense. Subject to evidentiary privileges, the right of an opposing party, including the government, to obtain evidence through discovery or subpoena is an important procedural right. The exercise of that right can be frustrated if relevant material is altered, concealed or destroyed. Applicable law in many jurisdictions makes it an offense to destroy material for purpose of impairing its availability in a pending proceeding or one whose commencement can be foreseen. Falsifying evidence is also generally a criminal offense. Paragraph (a) applies to evidentiary material generally, including computerized information. Applicable law may permit a lawyer to take temporary possession of physical evidence of client crimes for the purpose of conducting a limited examination that will not alter or destroy material characteristics of the evidence. In such a case, applicable law may require the lawyer to turn the evidence over to the police or other prosecuting authority, depending on the circumstances.

[3] With regard to paragraph (b), it is not improper to pay a witness's expenses or to compensate an expert witness on terms permitted by law. The common law rule in most jurisdictions is that it is improper to pay an occurrence witness any fee for testifying and that it is improper to pay an expert witness a contingent fee.

[4]   Paragraph (f) permits a lawyer to advise employees of a client to refrain from giving information to another party, for the employees may identify their interests with those of the client. See also Rule 4.2.

RULE 3.5: IMPARTIALITY AND DECORUM OF THE TRIBUNAL

A lawyer shall not:

(a) seek to influence a judge, juror, prospective juror or other official by means prohibited by law;

(b) communicate ex parte with such a person ~~except as permitted~~ **during the proceeding unless authorized to do so** ~~by~~ **law or court order;**

(c) communicate with a juror or prospective juror after discharge of the jury if:

(1) the communication is prohibited by law or court order;

(2) the juror has made known to the lawyer a desire not to communicate; or

(3) the communication involves misrepresentation, coercion, duress or harassment; or

~~(e)~~ **(d) engage in conduct intended to disrupt a tribunal.**

Comment

[1]   Many forms of improper influence upon a tribunal are proscribed by criminal law. Others are specified in the ABA Model Code of Judicial Conduct, with which an advocate should be familiar. A lawyer is required to avoid contributing to a violation of such provisions.

[2]   During a proceeding a lawyer may not communicate ex parte with persons serving in an official capacity in the proceeding, such as judges, masters or jurors, unless authorized to do so by law or court order.

[3]   A lawyer may on occasion want to communicate with a juror or prospective juror after the jury has been discharged. The lawyer may do so unless the communication is prohibited by law or a court order but must respect the desire of the juror not to talk with the lawyer. The lawyer may not engage in improper conduct during the communication.

~~[2]~~ [4] The advocate's function is to present evidence and argument so that the cause may be decided according to law. Refraining from abusive or obstreperous conduct is a corollary of the advocate's right to speak on behalf of litigants. A lawyer may stand firm against abuse by a judge but should avoid reciprocation; the judge's default is no justification for similar dereliction by an advocate. An advocate can present the cause, protect the record for subsequent review and preserve professional integrity by patient firmness no less effectively than by belligerence or theatrics.

[5]   The duty to refrain from disruptive conduct applies to any proceeding of a tribunal, including a deposition. See Rule 1.0(m).

RULE 3.6: TRIAL PUBLICITY

(a) A lawyer who is participating or has participated in the investigation or litigation of a matter shall not make an extrajudicial statement that ~~a reasonable person would expect to~~ the lawyer knows or reasonably should know will be disseminated by means of public communication ~~if the lawyer knows or reasonably should know that it~~ and will have a substantial likelihood of materially prejudicing an adjudicative proceeding in the matter.

(b) Notwithstanding paragraph (a), a lawyer may state:

(1) the claim, offense or defense involved and, except when prohibited by law, the identity of the persons involved;

(2) information contained in a public record;

(3) that an investigation of a matter is in progress;

(4) the scheduling or result of any step in litigation;

(5) a request for assistance in obtaining evidence and information necessary thereto;

(6) a warning of danger concerning the behavior of a person involved, when there is reason to believe that there exists the likelihood of substantial harm to an individual or to the public interest; and

(7) in a criminal case, in addition to subparagraphs (1) through (6):

(i) the identity, residence, occupation and family status of the accused;

(ii) if the accused has not been apprehended, information necessary to aid in apprehension of that person;

(iii) the fact, time and place of arrest; and

(iv) the identity of investigating and arresting officers or agencies and the length of the investigation.

(c) Notwithstanding paragraph (a), a lawyer may make a statement that a reasonable lawyer would believe is required to protect a client from the substantial undue prejudicial effect of recent publicity not initiated by the lawyer or the lawyer's client. A statement made pursuant to this paragraph shall be limited to such information as is necessary to mitigate the recent adverse publicity.

(d) No lawyer associated in a firm or government agency with a lawyer subject to paragraph (a) shall make a statement prohibited by paragraph (a).

Comment

[1] It is difficult to strike a balance between protecting the right to a fair trial and safeguarding the right of free expression. Preserving the right to a fair trial necessarily entails some curtailment of the information that may be disseminated about a party prior to trial, particularly where trial by jury is involved. If there were no such limits, the result would be the practical nullification of the protective effect of the rules of forensic decorum and the exclusionary rules of evidence. On the other hand, there are vital social interests served by the free dissemination of information about events having legal consequences and about legal proceedings themselves. The public has a right to know about threats to its safety and measures aimed at assuring its security. It also has a legitimate interest in the conduct of judicial proceedings, particularly in matters of general public concern. Furthermore, the subject matter of legal proceedings is often of direct significance in debate and deliberation over questions of public policy.

[2] Special rules of confidentiality may validly govern proceedings in juvenile, domestic relations and mental disability proceedings, and perhaps other types of litigation. Rule 3.4(c) requires compliance with such rules.

[3] The Rule sets forth a basic general prohibition against a lawyer's making statements that the lawyer knows or should know will have a substantial likelihood of materially prejudicing an adjudicative proceeding. Recognizing that the public value of informed commentary is great and the likelihood of prejudice to a proceeding by the commentary of a lawyer who is not involved in the proceeding is small, the rule applies only to lawyers who are, or who have been involved in the investigation or litigation of a case, and their associates.

[4] Paragraph (b) identifies specific matters about which a lawyer's statements would not ordinarily be considered to present a substantial likelihood of material prejudice, and should not in any event be considered prohibited by the general prohibition of paragraph (a). Paragraph (b) is not intended to be an exhaustive listing of the subjects upon which a lawyer may make a statement, but statements on other matters may be subject to paragraph (a).

[5] There are, on the other hand, certain subjects which are more likely than not to have a material prejudicial effect on a proceeding, particularly when they refer to a civil matter triable to a jury, a criminal matter, or any other proceeding that could result in incarceration. These subjects relate to:

(1) the character, credibility, reputation or criminal record of a party, suspect in a criminal investigation or witness, or the identity of a witness, or the expected testimony of a party or witness;

(2) in a criminal case or proceeding that could result in incarceration, the possibility of a plea of guilty to the offense or the existence or contents of any confession, admission, or statement given by a defendant or suspect or that person's refusal or failure to make a statement;

(3) the performance or results of any examination or test or the refusal or failure of a person to submit to an examination or test, or the identity or nature of physical evidence expected to be presented;

(4) any opinion as to the guilt or innocence of a defendant or suspect in a criminal case or proceeding that could result in incarceration;

(5) information that the lawyer knows or reasonably should know is likely to be inadmissible as evidence in a trial and that would, if disclosed, create a substantial risk of prejudicing an impartial trial; or

(6) the fact that a defendant has been charged with a crime, unless there is included therein a statement explaining that the charge is merely an accusation and that the defendant is presumed innocent until and unless proven guilty.

[6] Another relevant factor in determining prejudice is the nature of the proceeding involved. Criminal jury trials will be most sensitive to extrajudicial speech. Civil trials may be less sensitive. Non-jury hearings and arbitration proceedings may be even less affected. The Rule will still place limitations on prejudicial comments in these cases, but the likelihood of prejudice may be different depending on the type of proceeding.

[7] Finally, extrajudicial statements that might otherwise raise a question under this Rule may be permissible when they are made in response to statements made publicly by another party, another party's lawyer, or third persons, where a reasonable lawyer would believe a public response is required in order to avoid prejudice to the lawyer's client. When prejudicial statements have been publicly made by others, responsive statements may have the salutary effect of lessening any resulting adverse impact on the adjudicative proceeding. Such responsive statements should be limited to contain only such information as is necessary to mitigate undue prejudice created by the statements made by others.

[8] See Rule 3.8(f) for additional duties of prosecutors in connection with extrajudicial statements about criminal proceedings.

RULE 3.7: LAWYER AS WITNESS

(a) A lawyer shall not act as advocate at a trial in which the lawyer is likely to be a necessary witness ~~except where~~ unless:

(1) the testimony relates to an uncontested issue;

(2) the testimony relates to the nature and value of legal services rendered in the case; or

(3) disqualification of the lawyer would work substantial hardship on the client.

(b) A lawyer may act as advocate in a trial in which another lawyer in the lawyer's firm is likely to be called as a witness unless precluded from doing so by Rule 1.7 or Rule 1.9.

101

Comment

[1] Combining the roles of advocate and witness can prejudice <u>the tribunal and</u> the opposing party and can <u>also</u> involve a conflict of interest between the lawyer and client.

Advocate–Witness Rule

[2] <u>The tribunal has proper objection when the trier of fact may be confused or misled by a lawyer serving as both advocate and witness.</u> The opposing party has proper objection where the combination of roles may prejudice that party's rights in the litigation. A witness is required to testify on the basis of personal knowledge, while an advocate is expected to explain and comment on evidence given by others. It may not be clear whether a statement by an advocate-witness should be taken as proof or as an analysis of the proof.

[3] <u>To protect the tribunal, paragraph (a) prohibits a lawyer from simultaneously serving as advocate and necessary witness except in those circumstances specified in paragraphs (a)(1) through (a)(3).</u> Paragraph (a)(1) recognizes that if the testimony will be uncontested, the ambiguities in the dual role are purely theoretical. Paragraph (a)(2) recognizes that where the testimony concerns the extent and value of legal services rendered in the action in which the testimony is offered, permitting the lawyers to testify avoids the need for a second trial with new counsel to resolve that issue. Moreover, in such a situation the judge has firsthand knowledge of the matter in issue; hence, there is less dependence on the adversary process to test the credibility of the testimony.

[4] Apart from these two exceptions, paragraph (a)(3) recognizes that a balancing is required between the interests of the client and those of the tribunal and the opposing party. Whether the <u>tribunal is likely to be misled or the</u> opposing party is likely to suffer prejudice depends on the nature of the case, the importance and probable tenor of the lawyer's testimony, and the probability that the lawyer's testimony will conflict with that of other witnesses. Even if there is risk of such prejudice, in determining whether the lawyer should be disqualified, due regard must be given to the effect of disqualification on the lawyer's client. It is relevant that one or both parties could reasonably foresee that the lawyer would probably be a witness. The ~~principle of imputed disqualification~~ <u>conflict of interest principles</u> stated in ~~Rule~~ <u>Rules</u> 1.7, 1.9 and 1.10 ~~has~~ <u>have</u> no application to this aspect of the problem.

[5] <u>Because the tribunal is not likely to be misled when a lawyer acts as advocate in a trial in which another lawyer in the lawyer's firm will testify as a necessary witness, paragraph (b) permits the lawyer to do so except in situations involving a conflict of interest.</u>

Conflict of Interest

~~[5]~~ [6] ~~Whether the combination of roles involves an improper~~ <u>In determining if it is permissible to act as advocate in a trial in which the lawyer will</u>

be a necessary witness, the lawyer must also consider that the dual role may give rise to a conflict of interest ~~with respect to the client is determined by Rule~~ that will require compliance with Rules 1.7 or 1.9. For example, if there is likely to be substantial conflict between the testimony of the client and that of the lawyer ~~or a member of the lawyer's firm~~, the representation ~~is improper~~ involves a conflict of interest that requires compliance with Rule 1.7. This would be true even though the lawyer might not be prohibited by paragraph (a) from simultaneously serving as advocate and witness because the lawyer's disqualification would work a substantial hardship on the client. Similarly, a lawyer who might be permitted to simultaneously serve as an advocate and a witness by paragraph (a)(3) might be precluded from doing so by Rule 1.9. The problem can arise whether the lawyer is called as a witness on behalf of the client or is called by the opposing party. Determining whether or not such a conflict exists is primarily the responsibility of the lawyer involved. If there is a conflict of interest, the lawyer must secure the client's informed consent, confirmed in writing. In some cases, the lawyer will be precluded from seeking the client's consent. See ~~Comment to~~ Rule 1.7. ~~If a lawyer who is a member of a firm may not act as both advocate and witness by reason of conflict of interest, Rule 1.10 disqualifies the firm also.~~ See Rule 1.0(b) for the definition of "confirmed in writing" and Rule 1.0(e) for the definition of "informed consent."

[7] Paragraph (b) provides that a lawyer is not disqualified from serving as an advocate because a lawyer with whom the lawyer is associated in a firm is precluded from doing so by paragraph (a). If, however, the testifying lawyer would also be disqualified by Rule 1.7 or Rule 1.9 from representing the client in the matter, other lawyers in the firm will be precluded from representing the client by Rule 1.10 unless the client gives informed consent under the conditions stated in Rule 1.7.

RULE 3.8: SPECIAL RESPONSIBILITIES OF A PROSECUTOR

The prosecutor in a criminal case shall:

(a) refrain from prosecuting a charge that the prosecutor knows is not supported by probable cause;

(b) make reasonable efforts to assure that the accused has been advised of the right to, and the procedure for obtaining, counsel and has been given reasonable opportunity to obtain counsel;

(c) not seek to obtain from an unrepresented accused a waiver of important pretrial rights, such as the right to a preliminary hearing;

(d) make timely disclosure to the defense of all evidence or information known to the prosecutor that tends to negate the guilt of the accused or mitigates the offense, and, in connection with sentencing, disclose to the defense and to the tribunal all unprivileged mitigating information known to the prosecutor, except when the

prosecutor is relieved of this responsibility by a protective order of the tribunal;

~~(e) exercise reasonable care to prevent investigators, law enforcement personnel, employees or other persons assisting or associated with the prosecutor in a criminal case from making an extrajudicial statement that the prosecutor would be prohibited from making under Rule 3.6;~~

~~(f)~~ (e) not subpoena a lawyer in a grand jury or other criminal proceeding to present evidence about a past or present client unless the prosecutor reasonably believes:

    (1) the information sought is not protected from disclosure by any applicable privilege;

    (2) the evidence sought is essential to the successful completion of an ongoing investigation or prosecution; and

    (3) there is no other feasible alternative to obtain the information~~.~~;

~~(g)~~ (f) except for statements that are necessary to inform the public of the nature and extent of the prosecutor's action and that serve a legitimate law enforcement purpose, refrain from making extrajudicial comments that have a substantial likelihood of heightening public condemnation of the accused <u>and exercise reasonable care to prevent investigators, law enforcement personnel, employees or other persons assisting or associated with the prosecutor in a criminal case from making an extrajudicial statement that the prosecutor would be prohibited from making under Rule 3.6 or this Rule.</u>

Comment

[1]   A prosecutor has the responsibility of a minister of justice and not simply that of an advocate. This responsibility carries with it specific obligations to see that the defendant is accorded procedural justice and that guilt is decided upon the basis of sufficient evidence. Precisely how far the prosecutor is required to go in this direction is a matter of debate and varies in different jurisdictions. Many jurisdictions have adopted the ABA Standards of Criminal Justice Relating to the Prosecution Function, which in turn are the product of prolonged and careful deliberation by lawyers experienced in both criminal prosecution and defense. ~~See also Rule 3.3(d), governing ex parte proceedings, among which grand jury proceedings are included.~~ Applicable law may require other measures by the prosecutor and knowing disregard of those obligations or a systematic abuse of prosecutorial discretion could constitute a violation of Rule 8.4.

[2]   <u>In some jurisdictions, a defendant may waive a preliminary hearing and thereby lose a valuable opportunity to challenge probable cause. Accordingly, prosecutors should not seek to obtain waivers of preliminary hearings or other important pretrial rights from unrepresented accused persons.</u> Para-

graph (c) does not apply, however, to an accused appearing *pro se* with the approval of the tribunal. Nor does it forbid the lawful questioning of a an uncharged suspect who has knowingly waived the rights to counsel and silence.

[3] The exception in paragraph (d) recognizes that a prosecutor may seek an appropriate protective order from the tribunal if disclosure of information to the defense could result in substantial harm to an individual or to the public interest.

[4] Paragraph (f) (e) is intended to limit the issuance of lawyer subpoenas in grand jury and other criminal proceedings to those situations in which there is a genuine need to intrude into the client-lawyer relationship.

[5] Paragraph (g) (f) supplements Rule 3.6, which prohibits extrajudicial statements that have a substantial likelihood of prejudicing an adjudicatory proceeding. In the context of a criminal prosecution, a prosecutor's extrajudicial statement can create the additional problem of increasing public condemnation of the accused. Although the announcement of an indictment, for example, will necessarily have severe consequences for the accused, a prosecutor can, and should, avoid comments which have no legitimate law enforcement purpose and have a substantial likelihood of increasing public opprobrium of the accused. Nothing in this Comment is intended to restrict the statements which a prosecutor may make which comply with Rule 3.6(b) or 3.6(c).

[6] Like other lawyers, prosecutors are subject to Rules 5.1 and 5.3, which relate to responsibilities regarding lawyers and nonlawyers who work for or are associated with the lawyer's office. Paragraph (f) reminds the prosecutor of the importance of these obligations in connection with the unique dangers of improper extrajudicial statements in a criminal case. In addition, paragraph (f) requires a prosecutor to exercise reasonable care to prevent persons assisting or associated with the prosecutor from making improper extrajudicial statements, even when such persons are not under the direct supervision of the prosecutor. Ordinarily, the reasonable care standard will be satisfied if the prosecutor issues the appropriate cautions to law-enforcement personnel and other relevant individuals.

RULE 3.9: ADVOCATE IN NONADJUDICATIVE PROCEEDINGS

A lawyer representing a client before a legislative body or administrative tribunal agency in a nonadjudicative proceeding shall disclose that the appearance is in a representative capacity and shall conform to the provisions of Rules 3.3(a) through (c), 3.4(a) through (c), and 3.5.

Comment

[1] In representation before bodies such as legislatures, municipal councils, and executive and administrative agencies acting in a rule-making or

policy-making capacity, lawyers present facts, formulate issues and advance argument in the matters under consideration. The decision-making body, like a court, should be able to rely on the integrity of the submissions made to it. A lawyer appearing before such a body ~~should~~ <u>must</u> deal with ~~the tribunal~~ <u>it</u> honestly and in conformity with applicable rules of procedure. <u>See Rules 3.3(a) through (c), 3.4(a) through (c) and 3.5.</u>

[2]   Lawyers have no exclusive right to appear before nonadjudicative bodies, as they do before a court. The requirements of this Rule therefore may subject lawyers to regulations inapplicable to advocates who are not lawyers. However, legislatures and administrative agencies have a right to expect lawyers to deal with them as they deal with courts.

[3]   This Rule <u>only applies when a lawyer represents a client in connection with an official hearing or meeting of a governmental agency or a legislative body to which the lawyer or the lawyer's client is presenting evidence or argument. It</u> does not apply to representation of a client in a negotiation or other bilateral transaction with a governmental agency~~; representation~~ or in connection with an application for a license or other privilege <u>or the client's compliance with generally applicable reporting requirements, such as the filing of income-tax returns. Nor does it apply to the representation of a client in connection with an investigation or examination of the client's affairs conducted by government investigators or examiners. Representation</u> in such ~~a transaction~~ <u>matters</u> is governed by Rules 4.1 through 4.4.

TRANSACTIONS WITH PERSONS OTHER THAN CLIENTS

RULE 4.1: TRUTHFULNESS IN STATEMENTS TO OTHERS

In the course of representing a client a lawyer shall not knowingly:

(a) make a false statement of material fact or law to a third person; or

(b) fail to disclose a material fact when disclosure is necessary to avoid assisting a criminal or fraudulent act by a client, unless disclosure is prohibited by Rule 1.6.

Comment

Misrepresentation

[1]   A lawyer is required to be truthful when dealing with others on a client's behalf, but generally has no affirmative duty to inform an opposing party of relevant facts. A misrepresentation can occur if the lawyer incorporates or affirms a statement of another person that the lawyer knows is false. Misrepresentations can also occur by ~~failure to act~~ <u>partially true but misleading statements or omissions that are the equivalent of affirmative false statements. For dishonest conduct that does not amount to a false statement</u>

or for misrepresentations by a lawyer other than in the course of representing a client, see Rule 8.4.

Statements of Fact

[2] This Rule refers to statements of fact. Whether a particular statement should be regarded as one of fact can depend on the circumstances. Under generally accepted conventions in negotiation, certain types of statements ordinarily are not taken as statements of material fact. Estimates of price or value placed on the subject of a transaction and a party's intentions as to an acceptable settlement of a claim are ordinarily in this category, and so is the existence of an undisclosed principal except where nondisclosure of the principal would constitute fraud. Lawyers should be mindful of their obligations under applicable law to avoid criminal and tortious misrepresentation.

Crime or Fraud by Client

[3] Under Rule 1.2(d), a lawyer is prohibited from counseling or assisting a client in conduct that the lawyer knows is criminal or fraudulent. Paragraph (b) ~~recognizes that~~ states a specific application of the principle set forth in Rule 1.2(d) and addresses the situation where a client's crime or fraud takes the form of a lie or misrepresentation. Ordinarily, a lawyer can avoid assisting a client's crime or fraud by withdrawing from the representation. Sometimes it may be necessary for the lawyer to give notice of the fact of withdrawal and to disaffirm an opinion, document, affirmation or the like. In extreme cases, substantive law may require a lawyer to disclose ~~certain~~ information relating to the representation to avoid being deemed to have assisted the client's crime or fraud. ~~The requirement of~~ If the lawyer can avoid assisting a client's crime or fraud only by disclosing this information, then under paragraph (b) the lawyer is required to do so, unless the disclosure ~~created by this paragraph is, however, subject to the obligations created~~ is prohibited by Rule 1.6.

RULE 4.2: COMMUNICATION WITH PERSON REPRESENTED BY COUNSEL

In representing a client, a lawyer shall not communicate about the subject of the representation with a person the lawyer knows to be represented by another lawyer in the matter, unless the lawyer has the consent of the other lawyer or is authorized to do so by law ~~to do so~~ or a court order.

Comment

[1] This Rule contributes to the proper functioning of the legal system by protecting a person who has chosen to be represented by a lawyer in a matter against possible overreaching by other lawyers who are participating in the matter, interference by those lawyers with the client-lawyer relation-

ship and the uncounselled disclosure of information relating to the representation.

~~[3]~~ [2] This Rule ~~also~~ applies to communications with any person, ~~whether or not a party to a formal adjudicative proceeding, contract or negotiation,~~ who is represented by counsel concerning the matter to which the communication relates.

[3] The Rule applies even though the represented person initiates or consents to the communication. A lawyer must immediately terminate communication with a person if, after commencing communication, the lawyer learns that the person is one with whom communication is not permitted by this Rule.

~~[1]~~ [4] This Rule does not prohibit communication with a represented person, or an employee or agent of such a person, concerning matters outside the representation. For example, the existence of a controversy between a government agency and a private party, or between two organizations, does not prohibit a lawyer for either from communicating with nonlawyer representatives of the other regarding a separate matter. ~~Also, parties~~ Nor does this Rule preclude communication with a represented person who is seeking advice from a lawyer who is not otherwise representing a client in the matter. A lawyer may not make a communication prohibited by this Rule through the acts of another. See Rule 8.4(a). Parties to a matter may communicate directly with each other, and a lawyer is not prohibited from advising a client concerning a communication that the client is legally entitled to make. Also, a lawyer having independent justification or legal authorization for communicating with a represented person is permitted to do so. ~~Communications authorized by law include, for example, the right of a party to a controversy with a government agency to speak with government officials about the matter.~~

[5] Communications authorized by law may include communications by a lawyer on behalf of a client who is exercising a constitutional or other legal right to communicate with the government. ~~[2]~~ Communications authorized by law may also include ~~constitutionally permissible~~ investigative activities of lawyers representing governmental entities, directly or through investigative agents, prior to the commencement of criminal or civil enforcement proceedings, ~~when there is applicable judicial precedent that either has found the activity permissible under this Rule or has found this Rule inapplicable. However, the Rule imposes ethical restrictions that go beyond those imposed by constitutional provisions~~. When communicating with a accused in criminal matters, a government lawyer must comply with this Rule in addition to honoring the constitutional rights of the accused. The fact that a communication does not violate a state or federal constitutional right is insufficient to establish that the communication is permissible under this Rule.

[6] A lawyer who is uncertain whether a communication with a represented person is permissible may seek a court order. A lawyer may also seek a court order in exceptional circumstances to authorize a communication that

would otherwise be prohibited by this Rule, for example, where communication with a person represented by counsel is necessary to avoid reasonably certain injury.

[4] [7] In the case of ~~an~~ a represented organization, this Rule prohibits communications ~~by a lawyer for another person or entity concerning the matter in representation~~ with ~~persons having a managerial responsibility on behalf~~ a constituent of the organization, ~~and with any other person~~ who supervises, directs or regularly consults with the organization's lawyer concerning the matter or has authority to obligate the organization with respect to the matter or whose act or omission in connection with ~~that~~ the matter may be imputed to the organization for purposes of civil or criminal liability ~~or whose statement may constitute an admission on the part of the organization~~. Consent of the organization's lawyer is not required for communication with a former constituent. If ~~an agent or employee~~ a constituent of the organization is represented in the matter by his or her own counsel, the consent by that counsel to a communication will be sufficient for purposes of this Rule. Compare Rule 3.4(f). In communicating with a current or former constituent of an organization, a lawyer must not use methods of obtaining evidence that violate the legal rights of the organization. See Rule 4.4, Comment [2].

[5] [8] The prohibition on communications with a represented person only applies, ~~however,~~ in circumstances where the lawyer knows that the person is in fact represented in the matter to be discussed. This means that the lawyer has actual knowledge of the fact of the representation; but such actual knowledge may be inferred from the circumstances. See ~~Terminology~~ Rule 1.0(f). ~~Such an inference may arise in circumstances where there is substantial reason to believe that the person with whom communication is sought is represented in the matter to be discussed.~~ Thus, the lawyer cannot evade the requirement of obtaining the consent of counsel by closing eyes to the obvious.

[6] [9] In the event the person with whom the lawyer communicates is not known to be represented by counsel in the matter, the lawyer's communications are subject to Rule 4.3.

RULE 4.3: DEALING WITH UNREPRESENTED PERSON

In dealing on behalf of a client with a person who is not represented by counsel, a lawyer shall not state or imply that the lawyer is disinterested. When the lawyer knows or reasonably should know that the unrepresented person misunderstands the lawyer's role in the matter, the lawyer shall make reasonable efforts to correct the misunderstanding. The lawyer shall not give legal advice to an unrepresented person, other than the advice to secure counsel, if the lawyer knows or reasonably should know that the interests of such a person are or have a reasonable possibility of being in conflict with the interests of the client.

Comment

[1]   An unrepresented person, particularly one not experienced in deal-ing with legal matters, might assume that a lawyer is disinterested in loyalties or is a disinterested authority on the law even when the lawyer represents a client. ~~During the course of a lawyer's representation of a client, the lawyer should not give advice to an unrepresented person other than the advice to obtain counsel.~~ In order to avoid a misunderstanding, a lawyer will typically need to identify the lawyer's client and, where necessary, explain that the client has interests opposed to those of the unrepresented person. For misun-derstandings that sometimes arise when a lawyer for an organization deals with an unrepresented constituent, see Rule 1.13(d).

[2]   The Rule distinguishes between situations involving unrepresented persons whose interests may be adverse to those of the lawyer's client and those in which the person's interests are not in conflict with the client's. In the former situation, the possibility that the lawyer will compromise the unrepresented person's interests is so great that the Rule prohibits the giving of any advice, apart from the advice to obtain counsel. Whether a lawyer is giving impermissible advice may depend on the experience and sophistication of the unrepresented person, as well as the setting in which the behavior and comments occur. This Rule does not prohibit a lawyer from negotiating the terms of a transaction or settling a dispute with an unrepresented person. So long as the lawyer has explained that the lawyer represents an adverse party and is not representing the person, the lawyer may inform the person of the terms on which the lawyer's client will enter into an agreement or settle a matter, prepare documents that require the person's signature and explain the lawyer's own view of the meaning of the document or the lawyer's view of the underlying legal obligations.

RULE 4.4: RESPECT FOR RIGHTS OF THIRD PERSONS

(a) **In representing a client, a lawyer shall not use means that have no substantial purpose other than to embarrass, delay, or burden a third person, or use methods of obtaining evidence that violate the legal rights of such a person.**

(b) **A lawyer who receives a document and knows or reasonably should know that the document was inadvertently sent shall prompt-ly notify the sender.**

Comment

[1]   Responsibility to a client requires a lawyer to subordinate the interests of others to those of the client, but that responsibility does not imply that a lawyer may disregard the rights of third persons. It is impractical to catalogue all such rights, but they include legal restrictions on methods of obtaining evidence from third persons and unwarranted intrusions into privi-leged relationships, such as the client-lawyer relationship.

[2]   Paragraph (b) recognizes that lawyers sometimes receive documents that were mistakenly sent or produced by opposing parties or their lawyers. If a lawyer knows or reasonably should know that a document was sent inadvertently, then this Rule requires the lawyer to promptly notify the sender in order to permit that person to take protective measures. Whether the lawyer is required to take additional steps, such as returning the original document, is a matter of law beyond the scope of these Rules, as is the question of whether the privileged status of a document has been waived. Similarly, this Rule does not address the legal duties of a lawyer who receives a document that the lawyer knows or reasonably should know may have been wrongfully obtained by the sending person. For purposes of this Rule, "document" includes e-mail or other electronic modes of transmission subject to being read or put into readable form.

[3]   Some lawyers may choose to return a document unread, for example, when the lawyer learns before receiving the document that it was inadvertently sent to the wrong address. Where a lawyer is not required by applicable law to do so, the decision to voluntarily return such a document is a matter of professional judgment ordinarily reserved to the lawyer. See Rules 1.2 and 1.4.

LAW FIRMS AND ASSOCIATIONS

RULE 5.1: RESPONSIBILITIES OF A PARTNER OR PARTNERS, MANAGERS, AND SUPERVISORY LAWYER LAWYERS

(a) A partner in a law firm, and a lawyer who individually or together with other lawyers possesses comparable managerial authority in a law firm, shall make reasonable efforts to ensure that the firm has in effect measures giving reasonable assurance that all lawyers in the firm conform to the Rules of Professional Conduct.

(b) A lawyer having direct supervisory authority over another lawyer shall make reasonable efforts to ensure that the other lawyer conforms to the Rules of Professional Conduct.

(c) A lawyer shall be responsible for another lawyer's violation of the Rules of Professional Conduct if:

(1) the lawyer orders or, with knowledge of the specific conduct, ratifies the conduct involved; or

(2) the lawyer is a partner or has comparable managerial authority in the law firm in which the other lawyer practices, or has direct supervisory authority over the other lawyer, and knows of the conduct at a time when its consequences can be avoided or mitigated but fails to take reasonable remedial action.

Comment

[1]   Paragraphs Paragraph (a) and (b) refer applies to lawyers who have supervisory managerial authority over the professional work of a firm or legal

~~department of a government agency~~. See Rule 1.0(c). This includes members of a partnership, ~~and~~ the shareholders in a law firm organized as a professional corporation, and members of other associations authorized to practice law; lawyers having ~~supervisory~~ comparable managerial authority in ~~the~~ a legal services organization or a law department of an enterprise or government agency; and lawyers who have intermediate managerial responsibilities in a firm. Paragraph (b) applies to lawyers who have supervisory authority over the work of other lawyers in a firm.

[2] Paragraph (a) requires lawyers with managerial authority within a firm, and the firm, to make reasonable efforts to establish internal policies and procedures designed to provide reasonable assurance that all lawyers in the firm will conform to the Rules of Professional Conduct. Such policies and procedures include those designed to detect and resolve conflicts of interest, identify dates by which actions must be taken in pending matters, account for client funds and property, and ensure that inexperienced lawyers are properly supervised.

~~[2]~~ [3] ~~The~~ Other measures that may be required to fulfill the responsibility prescribed in ~~paragraphs~~ paragraph (a) ~~and (b)~~ can depend on the firm's structure and the nature of its practice. In a small firm of experienced lawyers, informal supervision and ~~occasional admonition~~ periodic review of compliance with the required systems ordinarily ~~might be sufficient~~ will suffice. In a large firm, or in practice situations in which ~~intensely~~ difficult ethical problems frequently arise, more elaborate ~~procedures~~ measures may be necessary. Some firms, for example, have a procedure whereby junior lawyers can make confidential referral of ethical problems directly to a designated senior partner or special committee. See Rule 5.2. Firms, whether large or small, may also rely on continuing legal education in professional ethics. In any event, the ethical atmosphere of a firm can influence the conduct of all its members and ~~a lawyer having authority over the work of another~~ the partners may not assume that ~~the subordinate lawyer~~ all lawyers associated with the firm will inevitably conform to the Rules.

~~[3]~~ [4] Paragraph (c)~~(1)~~ expresses a general principle of personal responsibility for acts of another. See also Rule 8.4(a).

~~[4]~~ [5] Paragraph (c)(2) defines the duty of a lawyer having direct supervisory authority over performance of specific legal work by another lawyer. Whether a lawyer has such supervisory authority in particular circumstances is a question of fact. Partners of a private firm have at least indirect responsibility for all work being done by the firm, while a partner in charge of a particular matter ordinarily has ~~direct authority over~~ responsibility for the work of other firm lawyers engaged in the matter. Appropriate remedial action by a partner would depend on the immediacy of the partner's involvement and the seriousness of the misconduct. The supervisor is required to intervene to prevent avoidable consequences of misconduct if the supervisor knows that the misconduct occurred. Thus, if a supervising lawyer knows that a subordinate misrepresented a matter to an opposing party in negotiation, the supervisor as well as the subordinate has a duty to correct the resulting misapprehension.

[5] [6] Professional misconduct by a lawyer under supervision could reveal a violation of paragraph (b) on the part of the supervisory lawyer even though it does not entail a violation of paragraph (c) because there was no direction, ratification or knowledge of the violation.

[6] [7] Apart from this Rule and Rule 8.4(a), a lawyer does not have disciplinary liability for the conduct of a partner, associate or subordinate. Whether a lawyer may be liable civilly or criminally for another lawyer's conduct is a question of law beyond the scope of these Rules.

[8] The duties imposed by this Rule on managing and supervising lawyers do not alter the personal duty of each lawyer in a firm to abide by the Rules of Professional Conduct. See Rule 5.2(a).

RULE 5.2: RESPONSIBILITIES OF A SUBORDINATE LAWYER

(a) A lawyer is bound by the Rules of Professional Conduct notwithstanding that the lawyer acted at the direction of another person.

(b) A subordinate lawyer does not violate the Rules of Professional Conduct if that lawyer acts in accordance with a supervisory lawyer's reasonable resolution of an arguable question of professional duty.

Comment

[1] Although a lawyer is not relieved of responsibility for a violation by the fact that the lawyer acted at the direction of a supervisor, that fact may be relevant in determining whether a lawyer had the knowledge required to render conduct a violation of the Rules. For example, if a subordinate filed a frivolous pleading at the direction of a supervisor, the subordinate would not be guilty of a professional violation unless the subordinate knew of the document's frivolous character.

[2] When lawyers in a supervisor-subordinate relationship encounter a matter involving professional judgment as to ethical duty, the supervisor may assume responsibility for making the judgment. Otherwise a consistent course of action or position could not be taken. If the question can reasonably be answered only one way, the duty of both lawyers is clear and they are equally responsible for fulfilling it. However, if the question is reasonably arguable, someone has to decide upon the course of action. That authority ordinarily reposes in the supervisor, and a subordinate may be guided accordingly. For example, if a question arises whether the interests of two clients conflict under Rule 1.7, the supervisor's reasonable resolution of the question should protect the subordinate professionally if the resolution is subsequently challenged.

RULE 5.3: RESPONSIBILITIES REGARDING
NONLAWYER ASSISTANTS

With respect to a nonlawyer employed or retained by or associated with a lawyer:

(a) a partner, a lawyer who individually or together with other lawyers possesses comparable managerial authority in a law firm, and the law firm shall make reasonable efforts to ensure that the firm has in effect measures giving reasonable assurance that the person's conduct is compatible with the professional obligations of the lawyer;

(b) a lawyer having direct supervisory authority over the nonlawyer shall make reasonable efforts to ensure that the person's conduct is compatible with the professional obligations of the lawyer; and

(c) a lawyer shall be responsible for conduct of such a person that would be a violation of the Rules of Professional Conduct if engaged in by a lawyer if:

(1) the lawyer orders or, with the knowledge of the specific conduct, ratifies the conduct involved; or

(2) the lawyer is a partner or has comparable managerial authority in the law firm in which the person is employed, or has direct supervisory authority over the person, and knows of the conduct at a time when its consequences can be avoided or mitigated but fails to take reasonable remedial action.

Comment

[1]   Lawyers generally employ assistants in their practice, including secretaries, investigators, law student interns, and paraprofessionals. Such assistants, whether employees or independent contractors, act for the lawyer in rendition of the lawyer's professional services. A lawyer ~~should~~ must give such assistants appropriate instruction and supervision concerning the ethical aspects of their employment, particularly regarding the obligation not to disclose information relating to representation of the client, and should be responsible for their work product. The measures employed in supervising nonlawyers should take account of the fact that they do not have legal training and are not subject to professional discipline.

[2]   Paragraph (a) requires lawyers with managerial authority within a law firm, and the firm itself, to make reasonable efforts to establish internal policies and procedures designed to provide reasonable assurance that nonlawyers in the firm will act in a way compatible with the Rules of Professional Conduct. See Comments [1] and [2] to Rule 5.1. Paragraphs (b) and (c) impose personal responsibility on lawyers who have supervisory authority over the performance of nonlawyers in the firm.

RULE 5.4: PROFESSIONAL INDEPENDENCE OF A LAWYER

(a) A lawyer or law firm shall not share legal fees with a nonlawyer, except that:

(1) an agreement by a lawyer with the lawyer's firm, partner, or associate may provide for the payment of money, over a reasonable period of time after the lawyer's death, to the lawyer's estate or to one or more specified persons;

(2) a lawyer who purchases the practice of a deceased, disabled, or disappeared lawyer may, pursuant to the provisions of Rule 1.17, pay to the estate or other representative of that lawyer the agreed-upon purchase price; ~~and~~

(3) a lawyer or law firm may include nonlawyer employees in a compensation or retirement plan, even though the plan is based in whole or in part on a profit-sharing arrangement; and

(4) a lawyer may share court-awarded legal fees with a nonprofit organization that employed, retained or recommended employment of the lawyer in the matter.

(b) A lawyer shall not form a partnership with a nonlawyer if any of the activities of the partnership consist of the practice of law.

(c) A lawyer shall not permit a person who recommends, employs, or pays the lawyer to render legal services for another to direct or regulate the lawyer's professional judgment in rendering such legal services.

(d) A lawyer shall not practice with or in the form of a professional corporation or association authorized to practice law for a profit, if:

(1) a nonlawyer owns any interest therein, except that a fiduciary representative of the estate of a lawyer may hold the stock or interest of the lawyer for a reasonable time during administration;

(2) a nonlawyer is a corporate director or officer thereof or occupies the position of similar responsibility in any form of association other than a corporation; or

(3) a nonlawyer has the right to direct or control the professional judgment of a lawyer.

Comment

[1] The provisions of this Rule express traditional limitations on sharing fees. These limitations are to protect the lawyer's professional independence of judgment. Where someone other than the client pays the lawyer's fee or salary, or recommends employment of the lawyer, that arrangement does not

modify the lawyer's obligation to the client. As stated in paragraph (c), such arrangements should not interfere with the lawyer's professional judgment.

[2] This Rule also expresses traditional limitations on permitting a third party to direct or regulate the lawyer's professional judgment in rendering legal services to another. See also Rule 1.8(f) (lawyer may accept compensation from a third party as long as there is no interference with the lawyer's independent professional judgment and the client gives informed consent).

RULE 5.5: UNAUTHORIZED PRACTICE OF LAW; MULTIJURISDICTIONAL PRACTICE OF LAW

~~A lawyer shall not:~~

(a) ~~practice law in a jurisdiction where doing so violates the regulation of the legal profession in that jurisdiction; or~~ A lawyer shall not practice law in a jurisdiction in violation of regulation of legal profession in that jurisdiction or assist another in doing so.

(b) ~~assist a person who is not a member of the bar in the performance of activity that constitutes the unauthorized practice of law.~~ A lawyer who is not admitted to practice in this jurisdiction shall not:

(1) except as authorized by these Rules or other law, establish an office or other systematic and continuous presence in this jurisdiction for the practice of law; or

(2) hold out to the public or otherwise represent that the lawyer is admitted to practice law in this jurisdiction.

(c) A lawyer admitted in another United States jurisdiction, and not disbarred or suspended from practice in any jurisdiction, may provide legal services on a temporary basis in this jurisdiction that:

(1) are undertaken in association with a lawyer who is admitted to practice in this jurisdiction and who actively participates in the matter;

(2) are in or reasonably related to a pending or potential proceeding before a tribunal in this or another jurisdiction, if the lawyer, or a person the lawyer is assisting, is authorized by law or order to appear in such proceeding or reasonably expects to be so authorized;

(3) are in or reasonably related to a pending or potential arbitration, mediation, or other alternative dispute resolution proceeding in this or another jurisdiction, if the services arise out of or are reasonably related to the lawyer's practice in a jurisdiction in which the lawyer is admitted to practice and are not services for which the forum requires pro hac vice admission; or

(4) are not within paragraphs (c)(2) or (c)(3) and arise out of or are reasonably related to the lawyer's practice in a jurisdiction in which the lawyer is admitted to practice.

(d) A lawyer admitted in another United States jurisdiction, and not disbarred or suspended from practice in any jurisdiction, may provide legal services in this jurisdiction that:

(1) are provided to the lawyer's employer or its organizational affiliates and are not services for which the forum requires pro hac vice admission; or

(2) are services that the lawyer is authorized to provide by federal law or other law of this jurisdiction.

Comment

[1] A lawyer may practice law only in a jurisdiction in which the lawyer is authorized to practice. A lawyer may be admitted to practice law in a jurisdiction on a regular basis or may be authorized by court rule or order or by law to practice for a limited purpose or on a restricted basis. Paragraph (a) applies to unauthorized practice of law by a lawyer, whether through the lawyer's direct action or by the lawyer assisting another person.

[1][2] The definition of the practice of law is established by law and varies from one jurisdiction to another. Whatever the definition, limiting the practice of law to members of the bar protects the public against rendition of legal services by unqualified persons. ~~Paragraph (b)~~ This Rule does not prohibit a lawyer from employing the services of paraprofessionals and delegating functions to them, so long as the lawyer supervises the delegated work and retains responsibility for their work. See Rule 5.3. ~~Likewise, it does not prohibit lawyers from providing professional advice and instruction to nonlawyers whose employment requires knowledge of law; for example, claims adjusters, employees of financial or commercial institutions, social workers, accountants and persons employed in government agencies. In addition, a lawyer may counsel nonlawyers who wish to proceed pro se~~.

[3] A Lawyer may provide professional advice and instruction to nonlawyers whose employment requires knowledge of the law; for example, claims adjusters, employees of financial or commercial institutions, social workers, accountants, and persons employed in government agencies. Lawyers also may assist independent nonlawyers, such as paraprofessionals, who are authorized by the law of a jurisdiction to provide particular law-related services. In addition, a lawyer may counsel nonlawyers who wish to proceed pro se.

[4] Other than as authorized by law or this Rule, a lawyer who is not admitted to practice generally in this jurisdiction violates paragraph (b) if the lawyer establishes an office or other systematic and continuous presence in this jurisdiction for the practice of law. Presence may be systematic and continuous even if the lawyer is not physically present here. Such a lawyer must not hold out to the public or otherwise represent that the lawyer is admitted to practice law in this jurisdiction. See also Rules 7.1(a) and 7.5(b).

[5]   There are occasions in which a lawyer admitted to practice in another United States jurisdiction, and not disbarred or suspended from practice in any jurisdiction, may provide legal services on a temporary basis in this jurisdiction under circumstances that do not create an unreasonable risk to the interests of their clients, the public or the courts. Paragraph (c) identifies four such circumstances. The fact that conduct is not so identified does not imply that the conduct is or is not authorized. With the exception of paragraphs (d)(1) and (d)(2), this Rule does not authorize a lawyer to establish an office or other systematic and continuous presence in this jurisdiction without being admitted to practice generally here.

[6]   There is no single test to determine whether a lawyer's services are provided on a "temporary basis" in this jurisdiction, and may therefore be permissible under paragraph (c). Services may be "temporary" even though the lawyer provides services in this jurisdiction on a recurring basis, or for an extended period of time, as when the lawyer is representing a client in a single lengthy negotiation or litigation.

[7]   Paragraphs (c) and (d) apply to lawyers who are admitted to practice law in any United States jurisdiction, which includes the District of Columbia and any state, territory or commonwealth of the United States. The word "admitted" in paragraph (c) contemplates that the lawyer is authorized to practice in the jurisdiction in which the lawyer is admitted and excludes a lawyer who while technically admitted is not authorized to practice, because, for example, the lawyer is on inactive status.

[8]   Paragraph (c)(1) recognizes that the interests of clients and the public are protected if a lawyer admitted only in another jurisdiction associates with a lawyer licensed to practice in this jurisdiction. For this paragraph to apply, however, the lawyer admitted to practice in this jurisdiction must actively participate in and share responsibility for the representation of the client.

[9]   Lawyers not admitted to practice generally in a jurisdiction may be authorized by law or order of a tribunal or an administrative agency to appear before the tribunal or agency. This authority may be granted pursuant to formal rules governing admission pro hac vice or pursuant to informal practice of the tribunal or agency. Under paragraph (c)(2), a lawyer does not violate this Rule when the lawyer appears before a tribunal or agency pursuant to such authority. To the extent that a court rule or other law of this jurisdiction requires a lawyer who is not admitted to practice in this jurisdiction to obtain admission pro hac vice before appearing before a tribunal or administrative agency, this Rule requires the lawyer to obtain that authority.

[10]   Paragraph (c)(2) also provides that a lawyer rendering services in this jurisdiction on a temporary basis does not violate this Rule when the lawyer engages in conduct in anticipation of a proceeding or hearing in a jurisdiction in which the lawyer is authorized to practice law or in which the lawyer reasonably expects to be admitted pro hac vice. Examples of such

118

conduct include meetings with the client, interviews of potential witnesses, and the review of documents. Similarly, a lawyer admitted only in another jurisdiction may engage in conduct temporarily in this jurisdiction in connection with pending litigation in another jurisdiction in which the lawyer is or reasonably expects to be authorized to appear, including taking depositions in this jurisdiction.

[11]   When a lawyer has been or reasonably expects to be admitted to appear before a court or administrative agency, paragraph (c)(2) also permits conduct by lawyers who are associated with that lawyer in the matter, but who do not expect to appear before the court or administrative agency. For example, subordinate lawyers may conduct research, review documents, and attend meetings with witnesses in support of the lawyer responsible for the litigation.

[12]   Paragraph (c)(3) permits a lawyer admitted to practice law in another jurisdiction to perform services on a temporary basis in this jurisdiction if those services are in or reasonably related to a pending or potential arbitration, mediation, or other alternative dispute resolution proceeding in this or another jurisdiction, if the services arise out of or are reasonably related to the lawyer's practice in a jurisdiction in which the lawyer is admitted to practice. The lawyer, however, must obtain admission pro hac vice in the case of a court-annexed arbitration or mediation or otherwise if court rules or law so require.

[13]   Paragraph (c)(4) permits a lawyer admitted in another jurisdiction to provide certain legal services on a temporary basis in this jurisdiction that arise out of or are reasonably related to the lawyer's practice in a jurisdiction in which the lawyer is admitted but are not within paragraphs (c)(2) or (c)(3). These services include both legal services and services that nonlawyers may perform but that are considered the practice of law when performed by lawyers.

[14]   Paragraphs (c)(3) and (c)(4) require that the services arise out of or be reasonably related to the lawyer's practice in a jurisdiction in which the lawyer is admitted. A variety of factors evidence such a relationship. The lawyer's client may have been previously represented by the lawyer, or may be resident in or have substantial contacts with the jurisdiction in which the lawyer is admitted. The matter, although involving other jurisdictions, may have a significant connection with that jurisdiction. In other cases, significant aspects of the lawyer's work might be conducted in that jurisdiction or a significant aspect of the matter may involve the law of that jurisdiction. The necessary relationship might arise when the client's activities or the legal issues involve multiple jurisdictions, such as when the officers of a multinational corporation survey potential business sites and seek the services of their lawyer in assessing the relative merits of each. In addition, the services may draw on the lawyer's recognized expertise developed through the regular practice of law on behalf of clients in matters involving a particular body of federal, nationally-uniform, foreign, or international law.

[15]   Paragraph (d) identifies two circumstances in which a lawyer who is admitted to practice in another United States jurisdiction, and is not disbarred or suspended from practice in any jurisdiction, may establish an office or other systematic and continuous presence in this jurisdiction for the practice of law as well as provide legal services on a temporary basis. Except as provided in paragraphs (d)(1) and (d)(2), a lawyer who is admitted to practice law in another jurisdiction and who establishes an office or other systematic or continuous presence in this jurisdiction must become admitted to practice law generally in this jurisdiction.

[16]   Paragraph (d)(1) applies to a lawyer who is employed by a client to provide legal services to the client or its organizational affiliates, i.e., entities that control, are controlled by, or are under common control with the employer. This paragraph does not authorize the provision of personal legal services to the employer's officers or employees. The paragraph applies to in-house corporate lawyers, government lawyers and others who are employed to render legal services to the employer. The lawyer's ability to represent the employer outside the jurisdiction in which the lawyer is licensed generally serves the interests of the employer and does not create an unreasonable risk to the client and others because the employer is well situated to assess the lawyer's qualifications and the quality of the lawyer's work.

[17]   If an employed lawyer establishes an office or other systematic presence in this jurisdiction for the purpose of rendering legal services to the employer, the lawyer may be subject to registration or other requirements, including assessments for client protection funds and mandatory continuing legal education.

[18]   Paragraph (d)(2) recognizes that a lawyer may provide legal services in a jurisdiction in which the lawyer is not licensed when authorized to do so by federal or other law, which includes statute, court rule, executive regulation or judicial precedent.

[19]   A lawyer who practices law in this jurisdiction pursuant to paragraphs (c) or (d) or otherwise is subject to the disciplinary authority of this jurisdiction. See Rule 8.5(a).

[20]   In some circumstances, a lawyer who practices law in this jurisdiction pursuant to paragraphs (c) or (d) may have to inform the client that the lawyer is not licensed to practice law in this jurisdiction. For example, that may be required when the representation occurs primarily in this jurisdiction and requires knowledge of the law of this jurisdiction. See Rule 1.4(b).

[21]   Paragraphs (c) and (d) do not authorize communications advertising legal services to prospective clients in this jurisdiction by lawyers who are admitted to practice in other jurisdictions. Whether and how lawyers may communicate the availability of their services to prospective clients in this jurisdiction is governed by Rules 7.1 to 7.5.

RULE 5.6: RESTRICTIONS ON RIGHT TO PRACTICE

A lawyer shall not participate in offering or making:

(a) a partnership, ~~or~~ shareholders, operating, employment, or other similar type of agreement that restricts the right of a lawyer to practice after termination of the relationship, except an agreement concerning benefits upon retirement; or

(b) an agreement in which a restriction on the lawyer's right to practice is part of the settlement of a client controversy ~~between private parties.~~

Comment

[1]   An agreement restricting the right of ~~partners or associates~~ lawyers to practice after leaving a firm not only limits their professional autonomy but also limits the freedom of clients to choose a lawyer. Paragraph (a) prohibits such agreements except for restrictions incident to provisions concerning retirement benefits for service with the firm.

[2]   Paragraph (b) prohibits a lawyer from agreeing not to represent other persons in connection with settling a claim on behalf of a client.

[3]   This Rule does not apply to prohibit restrictions that may be included in the terms of the sale of a law practice pursuant to Rule 1.17.

RULE 5.7: RESPONSIBILITIES REGARDING LAW–RELATED SERVICES

(a) A lawyer shall be subject to the Rules of Professional Conduct with respect to the provision of law-related services, as defined in paragraph (b), if the law-related services are provided:

(1) by the lawyer in circumstances that are not distinct from the lawyer's provision of legal services to clients; or

(2) in other circumstances by ~~a separate~~ an entity controlled by the lawyer individually or with others if the lawyer fails to take reasonable measures to assure that a person obtaining the law-related services knows that the services ~~of the separate entity~~ are not legal services and that the protections of the client-lawyer relationship do not exist.

(b) The term "law-related services" denotes services that might reasonably be performed in conjunction with and in substance are related to the provision of legal services, and that are not prohibited as unauthorized practice of law when provided by a nonlawyer.

Comment

[1]   When a lawyer performs law-related services or controls an organization that does so, there exists the potential for ethical problems. Principal

121

among these is the possibility that the person for whom the law-related services are performed fails to understand that the services may not carry with them the protections normally afforded as part of the client-lawyer relationship. The recipient of the law-related services may expect, for example, that the protection of client confidences, prohibitions against representation of persons with conflicting interests, and obligations of a lawyer to maintain professional independence apply to the provision of law-related services when that may not be the case.

[2]   Rule 5.7 applies to the provision of law-related services by a lawyer even when the lawyer does not provide any legal services to the person for whom the law-related services are performed and whether the law-related services are performed through a law firm or a separate entity. The Rule identifies the circumstances in which all of the Rules of Professional Conduct apply to the provision of law-related services. Even when those circumstances do not exist, however, the conduct of a lawyer involved in the provision of law-related services is subject to those Rules that apply generally to lawyer conduct, regardless of whether the conduct involves the provision of legal services. See, e.g., Rule 8.4.

[3]   When law-related services are provided by a lawyer under circumstances that are not distinct from the lawyer's provision of legal services to clients, the lawyer in providing the law-related services must adhere to the requirements of the Rules of Professional Conduct as provided in ~~Rule 5.7~~ paragraph (a)(1). Even when the law-related and legal services are provided in circumstances that are distinct from each other, for example through separate entities or different support staff within the law firm, the Rules of Professional Conduct apply to the lawyer as provided in paragraph (a)(2) unless the lawyer takes reasonable measures to assure that the recipient of the law-related services knows that the services are not legal services and that the protections of the client-lawyer relationship do not apply.

[4]   Law-related services also may be provided through an entity that is distinct from that through which the lawyer provides legal services. If the lawyer individually or with others has control of such an entity's operations, the Rule requires the lawyer to take reasonable measures to assure that each person using the services of the entity knows that the services provided by the entity are not legal services and that the Rules of Professional Conduct that relate to the client-lawyer relationship do not apply. A lawyer's control of an entity extends to the ability to direct its operation. Whether a lawyer has such control will depend upon the circumstances of the particular case.

[5]   When a client-lawyer relationship exists with a person who is referred by a lawyer to a separate law-related service entity controlled by the lawyer, individually or with others, the lawyer must comply with Rule 1.8(a).

[6]   In taking the reasonable measures referred to in paragraph (a)(2) to assure that a person using law-related services understands the practical effect or significance of the inapplicability of the Rules of Professional Conduct, the lawyer should communicate to the person receiving the law-related

services, in a manner sufficient to assure that the person understands the significance of the fact, that the relationship of the person to the business entity will not be a client-lawyer relationship. The communication should be made before entering into an agreement for provision of or providing law-related services, and preferably should be in writing.

[7] The burden is upon the lawyer to show that the lawyer has taken reasonable measures under the circumstances to communicate the desired understanding. For instance, a sophisticated user of law-related services, such as a publicly held corporation, may require a lesser explanation than someone unaccustomed to making distinctions between legal services and law-related services, such as an individual seeking tax advice from a lawyer-accountant or investigative services in connection with a lawsuit.

[8] Regardless of the sophistication of potential recipients of law-related services, a lawyer should take special care to keep separate the provision of law-related and legal services in order to minimize the risk that the recipient will assume that the law-related services are legal services. The risk of such confusion is especially acute when the lawyer renders both types of services with respect to the same matter. Under some circumstances the legal and law-related services may be so closely entwined that they cannot be distinguished from each other, and the requirement of disclosure and consultation imposed by paragraph (a)(2) of the Rule cannot be met. In such a case a lawyer will be responsible for assuring that both the lawyer's conduct and, to the extent required by Rule 5.3, that of nonlawyer employees in the distinct entity which the lawyer controls complies in all respects with the Rules of Professional Conduct.

[9] A broad range of economic and other interests of clients may be served by lawyers' engaging in the delivery of law-related services. Examples of law-related services include providing title insurance, financial planning, accounting, trust services, real estate counseling, legislative lobbying, economic analysis, social work, psychological counseling, tax preparation, and patent, medical or environmental consulting.

[10] When a lawyer is obliged to accord the recipients of such services the protections of those Rules that apply to the client-lawyer relationship, the lawyer must take special care to heed the proscriptions of the Rules addressing conflict of interest (Rules 1.7 through 1.11, especially Rules 1.7(b)(a)(2) and 1.8(a), (b) and (f)), and to scrupulously adhere to the requirements of Rule 1.6 relating to disclosure of confidential information. The promotion of the law-related services must also in all respects comply with Rules 7.1 through 7.3, dealing with advertising and solicitation. In that regard, lawyers should take special care to identify the obligations that may be imposed as a result of a jurisdiction's decisional law.

[11] When the full protections of all of the Rules of Professional Conduct do not apply to the provision of law-related services, principles of law external to the Rules, for example, the law of principal and agent, govern the legal duties owed to those receiving the services. Those other legal principles

may establish a different degree of protection for the recipient with respect to confidentiality of information, conflicts of interest and permissible business relationships with clients. See also Rule 8.4 (Misconduct).

PUBLIC SERVICE

RULE 6.1: VOLUNTARY PRO BONO PUBLICO SERVICE

Every lawyer has a professional responsibility to provide legal services to those unable to pay. A lawyer should aspire to render at least (50) hours of pro bono publico legal services per year. In fulfilling this responsibility, the lawyer should:

(a) provide a substantial majority of the (50) hours of legal services without fee or expectation of fee to:

(1) persons of limited means or

(2) charitable, religious, civic, community, governmental and educational organizations in matters which are designed primarily to address the needs of persons of limited means; and

(b) provide any additional services through:

(1) delivery of legal services at no fee or substantially reduced fee to individuals, groups or organizations seeking to secure or protect civil rights, civil liberties or public rights, or charitable, religious, civic, community, governmental and educational organizations in matters in furtherance of their organizational purposes, where the payment of standard legal fees would significantly deplete the organization's economic resources or would be otherwise inappropriate;

(2) delivery of legal services at a substantially reduced fee to persons of limited means; or

(3) participation in activities for improving the law, the legal system or the legal profession.

In addition, a lawyer should voluntarily contribute financial support to organizations that provide legal services to persons of limited means.

Comment

[1] Every lawyer, regardless of professional prominence or professional work load, has a responsibility to provide legal services to those unable to pay, and personal involvement in the problems of the disadvantaged can be one of the most rewarding experiences in the life of a lawyer. The American Bar Association urges all lawyers to provide a minimum of 50 hours of pro bono services annually. States, however, may decide to choose a higher or lower number of hours of annual service (which may be expressed as a percentage of a lawyer's professional time) depending upon local needs and local conditions.

It is recognized that in some years a lawyer may render greater or fewer hours than the annual standard specified, but during the course of his or her legal career, each lawyer should render on average per year, the number of hours set forth in this Rule. Services can be performed in civil matters or in criminal or quasi-criminal matters for which there is no government obligation to provide funds for legal representation, such as post-conviction death penalty appeal cases.

[2] Paragraphs (a)(1) and (2) recognize the critical need for legal services that exists among persons of limited means by providing that a substantial majority of the legal services rendered annually to the disadvantaged be furnished without fee or expectation of fee. Legal services under these paragraphs consist of a full range of activities, including individual and class representation, the provision of legal advice, legislative lobbying, administrative rule-making and the provision of free training or mentoring to those who represent persons of limited means. The variety of these activities should facilitate participation by government lawyers, even when restrictions exist on their engaging in the outside practice of law.

[3] Persons eligible for legal services under paragraphs (a)(1) and (2) are those who qualify for participation in programs funded by the Legal Services Corporation and those whose incomes and financial resources are slightly above the guidelines utilized by such programs but nevertheless, cannot afford counsel. Legal services can be rendered to individuals or to organizations such as homeless shelters, battered women's centers and food pantries that serve those of limited means. The term "governmental organizations" includes, but is not limited to, public protection programs and sections of governmental or public sector agencies.

[4] Because service must be provided without fee or expectation of fee, the intent of the lawyer to render free legal services is essential for the work performed to fall within the meaning of paragraphs (a)(1) and (2). Accordingly, services rendered cannot be considered pro bono if an anticipated fee is uncollected, but the award of statutory attorneys' fees in a case originally accepted as pro bono would not disqualify such services from inclusion under this section. Lawyers who do receive fees in such cases are encouraged to contribute an appropriate portion of such fees to organizations or projects that benefit persons of limited means.

[5] While it is possible for a lawyer to fulfill the annual responsibility to perform pro bono services exclusively through activities described in paragraphs (a)(1) and (2), to the extent that any hours of service remained unfulfilled, the remaining commitment can be met in a variety of ways as set forth in paragraph (b). Constitutional, statutory or regulatory restrictions may prohibit or impede government and public sector lawyers and judges from performing the pro bono services outlined in paragraphs (a)(1) and (2). Accordingly, where those restrictions apply, government and public sector lawyers and judges may fulfill their pro bono responsibility by performing services outlined in paragraph (b).

[6]   Paragraph (b)(1) includes the provision of certain types of legal services to those whose incomes and financial resources place them above limited means. It also permits the pro bono lawyer to accept a substantially reduced fee for services. Examples of the types of issues that may be addressed under this paragraph include First Amendment claims, Title VII claims and environmental protection claims. Additionally, a wide range of organizations may be represented, including social service, medical research, cultural and religious groups.

[7]   Paragraph (b)(2) covers instances in which lawyers agree to and receive a modest fee for furnishing legal services to persons of limited means. Participation in judicare programs and acceptance of court appointments in which the fee is substantially below a lawyer's usual rate are encouraged under this section.

[8]   Paragraph (b)(3) recognizes the value of lawyers engaging in activities that improve the law, the legal system or the legal profession. Serving on bar association committees, serving on boards of pro bono or legal services programs, taking part in Law Day activities, acting as a continuing legal education instructor, a mediator or an arbitrator and engaging in legislative lobbying to improve the law, the legal system or the profession are a few examples of the many activities that fall within this paragraph.

[9]   Because the provision of pro bono services is a professional responsibility, it is the individual ethical commitment of each lawyer. Nevertheless, there may be times when it is not feasible for a lawyer to engage in pro bono services. At such times a lawyer may discharge the pro bono responsibility by providing financial support to organizations providing free legal services to persons of limited means. Such financial support should be reasonably equivalent to the value of the hours of service that would have otherwise been provided. In addition, at times it may be more feasible to satisfy the pro bono responsibility collectively, as by a firm's aggregate pro bono activities.

[10]   Because the efforts of individual lawyers are not enough to meet the need for free legal services that exists among persons of limited means, the government and the profession have instituted additional programs to provide those services. Every lawyer should financially support such programs, in addition to either providing direct pro bono services or making financial contributions when pro bono service is not feasible.

[11]   Law firms should act reasonably to enable all lawyers in the firm to provide the pro bono legal services called for by this Rule.

[11] [12] The responsibility set forth in this Rule is not intended to be enforced through disciplinary process.

RULE 6.2: ACCEPTING APPOINTMENTS

A lawyer shall not seek to avoid appointment by a tribunal to represent a person except for good cause, such as:

(a) representing the client is likely to result in violation of the Rules of Professional Conduct or other law;

(b) representing the client is likely to result in an unreasonable financial burden on the lawyer; or

(c) the client or the cause is so repugnant to the lawyer as to be likely to impair the client-lawyer relationship or the lawyer's ability to represent the client.

Comment

[1] A lawyer ordinarily is not obliged to accept a client whose character or cause the lawyer regards as repugnant. The lawyer's freedom to select clients is, however, qualified. All lawyers have a responsibility to assist in providing pro bono publico service. See Rule 6.1. An individual lawyer fulfills this responsibility by accepting a fair share of unpopular matters or indigent or unpopular clients. A lawyer may also be subject to appointment by a court to serve unpopular clients or persons unable to afford legal services.

Appointed Counsel

[2] For good cause a lawyer may seek to decline an appointment to represent a person who cannot afford to retain counsel or whose cause is unpopular. Good cause exists if the lawyer could not handle the matter competently, see Rule 1.1, or if undertaking the representation would result in an improper conflict of interest, for example, when the client or the cause is so repugnant to the lawyer as to be likely to impair the client-lawyer relationship or the lawyer's ability to represent the client. A lawyer may also seek to decline an appointment if acceptance would be unreasonably burdensome, for example, when it would impose a financial sacrifice so great as to be unjust.

[3] An appointed lawyer has the same obligations to the client as retained counsel, including the obligations of loyalty and confidentiality, and is subject to the same limitations on the client-lawyer relationship, such as the obligation to refrain from assisting the client in violation of the Rules.

RULE 6.3: MEMBERSHIP IN LEGAL SERVICES ORGANIZATION

A lawyer may serve as a director, officer or member of a legal services organization, apart from the law firm in which the lawyer practices, notwithstanding that the organization serves persons having interests adverse to a client of the lawyer. The lawyer shall not knowingly participate in a decision or action of the organization:

(a) if participating in the decision or action would be incompatible with the lawyer's obligations to a client under Rule 1.7; or

(b) where the decision or action could have a material adverse effect on the representation of a client of the organization whose interests are adverse to a client of the lawyer.

Comment

[1] Lawyers should be encouraged to support and participate in legal service organizations. A lawyer who is an officer or a member of such an

organization does not thereby have a client-lawyer relationship with persons served by the organization. However, there is potential conflict between the interests of such persons and the interests of the lawyer's clients. If the possibility of such conflict disqualified a lawyer from serving on the board of a legal services organization, the profession's involvement in such organizations would be severely curtailed.

[2]   It may be necessary in appropriate cases to reassure a client of the organization that the representation will not be affected by conflicting loyalties of a member of the board. Established, written policies in this respect can enhance the credibility of such assurances.

RULE 6.4: LAW REFORM ACTIVITIES AFFECTING CLIENT INTERESTS

A lawyer may serve as a director, officer or member of an organization involved in reform of the law or its administration notwithstanding that the reform may affect the interests of a client of the lawyer. When the lawyer knows that the interests of a client may be materially benefitted by a decision in which the lawyer participates, the lawyer shall disclose that fact but need not identify the client.

Comment

[1]   Lawyers involved in organizations seeking law reform generally do not have a client-lawyer relationship with the organization. Otherwise, it might follow that a lawyer could not be involved in a bar association law reform program that might indirectly affect a client. See also Rule 1.2(b). For example, a lawyer specializing in antitrust litigation might be regarded as disqualified from participating in drafting revisions of rules governing that subject. In determining the nature and scope of participation in such activities, a lawyer should be mindful of obligations to clients under other Rules, particularly Rule 1.7. A lawyer is professionally obligated to protect the integrity of the program by making an appropriate disclosure within the organization when the lawyer knows a private client might be materially benefitted.

RULE 6.5: NON–PROFIT AND COURT–ANNEXED LIMITED LEGAL–SERVICE PROGRAMS

(a) A lawyer who, under the auspices of a program sponsored by a nonprofit organization or court, provides short-term limited legal services to a client without expectation by either the lawyer or the client that the lawyer will provide continuing representation in the matter:

(1) is subject to Rules 1.7 and 1.9(a) only if the lawyer knows that the representation of the client involves a conflict of interest; and

128

(2) is subject to Rule 1.10 only if the lawyer knows that another lawyer associated with the lawyer in a law firm is disqualified by Rule 1.7 or 1.9(a) with respect to the matter.

(b) Except as provided in paragraph (a)(2), Rule 1.10 is inapplicable to a representation governed by this Rule.

Comment

[1] Legal-service organizations, courts and various nonprofit organizations have established programs through which lawyers provide short-term limited legal services—such as advice or the completion of legal forms—that will assist persons to address their legal problems without further representation by a lawyer. In these programs, such as legal-advice hotlines, advice-only clinics or pro se counseling programs, a client-lawyer relationship is established, but there is no expectation that the lawyer's representation of the client will continue beyond the limited consultation. Such programs are normally operated under circumstances in which it is not feasible for a lawyer to systematically screen for conflicts of interest as is generally required before undertaking a representation. See, e.g., Rules 1.7, 1.9 and 1.10.

[2] A lawyer who provides short-term limited legal services pursuant to this Rule must secure the client's informed consent to the limited scope of the representation. See Rule 1.2(c). If a short-term limited representation would not be reasonable under the circumstances, the lawyer may offer advice to the client but must also advise the client of the need for further assistance of counsel. Except as provided in this Rule, the Rules of Professional Conduct, including Rules 1.6 and 1.9(c), are applicable to the limited representation.

[3] Because a lawyer who is representing a client in the circumstances addressed by this Rule ordinarily is not able to check systematically for conflicts of interest, paragraph (a) requires compliance with Rules 1.7 or 1.9(a) only if the lawyer knows that the representation presents a conflict of interest for the lawyer, and with Rule 1.10 only if the lawyer knows that another lawyer in the lawyer's firm is disqualified by Rules 1.7 or 1.9(a) in the matter.

[4] Because the limited nature of the services significantly reduces the risk of conflicts of interest with other matters being handled by the lawyer's firm, paragraph (b) provides that Rule 1.10 is inapplicable to a representation governed by this Rule except as provided by paragraph (a)(2). Paragraph (a)(2) requires the participating lawyer to comply with Rule 1.10 when the lawyer knows that the lawyer's firm is disqualified by Rules 1.7 or 1.9(a). By virtue of paragraph (b), however, a lawyer's participation in a short-term limited legal services program will not preclude the lawyer's firm from undertaking or continuing the representation of a client with interests adverse to a client being represented under the program's auspices. Nor will the personal disqualification of a lawyer participating in the program be imputed to other lawyers participating in the program.

[5] If, after commencing a short-term limited representation in accordance with this Rule, a lawyer undertakes to represent the client in the matter on an ongoing basis, Rules 1.7, 1.9(a) and 1.10 become applicable.

INFORMATION ABOUT LEGAL SERVICES

RULE 7.1: COMMUNICATIONS CONCERNING A LAWYER'S SERVICES

A lawyer shall not make a false or misleading communication about the lawyer or the lawyer's services. A communication is false or misleading if it: (a) contains a material misrepresentation of fact or law, or omits a fact necessary to make the statement considered as a whole not materially misleading;

(b) is likely to create an unjustified expectation about results the lawyer can achieve, or states or implies that the lawyer can achieve results by means that violate the Rules of Professional Conduct or other law; or

(c) compares the lawyer's services with other lawyers' services, unless the comparison can be factually substantiated.

Comment

[1] This Rule governs all communications about a lawyer's services, including advertising permitted by Rule 7.2. Whatever means are used to make known a lawyer's services, statements about them should must be truthful. The prohibition in paragraph (b) of statements that may create "unjustified expectations" would ordinarily preclude advertisements about results obtained on behalf of a client, such as the amount of a damage award or the lawyer's record in obtaining favorable verdicts, and advertisements containing client endorsements. Such information may create the unjustified expectation that similar results can be obtained for others without reference to the specific factual and legal circumstances.

[2] Truthful statements that are misleading are also prohibited by this Rule. A truthful statement is misleading if it omits a fact necessary to make the lawyer's communication considered as a whole not materially misleading. A truthful statement is also misleading if there is a substantial likelihood that it will lead a reasonable person to formulate a specific conclusion about the lawyer or the lawyer's services for which there is no reasonable factual foundation.

[3] An advertisement that truthfully reports a lawyer's achievements on behalf of clients or former clients may be misleading if presented so as to lead a reasonable person to form an unjustified expectation that the same results could be obtained for other clients in similar matters without reference to the specific factual and legal circumstances of each client's case. Similarly, an unsubstantiated comparison of the lawyer's services or fees with the services or fees of other lawyers may be misleading if presented with such specificity

as would lead a reasonable person to conclude that the comparison can be substantiated. The inclusion of an appropriate disclaimer or qualifying language may preclude a finding that a statement is likely to create unjustified expectations or otherwise mislead a prospective client.

[4] See also Rule 8.4(e) for the prohibition against stating or implying an ability to influence improperly a government agency or official or to achieve results by means that violate the Rules of Professional Conduct or other law.

RULE 7.2: ADVERTISING

(a) **Subject to the requirements of Rules 7.1 and 7.3, a lawyer may advertise services through** ~~public media, such as a telephone directory, legal directory, newspaper or other periodical, outdoor advertising, radio or television, or through~~ **written** ~~or~~**, recorded or electronic communication, including public media.**

(b) ~~A copy or recording of an advertisement or communication shall be kept for two years after its last dissemination along with a record of when and where it was used.~~

~~(c)~~ **(b) A lawyer shall not give anything of value to a person for recommending the lawyer's services except that a lawyer may**

(1) **pay the reasonable costs of advertisements or communications permitted by this Rule;**

(2) **pay the usual charges of a** ~~not-for-profit lawyer referral service or~~ **legal service** ~~organization~~ **plan or a not-a-profit or qualified lawyer referral service. A qualified lawyer referral service is a lawyer referral service that has been approved by the appropriate regulatory authority;** ~~and~~

(3) **pay for a law practice in accordance with Rule 1.17**~~.~~**; and**

(4) **refer clients to another lawyer or a nonlawyer professional pursuant to an agreement not otherwise prohibited under these Rules that provides for the other person to refer clients or customers to the lawyer, if**

(i) **the reciprocal referral agreement is not exclusive, and**

(ii) **the client is informed of the existence and nature of the agreement.**

~~(d)~~ **(c) Any communication made pursuant to this Rule shall include the name and office address of at least one lawyer or law firm responsible for its content.**

Comment

[1] To assist the public in obtaining legal services, lawyers should be allowed to make known their services not only through reputation but also

through organized information campaigns in the form of advertising. Advertising involves an active quest for clients, contrary to the tradition that a lawyer should not seek clientele. However, the public's need to know about legal services can be fulfilled in part through advertising. This need is particularly acute in the case of persons of moderate means who have not made extensive use of legal services. The interest in expanding public information about legal services ought to prevail over considerations of tradition. Nevertheless, advertising by lawyers entails the risk of practices that are misleading or overreaching.

[2] This Rule permits public dissemination of information concerning a lawyer's name or firm name, address and telephone number; the kinds of services the lawyer will undertake; the basis on which the lawyer's fees are determined, including prices for specific services and payment and credit arrangements; a lawyer's foreign language ability; names of references and, with their consent, names of clients regularly represented; and other information that might invite the attention of those seeking legal assistance.

[3] Questions of effectiveness and taste in advertising are matters of speculation and subjective judgment. Some jurisdictions have had extensive prohibitions against television advertising, against advertising going beyond specified facts about a lawyer, or against "undignified" advertising. Television is now one of the most powerful media for getting information to the public, particularly persons of low and moderate income; prohibiting television advertising, therefore, would impede the flow of information about legal services to many sectors of the public. Limiting the information that may be advertised has a similar effect and assumes that the bar can accurately forecast the kind of information that the public would regard as relevant. <u>Similarly, electronic media, such as the Internet, can be an important source of information about legal services, and lawful communication by electronic mail is permitted by this Rule. But see Rule 7.3(a) for the prohibition against the solicitation of a prospective client through a real-time electronic exchange that is not initiated by the prospective client.</u>

[4] Neither this Rule nor Rule 7.3 prohibits communications authorized by law, such as notice to members of a class in class action litigation.

Record of Advertising

[5] Paragraph (b) requires that a record of the content and use of advertising be kept in order to facilitate enforcement of this Rule. It does not require that advertising be subject to review prior to dissemination. Such a requirement would be burdensome and expensive relative to its possible benefits, and may be of doubtful constitutionality.

Paying Others to Recommend a Lawyer

[6] [5] A lawyer is allowed to pay for advertising permitted by this Rule and for the purchase of a law practice in accordance with the provisions of Rule 1.17, but otherwise is <u>Lawyers are</u> not permitted to pay <del>another person</del> <u>others</u> for channeling professional work. This restriction does not prevent an

~~organization or person other than the lawyer from advertising or recommend-~~
~~ing the lawyer's services. Thus, a legal aid agency or prepaid legal services~~
~~plan may pay to advertise legal services provided under its auspices. Likewise,~~
~~a lawyer may participate in not-for-profit lawyer referral programs and pay~~
~~the usual fees charged by such programs. Paragraph (c) does not prohibit~~
~~paying regular compensation to an assistant, such as a secretary, to prepare~~
~~communications permitted by this Rule.~~ Paragraph (b)(1), however, allows a
lawyer to pay for advertising and communications permitted by this Rule,
including the costs of print directory listings, on-line directory listings, newspaper ads, television and radio airtime, domain-name registrations, sponsor-
ship fees, banner ads, and group advertising. A lawyer may compensate
employees, agents and vendors who are engaged to provide marketing or
client-development services, such as publicists, public-relations personnel,
business-development staff and website designers. See Rule 5.3 for the duties
of lawyers and law firms with respect to the conduct of nonlawyers who
prepare marketing materials for them.

[6] A lawyer may pay the usual charges of a legal service plan or a not-
for-profit or qualified lawyer referral service. A legal service plan is a prepaid
or group legal service plan or a similar delivery system that assists prospective
clients to secure legal representation. A lawyer referral service, on the other
hand, is any organization that holds itself out to the public as a lawyer
referral service. Such referral services are understood by laypersons to be
consumer-oriented organizations that provide unbiased referrals to lawyers
with appropriate experience in the subject matter of the representation and
afford other client protections, such as complaint procedures or malpractice
insurance requirements. Consequently, this Rule only permits a lawyer to pay
the usual charges of a not-for-profit or qualified lawyer referral service. A
qualified lawyer referral service is one that is approved by an appropriate
regulatory authority as affording adequate protections for prospective clients.
See, e.g., the American Bar Association's Model Supreme Court Rules Governing Lawyer Referral Services and Model Lawyer Referral and Information
Service Quality Assurance Act (requiring that organizations that are identified as lawyer referral services (i) permit the participation or all lawyers who
are licensed and eligible to practice in the jurisdiction and who meet reasonable objective eligibility requirements as may be established by the referral
service for the protection of prospective clients; (ii) require each participating
lawyer to carry reasonably adequate malpractice insurance; (iii) act reasonably to assess client satisfaction and address client complaints; and (iv) do not
refer prospective clients to lawyers who own, operate or are employed by the
referral service.)

[7] A lawyer who accepts assignments or referrals from a legal service
plan or referrals from a lawyer referral service must act reasonably to assure
that the activities of the plan or service are compatible with the lawyer's
professional obligations. See Rule 5.3. Legal service plans and lawyer referral
services may communicate with prospective clients, but such communication
must be in conformity with these Rules. Thus, advertising must not be false

or misleading, as would be the case if the communications of a group advertising program or a group legal services plan would mislead prospective clients to think that it was a lawyer referral service sponsored by a state agency or bar association. Nor could the lawyer allow in-person, telephonic, or real-time contacts that would violate Rule 7.3.

[8] A lawyer also may agree to refer clients to another lawyer or a nonlawyer professional, in return for the undertaking of that person to refer clients or customers to the lawyer. Such reciprocal referral arrangements must not interfere with the lawyer's professional judgment as to making referrals or as to providing substantive legal services. See Rules 2.1 and 5.4(c). Except as provided in Rule 1.5(e), a lawyer who receives referrals from a lawyer or nonlawyer professional must not pay anything solely for the referral, but the lawyer does not violate paragraph (b) of this Rule by agreeing to refer clients to the other lawyer or nonlawyer professional, so long as the reciprocal referral agreement is not exclusive and the client is informed of the referral agreement. Conflicts of interest created by such arrangements are governed by Rule 1.7. Reciprocal referral agreements should not be of indefinite duration and should be reviewed periodically to determine whether they comply with these Rules. This Rule does not restrict referrals or divisions of revenues or net income among lawyers within firms comprised of multiple entities.

RULE 7.3: DIRECT CONTACT WITH PROSPECTIVE CLIENTS

(a) A lawyer shall not by in-person or, live telephone or real-time electronic contact solicit professional employment from a prospective client with whom the lawyer has no family or prior professional relationship when a significant motive for the lawyer's doing so is the lawyer's pecuniary gain, unless the person contacted:

(1) is a lawyer; or

(2) has a family, close personal, or prior professional relationship with the lawyer.

(b) A lawyer shall not solicit professional employment from a prospective client by written or, recorded or electronic communication or by in-person or, telephone or real-time electronic contact even when not otherwise prohibited by paragraph (a), if:

(1) the prospective client has made known to the lawyer a desire not to be solicited by the lawyer; or

(2) the solicitation involves coercion, duress or harassment.

(c) Every written or, recorded or electronic communication from a lawyer soliciting professional employment from a prospective client known to be in need of legal services in a particular matter, and with whom the lawyer has no family or prior professional relationship, shall include the words "Advertising Material" on the outside envelope, if any, and at the beginning and ending of any

recorded or electronic communication, unless the recipient of the communication is a person specified in paragraphs (a)(1) or (a)(2).

(d) Notwithstanding the prohibitions in paragraph (a), a lawyer may participate with a prepaid or group legal service plan operated by an organization not owned or directed by the lawyer which uses in-person or telephone contact to solicit memberships or subscriptions for the plan from persons who are not known to need legal services in a particular matter covered by the plan.

Comment

[1]   There is a potential for abuse inherent in direct in-person or, live telephone or real-time electronic contact by a lawyer with a prospective client known to need legal services. These forms of contact between a lawyer and a prospective client subject the layperson to the private importuning of the trained advocate in a direct interpersonal encounter. The prospective client, who may already feel overwhelmed by the circumstances giving rise to the need for legal services, may find it difficult fully to evaluate all available alternatives with reasoned judgment and appropriate self-interest in the face of the lawyer's presence and insistence upon being retained immediately. The situation is fraught with the possibility of undue influence, intimidation, and over-reaching.

[2]   This potential for abuse inherent in direct in-person or, live telephone or real-time electronic solicitation of prospective clients justifies its prohibition, particularly since lawyer advertising and written and recorded communication permitted under Rule 7.2 offer alternative means of conveying necessary information to those who may be in need of legal services. Advertising and written and recorded communications which may be mailed or autodialed make it possible for a prospective client to be informed about the need for legal services, and about the qualifications of available lawyers and law firms, without subjecting the prospective client to direct in-person or, telephone or real-time electronic persuasion that may overwhelm the client's judgment.

[3]   The use of general advertising and written and, recorded or electronic communications to transmit information from lawyer to prospective client, rather than direct in-person or, live telephone or real-time electronic contact, will help to assure that the information flows cleanly as well as freely. The contents of advertisements and communications permitted under Rule 7.2 are can be permanently recorded so that they cannot be disputed and may be shared with others who know the lawyer. This potential for informal review is itself likely to help guard against statements and claims that might constitute false and misleading communications, in violation of Rule 7.1. The contents of direct in-person or, live telephone or real-time electronic conversations between a lawyer to and a prospective client can be disputed and are may not be subject to third-party scrutiny. Consequently, they are much more likely to approach (and occasionally cross) the dividing line between accurate representations and those that are false and misleading.

[4]   There is far less likelihood that a lawyer would engage in abusive practices against an individual who is a former client, or with whom the lawyer has a ~~prior~~ close personal or ~~professional~~ family relationship, or ~~where~~ in situations in which the lawyer is motivated by considerations other than the lawyer's pecuniary gain. Nor is there a serious potential for abuse when the person contacted is a lawyer. Consequently, the general prohibition in Rule 7.3(a) and the requirements of Rule 7.3(c) are not applicable in those situations. Also, paragraph (a) is not intended to prohibit a lawyer from participating in constitutionally protected activities of public or charitable legal-service organizations or bona fide political, social, civic, fraternal, employee or trade organizations whose purposes include providing or recommending legal services to its members or beneficiaries.

[5]   But even permitted forms of solicitation can be abused. Thus, any solicitation which contains information which is false or misleading within the meaning of Rule 7.1, which involves coercion, duress or harassment within the meaning of Rule 7.3(b)(2), or which involves contact with a prospective client who has made known to the lawyer a desire not to be solicited by the lawyer within the meaning of Rule 7.3(b)(1) is prohibited. Moreover, if after sending a letter or other communication to a client as permitted by Rule 7.2 the lawyer receives no response, any further effort to communicate with the prospective client may violate the provisions of Rule 7.3(b).

[6]   This Rule is not intended to prohibit a lawyer from contacting representatives of organizations or groups that may be interested in establishing a group or prepaid legal plan for their members, insureds, beneficiaries or other third parties for the purpose of informing such entities of the availability of and details concerning the plan or arrangement which the lawyer or lawyer's firm is willing to offer. This form of communication is not directed to a prospective client. Rather, it is usually addressed to an individual acting in a fiduciary capacity seeking a supplier of legal services for others who may, if they choose, become prospective clients of the lawyer. Under these circumstances, the activity which the lawyer undertakes in communicating with such representatives and the type of information transmitted to the individual are functionally similar to and serve the same purpose as advertising permitted under Rule 7.2.

[7]   The requirement in Rule 7.3(c) that certain communications be marked "Advertising Material" does not apply to communications sent in response to requests of potential clients or their spokespersons or sponsors. General announcements by lawyers, including changes in personnel or office location, do not constitute communications soliciting professional employment from a client known to be in need of legal services within the meaning of this Rule.

[8]   Paragraph (d) of this Rule ~~would permit~~ permits a lawyer to participate with an organization which uses personal contact to solicit members for its group or prepaid legal service plan, provided that the personal contact is not undertaken by any lawyer who would be a provider of legal services through the plan. The organization ~~referred to in paragraph (d)~~ must not be

136

owned by or directed (whether as manager or otherwise) by any lawyer or law firm that participates in the plan. For example, paragraph (d) would not permit a lawyer to create an organization controlled directly or indirectly by the lawyer and use the organization for the in-person or telephone solicitation of legal employment of the lawyer through memberships in the plan or otherwise. The communication permitted by these organizations also must not be directed to a person known to need legal services in a particular matter, but is to be designed to inform potential plan members generally of another means of affordable legal services. Lawyers who participate in a legal service plan must reasonably assure that the plan sponsors are in compliance with Rules 7.1, 7.2 and 7.3(b). See 8.4(a).

RULE 7.4: COMMUNICATION OF FIELDS OF PRACTICE AND SPECIALIZATION

(a) A lawyer may communicate the fact that the lawyer does or does not practice in particular fields of law. ~~A lawyer shall not state or imply that the lawyer has been recognized or certified as a specialist in a particular field of law except as follows:~~

~~(a)~~ **(b)** ~~a~~ **A lawyer admitted to engage in patent practice before the United States Patent and Trademark Office may use the designation "Patent Attorney" or a substantially similar designation~~;~~.**

~~(b)~~ **(c)** ~~a~~ **A lawyer engaged in Admiralty practice may use the designation "Admiralty," "Proctor in Admiralty" or a substantially similar designation~~; and~~.**

~~(c) [for jurisdictions where there is a regulatory authority granting certification or approving organizations that grant certification] a lawyer may communicate the fact that the lawyer has been certified as a specialist in a field of law by a named organization or authority but only if:~~

~~(1) such certification is granted by the appropriate regulatory authority or by an organization which has been approved by the appropriate regulatory authority to grant such certification; or~~

~~(2) such certification is granted by an organization that has not yet been approved by, or has been denied the approval available from, the appropriate regulatory authority, and the absence or denial of approval is clearly stated in the communication, and in any advertising subject to Rule 7.2, such statement appears in the same sentence that communicates the certification.~~

~~(c) [for jurisdictions where there is no procedure either for certification of specialties or for approval of organizations granting certification] a lawyer may communicate the fact that the lawyer has been certified as a specialist in a field of law by a named organiza-~~

137

~~tion, provided that the communication clearly states that there is no~~ ~~procedure in this jurisdiction for approving certifying organizations.~~ ~~If, however, the named organization has been accredited by the~~ ~~American Bar Association to certify lawyers as specialists in a partic-~~ ~~ular field of law, the communication need not contain such a state-~~ ~~ment.~~

(d) A lawyer shall not state or imply that a lawyer is certified as a specialist in a particular field of law, unless:

(1) the lawyer has been certified as a specialist by an organization that has been approved by an appropriate state authority or that has been accredited by the American Bar Association; and

(2) the name of the certifying organization is clearly identified in the communication.

Comment

[1] ~~This~~ Paragraph (a) of this Rule permits a lawyer to indicate areas of practice in communications about the lawyer's services. If a lawyer practices only in certain fields, or will not accept matters except in a specified field or fields, the lawyer is permitted to so indicate. A lawyer is generally permitted to state that the lawyer is a "specialist," practices a "specialty," or "specializes in" particular fields, but such communications are subject to the "false and misleading" standard applied in Rule 7.1 to communications concerning a lawyer's services.

[2] ~~However, a lawyer may not communicate that the lawyer has been~~ ~~recognized or certified as a specialist in a particular field of law, except as~~ ~~provided by this Rule. Recognition of specialization in patent matters is a~~ ~~matter of~~ Paragraph (b) recognizes the long-established policy of the Patent and Trademark Office~~, as reflected in paragraph (a)~~ for the designation of lawyers practicing before the Office. Paragraph ~~(b)~~ (c) recognizes that designation of ~~admiralty~~ Admiralty practice has a long historical tradition associated with maritime commerce and the federal courts.

[3] Paragraph ~~(c) provides for certification~~ (d) permits a lawyer to state that the lawyer is certified as a specialist in a field of law ~~when a state~~ ~~authorizes an appropriate regulatory authority to grant such certification or~~ ~~when the state grants other organizations the right to grant certification~~ if such certification is granted by an organization approved by an appropriate state authority or accredited by the American Bar Association or another organization, such as a state bar association, that has been approved by the state authority to accredit organizations that certify lawyers as specialists. Certification ~~procedures imply~~ signifies that an objective entity has recognized ~~a lawyer's higher~~ an advanced degree of ~~specialized ability~~ knowledge and experience in the specialty area greater than is suggested by general licensure to practice law. ~~Those objective entities~~ Certifying organizations may be expected to apply standards of ~~competence,~~ experience ~~and~~, knowledge and

proficiency to insure that a lawyer's recognition as a specialist is meaningful and reliable. In order to insure that consumers can obtain access to useful information about an organization granting certification, the name of the certifying organization ~~or agency~~ must be included in any communication regarding the certification.

[4] ~~Lawyers may also be certified as specialists by organizations that either have not yet been approved to grant such certification or have been disapproved. In such instances, the consumer may be misled as to the significance of the lawyer's status as a certified specialist. The Rule therefore requires that a lawyer who chooses to communicate recognition by such an organization also clearly state the absence or denial of the organization's authority to grant such certification. Since lawyer advertising through public media and written or recorded communications invites the greatest danger of misleading consumers, the absence or denial of the organization's authority to grant certification must be clearly stated in such advertising in the same sentence that communicates the certification.~~

[5] ~~In jurisdictions where no appropriate regulatory authority has a procedure for approving organizations granting certification, the Rule requires that a lawyer clearly state such lack of procedure. If, however, the named organization has been accredited by the American Bar Association to certify lawyers as specialists in a particular field of law, the communication need not contain such a statement.~~

RULE 7.5: FIRM NAMES AND LETTERHEADS

(a) A lawyer shall not use a firm name, letterhead or other professional designation that violates Rule 7.1. A trade name may be used by a lawyer in private practice if it does not imply a connection with a government agency or with a public or charitable legal services organization and is not otherwise in violation of Rule 7.1.

(b) A law firm with offices in more than one jurisdiction may use the same name or other professional designation in each jurisdiction, but identification of the lawyers in an office of the firm shall indicate the jurisdictional limitations on those not licensed to practice in the jurisdiction where the office is located.

(c) The name of a lawyer holding a public office shall not be used in the name of a law firm, or in communications on its behalf, during any substantial period in which the lawyer is not actively and regularly practicing with the firm.

(d) Lawyers may state or imply that they practice in a partnership or other organization only when that is the fact.

Comment

[1] A firm may be designated by the names of all or some of its members, by the names of deceased members where there has been a

continuing succession in the firm's identity or by a trade name such as the "ABC Legal Clinic." A lawyer or law firm may also be designated by a distinctive website address or comparable professional designation. Although the United States Supreme Court has held that legislation may prohibit the use of trade names in professional practice, use of such names in law practice is acceptable so long as it is not misleading. If a private firm uses a trade name that includes a geographical name such as "Springfield Legal Clinic," an express disclaimer that it is a public legal aid agency may be required to avoid a misleading implication. It may be observed that any firm name including the name of a deceased partner is, strictly speaking, a trade name. The use of such names to designate law firms has proven a useful means of identification. However, it is misleading to use the name of a lawyer not associated with the firm or a predecessor of the firm.

[2] With regard to paragraph (d), lawyers sharing office facilities, but who are not in fact ~~partners~~ associated with each other in a law firm, may not denominate themselves as, for example, "Smith and Jones," for that title suggests ~~partnership in the practice of~~ that they are practicing law together in a firm.

RULE 7.6: POLITICAL CONTRIBUTIONS TO OBTAIN GOVERNMENT LEGAL ENGAGEMENTS OR APPOINTMENTS BY JUDGES

A lawyer or law firm shall not accept a government legal engagement or an appointment by a judge if the lawyer or law firm makes a political contribution or solicits political contributions for the purpose of obtaining or being considered for that type of legal engagement or appointment.

Comment

[1] Lawyers have a right to participate fully in the political process, which includes making and soliciting political contributions to candidates for judicial and other public office. Nevertheless, when lawyers make or solicit political contributions in order to obtain an engagement for legal work awarded by a government agency, or to obtain appointment by a judge, the public may legitimately question whether the lawyers engaged to perform the work are selected on the basis of competence and merit. In such a circumstance, the integrity of the profession is undermined.

[2] The term "political contribution" denotes any gift, subscription, loan, advance or deposit of anything of value made directly or indirectly to a candidate, incumbent, political party or campaign committee to influence or provide financial support for election to or retention in judicial or other government office. Political contributions in initiative and referendum elections are not included. For purposes of this Rule, the term "political contribution" does not include uncompensated services.

[3] Subject to the exceptions below, (i) the term "government legal engagement" denotes any engagement to provide legal services that a public official has the direct or indirect power to award; and (ii) the term "appointment by a judge" denotes an appointment to a position such as referee, commissioner, special master, receiver, guardian or other similar position that is made by a judge. Those terms do not, however, include (a) substantially uncompensated services; (b) engagements or appointments made on the basis of experience, expertise, professional qualifications and cost following a request for proposal or other process that is free from influence based upon political contributions; and (c) engagements or appointments made on a rotational basis from a list compiled without regard to political contributions.

[4] The term "lawyer or law firm" includes a political action committee or other entity owned or controlled by a lawyer or law firm.

[5] Political contributions are for the purpose of obtaining or being considered for a government legal engagement or appointment by a judge if, but for the desire to be considered for the legal engagement or appointment, the lawyer or law firm would not have made or solicited the contributions. The purpose may be determined by an examination of the circumstances in which the contributions occur. For example, one or more contributions that in the aggregate are substantial in relation to other contributions by lawyers or law firms, made for the benefit of an official in a position to influence award of a government legal engagement, and followed by an award of the legal engagement to the contributing or soliciting lawyer or the lawyer's firm would support an inference that the purpose of the contributions was to obtain the engagement, absent other factors that weigh against existence of the proscribed purpose. Those factors may include among others that the contribution or solicitation was made to further a political, social, or economic interest or because of an existing personal, family, or professional relationship with a candidate.

[6] If a lawyer makes or solicits a political contribution under circumstances that constitute bribery or another crime, Rule 8.4(b) is implicated.

MAINTAINING THE INTEGRITY OF THE PROFESSION

RULE 8.1: BAR ADMISSION AND DISCIPLINARY MATTERS

An applicant for admission to the bar, or a lawyer in connection with a bar admission application or in connection with a disciplinary matter, shall not:

(a) knowingly make a false statement of material fact; or

(b) fail to disclose a fact necessary to correct a misapprehension known by the person to have arisen in the matter, or knowingly fail to respond to a lawful demand for information from an admissions or disciplinary authority, except that this Rule does not require disclosure of information otherwise protected by Rule 1.6.

Comment

[1]   The duty imposed by this Rule extends to persons seeking admission to the bar as well as to lawyers. Hence, if a person makes a material false statement in connection with an application for admission, it may be the basis for subsequent disciplinary action if the person is admitted, and in any event may be relevant in a subsequent admission application. The duty imposed by this Rule applies to a lawyer's own admission or discipline as well as that of others. Thus, it is a separate professional offense for a lawyer to knowingly make a misrepresentation or omission in connection with a disciplinary investigation of the lawyer's own conduct. ~~This~~ Paragraph (b) of this Rule also requires correction of any prior misstatement in the matter that the applicant or lawyer may have made and affirmative clarification of any misunderstanding on the part of the admissions or disciplinary authority of which the person involved becomes aware.

[2]   This Rule is subject to the provisions of the fifth amendment of the United States Constitution and corresponding provisions of state constitutions. A person relying on such a provision in response to a question, however, should do so openly and not use the right of nondisclosure as a justification for failure to comply with this Rule.

[3]   A lawyer representing an applicant for admission to the bar, or representing a lawyer who is the subject of a disciplinary inquiry or proceeding, is governed by the rules applicable to the client-lawyer relationship, including Rule 1.6 and, in some cases, Rule 3.3.

RULE 8.2: JUDICIAL AND LEGAL OFFICIALS

(a) A lawyer shall not make a statement that the lawyer knows to be false or with reckless disregard as to its truth or falsity concerning the qualifications or integrity of a judge, adjudicatory officer or public legal officer, or of a candidate for election or appointment to judicial or legal office.

(b) A lawyer who is a candidate for judicial office shall comply with the applicable provisions of the Code of Judicial Conduct.

Comment

[1]   Assessments by lawyers are relied on in evaluating the professional or personal fitness of persons being considered for election or appointment to judicial office and to public legal offices, such as attorney general, prosecuting attorney and public defender. Expressing honest and candid opinions on such matters contributes to improving the administration of justice. Conversely, false statements by a lawyer can unfairly undermine public confidence in the administration of justice.

[2]   When a lawyer seeks judicial office, the lawyer should be bound by applicable limitations on political activity.

[3] To maintain the fair and independent administration of justice, lawyers are encouraged to continue traditional efforts to defend judges and courts unjustly criticized.

RULE 8.3: REPORTING PROFESSIONAL MISCONDUCT

(a) A lawyer ~~having knowledge~~ who knows that another lawyer has committed a violation of the Rules of Professional Conduct that raises a substantial question as to that lawyer's honesty, trustworthiness or fitness as a lawyer in other respects, shall inform the appropriate professional authority.

(b) A lawyer ~~having knowledge~~ who knows that a judge has committed a violation of applicable rules of judicial conduct that raises a substantial question as to the judge's fitness for office shall inform the appropriate authority.

(c) This Rule does not require disclosure of information otherwise protected by Rule 1.6 or information gained by a lawyer or judge while ~~serving as a member of~~ participating in an approved lawyers assistance program. ~~to the extent that such information would be confidential if it were communicated subject to the attorney-client privilege.~~

Comment

[1] Self-regulation of the legal profession requires that members of the profession initiate disciplinary investigation when they know of a violation of the Rules of Professional Conduct. Lawyers have a similar obligation with respect to judicial misconduct. An apparently isolated violation may indicate a pattern of misconduct that only a disciplinary investigation can uncover. Reporting a violation is especially important where the victim is unlikely to discover the offense.

[2] A report about misconduct is not required where it would involve violation of Rule 1.6. However, a lawyer should encourage a client to consent to disclosure where prosecution would not substantially prejudice the client's interests.

[3] If a lawyer were obliged to report every violation of the Rules, the failure to report any violation would itself be a professional offense. Such a requirement existed in many jurisdictions but proved to be unenforceable. This Rule limits the reporting obligation to those offenses that a self-regulating profession must vigorously endeavor to prevent. A measure of judgment is, therefore, required in complying with the provisions of this Rule. The term "substantial" refers to the seriousness of the possible offense and not the quantum of evidence of which the lawyer is aware. A report should be made to the bar disciplinary agency unless some other agency, such as a peer review agency, is more appropriate in the circumstances. Similar considerations apply to the reporting of judicial misconduct.

[4] The duty to report professional misconduct does not apply to a lawyer retained to represent a lawyer whose professional conduct is in question. Such a situation is governed by the Rules applicable to the client-lawyer relationship.

[5] Information about a lawyer's or judge's misconduct or fitness may be received by a lawyer in the course of that lawyer's participation in an approved lawyers or judges assistance program. In that circumstance, providing for ~~the confidentiality of such information~~ an exception to the reporting requirements of paragraphs (a) and (b) of this Rule encourages lawyers and judges to seek treatment through such a program. Conversely, without such ~~confidentiality~~ an exception, lawyers and judges may hesitate to seek assistance from these programs, which may then result in additional harm to their professional careers and additional injury to the welfare of clients and the public. ~~The Rule therefore exempts the lawyer from the reporting requirements of paragraphs (a) and (b) with respect to information that would be privileged if the relationship between the impaired lawyer or judge and the recipient of the information were that of a client and a lawyer. On the other hand, a lawyer who receives such information would nevertheless be required to comply with the Rule 8.3 reporting provisions to report misconduct if the impaired lawyer or judge indicates an intent to engage in illegal activity, for example, the conversion of client funds to his or her use.~~ These Rules do not otherwise address the confidentiality of information received by a lawyer or judge participating in an approved lawyers assistance program; such an obligation, however, may be imposed by the rules of the program or other law.

RULE 8.4: MISCONDUCT

It is professional misconduct for a lawyer to:

(a) violate or attempt to violate the Rules of Professional Conduct, knowingly assist or induce another to do so, or do so through the acts of another;

(b) commit a criminal act that reflects adversely on the lawyer's honesty, trustworthiness or fitness as a lawyer in other respects;

(c) engage in conduct involving dishonesty, fraud, deceit or misrepresentation;

(d) engage in conduct that is prejudicial to the administration of justice;

(e) state or imply an ability to influence improperly a government agency or official or to achieve results by means that violate the Rules of Professional Conduct or other law; or

(f) knowingly assist a judge or judicial officer in conduct that is a violation of applicable rules of judicial conduct or other law.

Comment

[1] Lawyers are subject to discipline when they violate or attempt to violate the Rules of Professional Conduct, knowingly assist or induce another

to do so or do so through the acts of another, as when they request or instruct an agent to do so on the lawyer's behalf. Paragraph (a), however, does not prohibit a lawyer from advising a client concerning action that the client is lawfully entitled to take.

{1} [2] Many kinds of illegal conduct reflect adversely on fitness to practice law, such as offenses involving fraud and the offense of willful failure to file an income tax return. However, some kinds of offenses carry no such implication. Traditionally, the distinction was drawn in terms of offenses involving "moral turpitude." That concept can be construed to include offenses concerning some matters of personal morality, such as adultery and comparable offenses, that have no specific connection to fitness for the practice of law. Although a lawyer is personally answerable to the entire criminal law, a lawyer should be professionally answerable only for offenses that indicate lack of those characteristics relevant to law practice. Offenses involving violence, dishonesty, breach of trust, or serious interference with the administration of justice are in that category. A pattern of repeated offenses, even ones of minor significance when considered separately, can indicate indifference to legal obligation.

{2} [3] A lawyer who, in the course of representing a client, knowingly manifests by words or conduct, bias or prejudice based upon race, sex, religion, national origin, disability, age, sexual orientation or socioeconomic status, violates paragraph (d) when such actions are prejudicial to the administration of justice. Legitimate advocacy respecting the foregoing factors does not violate paragraph (d). A trial judge's finding that peremptory challenges were exercised on a discriminatory basis does not alone establish a violation of this Rule.

{3} [4] A lawyer may refuse to comply with an obligation imposed by law upon a good faith belief that no valid obligation exists. The provisions of Rule 1.2(d) concerning a good faith challenge to the validity, scope, meaning or application of the law apply to challenges of legal regulation of the practice of law.

{4} [5] Lawyers holding public office assume legal responsibilities going beyond those of other citizens. A lawyer's abuse of public office can suggest an inability to fulfill the professional role of lawyers. The same is true of abuse of positions of private trust such as trustee, executor, administrator, guardian, agent and officer, director or manager of a corporation or other organization.

RULE 8.5: DISCIPLINARY AUTHORITY; CHOICE OF LAW

(a) Disciplinary Authority. A lawyer admitted to practice in this jurisdiction is subject to the disciplinary authority of this jurisdiction, regardless of where the lawyer's conduct occurs. A lawyer not admitted in this jurisdiction is also subject to the disciplinary authority of this jurisdiction if the lawyer renders or offers to render any legal services in this jurisdiction. A lawyer may be subject to the

disciplinary authority of both this jurisdiction and another jurisdiction ~~where the lawyer is admitted~~ for the same conduct.

(b) Choice of Law. In any exercise of the disciplinary authority of this jurisdiction, the rules of professional conduct to be applied shall be as follows:

(1) for conduct in connection with a ~~proceeding in~~ matter pending before a ~~court before which a lawyer has been admitted to practice (either generally or for purposes of that proceeding)~~ tribunal, the rules ~~to be applied shall be the rules~~ of the jurisdiction in which the ~~court~~ tribunal sits, unless the rules of the ~~court~~ tribunal provide otherwise; and

(2) for any other conduct, the rules of the jurisdiction in which the lawyer's conduct occurred, or, if the predominant effect of the conduct is in a different jurisdiction, the rules of that jurisdiction shall be applied to the conduct. A lawyer shall not be subject to discipline if the lawyer's conduct conforms to the rules of a jurisdiction in which the lawyer reasonably believes the predominant effect of the lawyer's conduct will occur

~~(i) if the lawyer is licensed to practice only in this jurisdiction, the rules to be applied shall be the rules of this jurisdiction, and~~

~~(ii) if the lawyer is licensed to practice in this and another jurisdiction, the rules to be applied shall be the rules of the admitting jurisdiction in which the lawyer principally practices; provided, however, that if particular conduct clearly has its predominant effect in another jurisdiction in which the lawyer is licensed to practice, the rules of that jurisdiction shall be applied to that conduct.~~

Comment

Disciplinary Authority

[1] ~~Paragraph (a) restates~~ It is longstanding law that conduct of a lawyer admitted to practice in this jurisdiction is subject to the disciplinary authority of this jurisdiction. Extension of the disciplinary authority of this jurisdiction to other lawyers who render or offer to render legal services in this jurisdiction is for the protection of the citizens of this jurisdiction. Reciprocal enforcement of a jurisdiction's disciplinary findings and sanctions will further advance the purposes of this Rule. See, Rules 6 and 22, ABA Model Rules for Lawyer Disciplinary Enforcement. A lawyer who is subject to the disciplinary authority of this jurisdiction under Rule 8.5(a) appoints an official to be designated by this Court to receive service of process in this jurisdiction. The fact that the lawyer is subject to the disciplinary authority of this jurisdiction may be a factor in determining whether personal jurisdiction may be asserted over the lawyer for civil matters.

Choice of Law

[2]   A lawyer may be potentially subject to more than one set of rules of professional conduct which impose different obligations. The lawyer may be licensed to practice in more than one jurisdiction with differing rules, or may be admitted to practice before a particular court with rules that differ from those of the jurisdiction or jurisdictions in which the lawyer is licensed to practice. ~~In the past, decisions have not developed clear or consistent guidance as to which rules apply in such circumstances.~~ Additionally, the lawyer's conduct might involve significant contacts with more than one jurisdiction.

[3]   Paragraph (b) seeks to resolve such potential conflicts. Its premise is that minimizing conflicts between rules, as well as uncertainty about which rules are applicable, is in the best interest of both clients and the profession (as well as the bodies having authority to regulate the profession). Accordingly, it takes the approach of (i) providing that any particular conduct of a lawyer shall be subject to only one set of rules of professional conduct, ~~and~~ (ii) making the determination of which set of rules applies to particular conduct as straightforward as possible, consistent with recognition of appropriate regulatory interests of relevant jurisdictions, and (iii) providing a safe harbor for lawyers who act reasonably in the face of uncertainty.

[4]   Paragraph (b)(1) provides that as to a lawyer's conduct relating to a proceeding ~~in~~ pending before a ~~court before which the lawyer is admitted to practice (either generally or pro hac vice)~~ tribunal, the lawyer shall be subject only to the rules of ~~professional conduct of that court~~ the jurisdiction in which the tribunal sits unless the rules of the tribunal, including its choice of law rule, provide otherwise. As to all other conduct, including conduct in anticipation of a proceeding not yet pending before a tribunal, paragraph (b)(2) provides that a lawyer ~~licensed to practice only in this jurisdiction shall be subject to the rules of professional conduct of this jurisdiction, and that a lawyer licensed in multiple jurisdictions shall be subject only to the rules of the jurisdiction where he or she (as an individual, not his or her firm) principally practices, but with one exception: if particular conduct clearly has its predominant effect in another admitting jurisdiction, then only the rules of that jurisdiction shall apply. The intention is for the latter exception to be a narrow one. It would be appropriately applied, for example, to a situation in which a lawyer admitted in, and principally practicing in, State A, but also admitted in State B, handled an acquisition by a company whose headquarters and operations were in State B of another, similar such company. The exception would not appropriately be applied, on the other hand, if the lawyer handled an acquisition by a company whose headquarters and operations were in State A of a company whose headquarters and main operations were in State A, but which also had some operations in State B~~ shall be subject to the rules of the jurisdiction in which the lawyer's conduct occurred, or, if the predominant effect of the conduct is in another jurisdiction, the rules of that jurisdiction shall be applied to the conduct. In the case of conduct in anticipation of a proceeding that is likely to be before a tribunal, the

predominant effect of such conduct could be where the conduct occurred, where the tribunal sits or in another jurisdiction.

[5] When a lawyer's conduct involves significant contacts with more than one jurisdiction, it may not be clear whether the predominant effect of the lawyer's conduct will occur in a jurisdiction other than the one in which the conduct occurred. So long as the lawyer's conduct conforms to the rules of a jurisdiction in which the lawyer reasonably believes the predominant effect will occur, the lawyer shall not be subject to discipline under this Rule.

[5] [6] If two admitting jurisdictions were to proceed against a lawyer for the same conduct, they should, applying this Rule, identify the same governing ethics rules. They should take all appropriate steps to see that they do apply the same rule to the same conduct, and in all events should avoid proceeding against a lawyer on the basis of two inconsistent rules.

[6] [7] The choice of law provision is not intended to apply to transnational practice. Choice of law in this context should be the subject of agreements between jurisdictions or of appropriate international law. applies to lawyers in transnational practice, unless international law, treaties or other agreements between competent regulatory authorities in the affected jurisdictions provide otherwise.

INDEX

A

INDEX

INDEX

D

INDEX

E

Employees of lawyer,
    Responsibility for, Rule 5.3

Estate planning,
    Conflicts of interest in, Rule 1.7 (Comment)

Evaluation,
    Confidential information used in preparing, Rule 2.3(b)
    Third person, prepared at client's request for, Rule 2.3

Evaluator,
    Lawyer as, Preamble

Evidence,
    Destruction of, Rule 3.4(a)
    Obstructing opposing party's access to, Rule 3.4(a)
    Offering false, Rule 3.3(a)(3)

Ex parte proceedings, Rule 3.3(d)

Expediting litigation, Rule 3.2

Expenses of litigation,
    Client's right to determine, Rule 1.2 (Comment)
    Indigent client, paying on behalf of, Rule 1.8(e)(2)
    Lawyer advancing to client, Rule 1.8(e)(1)

Expert witness, See Witness

Expertise,
    As relating to competent representation, Rule 1.1

F

Fairness to opposing party and counsel, Rule 3.4

False statement,
    Made to tribunal, Rule 3.3(a)(1)

Fees,
    Acquiring ownership interest in enterprise as, Rule 1.5 (Comment)
    Advance fee payments, Rule 1.5 (Comment)
    Advertising of, Rule 7.2 (Comment)
    Arbitration of, Rule 1.5 (Comment)
    Charged upon sale of law practice, Rule 1.17(d)
    Communication of to client, Rule 1.5(b)
    Contingent fee,
        Prohibited representations, Rule 1.5(d)
        Requirements of, Rule 1.5(c)
    Determination of, Rule 1.5(a)
    Disclosure of confidential information to collect, Rule 1.6(b)(3) and (Comment 9)
    Division of, Rule 1.5(e)
    Paid by one other than client, Rule 1.7 (Comment); Rule 1.8(f)

Firm,
    Defined, Terminology
    Disqualification, Rule 1.10 (Comment)

Firm name, Rule 7.5(a)

Former client, see Conflict of interest

Former government lawyer,
    "Confidential government information" defined, Rule 1.11(c)

153

INDEX

INDEX

Informed Consent,—Continued
    Defined as, Terminology
    Required for evaluation, Rule 2.3(b)
    Required if former judge, arbitrator, mediator, or third-party neutral, Rule 1.12(a)
    Required to inform client on basis of, Rule 1.42(a)(1)
    That of former clients, Rule 1.9(a)

Insurance representation,
    Conflict of interest, Rule 1.8(f), (Comment 11)

Intermediary,
    Lawyer as, Preamble

Intimidate,
    Law's procedures used to, Preamble

J

Judges,
    Appointments by judges and political contributions, Rule 7.6
    Duty to show respect for, Preamble
    Ex parte communication with, Rule 3.5(b)
    Former judge, disqualification, Rule 1.12
    Improper influence on, Rule 3.5(a)
    Reporting misconduct by, Rule 8.3(b)
    Statements about, Rule 8.2

Juror,
    Improper influence on, Rule 3.5(a)

Jury trial,
    Client's right to waive, Rule 1.2(a)

K

Know, Knows, Knowingly,
    Defined as, Rule 1.0(f)
    Legal knowledge required for competence, Rule 1.1

L

Law clerk,
    Negotiating for private employment, Rule 1.12(b)

Law firm,
    Ancillary services, Rule 5.7
    Defined, Terminology
    Nonlawyer assistants, responsibility for, Rule 5.3
    Responsibility of partner or supervisory lawyer, Rule 5.1
    Subordinate lawyer, responsibility of, Rule 5.2

Law reform activities,
    Affecting clients' interests, Rule 6.4

Lawyer referral service,
    Advertising by way of, Rule 7.2(c)(2)
    Financial support of, Rule 6.1 (Comment)
    Legal aid and, Rule 6.1 (Comment)

Law–related services, Rule 5.7

Legal education,
    Duty to work to strengthen, Preamble

INDEX

Legislature,
    Appearance before on behalf of client, Rule 3.9

Letterheads,
    False or misleading, Rule 7.5(a)
    Jurisdictional limitations of members, Rule 7.5(b)
    Public officials, Rule 7.5(c)

Liability to client,
    Agreements limiting, Rule 1.8(h)

Lien,
    To secure fees and expenses, Rule 1.8(i)(1)

Literary rights,
    Acquiring concerning representation, Rule 1.8(d)

Litigation,
    Expedite, duty to, Rule 3.2

Loyalty,
    Duty of to client, Rule 1.7 (Comment)

M

Malpractice,
    Limiting liability to client for, Rule 1.8(h)

Media rights,
    Acquiring concerning representation, Rule 1.8(d)

Meritorious claims and contentions, Rule 3.1

Military lawyers,
    Adverse interests, representation of, Rule 1.9 (Comment)

Misconduct,
    Forms of, Rule 8.4

Misleading legal argument, Rule 3.3 (Comment)

Misrepresentation,
    In advertisements, Rule 7.1
    To court, Rule 3.3 (Comment)

Multijurisdictional practice, Rule 5.5

Multiple representation, see Conflict of interest; Intermediary

N

Negotiation,
    Conflicting interest, representation of, Rule 1.7 (Comment)
    Statements made during, Rule 4.1 (Comment)

Negotiator,
    Lawyer as, Preamble

Neutral Party,
    Serve as, Preamble

Nonlawyers,
    Division of fees with, Rule 5.4(a)
    Partnership with, Rule 5.4(b)

INDEX

O

Objectives of the representation,
    Client's right to determine, Rule 1.2(a)
    Lawyer's right to limit, Rule 1.2(c)

Opposing party,
    Communications with represented party, Rule 4.2
    Duty of fairness to, Rule 3.4

Organization, representation of,
    Board of directors, lawyer for serving on, Rule 1.7 (Comment)
    Communication with, Rule 1.4 (Comment)
    Conflict of interest, Rule 1.7 (Comment)
    Conflicting interests among officers and employees, Rule 1.7 (Comment)
    Constituents, representing, Rule 1.13(e)
    Identity of client, Rule 1.13(a); Rule 1.13(d)
    Misconduct, client engaged in, Rule 1.13(b)

P

Partner,
    Defined, Rule 1.0(g)

Patent practice,
    Advertising, Rule 7.4(b)

Perjury,
    Criminal defendant, Rule 3.3 (Comment)
    Disclosure of, Rule 3.3(b)

Personal affairs of lawyer,
    Duty to conduct in compliance with law, Preamble

Plea bargain,
    Client's right to accept or reject, Rule 1.2(a)

Pleadings,
    Verification of, Rule 3.3 (Comment)

Political contributions to secure legal work, Rule 7.6

Positional conflicts, Rule 1.7 (Comment)

Precedent,
    Failure to disclose to court, Rule 3.3(a)(2)

Prepaid legal services,
    Advertising for, Rule 7.2 (Comment)

Pro bono publico service, Rule 6.1

Procedural law,
    Lawyer's professional responsibilities proscribed by, Preamble

Professional corporation,
    Ownership in, Rule 5.4(d)

Prompt,
    Lawyer's duty to be, Preamble

Property of client,
    Safekeeping, Rule 1.15

Prosecutor,
    Publicity, pre-trial and trial, Rule 3.6; Rule 3.8(f)
    Representing former defendant, Rule 1.9 (Comment)

INDEX

R

S

158

INDEX

Solicitation,
    By direct contact, Rule 7.3
    Prohibition on, Rule 7.3

Specialization, Rule 7.4
    Certification of, Rule 7.4(d)(1)

State's Attorney,
    Authority of, Scope

Statutes,
    Shape lawyer's role, Scope

Subpoenas by prosecutors, Rule 3.8(f)

Substantive law,
    Defines existence of client-lawyer relationship, Scope
    Lawyer's professional responsibilities proscribed by, Preamble

Supervising work of another lawyer,
    Responsibilities, Rule 5.1

T

Third persons,
    Respect for rights of, Rule 4.4
    Statements to, Rule 4.1

Transactions with persons other than client, see Third persons

Trial conduct,
    Allusion to irrelevant or inadmissable evidence, Rule 3.4(e)
    Disruptive conduct, Rule 3.5(d)
    Trial publicity, Rule 3.6; Rule 3.8(f)

Tribunal,
    Defined as, Rule 1.0(m)

Trust accounts,
    Maintain for client funds, Rule 1.15 (Comment)

U

Unauthorized practice of law,
    Assisting in, Rule 5.5(a)
    Engaging in, Rule 5.5(a)

W

Waiver,
    Prosecutor obtaining from criminal defendant, Rule 3.8(c)

Withdrawal,
    Conflict of interest, Rule 1.7 (Comment)
    Discharge, Rule 1.16(a)(3)
    Giving notice of fact of, Rule 1.6 (Comment)
    Incapacity, Rule 1.16(a)(2)
    Property of client, Rule 1.16(d)
    When client persists in criminal or fraudulent conduct, Rule 1.2 (Comment); Rule 1.6
        (Comment); Rule 1.16(b)(2); Rule 1.13(c)

Witness,
    Bribing, Rule 3.4(b)

INDEX

Witness,—Continued
Client's right to decide whether to testify, Rule 1.2(a)
Expenses, payment of, Rule 3.4 (Comment)
Expert, payment of, Rule 3.4 (Comment)
Lawyer as, Rule 3.7

Writing,
Defined as, Rule 1.0(n)

Work product privilege,
Rule 1.6 (Comment 3); Rule 5.3 (Comment 1)

Z

Zealous representation,
Opposing party well-represented, Preamble
Requirement of, Rule 1.3 (Comment)

APPENDIX A

Ethics Rules on Client Confidences*

Table of Contents

SECTION 1 Introduction

The attached chart analyzes in summary form the provisions of the ABA Model Code of Professional Responsibility (1969), the ABA Model Rules of Professional Conduct (2002), the various state versions of the Code and the Rules, and related comments, ethics opinions and case law that are applicable on the controversial "whistle-blowing" issue.

The chart indicates, with appropriate citations, whether a lawyer "May" or "Must" or "Must Not", as the case may be, reveal confidential client information relating to:

A. Client's intention to commit any crime.

B. Client's intention to commit a crime likely to result in death or bodily injury.

C. Client's intention to commit a *criminal* fraud likely to result in injury to the financial interest or property of another party.

D. Client's intention to commit a *non-criminal* fraud likely to result in injury to the financial interest or property of another party. (In some states, criminal statutes may be interpreted broadly, such that virtually any fraud likely to result in injury to the financial interest or property of another would be a crime.)

E. Client's prior commission of a crime or fraud, using the lawyer's services, resulting in injury to the financial interest or property of another party.

F. Client's prior or contemporaneous commission of perjury or other fraud on a tribunal.

G. Client's ongoing criminal or fraudulent act.

It must be emphasized that the attached chart is a somewhat cryptic summary intended to alert the reader to situations that raise the question whether disclosure of a client confidence or secret is discretionary, mandatory, or prohibited, and to direct the reader to the relevant provision and language in the Code or in the Rules and related authorities. There are many subtle distinctions and refinements that emerge when one compares the ABA Model Code, the ABA Model Rules, the Code or Rules of any particular state, the local rules of federal district courts, and a state's comments, ethics opinions and case law. There is no substitute for reading the relevant Rule and related authorities word for word. Unfortunately, in certain situations (as indicated by the notes following the chart) the applicable Rule and relevant ethics opinions and case law are ambiguous and, in some instances, incomprehensible.

The attached chart reflects amendments to the Model Code, the Model Rules and the relevant state Rules or Codes of which we are aware as of February 2002. We have not undertaken to determine the existence or effect of amendments effective after that date.

The ABA Commission on Evaluation of the Rules of Professional Conduct (the Ethics 2000 Commission) recommended changes that the Commission believed would broaden the scope of discretionary disclosure under Rule 1.6. The ABA House of Delegates adopted the proposed revision to Rule 1.6 that broadens a lawyer's discretion to disclose confidential information when death or substantial bodily harm is threatened, but rejected the Commission's proposal to broaden discretion to make disclosures when the threatened harm is to financial or property interests. The House of Delegates completed its work in early February 2002. The newly revised Model Rules will of course not take effect in any state until they are adopted by that state's supreme court.

Model Rule 3.3 was also revised in ways which may strengthen a lawyer's disclosure obligation in certain 'fraud on the court' situations.

The Restatement of the Law Governing Lawyers (2000) seems generally to support disclosures of client wrongdoing in a broader range of circumstances than do the Model Rules. Sections 59 through 67 of the Restatement deal generally with lawyer client confidentiality. Section 120 describes 'remedial measures', including revealing client confidences if necessary, that a lawyer should take upon learning that false evidence has been offered in litigation.

Below the line for Tennessee there appears in the chart an additional line for 'Proposed,' which refers to 'proposed rules.' This line is used if a state is considering new rules that might affect the outcome of situations covered in columns A through G.

SECTION 2 Chart of Ethics Rules on Client Confidences

See Section 1 For Full Explanation of Columns	A	B	C	D	E	F	G
	INTENT TO COMMIT/PREVENTION				RECTIFICATION		
	Any Crime	Death/Injury	Criminal Fraud	Non-Criminal Fraud	Prior Crime or Fraud Using Lawyer's Services	Prior Perjury/Fraud on Tribunal	Ongoing Client Crime or Fraud
ABA Model Rule (2002)	Must Not 1.6(a)	May 1.6(b)(1)	Must Not 1.6(a)	Must Not 1.6(a)	Must Not 1.6(a) [1]	Must 3.3(a)(1) (a)(3) and (b) [2]	Must 4.1(b) [3] See also 1.2(d)
ABA Model Code	May 4-101(C)(3)	May 4-101(C)(3)	May 4-101(C)(3)	Must Not 4-101(B)(1)	Must Not 7-102(B)(1) [4]	Must Not 7-102(B)(1) [4]	Must 7-102(A)(7) [5] and 2-110(B)(2) But see 7-102(B)(1) [4]
AL	Must Not 1.6(a)	May 1.6(b)(1)	Must Not 1.6(a)	Must Not 1.6(a)	Must Not 1.6(a) [1]	Must 3.3(a)(2)	Must 4.1(b) [3] See also 1.2(d)
AK	Must Not 1.6(a)	May 1.6(b)(1)	May 1.6(b)(1)	May 1.6(b)(1)	Must Not 1.6(a) [1]	Must 3.3(a)(2)	Must 4.1(b) [3] See also 1.2(d)
AZ	May 1.6(c)	Must 1.6(b)	May 1.6(c)	Must Not 1.6(a)	Must Not 1.6(a) [1]	Must 3.3(a)(2) [26]	Must 4.1(b) [3] See also 1.2(d)
AR	May 1.6(b)(1)	May 1.6(b)(1)	May 1.6(b)(1)	Must Not 1.6(a)	Must Not 1.6(a) [1]	Must 3.3(a)(2)	Must 4.1(b) [3] See also 1.2(d)
CA	Must Not §6068(e) Business and Professions Code [6]	Must Not §6068(e) Business and Professions Code [6]	Must Not §6068(e) Business and Professions Code [6]	Must Not §6068(e) Business and Professions Code [6]	Must Not §6068(e) Business and Professions Code [6]	Must Not §6068(e) Business and Professions Code [6]	Must Not §6068(e) Business and Professions Code [6]
CO	May 1.6(b)	May 1.6(b)	May 1.6(b)	Must Not 1.6(a)	Must Not 1.6(a) [1]	Must 3.3(a)(2)	Must 4.1(2) [3] See also 1.2(d)
CT	Must Not 1.6(a)	Must 1.6(b)	May 1.6(c)(1)	Must Not 1.6(a)	May 1.6(c)(2)	Must 3.3(a)(2)	Must 4.1(2) [3] See also 1.2 (d)
DE	Must Not 1.6(a)	May 1.6(b)(1)	Must Not 1.6(a)	Must Not 1.6(a)	Must Not 1.6(a) [1]	Must 3.3(a)(2)	Must 4.1(b) [3] See also 1.2 (d)
DC	Must Not 1.6(a)(1) [16]	May 1.6(c)(1)	Must Not 1.6(a)(1)	Must Not 1.6(a)(1)	Must Not 1.6(a)(1) [1]	Must Not 3.3(d) and 1.6(a)(1)	Must 4.1(b) [3] See also 1.2 (e)
FL	Must 4-1.6(b)(1)	Must 4-1.6(b)(2)	Must 4-1.6(b)(1)	Must Not 4-1.6(a)	Must Not 4-1.6(a) [1, 27]	Must 4-3.3(a)(2)	Must 4-4.1(b) [3] See also 4-1.2 (d)
GA	May 1.6(b)(1)(i) [21]	May 1.6(b)(1)(ii) [21]	May 1.6(b)(1)(i) [21]	Must Not 1.6(a)	Must Not 1.6(a) [1]	Must 3.3(a)(2), (b)	Must 4.1(b) [3] See also 1.2(d)

See Section 1 For Full Explanation of Columns	A	B	C	D	E	F	G
	INTENT TO COMMIT/PREVENTION				RECTIFICATION		
	Any Crime	Death/Injury	Criminal Fraud	Non-Criminal Fraud	Prior Crime or Fraud Using Lawyer's Services	Prior Perjury/Fraud on Tribunal	Ongoing Client Crime or Fraud
HI	Must Not 1.6(a)	May 1.6(c)(1)	May 1.6(c)(1)	May 1.6(c)(1)	Must 1.6(b) [15]	Must 3.3(a)(2)	Must 4.1(b) [9] See also 1.2(d)
ID	May 1.6(b)(1)	May 1.6(b)(1)	May 1.6(b)(1)	Must Not 1.6(a)	Must Not 1.6(a) [1]	Must 3.3(a)(2)	Must 4.1(b) [3] See also 1.2(d)
IL	May 1.6(c)(2)	Must 1.6(b)	May 1.6(c)(2)	Must Not 1.6(a)	Must Not 1.6(a) and 1.2(g)	Must 3.3(a)(2) [4]	Must 4.1(b) [3]
IN	May 1.6(b)(1)	May 1.6(b)(1)	May 1.6(b)(1)	Must Not 1.6(a)	Must Not 1.6(a) [1]	Must 3.3(a)(2)	Must 4.1(b) [3] See also 1.2(d)
IA	May 4-101(C)(3)	May 4-101(C)(3)	May 4-101(C)(3)	Must Not 4-101(B)(1)	Must Not 7-102(B)(1) [7]	Must Not 7-102(B)(1) [7]	Must 7-102(A)(7) [5] and 2-110(B)(2) But see 7-102(B)(1)
KS	May 1.6(b)(1)	May 1.6(b)(1)	May 1.6(b)(1)	Must Not 1.6(a)	Must Not 1.6(a) [1]	Must 3.3(a)(2)	Must 4.1(b) [3] See also 1.2(d)
KY	Must Not 1.6(a)	May 1.6(b)(1)	Must Not 1.6(a)	Must Not 1.6(a)	Must Not 1.6(a) [1]	Must 3.3(a)(2)	May See note 8 to this chart
LA	Must Not 1.6(a)	May 1.6(b)(1)	Must Not 1.6(a)	Must Not 1.6(a)	Must Not 1.6(a) [1]	Must 3.3(a)(2)	Must 4.1(b) [3] See also 1.2(c)
ME	May 3.6(H)(4)	May 3.6(H)(4)	May 3.6(H)(4)	Must Not 3.6(H)(1)	Must Not 3.6(B) [3]	Must Not 3.6(B) [4]	Must 3.6(D) and 3.5(B)(2)(ii) (see note 5 re Model Code counterparts of these two rules)
MD	Must Not 1.6(a)	May 1.6(b)(1)	May 1.6(b)(1)	May 1.6(b)(1)	May 1.6(b)(2)	Must 3.3(a)(2) [24]	Must 4.1(a)(2)and (b) [9] See also 1.2(d)
MA	Must Not 1.6(a)	May 1.6(b)(1) [17]	May 1.6(b)(1) [17]	May 1.6(b)(1) [17]	May 1.6(b)(3)	Must 3.3(a)(2) [18]	Must 4.1(b) [3] See also 1.2(d)
MI	May 1.6(c)(4)	May 1.6(c)(4)	May 1.6(c)(4)	Must Not 1.6(b)(1)	May 1.6(c)(3)	Must 3.3(a)(2)	Must 4.1 See also 1.2(c)
MN	May 1.6(b)(3)	May 1.6(b)(3)	May 1.6(b)(3)	Must Not 1.6(a)	May 1.6(b)(4)	Must 3.3(a)(2)	Must Resign 1.2(c) and 1.16(a)(1)
MS	May 1.6(b)(1)	May 1.6(b)(1)	May 1.6(b)(1)	Must Not 1.6(a)	Must Not 1.6(a) [1]	Must 3.3(a)(2)	Must 4.1(b) [3] See also 1.2(d)

See Section 1 For Full Explanation of Columns	A	B	C	D	E	F	G
	INTENT TO COMMIT/PREVENTION				RECTIFICATION		
	Any Crime	Death/Injury	Criminal Fraud	Non-Criminal Fraud	Prior Crime or Fraud Using Lawyer's Services	Prior Perjury/Fraud on Tribunal	Ongoing Client Crime or Fraud
MO	Must Not 1.6(a)	May 1.6(b)(1)	Must Not 1.6(a)	Must Not 1.6(a)	Must Not 1.6(a) [1]	Must 3.3(a)(2)	Must 4.1(b) [3] See also 1.2(d)
MT	Must Not 1.6(a)	May 1.6(b)(1)	Must Not 1.6(a)	Must Not 1.6(a)	Must Not 1.6(a) [1]	Must 3.3(a)(2)	Must 4.1(b) [3] See also 1.2(d)
NE	May 4-101(C)(3)	May 4-101(C)(3)	May 4-101(C)(3)	Must Not 4-101(B)(1)	Must Not 7-102(B)(1) [4]	Must Not 7-102(B)(1) [4]	Must 7-102(A)(7) [5] and 2-110(B)(2) But see 7-102(B)(1) [4]
NV	May 156(3)(a) [10]	Must 156(2)	May 156(3)(a) [10]	May 156(3)(a) [10]	May 156(3)(a) [10]	Must 172(1)(b) [30]	Must 181(2) [3] [equivalent of ABA Rule 4.1(b)] See also 152(4)
NH	Must Not 1.6(a)	May 1.6(b)(1)	May 1.6(b)(1)	Must Not 1.6(a)	Must Not 1.6(a) [1]	Must 3.3(a)(3) [23]	Must 4.1(b) [3] See also 1.2(d)
NJ	Must Not 1.6(a)	Must 1.6(b)(1) [11]	Must 1.6(b)(1) [11]	Must 1.6(b)(1) [11]	May 1.6(c)(1) [11]	Must 3.3(a)(2) [25]	Must 4.1(a)(2) and 4.1(b) [9] See also 1.2(d)
NM	Must Not 16-106(A)	"Should" 16-106(B)	May 16-106(C)	Must Not 16-106(A)	Must Not 16-106(A) [1]	Must 16-303(A)(2)	Must 16-401(B) [3] See also 16-102(D)
NY	May [12] 4-101(c)(3)	May 4-101(c)(3)	May [12] 4-101(c)(3)	Must Not [12] 4-101(b)(1)	Must Not [12] 7-102(b)(1) But see 4-101(c)(5)	Must Not 7-102(b) [4]	Must 7-102(a)(7) [5] and 2-110(b)(2) But see 7-102(b)(1)
NC	May 1.6(d)(4)	May 1.6(d)(4)	May 1.6(d)(4)	Must Not 1.6(c)(1)	May 1.6(d)(5)	Must 3.3(a)(2)	May 1.6(d)(5) [20] See also 1.2(d)
ND	Must Not 1.6 But see 1.6(d)	Must 1.6(a)	May 1.6(d)	May 1.6(d)	May 1.6(f)	Must Not 1.6 and 3.3(d)	May 1.6(f) See also 1.2(d)
OH	May 4-101(C)(3)	May 4-101(C)(3)	May 4-101(C)(3)	Must Not 4-101(B)(1)	Must 7-102(B)(1) [4]	Must 7-102(B)(1) [4, 13]	Must 7-102(A)(7) [5] and 7-102(B)(1) [4]
OK	May 1.6(b)(1)	May 1.6(b)(1)	May 1.6(b)(1)	Must Not 1.6(a)	May 1.6(b)(2)	Must 3.3(a)(2)	Must 4.1(b) [3] See also 1.2(c)
OR	May 4-101(C)(3)	May 4-101(C)(3)	May 4-101(C)(3)	Must Not 4-101(B)(1)	Must Not 7-102(B)(1) [4]	Must Not 7-102(B)(1) [4]	Must 7-102(A)(7) [5] and 2-110(B)(2) But see 7-102(B)(1) [4]

See Section 1 For Full Explanation of Columns	A	B	C	D	E	F	G
	INTENT TO COMMIT/PREVENTION				**RECTIFICATION**		
	Any Crime	Death/Injury	Criminal Fraud	Non-Criminal Fraud	Prior Crime or Fraud Using Lawyer's Services	Prior Perjury/Fraud on Tribunal	Ongoing Client Crime or Fraud
PA	May 1.6(c)(2) [14]	May 1.6(c)(1)	May 1.6(c)(1)	May 1.6(c)(2) [14]	May 1.6(c)(2)	Must 3.3(a)(2) [29] See also 1.6(b)	Must 4.1(b) [3] See also 1.2(d)
RI	Must Not 1.6(a)	May 1.6(b)(1)	Must Not 1.6(a)	Must Not 1.6(a)	Must Not 1.6(a) [1]	Must 3.3(a)(2)	Must 4.1(b) [3] See also 1.2(d)
SC	May 1.6(b)(1)	May 1.6(b)(1)	May 1.6(b)(1)	Must Not 1.6(a)	Must Not 1.6(a) [1]	Must 3.3(a)(2)	Must 4.1(b) [3] See also 1.2(d)
SD	Must Not 1.6(a)	May 1.6(b)(1)	Must Not 1.6(a)	Must Not 1.6(a)	May 1.6(b)(3)	Must 3.3(a)(2)	Must 4.1(b) [3] See also 1.2(d) and 1.6(b)(3)
TN	May 4-101(C)(3)	May 4-101(C)(3)	May 4-101(C)(3)	Must Not 4-101(B)(1)	Must Not 7-102(B)(1) [4]	Must Not 7-102(B)(1) [4]	Must Not 7-102(B)(1) [4]
Proposed	The proposed rules are under consideration by the Tennessee Supreme Court. For the current status of the proposed new Tennessee Rules, see www.tba.org/committees/conduct/index.html						
TX	May 1.05(c)(7)	Must 1.05(e)	May 1.05(c)(7)	May 1.05(c)(7)	May 1.05(c)(8)	Must 3.03(a)(2)	Must 4.01(b) [9] See also 1.02(c)
UT	Must Not 1.6(a)	May 1.6(b)(1)	May 1.6(b)(1)	May 1.6(b)(1)	May 1.6(b)(2)	Must 3.3(a)(2) [28]	Must 4.1(b) [3] See also 1.2(c)
VT	May 1.6(c)(1)	Must 1.6(b)(1)	May 1.6(c)(1)	Must Not 1.6(a)	Must Not See 1.6(b)(2) [22]	Must 3.3(a)(2)	Must Not See 1.6(b)(2) [22]
VA	Must 1.6(c)(1)	Must 1.6(c)(1)	Must 1.6(c)(1)	Must Not 1.6(a)	May 1.6(b)(3)	Must 1.6(c)(2) and 3.3(a)(2)	Must 4.1(b) [3] See also 1.2(c)
WA	May 1.6(b)(1)	May 1.6(b)(1)	May 1.6(b)(1)	Must Not 1.6(a)	Must Not 1.6(a) [1]	Must Not 3.3(a)(2) [19]	Must 4.1(b) [3] See also 1.2(d)
WV	May 1.6(b)	May 1.6(b)	May 1.6(b)	Must Not 1.6(a)	Must Not 1.6(a) [1]	Must 3.3(a)(2)	Must 4.1(b) [3] See also 1.2(d)
WI	Must Not 20:1.6(a)	Must 20:1.6(b)	Must 20:1.6(b)	Must 20:1.6(b)	May 20:1.6(c)(1)	Must 20:3.3(a)(2)	Must 20:4.1(b) [3] See also 20:1.2(d)
WY	May 1.6(b)(1)	May 1.6(b)(1)	May 1.6(b)(1)	Must Not 1.6(a)	Must Not 1.6(a) [1]	Must 3.3(a)(2)	Must 4.1(b) [3] See also 1.2(d)
TOTALS	**Must: 2** **May: 28** **Must Not: 21**	**Must: 11** **May: 38** **Must Not: 1** **"Should": 1**	**Must: 4** **May: 37** **Must Not: 10**	**Must: 2** **May: 9** **Must Not: 40**	**Must: 2** **May: 16** **Must Not: 33**	**Must: 41** **May: 0** **Must Not: 10**	**Must: 44** **May: 3** **Must Not: 3** **Must Resign: 1**

Section 3 Explanatory Notes to Chart

1. **"Noisy Withdrawal" Under Model Rule 1.6.** Model Rule 1.6 generated more controversy than any other Rule during the six-year (1977–83) Model Rules project. It is also generated substantial controversy during the Ethics 2000 deliberation. Although the black letter Rule emphasizes the obligation of confidentiality and generally prohibits "whistle-blowing" (except in cases of threatened death or substantial bodily harm), Official Comment [14] to Rule 1.6 (formerly Comment [16] to the 1983 version of Model Rule 1.6) is designed to permit under some circumstances what has been referred to as "flag-waving" by means of an abrupt and noisy resignation from the representation. The idea is that, although the lawyer is prohibited from disclosing any specifics about a client crime or fraud, the lawyer's resignation, accompanied by the "withdrawal" or "disaffirmance" of the lawyer's previous "opinion, document, affirmation, or the like," will in most instances signal the other parties involved in the transaction that the client may be engaged in wrongdoing. The portion of the official comment dealing with the lawyer's obligation to resign under certain circumstances, and specifying what "signals" the lawyer is permitted to give in connection with any such resignation notwithstanding the black letter Rule, is extraordinarily confusing. The text of the Official Comment to Rule 1.6 dealing with resignation/withdrawal is:

Withdrawal

[14] If the lawyer's services will be used by the client in materially furthering a course of criminal or fraudulent conduct, the lawyer must withdraw, as stated in Rule 1.16(a)(1). After withdrawal the lawyer is required to refrain from making disclosure of the client's confidences, except as otherwise permitted in Rule 1.6. Neither this Rule nor Rule 1.8(b) nor Rule 1.16(d) prevents the lawyer from giving notice of the fact of withdrawal, and the lawyer may also withdraw or disaffirm any opinion, document, affirmation, or the like. Where the client is an organization, the lawyer may be in doubt whether contemplated conduct will actually be carried out by the organization. Where necessary to guide conduct in connection with this Rule, the lawyer may make inquiry within the organization as indicated in Rule 1.13(b).

This so-called "noisy withdrawal" Comment is the subject of a comprehensive analysis in ABA Formal Opinion 92–366 (8/8/92).

2. **Disclosing Confidential Client Information To Avoid Perjury or Fraud on a Tribunal Under Model Rule 3.3.** The 2002 revisions to Rule 3.3 strengthened the disclosure obligations under that rule. Rules 3.3(a)(1), (a)(3) and (b) support the "must disclose" obligation under the Model Rules and in Model Rule jurisdictions. Rule 3.3(c) provides that the duties stated in Rule 3.3(a) and (b) apply even if compliance requires disclosure of information otherwise protected by Rule 1.6. *See* ABA Formal Opinion 87–353 (April 20, 1987). That Opinion was sharply criticized in Goldberg, *Heaven Help the Lawyer for a Civil Liar*, 2 Geo. J. Legal Ethics 885 (1989). *See also* ABA Formal Opinion 93–376 (August 6, 1993) discussing the application of Model Rule 3.3(a) to perjury of a client in a pre-trial deposition.

3. **Relationship of Model Rules 4.1(b) and 1.6.** Model Rule 4.1(b) provides that:

[i]n the course of representing a client a lawyer shall not knowingly: (b) fail to disclose a material fact to a third person when disclosure is necessary to avoid assisting a criminal or fraudulent act by a client, *unless disclosure is prohibited by Rule 1.6.* (Emphasis added.)

It has been suggested that the italicized clause, which was a last-minute addition during the final drafting process in 1983 in order to make Rule 4.1(b) consistent with the final lip-sealing version of Rule 1.6, has effectively negated the entire paragraph (b) of Rule 4.1. That is not a proper interpretation. Although the lawyer is prohibited by the final clause of the Rule from explicitly disclosing that the client is concealing or misrepresenting material facts, the lawyer in this situation is *required* by Rules 1.2(d) and 1.16(a)(1) to resign forthwith as counsel if the client cannot be persuaded to correct the record. Further, under Official Comment [14] to Rule 1.6 discussed in note 1 above, the lawyer after resigning may also noisily "withdraw or disaffirm" any fraudulent statement of the client with which the lawyer might be deemed to be associated by reason of the lawyer's prior presence in the transaction as the client's counsel. In other words, and similar to the situation under Rule 1.6 discussed in note 1 above, Rule 4.1(b) does not permit "whistle-blowing" in the normal sense, but (when interpreted in harmony with Rules 1.2(d) and 1.16(a)(1)) it clearly *requires* a certain amount of flag-waving that will alert even the most naive citizen to the fact that the lawyer's client has probably concealed or misrepresented material facts. Presumably the naive citizen, with assistance from his or her counsel, will promptly investigate and discover the truth, or at least some of the untruths, and will thus avoid being victimized. *See* Hazard and Hodes, *The Law of Lawyering* (3d ed.) §§ 9.30–31; Rotunda, *The Notice of Withdrawal and the New Model Rules of Professional Conduct: Blowing the Whistle and Waiving the Red Flag*, 63 Oregon Law Review 455 (1984). *See also* ABA Formal Opinion 93–375 (August 6, 1993) analyzing a lawyer's disclosure obligations in the context of representing a financial institution in connection with the statutory examination of the institution by the regulators. Additionally, where the client's behavior constitutes continuing misconduct, the permissive disclosure provisions of the many states that have adopted Rule 1.6 in modified form come into play (see Columns C and D on the chart). If disclosure of a client's intent to commit a crime or fraud is permitted under Rule 1.6, then such disclosure becomes mandatory under the "shall not knowingly fail to disclose" language of Rule 4.1(b) if the situation also meets the requirements of that Rule. For all these reasons the foregoing chart classifies this situation as a "Must" disclose case.

4. **Revealing Client Fraud Under Model Code DR 7–102(B)(1) and Various State Versions Thereof.** The ABA's original (1969) version of DR 7–102(B)(1) reads as follows:

DR 7–102 Representing a Client Within the Bounds of the Law

B. A lawyer who receives information clearly establishing that:

    1. His client has, in the course of the representation, perpetrated a fraud upon a person or tribunal shall promptly call upon his client to rectify the same, and if his client refuses or is unable to do so, he shall reveal the fraud to the affected person or tribunal.

This version of DR 7–102(B)(1) is referred to in this note as "Version 1." It was soon perceived that Version 1 was inconsistent with DR 4–101(B) because it literally obliterated both the attorney-client privilege and the ethical obligation of confidentiality, and *required* the lawyer to speak out in any case where, "in the course of the representation," the lawyer's client has perpetrated a fraud upon a person or a tribunal. The ABA, spurred in part by the pleas of securities lawyers (who in the aftermath of the National Student Marketing scandal were appre-

hensive about the SEC's threats to deputize them as securities law police), decided that result was not intended. In 1974 the ABA amended Version 1 by adding the following clause at the end as an important limitation on the applicability of Version 1: "except when the information is protected as a privileged communication." (The version of DR 7–102(B)(1) after the 1974 amendment is referred to in this footnote as "Version 2.") In drafting Version 2, the ABA again bungled the task by phrasing the exception to refer only to the relatively narrow testimonial attorney-client privilege, whereas the proponents of the 1974 amendment intended to protect *all* confidences and secrets of the client from the mandatory disclosure provisions of the first version of DR 7–102(B)(1). Thus, it was necessary for the ABA Committee on Ethics and Professional Responsibility to issue Formal Opinion 341 (September 30, 1975) holding that the term "privileged communication" included all confidences and secrets of the client, not merely the narrow class of confidences and secrets to which the attorney-client privilege applies.

The following should be noted about particular states and their adoption of Version 1 or Version 2 of DR 7–102(B)(1):

Maine, Nebraska, New York, Oregon: These four states have adopted the ABA's 1974 amendment to DR 7–102(B)(1), have declined to adopt any version of the Model Rules and therefore continue to have what is described above as Version 2 or the equivalent thereof. New York and Oregon have varied the wording of Version 2 slightly, but their wording is the functional equivalent of Version 2 as interpreted by ABA Formal Opinion 341. These states are classified in columns E and F of the foregoing chart as "Must Not" disclose states.

But in *People v. Depallo*, 96 N.Y.2d 437, 754 N.E.2d 751 (2001), the New York Court of Appeals may have been willing to take a narrow view of what constituted a "confidence or secret" that could not be disclosed. The defendant, appealing from a murder conviction, complained of ineffective assistance of counsel. After the defendant had taken the stand and testified (in narrative format) that he had not been at the scene of the crime, counsel advised the court in chambers that the defendant had previously told the lawyer that he had been involved in the crime. The lawyer did not refer to the defendant's testimony in closing, and the defendant was convicted.

The Court of Appeals affirmed the conviction based on DR 7–102(B)(1), finding that the intent to commit a crime is not a protected confidence or secret, and that admissions by the defendant in pre-trial hearings had lifted any confidentiality from his involvement in the crime. The court did warn in a footnote, however, that it did not have occasion to address whether a similar disclosure would be appropriate in a bench trial.

See also Nassau County (N.Y.) Bar Association Committee on Professional Ethics Opinion 01–8. (Information that client had filed false financial statement with court that was gained from client after conclusion of the engagement was not a protected confidence or secret, and must be revealed. Even if the information were a "confidence or secret" the lawyer would be required to withdraw his certification of the financial statements.)

Tennessee: Tennessee also adopted the ABA's 1974 amendment, has not adopted any version of the Model Rules (although it is actively considering doing so), and therefore has Version 2 of DR 7–102(B)(1). However, that provision has a history of varied interpretations by Tennessee ethics authorities. In Tennessee Formal Ethics Opinion 93–F–133 (12/10/93) the Board of Professional Responsibility of the Supreme Court of Tennessee opined that perjury enjoys "no protection by being a privileged communication" and must be disclosed. In late 1996, however, the Tennessee Supreme Court overruled that opinion to the extent that it required lawyers to disclose confidential information about client fraud. The ethics opinion reporting the Court's decision concludes: "Therefore, the ethical duty to protect client's confidences prevails over the duty to disclose client's [ongoing] fraud or perjury." Therefore, Tennessee is designated in columns F and G as a "Must Not" disclose state.

Ohio: Only Ohio still has Version 1 of DR 7–102(B)(1), and is therefore classified in columns F and G as a "Must" disclose state.

Illinois: Illinois adopted a modified version of the Model Rules in August 1990, but retained the substance of its prior Version 2 of DR 7–102(B)(1) as Illinois Rule 1.2(g). At the same time it adopted the substance of Model Rule 3.3(a)(2), which requires a lawyer to disclose to a tribunal material facts necessary to avoid assisting a client's crime or fraud. See Illinois State Bar Association Opinion No. 94–24 (May 17, 1995) for a discussion of the relationship between Illinois Rule 1.2(g) and Illinois Rule 3.3(a). As a result, Illinois is classified as "Must Not" disclose in column E and "Must" disclose in column F.

5. **Disclosing Prior Client Fraud and "Noisy Withdrawal" Under DR 7–102(A)(7).** This Model Code Disciplinary Rule basically says that a lawyer cannot commence to act *or continue to act* as counsel if the client is or will be engaged during the course of the representation in conduct that the lawyer knows is illegal or fraudulent. It is roughly the predecessor of Model Rules 1.2(d) and 4.1(b) referred to in note 3 above. Even in those states that have Version 2 of DR 7–102(B)(1) (see note 4 above), which severely limits the lawyer's authority to disclose a *prior* client fraud, the better view is that DR 7–102(A)(7), like its successor, Model Rule 4.1(b), speaks to *contemporaneous* concealment or misrepresentation by the client during the course of the representation and that, at a minimum, the lawyer is *required* to resign. See also on this point DR 2–110(B)(2). Thus, in all instances the foregoing chart classifies this situation as a "Must" disclose case. However, if Version 2 of DR 7–102(B)(1) is in effect, the disclosure cannot be an explicit revelation of a client confidence but has to be in the indirect form of an abrupt withdrawal as counsel from the transaction, followed by a disavowal by the lawyer of any fraudulent concealment or misrepresentation with which the lawyer might be deemed to be associated by reason of the lawyer's presence in the transaction at the time of the concealment or misrepresentation.

6. **California.** Lawyers' obligations to maintain client confidences in California are governed by § 6068(e) of the California Business and Professions Code, not by the California Rules of Professional Conduct. Section 6068(e) recognizes no exception to the obligation of secrecy in the context of this chart. While there had been several ethics opinions that suggested some implied exceptions (see, for example Opinions 414 [4/29/83] and 436 [4/15/85] of the Los Angeles County Bar Association, and Formal Opinion 1988–96 [undated] of the State Bar of California), a more recent opinion of the San Diego County Bar Association, 1990–1 (undated), is strongly anti-disclosure. In that opinion the Legal Ethics and Unlawful Practices Committee said that even when the client has expressed an intention to kill or injure someone, the lawyer may not "blow the whistle." The Committee relied principally upon the California Supreme Court's failure to adopt any such exception when it promulgated the revised Rules of Professional Conduct in 1988 (effective May 27, 1989).

More recently, in Formal Opinion 1996–146 [undated] the Standing Committee on Professional Responsibility and Conduct of the State Bar of California reiterated the duty of confidentiality in the context of a case in which a lawyer learns that a client general contractor is using inferior piping in violation of contractual warranties. The Opinion discusses steps a lawyer might take when faced with such conduct, but allows no room for disclosure of that conduct.

And in 2000, the Los Angeles County Bar Association Professional Responsibility and Ethics Committee opined that a lawyer representing a minor may not disclose information acquired in confidence that the minor is being sexually abused. (Formal Opinion 504, May 15, 2000) Even if the lawyer believes that the minor is not capable of an informed decision on the subject, the most the lawyer can do is seek appointment of a guardian ad litem, and make disclosure to that guardian.

In 2001, the California Court of Appeals held that a former in-house lawyer suing an employer for wrongful termination may disclose confidential and privileged information to her attorney in connection with her case. *Fox Searchlight Pictures, Inc. v. Paladeno*, 89 Cal. App. 4th 294, 106 Cal. Rptr. 2d 906 (2d Dist. 2001).

7. **Iowa**. To be protected from disclosure, the information in question must come within the definition of the attorney-client privilege contained in Iowa Code § 622.10. If the information is not privileged pursuant to that section, then these two situations are "Must" disclose cases. Section 622.10 prohibits "a practicing attorney," among other professions, "who obtains information by reason of the [attorney's] employment," from testifying about "any confidential communication properly entrusted to the [attorney] in the [attorney's] professional capacity, and necessary and proper to enable the [attorney] to discharge the function of the [attorney's] office according to the usual course of practice or discipline," unless the client waives the privilege.

8. **Kentucky.** The special drafting committee recommended that Rule 4.1(b) be deleted, stating that "sufficient guidance is provided by Rules 1.2(d), 1.6, and 1.16." The Kentucky Supreme Court adopted that recommendation. *See* note 3 above regarding Model Rule 4.1(b) generally. Since the Kentucky version of Rule 4.1 does not contain a counterpart to Model Rule 4.1(b), and thus places no affirmative obligation on the lawyer to disclose a material fact to avoid assisting a client crime or fraud, we have classified Kentucky as a "May" disclose state in column G.

9. **Disclosing Ongoing Client Fraud Under Rule 4.1 in Hawaii, Maryland, New Jersey and Texas.** The Hawaii, Maryland, New Jersey and Texas versions of Model Rule 4.1(b) do not contain the ABA's confusing limiting clause at the end ("unless disclosure is prohibited by Rule 1.6") referred to in note 3 above. (In Texas, the relevant rules are known as the Disciplinary Rules of Professional Conduct.) Therefore, in the context of an ongoing transaction where the lawyer's client has committed a criminal or fraudulent act by concealing or misrepresenting a material fact, the lawyer *must* disclose to the affected third parties the full truth. As a general proposition, the lawyer should first remonstrate with the client if practicable, then act affirmatively to reveal the client's deceit only if and after the client has refused to rectify the situation. In *Davin L.L.C. v. Daham*, 329 N.J. Super. 54, 746 A.2d 1034 (App. Div. 2000), the court reversed a summary judgment in favor of a landlord's lawyer in an action by a tenant for failure to disclose (or urge his client to disclose) during lease negotiations that the property was in foreclosure. The court cited Rule 4.1 in holding that the lawyer might have a duty of disclosure on the facts presented. The court's opinion includes some rather broad language about a lawyer's duty of candor.

10. **Nevada.** The Nevada Rules of Professional Conduct are part of the Nevada Supreme Court Rules beginning with Rule 150. In the situations described in columns A, C, D and E on the foregoing chart, disclosure is authorized, but not required, only if the "lawyer's services have been used" in connection with the transaction.

11. **New Jersey** In New Jersey the disclosure must or may, as the case may be, be made if the client's conduct is merely "illegal" but does not rise to the level of a crime or a fraud. In Opinion 677 (published 10/10/94) the Advisory Committee on Professional Ethics of the New Jersey Supreme Court opined that a supervisory and regulatory "department of the state of New Jersey" is a "tribunal" within the meaning of New Jersey's version of Rule 1.6, which requires a lawyer to blow the whistle on a client perpetrating a fraud on a tribunal.

12. **New York.** The Committee on Professional Ethics of the Association of the Bar of the City of New York has opined that a

lawyer who represents a limited partnership and the general partner on partnership and other matters *must* disclose wrongdoing by the general partner to the limited partners, Formal Opinion 1994–10 (10/21/94). *See also* Nassau County (N.Y.) Bar Association Committee on Professional Ethics, Opinion 01–7. (Client advises lawyer of intention to omit half-sibling from list of potential distributees in probate proceeding. Lawyer advises that would be improper, and client discharges lawyer before proceeding. Lawyer may disclose the fraud, but is not obligated to because lawyer had not assisted in the fraud.)

13. **Ohio.** In *Office of Disciplinary Counsel v. Heffernan*, 58 Ohio St. 3d 260, 569 N.E.2d 1027 (1991), the Ohio Supreme Court suspended a lawyer for six months because the lawyer had failed to inform a lower court upon learning "a few months" after the fact that the lawyer's client had perpetrated a fraud upon that court.

14. **Pennsylvania.** In these cases the disclosure is authorized only if the "lawyer's services are being or had been used" in the transaction.

15. **Hawaii.** Disclosure is required only "where the act [in furtherance of which the lawyer's services had been used] has resulted in substantial injury to the financial interests or property of another." Otherwise the lawyer "May" disclose under Rule 1.6(c)(2).

16. **District of Columbia.** A lawyer may reveal client confidences and secrets to prevent the bribery or intimidation of witnesses, juror, court officials, or other persons involved in proceedings before a tribunal. *See* Rule 1.6(c)(2).

17. **Massachusetts.** Massachusetts Rule 1.6(b)(1) also provides that a lawyer may reveal confidential information to prevent the wrongful execution or incarceration of another.

18. **Massachusetts.** *See* Massachusetts Rule 3.3(e) for an exception to Rule 3.3(a) that applies only in criminal cases. The Massachusetts Bar Association Committee on Professional Ethics has opined that a lawyer may disclose a client's believable threat of suicide to a family member or appropriate authorities. (Ethics Opinion 01–2.)

19. **Washington.** Washington generally adopts the ABA Model Rules, but Washington Rule 3.3(a)(2) differs from the Model Rule. The Washington rule provides that a lawyer shall not knowingly fail to disclose a material fact to a tribunal when disclosure is necessary to avoid assisting a criminal or fraudulent act by the client *unless* such disclosure is prohibited by Rule 1.6. The Washington rules do not have a provision equivalent to ABA Model Rule 3.3(b). Therefore, we have designated Washington as a "Must Not" disclose state in column F.

20. **North Carolina.** North Carolina Rule 1.6(d)(5) permits, but does not require, disclosure of a client's criminal or fraudulent acts "in the commission of which the lawyer's services were used." Therefore, we have designated North Carolina a "May" disclose state in column F.

21. **Georgia.** Rule 1.6(b)(1)(i) also permits disclosure to avoid or prevent harm or substantial financial loss to another as a result of third-party criminal conduct.

22. **Vermont.** We caution lawyers practicing in Vermont that the Vermont Supreme Court has not yet opined on this Rule. The Reporter's Note to Vermont Rule 4.1 states that the subject of Model Rule 4.1(b) was moved to Vermont Rule 1.6(b)(2) and changed to make the disclosure requirement absolute and not subject to the prohibition of Rule 1.6(a) or the discretion of Rule 1.6(c). However, we have designated columns E and G as "Must Not" because it is not clear that a lawyer must disclose when the crime or fraud is completed but the effects of the crime or fraud are continuing. Until the Vermont Supreme Court interprets Rule 1.6(b)(2), we cannot be certain of its application here.

23. **New Hampshire.** In *Feld's Case*, 737 A.2d 656 (N.H. 1999), the New Hampshire Supreme Court publicly censured a lawyer for failing to advise his client to correct false testimony in a civil deposition.

24. **Maryland.** In Maryland Ethics Opinion No. 86–28 (undated), the inquiring lawyer was a member of the Maryland and District of Columbia bars. The lawyer had introduced evidence in a court proceeding in the District of Columbia and subsequently learned that his client had forged the documents. The Maryland rule required disclosure, while the D.C. rule prohibited it. The Maryland State Bar Association Committee on Legal Ethics opined that when a Maryland lawyer acts in accordance with a foreign jurisdiction's ethics rules, his conduct is ethical *per se.*

25. **New Jersey.** In *In the Matter of Robert J. Forrest*, 158 N.J. 428, 730 A.2d 340

(1999), the New Jersey Supreme Court held that withholding a material fact from an arbitrator violates the duty of candor to a "tribunal" under New Jersey Rule 3.3(a).

26. **Arizona**. In Arizona State Bar Committee on the Rules of Professional Conduct Opinion 2000–02 (March 2000), the committee concluded that constitutional concerns might call for a different standard in criminal cases. Specifically, in responding to a series of hypothetical situations, the committee concluded that a lawyer is not required to disclose a client's factual misrepresentations to the court in connection with a plea bargain. The committee cautioned, however, that the lawyer cannot in any way become a party to, or endorse any misrepresentation

27. **Florida**. In *TransPetrol, Ltd. v. Radulovic*, 764 So.2d 868 (Fla. App. 2000), the court dismissed a claim against lawyers and accountants who had allegedly failed to disclose a client's fraudulent scheme to avoid payment of a debt. The court held that there was no duty of disclosure to a third party, and also rejected claims of aiding and abetting, and of RICO violations. The opinion does not refer to this rule.

28. **Utah**. *See* Utah State Bar Ethics Advisory Opinion Committee, Opinion 00–06 (September 29, 2000) (lawyer who hears client make unsworn false statement to court about his criminal past must first try to persuade client to correct the statement; second, failing that, ask leave to withdraw; third, if leave is denied, disclose the falsity to the court).

29. **Pennsylvania**. There is no obligation to disclose matters of which the lawyer does not learn until after the matter is closed, according to Philadelphia Bar Ass'n Professional Guidance Comm., Opinion 2001–2 (3/01).

30. **Nevada**. The Nevada State Bar Standing Committee on Ethics and Professional Responsibility concluded (Opinion 25, 1/01) that when a potential client receives advice from a lawyer, decides not to retain that lawyer, but uses the advice in furtherance of a fraud on the court, the lawyer may disclose the fraud if she learns of it, but is not obligated to do so.

APPENDIX B

Chart on Lawyer Screening*

The following chart analyzes in summary form the provisions of the ABA MODEL CODE OF PROFESSIONAL RESPONSIBILITY, the ABA MODEL RULES OF PROFESSIONAL CONDUCT, the RESTATEMENT, and the various state versions of the Code and Rules on the issue of imputed disqualification, and the sub-issues relating to screening generally, and the efficacy of an "Ethical Wall," without client consent.

The chart indicates, with appropriate citations, whether, in the case of movement from one law firm to another by a lawyer who is personally disqualified from a matter (in which both firms are involved) because of his or her participation in it at the previous firm, the second firm can avoid the general imputed disqualification rule by constructing an "Ethical Wall" or similar screening device. A "No" answer to that question on the attached chart means that the "Ethical Wall" or similar screening device is *not* sufficient by itself, and that, *in addition to the Ethical Wall*, the firm to which the lawyer is moving *must* seek and obtain the consent of the previous firm's client if the second firm is acting as counsel in the matter adverse to the previous firm's client. This must be done *before* the disqualified lawyer begins work at the new firm. Failure to recognize this rule and obtain consent of the previous firm's client ordinarily will subject the second firm to immediate disqualification. If that happens, a malpractice claim by the second firm's client is virtually inevitable. The obvious lesson that emerges from the chart is that the overwhelming majority of jurisdictions (44 out of 51) *do not* recognize screening of a tainted lawyer alone as a cure for imputed disqualification. As the notes to the chart demonstrate, federal courts may differ with courts and ethics committees of the states in which they sit.

This memorandum and the chart deal only with movement from one private employer (law firm, corporation, *etc.*) to another. In the case of a new lawyer who is a former member of the executive or judicial branch of government, some form of effective screening device is usually acceptable.

Lawyer Screening

Jurisdiction	Applicable rules	Screening by Rule?	Rule Provision	Note
ABA	Model Rules of Professional Conduct	No	1.9(b) and 1.10(a)	
ABA	Model Code of Professional Responsibility	No	5–105(D)	
Restatement of the Law Governing Lawyers		Limited	§ 124(2)	

Jurisdiction	Applicable rules	Screening by Rule?	Rule Provision	Note
AL	Rules of Professional Conduct	No	1.10(b)	1
AK	Rules of Professional Conduct	No	1.9(b) and 1.10(a)	
AZ	Rules of Professional Conduct	No	1.10(b)	2
AR	Rules of Professional Conduct	No	1.10(b)	3
CA	Rules of Professional Conduct	No		4
CO	Rules of Professional Conduct	No	1.9(b) and 1.10(a)	5
CT	Rules of Professional Conduct	No	1.10(b)	6
DE	Lawyers' Rules of Professional Conduct	No	1.10(b)	7
DC	Rules of Professional Conduct	No	1.10(b)	8
FL	Rules of Professional Conduct	No	4–1.10(b)	9
GA	Rules of Professional Conduct	No	1.9(b) and 1.10(a)	10
HI	Rules of Professional Conduct	No	1.9(b) and 1.10(a)	11
ID	Rules of Professional Conduct	No	1.10(b)	
IL	Rules of Professional Conduct	Yes	1.10(b)(2) and 1.10(e)	12
IN	Rules of Professional Conduct	No	1.10(b)	13
IA	Code of Professional Responsibility for Lawyers	No	5–105(E)	
KS	Rules of Professional Conduct	No	1.10(b)	14
KY	Rules of Professional Conduct	Yes	1.10(d)	
LA	Rules of Professional Conduct	No	1.10(b)	15
ME	Code of Professional Responsibility	No	3.4(k)	16
MD	Rules of Professional Conduct	Yes	1.10(b)	
MA	Rules of Professional Conduct	Limited	1.10(d)(2)	17
MI	Rules of Professional Conduct	Yes	1.10(b)(1)	18
MN	Rules of Professional Conduct	Limited	1.10(b)	19
MS	Rules of Professional Conduct	No	1.10(b)	20
MO	Rules of Professional Conduct	No	1.10(b)	21
MT	Rules of Professional Conduct	No	1.10(b)	
NE	Code of Professional Responsibility	No	5–105(D)	22
NV	Rules of Professional Conduct (Nevada Supreme Court Rule 160)	No	160(2)	23
NH	Rules of Professional Conduct	No	1.10(b)	
NJ	Rules of Professional Conduct	No	1.10(b)	24
NM	Rules of Professional Conduct	No	16–110(B)	
NY	Code of Professional Responsibility	No	5–105(D) and 5–108	25
NC	Revised Rules of Professional Conduct	No	1.9(b) and 1.10(a)	
ND	Rules of Professional Conduct	No	1.10(b)	26
OH	Code of Professional Responsibility	No	5–105(D)	27
OK	Rules of Professional Conduct	No	1.10(b)	
OR	Code of Professional Responsibility	Yes	5–105(I)	28
PA	Rules of Professional Conduct	Yes	1.10(b)(1) and (2)	29
RI	Rules of Professional Conduct	No	1.10(b)	30
SC	Rules of Professional Conduct	No	1.9(b) and 1.10(a)	31

174

Jurisdiction	Applicable rules	Screening by Rule?	Rule Provision	Note
SD	Rules of Professional Conduct	No	1.9(b) and 1.10(a)	
TN	Code of Professional Responsibility	Yes	5–105(D)	32
TN	Proposed Rules of Professional Conduct	Yes	1.10(D)	
TX	Disciplinary Rules of Professional Conduct	No	1.09(b)	33
UT	Rules of Professional Conduct	No	1.10(b)	34
VT	Rules of Professional Conduct	No	1.9(b) and 1.10(a)	35
VA	Rules of Professional Conduct	No	1.9(b)	36
WA	Rules of Professional Conduct	Yes	1.10(b)	
WV	Rules of Professional Conduct	No	1.10(b)	37
WI	Rules of Professional Conduct for Attorneys	No	20:1.10(b)	38
WY	Rules of Professional Conduct for Attorneys at Law	No	1.10(b)	

Notes for Chart

1. *See also Roberts v. Hutchins,* 572 So. 2d 1231 (Ala. 1990).

2. In *Towne Development of Chandler, Inc. v. Superior Court,* 173 Ariz. 364, 842 P.2d 1377 (Ariz. App. 1992), the court held that Arizona's Rule 1.10(b) means what it says and that screening will not work.

3. *See also Burnette v. Morgan,* 303 Ark. 150, 794 S.W.2d 145 (1990).

4. California has no ethics rule on this subject. In *County of Los Angeles v. United States Dist. Court,* 223 F.3d 990 (9th Cir. 2000), the Ninth Circuit refused to disqualify a firm that had established an adequate and timely screen, finding that the California Supreme Court had opened the door to screening in *People ex rel. Dep't of Corps. v. SpeeDee Oil Change Systems, Inc.,* 980 P.2d 371 (1999). It should not be assumed that California state courts will necessarily follow the Ninth Circuit's reasoning. In *SpeeDee Oil,* the California Supreme Court said that it need not address the screening issue, because in that case the law firm had not attempted to screen the tainted lawyer. Moreover, in 1992 an appellate panel held clearly that if the moving lawyer has confidential information about the case in question, an "ethical wall" will not save the entire second firm from disqualification. *Henriksen v. Great American Savings and Loan,* 11 Cal. App. 4th 109, 14 Cal. Rptr. 2d 184 (1992). Other cases demonstrating hostility to "ethical walls" are *Andric v. Calif.,* 55 F. Supp. 2d 1056 (C.D. Cal. 1999); *Employers Insurance of Wausau v. Albert D. Seeno Construction Co.,* 692 F. Supp. 1150 (N.D. Cal. 1988); and *In re Mortgage v. Realty Trust,* 195 Bankr. 740 (C.D. Cal. 1996). *Klein v. Superior Court of Santa Clara County,* 198 Cal. App. 3d 894, 244 Cal. Rptr. 226 (1988) implied that California courts *might* approve an "ethical wall" provided the new lawyer had not actually worked on the affected client's matter while at the previous firm.

5. Colorado's Rules of Professional Conduct replaced the former Code of Professional Responsibility effective January 1, 1993. Colorado Bar Ass'n Ethics Comm. Formal Opinion No. 88 (May 18, 1991) contains a comprehensive discussion of the use of "Ethical Walls." At footnote 7 the Committee specifically declined to predict how Colorado's proposed Rules of Professional Conduct would be applied. The Committee's conclusion under the then applicable Code of Professional Responsibility was that an "Ethical Wall" would work only if the moving lawyer had no confidences about the client of the old firm. In *Hunter Douglas, Inc. v. Home Fashions, Inc.* 811 F. Supp. 566 (D. Colo. 1992), a Colorado federal court, applying state ethics rules, found a lateral lawyer had been effectively screened.

6. *See* Connecticut Bar Association Committee on Professional Ethics, Informal Opinion 01–16 (Dec. 28, 2001). *But see Horch v. United of Omaha Life Insurance,* 25 Conn. L. Rptr. 18 (Super. 1999) where the Superior Court of Connecticut refused to disqualify a firm that hired a lawyer who had worked on the other side because it found the lawyer had been effectively screened from the matter and *Wellner v. Carroll,* 1995 Conn. Super. LEXIS 359 (Jan. 6, 1995) suggesting a screen might have avoided disqualification.

7. Opinion 1986–1 of the Delaware State Bar Association Committee on Professional Ethics (undated). The opinion relates specifically to non-lawyers; however, it relies, in part, on a case that extended the Rule 1.11(b) screening provisions to private lawyers. *Nemours Foundation v. Gilbane, Aetna, Federal Ins. Co.*, 632 F. Supp. 418 (D. Del. 1986).

8. *See* D.C. Bar Legal Ethics Committee Opinion 273 (Sept. 17, 1997). The former client may consent to the representation, however, and require screening as a condition of its consent under Rule 1.10(d). *Id.* Consent of the former client is not required under Rule 1.10(b) in the case of a new lawyer who was "tainted" solely because of work at a previous firm in the capacity of summer associate, law clerk, paralegal, or any other similar capacity "prior to becoming a lawyer" (*i.e.*, prior to becoming a "member of the Bar"). Of course, the second firm would be expected to take steps to assure that such persons do not have any involvement with, or make any improper disclosure regarding, any case in which they were previously involved (similar to the traditional requirement applicable to former judicial clerks). *See* D.C. Bar Legal Ethics Committee Opinion 279 (March 18, 1998). As to paralegals, secretaries and other non-lawyers, *see* D.C. Bar Legal Ethics Committee Opinion 227 (April 21, 1992) in which the D.C. ethics committee opined that screening is permissible.

9. *Birdsall v. Crowngap, Ltd.*, 575 So. 2d 231 (Fla. App. 1991); *Edward J. DeBartolo Corp. v. Petrin*, 516 So. 2d 6 (Fla. App. 1987); and *Nissan Motor Corp. v. Orozco*, 595 So. 2d 240 (Fla. App. 1992).

10. We are not aware of any state court or ethics committee ruling on screening in Georgia. A federal court said in *dicta* it would reject screening measures in *Amoco Chemicals Corp. v. McArthur*, 568 F. Supp. 42 (N.D. Ga. 1983).

11. *See Otaka, Inc. v. Klein*, 71 Haw. 376, 791 P.2d 713 (1990).

12. In *Van Jackson v. Check 'N Go of Illinois, Inc.*, 114 F. Supp. 2d 731 (N.D. Ill. 2000), the court recognized that the applicable rules of professional conduct allowed for screening, but nevertheless disqualified the firm because it had not provided sufficient detail as to how the lawyer was screened and because the small size of the firm indicated any screen would probably be ineffective. *See also Cromley v. Lockport Bd. of Educ.*, 17 F.3d 1059 (7th Cir. 1994); and *Miller v. Chicago and North*

Western Transportation Co., 938 F. Supp. 503 (N.D. Ill. 1996).

13. In *Chapman v. Chrysler Corp.*, 54 F. Supp. 2d 864 (S.D. Ind. 1999) and *Speedy v. Rexnord Corp.*, 54 F. Supp. 2d 867 (S.D. Ind. 1999), Indiana federal district courts found screening measures effective and, following Seventh Circuit precedent, refused to disqualify the law firm with the alleged conflict. Of course, an Indiana state court or ethics committee may not follow these federal court decisions.

14. *Lansing-Delaware Water Dist. v. Oak Lane Park, Inc.*, 248 Kan. 563, 808 P.2d 1369 (1991); *Parker v. Volkswagenwerk Aktiengesellschaft*, 245 Kan. 580, 781 P.2d 1099 (1989); *Graham v. Wyeth Laboratories*, 906 F.2d 1419 (10th Cir. 1990); *Pacific Employers Ins. Co. v. P.B. Hoidale Co.*, 796 F. Supp. 1428 (D. Kan. 1992). *See also* Kansas Bar Association Professional Ethics Advisory Committee Opinion 90–005 (Dec. 9, 1991) holding that screening is not permissible in the case of movement by a non-lawyer employee.

15. *But see Petrovich v. Petrovich*, 556 So. 2d 281 (La. App.), *cert. denied*, 559 So. 2d 1377 (1990) (upholding trial court's finding that lawyers had established "cone of silence" and therefore no disqualification). Federal courts in Louisiana follow Fifth Circuit precedent and refuse to allow the use of a screen to cure an imputed disqualification. *Green v. Administrators of Tulane Educational Fund*, 1998 U.S. Dist. LEXIS 769, 1998 WL 61041 (E.D. La. Jan. 22, 1998).

16. *See Casco Northern Bank v. JBI Assoc., Ltd.*, 667 A.2d 856 (Me. 1995).

17. *See United States Filter Corp. v. Ionics, Inc.*, 68 F. Supp. 2d 48 (D. Mass. 1999) (refusing to approve a screen because the Massachusetts Rule 1.10 (d)(2) requirements for a screen were not satisfied). Several decisions decided prior to the 1998 rule change allowed screening. *See First National Bank of Ipswich v. Peabody Gunner Hill, Inc.*, Massachusetts Superior Court, Civil Action No. 92–5172–J, Aug. 2, 1993; and *Thomalen v. Marriott Corp.*, 1994 U.S. Dist. LEXIS 13650, 1994 WL 524123 (D. Mass. 1994).

18. Opinion R–4, September 22, 1989, Michigan State Bar Committee on Professional and Judicial Ethics.

19. Under Rule 1.10(b), a lateral lawyer's conflict will not be imputed to others in the firm if 1) the lawyer does not have "significant" confidential information; 2)

the lawyer is screened; and 3) affected clients receive timely and adequate notice of the screen. *But see Lennartson v. Anoka–Hennepin Independent School District 11*, 638 N.W.2d 494, 499 (Minn. App. 2002) (holding Rule 1.10(b) should be interpreted to mean that a lateral lawyer's conflict will not be imputed if *either* the information communicated is unlikely to be significant *or* an ethical wall is erected *and* appropriate notice is given). *See also Jenson v. Touche Ross & Co.*, 335 N.W.2d 720 (Minn. 1983) (court approved a "Chinese wall," but opinion predates current rules).

20. *But see Mississippi State Dept. of Health v. Singing River Hospital*, No. 1998–CC–00968 (Miss S. Ct.) (denied disqualification motion where screen had been implemented).

21. *But see School District of Kansas City, Missouri v. ACandS, Inc.*, 1989 U.S. Dist. LEXIS 10009, 1989 WL 99138 (W.D. Mo. 1989); and *Hallmark Cards, Inc. v. Hallmark Dodge, Inc.*, 616 F. Supp. 516 (W.D. Mo. 1985).

22. *State of Nebraska ex rel. FirsTier Bank, N.A. v. Buckley*, 244 Neb. 36, 503 N.W.2d 838 (1993).

23. *Ogilvie v. Eighth Judicial District Court of Nevada*, No. 28374 (Nev. S. Ct. Nov. 7, 1996) (holding Nevada's screening procedures apply only to lawyers moving from government service to private employment and issuing writ of mandamus directing district court to disqualify law firm). *Cf. Ciaffone v. Eighth Judicial District Court of Nevada*, 945 P.2d 950 (Nev. 1997).

24. New Jersey Advisory Committee on Professional Ethics Opinion 667 (Nov. 2, 1992), discussed in the *Journal*, January 1993, page 23, appears to require consent as a condition precedent to screening. In *Cardona v. General Motors Corp.*, 945 F. Supp. 968 (D.N.J. 1996), the court affirmed that in New Jersey "ethics screens" have not been approved of as a device to preclude imputed disqualification. *See also Dewey v. R.J. Reynolds Tobacco Co.*, 109 N.J. 201, 536 A.2d 243 (1988).

25. *Kassis v. Teacher's Ins. & Annuity Ass'n*, 695 N.Y.S.2d 515, 717 N.E.2d 674 (1999) (if moving lawyer has information that is either "significant" or "material," screen will not work); *Alicea v. Bencivenga*, 704 N.Y.S.2d 578 (App. Div. 2000); *Cummin v. Cummin*, 695 N.Y.S.2d 346 (App. Div. 1999) (screen around lawyer with prelimi-

nary consultation conflict provided adequate safeguard); and *Trustco Bank v. Melino*, 164 Misc. 2d 999, 625 N.Y.S.2d 803 (S. Ct. 1995) (rejected screening). In *G.D. Searle & Co. v. Nutrapharm, Inc.*, 1999 U.S. Dist. LEXIS 5963, 1999 WL 249725 (S.D.N.Y. April 26, 1999); *Schwed v. General Electric Co.*, 990 F.Supp. 113 (N.D.N.Y. 1998); and *In re Del–Val Financial Corp. Securities Litigation*, 158 F.R.D. 270 (S.D.N.Y. 1994), New York federal courts approved screening measures. *But see Decora Inc. v. DW Wallcovering*, 899 F.Supp. 132 (S.D.N.Y. 1995) (new firm too small and screen erected too late).

26. *But see Ness, Motley, Loadholt, Richardson and Poole, P.A. v. Aetna Cas. & Surety Co.*, Civ. No. A3–88–157 (D.N.D. 1990).

27. The Ohio Supreme Court generally approved screening in *Kala v. Aluminum Smelting & Refining Co., Inc.*, 81 Ohio St. 3d 1, 688 N.E.2d 258 (1998), although on the basis of the particular facts of that case, it disqualified the law firm because of a strong appearance of impropriety. *See also* Opinion 89–013, May 30, 1989, Board of Commissioners on Grievances and Discipline, Supreme Court of Ohio; *In re McLaren*, Bankruptcy No. 889–0089 (N.D. Ohio 1990); *Legge Associates, Inc. v. The Dayton Power & Light Co.*, Case No. C–3–91–310 (S.D. Ohio 1993); and *Jurgens Real Estate Co. v. R.E.D. Construction Corp.*, Case No. 91 CV000842 (Ct. of Common Pleas, Clermont County, Ohio 1993).

28. In *Portland General Electric Co. v. Duncan, Weinberg, Miller & Pembroke*, 986 P.2d 35 (Or. App. 1999), the appellate court affirmed part of a judgment that allowed a firm's Washington, D.C. office to handle a matter that the firm's Portland office could not handle because of a conflict, provided an adequate screen was set up between the two offices. The appellate court agreed that the screen should be approved either by the lower court or by the ethics experts who testified in the matter. The parties in this case had previously consented to a screen on related matters.

29. Pennsylvania's Rule 1.10(b) specifically approves screening. Opinion 91–18, July 1991, Professional Guidance Committee, Philadelphia Bar Association, confirms that consent is not required where screening is used. The court applied that rule in *Dworkin v. General Motors Corp.*, 906 F. Supp. 273 (E.D. Pa. 1995). *See also James v. Teleflex, Inc.*, 1999 U.S. Dist. LEXIS

1961, 1999 WL 98559 (E.D. Pa. Feb. 24, 1999) (screen inadequate).

30. *See Falvey v. A.P.C. Sales Corp.*, 185 F.R.D. 120 (D.R.I. 1999); Rhode Island Supreme Court, Ethics Advisory Panel, Opinion 91–60 (Aug. 29, 1991). *But see Mearthane Products Corp. v. Lexmark Int'l, Inc.*, C.A. No. 00–245 ML (D.R.I. Nov. 21, 2001), where a magistrate judge disagreed with *Falvey* and held a screen rebutted the presumption that a lateral lawyer's conflict should be imputed to the rest of the firm.

31. South Carolina Bar Ethics Advisory Opinion 92–23 (Oct.1992).

32. In *Clinard v. Blackwood*, 46 S.W.3d 177 (Tenn. 2001), the Tennessee Supreme Court held that the screening provisions implemented by the lateral's new firm adequately rebutted the presumption of shared confidences. Nevertheless, the court disqualified the firm because of an appearance of impropriety. *See also Watson v. Ameredes*, 1997 Tenn. App. LEXIS 884, 1997 WL 772865 (Dec. 16, 1997) (under the particular circumstances, the court disqualified the new firm even though it had set up a screen); Bd. of Prof'l Responsibility of the Supreme Court of Tennessee Op. 89–F–118 (March 10, 1989) (approving screening). The Tennessee Bar Association has proposed new rules of professional conduct that specifically approve of screening. The Sixth Circuit also has approved of screening. *See Manning v. Waring, Cox, James, Sklar & Allen*, 849 F.2d 222 (6th Cir. 1988); *Vergos v. Timber Creek, Inc.*, 1996 U.S. Dist. LEXIS 16791, 1996 WL 535404 (W.D. Tenn. Aug. 26, 1996) (screening effective in bankruptcy matter); *In re Club Income Properties*, No. 92–11434 (E.D. Tenn. Sept. 13, 1993) (bankruptcy judge ruled that the law firm should not be disqualified). *But see Penn Mut. Life Ins. Co. v. Cleveland Mall Associates*, 841 F. Supp. 815 (E.D. Tenn. 1993), where on facts similar to those in *Club Income Properties*, a district judge ruled that the law firm should be disqualified.

33. *Phoenix Founders, Inc. v. Marshall*, 887 S.W.2d 831 (Tex. 1994); *Henderson v. Floyd*, 891 S.W.2d 252 (1995). *See* Hazard and Hodes § 14.11 for a discussion of *American Sterilizer v. Surgikos, Inc.*, (unreported) (N.D. Tex. 1992), which reportedly held that a moving lawyer with no knowledge may later be adverse to the client of the first firm. No lawyer in the new firm is disqualified.

34. *SLC Limited v. Bradford Group West, Inc.*, 999 F.2d 464 (10th Cir. 1993).

35. *See* Opinion 87–7 (undated), Committee on Professional Responsibility of the Vermont Bar Association.

36. Virginia State Bar, Standing Committee on Legal Ethics, Opinion 1428 (Feb. 22, 1992) specifically disapproves of screening without consent.

37. *Roberts & Schaefer Co. v. San–Con, Inc.*, 898 F. Supp. 356 (S.D.W. Va. 1995).

38. *But see Nelson v. Green Builders, Inc.*, 823 F. Supp. 1439 (E.D. Wis. 1993), where the court held, in effect, that a timely screen would have prevented disqualification. In *Nelson* the screen was not created until the disqualified firm was challenged by the other side; the court said that was too late to avoid disqualification.

APPENDIX C

When a Written Fee Agreement Is Required

The following chart analyzes in summary form the provisions of the ABA Model Code of Professional Responsibility (1969), the ABA Model Rules of Professional Conduct (1983), and the various state versions of the Code and Rules (in effect and proposed) on the question whether a lawyer *must* have a *written* fee agreement with a client in contingent fee matters and other circumstances or whether a written agreement is "preferred." The jurisdictions that require written fee agreements for all new clients are Connecticut, the District of Columbia, New Jersey, Pennsylvania and Utah. California requires written fee agreements for all non-corporate clients if fees will exceed $1,000, and Alaska requires a written fee agreement if fees will exceed $500. By court rule (not disciplinary rule) New York requires written engagement letters with new clients unless the fee is expected to be less than $3,000.

Several states have no provision relating to the need for written agreements in the *ethics* rules, but deal with the issue elsewhere in court rules or statutes. We have included the appropriate references where we are aware of them.

Generally, but not always, the "Others" column cites a provision that refers to a new client, noncontingent fee situation. The statutes and ethics codes rarely cover the case of a new matter for an existing client where the fee for that matter is not a contingent fee.

Chart on Written Fee Agreements

Jurisdiction	Applicable Rules	Contingent	Others
ABA	Model Rules of Professional Conduct	Must: 1.5(c)	Preferred: 1.5(b)
ABA	Model Code of Professional Responsibility	Preferred: EC 2–19	Preferred: EC 2–19
ALABAMA	Rules of Professional Conduct	Must: 1.5(c)	Preferred: 1.5(b)
ALASKA	Rules of Professional Conduct	Must: 1.5(c)	Must (if over $500) 1.5(b)
ARIZONA	Rules of Professional Conduct	Must: 1.5(c)	Preferred: 1.5(b)
ARKANSAS	Rules of Professional Conduct	Must: 1.5(c)	Preferred: 1.5(b)
CALIFORNIA	Statutory Provisions	Must: § 6147 of Business and Professions Code	Must: (If not a corporation and over $1000) § 6148 of Business and Professions Code
COLORADO	Rules of Professional Conduct and Court Rules	Must: Chapt. 23.3 Col. Court Rules, Rule 4(b)	Preferred: 1.5(b)

179

Jurisdiction	Applicable Rules	Contingent	Others
CONNECTICUT	Rules of Professional Conduct	Must: 1.5(c)	Must: 1.5(b)
DELAWARE	Lawyers' Rules of Professional Conduct	Must: 1.5(c)	Preferred: 1.5(b)
DIST. OF COLUMBIA	Rules of Professional Conduct	Must: 1.5(c)	Must: 1.5(b)
FLORIDA	Rules of Professional Conduct	Must: 4–1.5(f)	Preferred: 4–1.5(e)
GEORGIA	Rules of Professional Conduct	Must: 1.5(c)	Preferred: 1.5(b)
HAWAII	Rules of Professional Conduct	Must: 1.5(c)	Preferred: 1.5(b)
IDAHO	Rules of Professional Conduct	Must: 1.5(c)	Preferred: 1.5(b)
ILLINOIS	Rules of Professional Conduct	Must: 1.5(c)	No provision
INDIANA	Rules of Professional Conduct	Must: 1.5(c)	Preferred: 1.5(b)
IOWA	Code of Professional Responsibility for Lawyers	Preferred: EC 2–21	Preferred: EC 2–21
KANSAS	Rules of Professional Conduct	Must: 1.5(d)	Preferred: 1.5(b)
KENTUCKY	Rules of Professional Conduct	Must: 1.5(c)	Preferred: 1.5(b)
LOUISIANA	Rules of Professional Conduct	Must: 1.5(c)	Preferred: 1.5(b)
MAINE	Code of Professional Responsibility	Must: Maine Bar Rule 8(D)	No provision
MARYLAND	Rules of Professional Conduct	Must: 1.5(c)	Preferred: 1.5(b)
MASSACHUSETTS	Rules of Professional Conduct	Must: 1.5(c)	Preferred: 1.5(b)
MICHIGAN	Rules of Professional Conduct	Must: 1.5(c)	Preferred: 1.5(b)
MINNESOTA	Rules of Professional Conduct	Must: 1.5(c)	Preferred: 1.5(b)
MISSISSIPPI	Rules of Professional Conduct	Must: 1.5(c)	Preferred: 1.5(b)
MISSOURI	Rules of Professional Conduct	Must: 1.5(c)	Preferred: 1.5(b)
MONTANA	Rules of Professional Conduct	Must: 1.5(c)	Preferred: 1.5(b)
NEBRASKA	Code of Professional Responsibility	Preferred: EC 2–19	Preferred: EC 2–19
NEVADA	Rules of Professional Conduct (Nevada Supreme Court Rule 155)	Must: 155(3)	Preferred: 155(2)
NEW HAMPSHIRE	Rules of Professional Conduct	Must: 1.5(c)	Preferred: 1.5(b)
NEW JERSEY	Rules of Professional Conduct	Must: 1.5(c)	Must: 1.5(b)
NEW MEXICO	Rules of Professional Conduct	Must: 16–105(C)	Preferred: 16–105(B)
NEW YORK	Code of Professional Responsibility	Preferred: EC 2–19	Preferred: EC 2–19

Jurisdiction	Applicable Rules	Contingent	Others
	Official Compilation of Codes, Rules and Regulations of the State of New York, Title 22 Part 12.5	(Must provide statement of fee determination, DR 2–106(D).) Must unless fee is expected to be less than $3,000	(Must in domestic relations matters, DR 2–106(C)(2)(b).) Must unless fee is expected to be less than $3,000
NORTH CAROLINA	Revised Rules of Professional Conduct	Preferred: 1.5 (c)	Preferred: 1.5 (c)
NORTH DAKOTA	Rules of Professional Conduct	Must: 1.5(c)	No provision
OHIO	Code of Professional Responsibility	Must for tort claims: Tit. 47 § 4705.15(B)	Preferred: EC 2–18
OKLAHOMA	Rules of Professional Conduct	Must: 1.5(c)	Preferred: 1.5(b)
OREGON	Code of Professional Responsibility and Statutes	Must for personal injury and property damage claims: Oregon Revised Statutes, § 9.400(1)(a)	No provision
PENNSYLVANIA	Rules of Professional Conduct	Must: 1.5(c)	Must: 1.5(b)
RHODE ISLAND	Rules of Professional Conduct	Must: 1.5(c)	Must: 1.5(b)
SOUTH CAROLINA	Rules of Professional Conduct	Must: 1.5(c)	Preferred: 1.5(b)
SOUTH DAKOTA	Rules of Professional Conduct	Must: 1.5(c)	Preferred: 1.5(b)
TENNESSEE	Code of Professional Responsibility	Preferred: EC 2–19	Preferred: EC 2–19
TENNESSEE	Proposed Rules of Professional Conduct	Must: 1.5(c)	Preferred: 1.5(b)
TEXAS	Disciplinary Rules of Professional Conduct	Must: 1.04(d)	Preferred: 1.04(c)
UTAH	Rules of Professional Conduct	Must: 1.5(c)	Must: 1.5(b)
VERMONT	Rules of Professional Conduct	Must: 1.5(c)	Preferred: 1.5(b)
VIRGINIA	Rules of Professional Conduct	Must: 1.5(c)	Preferred: 1.5(b)
WASHINGTON	Rules of Professional Conduct	Must: 1.5(c)	Preferred: 1.5(b)
WEST VIRGINIA	Rules of Professional Conduct	Must: 1.5(c)	Preferred: 1.5(b)
WISCONSIN	Rules of Professional Conduct for Attorneys	Must: 20:1.5(c)	Preferred: 20:1.5(b)
WYOMING	Rules of Professional Conduct for Attorneys at Law	Must: 1.5(c)	Preferred: 1.5 Cmt. [1]

AMERICAN BAR ASSOCIATION
MODEL RULES OF PROFESSIONAL CONDUCT

The Model Rules of Professional Conduct
were adopted by the House of Delegates of the
American Bar Association on August 2, 1983

Copyright © 1983 by the American Bar Association.
All rights reserved. Permission to reprint granted
by the American Bar Association. Reprinted as amended
through August, 2001.

[Editor's Note: This is a "clean" version of the ABA Model Rules of Professional
Conduct as they read before the amendments that the ABA House of Delegates
approved in 2002. This is the version that underlies the rules of lawyer conduct
adopted by a majority of U.S. jurisdictions and the version that will continued to
be tested on the Multistate Professional Responsibility Examination (MPRE)
through 2003.]

Contents

CLIENT–LAWYER RELATIONSHIP

COUNSELOR

Preamble: A Lawyer's Responsibilities

[1] A lawyer is a representative of clients, an officer of the legal system and a public citizen having special responsibility for the quality of justice.

[2] As a representative of clients, a lawyer performs various functions. As advisor, a lawyer provides a client with an informed understanding of the client's legal rights and obligations and explains their practical implications. As advocate, a lawyer zealously asserts the client's position under the rules of the adversary system. As negotiator, a lawyer seeks a result advantageous to the client but consistent with requirements of honest dealing with others. As intermediary between clients, a lawyer seeks to reconcile their divergent interests as an advisor and, to a limited extent, as a spokesperson for each client. A lawyer acts as evaluator by examining a client's legal affairs and reporting about them to the client or to others.

[3] In all professional functions a lawyer should be competent, prompt and diligent. A lawyer should maintain communication with a client concerning the representation. A lawyer should keep in confidence information relating to representation of a client except so far as disclosure is required or permitted by the Rules of Professional Conduct or other law.

[4] A lawyer's conduct should conform to the requirements of the law, both in professional service to clients and in the lawyer's business and personal affairs. A lawyer should use the law's procedures only for legitimate purposes and not to harass or intimidate others. A lawyer should demonstrate respect for the legal system and for those who serve it, including judges, other lawyers and public officials. While it is a lawyer's duty, when necessary, to challenge the rectitude of official action, it is also a lawyer's duty to uphold legal process.

[5] As a public citizen, a lawyer should seek improvement of the law, the administration of justice and the quality of service rendered by the legal profession. As a member of a learned profession, a lawyer should cultivate knowledge of the law beyond its use for clients, employ that knowledge in reform of the law and work to strengthen legal education. A lawyer should be mindful of deficiencies in the administration of justice and of the fact that the poor, and sometimes persons who are not poor, cannot afford adequate legal assistance, and should therefore devote professional time and civic influence in their behalf. A lawyer should aid the legal profession in pursuing these objectives and should help the bar regulate itself in the public interest.

[6] Many of a lawyer's professional responsibilities are prescribed in the Rules of Professional Conduct, as well as substantive and procedural law. However, a lawyer is also guided by personal conscience and the approbation of professional peers. A lawyer should strive to attain the highest level of skill, to improve the law and the legal profession and to exemplify the legal profession's ideals of public service.

[7] A lawyer's responsibilities as a representative of clients, an officer of the legal system and a public citizen are usually harmonious. Thus, when an opposing party is well represented, a lawyer can be a zealous advocate on behalf of a client and at the same time assume that justice is being done. So also, a lawyer can be sure that preserving client confidences ordinarily serves the public interest because people are more likely to seek legal advice, and thereby heed their legal obligations, when they know their communications will be private.

[8]   In the nature of law practice, however, conflicting responsibilities are encountered.   Virtually all difficult ethical problems arise from conflict between a lawyer's responsibilities to clients, to the legal system and to the lawyer's own interest in remaining an upright person while earning a satisfactory living.   The Rules of Professional Conduct prescribe terms for resolving such conflicts.   Within the framework of these Rules many difficult issues of professional discretion can arise.   Such issues must be resolved through the exercise of sensitive professional and moral judgment guided by the basic principles underlying the Rules.

[9]   The legal profession is largely self-governing.   Although other professions also have been granted powers of self-government, the legal profession is unique in this respect because of the close relationship between the profession and the processes of government and law enforcement.   This connection is manifested in the fact that ultimate authority over the legal profession is vested largely in the courts.

[10]   To the extent that lawyers meet the obligations of their professional calling, the occasion for government regulation is obviated.   Self-regulation also helps maintain the legal profession's independence from government domination.   An independent legal profession is an important force in preserving government under law, for abuse of legal authority is more readily challenged by a profession whose members are not dependent on government for the right to practice.

[11]   The legal profession's relative autonomy carries with it special responsibilities of self-government.   The profession has a responsibility to assure that its regulations are conceived in the public interest and not in furtherance of parochial or self-interested concerns of the bar.   Every lawyer is responsible for observance of the Rules of Professional Conduct.   A lawyer should also aid in securing their observance by other lawyers.   Neglect of these responsibilities compromises the independence of the profession and the public interest which it serves.

[12]   Lawyers play a vital role in the preservation of society.   The fulfillment of this role requires an understanding by lawyers of their relationship to our legal system.   The Rules of Professional Conduct, when properly applied, serve to define that relationship.

Scope

[13]   The Rules of Professional Conduct are rules of reason.   They should be interpreted with reference to the purposes of legal representation and of the law itself. Some of the Rules are imperatives, cast in the terms "shall" or "shall not."   These define proper conduct for purposes of professional discipline.   Others, generally cast in the term "may," are permissive and define areas under the Rules in which the lawyer has professional discretion.   No disciplinary action should be taken when the lawyer chooses not to act or acts within the bounds of such discretion.   Other Rules define the nature of relationships between the lawyer and others.   The Rules are thus partly obligatory and disciplinary and partly constitutive and descriptive in that they define a lawyer's professional role.   Many of the Comments use the term "should."   Comments do not add obligations to the Rules but provide guidance for practicing in compliance with the Rules.

[14]   The Rules presuppose a larger legal context shaping the lawyer's role.   That context includes court rules and statutes relating to matters of licensure, laws defining specific obligations of lawyers and substantive and procedural law in general.   Compliance with the Rules, as with all law in an open society, depends primarily upon

understanding and voluntary compliance, secondarily upon reinforcement by peer and public opinion and finally, when necessary, upon enforcement through disciplinary proceedings. The Rules do not, however, exhaust the moral and ethical considerations that should inform a lawyer, for no worthwhile human activity can be completely defined by legal rules. The Rules simply provide a framework for the ethical practice of law.

[15] Furthermore, for purposes of determining the lawyer's authority and responsibility, principles of substantive law external to these Rules determine whether a client-lawyer relationship exists. Most of the duties flowing from the client-lawyer relationship attach only after the client has requested the lawyer to render legal services and the lawyer has agreed to do so. But there are some duties, such as that of confidentiality under Rule 1.6, that may attach when the lawyer agrees to consider whether a client-lawyer relationship shall be established. Whether a client-lawyer relationship exists for any specific purpose can depend on the circumstances and may be a question of fact.

[16] Under various legal provisions, including constitutional, statutory and common law, the responsibilities of government lawyers may include authority concerning legal matters that ordinarily reposes in the client in private client-lawyer relationships. For example, a lawyer for a government agency may have authority on behalf of the government to decide upon settlement or whether to appeal from an adverse judgment. Such authority in various respects is generally vested in the attorney general and the state's attorney in state government, and their federal counterparts, and the same may be true of other government law officers. Also, lawyers under the supervision of these officers may be authorized to represent several government agencies in intragovernmental legal controversies in circumstances where a private lawyer could not represent multiple private clients. They also may have authority to represent the "public interest" in circumstances where a private lawyer would not be authorized to do so. These Rules do not abrogate any such authority.

[17] Failure to comply with an obligation or prohibition imposed by a Rule is a basis for invoking the disciplinary process. The Rules presuppose that disciplinary assessment of a lawyer's conduct will be made on the basis of the facts and circumstances as they existed at the time of the conduct in question and in recognition of the fact that a lawyer often has to act upon uncertain or incomplete evidence of the situation. Moreover, the Rules presuppose that whether or not discipline should be imposed for a violation, and the severity of a sanction, depend on all the circumstances, such as the willfulness and seriousness of the violation, extenuating factors and whether there have been previous violations.

[18] Violation of a Rule should not give rise to a cause of action nor should it create any presumption that a legal duty has been breached. The Rules are designed to provide guidance to lawyers and to provide a structure for regulating conduct through disciplinary agencies. They are not designed to be a basis for civil liability. Furthermore, the purpose of the Rules can be subverted when they are invoked by opposing parties as procedural weapons. The fact that a Rule is a just basis for a lawyer's self-assessment, or for sanctioning a lawyer under the administration of a disciplinary authority, does not imply that an antagonist in a collateral proceeding or transaction has standing to seek enforcement of the Rule. Accordingly, nothing in the Rules should be deemed to augment any substantive legal duty of lawyers or the extra-disciplinary consequences of violating such a duty.

[19]   Moreover, these Rules are not intended to govern or affect judicial application of either the attorney-client or work product privilege.   Those privileges were developed to promote compliance with law and fairness in litigation.   In reliance on the attorney-client privilege, clients are entitled to expect that communications within the scope of the privilege will be protected against compelled disclosure.   The attorney-client privilege is that of the client and not of the lawyer.   The fact that in exceptional situations the lawyer under the Rules has a limited discretion to disclose a client confidence does not vitiate the proposition that, as a general matter, the client has a reasonable expectation that information relating to the client will not be voluntarily disclosed and that disclosure of such information may be judicially compelled only in accordance with recognized exceptions to the attorney-client and work product privileges.

[20]   The lawyer's exercise of discretion not to disclose information under Rule 1.6 should not be subject to reexamination.   Permitting such reexamination would be incompatible with the general policy of promoting compliance with law through assurances that communications will be protected against disclosure.

[21]   The Comment accompanying each Rule explains and illustrates the meaning and purpose of the Rule.   The Preamble and this note on Scope provide general orientation.   The Comments are intended as guides to interpretation, but the text of each Rule is authoritative.   Research notes were prepared to compare counterparts in the ABA Model Code of Professional Responsibility (adopted 1969, as amended) and to provide selected references to other authorities.   The notes have not been adopted, do not constitute part of the Model Rules, and are not intended to affect the application or interpretation of the Rules and Comments.

Terminology

[1]   "Belief" or "Believes" denotes that the person involved actually supposed the fact in question to be true.   A person's belief may be inferred from circumstances.

[2]   "Consult" or "Consultation" denotes communication of information reasonably sufficient to permit the client to appreciate the significance of the matter in question.

[3]   "Firm" or "Law firm" denotes a lawyer or lawyers in a private firm, lawyers employed in the legal department of a corporation or other organization and lawyers employed in a legal services organization.   See Comment, Rule 1.10.

[4]   "Fraud" or "Fraudulent" denotes conduct having a purpose to deceive and not merely negligent misrepresentation or failure to apprise another of relevant information.

[5]   "Knowingly," "Known," or "Knows" denotes actual knowledge of the fact in question.   A person's knowledge may be inferred from circumstances.

[6]   "Partner" denotes a member of a partnership and a shareholder in a law firm organized as a professional corporation.

[7]   "Reasonable" or "Reasonably" when used in relation to conduct by a lawyer denotes the conduct of a reasonably prudent and competent lawyer.

[8]   "Reasonable belief" or "Reasonably believes" when used in reference to a lawyer denotes that the lawyer believes the matter in question and that the circumstances are such that the belief is reasonable.

187

[9] "Reasonably should know" when used in reference to a lawyer denotes that a lawyer of reasonable prudence and competence would ascertain the matter in question.

[10] "Substantial" when used in reference to degree or extent denotes a material matter of clear and weighty importance.

MODEL RULES OF PROFESSIONAL CONDUCT
CLIENT–LAWYER RELATIONSHIP

RULE 1.1 Competence

A lawyer shall provide competent representation to a client. Competent representation requires the legal knowledge, skill, thoroughness and preparation reasonably necessary for the representation.

COMMENT:
Legal Knowledge and Skill

[1] In determining whether a lawyer employs the requisite knowledge and skill in a particular matter, relevant factors include the relative complexity and specialized nature of the matter, the lawyer's general experience, the lawyer's training and experience in the field in question, the preparation and study the lawyer is able to give the matter and whether it is feasible to refer the matter to, or associate or consult with, a lawyer of established competence in the field in question. In many instances, the required proficiency is that of a general practitioner. Expertise in a particular field of law may be required in some circumstances.

[2] A lawyer need not necessarily have special training or prior experience to handle legal problems of a type with which the lawyer is unfamiliar. A newly admitted lawyer can be as competent as a practitioner with long experience. Some important legal skills, such as the analysis of precedent, the evaluation of evidence and legal drafting, are required in all legal problems. Perhaps the most fundamental legal skill consists of determining what kind of legal problems a situation may involve, a skill that necessarily transcends any particular specialized knowledge. A lawyer can provide adequate representation in a wholly novel field through necessary study. Competent representation can also be provided through the association of a lawyer of established competence in the field in question.

[3] In an emergency a lawyer may give advice or assistance in a matter in which the lawyer does not have the skill ordinarily required where referral to or consultation or association with another lawyer would be impractical. Even in an emergency, however, assistance should be limited to that reasonably necessary in the circumstances, for ill considered action under emergency conditions can jeopardize the client's interest.

[4] A lawyer may accept representation where the requisite level of competence can be achieved by reasonable preparation. This applies as well to a lawyer who is appointed as counsel for an unrepresented person. See also Rule 6.2.

Thoroughness and Preparation

[5] Competent handling of a particular matter includes inquiry into and analysis of the factual and legal elements of the problem, and use of methods and procedures meeting the standards of competent practitioners. It also includes adequate preparation. The required attention and preparation are determined in part by what is at

stake; major litigation and complex transactions ordinarily require more elaborate treatment than matters of lesser consequence.

Maintaining Competence

[6] To maintain the requisite knowledge and skill, a lawyer should engage in continuing study and education. If a system of peer review has been established, the lawyer should consider making use of it in appropriate circumstances.

MODEL CODE COMPARISON

DR 6–101(A)(1) provided that a lawyer shall not handle a matter "which he knows or should know that he is not competent to handle, without associating himself with a lawyer who is competent to handle it;" DR 6–101(A)(2) required "preparation adequate in the circumstances." Rule 1.1 more fully particularizes the elements of competence. Whereas DR 6–101(A)(3) prohibited the "[n]eglect of a legal matter," Rule 1.1 does not contain such a prohibition. Instead, Rule 1.1 affirmatively requires the lawyer to be competent.

RULE 1.2   Scope of Representation

(a) A lawyer shall abide by a client's decisions concerning the objectives of representation, subject to paragraphs (c), (d) and (e), and shall consult with the client as to the means by which they are to be pursued. A lawyer shall abide by a client's decision whether to accept an offer of settlement of a matter. In a criminal case, the lawyer shall abide by the client's decision, after consultation with the lawyer, as to a plea to be entered, whether to waive jury trial and whether the client will testify.

(b) A lawyer's representation of a client, including representation by appointment, does not constitute an endorsement of the client's political, economic, social or moral views or activities.

(c) A lawyer may limit the objectives of the representation if the client consents after consultation.

(d) A lawyer shall not counsel a client to engage, or assist a client, in conduct that the lawyer knows is criminal or fraudulent, but a lawyer may discuss the legal consequences of any proposed course of conduct with a client and may counsel or assist a client to make a good faith effort to determine the validity, scope, meaning or application of the law.

(e) When a lawyer knows that a client expects assistance not permitted by the Rules of Professional Conduct or other law, the lawyer shall consult with the client regarding the relevant limitations on the lawyer's conduct.

COMMENT:

Scope of Representation

[1] Both lawyer and client have authority and responsibility in the objectives and means of representation. The client has ultimate authority to determine the purposes to be served by legal representation, within the limits imposed by law and the lawyer's professional obligations. Within those limits, a client also has a right to consult with the lawyer about the means to be used in pursuing those objectives. At the same time, a lawyer is not required to pursue objectives or employ means simply because a client may wish that the lawyer do so. A clear distinction between objectives and means

sometimes cannot be drawn, and in many cases the client-lawyer relationship partakes of a joint undertaking. In questions of means, the lawyer should assume responsibility for technical and legal tactical issues, but should defer to the client regarding such questions as the expense to be incurred and concern for third persons who might be adversely affected. Law defining the lawyer's scope of authority in litigation varies among jurisdictions.

[2] In a case in which the client appears to be suffering mental disability, the lawyer's duty to abide by the client's decisions is to be guided by reference to Rule 1.14.

Independence From Client's Views or Activities

[3] Legal representation should not be denied to people who are unable to afford legal services, or whose cause is controversial or the subject of popular disapproval. By the same token, representing a client does not constitute approval of the client's views or activities.

Services Limited in Objectives or Means

[4] The objectives or scope of services provided by a lawyer may be limited by agreement with the client or by the terms under which the lawyer's services are made available to the client. For example, a retainer may be for a specifically defined purpose. Representation provided through a legal aid agency may be subject to limitations on the types of cases the agency handles. When a lawyer has been retained by an insurer to represent an insured, the representation may be limited to matters related to the insurance coverage. The terms upon which representation is undertaken may exclude specific objectives or means. Such limitations may exclude objectives or means that the lawyer regards as repugnant or imprudent.

[5] An agreement concerning the scope of representation must accord with the Rules of Professional Conduct and other law. Thus, the client may not be asked to agree to representation so limited in scope as to violate Rule 1.1, or to surrender the right to terminate the lawyer's services or the right to settle litigation that the lawyer might wish to continue.

Criminal, Fraudulent and Prohibited Transactions

[6] A lawyer is required to give an honest opinion about the actual consequences that appear likely to result from a client's conduct. The fact that a client uses advice in a course of action that is criminal or fraudulent does not, of itself, make a lawyer a party to the course of action. However, a lawyer may not knowingly assist a client in criminal or fraudulent conduct. There is a critical distinction between presenting an analysis of legal aspects of questionable conduct and recommending the means by which a crime or fraud might be committed with impunity.

[7] When the client's course of action has already begun and is continuing, the lawyer's responsibility is especially delicate. The lawyer is not permitted to reveal the client's wrongdoing, except where permitted by Rule 1.6. However, the lawyer is required to avoid furthering the purpose, for example, by suggesting how it might be concealed. A lawyer may not continue assisting a client in conduct that the lawyer originally supposes is legally proper but then discovers is criminal or fraudulent. Withdrawal from the representation, therefore, may be required.

[8] Where the client is a fiduciary, the lawyer may be charged with special obligations in dealings with a beneficiary.

[9] Paragraph (d) applies whether or not the defrauded party is a party to the transaction. Hence, a lawyer should not participate in a sham transaction; for example, a transaction to effectuate criminal or fraudulent escape of tax liability. Paragraph (d) does not preclude undertaking a criminal defense incident to a general retainer for legal services to a lawful enterprise. The last clause of paragraph (d) recognizes that determining the validity or interpretation of a statute or regulation may require a course of action involving disobedience of the statute or regulation or of the interpretation placed upon it by governmental authorities.

MODEL CODE COMPARISON

[1] Paragraph (a) has no counterpart in the Disciplinary Rules of the Model Code. EC 7–7 stated: "In certain areas of legal representation not affecting the merits of the cause or substantially prejudicing the rights of a client, a lawyer is entitled to make decisions on his own. But otherwise the authority to make decisions is exclusively that of the client...." EC 7–8 stated that "[i]n the final analysis, however, the ... decision whether to forego legally available objectives or methods because of nonlegal factors is ultimately for the client.... In the event that the client in a nonadjudicatory matter insists upon a course of conduct that is contrary to the judgment and advice of the lawyer but not prohibited by Disciplinary Rules, the lawyer may withdraw from the employment." DR 7–101(A)(1) provided that a lawyer "shall not intentionally ... fail to seek the lawful objectives of his client through reasonably available means permitted by law.... A lawyer does not violate this Disciplinary Rule, however, by ... avoiding offensive tactics...."

[2] Paragraph (b) has no counterpart in the Model Code.

[3] With regard to paragraph (c), DR 7–101(B)(1) provided that a lawyer may, "where permissible, exercise his professional judgment to waive or fail to assert a right or position of his client."

[4] With regard to paragraph (d), DR 7–102(A)(7) provided that a lawyer shall not "counsel or assist his client in conduct that the lawyer knows to be illegal or fraudulent." DR 7–102(A)(6) provided that a lawyer shall not "participate in the creation or preservation of evidence when he knows or it is obvious that the evidence is false." DR 7–106 provided that a lawyer shall not "advise his client to disregard a standing rule of a tribunal or a ruling of a tribunal ... but he may take appropriate steps in good faith to test the validity of such rule or ruling." EC 7–5 stated that a lawyer "should never encourage or aid his client to commit criminal acts or counsel his client on how to violate the law and avoid punishment therefor."

[5] With regard to paragraph (e), DR 2–110(C)(1)(c) provided that a lawyer may withdraw from representation if a client "insists" that the lawyer engage in "conduct that is illegal or that is prohibited under the Disciplinary Rules." DR 9–101(C) provided that "a lawyer shall not state or imply that he is able to influence improperly ... any tribunal, legislative body or public official."

RULE 1.3 Diligence

A lawyer shall act with reasonable diligence and promptness in representing a client.

COMMENT:

[1] A lawyer should pursue a matter on behalf of a client despite opposition, obstruction or personal inconvenience to the lawyer, and may take whatever lawful

and ethical measures are required to vindicate a client's cause or endeavor. A lawyer should act with commitment and dedication to the interests of the client and with zeal in advocacy upon the client's behalf. However, a lawyer is not bound to press for every advantage that might be realized for a client. A lawyer has professional discretion in determining the means by which a matter should be pursued. See Rule 1.2. A lawyer's workload should be controlled so that each matter can be handled adequately.

[2] Perhaps no professional shortcoming is more widely resented than procrastination. A client's interests often can be adversely affected by the passage of time or the change of conditions; in extreme instances, as when a lawyer overlooks a statute of limitations, the client's legal position may be destroyed. Even when the client's interests are not affected in substance, however, unreasonable delay can cause a client needless anxiety and undermine confidence in the lawyer's trustworthiness.

[3] Unless the relationship is terminated as provided in Rule 1.16, a lawyer should carry through to conclusion all matters undertaken for a client. If a lawyer's employment is limited to a specific matter, the relationship terminates when the matter has been resolved. If a lawyer has served a client over a substantial period in a variety of matters, the client sometimes may assume that the lawyer will continue to serve on a continuing basis unless the lawyer gives notice of withdrawal. Doubt about whether a client-lawyer relationship still exists should be clarified by the lawyer, preferably in writing, so that the client will not mistakenly suppose the lawyer is looking after the client's affairs when the lawyer has ceased to do so. For example, if a lawyer has handled a judicial or administrative proceeding that produced a result adverse to the client but has not been specifically instructed concerning pursuit of an appeal, the lawyer should advise the client of the possibility of appeal before relinquishing responsibility for the matter.

MODEL CODE COMPARISON

DR 6–101(A)(3) required that a lawyer not "[n]eglect a matter entrusted to him." EC 6–4 stated that a lawyer should "give appropriate attention to his legal work." Canon 7 stated that "a lawyer should represent a client zealously within the bounds of law." DR 7–101(A)(1) provided that a lawyer "shall not intentionally ... fail to seek the lawful objectives of his client through reasonably available means permitted by law and the Disciplinary Rules...." DR 7–101(A)(3) provided that a lawyer "shall not intentionally ... [p]rejudice or damage his client during the course of the relationship...."

RULE 1.4 Communication

(a) A lawyer shall keep a client reasonably informed about the status of a matter and promptly comply with reasonable requests for information.

(b) A lawyer shall explain a matter to the extent reasonably necessary to permit the client to make informed decisions regarding the representation.

COMMENT:

[1] The client should have sufficient information to participate intelligently in decisions concerning the objectives of the representation and the means by which they are to be pursued, to the extent the client is willing and able to do so. For example, a lawyer negotiating on behalf of a client should provide the client with facts relevant to the matter, inform the client of communications from another party and take other

reasonable steps that permit the client to make a decision regarding a serious offer from another party. A lawyer who receives from opposing counsel an offer of settlement in a civil controversy or a proffered plea bargain in a criminal case should promptly inform the client of its substance unless prior discussions with the client have left it clear that the proposal will be unacceptable. See Rule 1.2(a). Even when a client delegates authority to the lawyer, the client should be kept advised of the status of the matter.

[2] Adequacy of communication depends in part on the kind of advice or assistance involved. For example, in negotiations where there is time to explain a proposal the lawyer should review all important provisions with the client before proceeding to an agreement. In litigation a lawyer should explain the general strategy and prospects of success and ordinarily should consult the client on tactics that might injure or coerce others. On the other hand, a lawyer ordinarily cannot be expected to describe trial or negotiation strategy in detail. The guiding principle is that the lawyer should fulfill reasonable client expectations for information consistent with the duty to act in the client's best interests, and the client's overall requirements as to the character of representation.

[3] Ordinarily, the information to be provided is that appropriate for a client who is a comprehending and responsible adult. However, fully informing the client according to this standard may be impracticable, for example, where the client is a child or suffers from mental disability. See Rule 1.14. When the client is an organization or group, it is often impossible or inappropriate to inform every one of its members about its legal affairs; ordinarily, the lawyer should address communications to the appropriate officials of the organization. See Rule 1.13. Where many routine matters are involved, a system of limited or occasional reporting may be arranged with the client. Practical exigency may also require a lawyer to act for a client without prior consultation.

Withholding Information

[4] In some circumstances, a lawyer may be justified in delaying transmission of information when the client would be likely to react imprudently to an immediate communication. Thus, a lawyer might withhold a psychiatric diagnosis of a client when the examining psychiatrist indicates that disclosure would harm the client. A lawyer may not withhold information to serve the lawyer's own interest or convenience. Rules or court orders governing litigation may provide that information supplied to a lawyer may not be disclosed to the client. Rule 3.4(c) directs compliance with such rules or orders.

MODEL CODE COMPARISON

Rule 1.4 has no direct counterpart in the Disciplinary Rules of the Model Code. DR 6–101(A)(3) provided that a lawyer shall not "[n]eglect a legal matter entrusted to him." DR 9–102(B)(1) provided that a lawyer shall "[p]romptly notify a client of the receipt of his funds, securities, or other properties." EC 7–8 stated that a lawyer "should exert his best efforts to insure that decisions of his client are made only after the client has been informed of relevant considerations." EC 9–2 stated that "a lawyer should fully and promptly inform his client of material developments in the matters being handled for the client."

RULE 1.5 Fees

(a) A lawyer's fee shall be reasonable. The factors to be considered in determining the reasonableness of a fee include the following:

(1) the time and labor required, the novelty and difficulty of the questions involved, and the skill requisite to perform the legal service properly;

(2) the likelihood, if apparent to the client, that the acceptance of the particular employment will preclude other employment by the lawyer;

(3) the fee customarily charged in the locality for similar legal services;

(4) the amount involved and the results obtained;

(5) the time limitations imposed by the client or by the circumstances;

(6) the nature and length of the professional relationship with the client;

(7) the experience, reputation, and ability of the lawyer or lawyers performing the services; and

(8) whether the fee is fixed or contingent.

(b) When the lawyer has not regularly represented the client, the basis or rate of the fee shall be communicated to the client, preferably in writing, before or within a reasonable time after commencing the representation.

(c) A fee may be contingent on the outcome of the matter for which the service is rendered, except in a matter in which a contingent fee is prohibited by paragraph (d) or other law. A contingent fee agreement shall be in writing and shall state the method by which the fee is to be determined, including the percentage or percentages that shall accrue to the lawyer in the event of settlement, trial or appeal, litigation and other expenses to be deducted from the recovery, and whether such expenses are to be deducted before or after the contingent fee is calculated. Upon conclusion of a contingent fee matter, the lawyer shall provide the client with a written statement stating the outcome of the matter and, if there is a recovery, showing the remittance to the client and the method of its determination.

(d) A lawyer shall not enter into an arrangement for, charge, or collect:

(1) any fee in a domestic relations matter, the payment or amount of which is contingent upon the securing of a divorce or upon the amount of alimony or support, or property settlement in lieu thereof; or

(2) a contingent fee for representing a defendant in a criminal case.

(e) A division of fee between lawyers who are not in the same firm may be made only if:

(1) the division is in proportion to the services performed by each lawyer or, by written agreement with the client, each lawyer assumes joint responsibility for the representation;

(2) the client is advised of and does not object to the participation of all the lawyers involved; and

(3) the total fee is reasonable.

COMMENT:

Basis or Rate of Fee

[1]   When the lawyer has regularly represented a client, they ordinarily will have evolved an understanding concerning the basis or rate of the fee. In a new client-lawyer relationship, however, an understanding as to the fee should be promptly established. It is not necessary to recite all the factors that underlie the basis of the fee, but only those that are directly involved in its computation. It is sufficient, for example, to state that the basic rate is an hourly charge or a fixed amount or an estimated amount, or to identify the factors that may be taken into account in finally fixing the fee. When developments occur during the representation that render an earlier estimate substantially inaccurate, a revised estimate should be provided to the client. A written statement concerning the fee reduces the possibility of misunderstanding. Furnishing the client with a simple memorandum or a copy of the lawyer's customary fee schedule is sufficient if the basis or rate of the fee is set forth.

Terms of Payment

[2]   A lawyer may require advance payment of a fee, but is obliged to return any unearned portion. See Rule 1.16(d). A lawyer may accept property in payment for services, such as an ownership interest in an enterprise, providing this does not involve acquisition of a proprietary interest in the cause of action or subject matter of the litigation contrary to Rule 1.8(j). However, a fee paid in property instead of money may be subject to special scrutiny because it involves questions concerning both the value of the services and the lawyer's special knowledge of the value of the property.

[3]   An agreement may not be made whose terms might induce the lawyer improperly to curtail services for the client or perform them in a way contrary to the client's interest. For example, a lawyer should not enter into an agreement whereby services are to be provided only up to a stated amount when it is foreseeable that more extensive services probably will be required, unless the situation is adequately explained to the client. Otherwise, the client might have to bargain for further assistance in the midst of a proceeding or transaction. However, it is proper to define the extent of services in light of the client's ability to pay. A lawyer should not exploit a fee arrangement based primarily on hourly charges by using wasteful procedures. When there is doubt whether a contingent fee is consistent with the client's best interest, the lawyer should offer the client alternative bases for the fee and explain their implications. Applicable law may impose limitations on contingent fees, such as a ceiling on the percentage.

Division of Fee

[4]   A division of fee is a single billing to a client covering the fee of two or more lawyers who are not in the same firm. A division of fee facilitates association of more than one lawyer in a matter in which neither alone could serve the client as well, and most often is used when the fee is contingent and the division is between a referring lawyer and a trial specialist. Paragraph (e) permits the lawyers to divide a fee on either the basis of the proportion of services they render or by agreement between the participating lawyers if all assume responsibility for the representation as a whole and the client is advised and does not object. It does not require disclosure to the client of the share that each lawyer is to receive. Joint responsibility for the representation entails the obligations stated in Rule 5.1 for purposes of the matter involved.

Disputes Over Fees

[5]   If a procedure has been established for resolution of fee disputes, such as an arbitration or mediation procedure established by the bar, the lawyer should conscientiously consider submitting to it.   Law may prescribe a procedure for determining a lawyer's fee, for example, in representation of an executor or administrator, a class or a person entitled to a reasonable fee as part of the measure of damages.   The lawyer entitled to such a fee and a lawyer representing another party concerned with the fee should comply with the prescribed procedure.

MODEL CODE COMPARISON

[1]   DR 2–106(A) provided that a lawyer "shall not enter into an agreement for, charge, or collect an illegal or clearly excessive fee."   DR 2–106(B) provided that a fee is "clearly excessive when, after a review of the facts, a lawyer of ordinary prudence would be left with a definite and firm conviction that the fee is in excess of a reasonable fee."   The factors of a reasonable fee in Rule 1.5(a) are substantially identical to those listed in DR 2–106(B).   EC 2–17 states that a lawyer "should not charge more than a reasonable fee. . . ."

[2]   There was no counterpart to paragraph (b) in the Disciplinary Rules of the Model Code.   EC 2–19 stated that it is "usually beneficial to reduce to writing the understanding of the parties regarding the fee, particularly when it is contingent."

[3]   There was also no counterpart to paragraph (c) in the Disciplinary Rules of the Model Code.   EC 2–20 provided that "[c]ontingent fee arrangements in civil cases have long been commonly accepted in the United States," but that "a lawyer generally should decline to accept employment on a contingent fee basis by one who is able to pay a reasonable fixed fee. . . ."

[4]   With regard to paragraph (d), DR 2–106(C) prohibited "a contingent fee in a criminal case."   EC 2–20 provided that "contingent fee arrangements in domestic relation cases are rarely justified."

[5]   With regard to paragraph (e), DR 2–107(A) permitted division of fees only if: "(1) The client consents to employment of the other lawyer after a full disclosure that a division of fees will be made.   (2) The division is in proportion to the services performed and responsibility assumed by each.   (3) The total fee does not exceed clearly reasonable compensation. . . ."   Paragraph (e) permits division without regard to the services rendered by each lawyer if they assume joint responsibility for the representation.

RULE 1.6   Confidentiality of Information *

(a) A lawyer shall not reveal information relating to representation of a client unless the client consents after consultation, except for disclosures

* Editors' Note: As previously proposed by the Kutak Commission, Rule 1.6 (Revised Final Draft, June 30, 1982) read as follows:

RULE 1.6   Confidentiality of Information

(a) A lawyer shall not reveal information relating to representation of a client unless the client consents after consultation, except for disclosures that are impliedly authorized in order to carry out the representation, and except as stated in paragraph (b).

(b) A lawyer may reveal such information to the extent the lawyer reasonably believes necessary:

(1) to prevent the client from committing a criminal or fraudulent act that the lawyer reasonably believes is likely to result in death or substantial bodily harm, or in substantial injury to the financial interests or property of another;

that are impliedly authorized in order to carry out the representation, and except as stated in paragraph (b).

(b) A lawyer may reveal such information to the extent the lawyer reasonably believes necessary:

(1) to prevent the client from committing a criminal act that the lawyer believes is likely to result in imminent death or substantial bodily harm; or

(2) to establish a claim or defense on behalf of the lawyer in a controversy between the lawyer and the client, to establish a defense to a criminal charge or civil claim against the lawyer based upon conduct in which the client was involved, or to respond to allegations in any proceeding concerning the lawyer's representation of the client.

COMMENT:

[1]   The lawyer is part of a judicial system charged with upholding the law. One of the lawyer's functions is to advise clients so that they avoid any violation of the law in the proper exercise of their rights.

[2]   The observance of the ethical obligation of a lawyer to hold inviolate confidential information of the client not only facilitates the full development of facts essential to proper representation of the client but also encourages people to seek early legal assistance.

[3]   Almost without exception, clients come to lawyers in order to determine what their rights are and what is, in the maze of laws and regulations, deemed to be legal and correct. The common law recognizes that the client's confidences must be protected from disclosure. Based upon experience, lawyers know that almost all clients follow the advice given, and the law is upheld.

[4]   A fundamental principle in the client-lawyer relationship is that the lawyer maintain confidentiality of information relating to the representation. The client is thereby encouraged to communicate fully and frankly with the lawyer even as to embarrassing or legally damaging subject matter.

[5]   The principle of confidentiality is given effect in two related bodies of law, the attorney-client privilege (which includes the work product doctrine) in the law of evidence and the rule of confidentiality established in professional ethics. The attorney-client privilege applies in judicial and other proceedings in which a lawyer may be called as a witness or otherwise required to produce evidence concerning a client. The rule of client-lawyer confidentiality applies in situations other than those where evidence is sought from the lawyer through compulsion of law. The confidentiality rule applies not merely to matters communicated in confidence by the client but

(2) to rectify the consequences of a client's criminal or fraudulent act in the furtherance of which the lawyer's services had been used;

(3) to establish a claim or defense on behalf of the lawyer in a controversy between the lawyer and the client, or to establish a defense to a criminal charge, civil claim or disciplinary complaint against the lawyer based upon conduct in which the client was involved; or

(4) to comply with other law.

In 1991, the ABA House of Delegates again rejected a proposal from its ethics committee to amend Rule 1.6(b) to add the rectification language found in subsection (b)(2) of the 1982 Revised Final Draft. As of the end of 1991, about a third of the states have adopted a rectification provision.

Please see: *State-by-State Analysis of Ethics Rules on Client Confidences*, reprinted after these Model Rules.

also to all information relating to the representation, whatever its source. A lawyer may not disclose such information except as authorized or required by the Rules of Professional Conduct or other law. See also Scope.

[6] The requirement of maintaining confidentiality of information relating to representation applies to government lawyers who may disagree with the policy goals that their representation is designed to advance.

Authorized Disclosure

[7] A lawyer is impliedly authorized to make disclosures about a client when appropriate in carrying out the representation, except to the extent that the client's instructions or special circumstances limit that authority. In litigation, for example, a lawyer may disclose information by admitting a fact that cannot properly be disputed, or in negotiation by making a disclosure that facilitates a satisfactory conclusion.

[8] Lawyers in a firm may, in the course of the firm's practice, disclose to each other information relating to a client of the firm, unless the client has instructed that particular information be confined to specified lawyers.

Disclosure Adverse to Client

[9] The confidentiality rule is subject to limited exceptions. In becoming privy to information about a client, a lawyer may foresee that the client intends serious harm to another person. However, to the extent a lawyer is required or permitted to disclose a client's purposes, the client will be inhibited from revealing facts which would enable the lawyer to counsel against a wrongful course of action. The public is better protected if full and open communication by the client is encouraged than if it is inhibited.

[10] Several situations must be distinguished.

[11] First, the lawyer may not counsel or assist a client in conduct that is criminal or fraudulent. See Rule 1.2(d). Similarly, a lawyer has a duty under Rule 3.3(a)(4) not to use false evidence. This duty is essentially a special instance of the duty prescribed in Rule 1.2(d) to avoid assisting a client in criminal or fraudulent conduct.

[12] Second, the lawyer may have been innocently involved in past conduct by the client that was criminal or fraudulent. In such a situation the lawyer has not violated Rule 1.2(d), because to "counsel or assist" criminal or fraudulent conduct requires knowing that the conduct is of that character.

[13] Third, the lawyer may learn that a client intends prospective conduct that is criminal and likely to result in imminent death or substantial bodily harm. As stated in paragraph (b)(1), the lawyer has professional discretion to reveal information in order to prevent such consequences. The lawyer may make a disclosure in order to prevent homicide or serious bodily injury which the lawyer reasonably believes is intended by a client. It is very difficult for a lawyer to "know" when such a heinous purpose will actually be carried out, for the client may have a change of mind.

[14] The lawyer's exercise of discretion requires consideration of such factors as the nature of the lawyer's relationship with the client and with those who might be injured by the client, the lawyer's own involvement in the transaction and factors that may extenuate the conduct in question. Where practical, the lawyer should seek to persuade the client to take suitable action. In any case, a disclosure adverse to the client's interest should be no greater than the lawyer reasonably believes necessary to

the purpose. A lawyer's decision not to take preventive action permitted by paragraph (b)(1) does not violate this Rule.

Withdrawal

[15] If the lawyer's services will be used by the client in materially furthering a course of criminal or fraudulent conduct, the lawyer must withdraw, as stated in Rule 1.16(a)(1).

[16] After withdrawal the lawyer is required to refrain from making disclosure of the clients' confidences, except as otherwise provided in Rule 1.6. Neither this Rule nor Rule 1.8(b) nor Rule 1.16(d) prevents the lawyer from giving notice of the fact of withdrawal, and the lawyer may also withdraw or disaffirm any opinion, document, affirmation, or the like.

[17] Where the client is an organization, the lawyer may be in doubt whether contemplated conduct will actually be carried out by the organization. Where necessary to guide conduct in connection with this Rule, the lawyer may make inquiry within the organization as indicated in Rule 1.13(b).

Dispute Concerning Lawyer's Conduct

[18] Where a legal claim or disciplinary charge alleges complicity of the lawyer in a client's conduct or other misconduct of the lawyer involving representation of the client, the lawyer may respond to the extent the lawyer reasonably believes necessary to establish a defense. The same is true with respect to a claim involving the conduct or representation of a former client. The lawyer's right to respond arises when an assertion of such complicity has been made. Paragraph (b)(2) does not require the lawyer to await the commencement of an action or proceeding that charges such complicity, so that the defense may be established by responding directly to a third party who has made such an assertion. The right to defend, of course, applies where a proceeding has been commenced. Where practicable and not prejudicial to the lawyer's ability to establish the defense, the lawyer should advise the client of the third party's assertion and request that the client respond appropriately. In any event, disclosure should be no greater than the lawyer reasonably believes is necessary to vindicate innocence, the disclosure should be made in a manner which limits access to the information to the tribunal or other persons having a need to know it, and appropriate protective orders or other arrangements should be sought by the lawyer to the fullest extent practicable.

[19] If the lawyer is charged with wrongdoing in which the client's conduct is implicated, the rule of confidentiality should not prevent the lawyer from defending against the charge. Such a charge can arise in a civil, criminal or professional disciplinary proceeding, and can be based on a wrong allegedly committed by the lawyer against the client, or on a wrong alleged by a third person; for example, a person claiming to have been defrauded by the lawyer and client acting together. A lawyer entitled to a fee is permitted by paragraph (b)(2) to prove the services rendered in an action to collect it. This aspect of the rule expresses the principle that the beneficiary of a fiduciary relationship may not exploit it to the detriment of the fiduciary. As stated above, the lawyer must make every effort practicable to avoid unnecessary disclosure of information relating to a representation, to limit disclosure to those having the need to know it, and to obtain protective orders or make other arrangements minimizing the risk of disclosure.

Disclosures Otherwise Required or Authorized

[20]   The attorney-client privilege is differently defined in various jurisdictions. If a lawyer is called as a witness to give testimony concerning a client, absent waiver by the client, Rule 1.6(a) requires the lawyer to invoke the privilege when it is applicable.   The lawyer must comply with the final orders of a court or other tribunal of competent jurisdiction requiring the lawyer to give information about the client.

[21]   The Rules of Professional Conduct in various circumstances permit or require a lawyer to disclose information relating to the representation.   See Rules 2.2, 2.3, 3.3 and 4.1.   In addition to these provisions, a lawyer may be obligated or permitted by other provisions of law to give information about a client.   Whether another provision of law supersedes Rule 1.6 is a matter of interpretation beyond the scope of these Rules, but a presumption should exist against such a supersession.

Former Client

[22]   The duty of confidentiality continues after the client-lawyer relationship has terminated.

MODEL CODE COMPARISON

[1]   Rule 1.6 eliminates the two-pronged duty under the Model Code in favor of a single standard protecting all information about a client "relating to the representation."   Under DR 4–101, the requirement applied only to information protected by the attorney-client privilege and to information "gained in" the professional relationship that "the client has requested be held inviolate or the disclosure of which would be embarrassing or would be likely to be detrimental to the client."   EC 4–4 added that the duty differed from the evidentiary privilege in that it existed "without regard to the nature or source of information or the fact that others share the knowledge." Rule 1.6 imposes confidentiality on information relating to the representation even if it is acquired before or after the relationship existed.   It does not require the client to indicate information that is to be confidential, or permit the lawyer to speculate whether particular information might be embarrassing or detrimental.

[2]   Paragraph (a) permits a lawyer to disclose information where impliedly authorized to do so in order to carry out the representation.   Under DR 4–101(B) and (C), a lawyer was not permitted to reveal "confidences" unless the client first consented after disclosure.

[3]   Paragraph (b) redefines the exceptions to the requirement of confidentiality. Regarding paragraph (b)(1), DR 4–101(C)(3) provided that a lawyer "may reveal . . . [t]he intention of his client to commit a crime and the information necessary to prevent the crime."   This option existed regardless of the seriousness of the proposed crime.

[4]   With regard to paragraph (b)(2), DR 4–101(C)(4) provided that a lawyer may reveal "[c]onfidences or secrets necessary to establish or collect his fee or to defend himself or his employers or associates against an accusation of wrongful conduct." Paragraph (b)(2) enlarges the exception to include disclosure of information relating to claims by the lawyer other than for the lawyer's fee; for example, recovery of property from the client.

RULE 1.7   Conflict of Interest: General Rule

(a) A lawyer shall not represent a client if the representation of that client will be directly adverse to another client, unless:

(1) the lawyer reasonably believes the representation will not adversely affect the relationship with the other client; and

(2) each client consents after consultation.

(b) A lawyer shall not represent a client if the representation of that client may be materially limited by the lawyer's responsibilities to another client or to a third person, or by the lawyer's own interests, unless:

(1) the lawyer reasonably believes the representation will not be adversely affected; and

(2) the client consents after consultation. When representation of multiple clients in a single matter is undertaken, the consultation shall include explanation of the implications of the common representation and the advantages and risks involved.

COMMENT:

Loyalty to a Client

[1]   Loyalty is an essential element in the lawyer's relationship to a client. An impermissible conflict of interest may exist before representation is undertaken, in which event the representation should be declined. The lawyer should adopt reasonable procedures, appropriate for the size and type of firm and practice, to determine in both litigation and non-litigation matters the parties and issues involved and to determine whether there are actual or potential conflicts of interest.

[2]   If such a conflict arises after representation has been undertaken, the lawyer should withdraw from the representation. See Rule 1.16. Where more than one client is involved and the lawyer withdraws because a conflict arises after representation, whether the lawyer may continue to represent any of the clients is determined by Rule 1.9. See also Rule 2.2(c). As to whether a client-lawyer relationship exists or, having once been established, is continuing, see Comment to Rule 1.3 and Scope.

[3]   As a general proposition, loyalty to a client prohibits undertaking representation directly adverse to that client without that client's consent. Paragraph (a) expresses that general rule. Thus, a lawyer ordinarily may not act as advocate against a person the lawyer represents in some other matter, even if it is wholly unrelated. On the other hand, simultaneous representation in unrelated matters of clients whose interests are only generally adverse, such as competing economic enterprises, does not require consent of the respective clients. Paragraph (a) applies only when the representation of one client would be directly adverse to the other.

[4]   Loyalty to a client is also impaired when a lawyer cannot consider, recommend or carry out an appropriate course of action for the client because of the lawyer's other responsibilities or interests. The conflict in effect forecloses alternatives that would otherwise be available to the client. Paragraph (b) addresses such situations. A possible conflict does not itself preclude the representation. The critical questions are the likelihood that a conflict will eventuate and, if it does, whether it will materially interfere with the lawyer's independent professional judgment in considering alternatives or foreclose courses of action that reasonably should be pursued on

behalf of the client. Consideration should be given to whether the client wishes to accommodate the other interest involved.

Consultation and Consent

[5] A client may consent to representation notwithstanding a conflict. However, as indicated in paragraph (a)(1) with respect to representation directly adverse to a client, and paragraph (b)(1) with respect to material limitations on representation of a client, when a disinterested lawyer would conclude that the client should not agree to the representation under the circumstances, the lawyer involved cannot properly ask for such agreement or provide representation on the basis of the client's consent. When more than one client is involved, the question of conflict must be resolved as to each client. Moreover, there may be circumstances where it is impossible to make the disclosure necessary to obtain consent. For example, when the lawyer represents different clients in related matters and one of the clients refuses to consent to the disclosure necessary to permit the other client to make an informed decision, the lawyer cannot properly ask the latter to consent.

Lawyer's Interests

[6] The lawyer's own interests should not be permitted to have adverse effect on representation of a client. For example, a lawyer's need for income should not lead the lawyer to undertake matters that cannot be handled competently and at a reasonable fee. See Rules 1.1 and 1.5. If the probity of a lawyer's own conduct in a transaction is in serious question, it may be difficult or impossible for the lawyer to give a client detached advice. A lawyer may not allow related business interests to affect representation, for example, by referring clients to an enterprise in which the lawyer has an undisclosed interest.

Conflicts in Litigation

[7] Paragraph (a) prohibits representation of opposing parties in litigation. Simultaneous representation of parties whose interests in litigation may conflict, such as co-plaintiffs or co-defendants, is governed by paragraph (b). An impermissible conflict may exist by reason of substantial discrepancy in the parties' testimony, incompatibility in positions in relation to an opposing party or the fact that there are substantially different possibilities of settlement of the claims or liabilities in question. Such conflicts can arise in criminal cases as well as civil. The potential for conflict of interest in representing multiple defendants in a criminal case is so grave that ordinarily a lawyer should decline to represent more than one codefendant. On the other hand, common representation of persons having similar interests is proper if the risk of adverse effect is minimal and the requirements of paragraph (b) are met. Compare Rule 2.2 involving intermediation between clients.

[8] Ordinarily, a lawyer may not act as advocate against a client the lawyer represents in some other matter, even if the other matter is wholly unrelated. However, there are circumstances in which a lawyer may act as advocate against a client. For example, a lawyer representing an enterprise with diverse operations may accept employment as an advocate against the enterprise in an unrelated matter if doing so will not adversely affect the lawyer's relationship with the enterprise or conduct of the suit and if both clients consent upon consultation. By the same token, government lawyers in some circumstances may represent government employees in proceedings in which a government agency is the opposing party. The propriety of concurrent representation can depend on the nature of the litigation. For example, a

suit charging fraud entails conflict to a degree not involved in a suit for a declaratory judgment concerning statutory interpretation.

[9] A lawyer may represent parties having antagonistic positions on a legal question that has arisen in different cases, unless representation of either client would be adversely affected. Thus, it is ordinarily not improper to assert such positions in cases pending in different trial courts, but it may be improper to do so in cases pending at the same time in an appellate court.

Interest of Person Paying for a Lawyer's Service

[10] A lawyer may be paid from a source other than the client, if the client is informed of that fact and consents and the arrangement does not compromise the lawyer's duty of loyalty to the client. See Rule 1.8(f). For example, when an insurer and its insured have conflicting interests in a matter arising from a liability insurance agreement, and the insurer is required to provide special counsel for the insured, the arrangement should assure the special counsel's professional independence. So also, when a corporation and its directors or employees are involved in a controversy in which they have conflicting interests, the corporation may provide funds for separate legal representation of the directors or employees, if the clients consent after consultation and the arrangement ensures the lawyer's professional independence.

Other Conflict Situations

[11] Conflicts of interest in contexts other than litigation sometimes may be difficult to assess. Relevant factors in determining whether there is potential for adverse effect include the duration and intimacy of the lawyer's relationship with the client or clients involved, the functions being performed by the lawyer, the likelihood that actual conflict will arise and the likely prejudice to the client from the conflict if it does arise. The question is often one of proximity and degree.

[12] For example, a lawyer may not represent multiple parties to a negotiation whose interests are fundamentally antagonistic to each other, but common representation is permissible where the clients are generally aligned in interest even though there is some difference of interest among them.

[13] Conflict questions may also arise in estate planning and estate administration. A lawyer may be called upon to prepare wills for several family members, such as husband and wife, and, depending upon the circumstances, a conflict of interest may arise. In estate administration the identity of the client may be unclear under the law of a particular jurisdiction. Under one view, the client is the fiduciary; under another view the client is the estate or trust, including its beneficiaries. The lawyer should make clear the relationship to the parties involved.

[14] A lawyer for a corporation or other organization who is also a member of its board of directors should determine whether the responsibilities of the two roles may conflict. The lawyer may be called on to advise the corporation in matters involving actions of the directors. Consideration should be given to the frequency with which such situations may arise, the potential intensity of the conflict, the effect of the lawyer's resignation from the board and the possibility of the corporation's obtaining legal advice from another lawyer in such situations. If there is material risk that the dual role will compromise the lawyer's independence of professional judgment, the lawyer should not serve as a director.

Conflict Charged by an Opposing Party

[15] Resolving questions of conflict of interest is primarily the responsibility of the lawyer undertaking the representation. In litigation, a court may raise the question when there is reason to infer that the lawyer has neglected the responsibility. In a criminal case, inquiry by the court is generally required when a lawyer represents multiple defendants. Where the conflict is such as clearly to call in question the fair or efficient administration of justice, opposing counsel may properly raise the question. Such an objection should be viewed with caution, however, for it can be misused as a technique of harassment. See Scope.

MODEL CODE COMPARISON

[1] DR 5–101(A) provided that "[e]xcept with the consent of his client after full disclosure, a lawyer shall not accept employment if the exercise of his professional judgment on behalf of the client will be or reasonably may be affected by his own financial, business, property, or personal interests." DR 5–105(A) provided that a lawyer "shall decline proffered employment if the exercise of his independent professional judgment in behalf of a client will be or is likely to be adversely affected by the acceptance of the proffered employment, or if it would be likely to involve him in representing differing interests, except to the extent permitted under DR 5–105(C)." DR 5–105(C) provided that "a lawyer may represent multiple clients if it is obvious that he can adequately represent the interest of each and if each consents to the representation after full disclosure of the possible effect of such representation on the exercise of his independent professional judgment on behalf on each." DR 5–107(B) provided that a lawyer "shall not permit a person who recommends, employs, or pays him to render legal services for another to direct or regulate his professional judgment in rendering such services."

[2] Rule 1.7 clarifies DR 5–105(A) by requiring that, when the lawyer's other interests are involved, not only must the client consent after consultation but also that, independent of such consent, the representation reasonably appears not to be adversely affected by the lawyer's other interests. This requirement appears to be the intended meaning of the provision in DR 5–105(C) that "it is obvious that he can adequately represent" the client, and was implicit in EC 5–2, which stated that a lawyer "should not accept proffered employment if his personal interests or desires will, or there is a reasonable possibility that they will, affect adversely the advice to be given or services to be rendered the prospective client."

RULE 1.8 Conflict of Interest: Prohibited Transactions

(a) A lawyer shall not enter into a business transaction with a client or knowingly acquire an ownership, possessory, security or other pecuniary interest adverse to a client unless:

    (1) the transaction and terms on which the lawyer acquires the interest are fair and reasonable to the client and are fully disclosed and transmitted in writing to the client in a manner which can be reasonably understood by the client;

    (2) the client is given a reasonable opportunity to seek the advice of independent counsel in the transaction; and

    (3) the client consents in writing thereto.

(b) A lawyer shall not use information relating to representation of a client to the disadvantage of the client unless the client consents after consultation, except as permitted or required by Rule 1.6 or Rule 3.3.

(c) A lawyer shall not prepare an instrument giving the lawyer or a person related to the lawyer as parent, child, sibling, or spouse any substantial gift from a client, including a testamentary gift, except where the client is related to the donee.

(d) Prior to the conclusion of representation of a client, a lawyer shall not make or negotiate an agreement giving the lawyer literary or media rights to a portrayal or account based in substantial part on information relating to the representation.

(e) A lawyer shall not provide financial assistance to a client in connection with pending or contemplated litigation, except that:

> (1) a lawyer may advance court costs and expenses of litigation, the repayment of which may be contingent on the outcome of the matter; and

> (2) a lawyer representing an indigent client may pay court costs and expenses of litigation on behalf of the client.

(f) A lawyer shall not accept compensation for representing a client from one other than the client unless:

> (1) the client consents after consultation;

> (2) there is no interference with the lawyer's independence of professional judgment or with the client–lawyer relationship; and

> (3) information relating to representation of a client is protected as required by rule 1.6.

(g) A lawyer who represents two or more clients shall not participate in making an aggregate settlement of the claims of or against the clients, or in a criminal case an aggregated agreement as to guilty or nolo contendere pleas, unless each client consents after consultation, including disclosure of the existence and nature of all the claims or pleas involved and of the participation of each person in the settlement.

(h) A lawyer shall not make an agreement prospectively limiting the lawyer's liability to a client for malpractice unless permitted by law and the client is independently represented in making the agreement, or settle a claim for such liability with an unrepresented client or former client without first advising that person in writing that independent representation is appropriate in connection therewith.

(i) A lawyer related to another lawyer as parent, child, sibling or spouse shall not represent a client in a representation directly adverse to a person who the lawyer knows is represented by the other lawyer except upon consent by the client after consultation regarding the relationship.

(j) A lawyer shall not acquire a proprietary interest in the cause of action or subject matter of litigation the lawyer is conducting for a client, except that the lawyer may:

> (1) acquire a lien granted by law to secure the lawyer's fee or expenses; and

(2) contract with a client for a reasonable contingent fee in a civil case.

COMMENT:

Transactions Between Client and Lawyer

[1]   As a general principle, all transactions between client and lawyer should be fair and reasonable to the client. In such transactions a review by independent counsel on behalf of the client is often advisable. Furthermore, a lawyer may not exploit information relating to the representation to the client's disadvantage. For example, a lawyer who has learned that the client is investing in specific real estate may not, without the client's consent, seek to acquire nearby property where doing so would adversely affect the client's plan for investment. Paragraph (a) does not, however, apply to standard commercial transactions between the lawyer and the client for products or services that the client generally markets to others, for example, banking or brokerage services, medical services, products manufactured or distributed by the client, and utilities services. In such transactions, the lawyer has no advantage in dealing with the client, and the restrictions in paragraph (a) are unnecessary and impracticable.

[2]   A lawyer may accept a gift from a client, if the transaction meets general standards of fairness. For example, a simple gift such as a present given at a holiday or as a token of appreciation is permitted. If effectuation of a substantial gift requires preparing a legal instrument such as a will or conveyance, however, the client should have the detached advice that another lawyer can provide. Paragraph (c) recognizes an exception where the client is a relative of the donee or the gift is not substantial.

Literary Rights

[3]   An agreement by which a lawyer acquires literary or media rights concerning the conduct of the representation creates a conflict between the interests of the client and the personal interests of the lawyer. Measures suitable in the representation of the client may detract from the publication value of an account of the representation. Paragraph (d) does not prohibit a lawyer representing a client in a transaction concerning literary property from agreeing that the lawyer's fee shall consist of a share in ownership in the property, if the arrangement conforms to Rule 1.5 and paragraph (j).

Person Paying for Lawyer's Services

[4]   Rule 1.8(f) requires disclosure of the fact that the lawyer's services are being paid for by a third party. Such an arrangement must also conform to the requirements of Rule 1.6 concerning confidentiality and Rule 1.7 concerning conflict of interest. Where the client is a class, consent may be obtained on behalf of the class by court-supervised procedure.

Limiting Liability

[5]   This Rule is not intended to apply to customary qualification and limitations in legal opinions and memoranda.

Family Relationships Between Lawyers

[6]   Rule 1.8(i) applies to related lawyers who are in different firms. Related lawyers in the same firm are governed by Rules 1.7, 1.9, and 1.10. The disqualifica-

tion stated in Rule 1.8(i) is personal and is not imputed to members of firms with whom the lawyers are associated.

Acquisition of Interest in Litigation

[7]   Paragraph (j) states the traditional general rule that lawyers are prohibited from acquiring a proprietary interest in litigation. This general rule, which has its basis in common law champerty and maintenance, is subject to specific exceptions developed in decisional law and continued in these Rules, such as the exception for reasonable contingent fees set forth in Rule 1.5 and the exception for certain advances of the costs of litigation set forth in paragraph (e).

MODEL CODE COMPARISON

[1]   With regard to paragraph (a), DR 5–104(A) provided that a lawyer "shall not enter into a business transaction with a client if they have differing interests therein and if the client expects the lawyer to exercise his professional judgment therein for the protection of the client, unless the client has consented after full disclosure." EC 5–3 stated that a lawyer "should not seek to persuade his client to permit him to invest in an undertaking of his client nor make improper use of his professional relationship to influence his client to invest in an enterprise in which the lawyer is interested."

[2]   With regard to paragraph (b), DR 4–101(B)(3) provided that a lawyer should not use "a confidence or secret of his client for the advantage of himself, or of a third person, unless the client consents after full disclosure."

[3]   There was no counterpart to paragraph (c) in the Disciplinary Rules of the Model Code. EC 5–5 stated that a lawyer "should not suggest to his client that a gift be made to himself or for his benefit. If a lawyer accepts a gift from his client, he is peculiarly susceptible to the charge that he unduly influenced or overreached the client. If a client voluntarily offers to make a gift to his lawyer, the lawyer may accept the gift, but before doing so, he should urge that the client secure disinterested advice from an independent, competent person who is cognizant of all the circumstances. Other than in exceptional circumstances, a lawyer should insist that an instrument in which his client desires to name him beneficially be prepared by another lawyer selected by the client."

[4]   Paragraph (d) is substantially similar to DR 5–104(B), but refers to "literary or media" rights, a more generally inclusive term than "publication" rights.

[5]   Paragraph (e)(1) is similar to DR 5–103(B), but eliminates the requirement that "the client remains ultimately liable for such expenses."

[6]   Paragraph (e)(2) has no counterpart in the Model Code.

[7]   Paragraph (f) is substantially identical to DR 5–107(A)(1).

[8]   Paragraph (g) is substantially identical to DR 5–106.

[9]   The first clause of paragraph (h) is similar to DR 6–102(A). There was no counterpart in the Model Code to the second clause of paragraph (h).

[10]   Paragraph (i) has no counterpart in the Model Code.

[11]   Paragraph (j) is substantially identical to DR 5–103(A).

RULE 1.9   Conflict of Interest: Former Client

(a) A lawyer who has formerly represented a client in a matter shall not thereafter represent another person in the same or a substantially related matter in which that person's interests are materially adverse to the interests of the former client unless the former client consents after consultation.

(b) A lawyer shall not knowingly represent a person in the same or a substantially related matter in which a firm with which the lawyer formerly was associated had previously represented a client

    (1) whose interests are materially adverse to that person; and

    (2) about whom the lawyer had acquired information protected by Rules 1.6 and 1.9(c) that is material to the matter;

unless the former client consents after consultation.

(c) A lawyer who has formerly represented a client in a matter or whose present or former firm has formerly represented a client in a matter shall not thereafter:

    (1) use information relating to the representation to the disadvantage of the former client except as Rule 1.6 or Rule 3.3 would permit or require with respect to a client, or when the information has become generally known; or

    (2) reveal information relating to the representation except as Rule 1.6 or Rule 3.3 would permit or require with respect to a client.

COMMENT:

[1]   After termination of a client-lawyer relationship, a lawyer may not represent another client except in conformity with this Rule. The principles in Rule 1.7 determine whether the interests of the present and former client are adverse. Thus, a lawyer could not properly seek to rescind on behalf of a new client a contract drafted on behalf of the former client. So also a lawyer who has prosecuted an accused person could not properly represent the accused in a subsequent civil action against the government concerning the same transaction.

[2]   The scope of a "matter" for purposes of this Rule may depend on the facts of a particular situation or transaction. The lawyer's involvement in a matter can also be a question of degree. When a lawyer has been directly involved in a specific transaction, subsequent representation of other clients with materially adverse interests clearly is prohibited. On the other hand, a lawyer who recurrently handled a type of problem for a former client is not precluded from later representing another client in a wholly distinct problem of that type even though the subsequent representation involves a position adverse to the prior client. Similar considerations can apply to the reassignment of military lawyers between defense and prosecution functions within the same military jurisdiction. The underlying question is whether the lawyer was so involved in the matter that the subsequent representation can be justly regarded as a changing of sides in the matter in question.

Lawyers Moving Between Firms

[3]   When lawyers have been associated within a firm but then end their association, the question of whether a lawyer should undertake representation is more complicated. There are several competing considerations. First, the client previously

represented by the former firm must be reasonably assured that the principle of loyalty to the client is not compromised. Second, the rule should not be so broadly cast as to preclude other persons from having reasonable choice of legal counsel. Third, the rule should not unreasonably hamper lawyers from forming new associations and taking on new clients after having left a previous association. In this connection, it should be recognized that today many lawyers practice in firms, that many lawyers to some degree limit their practice to one field or another, and that many move from one association to another several times in their careers. If the concept of imputation were applied with unqualified rigor, the result would be radical curtailment of the opportunity of lawyers to move from one practice setting to another and of the opportunity of clients to change counsel.

[4] Reconciliation of these competing principles in the past has been attempted under two rubrics. One approach has been to seek per se rules of disqualification. For example, it has been held that a partner in a law firm is conclusively presumed to have access to all confidences concerning all clients of the firm. Under this analysis, if a lawyer has been a partner in one law firm and then becomes a partner in another law firm, there may be a presumption that all confidences known by the partner in the first firm are known to all partners in the second firm. This presumption might properly be applied in some circumstances, especially where the client has been extensively represented, but may be unrealistic where the client was represented only for limited purposes. Furthermore, such a rigid rule exaggerates the difference between a partner and an associate in modern law firms.

[5] The other rubric formerly used for dealing with disqualification is the appearance of impropriety proscribed in Canon 9 of the ABA Model Code of Professional Responsibility. This rubric has a two fold problem. First, the appearance of impropriety can be taken to include any new client-lawyer relationship that might make a former client feel anxious. If that meaning were adopted, disqualification would become little more than a question of subjective judgment by the former client. Second, since "impropriety" is undefined, the term "appearance of impropriety" is question-begging. It therefore has to be recognized that the problem of disqualification cannot be properly resolved either by simple analogy to a lawyer practicing alone or by the very general concept of appearance of impropriety.

Confidentiality

[6] Preserving confidentiality is a question of access to information. Access to information, in turn, is essentially a question of fact in particular circumstances, aided by inferences, deductions or working presumptions that reasonably may be made about the way in which lawyers work together. A lawyer may have general access to files of all clients of a law firm and may regularly participate in discussions of their affairs; it should be inferred that such a lawyer in fact is privy to all information about all the firm's clients. In contrast, another lawyer may have access to the files of only a limited number of clients and participate in discussions of the affairs of no other clients; in the absence of information to the contrary, it should be inferred that such a lawyer in fact is privy to information about the clients actually served but not those of other clients.

[7] Application of paragraph (b) depends on a situation's particular facts. In such an inquiry, the burden of proof should rest upon the firm whose disqualification is sought.

[8] Paragraph (b) operates to disqualify the lawyer only when the lawyer involved has actual knowledge of information protected by Rules 1.6 and 1.9(b). Thus, if a lawyer while with one firm acquired no knowledge or information relating to a particular client of the firm, and that lawyer later joined another firm, neither the lawyer individually nor the second firm is disqualified from representing another client in the same or a related matter even though the interests of the two clients conflict. See Rule 1.10(b) for the restrictions on a firm once a lawyer has terminated association with the firm.

[9] Independent of the question of disqualification of a firm, a lawyer changing professional association has a continuing duty to preserve confidentiality of information about a client formerly represented. See Rules 1.6 and 1.9.

Adverse Positions

[10] The second aspect of loyalty to a client is the lawyer's obligation to decline subsequent representations involving positions adverse to a former client arising in substantially related matters. This obligation requires abstention from adverse representation by the individual lawyer involved, but does not properly entail abstention of other lawyers through imputed disqualification. Hence, this aspect of the problem is governed by Rule 1.9(a). Thus, if a lawyer left one firm for another, the new affiliation would not preclude the firms involved from continuing to represent clients with adverse interests in the same or related matters, so long as the conditions of paragraphs (b) and (c) concerning confidentiality have been met.

[11] Information acquired by the lawyer in the course of representing a client may not subsequently be used or revealed by the lawyer to the disadvantage of the client. However, the fact that a lawyer has once served a client does not preclude the lawyer from using generally known information about that client when later representing another client.

[12] Disqualification from subsequent representation is for the protection of former clients and can be waived by them. A waiver is effective only if there is disclosure of the circumstances, including the lawyer's intended role in behalf of the new client.

[13] With regard to an opposing party's raising a question of conflict of interest, see Comment to Rule 1.7. With regard to disqualification of a firm with which a lawyer is or was formerly associated, see Rule 1.10.

MODEL CODE COMPARISON

[1] There was no counterpart to this Rule in the Disciplinary Rules of the Model Code. Representation adverse to a former client was sometimes dealt with under the rubric of Canon 9 of the Model Code, which provided: "A lawyer should avoid even the appearance of impropriety." Also applicable were EC 4–6 which stated that the "obligation of a lawyer to preserve the confidences and secrets of his client continues after the termination of his employment" and Canon 5 which stated that "[a] lawyer should exercise independent professional judgment on behalf of a client."

[2] The provision for waiver by the former client in paragraphs (a) and (b) is similar to DR 5–105(C).

[3] The exception in the last clause of paragraph (c)(1) permits a lawyer to use information relating to a former client that is in the "public domain," a use that was also not prohibited by the Model Code, which protected only "confidences and secrets."

Since the scope of paragraphs (a) and (b) is much broader than "confidences and secrets," it is necessary to define when a lawyer may make use of information about a client after the client-lawyer relationship has terminated.

RULE 1.10   Imputed Disqualification: General Rule*

(a) While lawyers are associated in a firm, none of them shall knowingly represent a client when any one of them practicing alone would be prohibited from doing so by Rules 1.7, 1.8(c), 1.9 or 2.2.

(b) When a lawyer has terminated an association with a firm, the firm is not prohibited from thereafter representing a person with interests materially adverse to those of a client represented by the formerly associated lawyer and not currently represented by the firm, unless:

(1) the matter is the same or substantially related to that in which the formerly associated lawyer represented the client; and

(2) any lawyer remaining in the firm has information protected by Rules 1.6 and 1.9(c) that is material to the matter.

(c) A disqualification prescribed by this rule may be waived by the affected client under the conditions stated in Rule 1.7.

COMMENT:
Definition of "Firm"

[1]   For purposes of the Rules of Professional Conduct, the term "firm" includes lawyers in a private firm, and lawyers in the legal department of a corporation or other organization, or in a legal services organization. Whether two or more lawyers constitute a firm within this definition can depend on the specific facts. For example, two practitioners who share office space and occasionally consult or assist each other ordinarily would not be regarded as constituting a firm. However, if they present themselves to the public in a way suggesting that they are a firm or conduct themselves as a firm, they should be regarded as a firm for the purposes of the Rules. The terms of any formal agreement between associated lawyers are relevant in determining whether they are a firm, as is the fact that they have mutual access to information concerning the clients they serve. Furthermore, it is relevant in doubtful cases to consider the underlying purpose of the Rule that is involved. A group of lawyers could be regarded as a firm for purposes of the rule that the same lawyer should not represent opposing parties in litigation, while it might not be so regarded for purposes of the rule that information acquired by one lawyer is attributed to the other.

[2]   With respect to the law department of an organization, there is ordinarily no question that the members of the department constitute a firm within the meaning of the Rules of Professional Conduct. However, there can be uncertainty as to the identity of the client. For example, it may not be clear whether the law department of a corporation represents a subsidiary or an affiliated corporation, as well as the corporation by which the members of the department are directly employed. A similar question can arise concerning an unincorporated association and its local affiliates.

* Editor's Note: Please see Appendix: *Chart   Model Rules.*
on Lawyer Screening, reprinted following the

[3]   Similar questions can also arise with respect to lawyers in legal aid. Lawyers employed in the same unit of a legal service organization constitute a firm, but not necessarily those employed in separate units. As in the case of independent practitioners, whether the lawyers should be treated as associated with each other can depend on the particular rule that is involved, and on the specific facts of the situation.

[4]   Where a lawyer has joined a private firm after having represented the government, the situation is governed by Rule 1.11(a) and (b); where a lawyer represents the government after having served private clients, the situation is governed by Rule 1.11(c)(1). The individual lawyer involved is bound by the Rules generally, including Rules 1.6, 1.7 and 1.9.

[5]   Different provisions are thus made for movement of a lawyer from one private firm to another and for movement of a lawyer between a private firm and the government. The government is entitled to protection of its client confidences and, therefore, to the protections provided in Rules 1.6, 1.9 and 1.11. However, if the more extensive disqualification in Rule 1.10 were applied to former government lawyers, the potential effect on the government would be unduly burdensome. The government deals with all private citizens and organizations and, thus, has a much wider circle of adverse legal interests than does any private law firm. In these circumstances, the government's recruitment of lawyers would be seriously impaired if Rule 1.10 were applied to the government. On balance, therefore, the government is better served in the long run by the protections stated in Rule 1.11.

Principles of Imputed Disqualification

[6]   The rule of imputed disqualification stated in paragraph (a) gives effect to the principle of loyalty to the client as it applies to lawyers who practice in a law firm. Such situations can be considered from the premise that a firm of lawyers is essentially one lawyer for purposes of the rules governing loyalty to the client, or from the premise that each lawyer is vicariously bound by the obligation of loyalty owed by each lawyer with whom the lawyer is associated. Paragraph (a) operates only among the lawyers currently associated in a firm. When a lawyer moves from one firm to another, the situation is governed by Rules 1.9(b) and 1.10(b).

[7]   Rule 1.10(b) operates to permit a law firm, under certain circumstances, to represent a person with interests directly adverse to those of a client represented by a lawyer who formerly was associated with the firm. The Rule applies regardless of when the formerly associated lawyer represented the client. However, the law firm may not represent a person with interests adverse to those of a present client of the firm, which would violate Rule 1.7. Moreover, the firm may not represent the person where the matter is the same or substantially related to that in which the formerly associated lawyer represented the client and any other lawyer currently in the firm has material information protected by Rules 1.6 and 1.9(c).

MODEL CODE COMPARISON

DR 5–105(D) provided that "[i]f a lawyer is required to decline or to withdraw from employment under a Disciplinary Rule, no partner, or associate, or any other lawyer affiliated with him or his firm, may accept or continue such employment."

RULE 1.11   Successive Government and Private Employment

(a) Except as law may otherwise expressly permit, a lawyer shall not represent a private client in connection with a matter in which the lawyer

participated personally and substantially as a public officer or employee, unless the appropriate government agency consents after consultation. No lawyer in a firm with which that lawyer is associated may knowingly undertake or continue representation in such a matter unless:

(1) the disqualified lawyer is screened from any participation in the matter and is apportioned no part of the fee therefrom; and

(2) written notice is promptly given to the appropriate government agency to enable it to ascertain compliance with the provisions of this rule.

(b) Except as law may otherwise expressly permit, a lawyer having information that the lawyer knows is confidential government information about a person acquired when the lawyer was a public officer or employee, may not represent a private client whose interests are adverse to that person in a matter in which the information could be used to the material disadvantage of that person. A firm with which that lawyer is associated may undertake or continue representation in the matter only if the disqualified lawyer is screened from any participation in the matter and is apportioned no part of the fee therefrom.

(c) Except as law may otherwise expressly permit, a lawyer serving as a public officer or employee shall not:

(1) participate in a matter in which the lawyer participated personally and substantially while in private practice or nongovernmental employment, unless under applicable law no one is, or by lawful delegation may be, authorized to act in the lawyer's stead in the matter; or

(2) negotiate for private employment with any person who is involved as a party or as attorney for a party in a matter in which the lawyer is participating personally and substantially, except that a lawyer serving as a law clerk to a judge, other adjudicative officer or arbitrator may negotiate for private employment as permitted by Rule 1.12(b) and subject to the conditions stated in Rule 1.12(b).

(d) As used in this Rule, the term "matter" includes:

(1) any judicial or other proceeding, application, request for a ruling or other determination, contract, claim, controversy, investigation, charge, accusation, arrest or other particular matter involving a specific party or parties; and

(2) any other matter covered by the conflict of interest rules of the appropriate government agency.

(e) As used in this Rule, the term "confidential government information" means information which has been obtained under governmental authority and which, at the time this rule is applied, the government is prohibited by law from disclosing to the public or has a legal privilege not to disclose, and which is not otherwise available to the public.

COMMENT:

[1] This Rule prevents a lawyer from exploiting public office for the advantage of a private client. It is a counterpart of Rule 1.10(b), which applies to lawyers moving from one firm to another.

[2]   A lawyer representing a government agency, whether employed or specially retained by the government, is subject to the Rules of Professional Conduct, including the prohibition against representing adverse interests stated in Rule 1.7 and the protections afforded former clients in Rule 1.9.   In addition, such a lawyer is subject to Rule 1.11 and to statutes and government regulations regarding conflict of interest. Such statutes and regulations may circumscribe the extent to which the government agency may give consent under this Rule.

[3]   Where the successive clients are a public agency and a private client, the risk exists that power or discretion vested in public authority might be used for the special benefit of a private client.   A lawyer should not be in a position where benefit to a private client might affect performance of the lawyer's professional functions on behalf of public authority.   Also, unfair advantage could accrue to the private client by reason of access to confidential government information about the client's adversary obtainable only through the lawyer's government service.   However, the rules governing lawyers presently or formerly employed by a government agency should not be so restrictive as to inhibit transfer of employment to and from the government.   The government has a legitimate need to attract qualified lawyers as well as to maintain high ethical standards.   The provisions for screening and waiver are necessary to prevent the disqualification rule from imposing too severe a deterrent against entering public service.

[4]   When the client is an agency of one government, that agency should be treated as a private client for purposes of this Rule if the lawyer thereafter represents an agency of another government, as when a lawyer represents a city and subsequently is employed by a federal agency.

[5]   Paragraphs (a)(1) and (b) do not prohibit a lawyer from receiving a salary or partnership share established by prior independent agreement.   They prohibit directly relating the attorney's compensation to the fee in the matter in which the lawyer is disqualified.

[6]   Paragraph (a)(2) does not require that a lawyer give notice to the government agency at a time when premature disclosure would injure the client; a requirement for premature disclosure might preclude engagement of the lawyer.   Such notice is, however, required to be given as soon as practicable in order that the government agency will have a reasonable opportunity to ascertain that the lawyer is complying with Rule 1.11 and to take appropriate action if it believes the lawyer is not complying.

[7]   Paragraph (b) operates only when the lawyer in question has knowledge of the information, which means actual knowledge; it does not operate with respect to information that merely could be imputed to the lawyer.

[8]   Paragraphs (a) and (c) do not prohibit a lawyer from jointly representing a private party and a government agency when doing so is permitted by Rule 1.7 and is not otherwise prohibited by law.

[9]   Paragraph (c) does not disqualify other lawyers in the agency with which the lawyer in question has become associated.

MODEL CODE COMPARISON

[1]   Paragraph (a) is similar to DR 9–101(B), except that the latter used the terms "in which he had substantial responsibility while he was a public employee."

[2]   Paragraphs (b), (c), (d) and (e) have no counterparts in the Model Code.

RULE 1.12 Former Judge or Arbitrator

(a) Except as stated in paragraph (d), a lawyer shall not represent anyone in connection with a matter in which the lawyer participated personally and substantially as a judge or other adjudicative officer, arbitrator or law clerk to such a person, unless all parties to the proceeding consent after consultation.

(b) A lawyer shall not negotiate for employment with any person who is involved as a party or as attorney for a party in a matter in which the lawyer is participating personally and substantially as a judge or other adjudicative officer, or arbitrator. A lawyer serving as a law clerk to a judge, other adjudicative officer or arbitrator may negotiate for employment with a party or lawyer involved in a matter in which the clerk is participating personally and substantially, but only after the lawyer has notified the judge, other adjudicative officer or arbitrator.

(c) If a lawyer is disqualified by paragraph (a), no lawyer in a firm with which that lawyer is associated may knowingly undertake or continue representation in the matter unless:

(1) the disqualified lawyer is screened from any participation in the matter and is apportioned no part of the fee therefrom; and

(2) written notice is promptly given to the appropriate tribunal to enable it to ascertain compliance with the provisions of this Rule.

(d) An arbitrator selected as a partisan of a party in a multi-member arbitration panel is not prohibited from subsequently representing that party.

COMMENT:

[1] This Rule generally parallels Rule 1.11. The term "personally and substantially" signifies that a judge who was a member of a multi-member court, and thereafter left judicial office to practice law, is not prohibited from representing a client in a matter pending in the court, but in which the former judge did not participate. So also the fact that a former judge exercised administrative responsibility in a court does not prevent the former judge from acting as a lawyer in a matter where the judge had previously exercised remote or incidental administrative responsibility that did not affect the merits. Compare the Comment to Rule 1.11. The term "adjudicative officer" includes such officials as judges pro tempore, referees, special masters, hearing officers and other parajudicial officers, and also lawyers who serve as part-time judges. Compliance Canons A(2), B(2) and C of the Model Code of Judicial Conduct provide that a part-time judge, judge pro tempore or retired judge recalled to active service, may not "act as a lawyer in any proceeding in which he served as a judge or in any other proceeding related thereto." Although phrased differently from this Rule, those Rules correspond in meaning.

MODEL CODE COMPARISON

[1] Paragraph (a) is substantially similar to DR 9–101(A), which provided that a lawyer "shall not accept private employment in a matter upon the merits of which he has acted in a judicial capacity." Paragraph (a) differs, however, in that it is broader in scope and states more specifically the persons to whom it applies. There was no counterpart in the Model Code to paragraphs (b), (c) or (d).

[2] With regard to arbitrators, EC 5–20 stated that "a lawyer [who] has undertaken to act as an impartial arbitrator or mediator, . . . should not thereafter represent in the dispute any of the parties involved." DR 9–101(A) did not provide a waiver of the disqualification applied to former judges by consent of the parties. However, DR 5–105(C) was similar in effect and could be construed to permit waiver.

RULE 1.13 Organization as Client *

(a) A lawyer employed or retained by an organization represents the organization acting through its duly authorized constituents.

(b) If a lawyer for an organization knows that an officer, employee or other person associated with the organization is engaged in action, intends to act or refuses to act in a matter related to the representation that is a violation of a legal obligation to the organization, or a violation of law which reasonably might be imputed to the organization, and is likely to result in substantial injury to the organization, the lawyer shall proceed as is reason-

* Editors' Note: As previously proposed by the Kutak Commission, Rule 1.13 (Revised Final Draft, June 30, 1982) read as follows:

RULE 1.13 Organization as the Client

(a) A lawyer employed or retained to represent an organization represents the organization as distinct from its directors, officers, employees, members, shareholders or other constituents.

(b) If a lawyer for an organization knows that an officer, employee or other person associated with the organization is engaged in action, intends to act or refuses to act in a matter related to the representation that is a violation of a legal obligation to the organization, or a violation of law which reasonably might be imputed to the organization, and is likely to result in substantial injury to the organization, the lawyer shall proceed as is reasonably necessary in the best interest of the organization. In determining how to proceed, the lawyer shall give due consideration to the seriousness of the violation and its consequences, the scope and nature of the lawyer's representation, the responsibility in the organization and the apparent motivation of the person involved, the policies of the organization concerning such matters and any other relevant considerations. Any measures taken shall be designed to minimize disruption of the organization and the risk of revealing information relating to the representation to persons outside the organization. Such measures may include among others:

(1) asking reconsideration of the matter;

(2) advising that a separate legal opinion on the matter be sought for presentation to appropriate authority in the organization; and

(3) referring the matter to higher authority in the organization, including, if warranted by the seriousness of the matter, referral to the highest authority that can act in behalf of the organization as determined by applicable law.

(c) When the organization's highest authority insists upon action, or refuses to take action, that is clearly a violation of a legal obligation to the organization, or a violation of law which reasonably might be imputed to the organization, and is likely to result in substantial injury to the organization, the lawyer may take further remedial action that the lawyer reasonably believes to be in the best interest of organization. Such action may include revealing information otherwise protected by Rule 1.6 only if the lawyer reasonably believes that:

(1) the highest authority in the organization has acted to further the personal or financial interests of members of that authority which are in conflict with the interest of the organization; and

(2) revealing the information is necessary in the best interest of the organization.

(d) In dealing with an organization's directors, officers, employees, members, shareholders or other constituents, a lawyer shall explain the identity of the client when the lawyer believes that such explanation is necessary to avoid misunderstandings on their part.

(e) A lawyer representing an organization may also represent any of its directors, officers, employees, members, shareholders or other constituents, subject to the provisions of Rule 1.7. If the organization's consent to the dual representation is required by Rule 1.7, the consent shall be given by an appropriate official of the organization other than the individual who is to be represented or by the shareholders.

ably necessary in the best interest of the organization. In determining how to proceed, the lawyer shall give due consideration to the seriousness of the violation and its consequences, the scope and nature of the lawyer's representation, the responsibility in the organization and the apparent motivation of the person involved, the policies of the organization concerning such matters and any other relevant considerations. Any measures taken shall be designed to minimize disruption of the organization and the risk of revealing information relating to the representation to persons outside the organization. Such measures may include among others:

(1) asking reconsideration of the matter;

(2) advising that a separate legal opinion on the matter be sought for presentation to appropriate authority in the organization; and

(3) referring the matter to higher authority in the organization, including, if warranted by the seriousness of the matter, referral to the highest authority that can act in behalf of the organization as determined by applicable law.

(c) If, despite the lawyer's efforts in accordance with paragraph (b), the highest authority that can act on behalf of the organization insists upon action, or a refusal to act, that is clearly a violation of law and is likely to result in substantial injury to the organization, the lawyer may resign in accordance with rule 1.16.

(d) In dealing with an organization's directors, officers, employees, members, shareholders or other constituents, a lawyer shall explain the identity of the client when it is apparent that the organization's interests are adverse to those of the constituents with whom the lawyer is dealing.

(e) A lawyer representing an organization may also represent any of its directors, officers, employees, members, shareholders or other constituents, subject to the provisions of Rule 1.7. If the organization's consent to the dual representation is required by Rule 1.7, the consent shall be given by an appropriate official of the organization other than the individual who is to be represented, or by the shareholders.

COMMENT:

The Entity as the Client

[1]   An organizational client is a legal entity, but it cannot act except through its officers, directors, employees, shareholders and other constituents. Officers, directors, employees and shareholders are the constituents of the corporate organizational client. The duties defined in this Comment apply equally to unincorporated associations. "Other constituents" as used in this Comment means the positions equivalent to officers, directors, employees and shareholders held by persons acting for organizational clients that are not corporations.

[2]   When one of the constituents of an organizational client communicates with the organization's lawyer in that person's organizational capacity, the communication is protected by Rule 1.6. Thus, by way of example, if an organizational client requests its lawyer to investigate allegations of wrongdoing, interviews made in the course of that investigation between the lawyer and the client's employees or other constituents are covered by Rule 1.6. This does not mean, however, that constituents of an organizational client are the clients of the lawyer. The lawyer may not disclose to

such constituents information relating to the representation except for disclosures explicitly or impliedly authorized by the organizational client in order to carry out the representation or as otherwise permitted by Rule 1.6.

[3] When constituents of the organization make decisions for it, the decisions ordinarily must be accepted by the lawyer even if their utility or prudence is doubtful. Decisions concerning policy and operations, including ones entailing serious risk, are not as such in the lawyer's province. However, different considerations arise when the lawyer knows that the organization may be substantially injured by action of [a] constituent that is in violation of law. In such a circumstance, it may be reasonably necessary for the lawyer to ask the constituent to reconsider the matter. If that fails, or if the matter is of sufficient seriousness and importance to the organization, it may be reasonably necessary for the lawyer to take steps to have the matter reviewed by a higher authority in the organization. Clear justification should exist for seeking review over the head of the constituent normally responsible for it. The stated policy of the organization may define circumstances and prescribe channels for such review, and a lawyer should encourage the formulation of such a policy. Even in the absence of organization policy, however, the lawyer may have an obligation to refer a matter to higher authority, depending on the seriousness of the matter and whether the constituent in question has apparent motives to act at variance with the organization's interest. Review by the chief executive officer or by the board of directors may be required when the matter is of importance commensurate with their authority. At some point it may be useful or essential to obtain an independent legal opinion.

[4] In an extreme case, it may be reasonably necessary for the lawyer to refer the matter to the organization's highest authority. Ordinarily, that is the board of directors or similar governing body. However, applicable law may prescribe that under certain conditions highest authority reposes elsewhere; for example, in the independent directors of a corporation.

Relation to Other Rules

[5] The authority and responsibility provided in paragraph (b) are concurrent with the authority and responsibility provided in other Rules. In particular, this Rule does not limit or expand the lawyer's responsibility under Rules 1.6, 1.8, and 1.16, 3.3 or 4.1. If the lawyer's services are being used by an organization to further a crime or fraud by the organization, Rule 1.2(d) can be applicable.

Government Agency

[6] The duty defined in this Rule applies to governmental organizations. However, when the client is a governmental organization, a different balance may be appropriate between maintaining confidentiality and assuring that the wrongful official act is prevented or rectified, for public business is involved. In addition, duties of lawyers employed by the government or lawyers in military service may be defined by statutes and regulation. Therefore, defining precisely the identity of the client and prescribing the resulting obligations of such lawyers may be more difficult in the government context. Although in some circumstances the client may be a specific agency, it is generally the government as a whole. For example, if the action or failure to act involves the head of a bureau, either the department of which the bureau is a part or the government as a whole may be the client for purpose of this Rule. Moreover, in a matter involving the conduct of government officials, a government lawyer may have authority to question such conduct more extensively than that of a

lawyer for a private organization in similar circumstances. This Rule does not limit that authority. See note on Scope.

Clarifying the Lawyer's Role

[7] There are times when the organization's interest may be or become adverse to those of one or more of its constituents. In such circumstances the lawyer should advise any constituent, whose interest the lawyer finds adverse to that of the organization of the conflict or potential conflict of interest, that the lawyer cannot represent such constituent, and that such person may wish to obtain independent representation. Care must be taken to assure that the individual understands that, when there is such adversity of interest, the lawyer for the organization cannot provide legal representation for that constituent individual, and that discussions between the lawyer for the organization and the individual may not be privileged.

[8] Whether such a warning should be given by the lawyer for the organization to any constituent individual may turn on the facts of each case.

Dual Representation

[9] Paragraph (e) recognizes that a lawyer for an organization may also represent a principal officer or major shareholder.

Derivative Actions

[10] Under generally prevailing law, the shareholders or members of a corporation may bring suit to compel the directors to perform their legal obligations in the supervision of the organization. Members of unincorporated associations have essentially the same right. Such an action may be brought nominally by the organization, but usually is, in fact, a legal controversy over management of the organization.

[11] The question can arise whether counsel for the organization may defend such an action. The proposition that the organization is the lawyer's client does not alone resolve the issue. Most derivative actions are a normal incident of an organization's affairs, to be defended by the organization's lawyer like any other suit. However, if the claim involves serious charges of wrongdoing by those in control of the organization, a conflict may arise between the lawyer's duty to the organization and the lawyer's relationship with the board. In those circumstances, Rule 1.7 governs who should represent the directors and the organization.

MODEL CODE COMPARISON

There was no counterpart to this Rule in the Disciplinary Rules of the Model Code. EC 5–18 stated that "a lawyer employed or retained by a corporation or similar entity owes his allegiance to the entity and not to a stockholder, director, officer, employee, representative, or other person connected with the entity. In advising the entity, a lawyer should keep paramount its interests and his professional judgment should not be influenced by the personal desires of any person or organization. Occasionally, a lawyer for an entity is requested by a stockholder, director, officer, employee, representative, or other person connected with the entity to represent him in an individual capacity; in such case the lawyer may serve the individual only if the lawyer is convinced that differing interests are not present." EC 5–24 stated that although a lawyer "may be employed by a business corporation with non-lawyers serving as directors or officers, and they necessarily have the right to make decisions of business policy, a lawyer must decline to accept direction of his professional judgment from any layman." DR 5–107(B) provided that a lawyer "shall not permit a person who ... employs ... him to render legal services for another to direct or regulate his professional judgment in rendering such legal services."

RULE 1.14   Client Under a Disability

(a) When a client's ability to make adequately considered decisions in connection with the representation is impaired, whether because of minority, mental disability or for some other reason, the lawyer shall, as far as reasonably possible, maintain a normal client–lawyer relationship with the client.

(b) A lawyer may seek the appointment of a guardian or take other protective action with respect to a client, only when the lawyer reasonably believes that the client cannot adequately act in the client's own interest.

COMMENT:

[1]   The normal client-lawyer relationship is based on the assumption that the client, when properly advised and assisted, is capable of making decisions about important matters. When the client is a minor or suffers from a mental disorder or disability, however, maintaining the ordinary client-lawyer relationship may not be possible in all respects. In particular, an incapacitated person may have no power to make legally binding decisions. Nevertheless, a client lacking legal competence often has the ability to understand, deliberate upon, and reach conclusions about matters affecting the client's own well-being. Furthermore, to an increasing extent the law recognizes intermediate degrees of competence. For example, children as young as five or six years of age, and certainly those of ten or twelve, are regarded as having opinions that are entitled to weight in legal proceedings concerning their custody. So also, it is recognized that some persons of advanced age can be quite capable of handling routine financial matters while needing special legal protection concerning major transactions.

[2]   The fact that a client suffers a disability does not diminish the lawyer's obligation to treat the client with attention and respect. If the person has no guardian or legal representative, the lawyer often must act as de facto guardian. Even if the person does have a legal representative, the lawyer should as far as possible accord the represented person the status of client, particularly in maintaining communication.

[3]   If a legal representative has already been appointed for the client, the lawyer should ordinarily look to the representative for decisions on behalf of the client. If a legal representative has not been appointed, the lawyer should see to such an appointment where it would serve the client's best interests. Thus, if a disabled client has substantial property that should be sold for the client's benefit, effective completion of the transaction ordinarily requires appointment of a legal representative. In many circumstances, however, appointment of a legal representative may be expensive or traumatic for the client. Evaluation of these considerations is a matter of professional judgment on the lawyer's part.

[4]   If the lawyer represents the guardian as distinct from the ward, and is aware that the guardian is acting adversely to the ward's interest, the lawyer may have an obligation to prevent or rectify the guardian's misconduct. See Rule 1.2(d).

Disclosure of the Client's Condition

[5] Rules of procedure in litigation generally provide that minors or persons suffering mental disability shall be represented by a guardian or next friend if they do not have a general guardian. However, disclosure of the client's disability can adversely affect the client's interests. For example, raising the question of disability could, in some circumstances, lead to proceedings for involuntary commitment. The lawyer's position in such cases is an unavoidably difficult one. The lawyer may seek guidance from an appropriate diagnostician.

Emergency Legal Assistance

[6] In an emergency where the health, safety or a financial interest of a person under a disability is threatened with imminent and irreparable harm, a lawyer may take legal action on behalf of such a person even though the person is unable to establish a client-lawyer relationship or to make or express considered judgments about the matter, when the disabled person or another acting in good faith on that person's behalf has consulted the lawyer. Even in such an emergency, however, the lawyer should not act unless the lawyer reasonably believes that the person has no other lawyer, agent or other representative available. The lawyer should take legal action on behalf of the disabled person only to the extent reasonably necessary to maintain the status quo or otherwise avoid imminent and irreparable harm. A lawyer who undertakes to represent a person in such an exigent situation has the same duties under these Rules as the lawyer would with respect to a client.

[7] A lawyer who acts on behalf of a disabled person in an emergency should keep the confidences of the disabled person as if dealing with a client, disclosing them only to the extent necessary to accomplish the intended protective action. The lawyer should disclose to any tribunal involved and to any other counsel involved the nature of his or her relationship with the disabled person. The lawyer should take steps to regularize the relationship or implement other protective solutions as soon as possible. Normally, a lawyer would not seek compensation for such emergency actions taken on behalf of a disabled person.

MODEL CODE COMPARISON

There was no counterpart to this Rule in the Disciplinary Rules of the Model Code. EC 7–11 stated that the "responsibilities of a lawyer may vary according to the intelligence, experience, mental condition or age of a client. . . . Examples include the representation of an illiterate or an incompetent." EC 7–12 stated that "[a]ny mental or physical condition of a client that renders him incapable of making a considered judgment on his own behalf casts additional responsibilities upon his lawyer. Where an incompetent is acting through a guardian or other legal representative, a lawyer must look to such representative for those decisions which are normally the prerogative of the client to make. If a client under disability has no legal representative, his lawyer may be compelled in court proceedings to make decisions on behalf of the client. If the client is capable of understanding the matter in question or of contributing to the advancement of his interests, regardless of whether he is legally disqualified from performing certain acts, the lawyer should obtain from him all possible aid. If the disability of a client and the lack of a legal representative compel the lawyer to make decisions for his client, the lawyer should consider all circumstances then prevailing and act with care to safeguard and advance the interests of his client. But obviously a lawyer cannot perform any act or make any decision which the law requires his client to perform or make, either acting for himself if competent, or by a duly constituted representative if legally incompetent."

RULE 1.15   Safekeeping Property

(a) **A lawyer shall hold property of clients or third persons that is in a lawyer's possession in connection with a representation separate from the lawyer's own property. Funds shall be kept in a separate account maintained in the state where the lawyer's office is situated, or elsewhere with the consent of the client or third person. Other property shall be identified as such and appropriately safeguarded. Complete records of such account funds and other property shall be kept by the lawyer and shall be preserved for a period of [five years] after termination of the representation.**

(b) **Upon receiving funds or other property in which a client or third person has an interest, a lawyer shall promptly notify the client or third person. Except as stated in this rule or otherwise permitted by law or by agreement with the client, a lawyer shall promptly deliver to the client or third person any funds or other property that the client or third person is entitled to receive and, upon request by the client or third person, shall promptly render a full accounting regarding such property.**

(c) **When in the course of representation a lawyer is in possession of property in which both the lawyer and another person claim interests, the property shall be kept separate by the lawyer until there is an accounting and severance of their interests. If a dispute arises concerning their respective interests, the portion in dispute shall be kept separate by the lawyer until the dispute is resolved.**

COMMENT:

[1]   A lawyer should hold property of others with the care required of a professional fiduciary. Securities should be kept in a safe deposit box, except when some other form of safekeeping is warranted by special circumstances. All property which is the property of clients or third persons should be kept separate from the lawyer's business and personal property and, if monies, in one or more trust accounts. Separate trust accounts may be warranted when administering estate monies or acting in similar fiduciary capacities.

[2]   Lawyers often receive funds from third parties from which the lawyer's fee will be paid. If there is risk that the client may divert the funds without paying the fee, the lawyer is not required to remit the portion from which the fee is to be paid. However, a lawyer may not hold funds to coerce a client into accepting the lawyer's contention. The disputed portion of the funds should be kept in trust and the lawyer should suggest means for prompt resolution of the dispute, such as arbitration. The undisputed portion of the funds shall be promptly distributed.

[3]   Third parties, such as a client's creditors, may have just claims against funds or other property in a lawyer's custody. A lawyer may have a duty under applicable law to protect such third-party claims against wrongful interference by the client, and accordingly may refuse to surrender the property to the client. However, a lawyer should not unilaterally assume to arbitrate a dispute between the client and the third party.

[4]   The obligations of a lawyer under this Rule are independent of those arising from activity other than rendering legal services. For example, a lawyer who serves as

an escrow agent is governed by the applicable law relating to fiduciaries even though the lawyer does not render legal services in the transaction.

[5]   A "client's security fund" provides a means through the collective efforts of the bar to reimburse persons who have lost money or property as a result of dishonest conduct of a lawyer. Where such a fund has been established, a lawyer should participate.

MODEL CODE COMPARISON

[1]   With regard to paragraph (a), DR 9–102(A) provided that "funds of clients" are to be kept in an identifiable bank account in the state in which the lawyer's office is situated.   DR 9–102(B)(2) provided that a lawyer shall "identify and label securities and properties of a client ... and place them in ... safekeeping...."   DR 9–102(B)(3) required that a lawyer "[m]aintain complete records of all funds, securities, and other properties of a client...."   Rule 1.15(a) extends these requirements to property of a third person that is in the lawyer's possession in connection with the representation.

[2]   Paragraph (b) is substantially similar to DR 9–102(B)(1), (3) and (4).

[3]   Paragraph (c) is similar to DR 9–102(A)(2), except that the requirement concerning disputes applies to property concerning which an interest is claimed by a third person as well as by a client.

RULE 1.16   Declining or Terminating Representation

(a) Except as stated in paragraph (c), a lawyer shall not represent a client or, where representation has commenced, shall withdraw from the representation of a client if:

(1) the representation will result in violation of the rules of professional conduct or other law;

(2) the lawyer's physical or mental condition materially impairs the lawyer's ability to represent the client; or

(3) the lawyer is discharged.

(b) Except as stated in paragraph (c), a lawyer may withdraw from representing a client if withdrawal can be accomplished without material adverse effect on the interests of the client, or if:

(1) the client persists in a course of action involving the lawyer's services that the lawyer reasonably believes is criminal or fraudulent;

(2) the client has used the lawyer's services to perpetrate a crime or fraud;

(3) a client insists upon pursuing an objective that the lawyer considers repugnant or imprudent;

(4) the client fails substantially to fulfill an obligation to the lawyer regarding the lawyer's services and has been given reasonable warning that the lawyer will withdraw unless the obligation is fulfilled;

(5) the representation will result in an unreasonable financial burden on the lawyer or has been rendered unreasonably difficult by the client; or

(6) other good cause for withdrawal exists.

(c) When ordered to do so by a tribunal, a lawyer shall continue representation notwithstanding good cause for terminating the representation.

(d) Upon termination of representation, a lawyer shall take steps to the extent reasonably practicable to protect a client's interests, such as giving reasonable notice to the client, allowing time for employment of other counsel, surrendering papers and property to which the client is entitled and refunding any advance payment of fee that has not been earned. The lawyer may retain papers relating to the client to the extent permitted by other law.

COMMENT:

[1] A lawyer should not accept representation in a matter unless it can be performed competently, promptly, without improper conflict of interest and to completion.

Mandatory Withdrawal

[2] A lawyer ordinarily must decline or withdraw from representation if the client demands that the lawyer engage in conduct that is illegal or violates the Rules of Professional Conduct or other law. The lawyer is not obliged to decline or withdraw simply because the client suggests such a course of conduct; a client may make such a suggestion in the hope that a lawyer will not be constrained by a professional obligation.

[3] When a lawyer has been appointed to represent a client, withdrawal ordinarily requires approval of the appointing authority. See also Rule 6.2. Difficulty may be encountered if withdrawal is based on the client's demand that the lawyer engage in unprofessional conduct. The court may wish an explanation for the withdrawal, while the lawyer may be bound to keep confidential the facts that would constitute such an explanation. The lawyer's statement that professional considerations require termination of the representation ordinarily should be accepted as sufficient.

Discharge

[4] A client has a right to discharge a lawyer at any time, with or without cause, subject to liability for payment for the lawyer's services. Where future dispute about the withdrawal may be anticipated, it may be advisable to prepare a written statement reciting the circumstances.

[5] Whether a client can discharge appointed counsel may depend on applicable law. A client seeking to do so should be given a full explanation of the consequences. These consequences may include a decision by the appointing authority that appointment of successor counsel is unjustified, thus requiring self-representation by the client.

[6] If the client is mentally incompetent, the client may lack the legal capacity to discharge the lawyer, and in any event the discharge may be seriously adverse to the client's interests. The lawyer should make special effort to help the client consider the consequences and, in an extreme case, may initiate proceedings for a conservatorship or similar protection of the client. See Rule 1.14.

Optional Withdrawal

[7] A lawyer may withdraw from representation in some circumstances. The lawyer has the option to withdraw if it can be accomplished without material adverse effect on the client's interests. Withdrawal is also justified if the client persists in a

course of action that the lawyer reasonably believes is criminal or fraudulent, for a lawyer is not required to be associated with such conduct even if the lawyer does not further it. Withdrawal is also permitted if the lawyer's services were misused in the past even if that would materially prejudice the client. The lawyer also may withdraw where the client insists on a repugnant or imprudent objective.

[8] A lawyer may withdraw if the client refuses to abide by the terms of an agreement relating to the representation, such as an agreement concerning fees or court costs or an agreement limiting the objectives of the representation.

Assisting the Client Upon Withdrawal

[9] Even if the lawyer has been unfairly discharged by the client, a lawyer must take all reasonable steps to mitigate the consequences to the client. The lawyer may retain papers as security for a fee only to the extent permitted by law. Whether or not a lawyer for an organization may under certain unusual circumstances have a legal obligation to the organization after withdrawing or being discharged by the organization's highest authority is beyond the scope of these Rules.

MODEL CODE COMPARISON

[1] With regard to paragraph (a), DR 2–109(A) provided that a lawyer "shall not accept employment ... if he knows or it is obvious that [the prospective client] wishes to ... [b]ring a legal action ... or otherwise have steps taken for him, merely for the purpose of harassing or maliciously injuring any person...." Nor may a lawyer accept employment if the lawyer is aware that the prospective client wishes to "[p]resent a claim or defense ... that is not warranted under existing law, unless it can be supported by good faith argument for an extension, modification, or reversal of existing law." DR 2–110(B) provided that a lawyer "shall withdraw from employment ... if:

"(1) He knows or it is obvious that his client is bringing the legal action ... or is otherwise having steps taken for him, merely for the purpose of harassing or maliciously injuring any person.

"(2) He knows or it is obvious that his continued employment will result in violation of a Disciplinary Rule.

"(3) His mental or physical condition renders it unreasonably difficult for him to carry out the employment effectively.

"(4) He is discharged by his client."

[2] With regard to paragraph (b), DR 2–110(C) permitted withdrawal regardless of the effect on the client if:

"(1) His client: (a) Insists upon presenting a claim or defense that is not warranted under existing law and cannot be supported by good faith argument for an extension, modification, or reversal of existing law; (b) Personally seeks to pursue an illegal course of conduct; (c) Insists that the lawyer pursue a course of conduct that is illegal or that is prohibited under the Disciplinary Rules; (d) By other conduct renders it unreasonably difficult for the lawyer to carry out his employment effectively; (e) Insists, in a matter not pending before a tribunal, that the lawyer engage in conduct that is contrary to the judgment and advice of the lawyer but not prohibited under the Disciplinary Rules; (f) Deliberately disregards an agreement or obligation to the lawyer as to expenses and fees.

"(2) His continued employment is likely to result in a violation of a Disciplinary Rule.

"(3) His inability to work with co-counsel indicates that the best interest of the client likely will be served by withdrawal.

"(4) His mental or physical condition renders it difficult for him to carry out the employment effectively.

"(5) His client knowingly and freely assents to termination of his employment.

"(6) He believes in good faith, in a proceeding pending before a tribunal, that the tribunal will find the existence of other good cause for withdrawal."

[3] With regard to paragraph (c), DR 2–110(A)(1) provided: "If permission for withdrawal from employment is required by the rules of a tribunal, the lawyer shall not withdraw ... without its permission."

[4] The provisions of paragraph (d) are substantially identical to DR 2–110(A)(2) and (3).

RULE 1.17   Sale of Law Practice

A lawyer or a law firm may sell or purchase a law practice, including good will, if the following conditions are satisfied:

(a) The seller ceases to engage in the private practice of law [in the geographic area] [in the jurisdiction] (a jurisdiction may elect either version) in which the practice has been conducted;

(b) The practice is sold as an entirety to another lawyer or law firm;

(c) Actual written notice is given to each of the seller's clients regarding:

(1) the proposed sale;

(2) the terms of any proposed change in the fee arrangement authorized by paragraph (d);

(3) the client's right to retain other counsel or to take possession of the file; and

(4) the fact that the client's consent to the sale will be presumed if the client does not take any action or does not otherwise object within ninety (90) days of receipt of the notice.

If a client cannot be given notice, the representation of that client may be transferred to the purchaser only upon entry of an order so authorizing by a court having jurisdiction. The seller may disclose to the court in camera information relating to the representation only to the extent necessary to obtain an order authorizing the transfer of a file.

(d) The fees charged clients shall not be increased by reason of the sale. The purchaser may, however, refuse to undertake the representation unless the client consents to pay the purchaser fees at a rate not exceeding the fees charged by the purchaser for rendering substantially similar services prior to the initiation of the purchase negotiations.

COMMENT:

[1] The practice of law is a profession, not merely a business. Clients are not commodities that can be purchased and sold at will. Pursuant to this Rule, when a

lawyer or an entire firm ceases to practice and another lawyer or firm takes over the representation, the selling lawyer or firm may obtain compensation for the reasonable value of the practice as may withdrawing partners of law firms. See Rules 5.4 and 5.6.

Termination of Practice by the Seller

[2] The requirement that all of the private practice be sold is satisfied if the seller in good faith makes the entire practice available for sale to the purchaser. The fact that a number of the seller's clients decide not to be represented by the purchaser but take their matters elsewhere, therefore, does not result in a violation. Neither does a return to private practice as a result of an unanticipated change in circumstances result in a violation. For example, a lawyer who has sold the practice to accept an appointment to judicial office does not violate the requirement that the sale be attendant to cessation of practice if the lawyer later resumes private practice upon being defeated in a contested or a retention election for the office.

[3] The requirement that the seller cease to engage in the private practice of law does not prohibit employment as a lawyer on the staff of a public agency or a legal services entity which provides legal services to the poor, or as in-house counsel to a business.

[4] The Rule permits a sale attendant upon retirement from the private practice of law within the jurisdiction. Its provisions, therefore, accommodate the lawyer who sells the practice upon the occasion of moving to another state. Some states are so large that a move from one locale therein to another is tantamount to leaving the jurisdiction in which the lawyer has engaged in the practice of law. To also accommodate lawyers so situated, states may permit the sale of the practice when the lawyer leaves the geographic area rather than the jurisdiction. The alternative desired should be indicated by selecting one of the two provided for in Rule 1.17(a).

Single Purchaser

[5] The Rule requires a single purchaser. The prohibition against piecemeal sale of a practice protects those clients whose matters are less lucrative and who might find it difficult to secure other counsel if a sale could be limited to substantial fee-generating matters. The purchaser is required to undertake all client matters in the practice, subject to client consent. If, however, the purchaser is unable to undertake all client matters because of a conflict of interest in a specific matter respecting which the purchaser is not permitted by Rule 1.7 or another rule to represent the client, the requirement that there be a single purchaser is nevertheless satisfied.

Client Confidences, Consent and Notice

[6] Negotiations between seller and prospective purchaser prior to disclosure of information relating to a specific representation of an identifiable client no more violate the confidentiality provisions of Model Rule 1.6 than do preliminary discussions concerning the possible association of another lawyer or mergers between firms, with respect to which client consent is not required. Providing the purchaser access to client-specific information relating to the representation and to the file, however, requires client consent. The Rule provides that before such information can be disclosed by the seller to the purchaser the client must be given actual written notice of the contemplated sale, including the identity of the purchaser and any proposed change in the terms of future representation, and must be told that the decision to consent or make other arrangements must be made within 90 days. If nothing is heard from the client within that time, consent to the sale is presumed.

227

[7]   A lawyer or law firm ceasing to practice cannot be required to remain in practice because some clients cannot be given actual notice of the proposed purchase. Since these clients cannot themselves consent to the purchase or direct any other disposition of their files, the Rule requires an order from a court having jurisdiction authorizing their transfer or other disposition. The Court can be expected to determine whether reasonable efforts to locate the client have been exhausted, and whether the absent client's legitimate interests will be served by authorizing the transfer of the file so that the purchaser may continue the representation. Preservation of client confidences requires that the petition for a court order be considered in camera. (A procedure by which such an order can be obtained needs to be established in jurisdictions in which it presently does not exist.)

[8]   All the elements of client autonomy, including the client's absolute right to discharge a lawyer and transfer the representation to another, survive the sale of the practice.

Fee Arrangements Between Client and Purchaser

[9]   The sale may not be financed by increases in fees charged the clients of the practice. Existing agreements between the seller and the client as to fees and the scope of the work must be honored by the purchaser, unless the client consents after consultation. The purchaser may, however, advise the client that the purchaser will not undertake the representation unless the client consents to pay the higher fees the purchaser usually charges. To prevent client financing of the sale, the higher fee the purchaser may charge must not exceed the fees charged by the purchaser for substantially similar service rendered prior to the initiation of the purchase negotiations.

[10]   The purchaser may not intentionally fragment the practice which is the subject of the sale by charging significantly different fees in substantially similar matters. Doing so would make it possible for the purchaser to avoid the obligation to take over the entire practice by charging arbitrarily higher fees for less lucrative matters, thereby increasing the likelihood that those clients would not consent to the new representation.

Other Applicable Ethical Standards

[11]   Lawyers participating in the sale of a law practice are subject to the ethical standards applicable to involving another lawyer in the representation of a client. These include, for example, the seller's obligation to exercise competence in identifying a purchaser qualified to assume the practice and the purchaser's obligation to undertake the representation competently (see Rule 1.1); the obligation to avoid disqualifying conflicts, and to secure client consent after consultation for those conflicts which can be agreed to (see Rule 1.7); and the obligation to protect information relating to the representation (see Rules 1.6 and 1.9).

[12]   If approval of the substitution of the purchasing attorney for the selling attorney is required by the rules of any tribunal in which a matter is pending, such approval must be obtained before the matter can be included in the sale (see Rule 1.16).

Applicability of the Rule

[13]   This Rule applies to the sale of a law practice by representatives of a deceased, disabled or disappeared lawyer. Thus, the seller may be represented by a non-lawyer representative not subject to these Rules. Since, however, no lawyer may

participate in a sale of a law practice which does not conform to the requirements of this Rule, the representatives of the seller as well as the purchasing lawyer can be expected to see to it that they are met.

[14] Admission to or retirement from a law partnership or professional association, retirement plans and similar arrangements, and a sale of tangible assets of a law practice, do not constitute a sale or purchase governed by this Rule.

[15] This Rule does not apply to the transfers of legal representation between lawyers when such transfers are unrelated to the sale of a practice.

MODEL CODE COMPARISON

There was no counterpart to this Rule in the Model Code.

COUNSELOR

RULE 2.1   Advisor

In representing a client, a lawyer shall exercise independent professional judgment and render candid advice. In rendering advice, a lawyer may refer not only to law but to other considerations such as moral, economic, social and political factors, that may be relevant to the client's situation.

COMMENT:

Scope of Advice

[1] A client is entitled to straightforward advice expressing the lawyer's honest assessment. Legal advice often involves unpleasant facts and alternatives that a client may be disinclined to confront. In presenting advice, a lawyer endeavors to sustain the client's morale and may put advice in as acceptable a form as honesty permits. However, a lawyer should not be deterred from giving candid advice by the prospect that the advice will be unpalatable to the client.

[2] Advice couched in narrowly legal terms may be of little value to a client, especially where practical considerations, such as cost or effects on other people, are predominant. Purely technical legal advice, therefore, can sometimes be inadequate. It is proper for a lawyer to refer to relevant moral and ethical considerations in giving advice. Although a lawyer is not a moral advisor as such, moral and ethical considerations impinge upon most legal questions and may decisively influence how the law will be applied.

[3] A client may expressly or impliedly ask the lawyer for purely technical advice. When such a request is made by a client experienced in legal matters, the lawyer may accept it at face value. When such a request is made by a client inexperienced in legal matters, however, the lawyer's responsibility as advisor may include indicating that more may be involved than strictly legal considerations.

[4] Matters that go beyond strictly legal questions may also be in the domain of another profession. Family matters can involve problems within the professional competence of psychiatry, clinical psychology or social work; business matters can involve problems within the competence of the accounting profession or of financial specialists. Where consultation with a professional in another field is itself something a competent lawyer would recommend, the lawyer should make such a recommendation. At the same time, a lawyer's advice at its best often consists of recommending a course of action in the face of conflicting recommendations of experts.

229

Offering Advice

[5]   In general, a lawyer is not expected to give advice until asked by the client. However, when a lawyer knows that a client proposes a course of action that is likely to result in substantial adverse legal consequences to the client, duty to the client under Rule 1.4 may require that the lawyer act if the client's course of action is related to the representation.   A lawyer ordinarily has no duty to initiate investigation of a client's affairs or to give advice that the client has indicated is unwanted, but a lawyer may initiate advice to a client when doing so appears to be in the client's interest.

MODEL CODE COMPARISON

There was no direct counterpart to this Rule in the Disciplinary Rules of the Model Code.   DR 5–107(B) provided that a lawyer "shall not permit a person who recommends, employs, or pays him to render legal services for another to direct or regulate his professional judgment in rendering such legal services."   EC 7–8 stated that "[a]dvice of a lawyer to his client need not be confined to purely legal consider-ations. . . .   In assisting his client to reach a proper decision, it is often desirable for a lawyer to point out those factors which may lead to a decision that is morally just as well as legally permissible. . . .   In the final analysis, however, . . . the decision whether to forego legally available objectives or methods because of nonlegal factors is ultimately for the client. . . ."

RULE 2.2   Intermediary

(a) **A lawyer may act as intermediary between clients if:**

(1) **the lawyer consults with each client concerning the implications of the common representation, including the advantages and risks in-volved, and the effect on the attorney–client privileges, and obtains each client's consent to the common representation;**

(2) **the lawyer reasonably believes that the matter can be resolved on terms compatible with the clients' best interests, that each client will be able to make adequately informed decisions in the matter and that there is little risk of material prejudice to the interest of any of the clients if the contemplated resolution is unsuccessful;   and**

(3) **the lawyer reasonably believes that the common representation can be undertaken impartially and without improper effect on other responsibilities the lawyer has to any of the clients.**

(b) **While acting as intermediary, the lawyer shall consult with each client concerning the decisions to be made and the considerations relevant in making them, so that each client can make adequately informed decisions.**

(c) **A lawyer shall withdraw as intermediary if any of the clients so requests, or if any of the conditions stated in paragraph (a) is no longer satisfied.   Upon withdrawal, the lawyer shall not continue to represent any of the clients in the matter that was the subject of the intermediation.**

COMMENT:

[1]   A lawyer acts as intermediary under this Rule when the lawyer represents two or more parties with potentially conflicting interests.   A key factor in defining the relationship is whether the parties share responsibility for the lawyer's fee, but the common representation may be inferred from other circumstances.   Because confusion

can arise as to the lawyer's role where each party is not separately represented, it is important that the lawyer make clear the relationship.

[2]   The Rule does not apply to a lawyer acting as arbitrator or mediator between or among parties who are not clients of the lawyer, even where the lawyer has been appointed with the concurrence of the parties. In performing such a role the lawyer may be subject to applicable codes of ethics, such as the Code of Ethics for Arbitration in Commercial Disputes prepared by a joint Committee of the American Bar Association and the American Arbitration Association.

[3]   A lawyer acts as intermediary in seeking to establish or adjust a relationship between clients on an amicable and mutually advantageous basis; for example, in helping to organize a business in which two or more clients are entrepreneurs, working out the financial reorganization of an enterprise in which two or more clients have an interest, arranging a property distribution in settlement of an estate or mediating a dispute between clients. The lawyer seeks to resolve potentially conflicting interests by developing the parties' mutual interests. The alternative can be that each party may have to obtain separate representation, with the possibility in some situations of incurring additional cost, complication or even litigation. Given these and other relevant factors, all the clients may prefer that the lawyer act as intermediary.

[4]   In considering whether to act as intermediary between clients, a lawyer should be mindful that if the intermediation fails the result can be additional cost, embarrassment and recrimination. In some situations the risk of failure is so great that intermediation is plainly impossible. For example, a lawyer cannot undertake common representation of clients between whom contentious litigation is imminent or who contemplate contentious negotiations. More generally, if the relationship between the parties has already assumed definite antagonism, the possibility that the clients' interests can be adjusted by intermediation ordinarily is not very good.

[5]   The appropriateness of intermediation can depend on its form. Forms of intermediation range from informal arbitration, where each client's case is presented by the respective client and the lawyer decides the outcome, to mediation, to common representation where the clients' interests are substantially though not entirely compatible. One form may be appropriate in circumstances where another would not. Other relevant factors are whether the lawyer subsequently will represent both parties on a continuing basis and whether the situation involves creating a relationship between the parties or terminating one.

Confidentiality and Privilege

[6]   A particularly important factor in determining the appropriateness of intermediation is the effect on client-lawyer confidentiality and the attorney-client privilege. In a common representation, the lawyer is still required both to keep each client adequately informed and to maintain confidentiality of information relating to the representation. See Rules 1.4 and 1.6. Complying with both requirements while acting as intermediary requires a delicate balance. If the balance cannot be maintained, the common representation is improper. With regard to the attorney-client privilege, the prevailing rule is that as between commonly represented clients the privilege does not attach. Hence, it must be assumed that if litigation eventuates between the clients, the privilege will not protect any such communications, and the clients should be so advised.

[7]   Since the lawyer is required to be impartial between commonly represented clients, intermediation is improper when that impartiality cannot be maintained. For

231

example, a lawyer who has represented one of the clients for a long period and in a variety of matters might have difficulty being impartial between that client and one to whom the lawyer has only recently been introduced.

Consultation

[8]   In acting as intermediary between clients, the lawyer is required to consult with the clients on the implications of doing so, and proceed only upon consent based on such a consultation. The consultation should make clear that the lawyer's role is not that of partisanship normally expected in other circumstances.

[9]   Paragraph (b) is an application of the principle expressed in Rule 1.4. Where the lawyer is intermediary, the clients ordinarily must assume greater responsibility for decisions than when each client is independently represented.

Withdrawal

[10]   Common representation does not diminish the rights of each client in the client-lawyer relationship. Each has the right to loyal and diligent representation, the right to discharge the lawyer as stated in Rule 1.16, and the protection of Rule 1.9 concerning obligations to a former client.

MODEL CODE COMPARISON

There was no direct counterpart to this Rule in the Disciplinary Rules of the Model Code. EC 5–20 stated that a "lawyer is often asked to serve as an impartial arbitrator or mediator in matters which involve present or former clients. He may serve in either capacity if he first discloses such present or former relationships." DR 5–105(B) provided that a lawyer "shall not continue multiple employment if the exercise of his independent judgment in behalf of a client will be or is likely to be adversely affected by his representation of another client, or if it would be likely to involve him in representation of differing interests, except to the extent permitted under DR 5–105(C)." DR 5–105(C) provided that "a lawyer may represent multiple clients if it is obvious that he can adequately represent the interests of each and if each consents to the representation after full disclosure of the possible effect of such representation on the exercise of his independent professional judgment on behalf of each."

RULE 2.3   Evaluation for Use by Third Persons

(a) A lawyer may undertake an evaluation of a matter affecting a client for the use of someone other than the client if:

(1) the lawyer reasonably believes that making the evaluation is compatible with other aspects of the lawyer's relationship with the client; and

(2) the client consents after consultation.

(b) Except as disclosure is required in connection with a report of an evaluation, information relating to the evaluation is otherwise protected by rule 1.6.

COMMENT:

Definition

[1] An evaluation may be performed at the client's direction but for the primary purpose of establishing information for the benefit of third parties; for example, an opinion concerning the title of property rendered at the behest of a vendor for the information of a prospective purchaser, or at the behest of a borrower for the information of a prospective lender. In some situations, the evaluation may be required by a government agency; for example, an opinion concerning the legality of the securities registered for sale under the securities laws. In other instances, the evaluation may be required by a third person, such as a purchaser of a business.

[2] Lawyers for the government may be called upon to give a formal opinion on the legality of contemplated government agency action. In making such an evaluation, the government lawyer acts at the behest of the government as the client but for the purpose of establishing the limits of the agency's authorized activity. Such an opinion is to be distinguished from confidential legal advice given agency officials. The critical question is whether the opinion is to be made public.

[3] A legal evaluation should be distinguished from an investigation of a person with whom the lawyer does not have a client-lawyer relationship. For example, a lawyer retained by a purchaser to analyze a vendor's title to property does not have a client-lawyer relationship with the vendor. So also, an investigation into a person's affairs by a government lawyer, or by special counsel employed by the government, is not an evaluation as that term is used in this Rule. The question is whether the lawyer is retained by the person whose affairs are being examined. When the lawyer is retained by that person, the general rules concerning loyalty to client and preservation of confidences apply, which is not the case if the lawyer is retained by someone else. For this reason, it is essential to identify the person by whom the lawyer is retained. This should be made clear not only to the person under examination, but also to others to whom the results are to be made available.

Duty to Third Person

[4] When the evaluation is intended for the information or use of a third person, a legal duty to that person may or may not arise. That legal question is beyond the scope of this Rule. However, since such an evaluation involves a departure from the normal client-lawyer relationship, careful analysis of the situation is required. The lawyer must be satisfied as a matter of professional judgment that making the evaluation is compatible with other functions undertaken in behalf of the client. For example, if the lawyer is acting as advocate in defending the client against charges of fraud, it would normally be incompatible with that responsibility for the lawyer to perform an evaluation for others concerning the same or a related transaction. Assuming no such impediment is apparent, however, the lawyer should advise the client of the implications of the evaluation, particularly the lawyer's responsibilities to third persons and the duty to disseminate the findings.

Access to and Disclosure of Information

[5] The quality of an evaluation depends on the freedom and extent of the investigation upon which it is based. Ordinarily a lawyer should have whatever latitude of investigation seems necessary as a matter of professional judgment. Under some circumstances, however, the terms of the evaluation may be limited. For example, certain issues or sources may be categorically excluded, or the scope of search

may be limited by time constraints or the noncooperation of persons having relevant information. Any such limitations which are material to the evaluation should be described in the report. If after a lawyer has commenced an evaluation, the client refuses to comply with the terms upon which it was understood the evaluation was to have been made, the lawyer's obligations are determined by law, having reference to the terms of the client's agreement and the surrounding circumstances.

Financial Auditors' Requests for Information

[6] When a question concerning the legal situation of a client arises at the instance of the client's financial auditor and the question is referred to the lawyer, the lawyer's response may be made in accordance with procedures recognized in the legal profession. Such a procedure is set forth in the American Bar Association Statement of Policy Regarding Lawyers' Responses to Auditors' Requests for Information, adopted in 1975.

MODEL CODE COMPARISON

There was no counterpart to this Rule in the Model Code.

ADVOCATE

RULE 3.1 Meritorious Claims and Contentions

A lawyer shall not bring or defend a proceeding, or assert or controvert an issue therein, unless there is a basis for doing so that is not frivolous, which includes a good faith argument for an extension, modification or reversal of existing law. A lawyer for the defendant in a criminal proceeding, or the respondent in a proceeding that could result in incarceration, may nevertheless so defend the proceeding as to require that every element of the case be established.

COMMENT:

[1] The advocate has a duty to use legal procedure for the fullest benefit of the client's cause, but also a duty not to abuse legal procedure. The law, both procedural and substantive, establishes the limits within which an advocate may proceed. However, the law is not always clear and never is static. Accordingly, in determining the proper scope of advocacy, account must be taken of the law's ambiguities and potential for change.

[2] The filing of an action or defense or similar action taken for a client is not frivolous merely because the facts have not first been fully substantiated or because the lawyer expects to develop vital evidence only by discovery. Such action is not frivolous even though the lawyer believes that the client's position ultimately will not prevail. The action is frivolous, however, if the client desires to have the action taken primarily for the purpose of harassing or maliciously injuring a person or if the lawyer is unable either to make a good faith argument on the merits of the action taken or to support the action taken by a good faith argument for an extension, modification or reversal of existing law.

MODEL CODE COMPARISON

DR 7–102(A)(1) provided that a lawyer may not "[f]ile a suit, assert a position, conduct a defense, delay a trial, or take other action on behalf of his client when he knows or when it is obvious that such action would serve merely to harass or maliciously injure another." Rule 3.1 is to the same general effect as DR 7–102(A)(1), with three qualifications. First, the test of improper conduct is changed from "merely to harass or maliciously injure another" to the requirement that there be a basis for the litigation measure involved that is "not frivolous." This includes the concept stated in DR 7–102(A)(2) that a lawyer may advance a claim or defense unwarranted by existing law if "it can be supported by good faith argument for an extension, modification, or reversal of existing law." Second, the test in Rule 3.1 is an objective test, whereas DR 7–102(A)(1) applied only if the lawyer "knows or when it is obvious" that the litigation is frivolous. Third, Rule 3.1 has an exception that in a criminal case, or a case in which incarceration of the client may result (for example, certain juvenile proceedings), the lawyer may put the prosecution to its proof even if there is no nonfrivolous basis for defense.

RULE 3.2 Expediting Litigation

A lawyer shall make reasonable efforts to expedite litigation consistent with the interests of the client.

COMMENT:

Dilatory practices bring the administration of justice into disrepute. Delay should not be indulged merely for the convenience of the advocates, or for the purpose of frustrating an opposing party's attempt to obtain rightful redress or repose. It is not a justification that similar conduct is often tolerated by the bench and bar. The question is whether a competent lawyer acting in good faith would regard the course of action as having some substantial purpose other than delay. Realizing financial or other benefit from otherwise improper delay in litigation is not a legitimate interest of the client.

MODEL CODE COMPARISON

DR 7–101(A)(1) stated that a lawyer does not violate the lawyer's duty to represent a client zealously "by being punctual in fulfilling all professional commitments." DR 7–102(A)(1) provided that a lawyer "shall not ... file a suit, assert a position, conduct a defense [or] delay a trial ... when he knows or when it is obvious that such action would serve merely to harass or maliciously injure another."

RULE 3.3 Candor Toward the Tribunal

(a) A lawyer shall not knowingly:

(1) make a false statement of material fact or law to a tribunal;

(2) fail to disclose a material fact to a tribunal when disclosure is necessary to avoid assisting a criminal or fraudulent act by the client;

(3) fail to disclose to the tribunal legal authority in the controlling jurisdiction known to the lawyer to be directly adverse to the position of the client and not disclosed by opposing counsel; or

(4) offer evidence that the lawyer knows to be false. If a lawyer has offered material evidence and comes to know of its falsity, the lawyer shall take reasonable remedial measures.

(b) The duties stated in paragraph (a) continue to the conclusion of the proceeding, and apply even if compliance requires disclosure of information otherwise protected by Rule 1.6.

(c) A lawyer may refuse to offer evidence that the lawyer reasonably believes is false.

(d) In an ex parte proceeding, a lawyer shall inform the tribunal of all material facts known to the lawyer which will enable the tribunal to make an informed decision, whether or not the facts are adverse.

COMMENT:

[1] The advocate's task is to present the client's case with persuasive force. Performance of that duty while maintaining confidences of the client is qualified by the advocate's duty of candor to the tribunal. However, an advocate does not vouch for the evidence submitted in a cause; the tribunal is responsible for assessing its probative value.

Representations by a Lawyer

[2] An advocate is responsible for pleadings and other documents prepared for litigation, but is usually not required to have personal knowledge of matters asserted therein, for litigation documents ordinarily present assertions by the client, or by someone on the client's behalf, and not assertions by the lawyer. Compare Rule 3.1. However, an assertion purporting to be on the lawyer's own knowledge, as in an affidavit by the lawyer or in a statement in open court, may properly be made only when the lawyer knows the assertion is true or believes it to be true on the basis of a reasonably diligent inquiry. There are circumstances where failure to make a disclosure is the equivalent of an affirmative misrepresentation. The obligation prescribed in Rule 1.2(d) not to counsel a client to commit or assist the client in committing a fraud applies in litigation. Regarding compliance with Rule 1.2(d), see the Comment to that Rule. See also the Comment to Rule 8.4(b).

Misleading Legal Argument

[3] Legal argument based on a knowingly false representation of law constitutes dishonesty toward the tribunal. A lawyer is not required to make a disinterested exposition of the law, but must recognize the existence of pertinent legal authorities. Furthermore, as stated in paragraph (a)(3), an advocate has a duty to disclose directly adverse authority in the controlling jurisdiction which has not been disclosed by the opposing party. The underlying concept is that legal argument is a discussion seeking to determine the legal premises properly applicable to the case.

False Evidence

[4] When evidence that a lawyer knows to be false is provided by a person who is not the client, the lawyer must refuse to offer it regardless of the client's wishes.

[5] When false evidence is offered by the client, however, a conflict may arise between the lawyer's duty to keep the client's revelations confidential and the duty of candor to the court. Upon ascertaining that material evidence is false, the lawyer should seek to persuade the client that the evidence should not be offered or, if it has been offered, that its false character should immediately be disclosed. If the persuasion is ineffective, the lawyer must take reasonable remedial measures.

[6] Except in the defense of a criminal accused, the rule generally recognized is that, if necessary to rectify the situation, an advocate must disclose the existence of the client's deception to the court or to the other party. Such a disclosure can result in grave consequences to the client, including not only a sense of betrayal but also loss of the case and perhaps a prosecution for perjury. But the alternative is that the lawyer cooperate in deceiving the court, thereby subverting the truth-finding process which the adversary system is designed to implement. See Rule 1.2(d). Furthermore, unless it is clearly understood that the lawyer will act upon the duty to disclose the existence of false evidence, the client can simply reject the lawyer's advice to reveal the false evidence and insist that the lawyer keep silent. Thus the client could in effect coerce the lawyer into being a party to fraud on the court.

Perjury by a Criminal Defendant

[7] Whether an advocate for a criminally accused has the same duty of disclosure has been intensely debated. While it is agreed that the lawyer should seek to persuade the client to refrain from perjurious testimony, there has been dispute concerning the lawyer's duty when that persuasion fails. If the confrontation with the client occurs before trial, the lawyer ordinarily can withdraw. Withdrawal before trial may not be possible, however, either because trial is imminent, or because the confrontation with the client does not take place until the trial itself, or because no other counsel is available.

[8] The most difficult situation, therefore, arises in a criminal case where the accused insists on testifying when the lawyer knows that the testimony is perjurious. The lawyer's effort to rectify the situation can increase the likelihood of the client's being convicted as well as opening the possibility of a prosecution for perjury. On the other hand, if the lawyer does not exercise control over the proof, the lawyer participates, although in a merely passive way, in deception of the court.

[9] Three resolutions of this dilemma have been proposed. One is to permit the accused to testify by a narrative without guidance through the lawyer's questioning. This compromises both contending principles; it exempts the lawyer from the duty to disclose false evidence but subjects the client to an implicit disclosure of information imparted to counsel. Another suggested resolution, of relatively recent origin, is that the advocate be entirely excused from the duty to reveal perjury if the perjury is that of the client. This is a coherent solution but makes the advocate a knowing instrument of perjury.

[10] The other resolution of the dilemma is that the lawyer must reveal the client's perjury if necessary to rectify the situation. A criminal accused has a right to the assistance of an advocate, a right to testify and a right of confidential communication with counsel. However, an accused should not have a right to assistance of counsel in committing perjury. Furthermore, an advocate has an obligation, not only in professional ethics but under the law as well, to avoid implication in the commission of perjury or other falsification of evidence. See Rule 1.2(d).

Remedial Measures

[11] If perjured testimony or false evidence has been offered, the advocate's proper course ordinarily is to remonstrate with the client confidentially. If that fails, the advocate should seek to withdraw if that will remedy the situation. If withdrawal will not remedy the situation or is impossible, the advocate should make disclosure to the court. It is for the court then to determine what should be done—making a statement about the matter to the trier of fact, ordering a mistrial or perhaps nothing.

If the false testimony was that of the client, the client may controvert the lawyer's version of their communication when the lawyer discloses the situation to the court. If there is an issue whether the client has committed perjury, the lawyer cannot represent the client in resolution of the issue and a mistrial may be unavoidable. An unscrupulous client might in this way attempt to produce a series of mistrials and thus escape prosecution. However, a second such encounter could be construed as a deliberate abuse of the right to counsel and as such a waiver of the right to further representation.

Constitutional Requirements

[12]   The general rule—that an advocate must disclose the existence of perjury with respect to a material fact, even that of a client—applies to defense counsel in criminal cases, as well as in other instances. However, the definition of the lawyer's ethical duty in such a situation may be qualified by constitutional provisions for due process and the right to counsel in criminal cases. In some jurisdictions these provisions have been construed to require that counsel present an accused as a witness if the accused wishes to testify, even if counsel knows the testimony will be false. The obligation of the advocate under these Rules is subordinate to such a constitutional requirement.

Duration of Obligation

[13]   A practical time limit on the obligation to rectify the presentation of false evidence has to be established. The conclusion of the proceeding is a reasonably definite point for the termination of the obligation.

Refusing to Offer Proof Believed to Be False

[14]   Generally speaking, a lawyer has authority to refuse to offer testimony or other proof that the lawyer believes is untrustworthy. Offering such proof may reflect adversely on the lawyer's ability to discriminate in the quality of evidence and thus impair the lawyer's effectiveness as an advocate. In criminal cases, however, a lawyer may, in some jurisdictions, be denied this authority by constitutional requirements governing the right to counsel.

Ex Parte Proceedings

[15]   Ordinarily, an advocate has the limited responsibility of presenting one side of the matters that a tribunal should consider in reaching a decision; the conflicting position is expected to be presented by the opposing party. However, in an ex parte proceeding, such as an application for a temporary restraining order, there is no balance of presentation by opposing advocates. The object of an ex parte proceeding is nevertheless to yield a substantially just result. The judge has an affirmative responsibility to accord the absent party just consideration. The lawyer for the represented party has the correlative duty to make disclosures of material facts known to the lawyer and that the lawyer reasonably believes are necessary to an informed decision.

MODEL CODE COMPARISON

[1]   Paragraph (a)(1) is substantially identical to DR 7–102(A)(5), which provided that a lawyer shall not "knowingly make a false statement of law or fact."

[2]   Paragraph (a)(2) is implicit in DR 7–102(A)(3), which provided that "a lawyer shall not ... knowingly fail to disclose that which he is required by law to reveal."

[3]   Paragraph (a)(3) is substantially identical to DR 7–106(B)(1).

[4]   With regard to paragraph (a)(4), the first sentence of this subparagraph is similar to DR 7–102(A)(4), which provided that a lawyer shall not "knowingly use" perjured testimony or false evidence. The second sentence of paragraph (a)(4) resolves an ambiguity in the Model Code concerning the action required of a lawyer who discovers that the lawyer has offered perjured testimony or false evidence. DR 7–102(A)(4), quoted above, did not expressly deal with this situation, but the prohibition against "use" of false evidence can be construed to preclude carrying through with a case based on such evidence when that fact has become known during the trial. DR 7–102(B)(1), also noted in connection with Rule 1.6, provided that a lawyer "who receives information clearly establishing that ... his client has ... perpetrated a fraud upon ... a tribunal shall [if the client does not rectify the situation] ... reveal the fraud to the ... tribunal...." Since use of perjured testimony or false evidence is usually regarded as "fraud" upon the court, DR 7–102(B)(1) apparently required disclosure by the lawyer in such circumstances. However, some states have amended DR 7–102(B)(1) in conformity with an ABA-recommended amendment to provide that the duty of disclosure does not apply when the "information is protected as a privileged communication." This qualification may be empty, for the rule of attorney-client privilege has been construed to exclude communications that further a crime, including the crime of perjury. On this interpretation of DR 7–102(B)(1), the lawyer has a duty to disclose the perjury.

[5]   Paragraph (c) confers discretion on the lawyer to refuse to offer evidence that he "reasonably believes" is false. This gives the lawyer more latitude than DR 7–102(A)(4), which prohibited the lawyer from offering evidence the lawyer "knows" is false.

[6]   There was no counterpart in the Model Code to paragraph (d).

RULE 3.4   Fairness to Opposing Party and Counsel

A lawyer shall not:

(a) unlawfully obstruct another party's access to evidence or unlawfully alter, destroy or conceal a document or other material having potential evidentiary value. A lawyer shall not counsel or assist another person to do any such act;

(b) falsify evidence, counsel or assist a witness to testify falsely, or offer an inducement to a witness that is prohibited by law;

(c) knowingly disobey an obligation under the rules of a tribunal except for an open refusal based on an assertion that no valid obligation exists;

(d) in pretrial procedure, make a frivolous discovery request or fail to make reasonably diligent effort to comply with a legally proper discovery request by an opposing party;

(e) in trial, allude to any matter that the lawyer does not reasonably believe is relevant or that will not be supported by admissible evidence, assert personal knowledge of facts in issue except when testifying as a witness, or state a personal opinion as to the justness of a cause, the

credibility of a witness, the culpability of a civil litigant or the guilt or innocence of an accused; or

(f) request a person other than a client to refrain from voluntarily giving relevant information to another party unless:

(1) the person is a relative or an employee or other agent of a client; and

(2) the lawyer reasonably believes that the person's interests will not be adversely affected by refraining from giving such information.

COMMENT:

[1] The procedure of the adversary system contemplates that the evidence in a case is to be marshalled competitively by the contending parties. Fair competition in the adversary system is secured by prohibitions against destruction or concealment of evidence, improperly influencing witnesses, obstructive tactics in discovery procedure, and the like.

[2] Documents and other items of evidence are often essential to establish a claim or defense. Subject to evidentiary privileges, the right of an opposing party, including the government, to obtain evidence through discovery or subpoena is an important procedural right. The exercise of that right can be frustrated if relevant material is altered, concealed or destroyed. Applicable law in many jurisdictions makes it an offense to destroy material for purpose of impairing its availability in a pending proceeding or one whose commencement can be foreseen. Falsifying evidence is also generally a criminal offense. Paragraph (a) applies to evidentiary material generally, including computerized information.

[3] With regard to paragraph (b), it is not improper to pay a witness's expenses or to compensate an expert witness on terms permitted by law. The common law rule in most jurisdictions is that it is improper to pay an occurrence witness any fee for testifying and that it is improper to pay an expert witness a contingent fee.

[4] Paragraph (f) permits a lawyer to advise employees of a client to refrain from giving information to another party, for the employees may identify their interests with those of the client. See also Rule 4.2.

MODEL CODE COMPARISON

[1] With regard to paragraph (a), DR 7–109(A) provided that a lawyer "shall not suppress any evidence that he or his client has a legal obligation to reveal." DR 7–109(B) provided that a lawyer "shall not advise or cause a person to secrete himself . . . for the purpose of making him unavailable as a witness. . . ." DR 7–106(C)(7) provided that a lawyer shall not "[i]ntentionally or habitually violate any established rule of procedure or of evidence."

[2] With regard to paragraph (b), DR 7–102(A)(6) provided that a lawyer shall not participate "in the creation or preservation of evidence when he knows or it is obvious that the evidence is false." DR 7–109(C) provided that a lawyer "shall not pay, offer to pay, or acquiesce in the payment of compensation to a witness contingent on the content of his testimony or the outcome of the case. But a lawyer may advance, guarantee or acquiesce in the payment of: (1) Expenses reasonably incurred by a witness in attending or testifying; (2) Reasonable compensation to a witness for his loss of time in attending or testifying; [or] (3) A reasonable fee for the professional services of an expert witness." EC 7–28 stated that witnesses "should always testify

truthfully and should be free from any financial inducements that might tempt them to do otherwise."

[3]   Paragraph (c) is substantially similar to DR 7–106(A), which provided that a lawyer "shall not disregard . . . a standing rule of a tribunal or a ruling of a tribunal made in the course of a proceeding, but he may take appropriate steps in good faith to test the validity of such rule or ruling."

[4]   Paragraph (d) has no counterpart in the Model Code.

[5]   Paragraph (e) substantially incorporates DR 7–106(C)(1), (2), (3) and (4).   DR 7–106(C)(2) proscribed asking a question "intended to degrade a witness or other person," a matter dealt with in Rule 4.4.   DR 7–106(C)(5), providing that a lawyer shall not "[f]ail to comply with known local customs of courtesy or practice," was too vague to be a rule of conduct enforceable as law.

[6]   With regard to paragraph (f), DR 7–104(A)(2) provided that a lawyer shall not "[g]ive advice to a person who is not represented . . . other than the advice to secure counsel, if the interests of such person are or have a reasonable possibility of being in conflict with the interests of his client."

RULE 3.5   Impartiality and Decorum of the Tribunal

A lawyer shall not:

(a) seek to influence a judge, juror, prospective juror or other official by means prohibited by law;

(b) communicate ex parte with such a person except as permitted by law; or

(c) engage in conduct intended to disrupt a tribunal.

COMMENT:

[1]   Many forms of improper influence upon a tribunal are proscribed by criminal law.   Others are specified in the ABA Model Code of Judicial Conduct, with which an advocate should be familiar.   A lawyer is required to avoid contributing to a violation of such provisions.

[2]   The advocate's function is to present evidence and argument so that the cause may be decided according to law.   Refraining from abusive or obstreperous conduct is a corollary of the advocate's right to speak on behalf of litigants.   A lawyer may stand firm against abuse by a judge but should avoid reciprocation; the judge's default is no justification for similar dereliction by an advocate.   An advocate can present the cause, protect the record for subsequent review and preserve professional integrity by patient firmness no less effectively than by belligerence or theatrics.

MODEL CODE COMPARISON

[1]   With regard to paragraphs (a) and (b), DR 7–108(A) provided that "[b]efore the trial of a case a lawyer . . . shall not communicate with . . . anyone he knows to be a member of the venire. . . ."   DR 7–108(B) provided that during the trial of a case a lawyer "shall not communicate   . . . any member of the jury."   DR 7–110(B) provided that a lawyer shall not "communicate . . . as to the merits of the cause with a judge or an official before whom the proceeding is pending, except . . . upon adequate notice to opposing counsel," or as "otherwise authorized by law."

[2] With regard to paragraph (c), DR 7–106(C)(6) provided that a lawyer shall not engage in "undignified or discourteous conduct which is degrading to a tribunal."

RULE 3.6 Trial Publicity

(a) A lawyer who is participating or has participated in the investigation or litigation of a matter shall not make an extrajudicial statement that a reasonable person would expect to be disseminated by means of public communication if the lawyer knows or reasonably should know that it will have a substantial likelihood of materially prejudicing an adjudicative proceeding in the matter.

(b) Notwithstanding paragraph (a), a lawyer may state:

(1) the claim, offense or defense involved and, except when prohibited by law, the identity of the persons involved;

(2) information contained in a public record;

(3) that an investigation of a matter is in progress;

(4) the scheduling or result of any step in litigation;

(5) a request for assistance in obtaining evidence and information necessary thereto;

(6) a warning of danger concerning the behavior of a person involved, when there is reason to believe that there exists the likelihood of substantial harm to an individual or to the public interest; and

(7) in a criminal case, in addition to subparagraphs (1) through (6):

(i) the identity, residence, occupation and family status of the accused;

(ii) if the accused has not been apprehended, information necessary to aid in apprehension of that person;

(iii) the fact, time and place of arrest; and

(iv) the identity of investigating and arresting officers or agencies and the length of the investigation.

(c) Notwithstanding paragraph (a), a lawyer may make a statement that a reasonable lawyer would believe is required to protect a client from the substantial undue prejudicial effect of recent publicity not initiated by the lawyer or the lawyer's client. A statement made pursuant to this paragraph shall be limited to such information as is necessary to mitigate the recent adverse publicity.

(d) No lawyer associated in a firm or government agency with a lawyer subject to paragraph (a) shall make a statement prohibited by paragraph (a).

COMMENT:

[1] It is difficult to strike a balance between protecting the right to a fair trial and safeguarding the right of free expression. Preserving the right to a fair trial necessarily entails some curtailment of the information that may be disseminated about a party prior to trial, particularly where trial by jury is involved. If there were no such limits, the result would be the practical nullification of the protective effect of the rules of forensic decorum and the exclusionary rules of evidence. On the other

hand, there are vital social interests served by the free dissemination of information about events having legal consequences and about legal proceedings themselves. The public has a right to know about threats to its safety and measures aimed at assuring its security. It also has a legitimate interest in the conduct of judicial proceedings, particularly in matters of general public concern. Furthermore, the subject matter of legal proceedings is often of direct significance in debate and deliberation over questions of public policy.

[2] Special rules of confidentiality may validly govern proceedings in juvenile, domestic relations and mental disability proceedings, and perhaps other types of litigation. Rule 3.4(c) requires compliance with such rules.

[3] The Rule sets forth a basic general prohibition against a lawyer's making statements that the lawyer knows or should know will have a substantial likelihood of materially prejudicing an adjudicative proceeding. Recognizing that the public value of informed commentary is great and the likelihood of prejudice to a proceeding by the commentary of a lawyer who is not involved in the proceeding is small, the rule applies only to lawyers who are, or who have been involved in the investigation or litigation of a case, and their associates.

[4] Paragraph (b) identifies specific matters about which a lawyer's statements would not ordinarily be considered to present a substantial likelihood of material prejudice, and should not in any event be considered prohibited by the general prohibition of paragraph (a). Paragraph (b) is not intended to be an exhaustive listing of the subjects upon which a lawyer may make a statement, but statements on other matters may be subject to paragraph (a).

[5] There are, on the other hand, certain subjects which are more likely than not to have a material prejudicial effect on a proceeding, particularly when they refer to a civil matter triable to a jury, a criminal matter, or any other proceeding that could result in incarceration. These subjects relate to:

(1) the character, credibility, reputation or criminal record of a party, suspect in a criminal investigation or witness, or the identity of a witness, or the expected testimony of a party or witness;

(2) in a criminal case or proceeding that could result in incarceration, the possibility of a plea of guilty to the offense or the existence or contents of any confession, admission, or statement given by a defendant or suspect or that person's refusal or failure to make a statement;

(3) the performance or results of any examination or test or the refusal or failure of a person to submit to an examination or test, or the identity or nature of physical evidence expected to be presented;

(4) any opinion as to the guilt or innocence of a defendant or suspect in a criminal case or proceeding that could result in incarceration;

(5) information that the lawyer knows or reasonably should know is likely to be inadmissible as evidence in a trial and that would, if disclosed, create a substantial risk of prejudicing an impartial trial; or

(6) the fact that a defendant has been charged with a crime, unless there is included therein a statement explaining that the charge is merely an accusation and that the defendant is presumed innocent until and unless proven guilty.

[6] Another relevant factor in determining prejudice is the nature of the proceeding involved. Criminal jury trials will be most sensitive to extrajudicial speech. Civil

trials may be less sensitive. Non-jury hearings and arbitration proceedings may be even less affected. The Rule will still place limitations on prejudicial comments in these cases, but the likelihood of prejudice may be different depending on the type of proceeding.

[7] Finally, extrajudicial statements that might otherwise raise a question under this Rule may be permissible when they are made in response to statements made publicly by another party, another party's lawyer, or third persons, where a reasonable lawyer would believe a public response is required in order to avoid prejudice to the lawyer's client. When prejudicial statements have been publicly made by others, responsive statements may have the salutary effect of lessening any resulting adverse impact on the adjudicative proceeding. Such responsive statements should be limited to contain only such information as is necessary to mitigate undue prejudice created by the statements made by others.

MODEL CODE COMPARISON

Rule 3.6 is similar to DR 7–107, except as follows: First, Rule 3.6 adopts the general criterion of "substantial likelihood of materially prejudicing an adjudicative proceeding" to describe impermissible conduct. Second, Rule 3.6 makes clear that only attorneys who are, or have been involved in a proceeding, or their associates, are subject to the Rule. Third, Rule 3.6 omits the particulars in DR 7–107(b), transforming them instead into an illustrative compilation as part of the Rule's commentary that is intended to give fair notice of the kinds of statements that are generally thought to be more likely than other kinds of statements to pose unacceptable dangers to the fair administration of justice. Whether any statement will have a substantial likelihood of materially prejudicing an adjudicatory proceeding will depend upon the facts of each case. The particulars of DR 7–107(c) are retained in Rule 3.6(b), except DR 7–107(C)(7), which provided that a lawyer may reveal "[a]t the time of seizure, a description of the physical evidence seized, other than a confession, admission or statement." Such revelations may be substantially prejudicial and are frequently the subject of pretrial suppression motions whose success would be undermined by disclosure of the suppressed evidence to the press. Finally, Rule 3.6 authorizes a lawyer to protect a client by making a limited reply to adverse publicity substantially prejudicial to the client.

RULE 3.7   Lawyer as Witness

(a) A lawyer shall not act as advocate at a trial in which the lawyer is likely to be a necessary witness except where:

(1) the testimony relates to an uncontested issue;

(2) the testimony relates to the nature and value of legal services rendered in the case; or

(3) disqualification of the lawyer would work substantial hardship on the client.

(b) A lawyer may act as advocate in a trial in which another lawyer in the lawyer's firm is likely to be called as a witness unless precluded from doing so by Rule 1.7 or Rule 1.9.

COMMENT:

[1]   Combining the roles of advocate and witness can prejudice the opposing party and can involve a conflict of interest between the lawyer and client.

[2]   The opposing party has proper objection where the combination of roles may prejudice that party's rights in the litigation.   A witness is required to testify on the basis of personal knowledge, while an advocate is expected to explain and comment on evidence given by others.   It may not be clear whether a statement by an advocate-witness should be taken as proof or as an analysis of the proof.

[3]   Paragraph (a)(1) recognizes that if the testimony will be uncontested, the ambiguities in the dual role are purely theoretical.   Paragraph (a)(2) recognizes that where the testimony concerns the extent and value of legal services rendered in the action in which the testimony is offered, permitting the lawyers to testify avoids the need for a second trial with new counsel to resolve that issue.   Moreover, in such a situation the judge has first hand knowledge of the matter in issue; hence, there is less dependence on the adversary process to test the credibility of the testimony.

[4]   Apart from these two exceptions, paragraph (a)(3) recognizes that a balancing is required between the interests of the client and those of the opposing party. Whether the opposing party is likely to suffer prejudice depends on the nature of the case, the importance and probable tenor of the lawyer's testimony, and the probability that the lawyer's testimony will conflict with that of other witnesses.   Even if there is risk of such prejudice, in determining whether the lawyer should be disqualified due regard must be given to the effect of disqualification on the lawyer's client.   It is relevant that one or both parties could reasonably foresee that the lawyer would probably be a witness.   The principle of imputed disqualification stated in Rule 1.10 has no application to this aspect of the problem.

[5]   Whether the combination of roles involves an improper conflict of interest with respect to the client is determined by Rule 1.7 or 1.9.   For example, if there is likely to be substantial conflict between the testimony of the client and that of the lawyer or a member of the lawyer's firm, the representation is improper.   The problem can arise whether the lawyer is called as a witness on behalf of the client or is called by the opposing party.   Determining whether or not such a conflict exists is primarily the responsibility of the lawyer involved.   See Comment to Rule 1.7.   If a lawyer who is a member of a firm may not act as both advocate and witness by reason of conflict of interest, Rule 1.10 disqualifies the firm also.

MODEL CODE COMPARISON

[1]   DR 5–102(A) prohibited a lawyer, or the lawyer's firm, from serving as advocate if the lawyer "learns or it is obvious that he or a lawyer in his firm ought to be called as a witness on behalf of his client."   DR 5–102(B) provided that a lawyer, and the lawyer's firm, may continue representation if the "lawyer learns or it is obvious that he or a lawyer in his firm may be called as a witness other than on behalf of his client ... until it is apparent that his testimony is or may be prejudicial to his client."   DR 5–101(B) permitted a lawyer to testify while representing a client: "(1) If the testimony will relate solely to an uncontested matter; (2) If the testimony will relate solely to a matter of formality and there is no reason to believe that substantial evidence will be offered in opposition to the testimony; (3) If the testimony will relate solely to the nature and value of legal services rendered in the case by the lawyer or his firm to the client; (4) As to any matter if refusal would work a substantial

hardship on the client because of the distinctive value of the lawyer or his firm as counsel in the particular case."

[2]   The exception stated in paragraph (a)(1) consolidates provisions of DR 5–101(B)(1) and (2). Testimony relating to a formality, referred to in DR 5–101(B)(2), in effect defined the phrase "uncontested issue," and was redundant.

RULE 3.8   Special Responsibilities of a Prosecutor

The prosecutor in a criminal case shall:

(a) refrain from prosecuting a charge that the prosecutor knows is not supported by probable cause;

(b) make reasonable efforts to assure that the accused has been advised of the right to, and the procedure for obtaining, counsel and has been given reasonable opportunity to obtain counsel;

(c) not seek to obtain from an unrepresented accused a waiver of important pretrial rights, such as the right to a preliminary hearing;

(d) make timely disclosure to the defense of all evidence or information known to the prosecutor that tends to negate the guilt of the accused or mitigates the offense, and, in connection with sentencing, disclose to the defense and to the tribunal all unprivileged mitigating information known to the prosecutor, except when the prosecutor is relieved of this responsibility by a protective order of the tribunal;

(e) exercise reasonable care to prevent investigators, law enforcement personnel, employees or other persons assisting or associated with the prosecutor in a criminal case from making an extrajudicial statement that the prosecutor would be prohibited from making under Rule 3.6;

(f) not subpoena a lawyer in a grand jury or other criminal proceeding to present evidence about a past or present client unless the prosecutor reasonably believes:

(1) the information sought is not protected from disclosure by any applicable privilege;

(2) the evidence sought is essential to the successful completion of an ongoing investigation or prosecution; and

(3) there is no other feasible alternative to obtain the information.

(g) except for statements that are necessary to inform the public of the nature and extent of the prosecutor's action and that serve a legitimate law enforcement purpose, refrain from making extrajudicial comments that have a substantial likelihood of heightening public condemnation of the accused.

COMMENT:

[1]   A prosecutor has the responsibility of a minister of justice and not simply that of an advocate. This responsibility carries with it specific obligations to see that the defendant is accorded procedural justice and that guilt is decided upon the basis of sufficient evidence. Precisely how far the prosecutor is required to go in this direction is a matter of debate and varies in different jurisdictions. Many jurisdictions have adopted the ABA Standards of Criminal Justice Relating to Prosecution Function, which in turn are the product of prolonged and careful deliberation by lawyers

experienced in both criminal prosecution and defense. See also Rule 3.3(d), governing ex parte proceedings, among which grand jury proceedings are included. Applicable law may require other measures by the prosecutor and knowing disregard of those obligations or a systematic abuse of prosecutorial discretion could constitute a violation of Rule 8.4.

[2] Paragraph (c) does not apply to an accused appearing pro se with the approval of the tribunal. Nor does it forbid the lawful questioning of a suspect who has knowingly waived the rights to counsel and silence.

[3] The exception in paragraph (d) recognizes that a prosecutor may seek an appropriate protective order from the tribunal if disclosure of information to the defense could result in substantial harm to an individual or to the public interest.

[4] Paragraph (f) is intended to limit the issuance of lawyer subpoenas in grand jury and other criminal proceedings to those situations in which there is a genuine need to intrude into the client-lawyer relationship.

[5] Paragraph (g) supplements Rule 3.6, which prohibits extrajudicial statements that have a substantial likelihood of prejudicing an adjudicatory proceeding. In the context of a criminal prosecution, a prosecutor's extrajudicial statement can create the additional problem of increasing public condemnation of the accused. Although the announcement of an indictment, for example, will necessarily have severe consequences for the accused, a prosecutor can, and should, avoid comments which have no legitimate law enforcement purpose and have a substantial likelihood of increasing public opprobrium of the accused. Nothing in this Comment is intended to restrict the statements which a prosecutor may make which comply with Rule 3.6(b) or 3.6(c).

MODEL CODE COMPARISON

DR 7–103(A) provided that a "public prosecutor ... shall not institute ... criminal charges when he knows or it is obvious that the charges are not supported by probable cause." DR 7–103(B) provided that "[a] public prosecutor ... shall make timely disclosure ... of the existence of evidence, known to the prosecutor ... that tends to negate the guilt of the accused, mitigate the degree of the offense, or reduce the punishment."

RULE 3.9   Advocate in Nonadjudicative Proceedings

A lawyer representing a client before a legislative or administrative tribunal in a nonadjudicative proceeding shall disclose that the appearance is in a representative capacity and shall conform to the provisions of rules 3.3(a) through (c), 3.4(a) through (c), and 3.5.

COMMENT:

[1] In representation before bodies such as legislatures, municipal councils, and executive and administrative agencies acting in a rule-making or policy-making capacity, lawyers present facts, formulate issues and advance argument in the matters under consideration. The decision-making body, like a court, should be able to rely on the integrity of the submissions made to it. A lawyer appearing before such a body should deal with the tribunal honestly and in conformity with applicable rules of procedure.

[2] Lawyers have no exclusive right to appear before nonadjudicative bodies, as they do before a court. The requirements of this Rule therefore may subject lawyers to regulations inapplicable to advocates who are not lawyers. However, legislatures

and administrative agencies have a right to expect lawyers to deal with them as they deal with courts.

[3] This Rule does not apply to representation of a client in a negotiation or other bilateral transaction with a governmental agency; representation in such a transaction is governed by Rules 4.1 through 4.4.

MODEL CODE COMPARISON

EC 7–15 stated that a lawyer "appearing before an administrative agency, regardless of the nature of the proceeding it is conducting, has the continuing duty to advance the cause of his client within the bounds of the law." EC 7–16 stated that "[w]hen a lawyer appears in connection with proposed legislation, he ... should comply with applicable laws and legislative rules." EC 8–5 stated that "[f]raudulent, deceptive, or otherwise illegal conduct by a participant in a proceeding before a ... legislative body ... should never be participated in ... by lawyers." DR 7–106(B)(1) provided that "[i]n presenting a matter to a tribunal, a lawyer shall disclose ... [u]nless privileged or irrelevant, the identity of the clients he represents and of the persons who employed him."

TRANSACTIONS WITH PERSONS OTHER THAN CLIENTS

RULE 4.1   Truthfulness in Statements to Others

In the course of representing a client a lawyer shall not knowingly:

(a) make a false statement of material fact or law to a third person; or

(b) fail to disclose a material fact to a third person when disclosure is necessary to avoid assisting a criminal or fraudulent act by a client, unless disclosure is prohibited by rule 1.6.

COMMENT:

Misrepresentation

[1] A lawyer is required to be truthful when dealing with others on a client's behalf, but generally has no affirmative duty to inform an opposing party of relevant facts. A misrepresentation can occur if the lawyer incorporates or affirms a statement of another person that the lawyer knows is false. Misrepresentations can also occur by failure to act.

Statements of Fact

[2] This Rule refers to statements of fact. Whether a particular statement should be regarded as one of fact can depend on the circumstances. Under generally accepted conventions in negotiation, certain types of statements ordinarily are not taken as statements of material fact. Estimates of price or value placed on the subject of a transaction and a party's intentions as to an acceptable settlement of a claim are in this category, and so is the existence of an undisclosed principal except where nondisclosure of the principal would constitute fraud.

Fraud by Client

[3] Paragraph (b) recognizes that substantive law may require a lawyer to disclose certain information to avoid being deemed to have assisted the client's crime

or fraud. The requirement of disclosure created by this paragraph is, however, subject to the obligations created by Rule 1.6.

MODEL CODE COMPARISON

[1] Paragraph (a) is substantially similar to DR 7–102(A)(5), which stated that "[i]n his representation of a client, a lawyer shall not . . . [k]nowingly make a false statement of law or fact."

[2] With regard to paragraph (b), DR 7–102(A)(3) provided that a lawyer shall not "[c]onceal or knowingly fail to disclose that which he is required by law to reveal."

RULE 4.2   Communication With Person Represented by Counsel

In representing a client, a lawyer shall not communicate about the subject of the representation with a person the lawyer knows to be represented by another lawyer in the matter, unless the lawyer has the consent of the other lawyer or is authorized by law to do so.

COMMENT:

[1] This Rule does not prohibit communication with a represented person, or an employee or agent of such a person, concerning matters outside the representation. For example, the existence of a controversy between a government agency and a private party, or between two organizations, does not prohibit a lawyer for either from communicating with nonlawyer representatives of the other regarding a separate matter. Also, parties to a matter may communicate directly with each other and a lawyer having independent justification or legal authorization for communicating with a represented person is permitted to do so. Communications authorized by law include, for example, the right of a party to a controversy with a government agency to speak with government officials about the matter.

[2] Communications authorized by law also include constitutionally permissible investigative activities of lawyers representing governmental entities, directly or through investigative agents, prior to the commencement of criminal or civil enforcement proceedings, when there is applicable judicial precedent that either has found the activity permissible under this Rule or has found this Rule inapplicable. However, the Rule imposes ethical restrictions that go beyond those imposed by constitutional provisions.

[3] This rule applies to communications with any person, whether or not a party to a formal adjudicative proceeding, contract or negotiation, who is represented by counsel concerning the matter to which the communication relates.

[4] In the case of an organization, this Rule prohibits communications by a lawyer for another person or entity concerning the matter in representation with persons having a managerial responsibility on behalf of the organization, and with any other person whose act or omission in connection with that matter may be imputed to the organization for purposes of civil or criminal liability or whose statement may constitute an admission on the part of the organization. If an agent or employee of the organization is represented in the matter by his or her own counsel, the consent by that counsel to a communication will be sufficient for purposes of this Rule. Compare Rule 3.4(f).

[5] The prohibition on communications with a represented person only applies, however, in circumstances where the lawyer knows that the person is in fact repre-

sented in the matter to be discussed. This means that the lawyer has actual knowledge of the fact of the representation; but such actual knowledge may be inferred from the circumstances. See Terminology. Such an inference may arise in circumstances where there is substantial reason to believe that the person with whom communication is sought is represented in the matter to be discussed. Thus, a lawyer cannot evade the requirement of obtaining the consent of counsel by closing eyes to the obvious.

[6] In the event the person with whom the lawyer communicates is not known to be represented by counsel in the matter, the lawyer's communications are subject to Rule 4.3.

MODEL CODE COMPARISON

This Rule is substantially identical to DR 7–104(A)(1) except for the substitution of the term "person" for "party."

RULE 4.3 Dealing With Unrepresented Person

In dealing on behalf of a client with a person who is not represented by counsel, a lawyer shall not state or imply that the lawyer is disinterested. When the lawyer knows or reasonably should know that the unrepresented person misunderstands the lawyer's role in the matter, the lawyer shall make reasonable efforts to correct the misunderstanding.

COMMENT:

[1] An unrepresented person, particularly one not experienced in dealing with legal matters, might assume that a lawyer is disinterested in loyalties or is a disinterested authority on the law even when the lawyer represents a client. During the course of a lawyer's representation of a client, the lawyer should not give advice to an unrepresented person other than the advice to obtain counsel.

MODEL CODE COMPARISON

There is no direct counterpart to this Rule in the Model Code. DR 7–104(A)(2) provided that a lawyer shall not "[g]ive advice to a person who is not represented by a lawyer, other than the advice to secure counsel...."

RULE 4.4 Respect for Rights of Third Persons

In representing a client, a lawyer shall not use means that have no substantial purpose other than to embarrass, delay, or burden a third person, or use methods of obtaining evidence that violate the legal rights of such a person.

COMMENT:

[1] Responsibility to a client requires a lawyer to subordinate the interests of others to those of the client, but that responsibility does not imply that a lawyer may disregard the rights of third persons. It is impractical to catalogue all such rights, but they include legal restrictions on methods of obtaining evidence from third persons.

MODEL CODE COMPARISON

DR 7–106(C)(2) provided that a lawyer shall not "[a]sk any question that he has no reasonable basis to believe is relevant to the case and that is intended to degrade a witness or other person." DR 7–102(A)(1) provided that a lawyer shall not "take ... action on behalf of his client when he knows or when it is obvious that such action would serve merely to harass or maliciously injure another." DR 7–108(D) provided that "[a]fter discharge of the jury ... the lawyer shall not ask questions or make comments to a member of that jury that are calculated merely to harass or embarrass the juror...." DR 7–108(E) provided that a lawyer "shall not conduct ... a vexatious or harassing investigation of either a venireman or a juror."

LAW FIRMS AND ASSOCIATIONS

RULE 5.1   Responsibilities of a Partner or Supervisory Lawyer

(a) A partner in a law firm shall make reasonable efforts to ensure that the firm has in effect measures giving reasonable assurance that all lawyers in the firm conform to the Rules of Professional Conduct.

(b) A lawyer having direct supervisory authority over another lawyer shall make reasonable efforts to ensure that the other lawyer conforms to the Rules of Professional Conduct.

(c) A lawyer shall be responsible for another lawyer's violation of the Rules of Professional Conduct if:

(1) the lawyer orders or, with knowledge of the specific conduct, ratifies the conduct involved; or

(2) the lawyer is a partner in the law firm in which the other lawyer practices, or has direct supervisory authority over the other lawyer, and knows of the conduct at a time when its consequences can be avoided or mitigated but fails to take reasonable remedial action.

COMMENT:

[1]   Paragraphs (a) and (b) refer to lawyers who have supervisory authority over the professional work of a firm or legal department of a government agency. This includes members of a partnership and the shareholders in a law firm organized as a professional corporation; lawyers having supervisory authority in the law department of an enterprise or government agency; and lawyers who have intermediate managerial responsibilities in a firm.

[2]   The measures required to fulfill the responsibility prescribed in paragraphs (a) and (b) can depend on the firm's structure and the nature of its practice. In a small firm, informal supervision and occasional admonition ordinarily might be sufficient. In a large firm, or in practice situations in which intensely difficult ethical problems frequently arise, more elaborate procedures may be necessary. Some firms, for example, have a procedure whereby junior lawyers can make confidential referral of ethical problems directly to a designated senior partner or special committee. See Rule 5.2. Firms, whether large or small, may also rely on continuing legal education in professional ethics. In any event, the ethical atmosphere of a firm can influence the conduct of all its members and a lawyer having authority over the work of another may not assume that the subordinate lawyer will inevitably conform to the Rules.

[3] Paragraph (c)(1) expresses a general principle of responsibility for acts of another. See also Rule 8.4(a).

[4] Paragraph (c)(2) defines the duty of a lawyer having direct supervisory authority over performance of specific legal work by another lawyer. Whether a lawyer has such supervisory authority in particular circumstances is a question of fact. Partners of a private firm have at least indirect responsibility for all work being done by the firm, while a partner in charge of a particular matter ordinarily has direct authority over other firm lawyers engaged in the matter. Appropriate remedial action by a partner would depend on the immediacy of the partner's involvement and the seriousness of the misconduct. The supervisor is required to intervene to prevent avoidable consequences of misconduct if the supervisor knows that the misconduct occurred. Thus, if a supervising lawyer knows that a subordinate misrepresented a matter to an opposing party in negotiation, the supervisor as well as the subordinate has a duty to correct the resulting misapprehension.

[5] Professional misconduct by a lawyer under supervision could reveal a violation of paragraph (b) on the part of the supervisory lawyer even though it does not entail a violation of paragraph (c) because there was no direction, ratification or knowledge of the violation.

[6] Apart from this Rule and Rule 8.4(a), a lawyer does not have disciplinary liability for the conduct of a partner, associate or subordinate. Whether a lawyer may be liable civilly or criminally for another lawyer's conduct is a question of law beyond the scope of these Rules.

MODEL CODE COMPARISON

There was no direct counterpart to this Rule in the Model Code. DR 1–103(A) provided that a lawyer "possessing unprivileged knowledge of a violation of DR 1–102 shall report such knowledge to ... authority empowered to investigate or act upon such violation."

RULE 5.2 Responsibilities of a Subordinate Lawyer

(a) A lawyer is bound by the Rules of Professional Conduct notwithstanding that the lawyer acted at the direction of another person.

(b) A subordinate lawyer does not violate the Rules of Professional Conduct if that lawyer acts in accordance with a supervisory lawyer's reasonable resolution of an arguable question of professional duty.

COMMENT:

[1] Although a lawyer is not relieved of responsibility for a violation by the fact that the lawyer acted at the direction of a supervisor, that fact may be relevant in determining whether a lawyer had the knowledge required to render conduct a violation of the Rules. For example, if a subordinate filed a frivolous pleading at the direction of a supervisor, the subordinate would not be guilty of a professional violation unless the subordinate knew of the document's frivolous character.

[2] When lawyers in a supervisor-subordinate relationship encounter a matter involving professional judgment as to ethical duty, the supervisor may assume responsibility for making the judgment. Otherwise a consistent course of action or position could not be taken. If the question can reasonably be answered only one way, the duty of both lawyers is clear and they are equally responsible for fulfilling it.

However, if the question is reasonably arguable, someone has to decide upon the course of action. That authority ordinarily reposes in the supervisor, and a subordinate may be guided accordingly. For example, if a question arises whether the interests of two clients conflict under Rule 1.7, the supervisor's reasonable resolution of the question should protect the subordinate professionally if the resolution is subsequently challenged.

MODEL CODE COMPARISON

There was no counterpart to this Rule in the Model Code.

RULE 5.3   Responsibilities Regarding Nonlawyer Assistants

With respect to a nonlawyer employed or retained by or associated with a lawyer:

(a) a partner in a law firm shall make reasonable efforts to ensure that the firm has in effect measures giving reasonable assurance that the person's conduct is compatible with the professional obligations of the lawyer;

(b) a lawyer having direct supervisory authority over the nonlawyer shall make reasonable efforts to ensure that the person's conduct is compatible with the professional obligations of the lawyer; and

(c) a lawyer shall be responsible for conduct of such a person that would be a violation of the Rules of Professional Conduct if engaged in by a lawyer if:

(1) the lawyer orders or, with the knowledge of the specific conduct, ratifies the conduct involved; or

(2) the lawyer is a partner in the law firm in which the person is employed, or has direct supervisory authority over the person, and knows of the conduct at a time when its consequences can be avoided or mitigated but fails to take reasonable remedial action.

COMMENT:

[1]   Lawyers generally employ assistants in their practice, including secretaries, investigators, law student interns, and paraprofessionals. Such assistants, whether employees or independent contractors, act for the lawyer in rendition of the lawyer's professional services. A lawyer should give such assistants appropriate instruction and supervision concerning the ethical aspects of their employment, particularly regarding the obligation not to disclose information relating to representation of the client, and should be responsible for their work product. The measures employed in supervising nonlawyers should take account of the fact that they do not have legal training and are not subject to professional discipline.

MODEL CODE COMPARISON

There was no direct counterpart to this Rule in the Model Code. DR 4–101(D) provided that a lawyer "shall exercise reasonable care to prevent his employees, associates, and others whose services are utilized by him from disclosing or using confidences or secrets of a client...."   DR 7–107(J) provided that "[a] lawyer shall exercise reasonable care to prevent his employees and associates from making an extrajudicial statement that he would be prohibited from making under DR 7–107."

RULE 5.4 Professional Independence of a Lawyer

(a) A lawyer or law firm shall not share legal fees with a nonlawyer, except that:

(1) an agreement by a lawyer with the lawyer's firm, partner, or associate may provide for the payment of money, over a reasonable period of time after the lawyer's death, to the lawyer's estate or to one or more specified persons;

(2) a lawyer who purchases the practice of a deceased, disabled, or disappeared lawyer may, pursuant to the provisions of Rule 1.17, pay to the estate or other representative of that lawyer the agreed-upon purchase price; and

(3) a lawyer or law firm may include nonlawyer employees in a compensation or retirement plan, even though the plan is based in whole or in part on a profit-sharing arrangement.

(b) A lawyer shall not form a partnership with a nonlawyer if any of the activities of the partnership consist of the practice of law.

(c) A lawyer shall not permit a person who recommends, employs, or pays the lawyer to render legal services for another to direct or regulate the lawyer's professional judgment in rendering such legal services.

(d) A lawyer shall not practice with or in the form of a professional corporation or association authorized to practice law for a profit, if:

(1) a nonlawyer owns any interest therein, except that a fiduciary representative of the estate of a lawyer may hold the stock or interest of the lawyer for a reasonable time during administration;

(2) a nonlawyer is a corporate director or officer thereof; or

(3) a nonlawyer has the right to direct or control the professional judgment of a lawyer.

COMMENT:

[1] The provisions of this Rule express traditional limitations on sharing fees. These limitations are to protect the lawyer's professional independence of judgment. Where someone other than the client pays the lawyer's fee or salary, or recommends employment of the lawyer, that arrangement does not modify the lawyer's obligation to the client. As stated in paragraph (c), such arrangements should not interfere with the lawyer's professional judgment.

MODEL CODE COMPARISON

[1] Paragraph (a) is substantially identical to DR 3–102(A).

[2] Paragraph (b) is substantially identical to DR 3–103(A).

[3] Paragraph (c) is substantially identical to DR 5–107(B).

[4] Paragraph (d) is substantially identical to DR 5–107(C).

RULE 5.5 Unauthorized Practice of Law

A lawyer shall not:

(a) practice law in a jurisdiction where doing so violates the regulation of the legal profession in that jurisdiction; or

(b) assist a person who is not a member of the bar in the performance of activity that constitutes the unauthorized practice of law.

COMMENT:

[1]   The definition of the practice of law is established by law and varies from one jurisdiction to another.   Whatever the definition, limiting the practice of law to members of the bar protects the public against rendition of legal services by unqualified persons.   Paragraph (b) does not prohibit a lawyer from employing the services of paraprofessionals and delegating functions to them, so long as the lawyer supervises the delegated work and retains responsibility for their work.   See Rule 5.3.   Likewise, it does not prohibit lawyers from providing professional advice and instruction to nonlawyers whose employment requires knowledge of law; for example, claims adjusters, employees of financial or commercial institutions, social workers, accountants and persons employed in government agencies.   In addition, a lawyer may counsel nonlawyers who wish to proceed pro se.

MODEL CODE COMPARISON

[1]   With regard to paragraph (a), DR 3–101(B) of the Model Code provided that "[a] lawyer shall not practice law in a jurisdiction where to do so would be in violation of regulations of the profession in that jurisdiction."

[2]   With regard to paragraph (b), DR 3–101(A) of the Model Code provided that "[a] lawyer shall not aid a nonlawyer in the unauthorized practice of law."

RULE 5.6   Restrictions on Right to Practice

A lawyer shall not participate in offering or making:

(a) a partnership or employment agreement that restricts the right of a lawyer to practice after termination of the relationship, except an agreement concerning benefits upon retirement; or

(b) an agreement in which a restriction on the lawyer's right to practice is part of the settlement of a controversy between private parties.

COMMENT:

[1]   An agreement restricting the right of partners or associates to practice after leaving a firm not only limits their professional autonomy but also limits the freedom of clients to choose a lawyer.   Paragraph (a) prohibits such agreements except for restrictions incident to provisions concerning retirement benefits for service with the firm.

[2]   Paragraph (b) prohibits a lawyer from agreeing not to represent other persons in connection with settling a claim on behalf of a client.

[3]   This Rule does not apply to prohibit restrictions that may be included in the terms of the sale of a law practice pursuant to Rule 1.17.

MODEL CODE COMPARISON

This Rule is substantially similar to DR 2–108.

RULE 5.7   Responsibilities Regarding Law–Related Services

(a) A lawyer shall be subject to the Rules of Professional Conduct with respect to the provision of law-related services, as defined in paragraph (b), if the law-related services are provided:

(1) by the lawyer in circumstances that are not distinct from the lawyer's provision of legal services to clients; or

(2) by a separate entity controlled by the lawyer individually or with others if the lawyer fails to take reasonable measures to assure that a person obtaining the law-related services knows that the services of the separate entity are not legal services and that the protections of the client-lawyer relationship do not exist.

(b) The term "law-related services" denotes services that might reasonably be performed in conjunction with and in substance are related to the provision of legal services, and that are not prohibited as unauthorized practice of law when provided by a nonlawyer.

COMMENT

[1] When a lawyer performs law-related services or controls an organization that does so, there exists the potential for ethical problems. Principal among these is the possibility that the person for whom the law-related services are performed fails to understand that the services may not carry with them the protections normally afforded as part of the client-lawyer relationship. The recipient of the law-related services may expect, for example, that the protection of client confidences, prohibitions against representation of persons with conflicting interests, and obligations of a lawyer to maintain professional independence apply to the provision of law-related services when that may not be the case.

[2] Rule 5.7 applies to the provision of law-related services by a lawyer even when the lawyer does not provide any legal services to the person for whom the law-related services are performed. The Rule identifies the circumstances in which all of the Rules of Professional Conduct apply to the provision of law-related services. Even when those circumstances do not exist, however, the conduct of a lawyer involved in the provision of law-related services is subject to those Rules that apply generally to lawyer conduct, regardless of whether the conduct involves the provision of legal services. See, e.g., Rule 8.4.

[3] When law-related services are provided by a lawyer under circumstances that are not distinct from the lawyer's provision of legal services to clients, the lawyer in providing the law-related services must adhere to the requirements of the Rules of Professional Conduct as provided in Rule 5.7(a)(1).

[4] Law-related services also may be provided through an entity that is distinct from that through which the lawyer provides legal services. If the lawyer individually or with others has control of such an entity's operations, the Rule requires the lawyer to take reasonable measures to assure that each person using the services of the entity knows that the services provided by the entity are not legal services and that the Rules of Professional Conduct that relate to the client-lawyer relationship do not apply. A lawyer's control of an entity extends to the ability to direct its operation. Whether a lawyer has such control will depend upon the circumstances of the particular case.

[5] When a client-lawyer relationship exists with a person who is referred by a lawyer to a separate law-related service entity controlled by the lawyer, individually or with others, the lawyer must comply with Rule 1.8(a).

[6] In taking the reasonable measures referred to in paragraph (a)(2) to assure that a person using law-related services understands the practical effect or significance of the inapplicability of the Rules of Professional Conduct, the lawyer should communicate to the person receiving the law-related services, in a manner sufficient to assure that the person understands the significance of the fact, that the relationship of the person to the business entity will not be a client-lawyer relationship. The communication should be made before entering into an agreement for provision of or providing law-related services, and preferably should be in writing.

[7] The burden is upon the lawyer to show that the lawyer has taken reasonable measures under the circumstances to communicate the desired understanding. For instance, a sophisticated user of law-related services, such as a publicly held corporation, may require a lesser explanation than someone unaccustomed to making distinctions between legal services and law-related services, such as an individual seeking tax advice from a lawyer-accountant or investigative services in connection with a lawsuit.

[8] Regardless of the sophistication of potential recipients of law-related services, a lawyer should take special care to keep separate the provision of law-related and legal services in order to minimize the risk that the recipient will assume that the law-related services are legal services. The risk of such confusion is especially acute when the lawyer renders both types of services with respect to the same matter. Under some circumstances the legal and law-related services may be so closely entwined that they cannot be distinguished from each other, and the requirement of disclosure and consultation imposed by paragraph (a)(2) of the Rule cannot be met. In such a case a lawyer will be responsible for assuring that both the lawyer's conduct and, to the extent required by Rule 5.3, that of nonlawyer employees in the distinct entity which the lawyer controls complies in all respects with the Rules of Professional Conduct.

[9] A broad range of economic and other interests of clients may be served by lawyers' engaging in the delivery of law-related services. Examples of law-related services include providing title insurance, financial planning, accounting, trust services, real estate counseling, legislative lobbying, economic analysis, social work, psychological counseling, tax return preparation, and patent, medical or environmental consulting.

[10] When a lawyer is obliged to accord the recipients of such services the protections of those Rules that apply to the client-lawyer relationship, the lawyer must take special care to heed the proscriptions of the Rules addressing conflict of interest (Rules 1.7 through 1.11, especially Rules 1.7(b) and 1.8(a), (b) and (f)), and to scrupulously adhere to the requirements of Rule 1.6 relating to disclosure of confidential information. The promotion of the law-related services must also in all respects comply with Rules 7.1 through 7.3, dealing with advertising and solicitation. In that regard, lawyers should take special care to identify the obligations that may be imposed as a result of a jurisdiction's decisional law.

[11] When the full protections of all of the Rules of Professional Conduct do not apply to the provision of law-related services, principles of law external to the Rules, for example, the law of principal and agent, govern the legal duties owed to those receiving the services. Those other legal principles may establish a different degree of protection for the recipient with respect to confidentiality of information, conflicts of

interest and permissible business relationships with clients. See also Rule 8.4 (Misconduct).

MODEL CODE COMPARISON

There was no counterpart to this Rule in the Model Code.

PUBLIC SERVICE

RULE 6.1   Voluntary Pro Bono Publico Service

A lawyer should aspire to render at least (50) hours of pro bono publico legal services per year. In fulfilling this responsibility, the lawyer should:

(a) provide a substantial majority of the (50) hours of legal services without fee or expectation of fee to:

(1) persons of limited means or

(2) charitable, religious, civic, community, governmental and educational organizations in matters which are designed primarily to address the needs of persons of limited means; and

(b) provide any additional services through:

(1) delivery of legal services at no fee or substantially reduced fee to individuals, groups or organizations seeking to secure or protect civil rights, civil liberties or public rights, or charitably religious, civic, community, governmental and educational organizations in matters in furtherance of their organizational purposes, where the payment of standard legal fees would significantly deplete the organization's economic resources or would be otherwise inappropriate;

(2) delivery of legal services at a substantially reduced fee to persons of limited means; or

(3) participation in activities for improving the law, the legal system or the legal profession.

In addition, a lawyer should voluntarily contribute financial support to organizations that provide legal services to persons of limited means.

COMMENT

[1] Every lawyer, regardless of professional prominence or professional work load, has a responsibility to provide legal services to those unable to pay, and personal involvement in the problems of the disadvantaged can be one of the most rewarding experiences in the life of a lawyer. The American Bar Association urges all lawyers to provide a minimum of 50 hours of pro bono services annually. States, however, may decide to choose a higher or lower number of hours of annual service (which may be expressed as a percentage of a lawyer's professional time) depending upon local needs and local conditions. It is recognized that in some years a lawyer may render greater or fewer hours than the annual standard specified, but during the course of his or her legal career, each lawyer should render on average per year, the number of hours set forth in this Rule. Services can be performed in civil matters or in criminal or quasi-criminal matters for which there is no government obligation to provide funds for legal representation, such as post-conviction death penalty appeal cases.

[2] Paragraphs (a)(1) and (2) recognize the critical need for legal services that exists among persons of limited means by providing that a substantial majority of the legal services rendered annually to the disadvantaged be furnished without fee or expectation of fee. Legal services under these paragraphs consist of a full range of activities, including individual and class representation, the provision of legal advice, legislative lobbying, administrative rule making and the provision of free training or mentoring to those who represent persons of limited means. The variety of these activities should facilitate participation by government attorneys, even when restrictions exist on their engaging in the outside practice of law.

[3] Persons eligible for legal services under paragraphs (a)(1) and (2) are those who qualify for participation in programs funded by the Legal Services Corporation and those whose incomes and financial resources are slightly above the guidelines utilized by such programs but, nevertheless, cannot afford counsel. Legal services can be rendered to individuals or to organizations such as homeless shelters, battered women's centers and food pantries that serve those of limited means. The term "governmental organizations" includes, but is not limited to, public protection programs and sections of governmental or public sector agencies.

[4] Because service must be provided without fee or expectation of fee, the intent of the lawyer to render free legal services is essential for the work performed to fall within the meaning of paragraphs (a)(1) and (2). Accordingly, services rendered cannot be considered pro bono if an anticipated fee is uncollected, but the award of statutory attorneys' fees in a case originally accepted as pro bono would not disqualify such services from inclusion under this section. Lawyers who do receive fees in such cases are encouraged to contribute an appropriate portion of such fees to organizations or projects that benefit persons of limited means.

[5] While it is possible for a lawyer to fulfill the annual responsibility to perform pro bono services exclusively through activities described in paragraphs (a)(1) and (2), to the extent that any hours of service remained unfulfilled, the remaining commitment can be met in a variety of ways as set forth in paragraph (b). Constitutional, statutory or regulatory restrictions may prohibit or impede government and public sector lawyers and judges from performing services outlined in paragraph (b).

[6] Paragraph (b)(1) includes the provision of certain types of legal services to those whose incomes and financial resources place them above limited means. It also permits the pro bono attorney to accept a substantially reduced fee for services. Examples of the types of issues that may be addressed under this paragraph include First Amendment claims, Title VII claims and environmental protection claims. Additionally, a wide range of organizations may be represented, including social services, medical research, cultural and religious groups.

[7] Paragraph (b)(2) covers instances in which attorneys agree to and receive a modest fee for furnishing legal services to persons of limited means. Participation in judicare programs and acceptance of court appointments in which the fee is substantially below a lawyer's usual rate are encouraged under this section.

[8] Paragraph (b)(3) recognizes the value of lawyers engaging in activities that improve the law, the legal system or the legal profession. Serving on bar association committees, serving on boards of pro bono or legal services programs, taking part in Law Day activities, acting as a continuing legal education instructor, a mediator or an arbitrator and engaging in legislative lobbying to improve the law, the legal system or the profession are a few examples of the many activities that fall within this paragraph.

[9] Because the provision of pro bono services is a professional responsibility, it is the individual ethical commitment of each lawyer. Nevertheless, there may be times when it is not feasible for a lawyer to engage in pro bono services. At such times a lawyer may discharge the pro bono responsibility by providing financial support to organizations providing free legal services to persons of limited means. Such financial support should be reasonably equivalent to the value of the hours of service that would have otherwise been provided. In addition, at times it may be more feasible to satisfy the pro bono responsibility collectively, as by a firm's aggregate pro bono activities.

[10] Because the efforts of individual lawyers are not enough to meet the need for free legal services that exist among persons of limited means, the government and the profession have instituted additional programs to provide those services. Every lawyer should financially support such programs, in addition to either providing direct pro bono services or making financial contributions when pro bono service is not feasible.

[11] The responsibility set forth in this Rule is not intended to be enforced through disciplinary process.

MODEL CODE COMPARISON

There was no counterpart to this Rule in the Disciplinary Rules of the Model Code. EC 2–25 stated that the "basic responsibility for providing legal services for those unable to pay ultimately rests upon the individual lawyer.... Every lawyer, regardless of professional prominence or professional workload, should find time to participate in serving the disadvantaged." EC 8–9 stated that "[t]he advancement of our legal system is of vital importance in maintaining the rule of law ... [and] lawyers should encourage, and should aid in making, needed changes and improvements." EC 8–3 stated that "[t]hose persons unable to pay for legal services should be provided needed services."

RULE 6.2   Accepting Appointments

A lawyer shall not seek to avoid appointment by a tribunal to represent a person except for good cause, such as:

(a) representing the client is likely to result in violation of the Rules of Professional Conduct or other law;

(b) representing the client is likely to result in an unreasonable financial burden on the lawyer; or

(c) the client or the cause is so repugnant to the lawyer as to be likely to impair the client-lawyer relationship or the lawyer's ability to represent the client.

COMMENT:

[1]   A lawyer ordinarily is not obliged to accept a client whose character or cause the lawyer regards as repugnant. The lawyer's freedom to select clients is, however, qualified. All lawyers have a responsibility to assist in providing pro bono publico service. See Rule 6.1. An individual lawyer fulfills this responsibility by accepting a fair share of unpopular matters or indigent or unpopular clients. A lawyer may also be subject to appointment by a court to serve unpopular clients or persons unable to afford legal services.

Appointed Counsel

[2] For good cause a lawyer may seek to decline an appointment to represent a person who cannot afford to retain counsel or whose cause is unpopular. Good cause exists if the lawyer could not handle the matter competently, see Rule 1.1, or if undertaking the representation would result in an improper conflict of interest, for example, when the client or the cause is so repugnant to the lawyer as to be likely to impair the client-lawyer relationship or the lawyer's ability to represent the client. A lawyer may also seek to decline an appointment if acceptance would be unreasonably burdensome, for example, when it would impose a financial sacrifice so great as to be unjust.

[3] An appointed lawyer has the same obligations to the client as retained counsel, including the obligations of loyalty and confidentiality, and is subject to the same limitations on the client-lawyer relationship, such as the obligation to refrain from assisting the client in violation of the Rules.

MODEL CODE COMPARISON

There was no counterpart to this Rule in the Disciplinary Rules of the Model Code. EC 2–29 stated that when a lawyer is "appointed by a court or requested by a bar association to undertake representation of a person unable to obtain counsel, whether for financial or other reasons, he should not seek to be excused from undertaking the representation except for compelling reason. Compelling reasons do not include such factors as the repugnance of the subject matter of the proceeding, the identity or position of a person involved in the case, the belief of the lawyer that the defendant in a criminal proceeding is guilty, or the belief of the lawyer regarding the merits of the civil case." EC 2–30 stated that "a lawyer should decline employment if the intensity of his personal feelings, as distinguished from a community attitude, may impair his effective representation of a prospective client."

RULE 6.3   Membership in Legal Services Organization

A lawyer may serve as a director, officer or member of a legal services organization, apart from the law firm in which the lawyer practices, notwithstanding that the organization serves persons having interests adverse to a client of the lawyer. The lawyer shall not knowingly participate in a decision or action of the organization:

(a) if participating in the decision or action would be incompatible with the lawyer's obligations to a client under Rule 1.7; or

(b) where the decision or action could have a material adverse effect on the representation of a client of the organization whose interests are adverse to a client of the lawyer.

COMMENT:

[1] Lawyers should be encouraged to support and participate in legal service organizations. A lawyer who is an officer or a member of such an organization does not thereby have a client-lawyer relationship with persons served by the organization. However, there is potential conflict between the interests of such persons and the interests of the lawyer's clients. If the possibility of such conflict disqualified a lawyer from serving on the board of a legal services organization, the profession's involvement in such organizations would be severely curtailed.

[2]   It may be necessary in appropriate cases to reassure a client of the organization that the representation will not be affected by conflicting loyalties of a member of the board.   Established, written policies in this respect can enhance the credibility of such assurances.

MODEL CODE COMPARISON

There was no counterpart to this Rule in the Model Code.

RULE 6.4   Law Reform Activities Affecting Client Interests

A lawyer may serve as a director, officer or member of an organization involved in reform of the law or its administration notwithstanding that the reform may affect the interests of a client of the lawyer.   When the lawyer knows that the interests of a client may be materially benefitted by a decision in which the lawyer participates, the lawyer shall disclose that fact but need not identify the client.

COMMENT:

[1]   Lawyers involved in organizations seeking law reform generally do not have a client-lawyer relationship with the organization.   Otherwise, it might follow that a lawyer could not be involved in a bar association law reform program that might indirectly affect a client.   See also Rule 1.2(b).   For example, a lawyer specializing in antitrust litigation might be regarded as disqualified from participating in drafting revisions of rules governing that subject.   In determining the nature and scope of participation in such activities, a lawyer should be mindful of obligations to clients under other Rules, particularly Rule 1.7.   A lawyer is professionally obligated to protect the integrity of the program by making an appropriate disclosure within the organization when the lawyer knows a private client might be materially benefitted.

MODEL CODE COMPARISON

There was no counterpart to this Rule in the Model Code.

INFORMATION ABOUT LEGAL SERVICES

RULE 7.1   Communications Concerning a Lawyer's Services

A lawyer shall not make a false or misleading communication about the lawyer or the lawyer's services.   A communication is false or misleading if it:

(a) contains a material misrepresentation of fact or law, or omits a fact necessary to make the statement considered as a whole not materially misleading;

(b) is likely to create an unjustified expectation about results the lawyer can achieve, or states or implies that the lawyer can achieve results by means that violate the Rules of Professional Conduct or other law;   or

(c) compares the lawyer's services with other lawyers' services, unless the comparison can be factually substantiated.

COMMENT:

[1]   This Rule governs all communications about a lawyer's services, including advertising permitted by Rule 7.2.   Whatever means are used to make known a

lawyer's services, statements about them should be truthful. The prohibition in paragraph (b) of statements that may create "unjustified expectations" would ordinarily preclude advertisements about results obtained on behalf of a client, such as the amount of a damage award or the lawyer's record in obtaining favorable verdicts, and advertisements containing client endorsements. Such information may create the unjustified expectation that similar results can be obtained for others without reference to the specific factual and legal circumstances.

MODEL CODE COMPARISON

DR 2–101 provided that "[a] lawyer shall not ... use ... any form of public communication containing a false, fraudulent, misleading, deceptive, self-laudatory or unfair statement or claim." DR 2–101(B) provided that a lawyer "may publish or broadcast ... the following information ... in the geographic area or areas in which the lawyer resides or maintains offices or in which a significant part of the lawyer's clientele resides, provided that the information ... complies with DR 2–101(A), and is presented in a dignified manner...." DR 2–101(B) then specified 25 categories of information that may be disseminated. DR 2–101(C) provided that "[a]ny person desiring to expand the information authorized for disclosure in DR 2–101(B), or to provide for its dissemination through other forums may apply to [the agency having jurisdiction under state law].... The relief granted in response to any such application shall be promulgated as an amendment to DR 2–101(B), universally applicable to all lawyers."

RULE 7.2   Advertising

(a) **Subject to the requirements of Rules 7.1 and 7.3, a lawyer may advertise services through public media, such as a telephone directory, legal directory, newspaper or other periodical, outdoor advertising, radio or television, or through written or recorded communication.**

(b) **A copy or recording of an advertisement or communication shall be kept for two years after its last dissemination along with a record of when and where it was used.**

(c) **A lawyer shall not give anything of value to a person for recommending the lawyer's services except that a lawyer may**

(1) **pay the reasonable costs of advertisements or communications permitted by this Rule;**

(2) **pay the usual charges of a not-for-profit lawyer referral service or legal service organization; and**

(3) **pay for a law practice in accordance with Rule 1.17.**

(d) **Any communication made pursuant to this rule shall include the name of at least one lawyer responsible for its content.**

COMMENT:

[1] To assist the public in obtaining legal services, lawyers should be allowed to make known their services not only through reputation but also through organized information campaigns in the form of advertising. Advertising involves an active quest for clients, contrary to the tradition that a lawyer should not seek clientele. However, the public's need to know about legal services can be fulfilled in part through advertising. This need is particularly acute in the case of persons of moderate means

who have not made extensive use of legal services.   The interest in expanding public information about legal services ought to prevail over considerations of tradition. Nevertheless, advertising by lawyers entails the risk of practices that are misleading or overreaching.

[2]   This Rule permits public dissemination of information concerning a lawyer's name or firm name, address and telephone number; the kinds of services the lawyer will undertake; the basis on which the lawyer's fees are determined, including prices for specific services and payment and credit arrangements; a lawyer's foreign language ability;   names of references and, with their consent, names of clients regularly represented;   and other information that might invite the attention of those seeking legal assistance.

[3]   Questions of effectiveness and taste in advertising are matters of speculation and subjective judgment.   Some jurisdictions have had extensive prohibitions against television advertising, against advertising going beyond specified facts about a lawyer, or against "undignified" advertising.   Television is now one of the most powerful media for getting information to the public, particularly persons of low and moderate income; prohibiting television advertising, therefore, would impede the flow of information about legal services to many sectors of the public.   Limiting the information that may be advertised has a similar effect and assumes that the bar can accurately forecast the kind of information that the public would regard as relevant.

[4]   Neither this Rule nor Rule 7.3 prohibits communications authorized by law, such as notice to members of a class in class action litigation.

Record of Advertising

[5]   Paragraph (b) requires that a record of the content and use of advertising be kept in order to facilitate enforcement of this Rule.   It does not require that advertising be subject to review prior to dissemination.   Such a requirement would be burdensome and expensive relative to its possible benefits, and may be of doubtful constitutionality.

Paying Others to Recommend a Lawyer

[6]   A lawyer is allowed to pay for advertising permitted by this Rule and for the purchase of a law practice in accordance with the provisions of Rule 1.17, but otherwise is not permitted to pay another person for channeling professional work. This restriction does not prevent an organization or person other than the lawyer from advertising or recommending the lawyer's services.   Thus, a legal aid agency or prepaid legal services plan may pay to advertise legal services provided under its auspices.   Likewise, a lawyer may participate in not-for-profit lawyer referral programs and pay the usual fees charged by such programs.   Paragraph (c) does not prohibit paying regular compensation to an assistant, such as a secretary, to prepare communications permitted by this Rule.

MODEL CODE COMPARISON

[1]   With regard to paragraph (a), DR 2–101(B) provided that a lawyer "may publish or broadcast, subject to DR 2–103, ... in print media ... or television or radio...."

[2]   With regard to paragraph (b), DR 2–101(D) provided that if the advertisement is "communicated to the public over television or radio, ... a recording of the actual transmission shall be retained by the lawyer."

[3]   With regard to paragraph (c), DR 2–103(B) provided that a lawyer "shall not compensate or give anything of value to a person or organization to recommend or secure his employment ... except that he may pay the usual and reasonable fees or dues charged by any of the organizations listed in DR 2–103(D)." (DR 2–103(D) referred to legal aid and other legal services organizations.) DR 2–101(I) provided that a lawyer "shall not compensate or give anything of value to representatives of the press, radio, television, or other communication medium in anticipation of or in return for professional publicity in a news item."

[4]   There was no counterpart to paragraph (d) in the Model Code.

RULE 7.3   Direct Contact With Prospective Clients

(a) A lawyer shall not by in-person or live telephone contact solicit professional employment from a prospective client with whom the lawyer has no family or prior professional relationship when a significant motive for the lawyer's doing so is the lawyer's pecuniary gain.

(b) A lawyer shall not solicit professional employment from a prospective client by written or recorded communication or by in-person or telephone contact even when not otherwise prohibited by paragraph (a), if:

(1) the prospective client has made known to the lawyer a desire not to be solicited by the lawyer; or

(2) the solicitation involves coercion, duress or harassment.

(c) Every written or recorded communication from a lawyer soliciting professional employment from a prospective client known to be in need of legal services in a particular matter, and with whom the lawyer has no family or prior professional relationship, shall include the words "Advertising Material" on the outside envelope and at the beginning and ending of any recorded communication.

(d) Notwithstanding the prohibitions in paragraph (a), a lawyer may participate with a prepaid or group legal service plan operated by an organization not owned or directed by the lawyer which uses in-person or telephone contact to solicit memberships or subscriptions for the plan from persons who are not known to need legal services in a particular matter covered by the plan.

COMMENT:

[1]   There is a potential for abuse inherent in direct in-person or live telephone contact by a lawyer with a prospective client known to need legal services. These forms of contact between a lawyer and a prospective client subject the layperson to the private importuning of the trained advocate in a direct interpersonal encounter. The prospective client, who may already feel overwhelmed by the circumstances giving rise to the need for legal services, may find it difficult fully to evaluate all available alternatives with reasoned judgment and appropriate self-interest in the face of the lawyer's presence and insistence upon being retained immediately. The situation is fraught with the possibility of undue influence, intimidation, and over-reaching.

[2]   This potential for abuse inherent in direct in-person or live telephone solicitation of prospective clients justifies its prohibition, particularly since lawyer advertising and written and recorded communication permitted under Rule 7.2 offer alternative means of conveying necessary information to those who may be in need of

legal services. Advertising and written and recorded communications which may be mailed or autodialed make it possible for a prospective client to be informed about the need for legal services, and about the qualifications of available lawyers and law firms, without subjecting the prospective client to direct in-person or telephone persuasion that may overwhelm the client's judgment.

[3] The use of general advertising and written and recorded communications to transmit information from lawyer to prospective client, rather than direct in-person or live telephone contact, will help to assure that the information flows cleanly as well as freely. The contents of advertisements and communications permitted under Rule 7.2 are permanently recorded so that they cannot be disputed and may be shared with others who know the lawyer. This potential for informal review is itself likely to help guard against statements and claims that might constitute false and misleading communications, in violation of Rule 7.1. The contents of direct in-person or live telephone conversations between a lawyer to a prospective client can be disputed and are not subject to third-party scrutiny. Consequently, they are much more likely to approach (and occasionally cross) the dividing line between accurate representations and those that are false and misleading.

[4] There is far less likelihood that a lawyer would engage in abusive practices against an individual with whom the lawyer has a prior personal or professional relationship or where the lawyer is motivated by considerations other than the lawyer's pecuniary gain. Consequently, the general prohibition in Rule 7.3(a) and the requirements of Rule 7.3(c) are not applicable in those situations.

[5] But even permitted forms of solicitation can be abused. Thus, any solicitation which contains information which is false or misleading within the meaning of Rule 7.1, which involves coercion, duress or harassment within the meaning of Rule 7.3(b)(2), or which involves contact with a prospective client who has made known to the lawyer a desire not to be solicited by the lawyer within the meaning of Rule 7.3(b)(1) is prohibited. Moreover, if after sending a letter or other communication to a client as permitted by Rule 7.2 the lawyer receives no response, any further effort to communicate with the prospective client may violate the provisions of Rule 7.3(b).

[6] This Rule is not intended to prohibit a lawyer from contacting representatives of organizations or groups that may be interested in establishing a group or prepaid legal plan for their members, insureds, beneficiaries or other third parties for the purpose of informing such entities of the availability of and details concerning the plan or arrangement which the lawyer or lawyer's firm is willing to offer. This form of communication is not directed to a prospective client. Rather, it is usually addressed to an individual acting in a fiduciary capacity seeking a supplier of legal services for others who may, if they choose, become prospective clients of the lawyer. Under these circumstances, the activity which the lawyer undertakes in communicating with such representatives and the type of information transmitted to the individual are functionally similar to and serve the same purpose as advertising permitted under Rule 7.2.

[7] The requirement in Rule 7.3(c) that certain communications be marked "Advertising Material" does not apply to communications sent in response to requests of potential clients or their spokespersons or sponsors. General announcements by lawyers, including changes in personnel or office location, do not constitute communications soliciting professional employment from a client known to be in need of legal services within the meaning of this Rule.

[8]   Paragraph (d) of this Rule would permit an attorney to participate with an organization which uses personal contact to solicit members for its group or prepaid legal service plan, provided that the personal contact is not undertaken by any lawyer who would be a provider of legal services through the plan.   The organization referred to in paragraph (d) must not be owned by or directed (whether as manager or otherwise) by any lawyer or law firm that participates in the plan.   For example, paragraph (d) would not permit a lawyer to create an organization controlled directly or indirectly by the lawyer and use the organization for the in-person or telephone solicitation of legal employment of the lawyer through memberships in the plan or otherwise.   The communication permitted by these organizations also must not be directed to a person known to need legal services in a particular matter, but is to be designed to inform potential plan members generally of another means of affordable legal services.   Lawyers who participate in a legal service plan must reasonably assure that the plan sponsors are in compliance with Rules 7.1, 7.2 and 7.3(b).   See 8.4(a).

MODEL CODE COMPARISON

DR 2–104(A) provided with certain exceptions that "[a] lawyer who has given in-person unsolicited advice to a layperson that he should obtain counsel or take legal action shall not accept employment resulting from that advice...."   The exceptions include DR 2–104(A)(1), which provided that a lawyer "may accept employment by a close friend, relative, former client (if the advice is germane to the former employ-ment), or one whom the lawyer reasonably believes to be a client."   DR 2–104(A)(2) through DR 2–104(A)(5) provided other exceptions relating, respectively, to employ-ment resulting from public educational programs, recommendation by a legal assis-tance organization, public speaking or writing and representing members of a class in class action litigation.

RULE 7.4   Communication of Fields of Practice

A lawyer may communicate the fact that the lawyer does or does not practice in particular fields of law. A lawyer shall not state or imply that the lawyer is a specialist in a particular field of law except as follows:

(a) a lawyer admitted to engage in patent practice before the United States Patent and Trademark Office may use the designation "Patent Attor-ney" or a substantially similar designation;

(b) a lawyer engaged in Admiralty practice may use the designation "Admiralty," "Proctor in Admiralty" or a substantially similar designation; and

(c) [for jurisdictions where there is a regulatory authority granting certification or approving organizations that grant certification] a lawyer may communicate the fact that the lawyer has been certified as a specialist in a field of law by a named organization or authority but only if:

(1) such certification is granted by the appropriate regulatory au-thority or by an organization which has been approved by the appropri-ate regulatory authority to grant such certification; or

(2) such certification is granted by an organization that has not yet been approved by, or has been denied the approval available from, the appropriate regulatory authority, and the absence or denial of approval is clearly stated in the communication, and in any advertising subject to

Rule 7.2, such statement appears in the same sentence that communicates the certification.

(d) [for jurisdictions where there is no procedure either for certification
of specialties or for approval of organizations granting certification] a
lawyer may communicate the fact that the lawyer has been certified as a
specialist in a field of law by a named organization, provided that the
communication clearly states that there is no procedure in this jurisdiction
for approving certifying organizations. If, however, the named organization
has been accredited by the American Bar Association to certify lawyers as
specialists in a particular field of law, the communication need not contain
such a statement.

COMMENT

[1] This Rule permits a lawyer to indicate areas of practice in communications
about the lawyer's services. If a lawyer practices only in certain fields, or will not
accept matters in a specified field or fields, the lawyer is permitted to so indicate. The
lawyer is generally permitted to state that the lawyer is a "specialist," practices a
"specialty," or "specializes in" particular fields, but such communications are subject
to the "false and misleading" standard applied in Rule 7.1 to communications
concerning a lawyer's services.

[2] However, a lawyer may not communicate that the lawyer has been recognized
or certified as a specialist in a particular field of law, except as provided by this Rule.
Recognition of specialization in patent matters is a matter of long-established policy of
the Patent and Trademark Office, as reflected in paragraph (a). Paragraph (b)
recognizes that designation of admiralty practice has a long historical tradition
associated with maritime commerce and the federal courts.

[3] Paragraph (c) provides for certification as a specialist in a field of law when a
state authorizes an appropriate regulatory authority to grant such certification or
when the state grants other organizations the right to grant certification. Certification procedures imply that an objective entity has recognized a lawyer's higher degree
of specialized ability than is suggested by general licensure to practice law. Those
objective entities may be expected to apply standards of competence, experience and
knowledge to insure that a lawyer's recognition as a specialist is meaningful and
reliable. In order to insure that consumers can obtain access to useful information
about an organization granting certification, the name of the certifying organization or
agency must be included in any communication regarding the certification.

[4] Lawyers may also be certified as specialists by organizations that either have
not yet been approved to grant such certification or have been disapproved. In such
instances, the consumer may be misled as to the significance of the lawyer's status as a
certified specialist. The Rule therefore requires that a lawyer who chooses to communicate recognition by such an organization also clearly state the absence or denial of
the organization's authority to grant such certification. Since lawyer advertising
through public media and written or recorded communications invites the greatest
danger of misleading consumers, the absence or denial of the organization's authority
to grant certification must be clearly stated in such advertising in the same sentence
that communicates the certification.

[5] In jurisdictions where no appropriate regulatory authority has a procedure
for approving organizations granting certification, the Rule requires that a lawyer
clearly state such lack of procedure. If, however, the named organization has been

accredited by the American Bar Association to certify lawyers as specialists in a particular field of law, the communication need not contain such a statement.

MODEL CODE COMPARISON

[1]   DR 2–105(A) provided that a lawyer "shall not hold himself out publicly as a specialist, as practicing in certain areas of law or as limiting his practice . . . except as follows:

"(1) A lawyer admitted to practice before the United States Patent and Trademark Office may use the designation 'Patents,' 'Patent Attorney,' 'Patent Lawyer,' or 'Registered Patent Attorney' or any combination of those terms, on his letterhead and office sign.

"(2) A lawyer who publicly discloses fields of law in which the lawyer . . . practices or states his practice is limited to one or more fields of law shall do so by using designations and definitions authorized and approved by the [agency having jurisdiction of the subject under state law].

"(3) A lawyer who is certified as a specialist in a particular field of law or law practice by [the authority having jurisdiction under state law over the subject of specialization by lawyers] may hold himself out as such, but only in accordance with the rules prescribed by that authority."

[2]   EC 2–14 stated that "In the absence of state controls to insure the existence of special competence, a lawyer should not be permitted to hold himself out as a specialist, . . . other than in the fields of admiralty, trademark, and patent law where a holding out as a specialist historically has been permitted."

RULE 7.5   Firm Names and Letterheads

(a) A lawyer shall not use a firm name, letterhead or other professional designation that violates rule 7.1. A trade name may be used by a lawyer in private practice if it does not imply a connection with a government agency or with a public or charitable legal services organization and is not otherwise in violation of Rule 7.1.

(b) A law firm with offices in more than one jurisdiction may use the same name in each jurisdiction, but identification of the lawyers in an office of the firm shall indicate the jurisdictional limitations on those not licensed to practice in the jurisdiction where the office is located.

(c) The name of a lawyer holding a public office shall not be used in the name of a law firm, or in communications on its behalf, during any substantial period in which the lawyer is not actively and regularly practicing with the firm.

(d) Lawyers may state or imply that they practice in a partnership or other organization only when that is the fact.

COMMENT:

[1]   A firm may be designated by the names of all or some of its members, by the names of deceased members where there has been a continuing succession in the firm's identity or by a trade name such as the "ABC Legal Clinic." Although the United States Supreme Court has held that legislation may prohibit the use of trade names in professional practice, use of such names in law practice is acceptable so long as it is not misleading. If a private firm uses a trade name that includes a

geographical name such as "Springfield Legal Clinic," an express disclaimer that it is a public legal aid agency may be required to avoid a misleading implication. It may be observed that any firm name including the name of a deceased partner is, strictly speaking, a trade name. The use of such names to designate law firms has proven a useful means of identification. However, it is misleading to use the name of a lawyer not associated with the firm or a predecessor of the firm.

[2] With regard to paragraph (d), lawyers sharing office facilities, but who are not in fact partners, may not denominate themselves as, for example, "Smith and Jones," for that title suggests partnership in the practice of law.

MODEL CODE COMPARISON

[1] With regard to paragraph (a), DR 2–102(A) provided that "[a] lawyer ... shall not use ... professional cards ... letterheads, or similar professional notices, or devices, [except] ... if they are in dignified form...." DR 2–102(B) provided that "[a] lawyer in private practice shall not practice under a trade name, a name that is misleading as to the identity of the lawyer or lawyers practicing under such name, or a firm name containing names other than those of one or more of the lawyers in the firm, except that ... a firm may use as ... its name[,] the name or names of one or more deceased or retired members of the firm or of a predecessor firm in a continuing line of succession."

[2] With regard to paragraph (b), DR 2–102(D) provided that a partnership "shall not be formed or continued between or among lawyers licensed in different jurisdictions unless all enumerations of the members and associates of the firm on its letterhead and in other permissible listings make clear the jurisdictional limitations on those members and associates of the firm not licensed to practice in all listed jurisdictions; however, the same firm name may be used in each jurisdiction."

[3] With regard to paragraph (c), DR 2–102(B) provided that "[a] lawyer who assumes a judicial, legislative, or public executive or administrative post or office shall not permit his name to remain in the name of a law firm ... during any significant period in which he is not actively and regularly practicing law as a member of the firm...."

[4] Paragraph (d) is substantially identical to DR 2–102(C).

RULE 7.6   Political Contributions to Obtain Government Legal Engagements or Appointments by Judges*

A lawyer or law firm shall not accept a government legal engagement or an appointment by a judge if the lawyer or law firm makes a political contribution or solicits political contributions for the purpose of obtaining or being considered for that type of legal engagement or appointment.

COMMENT

[1] Lawyers have a right to participate fully in the political process, which includes making and soliciting political contributions to candidates for judicial and other public office. Nevertheless, when lawyers make or solicit political contributions in order to obtain an engagement for legal work awarded by a government agency, or to obtain appointment by a judge, the public may legitimately question whether the

* Adopted February 14, 2000.

lawyers engaged to perform the work are selected on the basis of competence and merit. In such a circumstance, the integrity of the profession is undermined.

[2] The term "political contribution" denotes any gift, subscription, loan, advance or deposit of anything of value made directly or indirectly to a candidate, incumbent, political party or campaign committee to influence or provide financial support for election to or retention in judicial or other government office. Political contributions in initiative and referendum elections are not included. For purposes of this Rule, the term "political contribution" does not include uncompensated services.

[3] Subject to the exceptions below, (i) the term "government legal engagement" denotes any engagement to provide legal services that a public official has the direct or indirect power to award; and (ii) the term "appointment by a judge" denotes an appointment to a position such as referee, commissioner, special master, receiver, guardian or other similar position that is made by a judge. Those terms do not, however, include (a) substantially uncompensated services; (b) engagements or appointments made on the basis of experience, expertise, professional qualifications and cost following a request for proposal or other process that is free from influence based upon political contributions; and (c) engagements or appointments made on a rotational basis from a list compiled without regard to political contributions.

[4] The term "lawyer or law firm" includes a political action committee or other entity owned or controlled by a lawyer or law firm.

[5] Political contributions are for the purpose of obtaining or being considered for a government legal engagement or appointment by a judge if, but for the desire to be considered for the legal engagement or appointment, the lawyer or law firm would not have made or solicited the contributions. The purpose may be determined by an examination of the circumstances in which the contributions occur. For example, one or more contributions that in the aggregate are substantial in relation to other contributions by lawyers or law firms, made for the benefit of an official in a position to influence award of a government legal engagement, and followed by an award of the legal engagement to the contributing or soliciting lawyer or the lawyer's firm would support an inference that the purpose of the contributions was to obtain the engagement, absent other factors that weigh against existence of the proscribed purpose. Those factors may include among others that the contribution or solicitation was made to further a political, social, or economic interest or because of an existing personal, family, or professional relationship with a candidate.

[6] If a lawyer makes or solicits a political contribution under circumstances that constitute bribery or another crime, Rule 8.4(b) is implicated.

MAINTAINING THE INTEGRITY
OF THE PROFESSION

RULE 8.1 Bar Admission and Disciplinary Matters

An applicant for admission to the bar, or a lawyer in connection with a bar admission application or in connection with a disciplinary matter, shall not:

(a) knowingly make a false statement of material fact; or

(b) fail to disclose a fact necessary to correct a misapprehension known by the person to have arisen in the matter, or knowingly fail to respond to a

lawful demand for information from an admissions or disciplinary authority, except that this rule does not require disclosure of information otherwise protected by Rule 1.6.

COMMENT:

[1] The duty imposed by this Rule extends to persons seeking admission to the bar as well as to lawyers. Hence, if a person makes a material false statement in connection with an application for admission, it may be the basis for subsequent disciplinary action if the person is admitted, and in any event may be relevant in a subsequent admission application. The duty imposed by this Rule applies to a lawyer's own admission or discipline as well as that of others. Thus, it is a separate professional offense for a lawyer to knowingly make a misrepresentation or omission in connection with a disciplinary investigation of the lawyer's own conduct. This Rule also requires affirmative clarification of any misunderstanding on the part of the admissions or disciplinary authority of which the person involved becomes aware.

[2] This Rule is subject to the provisions of the Fifth Amendment of the United States Constitution and corresponding provisions of state constitutions. A person relying on such a provision in response to a question, however, should do so openly and not use the right of nondisclosure as a justification for failure to comply with this Rule.

[3] A lawyer representing an applicant for admission to the bar, or representing a lawyer who is the subject of a disciplinary inquiry or proceeding, is governed by the rules applicable to the client-lawyer relationship.

MODEL CODE COMPARISON

DR 1–101(A) provided that a lawyer "is subject to discipline if he has made a materially false statement in, or if he has deliberately failed to disclose a material fact requested in connection with, his application for admission to the bar." DR 1–101(B) provided that a lawyer "shall not further the application for admission to the bar of another person known by him to be unqualified in respect to character, education, or other relevant attribute." With respect to paragraph (b), DR 1–102(A)(5) provided that a lawyer shall not engage in "conduct that is prejudicial to the administration of justice."

RULE 8.2 Judicial and Legal Officials

(a) A lawyer shall not make a statement that the lawyer knows to be false or with reckless disregard as to its truth or falsity concerning the qualifications or integrity of a judge, adjudicatory officer or public legal officer, or of a candidate for election or appointment to judicial or legal office.

(b) A lawyer who is a candidate for judicial office shall comply with the applicable provisions of the code of judicial conduct.

COMMENT:

[1] Assessments by lawyers are relied on in evaluating the professional or personal fitness of persons being considered for election or appointment to judicial office and to public legal offices, such as attorney general, prosecuting attorney and public defender. Expressing honest and candid opinions on such matters contributes to improving the administration of justice. Conversely, false statements by a lawyer can unfairly undermine public confidence in the administration of justice.

[2]   When a lawyer seeks judicial office, the lawyer should be bound by applicable limitations on political activity.

[3]   To maintain the fair and independent administration of justice, lawyers are encouraged to continue traditional efforts to defend judges and courts unjustly criticized.

MODEL CODE COMPARISON

[1]   With regard to paragraph (a), DR 8–102(A) provided that a lawyer "shall not knowingly make false statements of fact concerning the qualifications of a candidate for election or appointment to a judicial office." DR 8–102(B) provided that a lawyer "shall not knowingly make false accusations against a judge or other adjudicatory officer."

[2]   Paragraph (b) is substantially identical to DR 8–103.

RULE 8.3   Reporting Professional Misconduct

(a) A lawyer having knowledge that another lawyer has committed a violation of the Rules of Professional Conduct that raises a substantial question as to that lawyer's honesty, trustworthiness or fitness as a lawyer in other respects, shall inform the appropriate professional authority.

(b) A lawyer having knowledge that a judge has committed a violation of applicable rules of judicial conduct that raises a substantial question as to the judge's fitness for office shall inform the appropriate authority.

(c) This Rule does not require disclosure of information otherwise protected by Rule 1.6 or information gained by a lawyer or judge while serving as a member of an approved lawyers assistance program to the extent that such information would be confidential if it were communicated subject to the attorney-client privilege.

COMMENT:

[1]   Self-regulation of the legal profession requires that members of the profession initiate disciplinary investigation when they know of a violation of the Rules of Professional Conduct. Lawyers have a similar obligation with respect to judicial misconduct. An apparently isolated violation may indicate a pattern of misconduct that only a disciplinary investigation can uncover. Reporting a violation is especially important where the victim is unlikely to discover the offense.

[2]   A report about misconduct is not required where it would involve violation of Rule 1.6. However, a lawyer should encourage a client to consent to disclosure where prosecution would not substantially prejudice the client's interests.

[3]   If a lawyer were obliged to report every violation of the Rules, the failure to report any violation would itself be a professional offense. Such a requirement existed in many jurisdictions but proved to be unenforceable. This Rule limits the reporting obligation to those offenses that a self-regulating profession must vigorously endeavor to prevent. A measure of judgment is, therefore, required in complying with the provisions of this Rule. The term "substantial" refers to the seriousness of the possible offense and not the quantum of evidence of which the lawyer is aware. A report should be made to the bar disciplinary agency unless some other agency, such as a peer review agency, is more appropriate in the circumstances. Similar considerations apply to the reporting of judicial misconduct.

[4] The duty to report professional misconduct does not apply to a lawyer retained to represent a lawyer whose professional conduct is in question. Such a situation is governed by the rules applicable to the client-lawyer relationship.

[5] Information about a lawyer's or judge's misconduct or fitness may be received by a lawyer in the course of that lawyer's participation in an approved lawyers' or judges' assistance program. In that circumstance, providing for the confidentiality of such information encourages lawyers and judges to seek treatment through such program. Conversely, without such confidentiality, lawyers and judges may hesitate to seek assistance from these programs, which may then result in additional harm to their professional careers and additional injury to the welfare of clients and the public. The Rule therefore exempts the lawyer from the reporting requirements of paragraphs (a) and (b) with respect to information that would be privileged if the relationship between the impaired lawyer or judge and the recipient of the information were that of a client and a lawyer. On the other hand, a lawyer who receives such information would nevertheless be required to comply with the Rule 8.3 reporting provisions to report misconduct if the impaired lawyer or judge indicates an intent to engage in illegal activity, for example, the conversion of client funds to his or her use.

MODEL CODE COMPARISON

DR 1–103(A) provided that "[a] lawyer possessing unprivileged knowledge of a violation of [a Disciplinary Rule] shall report such knowledge to ... authority empowered to investigate or act upon such violation."

RULE 8.4 Misconduct

It is professional misconduct for a lawyer to:

(a) violate or attempt to violate the Rules of Professional Conduct, knowingly assist or induce another to do so, or do so through the acts of another;

(b) commit a criminal act that reflects adversely on the lawyer's honesty, trustworthiness or fitness as a lawyer in other respects;

(c) engage in conduct involving dishonesty, fraud, deceit or misrepresentation;

(d) engage in conduct that is prejudicial to the administration of justice;

(e) state or imply an ability to influence improperly a government agency or official; or

(f) knowingly assist a judge or judicial officer in conduct that is a violation of applicable rules of judicial conduct or other law.

COMMENT:

[1] Many kinds of illegal conduct reflect adversely on fitness to practice law, such as offenses involving fraud and the offense of willful failure to file an income tax return. However, some kinds of offense carry no such implication. Traditionally, the distinction was drawn in terms of offenses involving "moral turpitude." That concept can be construed to include offenses concerning some matters of personal morality, such as adultery and comparable offenses, that have no specific connection to fitness for the practice of law. Although a lawyer is personally answerable to the entire criminal law, a lawyer should be professionally answerable only for offenses that indicate lack of those characteristics relevant to law practice. Offenses involving

violence, dishonesty or breach of trust, or serious interference with the administration of justice are in that category. A pattern of repeated offenses, even ones of minor significance when considered separately, can indicate indifference to legal obligation.

[2] A lawyer who, in the course of representing a client, knowingly manifests by words or conduct, bias or prejudice based upon race, sex, religion, national origin, disability, age, sexual orientation or socioeconomic status, violates paragraph (d) when such actions are prejudicial to the administration of justice. Legitimate advocacy respecting the foregoing factors does not violate paragraph (d). A trial judge's finding that peremptory challenges were exercised on a discriminatory basis does not alone establish a violation of this rule.

[3] A lawyer may refuse to comply with an obligation imposed by law upon a good faith belief that no valid obligation exists. The provisions of Rule 1.2(d) concerning a good faith challenge to the validity, scope, meaning or application of the law apply to challenges of legal regulation of the practice of law.

[4] Lawyers holding public office assume legal responsibilities going beyond those of other citizens. A lawyer's abuse of public office can suggest an inability to fulfill the professional role of attorney. The same is true of abuse of positions of private trust such as trustee, executor, administrator, guardian, agent and officer, director or manager of a corporation or other organization.

MODEL CODE COMPARISON

[1] With regard to paragraphs (a) through (d), DR 1–102(A) provided that a lawyer shall not:

"(1) Violate a Disciplinary Rule.

"(2) Circumvent a Disciplinary Rule through actions of another.

"(3) Engage in illegal conduct involving moral turpitude.

"(4) Engage in conduct involving dishonesty, fraud, deceit, or misrepresentation.

"(5) Engage in conduct that is prejudicial to the administration of justice.

"(6) Engage in any other conduct that adversely reflects on his fitness to practice law."

[2] Paragraph (e) is substantially similar to DR 9–101(C).

[3] There is no direct counterpart to paragraph (f) in the Disciplinary Rules of the Model Code. EC 7–34 stated in part that "[a] lawyer ... is never justified in making a gift or a loan to a [judicial officer] except as permitted by ... the Code of Judicial Conduct." EC 9–1 stated that a lawyer "should promote public confidence in our [legal] system and in the legal profession."

RULE 8.5 Disciplinary Authority; Choice of Law

(a) *Disciplinary Authority.* **A lawyer admitted to practice in this jurisdiction is subject to the disciplinary authority of this jurisdiction, regardless of where the lawyer's conduct occurs. A lawyer may be subject to the disciplinary authority of both this jurisdiction and another jurisdiction where the lawyer is admitted for the same conduct.**

(b) *Choice of Law.* **In any exercise of the disciplinary authority of this jurisdiction, the rules of professional conduct to be applied shall be as follows:**

(1) for conduct in connection with a proceeding in a court before which a lawyer has been admitted to practice (either generally or for purposes of that proceeding), the rules to be applied shall be the rules of the jurisdiction in which the court sits, unless the rules of the court provide otherwise; and

(2) for any other conduct,

(i) if the lawyer is licensed to practice only in this jurisdiction, the rules to be applied shall be the rules of this jurisdiction, and

(ii) if the lawyer is licensed to practice in this and another jurisdiction, the rules to be applied shall be the rules of the admitting jurisdiction in which the lawyer principally practices; provided, however, that if particular conduct clearly has its predominant effect in another jurisdiction in which the lawyer is licensed to practice, the rules of that jurisdiction shall be applied to that conduct.

COMMENT

Disciplinary Authority

[1] Paragraph (a) restates longstanding law.

Choice of Law

[2] A lawyer may be potentially subject to more than one set of rules of professional conduct which impose different obligations. The lawyer may be licensed to practice in more than one jurisdiction with differing rules, or may be admitted to practice before a particular court with rules that differ from those of the jurisdiction or jurisdictions in which the lawyer is licensed to practice. In the past, decisions have not developed clear or consistent guidance as to which rules apply in such circumstances.

[3] Paragraph (b) seeks to resolve such potential conflicts. Its premise is that minimizing conflicts between rules, as well as uncertainty about which rules are applicable, is in the best interest of both clients and the profession (as well as the bodies having authority to regulate the profession). Accordingly, it takes the approach of (i) providing that any particular conduct of an attorney shall be subject to only one set of rules of professional conduct, and (ii) making the determination of which set of rules applies to particular conduct as straightforward as possible, consistent with recognition of appropriate regulatory interests of relevant jurisdictions.

[4] Paragraph (b) provides that as to a lawyer's conduct relating to a proceeding in a court before which the lawyer is admitted to practice (either generally or pro hac vice), the lawyer shall be subject only to the rules of professional conduct of that court. As to all other conduct, paragraph (b) provides that a lawyer licensed to practice only in this jurisdiction shall be subject to the rules of professional conduct of this jurisdiction, and that a lawyer licensed in multiple jurisdictions shall be subject only to the rules of the jurisdiction where he or she (as an individual, not his or her firm) principally practices, but with one exception: if particular conduct clearly has its predominant effect in another admitting jurisdiction, then only the rules of that jurisdiction shall apply. The intention is for the latter exception to be a narrow one.

It would be appropriately applied, for example, to a situation in which a lawyer admitted in, and principally practicing in, State A, but also admitted in State B, handled an acquisition by a company whose headquarters and operations were in State B of another, similar such company.   The exception would not appropriately be applied, on the other hand, if the lawyer handled an acquisition by a company whose headquarters and operations were in State A of a company whose headquarters and main operations were in State A, but which also had some operations in State B.

[5] If two admitting jurisdictions were to proceed against a lawyer for the same conduct, they should, applying this rule, identify the same governing ethics rules. They should take all appropriate steps to see that they do apply the same rule to the same conduct, and in all events should avoid proceeding against a lawyer on the basis of two inconsistent rules.

[6]   The choice of law provision is not intended to apply to transnational practice. Choice of law in this context should be the subject of agreements between jurisdictions or of appropriate international law.

MODEL CODE COMPARISON

There was no counterpart to this Rule in the Model Code.

AMERICAN BAR ASSOCIATION MODEL CODE OF PROFESSIONAL RESPONSIBILITY

As Amended

PREAMBLE AND PRELIMINARY STATEMENT

Preamble [1]

The continued existence of a free and democratic society depends upon recognition of the concept that justice is based upon the rule of law grounded in respect for the dignity of the individual and his capacity through reason for enlightened self-government.[2] Law so grounded makes justice possible, for only through such law does the dignity of the individual attain respect and protection. Without it, individual rights become subject to unrestrained power, respect for law is destroyed, and rational self-government is impossible.

Lawyers, as guardians of the law, play a vital role in the preservation of society.

The fulfillment of this role requires an understanding by lawyers of their relationship with and function in our legal system.[3] A consequent obligation of lawyers is to maintain the highest standards of ethical conduct.

In fulfilling his professional responsibilities, a lawyer necessarily assumes various roles that require the performance of many difficult tasks. Not every situation which he may encounter can be foreseen,[4] but fundamental ethical principles are always present to guide him. Within the framework of these principles, a lawyer must with courage and foresight be able and ready to shape the body of the law to the ever-changing relationships of society.[5]

1. The footnotes are intended merely to enable the reader to relate the provisions of this Code to the ABA Canons of Professional Ethics adopted in 1908, as amended, the Opinions of the ABA Committee on Professional Ethics, and a limited number of other sources; they are not intended to be an annotation of the views taken by the ABA Special Committee on Evaluation of Ethical Standards. Footnotes citing ABA Canons refer to the ABA Canons of Professional Ethics, adopted in 1908, as amended.

2. Cf. ABA Canons, Preamble.

3. "[T]he lawyer stands today in special need of a clear understanding of his obligations and of the vital connection between these obligations and the role his profession plays in society." *Professional Responsibility: Report of the Joint Conference,* 44 A.B.A.J. 1159, 1160 (1958).

4. "No general statement of the responsibilities of the legal profession can encompass all the situations in which the lawyer may be placed. Each position held by him makes its own peculiar demands. These demands the lawyer must clarify for himself in the light of the particular role in which he serves." *Professional Responsibility: Report of the Joint Conference,* 44 A.B.A.J. 1159, 1218 (1958).

5. "The law and its institutions change as social conditions change. They must change if they are to preserve, much less advance, the political and social values from which they derive their purposes and their life. This is true of the most important of legal institutions, the profession of law. The profession, too, must change when conditions change in order to preserve and advance the social values that are its reasons for being." Cheatham, *Avail-*

The Code of Professional Responsibility points the way to the aspiring and provides standards by which to judge the transgressor. Each lawyer must find within his own conscience the touchstone against which to test the extent to which his actions should rise above minimum standards. But in the last analysis it is the desire for the respect and confidence of the members of his profession and of the society which he serves that should provide to a lawyer the incentive for the highest possible degree of ethical conduct. The possible loss of that respect and confidence is the ultimate sanction. So long as its practitioners are guided by these principles, the law will continue to be a noble profession. This is its greatness and its strength, which permit of no compromise.

Preliminary Statement

In furtherance of the principles stated in the Preamble, the American Bar Association has promulgated this Code of Professional Responsibility, consisting of three separate but interrelated parts: Canons, Ethical Considerations, and Disciplinary Rules.[6] The Code is designed to be adopted by appropriate agencies both as an inspirational guide to the members of the profession and as a basis for disciplinary action when the conduct of a law-

yer falls below the required minimum standards stated in the Disciplinary Rules.

Obviously the Canons, Ethical Considerations, and Disciplinary Rules cannot apply to non-lawyers; however, they do define the type of ethical conduct that the public has a right to expect not only of lawyers but also of their non-professional employees and associates in all matters pertaining to professional employment. A lawyer should ultimately be responsible for the conduct of his employees and associates in the course of the professional representation of the client.

The Canons are statements of axiomatic norms, expressing in general terms the standards of professional conduct expected of lawyers in their relationships with the public, with the legal system, and with the legal profession. They embody the general concepts from which the Ethical Considerations and the Disciplinary Rules are derived.

The Ethical Considerations are aspirational in character and represent the objectives toward which every member of the profession should strive. They constitute a body of principles upon which the lawyer can rely for guidance in many specific situations.[7]

ability of Legal Services: The Responsibility of the Individual Lawyer and the Organized Bar, 12 U.C.L.A.L.Rev. 438, 440 (1965).

6. The Supreme Court of Wisconsin adopted a Code of Judicial Ethics in 1967. "The code is divided into standards and rules, the standards being statements of what the general desirable level of conduct should be, the rules being particular canons, the violation of which shall subject an individual judge to sanctions." In re Promulgation of a Code of Judicial Ethics, 36 Wis.2d 252, 255, 153 N.W.2d 873, 874 (1967).

The portion of the Wisconsin Code of Judicial Ethics entitled "Standards" states that "[t]he following standards set forth the significant qualities of the ideal judge . . . ." Id., 36 Wis.2d at 256, 153 N.W.2d at 875. The portion entitled "Rules" states that "[t]he court promulgates the following rules because the requirements of judicial conduct embodied

therein are of sufficient gravity to warrant sanctions if they are not obeyed. . . ." Id., 36 Wis.2d at 259, 153 N.W.2d at 876.

7. "Under the conditions of modern practice it is peculiarly necessary that the lawyer should understand, not merely the established standards of professional conduct, but the reasons underlying these standards. Today the lawyer plays a changing and increasingly varied role. In many developing fields the precise contribution of the legal profession is as yet undefined." *Professional Responsibility: Report of the Joint Conference,* 44 A.B.A.J. 1159 (1958).

"A true sense of professional responsibility must derive from an understanding of the reasons that lie back of specific restraints, such as those embodied in the Canons. The grounds for the lawyer's peculiar obligations are to be found in the nature of his calling. The lawyer who seeks a clear understanding of his duties

The Disciplinary Rules, unlike the Ethical Considerations, are mandatory in character. The Disciplinary Rules state the minimum level of conduct below which no lawyer can fall without being subject to disciplinary action. Within the framework of fair trial,[8] the Disciplinary Rules should be uniformly applied to all lawyers,[9] regardless of the nature of their professional activities.[10] The Code makes no attempt to prescribe either disciplinary procedures or penalties [11] for violation of a Disciplinary Rule,[12] nor does it undertake to define standards for civil liability of lawyers for professional conduct. The severity of judgment against one found guilty of violating a Disciplinary Rule should be determined by the character of the offense and the attendant circumstances.[13] An enforcing agency, in apply-

will be led to reflect on the special services his profession renders to society and the services it might render if its full capacities were realized. When the lawyer fully understands the nature of his office, he will then discern what restraints are necessary to keep that office wholesome and effective." *Id.*

8. "Disbarment, designed to protect the public, is a punishment or penalty imposed on the lawyer. *** He is accordingly entitled to procedural due process, which includes fair notice of the charge." In re Ruffalo, 390 U.S. 544, 550, 20 L.Ed.2d 117, 122, 88 S.Ct. 1222, 1226 (1968), rehearing denied, 391 U.S. 961, 20 L.Ed.2d 874, 88 S.Ct. 1833 (1968).

"A State cannot exclude a person from the practice of law or from any other occupation in a manner or for reasons that contravene the Due Process or Equal Protection Clause of the Fourteenth Amendment.... A State can require high standards of qualification ... but any qualification must have a rational connection with the applicant's fitness or capacity to practice law." Schware v. Bd. of Bar Examiners, 353 U.S. 232, 239, 1 L.Ed.2d 796, 801–02, 77 S.Ct. 752, 756 (1957).

"[A]n accused lawyer may expect that he will not be condemned out of a capricious self-righteousness or denied the essentials of a fair hearing." Kingsland v. Dorsey, 338 U.S. 318, 320, 94 L.Ed. 123, 126, 70 S.Ct. 123, 124–25 (1949).

"The attorney and counsellor being, by the solemn judicial act of the court, clothed with his office, does not hold it as a matter of grace and favor. The right which it confers upon him to appear for suitors, and to argue causes is something more than a mere indulgence, revocable at the pleasure of the court, or at the command of the legislature. It is a right of which he can only be deprived by the judgment of the court, for moral or professional delinquency." Ex parte Garland, 71 U.S. (4 Wall.) 333, 378–79, 18 L.Ed. 366, 370 (1866).

See generally Comment, *Procedural Due Process and Character Hearings for Bar Applicants,* 15 Stan.L.Rev. 500 (1963).

9. "The canons of professional ethics must be enforced by the Courts and must be respected by members of the Bar if we are to maintain public confidence in the integrity and impartiality of the administration of justice." In re Meeker, 76 N.M. 354, 357, 414 P.2d 862, 864 (1966), appeal dismissed, 385 U.S. 449 (1967).

10. See ABA Canon 45.

"The Canons of this Association govern all its members, irrespective of the nature of their practice, and the application of the Canons is not affected by statutes or regulations governing certain activities of lawyers which may prescribe less stringent standards." ABA Comm. on Professional Ethics, Opinions, No. 203 (1940) [hereinafter each Opinion is cited as "ABA Opinion"].

Cf. *ABA Opinion* 152 (1936).

11. "There is generally no prescribed discipline for any particular type of improper conduct. The disciplinary measures taken are discretionary with the courts, which may disbar, suspend, or merely censure the attorney as the nature of the offense and past indicia of character may warrant." Note, 43 Cornell L.Q. 489, 495 (1958).

12. The Code seeks only to specify conduct for which a lawyer should be disciplined. Recommendations as to the procedures to be used in disciplinary actions and the gravity of disciplinary measures appropriate for violations of the Code are within the jurisdiction of the American Bar Association Special Committee on Evaluation of Disciplinary Enforcement.

13. "The severity of the judgment of this court should be in proportion to the gravity of the offenses, the moral turpitude involved, and the extent that the defendant's acts and conduct affect his professional qualifications to practice law." Louisiana State Bar Ass'n v. Steiner, 204 La. 1073, 1092–93, 16 So.2d 843, 850 (1944) (Higgins, J., concurring in decree).

"Certainly an erring lawyer who has been disciplined and who having paid the penalty has given satisfactory evidence of repentance and has been rehabilitated and restored to his

ing the Disciplinary Rules, may find interpretive guidance in the basic principles embodied in the Canons and in the objectives reflected in the Ethical Considerations.

CANON 1

A Lawyer Should Assist in Maintaining the Integrity and Competence of the Legal Profession

ETHICAL CONSIDERATIONS

EC 1–1   A basic tenet of the professional responsibility of lawyers is that every person in our society should have ready access to the independent professional

place at the bar by the court which knows him best ought not to have what amounts to an order of permanent disbarment entered against him by a federal court solely on the basis of an earlier criminal record and without regard to his subsequent rehabilitation and present good character.... We think, therefore, that the district court should reconsider the appellant's application for admission and grant it unless the court finds it to be a fact that the appellant is not presently of good moral or professional character." In re Dreier, 258 F.2d 68, 69–70 (3d Cir.1958).

1. "[W]e cannot conclude that all educational restrictions [on bar admission] are unlawful. We assume that few would deny that a grammar school education requirement, before taking the bar examination, was reasonable. Or that an applicant had to be able to read or write. Once we conclude that *some* restriction is proper, then it becomes a matter of degree—the problem of drawing the line.

.   .   .

"We conclude the fundamental question here is whether Rule IV, Section 6 of the Rules Pertaining to Admission of Applicants to the State Bar of Arizona is 'arbitrary, capricious and unreasonable.' We conclude an educational requirement of graduation from an accredited law school is not." Hackin v. Lockwood, 361 F.2d 499, 503–04 (9th Cir.1966), cert. denied, 385 U.S. 960, 17 L.Ed.2d 305, 87 S.Ct. 396 (1966).

2. "Every state in the United States, as a prerequisite for admission to the practice of law, requires that applicants possess 'good moral character.' Although the requirement is of judicial origin, it is now embodied in legislation in most states." Comment, *Procedural Due Process and Character Hearings for Bar Applicants*, 15 Stan.L.Rev. 500 (1963).

services of a lawyer of integrity and competence. Maintaining the integrity and improving the competence of the bar to meet the highest standards is the ethical responsibility of every lawyer.

EC 1–2   The public should be protected from those who are not qualified to be lawyers by reason of a deficiency in education [1] or moral standards [2] or of other relevant factors [3] but who nevertheless seek to practice law. To assure the maintenance of high moral and educational standards of the legal profession, lawyers should affirmatively assist courts and other appropriate bodies in promulgating,

"Good character in the members of the bar is essential to the preservation of the integrity of the courts. The duty and power of the court to guard its portals against intrusion by men and women who are mentally and morally dishonest, unfit because of bad character, evidenced by their course of conduct, to participate in the administrative law, would seem to be unquestioned in the matter of preservation of judicial dignity and integrity." In re Monaghan, 126 Vt. 53, 222 A.2d 665, 670 (1966).

"Fundamentally, the question involved in both situations [i.e. admission and disciplinary proceedings] is the same—is the applicant for admission or the attorney sought to be disciplined a fit and proper person to be permitted to practice law, and that usually turns upon whether he has committed or is likely to continue to commit acts of moral turpitude. At the time of oral argument the attorney for respondent frankly conceded that the test for admission and for discipline is and should be the same. We agree with this concession." Hallinan v. Comm. of Bar Examiners, 65 Cal.2d 447, 453, 421 P.2d 76, 81, 55 Cal.Rptr. 228, 233 (1966).

3. "Proceedings to gain admission to the bar are for the purpose of protecting the public and the courts from the ministrations of persons unfit to practice the profession. Attorneys are officers of the court appointed to assist the court in the administration of justice. Into their hands are committed the property, the liberty and sometimes the lives of their clients. This commitment demands a high degree of intelligence, knowledge of the law, respect for its function in society, sound and faithful judgment and, above all else, integrity of character in private and professional conduct." In re Monaghan, 126 Vt. 53, 222 A.2d 665, 676 (1966) (Holden, C.J., dissenting).

enforcing, and improving requirements for admission to the bar.[4] In like manner, the bar has a positive obligation to aid in the continued improvement of all phases of pre-admission and post-admission legal education.

EC 1–3 Before recommending an applicant for admission, a lawyer should satisfy himself that the applicant is of good moral character. Although a lawyer should not become a self-appointed investigator or judge of applicants for admission, he should report to proper officials all unfavorable information he possesses relating to the character or other qualifications of an applicant.[5]

EC 1–4 The integrity of the profession can be maintained only if conduct of lawyers in violation of the Disciplinary Rules is brought to the attention of the proper officials. A lawyer should reveal voluntarily to those officials all unprivileged knowledge of conduct of lawyers which he believes clearly to be in violation of the Disciplinary Rules.[6] A lawyer should, upon request, serve on and assist commit-

4. "A bar composed of lawyers of good moral character is a worthy objective but it is unnecessary to sacrifice vital freedoms in order to obtain that goal. It is also important both to society and the bar itself that lawyers be unintimidated—free to think, speak, and act as members of an Independent Bar." Konigsberg v. State Bar, 353 U.S. 252, 273, 1 L.Ed.2d 810, 825, 77 S.Ct. 722, 733 (1957).

5. *See* ABA Canon 29.

6. ABA Canon 28 designates certain conduct as unprofessional and then states that: "A duty to the public and to the profession devolves upon every member of the Bar having knowledge of such practices upon the part of any practitioner immediately to inform thereof, to the end that the offender may be disbarred." ABA Canon 29 states a broader admonition: "Lawyers should expose without fear or favor before the proper tribunals corrupt or dishonest conduct in the profession."

7. "It is the obligation of the organized Bar and the individual lawyer to give unstinted cooperation and assistance to the highest court of the state in discharging its function and duty with respect to discipline and in purging the profession of the unworthy." *Report of the Special Committee on Disciplinary Procedures*, 80 A.B.A.Rep. 463, 470 (1955).

tees and boards having responsibility for the administration of the Disciplinary Rules.[7]

EC 1–5 A lawyer should maintain high standards of professional conduct and should encourage fellow lawyers to do likewise. He should be temperate and dignified, and he should refrain from all illegal and morally reprehensible conduct.[8] Because of his position in society, even minor violations of law by a lawyer may tend to lessen public confidence in the legal profession. Obedience to law exemplifies respect for law. To lawyers especially, respect for the law should be more than a platitude.

EC 1–6 An applicant for admission to the bar or a lawyer may be unqualified, temporarily or permanently, for other than moral and educational reasons, such as mental or emotional instability. Lawyers should be diligent in taking steps to see that during a period of disqualification such person is not granted a license or, if licensed, is not permitted to practice.[9] In like manner, when the disquali-

8. Cf. ABA Canon 32.

9. "We decline, on the present record, to disbar Mr. Sherman or to reprimand him—not because we condone his actions, but because, as heretofore indicated, we are concerned with whether he is mentally responsible for what he has done.

"The logic of the situation would seem to dictate the conclusion that, if he was mentally responsible for the conduct we have outlined, he should be disbarred; and, if he was not mentally responsible, he should not be permitted to practice law.

"However, the flaw in the logic is that he may have been mentally irresponsible [at the time of his offensive conduct] ..., and, yet, have sufficiently improved in the almost two and one-half years intervening to be able to capably and competently represent his clients....

. . .

"We would make clear that we are satisfied that a case has been made against Mr. Sherman, warranting a refusal to permit him to further practice law in this state unless he can establish his mental irresponsibility at the time

fication has terminated, members of the bar should assist such person in being licensed, or, if licensed, in being restored to his full right to practice.

DISCIPLINARY RULES

DR 1–101 Maintaining Integrity and Competence of the Legal Profession.

(A) A lawyer is subject to discipline if he has made a materially false statement in, or if he has deliberately failed to disclose a material fact requested in connection with, his application for admission to the bar.[10]

of the offenses charged. The burden of proof is upon him.

"If he establishes such mental irresponsibility, the burden is then upon him to establish his present capability to practice law." In re Sherman, 58 Wash.2d 1, 6–7, 354 P.2d 888, 890 (1960), cert. denied, 371 U.S. 951, 9 L.Ed.2d 499, 83 S.Ct. 506 (1963).

10. "This Court has the inherent power to revoke a license to practice law in this State, where such license was issued by this Court, and its issuance was procured by the fraudulent concealment, or by the false and fraudulent representation by the applicant of a fact which was manifestly material to the issuance of the license." North Carolina ex rel. Attorney General v. Gorson, 209 N.C. 320, 326, 183 S.E. 392, 395 (1936), cert. denied, 298 U.S. 662, 80 L.Ed. 1387, 56 S.Ct. 752 (1936).

See also Application of Patterson, 318 P.2d 907, 913 (Or.1957), cert. denied, 356 U.S. 947, 2 L.Ed.2d 822, 78 S.Ct. 795 (1958).

11. See ABA Canon 29.

12. In *ABA Opinion* 95 (1933), which held that a municipal attorney could not permit police officers to interview persons with claims against the municipality when the attorney knew the claimants to be represented by counsel, the Committee on Professional Ethics said:

"The law officer is, of course, responsible for the acts of those in his department who are under his supervision and control." *Opinion 85.* In re Robinson, 136 N.Y.S. 548 (affirmed 209 N.Y. 354–1912) held that it was a matter of disbarment for an attorney to adopt a general course of approving the unethical conduct of employees of his client, even though he did not actively participate therein.

(B) A lawyer shall not further the application for admission to the bar of another person known by him to be unqualified in respect to character, education, or other relevant attribute.[11]

DR 1–102 Misconduct.

(A) A lawyer shall not:

(1) Violate a Disciplinary Rule.

(2) Circumvent a Disciplinary Rule through actions of another.[12]

(3) Engage in illegal conduct involving moral turpitude.[13]

" '. . . The attorney should not advise or sanction acts by his client which he himself should not do.' *Opinion 75.*"

13. "The most obvious non-professional ground for disbarment is conviction for a felony. Most states make conviction for a felony grounds for automatic disbarment. Some of these states, including New York, make disbarment mandatory upon conviction for *any* felony, while others require disbarment only for those felonies which involve moral turpitude. There are strong arguments that some felonies, such as involuntary manslaughter, reflect neither on an attorney's fitness, trustworthiness, nor competence and, therefore, should not be grounds for disbarment, but most states tend to disregard these arguments and, following the common law rule, make disbarment mandatory on conviction for any felony." Note, 43 Cornell L.Q. 489, 490 (1958).

"Some states treat conviction for misdemeanors as grounds for automatic disbarment. . . . However, the vast majority, accepting the common law rule, require that the misdemeanor involve moral turpitude. While the definition of moral turpitude may prove difficult, it seems only proper that those minor offenses which do not affect the attorney's fitness to continue in the profession should not be grounds for disbarment. A good example is an assault and battery conviction which would not involve moral turpitude unless done with malice and deliberation." Id. at 491.

"The term 'moral turpitude' has been used in the law for centuries. It has been the subject of many decisions by the courts but has never been clearly defined because of the nature of the term. Perhaps the best general definition of the term 'moral turpitude' is that

(4) Engage in conduct involving dishonesty, fraud, deceit, or misrepresentation.

(5) Engage in conduct that is prejudicial to the administration of justice.

(6) Engage in any other conduct that adversely reflects on his fitness to practice law.[14]

DR 1–103   Disclosure of Information to Authorities.

(A) A lawyer possessing unprivileged knowledge of a violation of DR 1–102 shall report such knowledge to a tribunal or other authority empowered to investigate or act upon such violation.[15]

(B) A lawyer possessing unprivileged knowledge or evidence concern-

ing another lawyer or a judge shall reveal fully such knowledge or evidence upon proper request of a tribunal or other authority empowered to investigate or act upon the conduct of lawyers or judges.[16]

CANON 2

A Lawyer Should Assist the Legal Profession in Fulfilling Its Duty to Make Legal Counsel Available

ETHICAL CONSIDERATIONS

EC 2–1   The need of members of the public for legal services[1] is met only if they recognize their legal problems, appreciate the importance of seeking assistance,[2] and are able to obtain the services

---

it imports an act of baseness, vileness or depravity in the duties which one person owes to another or to society in general, which is contrary to the usual, accepted and customary rule of right and duty which a person should follow. 58 C.J.S. at page 1201. Although offenses against revenue laws have been held to be crimes of moral turpitude, it has also been held that the attempt to evade the payment of taxes due to the government or any subdivision thereof, while wrong and unlawful, does not involve moral turpitude. 58 C.J.S. at page 1205." Comm. on Legal Ethics v. Scherr, 149 W.Va. 721, 726–27, 143 S.E.2d 141, 145 (1965).

"The right and power to discipline an attorney, as one of its officers, is inherent in the court.... This power is not limited to those instances of misconduct wherein he has been employed, or has acted, in a professional capacity; but, on the contrary, this power may be exercised where his misconduct outside the scope of his professional relations shows him to be an unfit person to practice law." In re Wilson, 391 S.W.2d 914, 917–18 (Mo.1965).

14. "It is a fair characterization of the lawyer's responsibility in our society that he stands 'as a shield,' to quote Devlin, J., in defense of right and to ward off wrong. From a profession charged with these responsibilities there must be exacted those qualities of truthspeaking, of a high sense of honor, of granite discretion, of the strictest observance of fiduciary responsibility, that have, throughout the centuries, been compendiously described as 'moral character.'" Schware v. Bd. of Bar

Examiners, 353 U.S. 232, 1 L.Ed.2d 796, 806, 77 S.Ct. 752, 761 (1957) (Frankfurter, J., concurring).

"Particularly applicable here is Rule 4.47 providing that 'A lawyer should always maintain his integrity; and shall not willfully commit any act against the interest of the public; nor shall he violate his duty to the courts or his clients; *nor shall he, by any misconduct, commit any offense against the laws of Missouri or the United States of America, which amounts to a crime involving acts done by him contrary to justice, honesty, modesty or good morals;* nor shall he be guilty of any other misconduct whereby, for the protection of the public and those charged with the administration of justice, he should no longer be entrusted with the duties and responsibilities belonging to the office of an attorney.'" In re Wilson, 391 S.W.2d 914, 917 (Mo.1965).

15. See ABA Canon 29; cf. ABA Canon 28.

16. Cf. ABA Canons 28 and 29.

1. "Men have need for more than a system of law; they have need for a system of law which functions, and that means they have need for lawyers." Cheatham, *The Lawyer's Role and Surroundings*, 25 Rocky Mt.L.Rev. 405 (1953).

2. "Law is not self-applying; men must apply and utilize it in concrete cases. But the ordinary man is incapable. He cannot know the principles of law or the rules guiding the machinery of law administration; he does not

of acceptable legal counsel.[3]   Hence, important functions of the legal profession are to educate laymen to recognize their problems, to facilitate the process of intelligent selection of lawyers, and to assist in making legal services fully available.[4]

Recognition of Legal Problems

EC 2–2   The legal profession should assist lay-persons to recognize legal problems because such problems may not be self-revealing and often are not timely noticed.   Therefore, lawyers should encourage and participate in educational and public relations programs concerning our legal system with particular reference to legal problems that frequently arise. Preparation of advertisements and professional articles for lay publications [5] and participation in seminars, lectures, and civic programs should be motivated by a desire to educate the public to an aware-

ness of legal needs and to provide information relevant to the selection of the most appropriate counsel rather than to obtain publicity for particular lawyers. The problems of advertising on television require special consideration, due to the style, cost, and transitory nature of such media.   If the interests of laypersons in receiving relevant lawyer advertising are not adequately served by print media and radio advertising, and if adequate safeguards to protect the public can reasonably be formulated, television advertising may serve a public interest.

EC 2–3   Whether a lawyer acts properly in volunteering in-person advice to a layperson to seek legal services depends upon the circumstances.[6]   The giving of advice that one should take legal action could well be in fulfillment of the duty of the legal profession to assist laypersons in

know how to formulate his desires with precision and to put them into writing; he is ineffective in the presentation of his claims." Cheatham, *The Lawyer's Role and Surroundings,* 25 Rocky Mt.L.Rev. 405 (1953).

3.   "This need [to provide legal services] was recognized by ... Mr. [Lewis F.] Powell [Jr., President, American Bar Association, 1963–64], who said: 'Looking at contemporary America realistically, we must admit that despite all our efforts to date (and these have not been insignificant), far too many persons are not able to obtain equal justice under law. This usually results because their poverty or their ignorance has prevented them from obtaining legal counsel.' "   Address by E. Clinton Bamberger, Association of American Law Schools 1965 Annual Meeting, Dec. 28, 1965, in Proceedings, Part II, 1965, 61, 63–64 (1965).

"A wide gap separates the need for legal services and its satisfaction, as numerous studies reveal.   Looked at from the side of the layman, one reason for the gap is poverty and the consequent inability to pay legal fees.   Another set of reasons is ignorance of the need for and the value of legal services, and ignorance of where to find a dependable lawyer. There is fear of the mysterious processes and delays of the law, and there is fear of overreaching and overcharging by lawyers, a fear stimulated by the occasional exposure of shysters."   Cheatham, *Availability of Legal Services: The Responsibility of the Individual*

Lawyer and of the Organized Bar, 12 U.C.L.A.L.Rev. 438 (1965).

4.   "It is not only the right but the duty of the profession as a whole to utilize such methods as may be developed to bring the services of its members to those who need them, so long as this can be done ethically and with dignity."   *ABA Opinion* 320 (1968).

"[T]here is a responsibility on the bar to make legal services available to those who need them.   The maxim, 'privilege brings responsibilities,' can be expanded to read, exclusive privilege to render public service brings responsibility to assure that the service is available to those in need of it."   Cheatham, *Availability of Legal Services: The Responsibility of the Individual Lawyer and of the Organized Bar,* 12 U.C.L.A.L.Rev. 438, 443 (1965).

"The obligation to provide legal services for those actually caught up in litigation carries with it the obligation to make preventive legal advice accessible to all.   It is among those unaccustomed to business affairs and fearful of the ways of the law that such advice is often most needed.   If it is not received in time, the most valiant and skillful representation in court may come too late."   *Professional Responsibility: Report of the Joint Conference,* 44 A.B.A.J. 1159, 1216 (1958).

5.   "A lawyer may with propriety write articles for publications in which he gives information upon the law...."   A.B.A. Canon 40.

6.   See ABA Canon 28.

recognizing legal problems.[7] The advice is proper only if motivated by a desire to protect one who does not recognize that he may have legal problems or who is ignorant of his legal rights or obligations. It is improper if motivated by a desire to obtain personal benefit, secure personal publicity, or cause legal action to be taken merely to harass or injure another. A lawyer should not initiate an in-person contact with a non-client, personally or through a representative, for the purpose of being retained to represent him for compensation.

EC 2–4 Since motivation is subjective and often difficult to judge, the motives of a lawyer who volunteers in-person advice likely to produce legal controversy may well be suspect if he receives professional employment or other benefits as a result.[8] A lawyer who volunteers in-person advice that one should obtain the services of a lawyer generally should not himself ac-

cept employment, compensation, or other benefit in connection with that matter. However, it is not improper for a lawyer to volunteer such advice and render resulting legal services to close friends, relatives, former clients (in regard to matters germane to former employment), and regular clients.[9]

EC 2–5 A lawyer who writes or speaks for the purpose of educating members of the public to recognize their legal problems should carefully refrain from giving or appearing to give a general solution applicable to all apparently similar individual problems,[10] since slight changes in fact situations may require a material variance in the applicable advice; otherwise, the public may be mislead and misadvised. Talks and writings by lawyers for laypersons should caution them not to attempt to solve individual problems upon the basis of the information contained

7. This question can assume constitutional dimensions: "We meet at the outset the contention that 'solicitation' is wholly outside the area of freedoms protected by the First Amendment. To this contention there are two answers. The first is that a State cannot foreclose the exercise of constitutional rights by mere labels. The second is that abstract discussion is not the only species of communication which the Constitution protects; the First Amendment also protects vigorous advocacy, certainly of lawful ends, against governmental intrusion. . . .

. . . .

"However valid may be Virginia's interest in regulating the traditionally illegal practice of barratry, maintenance and champerty, that interest does not justify the prohibition of the NAACP activities disclosed by this record. Malicious intent was of the essence of the common-law offenses of fomenting or stirring up litigation. And whatever may be or may have been true of suits against governments in other countries, the exercise in our own, as in this case of First Amendment rights to enforce Constitutional rights through litigation, as a matter of law, cannot be deemed malicious." NAACP v. Button, 371 U.S. 415, 429, 439–40, 9 L.Ed.2d 405, 415–16, 422, 83 S.Ct. 328, 336, 341 (1963).

8. It is disreputable for an attorney to breed litigation by seeking out those who have

claims for personal injuries or other grounds of action in order to secure them as clients, or to employ agents or runners, or to reward those who bring or influence the bringing of business to his office. . . . Moreover, it tends quite easily to the institution of baseless litigation and the manufacture of perjured testimony. From early times, this danger has been recognized in the law by the condemnation of the crime of common barratry, or the stirring up of suits or quarrels between individuals at law or otherwise." In re Ades, 6 F.Supp. 467, 474–75 (D.Md.1934).

9. "*Rule 2.*

"§ a. . . .

"[A] member of the State Bar shall not solicit professional employment by

"(1) Volunteering counsel or advice except where ties of blood relationship or trust make it appropriate." Cal.Business and Professions Code § 6076 (West 1962).

10. "*Rule 18* . . . A member of the State Bar shall not advise inquirers or render opinions to them through or in connection with a newspaper, radio or other publicity medium of any kind in respect to their specific legal problems, whether or not such attorney shall be compensated for his services." Cal.Business and Professions Code § 6076 (West 1962).

therein.[11]

Selection of a Lawyer

EC 2–6 Formerly a potential client usually knew the reputations of local lawyers for competency and integrity and therefore could select a practitioner in whom he had confidence. This traditional selection process worked well because it was initiated by the client and the choice was an informed one.

EC 2–7 Changed conditions, however, have seriously restricted the effectiveness of the traditional selection process. Often the reputations of lawyers are not sufficiently known to enable laypersons to make intelligent choices.[12] The law has become increasingly complex and specialized. Few lawyers are willing and competent to deal with every kind of legal matter, and many laypersons have difficulty in determining the competence of lawyers to render different types of legal services. The selection of legal counsel is particularly difficult for transients, persons moving into new areas, persons of limited education or means, and others who have little or no contact with lawyers.[13] Lack of information about the availability of lawyers, the qualifications of particular lawyers, and the expense of legal representation leads laypersons to avoid seeking legal advice.

EC 2–8 Selection of a lawyer by a layperson should be made on an informed basis. Advice and recommendation of third parties—relatives, friends, acquaintances, business associates, or other lawyers—and disclosure of relevant information about the lawyer and his practice may be helpful. A layperson is best served if the recommendation is disinterested and informed. In order that the recommendation be disinterested, a lawyer should not seek to influence another to recommend his employment. A lawyer should not compensate another person for recommending him, for influencing a prospective client to employ him, or to encourage future recommendations.[14] Advertisements and public communications, whether in law lists, telephone directories, newspapers, other forms of print media, television or radio, should be formulated to convey only information that is necessary to make an appropriate selection. Such information includes: (1) office information, such as, name, including name of law firm and names of professional associates; addresses; telephone numbers; credit card acceptability; fluency in foreign languages; and office hours; (2) relevant biographical information; (3) description of the practice, but only by using designations and definitions authorized by [the agency having jurisdiction of the subject under state law], for example, one or more fields of law in which the lawyer or law firm practices; a statement that practice is limited to one or more fields of law; and/or a statement that the lawyer or law firm specializes in a particular field of law practice, but only by using designations, definitions and standards authorized by [the agency having jurisdiction of the subject under state

11. "In any case where a member might well apply the advice given in the opinion to his individual affairs, the lawyer rendering the opinion [concerning problems common to members of an association and distributed to the members through a periodic bulletin] should specifically state that this opinion should not be relied on by any member as a basis for handling his individual affairs, but that in every case he should consult his counsel. In the publication of the opinion the association should make a similar statement." *ABA Opinion* 273 (1946).

12. "A group of recent interrelated changes bears directly on the availability of legal services. . . . [One] change is the constantly accelerating urbanization of the country and the decline of personal and neighborhood knowledge of whom to retain as a professional man." Cheatham, *Availability of Legal Services: The Responsibility of the Individual Lawyer and of the Organized Bar,* 12 U.C.L.A.L.Rev. 438, 440 (1965).

13. Cf. Cheatham, *A Lawyer When Needed: Legal Services for the Middle Classes,* 63 Colum.L.Rev. 973, 974 (1963).

14. See ABA Canon 28.

law]; and (4) permitted fee information. Self-laudation should be avoided.

Selection of a Lawyer: Lawyer Advertising

EC 2–9 The lack of sophistication on the part of many members of the public concerning legal services, the importance of the interests affected by the choice of a lawyer and prior experience with unrestricted lawyer advertising, require that special care be taken by lawyers to avoid misleading the public and to assure that the information set forth in any advertising is relevant to the selection of a lawyer. The lawyer must be mindful that the benefits of lawyer advertising depend upon its reliability and accuracy. Examples of information in lawyer advertising that would be deceptive include misstatements of fact, suggestions that the ingenuity or prior record of a lawyer rather than the justice of the claim are the principal factors likely to determine the result, inclusion of information irrelevant to selecting a lawyer, and representations concerning the quality of service, which cannot be measured or verified. Since lawyer advertising is calculated and not spontaneous, reasonable regulation of lawyer advertising designed to foster compliance with appropriate standards serves the public interest without impeding the flow of useful, meaningful, and relevant information to the public.

EC 2–10 A lawyer should ensure that the information contained in any advertising which the lawyer publishes, broadcasts or causes to be published or broadcast is relevant, is disseminated in an objective and understandable fashion, and would facilitate the prospective client's ability to compare the qualifications of the lawyers available to represent him. A lawyer should strive to communicate such information without undue emphasis upon style and advertising stratagems which serve to hinder rather than to facilitate intelligent selection of counsel. Be-

cause technological change is a recurrent feature of communications forms, and because perceptions of what is relevant in lawyer selection may change, lawyer advertising regulations should not be cast in rigid, unchangeable terms. Machinery is therefore available to advertisers and consumers for prompt consideration of proposals to change the rules governing lawyer advertising. The determination of any request for such change should depend upon whether the proposal is necessary in light of existing Code provisions, whether the proposal accords with standards of accuracy, reliability and truthfulness, and whether the proposal would facilitate informed selection of lawyers by potential consumers of legal services. Representatives of lawyers and consumers should be heard in addition to the applicant concerning any proposed change. Any change which is approved should be promulgated in the form of an amendment to the Code so that all lawyers practicing in the jurisdiction may avail themselves of its provisions.

EC 2–11 The name under which a lawyer conducts his practice may be a factor in the selection process.[15] The use of a trade name or an assumed name could mislead laypersons concerning the identity, responsibility, and status of those practicing thereunder.[16] Accordingly, a lawyer in private practice should practice only under a designation containing his own name, the name of a lawyer employing him, the name of one or more of the lawyers practicing in a partnership, or, if permitted by law, the name of a professional legal corporation, which should be clearly designated as such. For many years some law firms have used a firm name retaining one or more names of deceased or retired partners and such practice is not improper if the firm is a bona fide successor of a firm in which the deceased or retired person was a member, if the use of the name is authorized by

---

15. *Cf. ABA Opinion* 303 (1961).

16. *See* ABA Canon 33.

law or by contract, and if the public is not misled thereby.[17]   However, the name of a partner who withdraws from a firm but continues to practice law should be omitted from the firm name in order to avoid misleading the public.

EC 2–12   A lawyer occupying a judicial, legislative, or public executive or administrative position who has the right to practice law concurrently may allow his name to remain in the name of the firm if he actively continues to practice law as a member thereof.   Otherwise, his name should be removed from the firm name,[18] and he should not be identified as a past or present member of the firm; and he should not hold himself out as being a practicing lawyer.

EC 2–13   In order to avoid the possibility of misleading persons with whom he

deals, a lawyer should be scrupulous in the representation of his professional status.[19]   He should not hold himself out as being a partner or associate of a law firm if he is not one in fact,[20] and thus should not hold himself out as partner or associate if he only shares offices with another lawyer.[21]

EC 2–14   In some instances a lawyer confines his practice to a particular field of law.[22]   In the absence of state controls to insure the existence of special competence, a lawyer should not be permitted to hold himself out as a specialist or as having official recognition as a specialist, other than in the fields of admiralty, trademark, and patent law where a holding out as a specialist historically has been permitted.   A lawyer may, however, indicate in permitted advertising, if it is

---

17. Id.

"The continued use of a firm name by one or more surviving partners after the death of a member of the firm whose name is in the firm title is expressly permitted by the Canons of Ethics.   The reason for this is that all of the partners have by their joint and several efforts over a period of years contributed to the good will attached to the firm name.   In the case of a firm having widespread connections, this good will is disturbed by a change in firm name every time a name partner dies, and that reflects a loss in some degree of the good will to the building up of which the surviving partners have contributed their time, skill and labor through a period of years.   To avoid this loss the firm name is continued, and to meet the requirements of the Canon the individuals constituting the firm from time to time are listed."   *ABA Opinion* 267 (1945).

"Accepted local custom in New York recognizes that the name of a law firm does not necessarily identify the individual members of the firm, and hence the continued use of a firm name after the death of one or more partners is not a deception and is permissible....   The continued use of a deceased partner's name in the firm title is not affected by the fact that another partner withdraws from the firm and his name is dropped, or the name of the new partner is added to the firm name."   *Opinion* No. 45, Committee on Professional Ethics, New York State Bar Ass'n, 39 N.Y.St.B.J. 455 (1967).

Cf. *ABA Opinion* 258 (1943).

18. Cf. ABA Canon 33 and *ABA Opinion* 315 (1965).

19. Cf. *ABA Opinions* 283 (1950) and 81 (1932).

20. See *ABA Opinion* 316 (1967).

21. "The word 'associates' has a variety of meanings.   Principally through custom the word when used on the letterheads of law firms has come to be regarded as describing those who are employees of the firm.   Because the word has acquired this special significance in connection with the practice of the law the use of the word to describe lawyer relationships other than employer-employee is likely to be misleading."   In re Sussman and Tanner, 241 Ore. 246, 248, 405 P.2d 355, 356 (1965).

According to *ABA Opinion* 310 (1963), use of the term "associates" would be misleading in two situations: (1) where two lawyers are partners and they share both responsibility and liability for the partnership; and (2) where two lawyers practice separately, sharing no responsibility or liability, and only share a suite of offices and some costs.

22. "For a long time, many lawyers have, of necessity, limited their practice to certain branches of law.   The increasing complexity of the law and the demand of the public for more expertness on the part of the lawyer has, in the past few years—particularly in the last ten years—brought about specialization on an increasing scale."   *Report of the Special Committee on Specialization and Specialized Legal Services,* 79 A.B.A.Rep. 582, 584 (1954).

factual, a limitation of his practice or one or more particular areas or fields of law in which he practices using designations and definitions authorized for that purpose by [the state agency having jurisdiction]. A lawyer practicing in a jurisdiction which certifies specialists must also be careful not to confuse laypersons as to his status. If a lawyer discloses areas of law in which he practices or to which he limits his practice, but is not certified in [the jurisdiction], he, and the designation authorized in [the jurisdiction], should avoid any implication that he is in fact certified.

EC 2–15 The legal profession has developed lawyer referral systems designed to aid individuals who are able to pay fees but need assistance in locating lawyers competent to handle their particular problems. Use of a lawyer referral system enables a layman to avoid an uninformed selection of a lawyer because such a system makes possible the employment of competent lawyers who have indicated an interest in the subject matter involved. Lawyers should support the principle of lawyer referral systems and should encourage the evolution of other ethical plans which aid in the selection of qualified counsel.

Financial Ability to Employ Counsel: Generally

EC 2–16 The legal profession cannot remain a viable force in fulfilling its role in our society unless its members receive adequate compensation for services rendered, and reasonable fees [23] should be charged in appropriate cases to clients able to pay them. Nevertheless, persons unable to pay all or a portion of a reasonable fee should be able to obtain necessary legal services,[24] and lawyers should support and participate in ethical activities designed to achieve that objective.[25]

Financial Ability to Employ Counsel: Persons Able to Pay Reasonable Fees

EC 2–17 The determination of a proper fee requires consideration of the interests of both client and lawyer.[26] A lawyer should not charge more than a reasonable fee,[27] for excessive cost of legal service would deter laymen from utilizing the legal system in protection of their rights. Furthermore, an excessive charge abuses the professional relationship between lawyer and client. On the other hand, adequate compensation is necessary in order to enable the lawyer to serve his client effectively and to preserve the integrity and independence of the profession.[28]

EC 2–18 The determination of the reasonableness of a fee requires consideration of all relevant circumstances,[29] including those stated in the Disciplinary Rules. The fees of a lawyer will vary according to many factors, including the time required, his experience, ability, and reputation, the nature of the employment, the responsibility involved, and the results obtained. It is a commendable and long-standing tradition of the bar that special consideration is given in the fixing of any fee for services rendered a brother lawyer or a member of his immediate family.

23. See ABA Canon 12.

24. Cf. ABA Canon 12.

25. "If there is any fundamental proposition of government on which all would agree, it is that one of the highest goals of society must be to achieve and maintain equality before the law. Yet this ideal remains an empty form of words unless the legal profession is ready to provide adequate representation for those unable to pay the usual fees." *Professional Representation: Report of the Joint Conference*, 44 A.B.A.J. 1159, 1216 (1958).

26. See ABA Canon 12.

27. Cf. ABA Canon 12.

28. "When members of the Bar are induced to render legal services for inadequate compensation as a consequence the quality of the service rendered may be lowered, the welfare of the profession injured and the administration of justice made less efficient." *ABA Opinion* 302 (1961).

Cf. *ABA Opinion* 307 (1962).

29. See ABA Canon 12.

EC 2–19 As soon as feasible after a lawyer has been employed, it is desirable that he reach a clear agreement with his client as to the basis of the fee charges to be made. Such a course will not only prevent later misunderstanding but will also work for good relations between the lawyer and the client. It is usually beneficial to reduce to writing the understanding of the parties regarding the fee, particularly when it is contingent. A lawyer should be mindful that many persons who desire to employ him may have had little or no experience with fee charges of lawyers, and for this reason he should explain fully to such persons the reasons for the particular fee arrangement he proposes.

EC 2–20 Contingent fee arrangements [30] in civil cases have long been commonly accepted in the United States in proceedings to enforce claims. The historical bases of their acceptance are that (1) they often, and in a variety of circumstances, provide the only practical means by which one having a claim against another can economically afford, finance, and obtain the services of a competent lawyer to prosecute his claim, and (2) a successful prosecution of the claim produces a *res* out of which the fee can be paid.[31] Although a lawyer generally should decline to accept employment on a contingent fee basis by one who is able to pay a reasonable fixed fee, it is not necessarily improper for a lawyer, where justified by the particular circumstances of a case, to enter into a contingent fee contract in a civil case with any client who, after being fully informed of all relevant factors, desires that arrangement. Because of the human relationships involved and the unique character of the proceedings, contingent fee arrangements in domestic relation cases are rarely justified. In administrative agency proceedings contingent fee contracts should be governed by the same consideration as in other civil cases. Public policy properly condemns contingent fee arrangements in criminal cases, largely on the ground that legal services in criminal cases do not produce a *res* with which to pay the fee.

EC 2–21 A lawyer should not accept compensation or any thing of value incident to his employment or services from one other than his client without the knowledge and consent of his client after full disclosure.[32]

EC 2–22 Without the consent of his client, a lawyer should not associate in a particular matter another lawyer outside his firm. A fee may properly be divided between lawyers [33] properly associated if the division is in proportion to the services performed and the responsibility assumed by each lawyer [34] and if the total fee is reasonable.

30. See ABA Canon 13; see also MacKinnon, Contingent Fees for Legal Services (1964) (A report of the American Bar Foundation).

"A contract for a reasonable contingent fee where sanctioned by law is permitted by *Canon 13*, but the client must remain responsible to the lawyer for expenses advanced by the latter. 'There is to be no barter of the privilege of prosecuting a cause for gain in exchange for the promise of the attorney to prosecute at his own expense.' (Cardozo, C.J. In Matter of Gilman, 251 N.Y. 265, 270–271.)" *ABA Opinion* 246 (1942).

31. See Comment, *Providing Legal Services for the Middle Class in Civil Matters: The Problem, the Duty and a Solution,* 26 U.Pitt.L.Rev. 811, 829 (1965).

32. See ABA Canon 38.

"Of course, as ... [Informal Opinion 679] points out, there must be full disclosure of the arrangement [that an entity other than the client pays the attorney's fee] by the attorney to the client...." *ABA Opinion* 320 (1968).

33. "Only lawyers may share in ... a division of fees, but ... it is not necessary that both lawyers be admitted to practice in the same state, so long as the division was based on the division of services or responsibility." *ABA Opinion* 316 (1967).

34. See ABA Canon 34.

"We adhere to our previous rulings that where a lawyer merely brings about the employment of another lawyer *but renders no service and assumes no responsibility in the matter,* a division of the latter's fee is improper. *(Opinions 18 and 153).*

EC 2–23 A lawyer should be zealous in his efforts to avoid controversies over fees with clients [35] and should attempt to resolve amicably any differences on the subject.[36] He should not sue a client for a fee unless necessary to prevent fraud or gross imposition by the client.[37]

Financial Ability to Employ Counsel: Persons Unable to Pay Reasonable Fees

EC 2–24 A layman whose financial ability is not sufficient to permit payment of any fee cannot obtain legal services, other than in cases where a contingent fee is appropriate, unless the services are provided for him. Even a person of moderate means may be unable to pay a reasonable fee which is large because of the complexity, novelty, or difficulty of the problem or similar factors.[38]

"It is assumed that the bar, generally, understands what acts or conduct of a lawyer may constitute 'services' to a client within the intendment of *Canon 12.* Such acts or conduct invariably, if not always, involve 'responsibility' on the part of the lawyer, whether the word 'responsibility' be construed to denote the possible resultant legal or moral liability on the part of the lawyer to the client or to others, or the onus of deciding what should or should not be done in behalf of the client. The word 'services' in *Canon 12* must be construed in this broad sense and may apply to the selection and retainer of associate counsel as well as to others acts or conduct in the client's behalf." *ABA Opinion* 204 (1940).

  35. See ABA Canon 14.

  36. Cf. *ABA Opinion* 320 (1968).

  37. See ABA Canon 14.

"Ours is a learned profession, not a mere money-getting trade.... Suits to collect fees should be avoided. Only where the circumstances imperatively require, should resort be had to a suit to compel payment. And where a lawyer does resort to a suit to enforce payment of fees which involves a disclosure, he should carefully avoid any disclosure not clearly necessary to obtaining or defending his rights." *ABA Opinion* 250 (1943).

  But cf. *ABA Opinion* 320 (1968).

  38. "As a society increases in size, sophistication and technology, the body of laws which is required to control that society also increases in size, scope and complexity. With this growth, the law directly affects more and more

EC 2–25 Historically, the need for legal services of those unable to pay reasonable fees has been met in part by lawyers who donated their services or accepted court appointments on behalf of such individuals. The basic responsibility for providing legal services for those unable to pay ultimately rests upon the individual lawyer, and personal involvement in the problems of the disadvantaged can be one of the most rewarding experiences in the life of a lawyer. Every lawyer, regardless of professional prominence or professional workload, should find time to participate in serving the disadvantaged. The rendition of free legal services to those unable to pay reasonable fees continues to be an obligation of each lawyer, but the efforts of individual lawyers are often not enough to meet the need.[39] Thus it has

facets of individual behavior, creating an expanding need for legal services on the part of the individual members of the society.... As legal guidance in social and commercial behavior increasingly becomes necessary, there will come a concurrent demand from the layman that such guidance be made available to him. This demand will not come from those who are able to employ the best legal talent, nor from those who can obtain legal assistance at little or no cost. It will come from the large 'forgotten middle income class,' who can neither afford to pay proportionately large fees nor qualify for ultra-low-cost services. The legal profession must recognize this inevitable demand and consider methods whereby it can be satisfied. If the profession fails to provide such methods, the laity will." Comment, *Providing Legal Services for the Middle Class in Civil Matters: The Problem, the Duty and a Solution,* 26 U.Pitt.L.Rev. 811, 811–12 (1965).

"The issue is not whether we shall do something or do nothing. The demand for ordinary everyday legal justice is so great and the moral nature of the demand is so strong that the issue has become whether we devise, maintain, and support suitable agencies able to satisfy the demand or, by our own default, force the government to take over the job, supplant us, and ultimately dominate us." Smith, *Legal Service Offices for Persons of Moderate Means,* 1949 Wis.L.Rev. 416, 418 (1949).

  39. "Lawyers have peculiar responsibilities for the just administration of the law, and these responsibilities include providing advice

been necessary for the profession to institute additional programs to provide legal services.[40]   Accordingly, legal aid offices,[41] lawyer referral services, and other related programs have been developed, and others will be developed, by the profession.[42]   Every lawyer should support all proper efforts to meet this need for legal services.[43]

Acceptance and Retention of Employment

EC 2-26   A lawyer is under no obligation to act as advisor or advocate for every person who may wish to become his client; but in furtherance of the objective

of the bar to make legal services fully available, a lawyer should not lightly decline proffered employment.   The fulfillment of this objective requires acceptance by a lawyer of his share of tendered employment which may be unattractive both to him and the bar generally.[44]

EC 2-27   History is replete with instances of distinguished and sacrificial services by lawyers who have represented unpopular clients and causes.   Regardless of his personal feelings, a lawyer should not decline representation because a client or a cause is unpopular or community reaction is adverse.[45]

and representation for needy persons. To a degree not always appreciated by the public at large, the bar has performed these obligations with zeal and devotion. The Committee is persuaded, however, that a system of justice that attempts, in mid-twentieth century America, to meet the needs of the financially incapacitated accused through primary or exclusive reliance on the uncompensated services of counsel will prove unsuccessful and inadequate. . . .   A system of adequate representation, therefore, should be structured and financed in a manner reflecting its public importance. . . .   We believe that fees for private appointed counsel should be set by the court within maximum limits established by the statute."   Report of the Att'y Gen's Comm. on Poverty and the Administration of Criminal Justice 41–43 (1963).

40. "At present this representation [of those unable to pay usual fees] is being supplied in some measure through the spontaneous generosity of individual lawyers, through legal aid societies, and—increasingly—through the organized efforts of the Bar. If those who stand in need of this service know of its availability and their need is in fact adequately met, the precise mechanism by which this service is provided becomes of secondary importance. It is of great importance, however, that both the impulse to render this service, and the plan for making that impulse effective, should arise within the legal profession itself."   *Professional Responsibility: Report of the Joint Conference*, 44 A.B.A.J. 1159, 1216 (1958).

41. "Free legal clinics carried on by the organized bar are not ethically objectionable. On the contrary, they serve a very worthwhile purpose and should be encouraged."   *ABA Opinion* 191 (1939).

42. "Whereas the American Bar Association believes that it is a fundamental duty of

the bar to see to it that all persons requiring legal advice be able to attain it, irrespective of their economic status . . . .

"Resolved, that the Association approves and sponsors the setting up by state and local bar associations of lawyer referral plans and low-cost legal service methods for the purpose of dealing with cases of persons who might not otherwise have the benefit of legal advice. . . ."   *Proceedings of the House of Delegates of the American Bar Association*, Oct. 30, 1946, 71 A.B.A.Rep. 103, 109–10 (1946).

43. "The defense of indigent citizens, without compensation, is carried on throughout the country by lawyers representing legal aid societies, not only with the approval, but with the commendation of those acquainted with the work. Not infrequently services are rendered out of sympathy or for other philanthropic reasons, by individual lawyers who do not represent legal aid societies. There is nothing whatever in the Canons to prevent a lawyer from performing such an act, nor should there be."   *ABA Opinion* 148 (1935).

44. But cf. ABA Canon 31.

45. "One of the highest services the lawyer can render to society is to appear in court on behalf of clients whose causes are in disfavor with the general public."   *Professional Responsibility: Report of the Joint Conference*, 44 A.B.A.J. 1159, 1216 (1958).

One author proposes the following proposition to be included in "A Proper Oath for Advocates": "I recognize that it is sometimes difficult for clients with unpopular causes to obtain proper legal representation. I will do all that I can to assure that the client with the unpopular cause is properly represented, and that the lawyer representing such a client re-

EC 2–28 The personal preference of a lawyer to avoid adversary alignment against judges, other lawyers,[46] public officials, or influential members of the community does not justify his rejection of tendered employment.

EC 2–29 When a lawyer is appointed by a court or requested by a bar association to undertake representation of a person unable to obtain counsel, whether for financial or other reasons, he should not seek to be excused from undertaking the representation except for compelling reasons.[47] Compelling reasons do not include such factors as the repugnance of the subject matter of the proceeding, the identity [48] or position of a person involved in the case, the belief of the lawyer that the defendant in a criminal proceeding is guilty,[49] or the belief of the lawyer regarding the merits of the civil case.[50]

EC 2–30 Employment should not be accepted by a lawyer when he is unable to render competent service [51] or when he knows or it is obvious that the person seeking to employ him desires to institute or maintain an action merely for the purpose of harassing or maliciously injuring another.[52] Likewise, a lawyer should decline employment if the intensity of his personal feeling, as distinguished from a community attitude, may impair his effective representation of a prospective client. If a lawyer knows a client has previously obtained counsel, he should not accept employment in the matter unless the other counsel approves [53] or withdraws, or the client terminates the prior employment.[54]

ceives credit from and support of the bar for handling such a matter." Thode, *The Ethical Standard for the Advocate,* 39 Texas L.Rev. 575, 592 (1961).

"§ 6068. ... It is the duty of an attorney:

. . .

"(h) Never to reject, for any consideration personal to himself, the cause of the defenseless or the oppressed." Cal.Business and Professions Code § 6068 (West 1962). Virtually the same language is found in the Oregon statutes at Ore.Rev.Stats. Ch. 9, § 9.460(8).

See Rostow, *The Lawyer and His Client,* 48 A.B.A.J. 25 and 146 (1962).

46. See ABA Canons 7 and 29.

"We are of the opinion that it is not professionally improper for a lawyer to accept employment to compel another lawyer to honor the just claim of a layman. On the contrary, it is highly proper that he do so. Unfortunately, there appears to be a widespread feeling among laymen that it is difficult, if not impossible, to obtain justice when they have claims against members of the Bar because other lawyers will not accept employment to proceed against them. The honor of the profession, whose members proudly style themselves officers of the court, must surely be sullied if its members bind themselves by custom to refrain from enforcing just claims of laymen against lawyers." *ABA Opinion* 144 (1935).

47. ABA Canon 4 uses a slightly different test, saying, "A lawyer assigned as counsel for an indigent prisoner ought not to ask to be excused for any trivial reason...."

48. Cf. ABA Canon 7.

49. See ABA Canon 5.

50. Dr. Johnson's reply to Boswell upon being asked what he thought of "supporting a cause which you know to be bad" was: "Sir, you do not know it to be good or bad till the Judge determines it. I have said that you are to state facts fairly; so that your thinking, or what you call knowing, a cause to be bad, must be from reasoning, must be from supposing your arguments to be weak and inconclusive. But, Sir, that is not enough. An argument which does not convince yourself, may convince the Judge to whom you urge it; and if it does convince him, why, then, Sir, you are wrong, and he is right." 2 Boswell, The Life of Johnson 47–48 (Hill ed. 1887).

51. "The lawyer deciding whether to undertake a case must be able to judge objectively whether he is capable of handling it and whether he can assume its burdens without prejudice to previous commitments....." *Professional Responsibility: Report of the Joint Conference,* 44 A.B.A.J. 1158, 1218 (1958).

52. "The lawyer must decline to conduct a civil cause or to make a defense when convinced that it is intended merely to harass or to injure the opposite party or to work oppression or wrong." ABA Canon 30.

53. See ABA Canon 7.

54. Id.

"From the facts stated we assume that the client has discharged the first attorney and

EC 2–31 Full availability of legal counsel requires both that persons be able to obtain counsel and that lawyers who undertake representation complete the work involved. Trial counsel for a convicted defendant should continue to represent his client by advising whether to take an appeal and, if the appeal is prosecuted, by representing him through the appeal unless new counsel is substituted or withdrawal is permitted by the appropriate court.

EC 2–32 A decision by a lawyer to withdraw should be made only on the basis of compelling circumstances,[55] and in a matter pending before a tribunal he must comply with the rules of the tribunal regarding withdrawal. A lawyer should not withdraw without considering carefully and endeavoring to minimize the possible adverse effect on the rights of his client and the possibility of prejudice to his client [56] as a result of his withdrawal. Even when he justifiably withdraws, a lawyer should protect the welfare of his client by giving due notice of his withdrawal,[57] suggesting employment of other counsel, delivering to the client all papers and property to which the client is entitled, cooperating with counsel subsequently employed, and otherwise endeavoring to minimize the possibility of harm. Further, he should refund to the client any compensation not earned during the employment.[58]

EC 2–33 As a part of the legal profession's commitment to the principle that high quality legal services should be available to all, attorneys are encouraged to cooperate with qualified legal assistance organizations providing prepaid legal services. Such participation should at all times be in accordance with the basic tenets of the profession: independence, integrity, competence and devotion to the interests of individual clients. An attorney so participating should make certain that his relationship with a qualified legal assistance organization in no way interferes with his independent, professional representation of the interests of the individual client. An attorney should avoid situations in which officials of the organization who are not lawyers attempt to direct attorneys concerning the manner in which legal services are performed for individual members, and should also avoid situations in which considerations of economy are given undue weight in determining the attorneys employed by an organization or the legal services to be performed for the member or beneficiary rather than competence and quality of service. An attorney interested in maintaining the historic traditions of the profession and preserving the function of a lawyer as a trusted and independent advisor to individual members of society should carefully assess such factors when accepting employment by, or otherwise participating in, a particular qualified legal assistance organization, and while so participating should adhere to the highest professional standards of effort and competence.

DISCIPLINARY RULES

DR 2–101 Publicity.

(A) A lawyer shall not, on behalf of himself, his partner, associate or

given notice of the discharge. Such being the case, the second attorney may properly accept employment. *Canon 7; Opinions 10, 130, 149.*" ABA *Opinion* 209 (1941).

55. See ABA Canon 44.

"I will carefully consider, before taking a case, whether it appears that I can fully represent the client within the framework of law. If the decision is in the affirmative, then it will take extreme circumstances to cause me to decide later that I cannot so represent him." Thode, *The Ethical Standard for the Advocate,* 39 Texas L.Rev. 575, 592 (1961) (from "A Proper Oath for Advocates").

56. *ABA Opinion* 314 (1965) held that a lawyer should not disassociate himself from a cause when "it is obvious that the very act of disassociation would have the effect of violating *Canon 37.*"

57. ABA Canon 44 enumerates instances in which "... the lawyer may be warranted in withdrawing on due notice to the client, allowing him time to employ another lawyer."

58. *See* ABA Canon 44.

any other lawyer affiliated with him or his firm, use or participate in the use of any form of public communication containing a false, fraudulent, misleading, deceptive, self-laudatory or unfair statement or claim.

(B) In order to facilitate the process of informed selection of a lawyer by potential consumers of legal services, a lawyer may publish or broadcast, subject to DR 2–103, the following information in print media distributed or over television or radio broadcast in the geographic area or areas in which the lawyer resides or maintains offices or in which a significant part of the lawyer's clientele resides, provided that the information disclosed by the lawyer in such publication or broadcast complies with DR 2–101(A), and is presented in a dignified manner:

(1) Name, including name of law firm and names of professional associates; addresses and telephone numbers;

(2) One or more fields of law in which the lawyer or law firm practices, a statement that practice is limited to one or more fields of law, or a statement that the lawyer or law firm specializes in a particular field of law practice, to the extent authorized under DR 2–105;

(3) Date and place of birth;

(4) Date and place of admission to the bar of state and federal courts;

(5) Schools attended, with dates of graduation, degrees and other scholastic distinctions;

(6) Public or quasi-public offices;

(7) Military service;

(8) Legal authorships;

(9) Legal teaching positions;

(10) Memberships, offices, and committee assignments, in bar associations;

(11) Membership and offices in legal fraternities and legal societies;

(12) Technical and professional licenses;

(13) Memberships in scientific, technical and professional associations and societies;

(14) Foreign language ability;

(15) Names and addresses of bank references;

(16) With their written consent, names of clients regularly represented;

(17) Prepaid or group legal services programs in which the lawyer participates;

(18) Whether credit cards or other credit arrangements are accepted;

(19) Office and telephone answering service hours;

(20) Fee for an initial consultation;

(21) Availability upon request of a written schedule of fees and/or an estimate of the fee to be charged for specific services;

(22) Contingent fee rates subject to DR 2–106(C), provided that the statement discloses whether percentages are computed before or after deduction of costs;

(23) Range of fees for services, provided that the statement discloses that the specific

296

fee within the range which will be charged will vary depending upon the particular matter to be handled for each client and the client is entitled without obligation to an estimate of the fee within the range likely to be charged, in print size equivalent to the largest print used in setting forth the fee information;

(24) Hourly rate, provided that the statement discloses that the total fee charged will depend upon the number of hours which must be devoted to the particular matter to be handled for each client and the client is entitled to without obligation an estimate of the fee likely to be charged, in print size at least equivalent to the largest print used in setting forth the fee information;

(25) Fixed fees for specific legal services,* the description of which would not be misunderstood or be deceptive, provided that the statement discloses that the quoted fee will be available only to clients whose matters fall into the services described and that the client is entitled without obligation to a specific estimate of the fee likely to be charged in print size at least equivalent to the largest print used in setting forth the fee information.

(C) Any person desiring to expand the information authorized for disclosure in DR 2-101(B), or to provide for its dissemination through other forums may apply to [the agency having jurisdiction under state law]. Any such application shall be served upon [the agencies having jurisdiction under state law over the regulation of the legal profession and consumer matters] who shall be heard, together with the applicant, on the issue of whether the proposal is necessary in light of the existing provisions of the Code, accords with standards of accuracy, reliability and truthfulness, and would facilitate the process of informed selection of lawyers by potential consumers of legal services. The relief granted in response to any such application shall be promulgated as an amendment to DR 2-101(B), universally applicable to all lawyers.**

(D) If the advertisement is communicated to the public over television or radio, it shall be prerecorded, approved for broadcast by the lawyer, and a recording of the actual transmission shall be retained by the lawyer.

(E) If a lawyer advertises a fee for a service, the lawyer must render that service for no more than the fee advertised.

(F) Unless otherwise specified in the advertisement if a lawyer publishes any fee information authorized under DR 2-101(B) in a publication that is published more frequently than one time per month, the lawyer shall be bound by any representation made therein for a period of not less than 30 days after such publication. If a lawyer publishes

---

* The agency having jurisdiction under state law may desire to issue appropriate guidelines defining "specific legal services."

** The agency having jurisdiction under state law should establish orderly and expeditious procedures for ruling on such applications.

any fee information authorized under DR 2–101(B) in a publication that is published once a month or less frequently, he shall be bound by any representation made therein until the publication of the succeeding issue. If a lawyer publishes any fee information authorized under DR 2–101(B) in a publication which has no fixed date for publication of a succeeding issue, the lawyer shall be bound by any representation made therein for a reasonable period of time after publication but in no event less than one year.

(G) Unless otherwise specified, if a lawyer broadcasts any fee information authorized under DR 2–101(B), the lawyer shall be bound by any representation made therein for a period of not less than 30 days after such broadcast.

(H) This rule does not prohibit limited and dignified identification of a lawyer as a lawyer as well as by name:

(1) In political advertisements when his professional status is germane to the political campaign or to a political issue.

(2) In public notices when the name and profession of a lawyer are required or authorized by law or are reasonably pertinent for a purpose other than the attraction of potential clients.

(3) In routine reports and announcements of a bona fide business, civic, professional, or political organization in which he serves as a director or officer.

(4) In and on legal documents prepared by him.

(5) In and on legal textbooks, treatises, and other legal publications, and in dignified advertisements thereof.

(I) A lawyer shall not compensate or give any thing of value to representatives of the press, radio, television, or other communication medium in anticipation of or in return for professional publicity in a news item.

DR 2–102 Professional Notices, Letterheads and Offices.

(A) A lawyer or law firm shall not use or participate in the use of professional cards, professional announcement cards, office signs, letterheads, or similar professional notices or devices, except that the following may be used if they are in dignified form:

(1) A professional card of a lawyer identifying him by name and as a lawyer, and giving his addresses, telephone numbers, the name of his law firm, and any information permitted under DR 2–105. A professional card of a law firm may also give the names of members and associates. Such cards may be used for identification.

(2) A brief professional announcement card stating new or changed associations or addresses, change of firm name, or similar matters pertaining to the professional offices of a lawyer or law firm, which may be mailed to lawyers, clients, former clients, personal friends, and relatives.[59] It shall not state bio-

59. See *ABA Opinion* 301 (1961).

graphical data except to the extent reasonably necessary to identify the lawyer or to explain the change in his association, but it may state the immediate past position of the lawyer.[60] It may give the names and dates of predecessor firms in a continuing line of succession. It shall not state the nature of the practice except as permitted under DR 2–105.[61]

(3) A sign on or near the door of the office and in the building directory identifying the law office. The sign shall not state the nature of the practice, except as permitted under DR 2–105.

(4) A letter head of a lawyer identifying him by name and as a lawyer, and giving his addresses, telephone numbers, the name of his law firm, associates and any information permitted under DR 2–105. A letterhead of a law firm may also give the names of members and associates,[62] and names and dates relating to deceased and retired members.[63] A lawyer may be designated "Of Counsel" on a letterhead if he has a continuing relationship with a lawyer or law firm, other than as a partner or associate. A lawyer or law firm may be designated as "General Counsel" or by similar professional reference on stationary of a client if he or the firm devotes a substantial amount of professional time in the representation of that client.[64] The letterhead of a law firm may give the names and dates of predecessor firms in a continuing line of succession.

(B) A lawyer in private practice shall not practice under a trade name, a name that is misleading as to the identity of the lawyer or lawyers practicing under such name, or a firm name containing names other than those of one or more of the lawyers in the firm, except that the name of a professional corporation or professional association may contain "P.C." or "P.A." or similar symbols indicating the nature of the organization, and if otherwise lawful a firm may use as, or continue to include in, its name the name or names of one or more deceased or retired members of the firm or of a predecessor firm in a continuing line of succession.[65] A lawyer who assumes a judicial, legislative, or public executive or administrative post or

---

60. "[I]t has become commonplace for many lawyers to participate in government service; to deny them the right, upon their return to private practice, to refer to their prior employment in a brief and dignified manner, would place an undue limitation upon a large element of our profession. It is entirely proper for a member of the profession to explain his absence from private practice, where such is the primary purpose of the announcement, by a brief and dignified reference to the prior employment.

"... [A]ny such announcement should be limited to the immediate past connection of the lawyer with the government, made upon his leaving that position to enter private practice." *ABA Opinion* 301 (1961).

61. See *ABA Opinion* 251 (1943).

62. "Those lawyers who are working for an individual lawyer or a law firm may be designated on the letterhead and in other appropriate places as 'associates'." *ABA Opinion* 310 (1963).

63. See ABA Canon 33.

64. But see *ABA Opinion* 285 (1951).

65. See ABA Canon 33; cf. *ABA Opinions* 318 (1967), 267 (1945), 219 (1941), 208 (1940), 192 (1939), 97 (1933), and 6 (1925).

office shall not permit his name to remain in the name of a law firm or to be used in professional notices of the firm during any significant period in which he is not actively and regularly practicing law as a member of the firm,[66] and during such period other members of the firm shall not use his name in the firm name or in professional notices of the firm.[67]

(C) A lawyer shall not hold himself out as having a partnership with one or more other lawyers or professional corporations unless they are in fact partners.[68]

(D) A partnership shall not be formed or continued between or among lawyers licensed in different jurisdictions unless all enumerations of the members and associates of the firm on its letterhead and in other permissible listings make clear the jurisdictional limitations on those members and associates of the firm not licensed to practice in all listed jurisdictions; [69] however,

the same firm name may be used in each jurisdiction.

(E) Nothing contained herein shall prohibit a lawyer from using or permitting the use of, in connection with his name, an earned degree or title derived therefrom indicating his training in the law.

DR 2–103 Recommendation of Professional Employment.[70]

(A) A lawyer shall not, except as authorized in DR 2–101(B), recommend employment as a private practitioner,[71] of himself, his partner, or associate to a layperson who has not sought his advice regarding employment of a lawyer.[72]

(B) A lawyer shall not compensate or give anything of value to a person or organization to recommend or secure his employment [73] by a client, or as a reward for having made a recommendation resulting in his employment [74] by a client, ex-

---

66. *ABA Opinion* 318 (1967) held, "anything to the contrary in Formal Opinion 315 or in the other opinions cited notwithstanding that: "Where a partner whose name appears in the name of a law firm is elected or appointed to high local, state or federal office, which office he intends to occupy only temporarily, at the end of which time he intends to return to his position with the firm, and provided that he is not precluded by holding such office from engaging in the practice of law and does not in fact sever his relationship with the firm but only takes a leave of absence, and provided that there is no local law, statute or custom to the contrary, his name may be retained in the firm name during his term or terms of office, but only if proper precautions are taken not to mislead the public as to his degree of participation in the firm's affairs."

Cf. *ABA Opinion* 143 (1935). New York County Opinion 67, and New York City Opinions 36 and 798; but cf. *ABA Opinion* 192 (1939) and Michigan Opinion 164.

67. Cf. ABA Canon 33.

68. See *ABA Opinion* 277 (1948); cf. ABA Canon 33 and *ABA Opinions* 318 (1967), 126 (1935), 115 (1934), and 106 (1934).

69. See *ABA Opinions* 318 (1967) and 316 (1967); cf. ABA Canon 33.

70. Cf. ABA Canon 28.

71. "We think it clear that a lawyer's seeking employment in an ordinary law office, or appointment to a civil service position, is not prohibited by ... [Canon 27]." *ABA Opinion* 197 (1939).

72. "[A] lawyer may not seek from persons not his clients the opportunity to perform ... a [legal] checkup." *ABA Opinion* 307 (1962).

73. Cf. *ABA Opinion* 78 (1932).

74. " 'No financial connection of any kind between the Brotherhood and any lawyer is permissible. No lawyer can properly pay any amount whatsoever to the Brotherhood or any of its departments, officers or members as compensation, reimbursement of expenses or gratuity in connection with the procurement of a case.' " In re Brotherhood of R.R. Trainmen,

300

cept that he may pay the usual and reasonable fees or dues charged by any of the organizations listed in DR 2–103(D).

(C) A lawyer shall not request a person or organization to recommend or promote the use of his services or those of his partner or associate, or any other lawyer affiliated with him or his firm, as a private practitioner,[75] except as authorized in DR 2–101, and except that

(1) He may request referrals from a lawyer referral service operated, sponsored, or approved by a bar association and may pay its fees incident thereto.[76]

(2) He may cooperate with the legal service activities of any of the offices or organizations enumerated in DR 2–103(D)(1) through (4) and may perform legal services for those to whom he was recommended by it to do such work if:

(a) The person to whom the recommendation is made is a member or beneficiary of such office or organization; and

(b) The lawyer remains free to exercise his independent professional judgment on behalf of his client.

(D) A lawyer or his partner or associate or any other lawyer affiliated with him or his firm may be recommended, employed or paid by, or may cooperate with, one of the following offices or organizations that promote the use of his services or those of his partner or associate or any other lawyer affiliated with him or his firm if there is no interference with the exercise of independent professional judgment in behalf of his client:

(1) A legal aid office or public defender office:

(a) Operated or sponsored by a duly accredited law school.

(b) Operated or sponsored by a bona fide nonprofit community organization.

(c) Operated or sponsored by a governmental agency.

(d) Operated, sponsored, or approved by a bar association.[77]

(2) A military legal assistance office.

(3) A lawyer referral service operated, sponsored, or approved by a bar association.

(4) Any bona fide organization that recommends, furnishes or pays for legal services to its members or beneficiaries[78] provided the following conditions are satisfied:

13 Ill.2d 391, 398, 150 N.E.2d 163, 167 (1958), quoted in In re Ratner, 194 Kan. 362, 372, 399 P.2d 865, 873 (1956).

See *ABA Opinion* 147 (1935).

75. "This Court has condemned the practice of ambulance chasing through the media of runners and touters. In similar fashion we have with equal emphasis condemned the practice of direct solicitation by a lawyer. We have classified both offenses as serious breaches of the Canons of Ethics demanding severe treat-

ment of the offending lawyer." State v. Dawson, 111 So.2d 427, 431 (Fla.1959).

76. "Registrants [of a lawyer referral plan] may be required to contribute to the expense of operating it by a reasonable registration charge or by a reasonable percentage of fees collected by them." *ABA Opinion* 291 (1956).

Cf. *ABA Opinion* 227 (1941).

77. Cf. *ABA Opinion* 148 (1935).

78. United Mine Workers v. Ill. State Bar Ass'n., 389 U.S. 217, 19 L.Ed.2d 426, 88 S.Ct.

(a) Such organization, including any affiliate, is so organized and operated that no profit is derived by it from the rendition of legal services by lawyers, and that, if the organization is organized for profit, the legal services are not rendered by lawyers employed, directed, supervised or selected by it except in connection with matters where such organization bears ultimate liability of its member or beneficiary.

(b) Neither the lawyer, nor his partner, nor associate, nor any other lawyer affiliated with him or his firm, nor any non-lawyer, shall have initiated or promoted such organization for the primary purpose of providing financial or other benefit to such lawyer, partner, associate or affiliated lawyer.

(c) Such organization is not operated for the purpose of procuring legal work or financial benefit for any lawyer as a private practitioner outside of the legal services program of the organization.

(d) The member or beneficiary to whom the legal services are furnished, and not such organization, is recognized as the client of the lawyer in the matter.

(e) Any member or beneficiary who is entitled to have legal services furnished or paid for by the organization may, if such member or beneficiary so desires, select counsel other than that furnished, selected or approved by the organization for the particular matter involved; and the legal service plan of such organization provides appropriate relief for any member or beneficiary who asserts a claim that representation by counsel furnished, selected or approved would be unethical, improper or inadequate under the circumstances of the matter involved and the plan provides an appropriate procedure for seeking such relief.

(f) The lawyer does not know or have cause to know that such organization is in violation of applicable laws, rules of court and other legal requirements that govern its legal service operations.

(g) Such organization has filed with the appropriate disciplinary authority at least annually a report with respect to its legal service plan, if any, showing its terms, its schedule of benefits, its subscription charges, agreements with counsel, and financial results of its legal service activities or, if it has failed to do so, the lawyer does not know or have cause to know of such failure.

(E) A lawyer shall not accept employment when he knows or it is

353 (1967); Brotherhood of R.R. Trainmen v. Virginia, 377 U.S. 1, 12 L.Ed.2d 89, 84 S.Ct. 1113 (1964); NAACP v. Button, 371 U.S. 415, 9 L.Ed.2d 405, 83 S.Ct. 328 (1963).

obvious that the person who seeks his services does so as a result of conduct prohibited under this Disciplinary Rule.

DR 2–104 Suggestion of Need of Legal Services.[79, 80]

(A) A lawyer who has given in-person unsolicited advice to a layperson that he should obtain counsel or take legal action shall not accept employment resulting from that advice,[81] except that:

(1) A lawyer may accept employment by a close friend, relative, former client (if the advice is germane to the former employment), or one whom the lawyer reasonably believes to be a client.[82]

(2) A lawyer may accept employment that results from his participation in activities designed to educate laypersons to recognize legal problems, to make intelligent selection of counsel, or to utilize available legal services if such activities are conducted or sponsored by a qualified legal assistance organization.

(3) A lawyer who is recommended, furnished or paid by a qualified legal assistance organization enumerated in DR 2–103(D)(1) through (4) may represent a member or beneficiary thereof, to the extent and under the conditions prescribed therein.

(4) Without affecting his right to accept employment, a lawyer may speak publicly or write for publication on legal topics [83] so long as he does not emphasize his own professional experience or reputation and does not undertake to give individual advice.

(5) If success in asserting rights or defenses of his client in litigation in the nature of a class action is dependent upon the joinder of others, a lawyer may accept, but shall not seek, employment from those contacted for the purpose of obtaining their joinder.[84]

DR 2–105 Limitation of Practice.[85]

(A) A lawyer shall not hold himself out publicly as a specialist, as

---

79. "If a bar association has embarked on a program of institutional advertising for an annual legal check-up and provides brochures and reprints, it is not improper to have these available in the lawyer's office for persons to read and take." *ABA Opinion* 307 (1962).

Cf. *ABA Opinion* 121 (1934).

80. ABA Canon 28.

81. Cf. *ABA Opinions* 229 (1941) and 173 (1937).

82. "It certainly is not improper for a lawyer to advise his regular clients of new statutes, court decisions, and administrative rulings, which may affect the client's interests, provided the communication is strictly limited to such information. . . ."

"When such communications go to concerns or individuals other than regular clients of the lawyer, they are thinly disguised advertisements for professional employment, and are

obviously improper." *ABA Opinion* 213 (1941).

"It is our opinion that where the lawyer has no reason to believe that he has been supplanted by another lawyer, it is not only his right, but it might even be his duty to advise his client of any change of fact or law which might defeat the client's testamentary purpose as expressed in the will.

"Periodic notices might be sent to the client for whom a lawyer has drawn a will, suggesting that it might be wise for the client to reexamine his will to determine whether or not there has been any change in his situation requiring a modification of his will." *ABA Opinion* 210 (1941).

Cf. ABA Canon 28.

83. Cf. *ABA Opinion* 168 (1937).

84. But cf. *ABA Opinion* 111 (1934).

85. See ABA Canon 45; cf. ABA Canons 43, and 46.

practicing in certain areas of law or as limiting his practice permitted under DR 2–101(B), except as follows:

(1) A lawyer admitted to practice before the United States Patent and Trademark Office may use the designation "Patents," "Patent Attorney," "Patent Lawyer," or "Registered Patent Attorney" or any combination of those terms, on his letterhead and office sign.

(2) A lawyer who publicly discloses fields of law in which the lawyer or the law firm practices or states that his practice is limited to one or more fields of law shall do so by using designations and definitions authorized and approved by [the agency having jurisdiction of the subject under state law].

(3) A lawyer who is certified as a specialist in a particular field of law or law practice by [the authority having jurisdiction under state law over the subject of specialization by lawyers] may hold himself out as such, but only in accordance with the rules prescribed by that authority.[86]

DR 2–106   Fees for Legal Services.[87]

(A) A lawyer shall not enter into an agreement for, charge, or collect an illegal or clearly excessive fee.[88]

(B) A fee is clearly excessive when, after a review of the facts, a lawyer of ordinary prudence would be left with a definite and firm conviction that the fee is in excess of a reasonable fee. Factors to be considered as guides in determining the reasonableness of a fee include the following:

(1) The time and labor required, the novelty and difficulty of the questions involved, and the skill requisite to perform the legal service properly.

(2) The likelihood, if apparent to the client, that the acceptance of the particular employment will preclude other employment by the lawyer.

(3) The fee customarily charged in the locality for similar legal services.

(4) The amount involved and the results obtained.

(5) The time limitations imposed by the client or by the circumstances.

(6) The nature and length of the professional relationship with the client.

(7) The experience, reputation, and ability of the lawyer or lawyers performing the services.

(8) Whether the fee is fixed or contingent.[89]

---

86. This provision is included to conform to action taken by the ABA House of Delegates at the Mid-Winter Meeting, January, 1969.

87. See ABA Canon 12.

88. The charging of a "clearly excessive fee" is a ground for discipline. State ex rel. Nebraska State Bar Ass'n. v. Richards, 165 Neb. 80, 90, 84 N.W.2d 136, 143 (1957).

"An attorney has the right to contract for any fee he chooses so long as it is not excessive (see Opinion 190), and this Committee is not concerned with the amount of such fees unless so excessive as to constitute a misappropriation of the client's funds (see Opinion 27)." *ABA Opinion* 320 (1968).

Cf. *ABA Opinions* 209 (1940), 190 (1939), and 27 (1930) and State ex rel. Lee v. Buchanan, 191 So.2d 33 (Fla.1966).

89. Cf. ABA Canon 13; see generally MacKinnon, Contingent Fees for Legal Services (1964) (A Report of the American Bar Foundation).

(C) A lawyer shall not enter into an arrangement for, charge, or collect a contingent fee for representing a defendant in a criminal case.[90]

DR 2–107 Division of Fees Among Lawyers

(A) A lawyer shall not divide a fee for legal services with another lawyer who is not a partner in or associate of his law firm or law office, unless:

(1) The client consents to employment of the other lawyer after a full disclosure that a division of fees will be made.

(2) The division is made in proportion to the services performed and responsibility assumed by each.[91]

(3) The total fee of the lawyers does not clearly exceed reasonable compensation for all legal services they rendered the client.[92]

(B) This Disciplinary Rule does not prohibit payment to a former partner or associate pursuant to a separation or retirement agreement.

DR 2–108 Agreements Restricting the Practice of a Lawyer.

(A) A lawyer shall not be a party to or participate in a partnership or employment agreement with another lawyer that restricts the right of a lawyer to practice law after the termination of a relationship created by the agreement, except as a condition to payment of retirement benefits.[93]

(B) In connection with the settlement of a controversy or suit, a lawyer shall not enter into an agreement that restricts his right to practice law.

DR 2–109 Acceptance of Employment.

(A) A lawyer shall not accept employment on behalf of a person if

90. "Contingent fees, whether in civil or criminal cases, are a special concern of the law.....

"In criminal cases, the rule is stricter because of the danger of corrupting justice. The second part of Section 542 of the Restatement [of Contracts] reads: 'A bargain to conduct a criminal case . . . in consideration of a promise of a fee contingent on success is illegal....'" Peyton v. Margiotti, 398 Pa. 86, 156 A.2d 865, 967 (1959).

"The third area of practice in which the use of the contingent fee is generally considered to be prohibited is the prosecution and defense of criminal cases. However, there are so few cases, and these are predominantly old, that it is doubtful that there can be said to be any current law on the subject.... In the absence of cases on the validity of contingent fees for defense attorneys, it is necessary to rely on the consensus among commentators that such a fee is void as against public policy. The nature of criminal practice itself makes unlikely the use of contingent fee contracts." MacKinnon,

Contingent Fees for Legal Services 52 (1964) (A Report of the American Bar Foundation).

91. See ABA Canon 34 and *ABA Opinions* 316 (1967) and 294 (1958); see generally *ABA Opinions* 265 (1945), 204 (1940), 190 (1939), 171 (1937), 153 (1936), 97 (1933), 63 (1932), 28 (1930), 27 (1930), and 18 (1930).

92. "*Canon 12* contemplates that a lawyer's fee should not exceed *the value of the services* rendered....

"*Canon 12* applies, whether joint or separate fees are charged [by associate attorneys] ...." *ABA Opinion* 204 (1940).

93. "[A] general covenant restricting an employed lawyer, after leaving the employment, from practicing in the community for a stated period, appears to this Committee to be an unwarranted restriction on the right of a lawyer to choose where he will practice and inconsistent with our professional status. Accordingly, the Committee is of the opinion it would be improper for the employing lawyer to require the covenant and likewise for the em-

he knows or it is obvious that such person wishes to:

(1) Bring a legal action, conduct a defense, or assert a position in litigation, or otherwise have steps taken for him, merely for the purpose of harassing or maliciously injuring any person.[94]

(2) Present a claim or defense in litigation that is not warranted under existing law, unless it can be supported by good faith argument for an extension, modification, or reversal of existing law.

DR 2–110 Withdrawal from Employment.[95]

(A) In general.

(1) If permission for withdrawal from employment is required by the rules of a tribunal, a lawyer shall not withdraw from employment in a proceeding before that tribunal without its permission.

(2) In any event, a lawyer shall not withdraw from employment until he has taken reasonable steps to avoid foreseeable prejudice to the rights of his client, including giving due notice to his client, allowing time for employment of other counsel, delivering to the client all papers and property to which the client is entitled, and complying with applicable laws and rules.

(3) A lawyer who withdraws from employment shall refund promptly any part of a fee paid in advance that has not been earned.

(B) Mandatory Withdrawal.

A lawyer representing a client before a tribunal, with its permission if required by its rules, shall withdraw from employment, and a lawyer representing a client in other matters shall withdraw from employment, if:

(1) He knows or it is obvious that his client is bringing the legal action, conducting the defense, or asserting a position in the litigation, or is otherwise having steps taken for him, merely for the purpose of harassing or maliciously injuring any person.

(2) He knows or it is obvious that his continued employment will result in violation of a Disciplinary Rule.[96]

(3) His mental or physical condition renders it unreasonably difficult for him to carry out the employment effectively.

(4) He is discharged by his client.

(C) Permissive withdrawal.[97]

If DR 2–110(B) is not applicable, a lawyer may not request permission to withdraw in matters pending before a tribunal, and may not withdraw in other matters, unless such request or such withdrawal is because:

ployed lawyer to agree to it." *ABA Opinion* 300 (1961).

94. See ABA Canon 30.

"*Rule 13.* . . . A member of the State Bar shall not accept employment to prosecute or defend a case solely out of spite, or solely for the purpose of harassing or delaying another. . . ." Cal.Business and Professions Code § 6067 (West 1962).

95. Cf. ABA Canon 44.

96. See also Code of Professional Responsibility, DR 5–102 and DR 5–105.

97. Cf. ABA Canon 4.

(1) His client:

(a) Insists upon presenting a claim or defense that is not warranted under existing law and cannot be supported by good faith argument for an extension, modification, or reversal of existing law.[98]

(b) Personally seeks to pursue an illegal course of conduct.

(c) Insists that the lawyer pursue a course of conduct that is illegal or that is prohibited under the Disciplinary Rules.

(d) By other conduct renders it unreasonably difficult for the lawyer to carry out his employment effectively.

(e) Insists, in a matter not pending before a tribunal, that the lawyer engage in conduct that is contrary to the judgment and advice of the lawyer but not prohibited under the Disciplinary Rules.

(f) Deliberately disregards an agreement or obligation to the lawyer as to expenses or fees.

(2) His continued employment is likely to result in a violation of a Disciplinary Rule.

(3) His inability to work with co-counsel indicates that the best interests of the client likely will be served by withdrawal.

(4) His mental or physical condition renders it difficult for him to carry out the employment effectively.

(5) His client knowingly and freely assents to termination of his employment.

(6) He believes in good faith, in a proceeding pending before a tribunal, that the tribunal will find the existence of other good cause for withdrawal.

CANON 3

A Lawyer Should Assist in Preventing the Unauthorized Practice of Law

ETHICAL CONSIDERATIONS

EC 3–1 The prohibition against the practice of law by a layman is grounded in the need of the public for integrity and competence of those who undertake to render legal services. Because of the fiduciary and personal character of the lawyer-client relationship and the inherently complex nature of our legal system, the public can better be assured of the requisite responsibility and competence if the practice of law is confined to those who are subject to the requirements and regulations imposed upon members of the legal profession.

EC 3–2 The sensitive variations in the considerations that bear on legal determinations often make it difficult even for a lawyer to exercise appropriate professional judgment, and it is therefore essential that the personal nature of the relationship of client and lawyer be preserved. Competent professional judgment is the product of a trained familiarity with law and legal processes, a disciplined, analytical approach to legal problems, and a firm ethical commitment.

EC 3–3 A non-lawyer who undertakes to handle legal matters is not governed as to integrity or legal competence by the same rules that govern the conduct of a lawyer. A lawyer is not only subject to that regulation but also is committed to

---

98. Cf. Anders v. California, 386 U.S. 738, 18 L.Ed.2d 493, 87 S.Ct. 1396 (1967), rehearing denied, 388 U.S. 924, 18 L.Ed.2d 1377, 87 S.Ct. 2094 (1967).

high standards of ethical conduct. The public interest is best served in legal matters by a regulated profession committed to such standards.[1] The Disciplinary Rules protect the public in that they prohibit a lawyer from seeking employment by improper overtures, from acting in cases of divided loyalties, and from submitting to the control of others in the exercise of his judgment. Moreover, a person who entrusts legal matters to a lawyer is protected by the attorney-client privilege and by the duty of the lawyer to hold inviolate the confidences and secrets of his client.

EC 3–4 A layman who seeks legal services often is not in a position to judge whether he will receive proper professional attention. The entrustment of a legal matter may well involve the confidences, the reputation, the property, the freedom, or even the life of the client. Proper protection of members of the public demands that no person be permitted to act in the confidential and demanding capacity of a lawyer unless he is subject to the regulations of the legal profession.

EC 3–5 It is neither necessary nor desirable to attempt the formulation of a single, specific definition of what constitutes the practice of law.[2] Functionally, the practice of law relates to the rendition of services for others that call for the professional judgment of a lawyer. The essence of the professional judgment of the lawyer is his educated ability to relate the general body and philosophy of law to a specific legal problem of a client; and thus, the public interest will be better served if only lawyers are permitted to act in matters involving professional judgment. Where this professional judgment is not involved, non-lawyers, such as court clerks, police officers, abstracters, and many governmental employees, may engage in occupations that require a special knowledge of law in certain areas. But the services of a lawyer are essential in the public interest whenever the exercise of professional legal judgment is required.

EC 3–6 A lawyer often delegates tasks to clerks, secretaries, and other lay persons. Such delegation is proper if the lawyer maintains a direct relationship with his client, supervises the delegated work, and has complete professional responsibility for the work product.[3] This

1. "The condemnation of the unauthorized practice of law is designed to protect the public from legal services by persons unskilled in the law. The prohibition of lay intermediaries is intended to insure the loyalty of the lawyer to the client unimpaired by intervening and possibly conflicting interests." Cheatham, *Availability of Legal Services: The Responsibility of the Individual Lawyer and of the Organized Bar*, 12 U.C.L.A.L.Rev. 438, 439 (1965).

2. "What constitutes unauthorized practice of the law in a particular jurisdiction is a matter for determination by the courts of that jurisdiction." *ABA Opinion* 198 (1939).

"In the light of the historical development of the lawyer's functions, it is impossible to lay down an exhaustive definition of 'the practice of law' by attempting to enumerate every conceivable act performed by lawyers in the normal course of their work." State Bar of Arizona v. Arizona Land Title & Trust Co., 90 Ariz. 76, 87, 366 P.2d 1, 8–9 (1961), modified, 91 Ariz. 293, 371 P.2d 1020 (1962).

3. "A lawyer can employ lay secretaries, lay investigators, lay detectives, lay researchers, accountants, lay scriveners, nonlawyer draftsmen or nonlawyer researchers. In fact, he may employ nonlawyers to do any task for him except counsel clients about law matters, engage directly in the practice of law, appear in court or appear in formal proceedings a part of the judicial process, so long as it is he who takes the work and vouches for it to the client and becomes responsible to the client." *ABA Opinion* 316 (1967).

ABA Opinion 316 (1967) also stated that if a lawyer practices law as part of a law firm which includes lawyers from several states, he may delegate tasks to firm members in other states so long as he "is the person who, on behalf of the firm, vouched for the work of all of the others and, with the client and in the courts, did the legal acts defined by that state as the practice of law."

"A lawyer cannot delegate his professional responsibility to a law student employed in his office. He may avail himself of the assistance of the student in many of the fields of the lawyer's work, such as examination of case

delegation enables a lawyer to render legal service more economically and efficiently.

EC 3-7 The prohibition against a nonlawyer practicing law does not prevent a layman from representing himself, for then he is ordinarily exposing only himself to possible injury. The purpose of the legal profession is to make educated legal representation available to the public; but anyone who does not wish to avail himself of such representation is not required to do so. Even so, the legal profession should help members of the public to recognize legal problems and to understand why it may be unwise for them to act for themselves in matters having legal consequences.

EC 3-8 Since a lawyer should not aid or encourage a layman to practice law, he should not practice law in association with a layman or otherwise share legal

fees with a layman.[4] This does not mean, however, that the pecuniary value of the interest of a deceased lawyer in his firm or practice may not be paid to his estate or specified persons such as his widow or heirs.[5] In like manner, profit-sharing retirement plans of a lawyer or law firm which include non-lawyer office employees are not improper.[6] These limited exceptions to the rule against sharing legal fees with laymen are permissible since they do not aid or encourage laymen to practice law.

EC 3-9 Regulation of the practice of law is accomplished principally by the respective states.[7] Authority to engage in the practice of law conferred in any jurisdiction is not per se a grant of the right to practice elsewhere, and it is improper for a lawyer to engage in practice where he is not permitted by law or by court order to do so. However, the demands of business

law, finding and interviewing witnesses, making collections of claims, examining court records, delivering papers, conveying important messages, and other similar matters. But the student is not permitted, until he is admitted to the Bar, to perform the professional functions of a lawyer, such as conducting court trials, giving professional advice to clients or drawing legal documents for them. The student in all his work must act as agent for the lawyer employing him, who must supervise his work and be responsible for his good conduct." *ABA Opinion* 85 (1932).

4. "No division of fees for legal services is proper, except with another lawyer...." ABA Canon 34. Otherwise, according to *ABA Opinion* 316 (1967), "[t]he Canons of Ethics do not examine into the method by which such persons are remunerated by the lawyer.... They may be paid a salary, a per diem charge, a flat fee, a contract price, etc."

See ABA Canons 33 and 47.

5. "Many partnership agreements provide that the active partners, on the death of any one of them, are to make payments to the estate or to the nominee of a deceased partner on a pre-determined formula. It is only where the effect of such an arrangement is to make the estate or nominee a member of the partnership along with the surviving partners that

it is prohibited by *Canon 34*. Where the payments are made in accordance with a pre-existing agreement entered into by the deceased partner during his lifetime and providing for a fixed method for determining their amount based upon the value of services rendered during the partner's lifetime and providing for a fixed period over which the payments are to be made, this is not the case. Under these circumstances, whether the payments are considered to be delayed payment of compensation earned but withheld during the partner's lifetime, or whether they are considered to be an approximation of his interest in matters pending at the time of his death, is immaterial. In either event, as Henry S. Drinker says in his book, Legal Ethics, at page 189: 'It would seem, however, that a reasonable agreement to pay the estate a proportion of the receipts for a reasonable period is a proper practical settlement for the lawyer's services to his retirement or death.' " *ABA Opinion* 308 (1963).

6. Cf. ABA Opinion 311 (1964).

7. "That the States have broad power to regulate the practice of law is, of course, beyond question." United Mine Workers v. Ill. State Bar Ass'n, 389 U.S. 217, 222 (1967).

"It is a matter of law, not of ethics, as to where an individual may practice law. Each

and the mobility of our society pose distinct problems in the regulation of the practice of law by the states.[8] In furtherance of the public interest, the legal profession should discourage regulation that unreasonably imposes territorial limitations upon the right of a lawyer to handle the legal affairs of his client or upon the opportunity of a client to obtain the services of a lawyer of his choice in all matters including the presentation of a contested matter in a tribunal before which the lawyer is not permanently admitted to practice.[9]

DISCIPLINARY RULES

DR 3–101 Aiding   Unauthorized Practice of Law.[10]

(A) A lawyer shall not aid a non-lawyer in the unauthorized practice of law.[11]

(B) A lawyer shall not practice law in a jurisdiction where to do so would be in violation of regulations of the profession in that jurisdiction.[12]

state has its own rules." *ABA Opinion* 316 (1967).

8. "Much of clients' business crosses state lines. People are mobile, moving from state to state. Many metropolitan areas cross state lines. It is common today to have a single economic and social community involving more than one state. The business of a single client may involve legal problems in several states." *ABA Opinion* 316 (1967).

9. "[W]e reaffirmed the general principle that legal services to New Jersey residents with respect to New Jersey matters may ordinarily be furnished only by New Jersey counsel; but we pointed out that there may be multistate transactions where strict adherence to this thesis would not be in the public interest and that, under the circumstances, it would have been not only more costly to the client but also 'grossly impractical and inefficient' to have had the settlement negotiations conducted by separate lawyers from different states." In re Estate of Waring, 47 N.J. 367, 376, 221 A.2d 193, 197 (1966).

Cf. *ABA Opinion* 316 (1967).

DR 3–102 Dividing Legal Fees with a Non-Lawyer.

(A) A lawyer or law firm shall not share legal fees with a non-lawyer,[13] except that:

(1) An agreement by a lawyer with his firm, partner, or associate may provide for the payment of money, over a reasonable period of time after his death, to his estate or to one or more specified persons.[14]

(2) A lawyer who undertakes to complete unfinished legal business of a deceased lawyer may pay to the estate of the deceased lawyer that proportion of the total compensation which fairly represents the services rendered by the deceased lawyer.

(3) A lawyer or law firm may include non-lawyer employees in a compensation or retirement plan, even though the plan is based in whole or in part on a profit-sharing arrangement [15] providing such

10. Conduct permitted by the Disciplinary Rules of Canons 2 and 5 does not violate DR 3–101.

11. See ABA Canon 47.

12. It should be noted, however, that a lawyer may engage in conduct, otherwise prohibited by this Disciplinary Rule, where such conduct is authorized by preemptive federal legislation. See Sperry v. Florida, 373 U.S. 379, 10 L.Ed.2d 428, 83 S.Ct. 1322 (1963).

13. See ABA Canon 34 and *ABA Opinions* 316 (1967), 180 (1938), and 48 (1931).

"The receiving attorney shall not under any guise or form share his fee for legal services with a lay agency, personal or corporate, without prejudice, however, to the right of the lay forwarder to charge and collect from the creditor proper compensation for non-legal services rendered by the law [*sic*] forwarder which are separate and apart from the services performed by the receiving attorney." *ABA Opinion* 294 (1958).

14. See *ABA Opinion* 266 (1945).

15. Cf. *ABA Opinion* 311 (1964).

plan does not circumvent another disciplinary rule.[16]

DR 3-103 Forming a Partnership with a Non-Lawyer.

(A) A lawyer shall not form a partnership with a non-lawyer if any of the activities of the partnership consist of the practice of law.[17]

CANON 4

A Lawyer Should Preserve the Confidences and Secrets of a Client

ETHICAL CONSIDERATIONS

EC 4-1 Both the fiduciary relationship existing between lawyer and client and the proper functioning of the legal system require the preservation by the lawyer of confidences and secrets of one who has

employed or sought to employ him.[1] A client must feel free to discuss whatever he wishes with his lawyer and a lawyer must be equally free to obtain information beyond that volunteered by his client.[2] A lawyer should be fully informed of all the facts of the matter he is handling in order for his client to obtain the full advantage of our legal system. It is for the lawyer in the exercise of his independent professional judgment to separate the relevant and important from the irrelevant and unimportant. The observance of the ethical obligation of a lawyer to hold inviolate the confidences and secrets of his client not only facilitates the full development of facts essential to proper representation of the client but also encourages laymen to seek early legal assistance.

EC 4-2 The obligation to protect confidences and secrets obviously does not pre-

---

16. See ABA Informal Opinion 1440 (1979).

17. See ABA Canon 33; cf. *ABA Opinions* 239 (1942) and 201 (1940).

ABA Opinion 316 (1967) states that lawyers licensed in different jurisdictions may, under certain conditions, enter "into an arrangement for the practice of law" and that a lawyer licensed in State A is not, for such purpose a layman in State B.

1. See ABA Canons 6 and 37 and *ABA Opinion* 287 (1953). "The reason underlying the rule with respect to confidential communications between attorney and client is well stated in Mechem on Agency, 2d Ed., Vol. 2, § 2297, as follows: 'The purposes and necessities of the relation between a client and his attorney require, in many cases, on the part of the client, the fullest and freest disclosures to the attorney of the client's objectives, motives and acts. This disclosure is made in the strictest confidence, relying upon the attorney's honor and fidelity. To permit the attorney to reveal to others what is so disclosed, would be not only a gross violation of a sacred trust upon his part, but it would utterly destroy and prevent the usefulness and benefits to be derived from professional assistance. Based upon considerations of public policy, therefore, the law wisely declares that all confidential communications and disclosures, made by a client to his legal adviser for the purpose of obtaining his professional aid or advice, shall be strictly privileged:—that the attorney shall not be permitted, without the consent of his

client,—and much less will he be compelled—to reveal or disclose communications made to him under such circumstances.' " *ABA Opinion* 250 (1943).

"While it is true that complete revelation of relevant facts should be encouraged for trial purposes, nevertheless an attorney's dealings with his client, if both are sincere, and if the dealings involve more than mere technical matters, should be immune to discovery proceedings. There must be freedom from fear of revealment of matters disclosed to an attorney because of the peculiarly intimate relationship existing." Ellis-Foster Co. v. Union Carbide & Carbon Corp., 159 F.Supp. 917, 919 (D.N.J. 1958).

Cf. *ABA Opinions* 314 (1965), 274 (1946) and 268 (1945).

2. "While it is the great purpose of law to ascertain the truth, there is the countervailing necessity of insuring the right of every person to freely and fully confer and confide in one having knowledge of the law, and skilled in its practice, in order that the former may have adequate advice and a proper defense. This assistance can be made safely and readily available only when the client is free from the consequences of apprehension of disclosure by reason of the subsequent statements of the skilled lawyer." Baird v. Koerner, 279 F.2d 623, 629–30 (9th Cir.1960).

Cf. *ABA Opinion* 150 (1936).

clude a lawyer from revealing information when his client consents after full disclosure,[3] when necessary to perform his professional employment, when permitted by a Disciplinary Rule, or when required by law. Unless the client otherwise directs, a lawyer may disclose the affairs of his client to partners or associates of his firm. It is a matter of common knowledge that the normal operation of a law office exposes confidential professional information to non-lawyer employees of the office, particularly secretaries and those having access to the files; and this obligates a lawyer to exercise care in selecting and training his employees so that the sanctity of all confidences and secrets of his clients may be preserved. If the obligation extends to two or more clients as to the same information, a lawyer should obtain the permission of all before revealing the information. A lawyer must always be sensitive to the rights and wishes of his client and act scrupulously in the making of decisions which may involve the disclosure of information obtained in his professional relationship.[4] Thus, in the absence of consent of his client after full disclosure, a lawyer should not associate another lawyer in the handling of a matter; nor should he, in the absence of consent, seek counsel from another lawyer if there is a reasonable possibility that the identity of the client or his confidences or secrets would be revealed to such lawyer. Both social amenities and professional duty should cause a lawyer to shun indiscreet conversations concerning his clients.

EC 4-3 Unless the client otherwise directs, it is not improper for a lawyer to give limited information from his files to an outside agency necessary for statistical, bookkeeping, accounting, data processing, banking, printing, or other legitimate purposes, provided he exercises due care in the selection of the agency and warns the agency that the information must be kept confidential.

EC 4-4 The attorney-client privilege is more limited than the ethical obligation of a lawyer to guard the confidences and secrets of his client. This ethical precept, unlike the evidentiary privilege, exists without regard to the nature or source of information or the fact that others share the knowledge. A lawyer should endeavor to act in a manner which preserves the evidentiary privilege; for example, he should avoid professional discussions in the presence of persons to whom the privilege does not extend. A lawyer owes an obligation to advise the client of the attorney-client privilege and timely to assert the privilege unless it is waived by the client.

EC 4-5 A lawyer should not use information acquired in the course of the representation of a client to the disadvantage of the client and a lawyer should not use, except with the consent of his client after full disclosure, such information for his own purposes.[5] Likewise, a lawyer should be diligent in his efforts to prevent the misuse of such information by his employees and associates.[6] Care should be exercised by a lawyer to prevent the disclosure of the confidences and secrets of one client to another,[7] and no employ-

3. "Where ... [a client] knowingly and after full disclosure participates in a [legal fee] financing plan which requires the furnishing of certain information to the bank, clearly by his conduct he has waived any privilege as to that information." *ABA Opinion* 320 (1968).

4. "The lawyer must decide when he takes a case whether it is a suitable one for him to undertake and after this decision is made, he is not justified in turning against his client by exposing injurious evidence entrusted to him.... [D]oing something intrinsically re-

grettable, because the only alternative involves worse consequences, is a necessity in every profession." Williston, Life and Law 271 (1940).

Cf. *ABA Opinions* 177 (1938) and 83 (1932).

5. See ABA Canon 11.

6. See ABA Canon 37.

7. See ABA Canons 6 and 37.

"[A]n attorney must not accept professional employment against a client or a former client

ment should be accepted that might require such disclosure.

EC 4-6 The obligation of a lawyer to preserve the confidences and secrets of his client continues after the termination of his employment.[8] Thus a lawyer should not attempt to sell a law practice as a going business because, among other reasons, to do so would involve the disclosure of confidences and secrets.[9] A lawyer should also provide for the protection of the confidences and secrets of his client following the termination of the practice of the lawyer, whether termination is due to death, disability, or retirement. For example, a lawyer might provide for the personal papers of the client to be returned to him and for the papers of the lawyer to be delivered to another lawyer or to be destroyed. In determining the method of disposition, the instructions and wishes of the client should be a dominant consideration.

DISCIPLINARY RULES

DR 4-101 Preservation of Confidences and Secrets of a Client.[10]

(A) "Confidence" refers to information protected by the attorney-client privilege under applicable law, and "secret" refers to other information gained in the professional relationship that the client has requested be held inviolate or the disclosure of which would be embarrassing or would be likely to be detrimental to the client.

(B) Except when permitted under DR 4-101(C), a lawyer shall not knowingly:

(1) Reveal a confidence or secret of his client.[11]

(2) Use a confidence or secret of his client to the disadvantage of the client.

(3) Use a confidence or secret of his client for the advantage of himself [12] or of a third per-

---

which will, or even *may* require him to use confidential information obtained by the attorney in the course of his professional relations with such client regarding the subject matter of the employment...." *ABA Opinion* 165 (1936).

8. See ABA Canon 37.

"Confidential communications between an attorney and his client, made because of the relationship and concerning the subject-matter of the attorney's employment, are generally privileged from disclosure without the consent of the client, and this privilege outlasts the attorney's employment. *Canon 37.*" *ABA Opinion* 154 (1936).

9. Cf. *ABA Opinion* 266 (1945).

10. See ABA Canon 37; cf. ABA Canon 6.

11. "§ 6068 ... It is the duty of an attorney: ....

"(e) To maintain inviolate the confidence, and at every peril to himself to preserve the secrets, of his client." Cal. Business and Professions Code § 6068 (West 1962). Virtually the same provision is found in the Oregon statutes. Ore.Rev.Stat. ch. 9, § 9.460(5).

"Communications between lawyer and client are privileged (Wigmore on Evidence, 3d Ed., Vol. 8, §§ 2290–2329). The modern theory underlying the privilege is subjective and is to give the client freedom of apprehension in consulting his legal advisor (ibid., § 2290, p. 548). The privilege applies to communications made in seeking legal advice for any purpose (ibid., § 2294, p. 563). The mere circumstance that the advice is given without charge therefore does not nullify the privilege (ibid., § 2303)." *ABA Opinion* 216 (1941).

"It is the duty of an attorney to maintain the confidence and preserve inviolate the secrets of his client...." *ABA Opinion* 155 (1936).

12. See ABA Canon 11.

"The provision respecting employment is in accord with the general rule announced in the adjudicated cases that a lawyer may not make use of knowledge or information acquired by him through his professional relations with his client, or in the conduct of his client's business, to his own advantage or profit (7 C.J.S., § 125, p. 958; Healy v. Gray, 184 Iowa 111, 168 N.W. 222; Baumgardner v. Hudson, D.C.App., 277 F. 552; Goodrum v. Clement, D.C.App., 277 F. 586)." *ABA Opinion* 250 (1943).

son,[13] **unless the client consents after full disclosure.**

(C) A lawyer may reveal:

(1) Confidences or secrets with the consent of the client or clients affected, but only after a full disclosure to them.[14]

(2) Confidences or secrets when permitted under Disciplinary Rules or required by law or court order.[15]

(3) The intention of his client to commit a crime [16] and the information necessary to prevent the crime.[17]

(4) Confidences or secrets necessary to establish or collect his fee [18] or to defend himself or his employees or associates against an accusation of wrongful conduct.[19]

---

13. See *ABA Opinion* 177 (1938).

14. "[A lawyer] may not divulge confidential communications, information, and secrets imparted to him by the client or acquired during their professional relations, unless he is authorized to do so by the client (People v. Gerold, 265 Ill. 448, 107 N.E. 165, 178; Murphy v. Riggs, 238 Mich. 151, 213 N.W. 110, 112; Opinion of this Committee, No. 91)." *ABA Opinion* 202 (1940).

Cf. *ABA Opinion* 91 (1933).

15. "A defendant in a criminal case when admitted to bail is not only regarded as in the custody of his bail, but he is also in the custody of the law, and admission to bail does not deprive the court of its inherent power to deal with the person of the prisoner. Being in lawful custody, the defendant is guilty of an escape when he gains his liberty before he is delivered in due process of law, and is guilty of a separate offense for which he may be punished. In failing to disclose his client's whereabouts as a fugitive under these circumstances the attorney would not only be aiding his client to escape trial on the charge for which he was indicted, but would likewise be aiding him in evading prosecution for the additional offense of escape.

"It is the opinion of the committee that under such circumstances the attorney's knowledge of his client's whereabouts is not privileged, and that he may be disciplined for failing to disclose that information to the proper authorities...." *ABA Opinion* 155 (1936).

"We held in *Opinion* 155 that a communication by a client to his attorney in respect to the future commission of an unlawful act or to a continuing wrong is not privileged from disclosure. Public policy forbids that the relation of attorney and client should be used to conceal wrongdoing on the part of the client.

. . .

"When an attorney representing a defendant in a criminal case applies on his behalf for probation or suspension of sentence, he represents to the court, by implication at least, that

his client will abide by the terms and conditions of the court's order. When that attorney is later advised of a violation of that order, it is his duty to advise his client of the consequences of his act, and endeavor to prevent a continuance of the wrongdoing. If his client thereafter persists in violating the terms and conditions of his probation, it is the duty of the attorney as an officer of the court to advise the proper authorities concerning his client's conduct. Such information, even though coming to the attorney from the client in the course of his professional relations with respect to other matters in which he represents the defendant, is not privileged from disclosure...." *ABA Opinion* 156 (1936).

See *ABA Opinion* 155 (1936).

16. *ABA Opinion* 314 (1965) indicates that a lawyer must disclose even the confidences of his clients if "the facts in the attorney's possession indicate beyond reasonable doubt that a crime will be committed."

See *ABA Opinion* 155 (1936).

17. See ABA Canon 37 and *ABA Opinion* 202 (1940).

18. Cf. *ABA Opinion* 250 (1943).

19. See ABA Canon 37 and *ABA Opinions* 202 (1940) and 19 (1930).

"[T]he adjudicated cases recognize an exception to the rule [that a lawyer shall not reveal the confidences of his client], where disclosure is necessary to protect the attorney's interests arising out of the relation of attorney and client in which disclosure was made.

"The exception is stated in Mechem on Agency, 2d Ed., Vol. 2, § 2313, as follows: 'But the attorney may disclose information received from the client when it becomes necessary for his own protection, as if the client should bring an action against the attorney for negligence or misconduct, and it became necessary for the attorney to show what his instructions were, or what was the nature of the duty which the

(D) **A lawyer shall exercise reasonable care to prevent his employees, associates, and others whose services are utilized by him from disclosing or using confidences or secrets of a client, except that a lawyer may reveal the information allowed by DR 4–101(C) through an employee.**

CANON 5

A Lawyer Should Exercise Independent Professional Judgment on Behalf of a Client

ETHICAL CONSIDERATIONS

EC 5–1 The professional judgment of a lawyer should be exercised, within the

client expected him to perform. So if it became necessary for the attorney to bring an action against the client, the client's privilege could not prevent the attorney from disclosing what was essential as a means of obtaining or defending his own rights.'

"Mr. Jones, in his Commentaries on Evidence, 2d Ed., Vol. 5, § 2165, states the exception thus: 'It has frequently been held that the rule as to privileged communications does not apply when litigation arises between attorney and client to the extent that their communications are relevant to the issue. In such cases, if the disclosure of privileged communications becomes necessary to protect the attorney's rights, he is released from those obligations of secrecy which the law places upon him. He should not, however, disclose more than is necessary for his own protection. It would be a manifest injustice to allow the client to take advantage of the rule of exclusion as to professional confidence to the prejudice of his attorney, or that it should be carried to the extent of depriving the attorney of the means of obtaining or defending his own rights. In such cases the attorney is exempted from the obligations of secrecy.'" *ABA Opinion* 250 (1943).

1. Cf. ABA Canon 35.

"[A lawyer's] fiduciary duty is of the highest order and he must not represent interests adverse to those of the client. It is true that because of his professional responsibility and the confidence and trust which his client may legitimately repose in him, he must adhere to a high standard of honesty, integrity and good faith in dealing with his client. He is not permitted to take advantage of his position or superior knowledge to impose upon the client; nor to conceal facts or law, nor in any way

bounds of the law, solely for the benefit of his client and free of compromising influences and loyalties.[1] Neither his personal interests, the interests of other clients, nor the desires of third persons should be permitted to dilute his loyalty to his client.

Interests of a Lawyer That May Affect His Judgment

EC 5–2 A lawyer should not accept proffered employment if his personal interests or desires will, or there is a reasonable probability that they will, affect adversely the advice to be given or services to be rendered the prospective client.[2] After accepting employment, a

deceive him without being held responsible therefor." Smoot v. Lund, 13 Utah 2d 168, 172, 369 P.2d 933, 936 (1962).

"When a client engages the services of a lawyer in a given piece of business he is entitled to feel that, until that business is finally disposed of in some manner, he has the undivided loyalty of the one upon whom he looks as his advocate and champion. If, as in this case, he is sued and his home attached by his own attorney, who is representing him in another matter, all feeling of loyalty is necessarily destroyed, and the profession is exposed to the charge that it is interested only in money." Grievance Comm. v. Rattner, 152 Conn. 59, 65, 203 A.2d 82, 84 (1964).

"One of the cardinal principles confronting every attorney in the representation of a client is the requirement of complete loyalty and service in good faith to the best of his ability. In a criminal case the client is entitled to a fair trial, but not a perfect one. These are fundamental requirements of due process under the Fourteenth Amendment.... The same principles are applicable in Sixth Amendment cases (not pertinent herein) and suggest that an attorney should have no conflict of interest and that he must devote his full and faithful efforts toward the defense of his client." Johns v. Smyth, 176 F.Supp. 949, 952 (E.D.Va.1959), modified, United States ex rel. Wilkins v. Banmiller, 205 F.Supp. 123, 128 n. 5 (E.D.Pa. 1962), aff'd 325 F.2d 514 (3d Cir.1963), cert. denied, 379 U.S. 847, 13 L.Ed.2d 51, 85 S.Ct. 87 (1964).

2. "Attorneys must not allow their private interests to conflict with those of their clients.... They owe their entire devotion to

lawyer carefully should refrain from acquiring a property right or assuming a position that would tend to make his judgment less protective of the interests of his client.

EC 5–3 The self-interest of a lawyer resulting from his ownership of property in which his client also has an interest or which may affect property of his client may interfere with the exercise of free judgment on behalf of his client. If such interference would occur with respect to a prospective client, a lawyer should decline employment proffered by him. After accepting employment, a lawyer should not acquire property rights that would adversely affect his professional judgment in the representation of his client. Even if the property interests of a lawyer do not presently interfere with the exercise of his independent judgment, but the likelihood of interference can reasonably be foreseen by him, a lawyer should explain the situation to his client and should decline employment or withdraw unless the client consents to the continuance of the relationship after full disclosure. A lawyer should not seek to persuade his client to permit him to invest in an undertaking of his client nor make improper use of his professional relationship to influence his client to invest in an enterprise in which the lawyer is interested.

the interests of their clients." United States v. Anonymous, 215 F.Supp. 111, 113 (E.D.Tenn.1963).

"[T]he court [below] concluded that a firm may not accept any action against a person whom they are presently representing even though there is no relationship between the two cases. In arriving at this conclusion, the court cites an opinion of the Committee on Professional Ethics of the New York County Lawyers' Association which stated in part: 'While under the circumstances ... there may be no actual conflict of interest ... "maintenance of public confidence in the Bar requires an attorney who has accepted representation of a client to decline, while representing such client, any employment from an adverse party in any matter even though wholly unrelated to the original retainer." See Question and An-

EC 5–4 If, in the course of his representation of a client, a lawyer is permitted to receive from his client a beneficial ownership in publication rights relating to the subject matter of the employment, he may be tempted to subordinate the interests of his client to his own anticipated pecuniary gain. For example, a lawyer in a criminal case who obtains from his client television, radio, motion picture, newspaper, magazine, book, or other publication rights with respect to the case may be influenced, consciously or unconsciously, to a course of conduct that will enhance the value of his publication rights to the prejudice of his client. To prevent these potentially differing interests, such arrangements should be scrupulously avoided prior to the termination of all aspects of the matter giving rise to the employment, even though his employment has previously ended.

EC 5–5 A lawyer should not suggest to his client that a gift be made to himself or for his benefit. If a lawyer accepts a gift from his client, he is peculiarly susceptible to the charge that he unduly influenced or over-reached the client. If a client voluntarily offers to make a gift to his lawyer, the lawyer may accept the gift, but before doing so, he should urge that his client secure disinterested advice from an independent, competent person who is cognizant of all the circumstances.[3] Other than in exceptional cir-

swer No. 350, N.Y. County L. Ass'n, Question and Answer No. 450 (June 21, 1956).' " Grievance Comm. v. Rottner, 152 Conn. 59, 65, 203 A.2d 82, 84 (1964).

3. "Courts of equity will scrutinize with jealous vigilance transactions between parties occupying fiduciary relations toward each other.... A deed will not be held invalid, however, if made by the grantor with full knowledge of its nature and effect, and because of the deliberate, voluntary and intelligent desire of the grantor.... Where a fiduciary relation exists, the burden of proof is on the grantee or beneficiary of an instrument executed during the existence of such relationship to show the fairness of the transaction, that it was equitable and just and that it did not proceed from undue influence.... The same rule has application where an attorney engages in a transac-

cumstances, a lawyer should insist that an instrument in which his client desires to name him beneficially be prepared by another lawyer selected by the client.[4]

EC 5-6 A lawyer should not consciously influence a client to name him as executor, trustee, or lawyer in an instrument. In those cases where a client wishes to name his lawyer as such, care should be taken by the lawyer to avoid even the appearance of impropriety.[5]

EC 5-7 The possibility of an adverse effect upon the exercise of free judgment by a lawyer on behalf of his client during litigation generally makes it undesirable for the lawyer to acquire a proprietary interest in the cause of his client or otherwise to become financially interested in the outcome of the litigation.[6] However, it is not improper for a lawyer to protect his right to collect a fee for his services by the assertion of legally permissible liens, even though by doing so he may acquire an interest in the outcome of litigation. Although a contingent fee arrangement[7] gives a lawyer a financial interest in the outcome of litigation, a reasonable contingent fee is permissible in civil cases because it may be the only means by which a layman can obtain the services of a

lawyer of his choice. But a lawyer, because he is in a better position to evaluate a cause of action, should enter into a contingent fee arrangement only in those instances where the arrangement will be beneficial to the client.

EC 5-8 A financial interest in the outcome of litigation also results if monetary advances are made by the lawyer to his client.[8] Although this assistance generally is not encouraged, there are instances when it is not improper to make loans to a client. For example, the advancing or guaranteeing of payment of the costs and expenses of litigation by a lawyer may be the only way a client can enforce his cause of action,[9] but the ultimate liability for such costs and expenses must be that of the client.

EC 5-9 Occasionally a lawyer is called upon to decide in a particular case whether he will be a witness or an advocate. If a lawyer is both counsel and witness, he becomes more easily impeachable for interest and thus may be a less effective witness. Conversely, the opposing counsel may be handicapped in challenging the credibility of the lawyer when the lawyer also appears as an advocate in the case. An advocate who becomes a wit-

tion with a client during the existence of the relation and is benefited thereby.... Conversely, an attorney is not prohibited from dealing with his client or buying his property, and such contracts, if open, fair and honest, when deliberately made, are as valid as contracts between other parties.... [I]mportant factors in determining whether a transaction is fair include a showing by the fiduciary (1) that he made a full and frank disclosure of all the relevant information that he had; (2) that the consideration was adequate; and (3) that the principal had independent advice before completing the transaction." McFail v. Braden, 19 Ill.2d 108, 117–18, 166 N.E.2d 46, 52 (1960).

4. See State ex rel. Nebraska State Bar Ass'n v. Richards, 165 Neb. 80, 94–95, 84 N.W.2d 136, 146 (1957).

5. See ABA Canon 9.

6. See ABA Canon 10.

7. See Code of Professional Responsibility, EC 2–20.

8. See ABA Canon 42.

9. "*Rule 3a.* ... A member of the State Bar shall not directly or indirectly pay or agree to pay, or represent or sanction the representation that he will pay, medical, hospital or nursing bills or other personal expenses incurred by or for a client, prospective or existing; provided this rule shall not prohibit a member:

"(1) with the consent of the client, from paying or agreeing to pay to third persons such expenses from funds collected or to be collected for the client; or

"(2) after he has been employed, from lending money to his client upon the client's promise in writing to repay such loan; or

"(3) from advancing the costs of prosecuting or defending a claim or action. Such costs within the meaning of this subparagraph (3) include all taxable costs or disbursements, costs of investigation and costs of obtaining and presenting evidence." Cal. Business and Professions Code § 6076 (West Supp.1967).

ness is in the unseemly and ineffective position of arguing his own credibility. The roles of an advocate and of a witness are inconsistent; the function of an advocate is to advance or argue the cause of another, while that of a witness is to state facts objectively.

EC 5–10 Problems incident to the lawyer-witness relationship arise at different stages; they relate either to whether a lawyer should accept employment or should withdraw from employment.[10] Regardless of when the problem arises, his decision is to be governed by the same basic considerations. It is not objectionable for a lawyer who is a potential witness to be an advocate if it is unlikely that he will be called as a witness because his testimony would be merely cumulative or if his testimony will relate only to an uncontested issue.[11] In the exceptional situation where it will be manifestly unfair to the client for the lawyer to refuse employment or to withdraw when he will likely be a witness on a contested issue,

he may serve as advocate even though he may be a witness.[12] In making such decision, he should determine the personal or financial sacrifice of the client that may result from his refusal of employment or withdrawal therefrom, the materiality of his testimony, and the effectiveness of his representation in view of his personal involvement. In weighing these factors, it should be clear that refusal or withdrawal will impose an unreasonable hardship upon the client before the lawyer accepts or continues the employment.[13] Where the question arises, doubts should be resolved in favor of the lawyer testifying and against his becoming or continuing as an advocate.[14]

EC 5–11 A lawyer should not permit his personal interests to influence his advice relative to a suggestion by his client that additional counsel be employed.[15] In like manner, his personal interests should not deter him from suggesting that additional counsel be employed; on the contrary, he should be alert to the desirabili-

---

10. "When a lawyer knows, prior to trial, that he will be a necessary witness, except as to merely formal matters such as identification or custody of a document or the like, neither he nor his firm or associates should conduct the trial. If, during the trial, he discovers that the ends of justice require his testimony, he should, from that point on, if feasible and not prejudicial to his client's case, leave further conduct of the trial to other counsel. If circumstances do not permit withdrawal from the conduct of the trial, the lawyer should not argue the credibility of his own testimony." *A Code of Trial Conduct: Promulgated by the American College of Trial Lawyers,* 43 A.B.A.J. 223, 224–25 (1957).

11. Cf. Canon 19: "When a lawyer is a witness for his client, except as to merely formal matters, such as the attestation or custody of an instrument and the like, he should leave the trial of the case to other counsel."

12. "It is the general rule that a lawyer may not testify in litigation in which he is an advocate unless circumstances arise which could not be anticipated and it is necessary to prevent a miscarriage of justice. In those rare cases where the testimony of an attorney is needed to protect his client's interests, it is not only proper but mandatory that it be forthcom-

ing." Schwartz v. Wenger, 267 Minn. 40, 43–44, 124 N.W.2d 489, 492 (1963).

13. "The great weight of authority in this country holds that the attorney who acts as counsel and witness, in behalf of his client, in the same cause on a material matter, not of a merely formal character, and not in an emergency, but having knowledge that he would be required to be a witness in ample time to have secured other counsel and given up his service in the case, violates a highly important provision of the Code of Ethics and a rule of professional conduct, but does not commit a legal error in so testifying, as a result of which a new trial will be granted." Erwin M. Jennings Co. v. DiGenova, 107 Conn. 491, 499, 141 A. 866, 869 (1928).

14. "[C]ases may arise, and in practice often do arise, in which there would be a failure of justice should the attorney withhold his testimony. In such a case it would be a vicious professional sentiment which would deprive the client of the benefit of his attorney's testimony." Connolly v. Straw, 53 Wis. 645, 649, 11 N.W. 17, 19 (1881).

But see canon 19: "Except when essential to the ends of justice, a lawyer should avoid testifying in court in behalf of his client."

15. Cf. ABA Canon 7.

ty of recommending additional counsel when, in his judgment, the proper representation of his client requires it. However, a lawyer should advise his client not to employ additional counsel suggested by the client if the lawyer believes that such employment would be a disservice to the client, and he should disclose the reasons for his belief.

EC 5–12 Inability of co-counsel to agree on a matter vital to the representation of their client requires that their disagreement be submitted by them jointly to their client for his resolution, and the decision of the client shall control the action to be taken.[16]

EC 5–13 A lawyer should not maintain membership in or be influenced by any organization of employees that undertakes to prescribe, direct, or suggest when or how he should fulfill his professional obligations to a person or organization that employs him as a lawyer. Although it is not necessarily improper for a lawyer employed by a corporation or similar entity to be a member of an organization of employees, he should be vigilant to safeguard his fidelity as a lawyer to his employer, free from outside influences.

Interests of Multiple Clients

EC 5–14 Maintaining the independence of professional judgment required of a lawyer precludes his acceptance or continuation of employment that will adversely affect his judgment on behalf of or dilute his loyalty to a client.[17] This problem arises whenever a lawyer is asked to represent two or more clients who may have differing interests, whether such interests be conflicting, inconsistent, diverse, or otherwise discordant.[18]

EC 5–15 If a lawyer is requested to undertake or to continue representation of multiple clients having potentially differing interests, he must weigh carefully the possibility that his judgment may be impaired or his loyalty divided if he accepts or continues the employment. He should resolve all doubts against the propriety of the representation. A lawyer should never represent in litigation multiple clients with differing interests;[19] and there are few situations in which he would be justified in representing in litigation multiple clients with potentially differing interests. If a lawyer accepted such employment and the interests did become actually differing, he would have to withdraw from employment with likelihood of resulting hardship on the clients; and for this rea-

16. See ABA Canon 7.

17. See ABA Canon 6; cf. *ABA Opinions* 261 (1944), 242 (1942), 142 (1935), and 30 (1931).

18. The ABA Canons speak of "conflicting interests" rather than "differing interests" but make no attempt to define such other than the statement in Canon 6: "Within the meaning of this canon, a lawyer represents conflicting interests when, in behalf of one client, it is his duty to contend for that which duty to another client requires him to oppose."

19. "Canon 6 of the Canons of Professional Ethics, adopted by the American Bar Association on September 30, 1937, and by the Pennsylvania Bar Association on January 7, 1938, provides in part that 'It is unprofessional to represent conflicting interests, except by express consent of all concerned given after a full disclosure of the facts. Within the meaning of this Canon, a lawyer represents conflicting interests when, in behalf of one client, it is his duty to contend for that which duty to another

client requires him to oppose.' The full disclosure required by this canon contemplates that the possibly adverse effect of the conflict be fully explained by the attorney to the client to be affected and by him thoroughly understood. . . .

"The foregoing canon applies to cases where the circumstances are such that possibly conflicting interests may permissibly be represented by the same attorney. But manifestly, there are instances where the conflicts of interest are so critically adverse as not to admit of one attorney's representing both sides. Such is the situation which this record presents. No one could conscionably contend that the same attorney may represent both the plaintiff and defendant in an adversary action. Yet, that is what is being done in this case." Jedwabny v. Philadelphia Transportation Co., 390 Pa. 231, 235, 135 A.2d 252, 254 (1957), cert. denied, 355 U.S. 966, 2 L.Ed.2d 541, 78 S.Ct. 557 (1958).

son it is preferable that he refuse the employment initially. On the other hand, there are many instances in which a lawyer may properly serve multiple clients having potentially differing interests in matters not involving litigation. If the interests vary only slightly, it is generally likely that the lawyer will not be subjected to an adverse influence and that he can retain his independent judgment on behalf of each client; and if the interests become differing, withdrawal is less likely to have a disruptive effect upon the causes of his clients.

EC 5–16 In those instances in which a lawyer is justified in representing two or more clients having differing interests, it is nevertheless essential that each client be given the opportunity to evaluate his need for representation free of any potential conflict and to obtain other counsel if he so desires.[20] Thus before a lawyer may represent multiple clients, he should explain fully to each client the implications of the common representation and

20. "Glasser wished the benefit of the undivided assistance of counsel of his own choice. We think that such a desire on the part of an accused should be respected. Irrespective of any conflict of interest, the additional burden of representing another party may conceivably impair counsel's effectiveness.

"To determine the precise degree of prejudice sustained by Glasser as a result of the court's appointment of Stewart as counsel for Kretske is at once difficult and unnecessary. The right to have the assistance of counsel is too fundamental and absolute to allow courts to indulge in nice calculations as to the amount of prejudice arising from its denial." Glasser v. United States, 315 U.S. 60, 75–76, 86 L.Ed. 680, 62 S.Ct. 457, 467 (1942).

21. See ABA Canon 6.

22. Id.

23. Cf. *ABA Opinion* 282 (1950).

"When counsel, although paid by the casualty company, undertakes to represent the policyholder and files his notice of appearance, he owes to his client, the assured, an undeviating and single allegiance. His fealty embraces the requirement to produce in court all witnesses, fact and expert, who are available and necessary for the proper protection of the rights of his client...."

should accept or continue employment only if the clients consent.[21] If there are present other circumstances that might cause any of the multiple clients to question the undivided loyalty of the lawyer, he should also advise all of the clients of those circumstances.[22]

EC 5–17 Typically recurring situations involving potentially differing interests are those in which a lawyer is asked to represent co-defendants in a criminal case, co-plaintiffs in a personal injury case, an insured and his insurer,[23] and beneficiaries of the estate of a decedent. Whether a lawyer can fairly and adequately protect the interests of multiple clients in these and similar situations depends upon an analysis of each case. In certain circumstances, there may exist little chance of the judgment of the lawyer being adversely affected by the slight possibility that the interests will become actually differing; in other circumstances, the chance of adverse effect upon his judgment is not unlikely.

"... The Canons of Professional Ethics make it pellucid that there are not two standards, one applying to counsel privately retained by a client, and the other to counsel paid by an insurance carrier." American Employers Ins. Co. v. Goble Aircraft Specialties, 205 Misc. 1066, 1075, 131 N.Y.S.2d 393, 401 (1954), motion to withdraw appeal granted, 1 App.Div.2d 1008, 154 N.Y.S.2d 835 (1956).

"[C]ounsel, selected by State Farm to defend Dorothy Walker's suit for $50,000 damages, was apprised by Walker that his earlier version of the accident was untrue and that actually the accident occurred because he lost control of his car in passing a Cadillac just ahead. At that point, Walker's counsel should have refused to participate further in view of the conflict of interest between Walker and State Farm.... Instead he participated in the ensuing deposition of the Walkers, even took an *ex parte* sworn statement from Mr. Walker in order to advise State Farm what action it should take, and later used the statement against Walker in the District Court. This action appears to contravene an Indiana attorney's duty 'at every peril to himself, to preserve the secrets of his client' ...." State Farm Mut. Auto Ins. Co. v. Walker, 382 F.2d 548, 552 (1967), cert. denied, 389 U.S. 1045, 19 L.Ed.2d 837, 88 S.Ct. 789 (1968).

EC 5–18 A lawyer employed or retained by a corporation or similar entity owes his allegiance to the entity and not to a stockholder, director, officer, employee, representative, or other person connected with the entity. In advising the entity, a lawyer should keep paramount its interests and his professional judgment should not be influenced by the personal desires of any person or organization. Occasionally a lawyer for an entity is requested by a stockholder, director, officer, employee, representative, or other person connected with the entity to represent him in an individual capacity; in such case the lawyer may serve the individual only if the lawyer is convinced that differing interests are not present.

EC 5–19 A lawyer may represent several clients whose interests are not actually or potentially differing. Nevertheless, he should explain any circumstances that might cause a client to question his undivided loyalty.[24] Regardless of the belief of a lawyer that he may properly represent multiple clients, he must defer to a client who holds the contrary belief and withdraw from representation of that client.

EC 5–20 A lawyer is often asked to serve as an impartial arbitrator or mediator in matters which involve present or former clients. He may serve in either capacity if he first discloses such present or former relationships. After a lawyer has undertaken to act as an impartial arbitrator or mediator, he should not thereafter represent in the dispute any of the parties involved.

24. See ABA Canon 6.

25. See ABA Canon 35.

"Objection to the intervention of a lay intermediary, who may control litigation or otherwise interfere with the rendering of legal services in a confidential relationship, ... derives from the element of pecuniary gain. Fearful of dangers thought to arise from that element, the courts of several States have sustained regulations aimed at these activities. We intimate no view one way or the other as to the merits of those decisions with respect to the

Desires of Third Persons

EC 5–21 The obligation of a lawyer to exercise professional judgment solely on behalf of his client requires that he disregard the desires of others that might impair his free judgment.[25] The desires of a third person will seldom adversely affect a lawyer unless that person is in a position to exert strong economic, political, or social pressures upon the lawyer. These influences are often subtle, and a lawyer must be alert to their existence. A lawyer subjected to outside pressures should make full disclosure of them to his client;[26] and if he or his client believes that the effectiveness of his representation has been or will be impaired thereby, the lawyer should take proper steps to withdraw from representation of his client.

EC 5–22 Economic, political, or social pressures by third persons are less likely to impinge upon the independent judgment of a lawyer in a matter in which he is compensated directly by his client and his professional work is exclusively with his client. On the other hand, if a lawyer is compensated from a source other than his client, he may feel a sense of responsibility to someone other than his client.

EC 5–23 A person or organization that pays or furnishes lawyers to represent others possesses a potential power to exert strong pressures against the independent judgment of those lawyers. Some employers may be interested in furthering their own economic, political, or social goals without regard to the professional

particular arrangements against which they are directed. It is enough that the superficial resemblance in form between those arrangements and that at bar cannot obscure the vital fact that here the entire arrangement employs constitutionally privileged means of expression to secure constitutionally guaranteed civil rights." NAACP v. Button, 371 U.S. 415, 441–42, 9 L.Ed.2d 405, 423–24, 83 S.Ct. 328, 342–43 (1963).

26. Cf. ABA Canon 38.

responsibility of the lawyer to his individual client. Others may be far more concerned with establishment or extension of legal principles than in the immediate protection of the rights of the lawyer's individual client. On some occasions, decisions on priority of work may be made by the employer rather than the lawyer with the result that prosecution of work already undertaken for clients is postponed to their detriment. Similarly, an employer may seek, consciously or unconsciously, to further its own economic interests through the action of the lawyers employed by it. Since a lawyer must always be free to exercise his professional judgment without regard to the interests or motives of a third person, the lawyer who is employed by one to represent another must constantly guard against erosion of his professional freedom.[27]

EC 5–24 To assist a lawyer in preserving his professional independence, a number of courses are available to him. For example, a lawyer should not practice with or in the form of a professional legal corporation, even though the corporate form is permitted by law,[28] if any director, officer, or stockholder of it is a non-lawyer. Although a lawyer may be employed by a business corporation with non-lawyers serving as directors or officers, and they necessarily have the right to make decisions of business policy, a lawyer must decline to accept direction of his professional judgment from any layman. Various types of legal aid offices

are administered by boards of directors composed of lawyers and laymen. A lawyer should not accept employment from such an organization unless the board sets only broad policies and there is no interference in the relationship of the lawyer and the individual client he serves. Where a lawyer is employed by an organization, a written agreement that defines the relationship between him and the organization and provides for his independence is desirable since it may serve to prevent misunderstanding as to their respective roles. Although other innovations in the means of supplying legal counsel may develop, the responsibility of the lawyer to maintain his professional independence remains constant, and the legal profession must insure that changing circumstances do not result in loss of the professional independence of the lawyer.

DISCIPLINARY RULES

DR 5–101 Refusing Employment When the Interests of the Lawyer May Impair His Independent Professional Judgment.

(A) Except with the consent of his client after full disclosure, a lawyer shall not accept employment if the exercise of his professional judgment on behalf of his client will be or reasonably may be affected by his own financial, business, property, or personal inter-

---

27. "Certainly it is true that 'the professional relationship between an attorney and his client is highly personal, involving an intimate appreciation of each individual client's particular problem.' And this Committee does not condone practices which interfere with that relationship. However, the mere fact the lawyer is actually paid by some entity other than the client does not affect that relationship, so long as the lawyer is selected by and is directly responsible to the client. See Informal Opinions 469 and 679. Of course, as the latter decision points out, there must be full disclosure of the arrangement by the attorney to the client...." *ABA Opinion* 320 (1968).

"[A] third party may pay the cost of legal services as long as control remains in the client and the responsibility of the lawyer is solely to the client. Informal Opinions 469 ad [*sic*] 679. See also *Opinion* 237." Id.

28. *ABA Opinion* 303 (1961) recognized that "[s]tatutory provisions now exist in several states which are designed to make [the practice of law in a form that will be classified as a corporation for federal income tax purposes] legally possible, either as a result of lawyers incorporating or forming associations with various corporate characteristics."

ests.[29]

(B) A lawyer shall not accept employment in contemplated or pending litigation if he knows or it is obvious that he or a lawyer in his firm ought to be called as a witness, except that he may undertake the employment and he or a lawyer in his firm may testify:

(1) If the testimony will relate solely to an uncontested matter.

(2) If the testimony will relate solely to a matter of formality and there is no reason to believe that substantial evidence will be offered in opposition to the testimony.

(3) If the testimony will relate solely to the nature and value of legal services rendered in the case by the lawyer or his firm to the client.

(4) As to any matter, if refusal would work a substantial hardship on the client because of the distinctive value of the lawyer or his firm as counsel in the particular case.

DR 5–102 Withdrawal as Counsel When the Lawyer Becomes a Witness.[30]

(A) If, after undertaking employment in contemplated or pending litigation, a lawyer learns or it is obvious that he or a lawyer in his firm ought to be called as a witness on behalf of his client, he shall withdraw from the conduct of the trial and his firm, if any, shall not continue representation in the trial, except that he may continue the representation and he or a lawyer in his firm may testify in the circumstances enumerated in DR 5–101(B)(1) through (4).

(B) If, after undertaking employment in contemplated or pending litigation, a lawyer learns or it is obvious that he or a lawyer in his firm may be called as a witness other than on behalf of his client, he may continue the representation until it is apparent that his testimony is or may be prejudicial to his client.[31]

29. Cf. ABA Canon 6 and *ABA Opinions* 181 (1938), 104 (1934), 103 (1933), 72 (1932), 50 (1931), 49 (1931), and 33 (1931).

"New York County [Opinion] 203.... [A lawyer] should not advise a client to employ an investment company in which he is interested, without informing him of this." Drinker, *Legal Ethics* 956 (1953).

"In *Opinions* 72 and 49 this Committee held: The relations of partners in a law firm are such that neither the firm nor any member or associate thereof, may accept any professional employment which any member of the firm cannot properly accept.

"In *Opinion* 16 this Committee held that a member of a law firm could not represent a defendant in a criminal case which was being prosecuted by another member of the firm who was public prosecuting attorney. The Opinion stated that it was clearly unethical for one member of the firm to oppose the interest of the state while another member represented those interests.... Since the prosecutor himself could not represent both the public and the defendant, no member of his law firm could either." *ABA Opinion* 296 (1959).

30. Cf. ABA Canon 19 and *ABA Opinions* 220 (1941), 185 (1938), 50 (1931), and 33 (1931); but cf. Erwin M. Jennings Co. v. DiGenova, 107 Conn. 491, 498–99, 141 A. 866, 868 (1928).

31. "This *Canon* [19] *of Ethics* needs no elaboration to be applied to the facts here. Apparently, the object of this precept is to avoid putting a lawyer in the obviously embarrassing predicament of testifying and then having to argue the credibility and effect of his own testimony. It was not designed to permit a lawyer to call opposing counsel as a witness and thereby disqualify him as counsel." Galarowicz v. Ward, 119 Utah 611, 620, 230 P.2d 576, 580 (1951).

DR 5–103 Avoiding Acquisition of Interest in Litigation.

(A) A lawyer shall not acquire a proprietary interest in the cause of action or subject matter of litigation he is conducting for a client,[32] except that he may:

(1) Acquire a lien granted by law to secure his fee or expenses.

(2) Contract with a client for a reasonable contingent fee in a civil case.[33]

(B) While representing a client in connection with contemplated or pending litigation, a lawyer shall not advance or guarantee financial assistance to his client,[34] except that a lawyer may advance or guarantee the expenses of litigation, including court costs, expenses of investigation, expenses of medical examination, and costs of obtaining and presenting evidence, provided the client remains ultimately liable for such expenses.

DR 5–104 Limiting Business Relations With a Client.

(A) A lawyer shall not enter into a business transaction with a client if they have differing interests therein and if the client expects the lawyer to exercise his professional judgment therein for the protection of the client, unless the client has consented after full disclosure.

(B) Prior to conclusion of all aspects of the matter giving rise to his employment, a lawyer shall not enter into any arrangement or understanding with a client or a prospective client by which he acquires an interest in publication rights with respect to the subject matter of his employment or proposed employment.

DR 5–105 Refusing to Accept or Continue Employment if the Interests of Another Client May Impair the Independent Professional Judgment of the Lawyer.

(A) A lawyer shall decline proffered employment if the exercise of his independent professional judgment in behalf of a client will be or is likely to be adversely affected by the acceptance of the proffered employment,[35] or if it would be likely to involve him in representing differing interests, except to the extent permitted under DR 5–105(C).[36]

(B) A lawyer shall not continue multiple employment if the exercise of his independent professional judgment in behalf of a client will be or is likely to be adversely affected by his representation of another client, or if it would be likely to involve him in representing differing interests, except to the extent permitted under DR 5–105(C).[37]

32. ABA Canon 10 and *ABA Opinions* 279 (1949), 246 (1942) and 176 (1938).

33. See Code of Professional Responsibility, DR 2–106(C).

34. See ABA Canon 42; cf. *ABA Opinion* 288 (1954).

35. See ABA Canon 6; cf. *ABA Opinions* 167 (1937), 60 (1931), and 40 (1931).

36. *ABA Opinion* 247 (1942) held that an attorney could not investigate a night club shooting on behalf of one of the owner's liability insurers, obtaining the cooperation of the owner, and later represent the injured patron in an action against the owner and a different insurance company unless the attorney obtain the "express consent of all concerned given after a full disclosure of the facts," since to do so would be to represent conflicting interests.

See *ABA Opinions* 247 (1942), 224 (1941), 222 (1941), 218 (1941), 112 (1934), 83 (1932), and 86 (1932).

37. Cf. *ABA Opinions* 231 (1941) and 160 (1936).

(C) In the situations covered by DR 5–105(A) and (B), a lawyer may represent multiple clients if it is obvious that he can adequately represent the interest of each and if each consents to the representation after full disclosure of the possible effect of such representation on the exercise of his independent professional judgment on behalf of each.5h

(D) If a lawyer is required to decline employment or to withdraw from employment under a Disciplinary Rule, no partner or associate, or any other lawyer affiliated with him or his firm may accept or continue such employment.

DR 5–106 Settling Similar Claims of Clients.[38]

(A) A lawyer who represents two or more clients shall not make or participate in the making of an aggregate settlement of the claims of or against his clients, unless each client has consented to the settlement after being advised of the existence and nature of all the claims involved in the proposed settlement, of the total amount of the settlement, and of the participation of each person in the settlement.

DR 5–107 Avoiding Influence by Others Than the Client.

(A) Except with the consent of his client after full disclosure, a lawyer shall not:

   (1) Accept compensation for his legal services from one other than his client.

   (2) Accept from one other than his client any thing of value related to his representation of or his employment by his client.[39]

(B) A lawyer shall not permit a person who recommends, employs, or pays him to render legal services for another to direct or regulate his professional judgment in rendering such legal services.[40]

(C) A lawyer shall not practice with or in the form of a professional corporation or association authorized to practice law for a profit, if:

   (1) A non-lawyer owns any interest therein,[41] except that a fiduciary representative of the estate of a lawyer may hold the stock or interest of the lawyer for a reasonable time during administration;

   (2) A non-lawyer is a corporate director or officer thereof;[42] or

38. Cf. *ABA Opinions* 243 (1942) and 235 (1941).

39. See ABA Canon 38.

"A lawyer who receives a commission (whether delayed or not) from a title insurance company or guaranty fund for recommending or selling the insurance to his client, or for work done for the client or the company, without either fully disclosing to the client his financial interest in the transaction, or crediting the client's bill with the amount thus received, is guilty of unethical conduct." *ABA Opinion* 304 (1962).

40. See ABA Canon 35; cf. *ABA Opinion* 237 (1941).

"When the lay forwarder, as agent for the creditor, forwards a claim to an attorney, the direct relationship of attorney and client shall then exist between the attorney and the creditor, and the forwarder shall not interpose itself as an intermediary to control the activities of the attorney." *ABA Opinion* 294 (1958).

41. "Permanent beneficial and voting rights in the organization set up to practice law, whatever its form, must be restricted to lawyers while the organization is engaged in the practice of law." *ABA Opinion* 303 (1961).

42. "*Canon 33* ... promulgates underlying principles that must be observed no matter in what form of organization lawyers practice

(3) A non-lawyer has the right to direct or control the professional judgment of a lawyer.[43]

CANON 6

A Lawyer Should Represent a Client Competently

ETHICAL CONSIDERATIONS

EC 6–1 Because of his vital role in the legal process, a lawyer should act with competence and proper care in representing clients. He should strive to become and remain proficient in his practice[1] and should accept employment only in matters which he is or intends to become competent to handle.

EC 6–2 A lawyer is aided in attaining and maintaining his competence by keeping abreast of current legal literature and developments, participating in continuing legal education programs,[2] concentrating in particular areas of the law, and by utilizing other available means. He has the additional ethical obligation to assist in improving the legal profession, and he may do so by participating in bar activities intended to advance the quality and standards of members of the profession. Of particular importance is the careful training of his younger associates and the giving of sound guidance to all lawyers who consult him. In short, a lawyer should strive at all levels to aid the legal profession in advancing the highest possible standards of integrity and competence and to meet those standards himself.

EC 6–3 While the licensing of a lawyer is evidence that he has met the standards then prevailing for admission to the bar, a

law. Its requirement that no person shall be admitted or held out as a practitioner or member who is not a member of the legal profession duly authorized to practice, and amendable to professional discipline, makes it clear that any centralized management must be in lawyers to avoid a violation of this Canon." *ABA Opinion* 303 (1961).

43. "There is no intervention of any lay agency between lawyer and client when centralized management provided only by lawyers may give guidance or direction to the services being rendered by a lawyer-member of the organization to a client. The language in *Canon 35* that a lawyer should avoid all relations which direct the performance of his duties by or in the interest of an intermediary refers to lay intermediaries and not lawyer intermediaries with whom he is associated in the practice of law." *ABA Opinion* 303 (1961).

1. "[W]hen a citizen is faced with the need for a lawyer, he wants, and is entitled to, the best informed counsel he can obtain. Changing times produce changes in our laws and legal procedures. The natural complexities of law require continuing intensive study by a lawyer if he is to render his clients a maximum of efficient service. And, in so doing, he maintains the high standards of the legal profession; and he also increases respect and confidence by the general public." Rochelle & Payne, *The Struggle for Public Understanding*, 25 Texas B.J. 109, 160 (1962).

"We have undergone enormous changes in the last fifty years within the lives of most of the adults living today who may be seeking advice. Most of these changes have been accompanied by changes and developments in the law.... Every practicing lawyer encounters these problems and is often perplexed with his own inability to keep up, not only with changes in the law, but also with changes in the lives of his clients and their legal problems.

"To be sure, no client has a right to expect that his lawyer will have all of the answers at the end of his tongue or even in the back of his head at all times. But the client does have the right to expect that the lawyer will have devoted his time and energies to maintaining and improving his competence to know where to look for the answers, to know how to deal with the problems, and to know how to advise to the best of his legal talents and abilities." Levy & Sprague, *Accounting and Law: Is Dual Practice in the Public Interest?*, 52 A.B.A.J. 1110, 1112 (1966).

2. "The whole purpose of continuing legal education, so enthusiastically supported by the ABA, is to make it possible for lawyers to make themselves better lawyers. But there are no nostrums for proficiency in the law; it must come through the hard work of the lawyer himself. To the extent that that work, whether it be in attending institutes or lecture courses, in studying after hours or in the actual day in and day out practice of his profession, can be concentrated within a limited field, the greater the proficiency and expertness that can be developed." *Report of the Special Committee on Specialization and Specialized Legal Education*, 79 A.B.A.Rep. 582, 588 (1954).

lawyer generally should not accept employment in any area of the law in which he is not qualified.[3] However, he may accept such employment if in good faith he expects to become qualified through study and investigation, as long as such preparation would not result in unreasonable delay or expense to his client. Proper preparation and representation may require the association by the lawyer of professionals in other disciplines. A lawyer offered employment in a matter in which he is not and does not expect to become so qualified should either decline the employment or, with the consent of his client, accept the employment and associate a lawyer who is competent in the matter.

EC 6–4 Having undertaken representation, a lawyer should use proper care to safeguard the interests of his client. If a lawyer has accepted employment in a matter beyond his competence but in which he expected to become competent, he should diligently undertake the work and study necessary to qualify himself. In addition to being qualified to handle a particular matter, his obligation to his client requires him to prepare adequately for and give appropriate attention to his legal work.

EC 6–5 A lawyer should have pride in his professional endeavors. His obligation to act competently calls for higher motivation than that arising from fear of civil liability or disciplinary penalty.

EC 6–6 A lawyer should not seek, by contract or other means, to limit his individual liability to his client for his malpractice. A lawyer who handles the affairs of his client properly has no need to attempt to limit his liability for his professional activities and one who does not handle the affairs of his client properly should not be permitted to do so. A lawyer who is a stockholder in or is associated with a professional legal corporation may, however, limit his liability for malpractice of his associates in the corporation, but only to the extent permitted by law.[4]

DISCIPLINARY RULES

DR 6–101 Failing to Act Competently.

(A) A lawyer shall not:

    (1) Handle a legal matter which he knows or should know that he is not competent to handle, without associating with him a lawyer who is competent to handle it.

    (2) Handle a legal matter without preparation adequate in the circumstances.

    (3) Neglect a legal matter entrusted to him.[5]

DR 6–102 Limiting Liability to Client.

(A) A lawyer shall not attempt to exonerate himself from or limit his liability to his client for his personal malpractice.

CANON 7

A Lawyer Should Represent a Client Zealously Within the Bounds of the Law

ETHICAL CONSIDERATIONS

EC 7–1 The duty of a lawyer, both to

---

3. "If the attorney is not competent to skillfully and properly perform the work, he should not undertake the service." Degen v. Steinbrink, 202 App.Div. 477, 481, 195 N.Y.S. 810, 814 (1922), aff'd mem., 236 N.Y. 669, 142 N.E. 328 (1923).

4. See *ABA Opinion* 303 (1961); cf. Code of Professional Responsibility EC 2–11.

5. The annual report for 1967–1968 of the Committee on Grievances of the Association of the Bar of the City of New York showed a receipt of 2,232 complaints; of the 828 offenses against clients, 76 involved conversion, 49 involved "overreaching," and 452, or more than half of all such offenses, involved neglect. *Annual Report of the Committee on Grievances of the Association of the Bar of the City of New York*, N.Y.L.J., Sept. 12, 1968, at 4, col. 5.

his client [1] and to the legal system, is to

1. "The right to be heard would be, in many cases, of little avail if it did not comprehend the right to be heard by counsel. Even the intelligent and educated layman has small and sometimes no skill in the science of law." Powell v. Alabama, 287 U.S. 45, 68–69, 77 L.Ed. 158, 170, 53 S.Ct. 55, 64 (1932).

2. Cf. ABA Canon 4.

"At times . . . [the tax lawyer] will be wise to discard some arguments and he should exercise discretion to emphasize the arguments which in his judgment are most likely to be persuasive. But this process involves legal judgment rather than moral attitudes. The tax lawyer should put aside private disagreements with Congressional and Treasury policies. His own notions of policy, and his personal view of what the law should be, are irrelevant. The job entrusted to him by his client is to use all his learning and ability to protect his client's rights, not to help in the process of promoting a better tax system. The tax lawyer need not accept his client's economic and social opinions, but the client is paying for technical attention and undivided concentration upon his affairs. He is equally entitled to performance unfettered by his attorney's economic and social predilections." Paul, *The Lawyer as a Tax Advisor*, 25 Rocky Mt.L.Rev. 412, 418 (1953).

3. See ABA Canons 15 and 32.

ABA Canon 5, although only speaking of one accused of crime, imposes a similar obligation on the lawyer: "[T]he lawyer is bound, by all fair and honorable means, to present every defense that the law of the land permits, to the end that no person may be deprived of life or liberty, but by due process of law."

"Any persuasion or pressure on the advocate which deters him from planning and carrying out the litigation on the basis of 'what, within the framework of the law, is best for my client's interest?' interferes with the obligation to represent the client fully within the law.

"This obligation, in its fullest sense, is the heart of the adversary process. Each attorney, as an advocate, acts for and seeks that which in his judgment is best for his client, within the bounds authoritatively established. The advocate does not *decide* what is just in this case—he would be usurping the function of the judge and jury—he acts for and seeks for his client that which he is entitled to under the law. He can do no less and properly represent the client." Thode, *The Ethical Standard for the Advocate*, 39 Texas L.Rev. 575, 584 (1961).

"The [Texas public opinion] survey indicates that distrust of the lawyer can be traced direct-

represent his client zealously [2] within the bounds of the law,[3] which includes Disci-ly to certain factors. Foremost of these is a basic misunderstanding of the function of the lawyer as an advocate in an adversary system.

"Lawyers are accused of taking advantage of 'loopholes' and 'technicalities' to win. Persons who make this charge are unaware, or do not understand, that the lawyer is hired to win, and if he does not exercise every legitimate effort in his client's behalf, then he is betraying a sacred trust." Rochelle & Payne, *The Struggle for Public Understanding*, 25 Texas B.J. 109, 159 (1962).

"The importance of the attorney's undivided allegiance and faithful service to one accused of crime, irrespective of the attorney's personal opinion as to the guilt of his client, lies in Canon 5 of the American Bar Association Canon of Ethics.

"The difficulty lies, of course, in ascertaining whether the attorney has been guilty of an error of judgment, such as an election with respect to trial tactics, or has otherwise been actuated by his conscience or belief that his client should be convicted in any event. All too frequently courts are called upon to review actions of defense counsel which are, at the most, errors of judgment, not properly reviewable on habeas corpus unless the trial is a farce and a mockery of justice which requires the court to intervene. . . . But when defense counsel, in a truly adverse proceeding, admits that his conscience would not permit him to adopt certain customary trial procedures, this extends beyond the realm of judgment and strongly suggests an invasion of constitutional rights." Johns v. Smyth, 176 F.Supp. 949, 952 (E.D.Va.1959), modified, United States ex rel. Wilkins v. Banmiller, 205 F.Supp. 123, 128, n. 5 (E.D. Pa.1962), aff'd 325 F.2d 514 (3d Cir. 1963), cert. denied, 379 U.S. 847, 13 L.Ed.2d 51, 85 S.Ct. 87 (1964).

"The adversary system in law administration bears a striking resemblance to the competitive economic system. In each we assume that the individual through partisanship or through self-interest will strive mightily for his side, and that kind of striving we must have. But neither system would be tolerable without restraints and modifications, and at times without outright departures from the system itself. Since the legal profession is entrusted with the system of law administration, a part of its task is to develop in its members appropriate restraints without impairing the values of partisan striving. An accompanying task is to aid in the modification of the adversary system or departure from it in areas to which

plinary Rules and enforceable professional regulations.[4] The professional responsibility of a lawyer derives from his membership in a profession which has the duty of assisting members of the public to secure and protect available legal rights and benefits. In our government of laws and not of men, each member of our society is entitled to have his conduct judged and regulated in accordance with the law;[5] to seek any lawful objective[6] through legally permissible means;[7] and to present for adjudication any lawful claim, issue, or defense.

EC 7-2 The bounds of the law in a given case are often difficult to ascertain.[8] The language of legislative enactments and judicial opinions may be uncertain as

applied to varying factual situations. The limits and specific meaning of apparently relevant law may be made doubtful by changing or developing constitutional interpretations, inadequately expressed statutes or judicial opinions, and changing public and judicial attitudes. Certainty of law ranges from well-settled rules through areas of conflicting authority to areas without precedent.

EC 7-3 Where the bounds of law are uncertain, the action of a lawyer may depend on whether he is serving as advocate or adviser. A lawyer may serve simultaneously as both advocate and adviser, but the two roles are essentially different.[9] In asserting a position on be-

the system is unsuited." Cheatham, *The Lawyer's Role and Surroundings*, 25 Rocky Mt. L.Rev. 405, 410 (1953).

4. "Rule 4.15 prohibits, in the pursuit of a client's cause, 'any manner of fraud or chicane'; Rule 4.22 requires 'candor and fairness' in the conduct of the lawyer, and forbids the making of knowing misquotations; Rule 4.47 provides that a lawyer 'should always maintain his integrity,' and generally forbids all misconduct injurious to the interests of the public, the courts, or his clients, and acts contrary to 'justice, honesty, modesty or good morals.' Our Commissioner has accurately paraphrased these rules as follows: 'An attorney does not have the duty to do all and whatever he can that may enable him to win his client's cause or to further his client's interest. His duty and efforts in these respects, although they should be prompted by his "entire devotion" to the interest of his client, must be within and not without the bounds of the law.'" In re Wines, 370 S.W.2d 328, 333 (Mo.1963).

See Note, 38 Texas L.Rev. 107, 110 (1959).

5. "Under our system of government the process of adjudication is surrounded by safeguards evolved from centuries of experience. These safeguards are not designed merely to lend formality and decorum to the trial of causes. They are predicated on the assumption that to secure for any controversy a truly informed and dispassionate decision is a difficult thing, requiring for its achievement a special summoning and organization of human effort and the adoption of measures to exclude the biases and prejudgments that have free play outside the courtroom. All of this goes for naught if the man with an unpopular cause is unable to find a competent lawyer coura-

geous enough to represent him. His chance to have his day in court loses much of its meaning if his case is handicapped from the outset by the very kind of prejudgment our rules of evidence and procedure are intended to prevent." *Professional Responsibility: Report of the Joint Conference*, 44 A.B.A.J. 1159, 1216 (1958).

6. "[I]t is ... [the tax lawyer's] positive duty to show the client how to avail himself to the full of what the law permits. He is not the keeper of the Congressional conscience." Paul, *The Lawyer as a Tax Adviser*, 25 Rocky Mt.L.Rev. 412, 418 (1953).

7. See ABA Canons 15 and 30.

8. "The fact that it desired to evade the law, as it is called, is immaterial, because the very meaning of a line in the law is that you intentionally may go as close to it as you can if you do not pass it .... It is a matter of proximity and degree as to which minds will differ...." Justice Holmes, in Superior Oil Co. v. Mississippi, 280 U.S. 390, 395-96, 74 L.Ed. 504, 508, 50 S.Ct. 169, 170 (1930).

9. "Today's lawyers perform two distinct types of functions, and our ethical standards should, but in the main do not, recognize these two functions. Judge Philbrick McCoy recently reported to the American Bar Association the need for a reappraisal of the Canons in light of the new and distinct function of counselor, as distinguished from advocate, which today predominates in the legal profession....

"... In the first place, any revision of the canons must take into account and speak to this new and now predominant function of the lawyer.... It is beyond the scope of this pa-

half of his client, an advocate for the most part deals with past conduct and must take the facts as he finds them. By contrast, a lawyer serving as adviser primarily assists his client in determining the course of future conduct and relationships. While serving as advocate, a lawyer should resolve in favor of his client doubts as to the bounds of the law.[10] In serving a client as adviser, a lawyer in appropriate circumstances should give his professional opinion as to what the ultimate decisions of the courts would likely be as to the applicable law.

per to discuss the ethical standards to be applied to the counselor except to state that in my opinion such standards should require a greater recognition and protection for the interest of the public generally than is presently expressed in the canons. Also, the counselor's obligation should extend to requiring him to inform and to impress upon the client a just solution of the problem, considering all interests involved." Thode, *The Ethical Standard for the Advocate*, 39 Texas L.Rev. 575, 578–79 (1961).

"The man who has been called into court to answer for his own actions is entitled to fair hearing. Partisan advocacy plays its essential part in such a hearing, and the lawyer pleading his client's case may properly present it in the most favorable light. A similar resolution of doubts in one direction becomes inappropriate when the lawyer acts as counselor. The reasons that justify and even require partisan advocacy in the trial of a cause do not grant any license to the lawyer to participate as legal advisor in a line of conduct that is immoral, unfair, or of doubtful legality. In saving himself from this unworthy involvement, the lawyer cannot be guided solely by an unreflective inner sense of good faith; he must be at pains to preserve a sufficient detachment from his client's interests so that he remains capable of a sound and objective appraisal of the propriety of what his client proposes to do." *Professional Responsibility: Report of the Joint Conference*, 44 A.B.J. 1159, 1161 (1958).

10. "[A] lawyer who is asked to advise his client ... may freely urge the statement of positions most favorable to the client just as long as there is reasonable basis for those positions." *ABA Opinion* 314 (1965).

11. "The lawyer ... is not an umpire, but an advocate. He is under no duty to refrain from making every proper argument in support of any legal point because he is not convinced

Duty of the Lawyer to a Client

EC 7–4 The advocate may urge any permissible construction of the law favorable to his client, without regard to his professional opinion as to the likelihood that the construction will ultimately prevail.[11] His conduct is within the bounds of the law, and therefore permissible, if the position taken is supported by the law or is supportable by a good faith argument for an extension, modification, or reversal of the law. However, a lawyer is not justified in asserting a position in litigation that is frivolous.[12]

of its inherent soundness.... His personal belief in the soundness of his cause or of the authorities supporting it, is irrelevant." *ABA Opinion* 280 (1949).

"Counsel apparently misconceived his role. It was his duty to honorably present his client's contentions in the light most favorable to his client. Instead he presumed to advise the court as to the validity and sufficiency of prisoner's motion, by letter. We therefore conclude that the prisoner had no effective assistance of counsel and remand this case to the District Court with instructions to set aside the Judgment, appoint new counsel to represent the prisoner if he makes no objection thereto, and proceed anew." *McCartney v. United States*, 343 F.2d 471, 472 (9th Cir. 1965).

12. "Here the court-appointed counsel had the transcript but refused to proceed with the appeal because he found no merit in it.... We cannot say that there was a finding of frivolity by either of the California courts or that counsel acted in any greater capacity than merely as *amicus curiae* which was condemned in *Ellis*, supra. Hence California's procedure did not furnish petitioner with counsel acting in the role of an advocate nor did it provide that full consideration and resolution of the matter as is obtained when counsel is acting in that capacity....

"The constitutional requirement of substantial equality and fair process can only be attained where counsel acts in the role of an active advocate in behalf of his client, as opposed to that of *amicus curiae*. The no-merit letter and the procedure it triggers do not reach that dignity. Counsel should, and can with honor and without conflict, be of more assistance to his client and to the court. His role as advocate requires that he support his

EC 7–5 A lawyer as adviser furthers the interest of his client by giving his professional opinion as to what he believes would likely be the ultimate decision of the courts on the matter at hand and by informing his client of the practical effect of such decision.[13] He may continue in the representation of his client even though his client has elected to pursue a course of conduct contrary to the advice of the lawyer so long as he does not thereby knowingly assist the client to engage in illegal conduct or to take a frivolous legal position. A lawyer should never encourage or aid his client to commit criminal acts or counsel his client on how to violate the law and avoid punishment therefor.[14]

EC 7–6 Whether the proposed action of a lawyer is within the bounds of the law may be a perplexing question when his client is contemplating a course of conduct having legal consequences that vary according to the client's intent, motive, or desires at the time of the action. Often a lawyer is asked to assist his client in developing evidence relevant to the state of mind of the client at a particular time. He may properly assist his client in the development and preservation of evidence of existing motive, intent, or desire; obviously, he may not do anything furthering the creation or preservation of false evidence. In many cases a lawyer may not be certain as to the state of mind of his client, and in those situations he should resolve reasonable doubts in favor of his client.

EC 7–7 In certain areas of legal representation not affecting the merits of the cause or substantially prejudicing the rights of a client, a lawyer is entitled to make decisions on his own. But otherwise the authority to make decisions is exclusively that of the client and, if made within the framework of the law, such decisions are binding on his lawyer. As typical examples in civil cases, it is for the client to decide whether he will accept a settlement offer or whether he will waive his right to plead an affirmative defense. A defense lawyer in a criminal case has the duty to advise his client fully on whether a particular plea to a charge appears to be desirable and as to the prospects of success on appeal, but it is for the client to decide what plea should be entered and whether an appeal should

---

client's appeal to the best of his ability. Of course, if counsel finds his case to be wholly frivolous, after a conscientious examination of it, he should so advise the court and request permission to withdraw. That request must, however, be accompanied by a brief referring to anything in the record that might arguably support the appeal. A copy of counsel's brief should be furnished the indigent and time allowed him to raise any points that he chooses; the court—not counsel—then proceeds, after a full examination of all the proceedings, to decide whether the case is wholly frivolous. If it so finds it may grant counsel's request to withdraw and dismiss the appeal insofar as federal requirements are concerned, or proceed to a decision on the merits, if state law so requires. On the other hand, if it finds any of the legal points arguable on their merits (and therefore not frivolous) it must, prior to decision, afford the indigent the assistance of counsel to argue the appeal." *Anders v. California*, 386 U.S. 738, 744, 18 L.Ed.2d 493, 498, 87 S.Ct. 1396, 1399–1400 (1967), rehearing denied, 388 U.S. 924, 18 L.Ed.2d 1377, 87 S.Ct. 2094 (1967).

See Paul, *The Lawyer As a Tax Adviser*, 25 Rocky Mt.L.Rev. 412, 432 (1953).

13. See ABA Canon 32.

14. "For a lawyer to represent a syndicate notoriously engaged in the violation of the law for the purpose of advising the members how to break the law and at the same time escape it, is manifestly improper. While a lawyer may see to it that anyone accused of crime, no matter how serious and flagrant, has a fair trial, and present all available defenses, he may not co-operate in planning violations of the law. There is a sharp distinction, of course, between advising what can lawfully be done and advising how unlawful acts can be done in a way to avoid conviction. Where a lawyer accepts a retainer from an organization, known to be unlawful, and agrees in advance to defend its members when from time to time they are accused of crime arising out of its unlawful activities, this is equally improper."

"See also *Opinion* 155." *ABA Opinion* 281 (1952).

be taken.[15]

EC 7–8 A lawyer should exert his best efforts to insure that decisions of his client are made only after the client has been informed of relevant considerations. A lawyer ought to initiate this decision-making process if the client does not do so. Advice of a lawyer to his client need not be confined to purely legal considerations.[16] A lawyer should advise his client of the possible effect of each legal alternative.[17] A lawyer should bring to bear upon this decision-making process the fullness of his experience as well as his objective viewpoint.[18] In assisting his client to reach a proper decision, it is often desirable for a lawyer to point out those factors which may lead to a decision that is morally just as well as legally permissible.[19] He may emphasize the possibility of harsh consequences that might result from assertion of legally permissible positions. In the final analysis, however, the lawyer should always remember that the decision whether to forego legally available objectives or methods because of non-legal factors is ultimately for the client and not for himself. In the event that the client in a non-adjudicatory matter insists upon a course of conduct that is contrary to the judgment and advice of the lawyer but not prohibited by Disciplinary Rules, the lawyer may withdraw from the employment.[20]

EC 7–9 In the exercise of his professional judgment on those decisions which are for his determination in the handling of a legal matter,[21] a lawyer should always act in a manner consistent with the

15. See ABA Special Committee on Minimum Standards for the Administration of Criminal Justice, *Standards Relating to Pleas of Guilty,* pp. 69–70 (1968).

16. "First of all, a truly great lawyer is a wise counselor to all manner of men in the varied crises of their lives when they most need disinterested advice. Effective counseling necessarily involves a thoroughgoing knowledge of the principles of the law not merely as they appear in the books but as they actually operate in action." Vanderbilt, *The Five Functions of the Lawyer: Service to Clients and the Public,* 40 A.B.A.J. 31 (1954).

17. "A lawyer should endeavor to obtain full knowledge of his client's cause before advising thereon...." ABA Canon 8.

18. "[I]n devising charters of collaborative effort the lawyer often acts where all of the affected parties are present as participants. But the lawyer also performs a similar function in situations where this is not so, as, for example, in planning estates and drafting wills. Here the instrument defining the terms of collaboration may affect persons not present and often not born. Yet here, too, the good lawyer does not serve merely as a legal conduit for his client's desires, but as a wise counselor, experienced in the art of devising arrangements that will put in workable order the entangled affairs and interests of human beings." *Professional Responsibility: Report of the Joint Conference,* 44 A.B.A.J. 1159, 1162 (1958).

19. See ABA Canon 8.

"Vital as is the lawyer's role in adjudication, it should not be thought that it is only as an advocate pleading in open court that he contributes to the administration of the law. The most effective realization of the law's aims often takes place in the attorney's office, where litigation is forestalled by anticipating its outcome, where the lawyer's quiet counsel takes the place of public force. Contrary to popular belief, the compliance with the law thus brought about is not generally lip-serving and narrow, for by reminding him of its long-run costs the lawyer often deters his client from a course of conduct technically permissible under existing law, though inconsistent with its underlying spirit and purpose." *Professional Responsibility: Report of the Joint Conference,* 44 A.B.A.J. 1159, 1161 (1958).

20. "My summation of Judge Sharswood's view of the advocate's duty to the client is that he owes to the client the duty to use all legal means in support of the client's case. However, at the same time Judge Sharswood recognized that many advocates would find this obligation unbearable if applicable without exception. Therefore, the individual lawyer is given the choice of representing his client fully within the bounds set by the law *or of telling his client that he cannot do so,* so that the client may obtain another attorney if he wishes." Thode, *The Ethical Standard for the Advocate,* 39 Texas L.Rev. 575, 582 (1961).

Cf. Code of Professional Responsibility, DR 2–110(C).

21. See ABA Canon 24.

best interests of his client.[22] However, when an action in the best interest of his client seems to him to be unjust, he may ask his client for permission to forego such action.[23]

EC 7–10 The duty of a lawyer to represent his client with zeal does not militate against his concurrent obligation to treat with consideration all persons involved in the legal process and to avoid the infliction of needless harm.

EC 7–11 The responsibilities of a lawyer may vary according to the intelligence, experience, mental condition or age of a client, the obligation of a public officer, or the nature of a particular proceeding. Examples include the representation of an illiterate or an incompetent, service as a public prosecutor or other government lawyer, and appearances before administrative and legislative bodies.

EC 7–12 Any mental or physical condition of a client that renders him incapable of making a considered judgment on his own behalf casts additional responsibilities upon his lawyer. Where an incompetent is acting through a guardian or other legal representative, a lawyer must look to such representative for those decisions which are normally the prerogative of the client to make. If a client under disability has no legal representative, his lawyer may be compelled in court proceedings to make decisions on behalf of the client. If the client is capable of understanding the matter in question or of contributing to

the advancement of his interests, regardless of whether he is legally disqualified from performing certain acts, the lawyer should obtain from him all possible aid. If the disability of a client and the lack of a legal representative compel the lawyer to make decisions for his client, the lawyer should consider all circumstances then prevailing and act with care to safeguard and advance the interests of his client. But obviously a lawyer cannot perform any act or make any decision which the law requires his client to perform or make, either acting for himself if competent, or by a duly constituted representative if legally incompetent.

EC 7–13 The responsibility of a public prosecutor differs from that of the usual advocate; his duty is to seek justice, not merely to convict.[24] This special duty exists because: (1) the prosecutor represents the sovereign and therefore should use restraint in the discretionary exercise of governmental powers, such as in the selection of cases to prosecute; (2) during trial the prosecutor is not only an advocate but he also may make decisions normally made by an individual client, and those affecting the public interest should be fair to all; and (3) in our system of criminal justice the accused is to be given the benefit of all reasonable doubts. With respect to evidence and witnesses, the prosecutor has responsibilities different from those of a lawyer in private

22. Thode, *The Ethical Standard for the Advocate*, 39 Texas L.Rev. 575, 592 (1961).

23. Cf. *ABA Opinions* 253 (1946) and 178 (1938).

24. See ABA Canon 5 and Berger v. United States, 295 U.S. 78, 79 L.Ed. 1314, 55 S.Ct. 629 (1935).

"The public prosecutor cannot take as a guide for the conduct of his office the standards of an attorney appearing on behalf of an individual client. The freedom elsewhere wisely granted to a partisan advocate must be severely curtailed if the prosecutor's duties are to be properly discharged. The public prosecutor must recall that he occupies a dual role, being obligated, on the one hand, to furnish

that adversary element essential to the informed decision of any controversy, but being possessed, on the other, of important governmental powers that are pledged to the accomplishment of one objective only, that of impartial justice. Where the prosecutor is recreant to the trust implicit in his office, he undermines confidence, not only in his profession, but in government and the very ideal of justice itself." *Professional Responsibility: Report of the Joint Conference*, 44 A.B.A.J. 1159, 1218 (1958).

"The prosecuting attorney is the attorney for the state, and it is his primary duty not to convict but to see that justice is done." *ABA Opinion* 150 (1936).

practice; the prosecutor should make timely disclosure to the defense of available evidence, known to him, that tends to negate the guilt of the accused, mitigate the degree of the offense, or reduce the punishment. Further, a prosecutor should not intentionally avoid pursuit of evidence merely because he believes it will damage the prosecutor's case or aid the accused.

EC 7–14 A government lawyer who has discretionary power relative to litigation should refrain from instituting or continuing litigation that is obviously unfair. A government lawyer not having such discretionary power who believes there is lack of merit in a controversy submitted to him should so advise his superiors and recommend the avoidance of unfair litigation. A government lawyer in a civil action or administrative proceeding has the responsibility to seek justice and to develop a full and fair record, and he should not use his position or the economic power of the government to harass parties or to bring about unjust settlements or results.

EC 7–15 The nature and purpose of proceedings before administrative agencies vary widely. The proceedings may be legislative or quasi-judicial, or a combination of both. They may be *ex parte* in character, in which event they may originate either at the instance of the agency or upon motion of an interested party. The scope of an inquiry may be purely investigative or it may be truly adversary looking toward the adjudication of specific rights of a party or of classes of parties. The foregoing are but examples of some of the types of proceedings conducted by administrative agen-

cies. A lawyer appearing before an administrative agency,[25] regardless of the nature of the proceeding it is conducting, has the continuing duty to advance the cause of his client within the bounds of the law.[26] Where the applicable rules of the agency impose specific obligations upon a lawyer, it is his duty to comply therewith, unless the lawyer has a legitimate basis for challenging the validity thereof. In all appearances before administrative agencies, a lawyer should identify himself, his client if identity of his client is not privileged,[27] and the representative nature of his appearance. It is not improper, however, for a lawyer to seek from an agency information available to the public without identifying his client.

EC 7–16 The primary business of a legislative body is to enact laws rather than to adjudicate controversies, although on occasion the activities of a legislative body may take on the characteristics of an adversary proceeding, particularly in investigative and impeachment matters. The role of a lawyer supporting or opposing proposed legislation normally is quite different from his role in representing a person under investigation or on trial by a legislative body. When a lawyer appears in connection with proposed legislation, he seeks to affect the lawmaking process, but when he appears on behalf of a client in investigatory or impeachment proceedings, he is concerned with the protection of the rights of his client. In either event, he should identify himself and his client, if identity of his client is not privileged, and should comply with

25. As to appearances before a department of government, Canon 26 provides: "A lawyer openly ... may render professional services ... in advocacy of claims before departments of government, upon the same principles of ethics which justify his appearance before the Courts ...."

26. "But as an advocate before a service which itself represents the adversary point of view, where his client's case is fairly arguable,

a lawyer is under no duty to disclose its weaknesses, any more than he would be to make such a disclosure to a brother lawyer. The limitations within which he must operate are best expressed in Canon 22...." *ABA Opinion* 314 (1965).

27. See Baird v. Koerner, 279 F.2d 623 (9th Cir.1960).

applicable laws and legislative rules.[28]

EC 7-17 The obligation of loyalty to his client applies only to a lawyer in the discharge of his professional duties and implies no obligation to adopt a personal viewpoint favorable to the interests or desires of his client[29] While a lawyer must act always with circumspection in order that his conduct will not adversely affect the rights of a client in a matter he is then handling, he may take positions on public issues and espouse legal reforms he favors without regard to the individual views of any client.

EC 7-18 The legal system in its broadest sense functions best when persons in need of legal advice or assistance are represented by their own counsel. For this reason a lawyer should not communicate on the subject matter of the representation of his client with a person he knows to be represented in the matter by a lawyer, unless pursuant to law or rule of court or unless he has the consent of the lawyer for that person.[30] If one is not represented by counsel, a lawyer representing another may have to deal directly with the unrepresented person; in such an instance, a lawyer should not undertake to give advice to the person who is attempting to represent himself,[31] except that he may advise him to obtain a lawyer.

Duty of the Lawyer to the Adversary System of Justice

EC 7-19 Our legal system provides for the adjudication of disputes governed by the rules of substantive, evidentiary, and procedural law. An adversary presentation counters the natural human tendency to judge too swiftly in terms of the familiar that which is not yet fully known;[32] the advocate, by his zealous preparation and presentation of facts and law, enables the tribunal to come to the hearing with an open and neutral mind and to render impartial judgments.[33] The duty of a lawyer to his client and his duty to the legal system are the same: to represent his client zealously within the

28. See ABA Canon 26.

29. "Law should be so practiced that the lawyer remains free to make up his own mind how he will vote, what causes he will support, what economic and political philosophy he will espouse. It is one of the glories of the profession that it admits of this freedom. Distinguished examples can be cited of lawyers whose views were at variance from those of their clients, lawyers whose skill and wisdom make them valued advisers to those who had little sympathy with their views as citizens." *Professional Responsibility: Report of the Joint Conference,* 44 A.B.A.J. 1159, 1217 (1958).

"No doubt some tax lawyers feel constrained to abstain from activities on behalf of a better tax system because they think that their clients may object. Clients have no right to object if the tax adviser handles their affairs competently and faithfully and independently of his private views as to tax policy. They buy his expert services, not his private opinions or his silence on issues that gravely affect the public interest." Paul, *The Lawyer as a Tax Adviser,* 25 Rocky Mt.L.Rev. 412, 434 (1953).

30. See ABA Canon 9.

31. Id.

32. See *Professional Responsibility: Report of the Joint Conference,* 44 A.B.A.J. 1159, 1160 (1958).

33. "Without the participation of someone who can act responsibly for each of the parties, this essential narrowing of the issues [by exchange of written pleadings or stipulations of counsel] becomes impossible. But here again the true significance of partisan advocacy lies deeper, touching once more the integrity of the adjudicative process itself. It is only through the advocate's participation that the hearing may remain in fact what it purports to be in theory: a public trial of the facts and issues. Each advocate comes to the hearing prepared to present his proofs and arguments, knowing at the same time that his arguments may fail to persuade and that his proof may be rejected as inadequate.... The deciding tribunal, on the other hand, comes to the hearing uncommitted. It has not represented to the public that any fact can be proved, that any argument is sound, or that any particular way of stating a litigant's case is the most effective expression of its merits." *Professional Responsibility: Report of the Joint Conference,* 44 A.B.A.J. 1159, 1160–61 (1958).

bounds of the law.[34]

EC 7–20 In order to function properly, our adjudicative process requires an informed, impartial tribunal capable of administering justice promptly and efficiently [35] according to procedures that command public confidence and respect.[36] Not only must there be competent, adverse presentation of evidence and issues, but a tribunal must be aided by rules appropriate to an effective and dignified process. The procedures under which tribunals operate in our adversary system have been prescribed largely by legislative enactments, court rules and decisions, and administrative rules. Through the years certain concepts of proper professional conduct have become rules of law applicable to the adversary adjudicative process. Many of these concepts are the bases for standards of professional conduct set forth in the Disciplinary Rules.

EC 7–21 The civil adjudicative process is primarily designed for the settlement of disputes between parties, while the criminal process is designed for the protection of society as a whole. Threatening to use, or using, the criminal process to coerce adjustment of private civil claims or controversies is a subversion of that process; [37] further, the person against whom the criminal process is so misused may be deterred from asserting his legal rights and thus the usefulness of the civil process in settling private disputes is impaired. As in all cases of abuse of judicial process, the improper use of criminal process tends to diminish public confidence in our legal system.

EC 7–22 Respect for judicial rulings is essential to the proper administration of justice; however, a litigant or his lawyer may, in good faith and within the framework of the law, take steps to test the correctness of a ruling of a tribunal.[38]

EC 7–23 The complexity of law often makes it difficult for a tribunal to be fully informed unless the pertinent law is presented by the lawyers in the cause. A tribunal that is fully informed on the applicable law is better able to make a fair and accurate determination of the matter before it. The adversary system contemplates that each lawyer will present and argue the existing law in the light most favorable to his client.[39] Where a lawyer knows of legal authority in the controlling jurisdiction directly adverse to the position of his client, he should inform the tribunal of its existence unless his adversary has done so; but, having made such disclosure, he may challenge

---

34. Cf. ABA Canons 15 and 32.

35. Cf. ABA Canon 21.

36. See *Professional Responsibility: Report of the Joint Conference,* 44 A.B.A.J. 1159, 1216 (1958).

37. "We are of the opinion that the letter in question was improper, and that in writing and sending it respondent was guilty of unprofessional conduct. This court has heretofore expressed its disapproval of using threats of criminal prosecution as a means of forcing settlement of civil claims. . . .

"Respondent has been guilty of a violation of a principle which condemns any confusion of threats of criminal prosecution with the enforcement of civil claims. For this misconduct he should be severely censured." Matter of Gelman, 230 App.Div. 524, 527, 245 N.Y.S. 416, 419 (1930).

38. "An attorney has the duty to protect the interests of his client. He has a right to press legitimate argument and to protest an erroneous ruling." Gallagher v. Municipal Court, 31 Cal.2d 784, 796, 192 P.2d 905, 913 (1948).

"There must be protection, however, in the far more frequent case of the attorney who stands on his rights and combats the order in good faith and without disrespect believing with good cause that it is void, for it is here that the independence of the bar becomes valuable." Note, 39 Colum.L.Rev. 433, 438 (1939).

39. "Too many do not understand that accomplishment of the layman's abstract ideas of justice is the function of the judge and jury, and that it is the lawyer's sworn duty to portray his client's case in its most favorable light." Rochelle and Payne, *The Struggle for Public Understanding,* 25 Texas B.J. 109, 159 (1962).

its soundness in whole or in part.[40]

EC 7–24 In order to bring about just and informed decisions, evidentiary and procedural rules have been established by tribunals to permit the inclusion of relevant evidence and argument and the exclusion of all other considerations. The expression by a lawyer of his personal opinion as to the justness of a cause, as to the credibility of a witness, as to the culpability of a civil litigant, or as to the guilt or innocence of an accused is not a proper subject for argument to the trier of fact.[41] It is improper as to factual matters because admissible evidence possessed by a lawyer should be presented only as sworn testimony. It is improper as to all other matters because, were the rule otherwise, the silence of a lawyer on a given occasion could be construed unfavorably to his client. However, a lawyer may argue, on his analysis of the evidence, for any position or conclusion with respect to any of the foregoing matters.

EC 7–25 Rules of evidence and procedure are designed to lead to just decisions and are part of the framework of the law. Thus while a lawyer may take steps in good faith and within the framework of the law to test the validity of rules, he is not justified in consciously violating such rules and he should be diligent in his efforts to guard against his unintentional

violation of them.[42] As examples, a lawyer should subscribe to or verify only those pleadings that he believes are in compliance with applicable law and rules; a lawyer should not make any prefatory statement before a tribunal in regard to the purported facts of the case on trial unless he believes that his statement will be supported by admissible evidence; a lawyer should not ask a witness a question solely for the purpose of harassing or embarrassing him; and a lawyer should not by subterfuge put before a jury matters which it cannot properly consider.

EC 7–26 The law and Disciplinary Rules prohibit the use of fraudulent, false, or perjured testimony or evidence.[43] A lawyer who knowingly [44] participates in introduction of such testimony or evidence is subject to discipline. A lawyer should, however, present any admissible evidence his client desires to have presented unless he knows, or from facts within his knowledge should know, that such testimony or evidence is false, fraudulent, or perjured.[45]

EC 7–27 Because it interferes with the proper administration of justice, a lawyer should not suppress evidence that he or his client has a legal obligation to reveal or produce. In like manner, a lawyer should not advise or cause a person to

---

40. "We are of the opinion that this Canon requires the lawyer to disclose such decisions [that are adverse to his client's contentions] to the court. He may, of course, after doing so, challenge the soundness of the decisions or present reasons which he believes would warrant the court in not following them in the pending case." *ABA Opinion* 146 (1935).

Cf. *ABA Opinion* 280 (1949) and Thode, *The Ethical Standard for the Advocate,* 39 Texas L.Rev. 575, 585–86 (1961).

41. See ABA Canon 15.

"The traditional duty of an advocate is that he honorably uphold the contentions of his client. He should not voluntarily undermine them." Harders v. State of California, 373 F.2d 839, 842 (9th Cir.1967).

42. See ABA Canon 22.

43. Id. Cf. ABA Canon 41.

44. See generally *ABA Opinion* 287 (1953) as to a lawyer's duty when he unknowingly participates in introducing perjured testimony.

45. "Under any standard of proper ethical conduct an attorney should not sit by silently and permit his client to commit what may have been perjury, and which certainly would mislead the court and the opposing party on a matter vital to the issue under consideration. . . .

. . . .

"Respondent next urges that it was his duty to observe the utmost good faith toward his client, and therefore he could not divulge any confidential information. This duty to the client of course does not extend to the point of authorizing collaboration with him in the commission of fraud." In re Carroll, 244 S.W.2d 474, 474–75 (Ky.1951).

secrete himself or to leave the jurisdiction of a tribunal for the purpose of making him unavailable as a witness therein.[46]

EC 7–28 Witnesses should always testify truthfully[47] and should be free from any financial inducements that might tempt them to do otherwise.[48] A lawyer should not pay or agree to pay a non-expert witness an amount in excess of reimbursement for expenses and financial loss incident to his being a witness; however, a lawyer may pay or agree to pay an expert witness a reasonable fee for his services as an expert. But in no event should a lawyer pay or agree to pay a contingent fee to any witness. A lawyer should exercise reasonable diligence to see that his client and lay associates conform to these standards.[49]

EC 7–29 To safeguard the impartiality that is essential to the judicial process, veniremen and jurors should be protected against extraneous influences.[50] When impartiality is present, public confidence in the judicial system is enhanced. There should be no extrajudicial communication with veniremen prior to trial or with jurors during trial by or on behalf of a lawyer connected with the case. Furthermore, a lawyer who is not connected with the case should not communicate with or cause another to communicate with a venireman or a juror about the case. After the trial, communication by a lawyer with jurors is permitted so long as he refrains from asking questions or making comments that tend to harass or embarrass the juror[51] or to influence actions of the juror in future cases. Were a lawyer to be prohibited from communicating after a trial with a juror, he could not ascertain if the verdict might be subject to legal challenge, in which event the invalidity of a verdict might go undetected.[52] When an extrajudicial communication by a lawyer with a juror is permitted by law, it should be made considerately and with deference to the personal feelings of the juror.

46. See ABA Canon 5; cf. *ABA Opinion* 131 (1935).

47. Cf. ABA Canon 39.

48. "The prevalence of perjury is a serious menace to the administration of justice, to prevent which no means have as yet been satisfactorily devised. But there certainly can be no greater incentive to perjury than to allow a party to make payments to its opponents witnesses under any guise or on any excuse, and at least attorneys who are officers of the court to aid it in the administration of justice, must keep themselves clear of any connection which in the slightest degree tends to induce witnesses to testify in favor of their clients." In re Robinson, 151 App.Div. 589, 600, 136 N.Y.S. 548, 556–57 (1912), aff'd, 209 N.Y. 354, 103 N.E. 160 (1913).

49. "It will not do for an attorney who seeks to justify himself against charges of this kind to show that he has escaped criminal responsibility under the Penal Law, nor can he blindly shut his eyes to a system which tends to suborn witnesses, to produce perjured testimony, and to suppress the truth. He has an active affirmative duty to protect the administration of justice from perjury and fraud, and that duty is not performed by allowing his subordinates and assistants to attempt to subvert justice and procure results for his clients based upon false testimony and perjured witnesses." Id., 151 App.Div. at 592, 136 N.Y.S. at 551.

50. See ABA Canon 23.

51. "[I]t is unfair to jurors to permit a disappointed litigant to pick over their private associations in search of something to discredit them and their verdict. And it would be unfair to the public too if jurors should understand that they cannot convict a man of means without risking an inquiry of that kind by paid investigators, with, to boot, the distortions an inquiry of that kind can produce." State v. LaFera, 42 N.J. 97, 107, 199 A.2d 630, 636 (1964).

52. *ABA Opinion* 319 (1968) points out that "[m]any courts today, and the trend is in this direction, allow the testimony of jurors as to all irregularities in and out of the courtroom except those irregularities whose existence can be determined only by exploring the consciousness of a single particular juror, New Jersey v. Kociolek, 20 N.J. 92, 118 A.2d 812 (1955). Model Code of Evidence Rule 301. Certainly as to states in which the testimony and affidavits of jurors may be received in support of or against a motion for new trial, a lawyer, in his obligation to protect his client, must have the tools for ascertaining whether or not grounds for a new trial exist and it is not unethical for him to talk to and question jurors."

EC 7-30 Vexatious or harassing investigations of veniremen or jurors seriously impair the effectiveness of our jury system. For this reason, a lawyer or anyone on his behalf who conducts an investigation of veniremen or jurors should act with circumspection and restraint.

EC 7-31 Communications with or investigations of members of families of veniremen or jurors by a lawyer or by anyone on his behalf are subject to the restrictions imposed upon the lawyer with respect to his communications with or investigations of veniremen and jurors.

EC 7-32 Because of his duty to aid in preserving the integrity of the jury system, a lawyer who learns of improper

conduct by or towards a venireman, a juror, or a member of the family of either should make a prompt report to the court regarding such conduct.

EC 7-33 A goal of our legal system is that each party shall have his case, criminal or civil, adjudicated by an impartial tribunal. The attainment of this goal may be defeated by dissemination of news or comments which tend to influence judge or jury.[53] Such news or comments may prevent prospective jurors from being impartial at the outset of the trial [54] and may also interfere with the obligation of jurors to base their verdict solely upon the evidence admitted in the trial.[55] The release by a lawyer of out-of-

53. Generally see ABA Advisory Committee on Fair Trial and Free Press, Standards Relating to Fair Trial and Free Press (1966).

"[T]he trial court might well have proscribed extrajudicial statements by any lawyer, party, witness, or court official which divulged prejudicial matters.... See State v. Van Dwyne, 43 N.J. 369, 389, 204 A.2d 841, 852 (1964), in which the court interpreted Canon 20 of the American Bar Association's Canons of Professional Ethics to prohibit such statements. Being advised of the great public interest in the case, the mass coverage of the press, and the potential prejudicial impact of publicity, the court could also have requested the appropriate city and county officials to promulgate a regulation with respect to dissemination of information about the case by their employees. In addition, reporters who wrote or broadcast prejudicial stories, could have been warned as to the impropriety of publishing material not introduced in the proceedings.... In this manner, Sheppard's right to a trial free from outside interference would have been given added protection without corresponding curtailment of the news media. Had the judge, the other officers of the court, and the police placed the interest of justice first, the news media would have soon learned to be content with the task of reporting the case as it unfolded in the courtroom—not pieced together from extrajudicial statements." Sheppard v. Maxwell, 384 U.S. 333, 361–62, 16 L.Ed.2d 600, 619–20, 86 S.Ct. 1507, 1521–22 (1966).

"Court proceedings are held for the solemn purpose of endeavoring to ascertain the truth which is the *sine qua non* of a fair trial. Over the centuries Anglo-American courts have devised careful safeguards by rule and otherwise

to protect and facilitate the performance of this high function. As a result, at this time those safeguards do not permit the televising and photographing of a criminal trial, save in two States and there only under restrictions. The federal courts prohibit it by specific rule. This is weighty evidence that our concepts of a fair trial do not tolerate such an indulgence. We have always held that the atmosphere essential to the preservation of a fair trial—the most fundamental of all freedoms—must be maintained at all costs." Estes v. State of Texas, 381 U.S. 532, 540, 14 L.Ed.2d 543, 549, 85 S.Ct. 1628, 1631–32 (1965), rehearing denied, 382 U.S. 875, 15 L.Ed.2d 118, 86 S.Ct. 18 (1965).

54. "Pretrial can create a major problem for the defendant in a criminal case. Indeed, it may be more harmful than publicity during the trial for it may well set the community opinion as to guilt or innocence.... The trial witnesses present at the hearing, as well as the original jury panel, were undoubtedly made aware of the peculiar public importance of the case by the press and television coverage being provided, and by the fact that they themselves were televised live and their pictures rebroadcast on the evening show." Id., 381 U.S. at 536–37, 14 L.Ed.2d at 546–47, 85 S.Ct. at 1629–30.

55. "The undeviating rule of this Court was expressed by Mr. Justice Holmes over half a century ago in Patterson v. Colorado, 205 U.S. 454, 462 (1907):

"The theory of our system is that the conclusions to be reached in a case will be induced only by evidence and argument in open

court statements regarding an anticipated or pending trial may improperly affect the impartiality of the tribunal.[56] For these reasons, standards for permissible and prohibited conduct of a lawyer with respect to trial publicity have been established.

EC 7–34 The impartiality of a public servant in our legal system may be impaired by the receipt of gifts or loans. A lawyer,[57] therefore, is never justified in making a gift or a loan to a judge, a hearing officer, or an official or employee of a tribunal, except as permitted by Section C(4) of Canon 5 of the Code of Judi-

cial Conduct, but a lawyer may make a contribution to the campaign fund of a candidate for judicial office in conformity with Section B(2) under Canon 7 of the Code of Judicial Conduct.[58]

EC 7–35 All litigants and lawyers should have access to tribunals on an equal basis. Generally, in adversary proceedings a lawyer should not communicate with a judge relative to a matter pending before, or which is to be brought before, a tribunal over which he presides in circumstances which might have the effect or give the appearance of granting

---

court, and not by any outside influence, whether of private talk or public print."
Sheppard v. Maxwell, 384 U.S. 333, 351, 16 L.Ed.2d 600, 614, 86 S.Ct. 1507, 1516 (1966).

"The trial judge has a large discretion in ruling on the issue of prejudice resulting from the reading by jurors of news articles concerning the trial.... Generalizations beyond that statement are not profitable, because each case must turn on its special facts. We have here the exposure of jurors to information of a character which the trial judge ruled was so prejudicial it could not be directly offered as evidence. The prejudice to the defendant is almost certain to be as great when that evidence reaches the jury through news accounts as when it is a part of the prosecution's evidence.... It may indeed be greater for it is then not tempered by protective procedures." Marshall v. United States, 360 U.S. 310, 312–13, 3 L.Ed.2d 1250, 1252, 79 S.Ct. 1171, 1173 (1959).

"The experienced trial lawyer knows that an adverse public opinion is a tremendous disadvantage to the defense of his client. Although grand jurors conduct their deliberations in secret, they are selected from the body of the public. They are likely to know what the general public knows and to reflect the public attitude. Trials are open to the public, and aroused public opinion respecting the merits of a legal controversy creates a court room atmosphere which, without any vocal expression in the presence of the petit jury, makes itself felt and has its effect upon the action of the petit jury. Our fundamental concepts of justice and our American sense of fair play requires that the petit jury shall be composed of persons with fair and impartial minds and without preconceived views as to the merits of the controversy, and that it shall determine the issues presented to it solely upon the evidence

adduced at the trial and according to the law given in the instructions of the trial judge.

"While we may doubt that the effect of public opinion would sway or bias the judgment of the trial judge in an equity proceeding, the defendant should not be called upon to run that risk and the trial court should not have his work made more difficult by any dissemination of statements to the public that would be calculated to create a public demand for a particular judgment in a prospective or pending case." *ABA Opinion* 199 (1940).

Cf. Estes v. State of Texas, 381 U.S. 532, 544–45, 14 L.Ed.2d 543, 551, 85 S.Ct. 1628, 1634 (1965), rehearing denied, 382 U.S. 875, 15 L.Ed.2d 118, 86 S.Ct. 18 (1965).

56. See ABA Canon 20.

57. Canon 3 observes that a lawyer "deserves rebuke and denunciation for any device or attempt to gain from a Judge special personal consideration or favor."

See ABA Canon 32.

58. "*Judicial Canon 32* provides:

" 'A judge should not accept any presents or favors from litigants, or from lawyers practicing before him or from others whose interests are likely to be submitted to him for judgment.'

"The language of this Canon is perhaps broad enough to prohibit campaign contributions by lawyers, practicing before the court upon which the candidate hopes to sit. However, we do not think it was intended to prohibit such contributions when the candidate is obligated, by force of circumstances over which he has no control, to conduct a campaign, the expense of which exceeds that which he should reasonably be expected to personally bear!" *ABA Opinion* 226 (1941).

undue advantage to one party.[59] For example, a lawyer should not communicate with a tribunal by a writing unless a copy thereof is promptly delivered to opposing counsel or to the adverse party if he is not represented by a lawyer. Ordinarily an oral communication by a lawyer with a judge or hearing officer should be made only upon adequate notice to opposing counsel, or, if there is none, to the opposing party. A lawyer should not condone or lend himself to private importunities by another with a judge or hearing officer on behalf of himself or his client.

EC 7–36 Judicial hearings ought to be conducted through dignified and orderly procedures designed to protect the rights of all parties. Although a lawyer has the duty to represent his client zealously, he should not engage in any conduct that offends the dignity and decorum of proceedings.[60] While maintaining his independence, a lawyer should be respectful, courteous, and above-board in his relations with a judge or hearing officer before whom he appears.[61] He should avoid undue solicitude for the comfort or convenience of judge or jury and should avoid any other conduct calculated to gain special consideration.

EC 7–37 In adversary proceedings, clients are litigants and though ill feeling may exist between clients, such ill feeling should not influence a lawyer in his conduct, attitude, and demeanor towards opposing lawyers.[62] A lawyer should not make unfair or derogatory personal reference to opposing counsel. Haranguing and offensive tactics by lawyers interfere with the orderly administration of justice and have no proper place in our legal system.

EC 7–38 A lawyer should be courteous to opposing counsel and should accede to reasonable requests regarding court proceedings, settings, continuances, waiver of procedural formalities, and similar matters which do not prejudice the rights of his client.[63] He should follow local customs of courtesy or practice, unless he gives timely notice to opposing counsel of his intention not to do so.[64] A lawyer should be punctual in fulfilling all professional commitments.[65]

EC 7–39 In the final analysis, proper functioning of the adversary system depends upon cooperation between lawyers and tribunals in utilizing procedures which will preserve the impartiality of tribunals and make their decisional processes prompt and just, without impinging upon the obligation of lawyers to represent their clients zealously within the framework of the law.

DISCIPLINARY RULES

DR 7–101 Representing a Client Zealously.

(A) **A lawyer shall not intentionally:**[66]

(1) **Fail to seek the lawful objectives of his client through reasonably available means**[67] **permitted by law and the Disciplinary Rules, except as provided by DR 7–101(B). A lawyer does not violate this Disciplinary Rule, however, by acceding to reasonable requests of opposing counsel which do not prejudice the rights of his client, by being punctual in fulfilling all professional commitments, by avoiding offensive tactics, or by treating with courtesy and**

---

59. See ABA Canons 3 and 32.
60. Cf. ABA Canon 18.
61. See ABA Canons 1 and 3.
62. See ABA Canon 17.
63. See ABA Canon 24.

64. See ABA Canon 25.
65. See ABA Canon 21.
66. See ABA Canon 15.
67. See ABA Canons 5 and 15; cf. ABA Canons 4 and 32.

consideration all persons involved in the legal process.

(2) Fail to carry out a contract of employment entered into with a client for professional services, but he may withdraw as permitted under DR 2–110, DR 5–102, and DR 5–105.

(3) Prejudice or damage his client during the course of the professional relationship [68] except as required under DR 7–102(B).

(B) In his representation of a client, a lawyer may:

(1) Where permissible, exercise his professional judgment to waive or fail to assert a right or position of his client.

(2) Refuse to aid or participate in conduct that he believes to be unlawful, even though there is some support for an argument that the conduct is legal.

DR 7–102 Representing a Client Within the Bounds of the Law.

(A) In his representation of a client, a lawyer shall not:

(1) File a suit, assert a position, conduct a defense, delay a trial, or take other action on behalf of his client when he knows or when it is obvious that such action would serve merely to harass or maliciously injure another.[69]

(2) Knowingly advance a claim or defense that is unwarranted under existing law, except that he may advance such claim or defense if it can be supported by good faith argument for an extension, modification, or reversal of existing law.

(3) Conceal or knowingly fail to disclose that which he is required by law to reveal.

(4) Knowingly use perjured testimony or false evidence.[70]

(5) Knowingly make a false statement of law or fact.

(6) Participate in the creation or preservation of evidence when he knows or it is obvious that the evidence is false.

(7) Counsel or assist his client in conduct that the lawyer knows to be illegal or fraudulent.

(8) Knowingly engage in other illegal conduct or conduct contrary to a Disciplinary Rule.

(B) A lawyer who receives information clearly establishing that:

(1) His client has, in the course of the representation, perpetrated a fraud upon a person or tribunal shall promptly call upon his client to rectify the same, and if his client refuses or is unable to do so, he shall reveal the fraud to the affected person or tribunal, except when the information is protected as a privileged communication.[71]

(2) A person other than his client has perpetrated a fraud upon a tribunal shall promptly reveal the fraud to the tri-

68. Cf. ABA Canon 24.

69. See ABA Canon 30.

70. Cf. ABA Canons 22 and 29.

71. See ABA Canon 41; cf. Hinds v. State Bar, 19 Cal.2d 87, 92–93, 119 P.2d 134, 137 (1941); but see *ABA Opinion* 287 (1953) and Texas Canon 38. Also see Code of Professional Responsibility. DR 4–101(C)(2).

bunal.[72]

DR 7-103 Performing the Duty of Public Prosecutor or Other Government Lawyer.[73]

(A) A public prosecutor or other government lawyer shall not institute or cause to be instituted criminal charges when he knows or it is obvious that the charges are not supported by probable cause.

(B) A public prosecutor or other government lawyer in criminal litigation shall make timely disclosure to counsel for the defendant, or to the defendant if he has no counsel, of the existence of evidence, known to the prosecutor or other government lawyer, that tends to negate the guilt of the accused, mitigate the degree of the offense, or reduce the punishment.

DR 7-104 Communicating With One of Adverse Interest.[74]

(A) During the course of his representation of a client a lawyer shall not:

(1) Communicate or cause another to communicate on the subject of the representation with a party he knows to be represented by a lawyer in that matter unless he has the prior consent of the lawyer representing such other party[75] or is authorized by law to do so.

(2) Give advice to a person who is not represented by a lawyer, other than the advice to secure counsel,[76] if the interests of such person are or have a reasonable possibility of being in conflict with the interests of his client.[77]

DR 7-105 Threatening Criminal Prosecution.

(A) A lawyer shall not present, participate in presenting, or threaten to present criminal charges solely to obtain an advantage in a civil matter.

DR 7-106 Trial Conduct.

(A) A lawyer shall not disregard or advise his client to disregard a standing rule of a tribunal or a ruling of a tribunal made in the course of a proceeding, but he may take appropriate steps in good faith to test the validity of such rule or ruling.

(B) In presenting a matter to a tribunal, a lawyer shall disclose:[78]

(1) Legal authority in the controlling jurisdiction known to him to be directly adverse to the position of his client and

---

72. See Precision Inst. Mfg. Co. v. Automotive M.M. Co., 324 U.S. 806, 89 L.Ed. 1381, 65 S.Ct. 993 (1945).

73. Cf. ABA Canon 5.

74. *"Rule 12.* . . . A member of the State Bar shall not communicate with a party represented by counsel upon a subject of controversy, in the absence and without the consent of such counsel. This rule shall not apply to communications with a public officer, board, committee or body." Cal. Business and Professions Code § 6076 (West 1962).

75. See ABA Canon 9; cf. *ABA Opinions* 124 (1934), 108 (1934), 95 (1933), and 75

(1932); also see In re Schwabe, 242 Or. 169, 174–75, 408 P.2d 922, 924 (1965).

"It is clear from the earlier opinions of this committee that *Canon 9* is to be construed literally and does not allow a communication with an opposing party, without the consent of his counsel, though the purpose merely be to investigate the facts. *Opinions 117, 55, 66,*" *ABA Opinion* 187 (1938).

76. Cf. *ABA Opinion* 102 (1933).

77. Cf. ABA Canon 9 and *ABA Opinion* 58 (1931).

78. Cf. Note, 38 Texas L.Rev. 107, 108–09 (1959).

which is not disclosed by opposing counsel.[79]

(2) Unless privileged or irrelevant, the identities of the clients he represents and of the persons who employed him.[80]

(C) In appearing in his professional capacity before a tribunal, a lawyer shall not:

(1) State or allude to any matter that he has no reasonable basis to believe is relevant to the case or that will not be supported by admissible evidence.[81]

(2) Ask any question that he has no reasonable basis to believe is relevant to the case and that is intended to degrade a witness or other person.[82]

(3) Assert his personal knowledge of the facts in issue, except when testifying as a witness.

(4) Assert his personal opinion as to the justness of a cause, as to the credibility of a witness, as to the culpability of a civil litigant, or as to the guilt or innocence of an accused;[83]

---

79. "In the brief summary in the 1947 edition of the Committee's decisions (p. 17), *Opinion 146* was thus summarized: *Opinion 146*— A lawyer should disclose to the court a decision directly adverse to his client's case that is unknown to his adversary.

. . .

"We would not confine the Opinion to 'controlling authorities'—i.e., those decisive of the pending case—but, in accordance with the tests hereafter suggested, would apply it to a decision directly adverse to any proposition of law on which the lawyer expressly relies, which would reasonably be considered important by the judge sitting on the case.

. . .

". . . The test in every case should be: Is the decision which opposing counsel has overlooked one which the court should clearly consider in deciding the case? Would a reasonable judge properly feel that a lawyer who advanced, as the law, a proposition adverse to the undisclosed decision, was lacking in candor and fairness to him? Might the judge consider himself misled by an implied representation that the lawyer knew of no adverse authority?" *ABA Opinion* 280 (1949).

80. "The authorities are substantially uniform against any privilege as applied to the fact of retainer or identity of the client. The privilege is limited to confidential communications, and a retainer is not a confidential communication, although it cannot come into existence without some communication between the attorney and the—at that stage prospective—client." United States v. Pape, 144 F.2d 778, 782 (2d Cir. 1944), cert. denied, 323 U.S. 752, 89 L.Ed.2d 602, 65 S.Ct. 86 (1944).

"To be sure, there may be circumstances under which the identification of a client may amount to the prejudicial disclosure of a confidential communication, as where the substance of a disclosure has already been revealed but not its source." Colton v. United States, 306 F.2d 633, 637 (2d Cir. 1962).

81. See ABA Canon 22; cf. ABA Canon 17.

"The rule allowing counsel when addressing the jury the widest latitude in discussing the evidence and presenting the client's theories falls far short of authorizing the statement by counsel of matter not in evidence, or indulging in argument founded on no proof, or demanding verdicts for purposes other than the just settlement of the matters at issue between the litigants, or appealing to prejudice or passion. The rule confining counsel to legitimate argument is not based on etiquette, but on justice. Its violation is not merely an overstepping of the bounds of propriety, but a violation of a party's rights. The jurors must determine the issues upon the evidence. Counsel's address should help them do this, not tend to lead them astray." Cherry Creek Nat. Bank v. Fidelity & Cas. Co., 207 App.Div. 787, 790–91, 202 N.Y.S. 611, 614 (1924).

82. Cf. ABA Canon 18.

§ 6068.   . . . It is the duty of an attorney:

. . .

"(f) To abstain from all offensive personality, and to advance no fact prejudicial to the honor or reputation of a party or witness, unless required by the justice of the cause with which he is charged." Cal.Business and Professions Code § 6068 (West 1962).

83. "The record in the case at bar was silent concerning the qualities and character of the deceased. It is especially improper, in ad-

but he may argue, on his analysis of the evidence, for any position or conclusion with respect to the matters stated herein.

(5) Fail to comply with known local customs of courtesy or practice of the bar or a particular tribunal without giving to opposing counsel timely notice of his intent not to comply.[84]

(6) Engage in undignified or discourteous conduct which is degrading to a tribunal.

(7) Intentionally or habitually violate any established rule of procedure or of evidence.

DR 7-107 Trial Publicity.[85]

(A) A lawyer participating in or associated with the investigation of a criminal matter shall not make or participate in making an ex-

trajudicial statement that a reasonable person would expect to be disseminated by means of public communication and that does more than state without elaboration:

(1) Information contained in a public record.

(2) That the investigation is in progress.

(3) The general scope of the investigation including a description of the offense and, if permitted by law, the identity of the victim.

(4) A request for assistance in apprehending a suspect or assistance in other matters and the information necessary thereto.

(5) A warning to the public of any dangers.

dressing the jury in a murder case, for the prosecuting attorney to make reference to his knowledge of the good qualities of the deceased where there is no evidence in the record bearing upon his character.... A prosecutor should never inject into his argument evidence not introduced at the trial." People v. Dukes, 12 Ill.2d 334, 341, 146 N.E.2d 14, 17–18 (1957).

84. "A lawyer should not ignore known customs or practice of the Bar or of a particular Court, even when the law permits, without giving timely notice to the opposing counsel." ABA Canon 25.

85. The provisions of Sections (A), (B), (C), and (D) of this Disciplinary Rule incorporate the fair trial-free press standards which apply to lawyers as adopted by the ABA House of Delegates, Feb. 19, 1968, upon the recommendation of the Fair Trial and Free Press Advisory Committee of the ABA Special Committee on Minimum Standards for the Administration of Criminal Justice.

Cf. ABA Canon 20; see generally ABA Advisory Committee on Fair Trial and Free Press, Standards Relating to Fair Trial and Free Press (1966).

"From the cases coming here we note that unfair and prejudicial news comment on pending trials has become increasingly prevalent.

Due process requires that the accused receive a trial by an impartial jury free from outside influences. Given the pervasiveness of modern communications and the difficulty of effacing prejudicial publicity from the minds of the jurors, the trial courts must take strong measures to ensure that the balance is never weighed against the accused. And appellate tribunals have the duty to make an independent evaluation of the circumstances. Of course, there is nothing that prescribes the press from reporting events that transpire in the courtroom. But where there is a reasonable likelihood that prejudicial news prior to trial will prevent a fair trial, the judge should continue the case until the threat abates, or transfer it to another county not so permeated with publicity.... The courts must take such steps by rule and regulation that will protect their processes from prejudicial outside interferences. Neither prosecutors, counsel for defense, the accused, witnesses, court staff nor enforcement officers coming under the jurisdiction of the court should be permitted to frustrate its function. Collaboration between counsel and the press as to information affecting the fairness of a criminal trial is not only subject to regulation, but is highly censurable and worthy of disciplinary measures." Sheppard v. Maxwell, 384 U.S. 333, 362–63, 16 L.Ed.2d 600, 620, 86 S.Ct. 1507, 1522 (1966).

(B) A lawyer or law firm associated with the prosecution or defense of a criminal matter shall not, from the time of the filing of a complaint, information, or indictment, the issuance of an arrest warrant, or arrest until the commencement of the trial or disposition without trial, make or participate in making an extrajudicial statement that a reasonable person would expect to be disseminated by means of public communication and that relates to:

    (1) The character, reputation, or prior criminal record (including arrests, indictments, or other charges of crime) of the accused.

    (2) The possibility of a plea of guilty to the offense charged or to a lesser offense.

    (3) The existence or contents of any confession, admission, or statement given by the accused or his refusal or failure to make a statement.

    (4) The performance or results of any examinations or tests or the refusal or failure of the accused to submit to examinations or tests.

    (5) The identity, testimony, or credibility of a prospective witness.

    (6) Any opinion as to the guilt or innocence of the accused, the evidence, or the merits of the case.

(C) DR 7–107(B) does not preclude a lawyer during such period from announcing:

    (1) The name, age, residence, occupation, and family status of the accused.

    (2) If the accused has not been apprehended, any information necessary to aid in his apprehension or to warn the public of any dangers he may present.

    (3) A request for assistance in obtaining evidence.

    (4) The identity of the victim of the crime.

    (5) The fact, time, and place of arrest, resistance, pursuit, and use of weapons.

    (6) The identity of investigating and arresting officers or agencies and the length of the investigation.

    (7) At the time of seizure, a description of the physical evidence seized, other than a confession, admission, or statement.

    (8) The nature, substance, or text of the charge.

    (9) Quotations from or references to public records of the court in the case.

    (10) The scheduling or result of any step in the judicial proceedings.

    (11) That the accused denies the charges made against him.

(D) During the selection of a jury or the trial of a criminal matter, a lawyer or law firm associated with the prosecution or defense of a criminal matter shall not make or participate in making an extra-judicial statement that a reasonable person would expect to be disseminated by means of public communication and that relates to the trial, parties, or issues in the trial or other matters that are reasonably likely to interfere with a fair trial, except that he may quote from or refer without comment to public records of the court in the case.

(E) After the completion of a trial or disposition without trial of a criminal matter and prior to the imposition of sentence, a lawyer or law firm associated with the prosecution or defense shall not make or participate in making an extra-judicial statement that a reasonable person would expect to be disseminated by public communication and that is reasonably likely to affect the imposition of sentence.

(F) The foregoing provisions of DR 7–107 also apply to professional disciplinary proceedings and juvenile disciplinary proceedings when pertinent and consistent with other law applicable to such proceedings.

(G) A lawyer or law firm associated with a civil action shall not during its investigation or litigation make or participate in making an extra-judicial statement, other than a quotation from or reference to public records, that a reasonable person would expect to be disseminated by means of public communication and that relates to:

(1) Evidence regarding the occurrence or transaction involved.

(2) The character, credibility, or criminal record of a party, witness, or prospective witness.

(3) The performance or results of any examinations or tests or the refusal or failure of a party to submit to such.

(4) His opinion as to the merits of the claims or defenses of a party, except as required by law or administrative rule.

(5) Any other matter reasonably likely to interfere with a fair trial of the action.

(H) During the pendency of an administrative proceeding, a lawyer or law firm associated therewith shall not make or participate in making a statement, other than a quotation from or reference to public records, that a reasonable person would expect to be disseminated by means of public communication if it is made outside the official course of the proceeding and relates to:

(1) Evidence regarding the occurrence or transaction involved.

(2) The character, credibility, or criminal record of a party, witness, or prospective witness.

(3) Physical evidence or the performance or results of any examinations or tests or the refusal or failure of a party to submit to such.

(4) His opinion as to the merits of the claims, defenses, or positions of an interested person.

(5) Any other matter reasonably likely to interfere with a fair hearing.

(I) The foregoing provisions of DR 7–107 do not preclude a lawyer from replying to charges of misconduct publicly made against him or from participating in the proceedings of legislative, administrative, or other investigative bodies.

(J) A lawyer shall exercise reasonable care to prevent his employees and associates from making an extra-judicial statement that he would be prohibited from making under DR 7-107.

DR 7-108 Communication with or Investigation of Jurors.

(A) Before the trial of a case a lawyer connected therewith shall not communicate with or cause another to communicate with anyone he knows to be a member of the venire from which the jury will be selected for the trial of the case.

(B) During the trial of a case:

(1) A lawyer connected therewith shall not communicate with or cause another to communicate with any member of the jury.[86]

(2) A lawyer who is not connected therewith shall not communicate with or cause another to communicate with a juror concerning the case.

(C) DR 7-108(A) and (B) do not prohibit a lawyer from communicating with veniremen or jurors in the course of official proceedings.

(D) After discharge of the jury from further consideration of a case with which the lawyer was connected, the lawyer shall not ask questions of or make comments to a member of that jury that are calculated merely to harass or embarrass the juror or to influence his actions in future jury service.[87]

(E) A lawyer shall not conduct or cause, by financial support or otherwise, another to conduct a vexatious or harassing investigation of either a venireman or a juror.

(F) All restrictions imposed by DR 7-108 upon a lawyer also apply to communications with or investigations of members of a family of a venireman or a juror.

(G) A lawyer shall reveal promptly to the court improper conduct by a venireman or a juror, or by another toward a venireman or a juror or a member of his family, of which the lawyer has knowledge.

DR 7-109 Contact With Witnesses.

(A) A lawyer shall not suppress any evidence that he or his client has a legal obligation to reveal or produce.[88]

(B) A lawyer shall not advise or cause a person to secrete himself or to leave the jurisdiction of a tribunal for the purpose of making him unavailable as a witness therein.[89]

(C) A lawyer shall not pay, offer to pay, or acquiesce in the payment of compensation to a witness contingent upon the content of his testimony or the outcome of the case.[90] But a lawyer may advance, guarantee, or acquiesce in the payment of:

(1) Expenses reasonably incurred by a witness in attending or testifying.

86. See ABA Canon 23.

87. "[I]t would be unethical for a lawyer to harass, entice, induce or exert influence on a juror to obtain his testimony." *ABA Opinion* 319 (1968).

88. See ABA Canon 5.

89. Cf. ABA Canon 5.

"*Rule 15.* ... A member of the State Bar shall not advise a person, whose testimony could establish or tend to establish a material fact, to avoid service of process, or secrete himself, or otherwise to make his testimony unavailable." Cal.Business and Professions Code § 6076 (West 1962).

90. See In re O'Keefe, 49 Mont. 369, 142 P. 638 (1914).

(2) **Reasonable compensation to a witness for his loss of time in attending or testifying.**

(3) **A reasonable fee for the professional services of an expert witness.**

DR 7-110   Contact With Officials.[91]

(A) **A lawyer shall not give or lend any thing of value to a judge, official, or employee of a tribunal, except as permitted by Section C(4) of Canon 5 of the Code of Judicial Conduct, but a lawyer may make a contribution to the campaign fund of a candidate for judicial office in conformity with Section B(2) under Canon 7 of the Code of Judicial Conduct.**

(B) **In an adversary proceeding, a lawyer shall not communicate, or cause another to communicate, as to the merits of the cause with a judge or an official before whom the proceeding is pending, except:**

(1) **In the course of official proceedings in the cause.**

(2) **In writing if he promptly delivers a copy of the writing to opposing counsel or to the ad-**

verse party if he is not represented by a lawyer.

(3) **Orally upon adequate notice to opposing counsel or to the adverse party if he is not represented by a lawyer.**

(4) **As otherwise authorized by law, or by Section A(4) under Canon 3 of the Code of Judicial Conduct.[92]**

CANON 8

A Lawyer Should Assist in Improving the Legal System

ETHICAL CONSIDERATIONS

EC 8-1   Changes in human affairs and imperfections in human institutions make necessary constant efforts to maintain and improve our legal system.[1] This system should function in a manner that commands public respect and fosters the use of legal remedies to achieve redress of grievances. By reason of education and experience, lawyers are especially qualified to recognize deficiencies in the legal system and to initiate corrective measures therein. Thus they should participate in proposing and supporting legislation and programs to improve the system,[2] without regard to the general

---

91. Cf. ABA Canon 3.

92. *"Rule 16. . . .* A member of the State Bar shall not, in the absence of opposing counsel, communicate with or argue to a judge or judicial officer except in open court upon the merits of a contested matter pending before such judge or judicial officer; nor shall he, without furnishing opposing counsel with a copy thereof, address a written communication to a judge or judicial officer concerning the merits of a contested matter pending before such judge or judicial officer. This rule shall not apply to ex parte matters." Cal.Business and Professions Code § 6076 (West 1962).

1. ". . . [Another] task of the great lawyer is to do his part individually and as a member of the organized bar to improve his profession, the courts, and the law. As President Theodore Roosevelt aptly put it, 'Every man owes some of his time to the upbuilding of the profession to which he belongs.' Indeed, this

obligation is one of the great things which distinguishes a profession from a business. The soundness and the necessity of President Roosevelt's admonition insofar as it relates to the legal profession cannot be doubted. The advances in natural science and technology are so startling and the velocity of change in business and in social life is so great that the law along with the other social sciences, and even human life itself, is in grave danger of being extinguished by new gods of its own invention if it does not awake from its lethargy. Vanderbilt, *The Five Functions of the Lawyer: Service to Clients and the Public,* 40 A.B.A.J. 31, 31–32 (1954).

2. See ABA Cannon 29; Cf. Cheatham, *The Lawyer's Role and Surroundings,* 25 Rocky Mt.L.Rev. 405, 406–07 (1953).

"The lawyer tempted by repose should recall the heavy costs paid by his profession when needed legal reform has to be accomplished

interests or desires of clients or former clients.[3]

EC 8–2 Rules of law are deficient if they are not just, understandable, and responsive to the needs of society. If a lawyer believes that the existence or absence of a rule of law, substantive or procedural, causes or contributes to an unjust result, he should endeavor by lawful means to obtain appropriate changes in the law. He should encourage the simplification of laws and the repeal or amendment of laws that are outmoded.[4] Likewise, legal procedures should be improved whenever experience indicates a change is needed.

EC 8–3 The fair administration of justice requires the availability of competent lawyers. Members of the public should be educated to recognize the existence of legal problems and the resultant need for legal services, and should be provided methods for intelligent selection of counsel. Those persons unable to pay for legal services should be provided needed services. Clients and lawyers should not be penalized by undue geographical restraints upon representation in legal matters, and the bar should address itself to improvements in licensing, reciprocity, and admission procedures consistent with the needs of modern commerce.

EC 8–4 Whenever a lawyer seeks legislative or administrative changes, he should identify the capacity in which he appears, whether on behalf of himself, a client, or the public.[5] A lawyer may advocate such changes on behalf of a client even though he does not agree with them. But when a lawyer purports to act on behalf of the public, he should espouse only those changes which he conscientiously believes to be in the public interest.

EC 8–5 Fraudulent, deceptive, or otherwise illegal conduct by a participant in a proceeding before a tribunal or legislative body is inconsistent with fair administration of justice, and it should never be participated in or condoned by lawyers. Unless constrained by his obligation to preserve the confidences and secrets of his client, a lawyer should reveal to appropriate authorities any knowledge he may have of such improper conduct.

EC 8–6 Judges and administrative officials having adjudicatory powers ought to be persons of integrity, competence, and suitable temperament. Generally, lawyers are qualified, by personal observation or investigation, to evaluate the qualifications of persons seeking or being considered for such public offices, and for this reason they have a special responsibility to aid in the selection of only those

through the initiative of public-spirited laymen. Where change must be thrust from without upon an unwilling Bar, the public's least flattering picture of the lawyer seems confirmed. The lawyer concerned for the standing of his profession will, therefore, interest himself actively in the improvement of the law. In doing so he will not only help to maintain confidence in the Bar, but will have the satisfaction of meeting a responsibility inhering in the nature of his calling." *Professional Responsibility: Report of the Joint Conference,* 44 A.B.A.J. 1159, 1217 (1958).

3. See Stayton, *Cum Honore Officium,* 19 Tex.B.J. 765, 766 (1956); *Professional Responsibility: Report of the Joint Conference,* 44 A.B.A.J. 1159, 1162 (1958); and Paul, *The Lawyer as a Tax Adviser,* 25 Rocky Mt.L.Rev. 412, 433–34 (1953).

4. "There are few great figures in the history of the Bar who have not concerned themselves with the reform and improvement of the law. The special obligation of the profession with respect to legal reform rests on considerations too obvious to require enumeration. Certainly it is the lawyer who has both the best chance to know when the law is working badly and the special competence to put it in order." *Professional Responsibility: Report of the Joint Conference,* 44 A.B.A.J. 1159, 1217 (1958).

5. "*Rule 14.* ... A member of the State Bar shall not communicate with, or appear before, a public officer, board, committee or body, in his professional capacity, without first disclosing that he is an attorney representing interests that may be affected by action of such officer, board, committee or body." Cal.Business and Professions Code § 6076 (West 1962).

who are qualified.[6] It is the duty of lawyers to endeavor to prevent political considerations from outweighing judicial fitness in the selection of judges. Lawyers should protest earnestly against the appointment or election of those who are unsuited for the bench and should strive to have elected[7] or appointed thereto only those who are willing to forego pursuits, whether of a business, political, or other nature, that may interfere with the free and fair consideration of questions presented for adjudication. Adjudicatory officials, not being wholly free to defend themselves, are entitled to receive the support of the bar against unjust criticism.[8] While a lawyer as a citizen has a right to criticize such officials publicly,[9] he should be certain of the merit of his complaint, use appropriate language, and avoid petty criticisms, for unrestrained and intemperate statements tend to lessen public confidence in our legal sys-

tem.[10] Criticisms motivated by reasons other than a desire to improve the legal system are not justified.

EC 8–7 Since lawyers are a vital part of the legal system, they should be persons of integrity, of professional skill, and of dedication to the improvement of the system. Thus a lawyer should aid in establishing, as well as enforcing, standards of conduct adequate to protect the public by insuring that those who practice law are qualified to do so.

EC 8–8 Lawyers often serve as legislators or as holders of other public offices. This is highly desirable, as lawyers are uniquely qualified to make significant contributions to the improvement of the legal system. A lawyer who is a public officer, whether full or part-time, should not engage in activities in which his personal or professional interests are or fore-

6. See ABA Canon 2.

"Lawyers are better able than laymen to appraise accurately the qualifications of candidates for judicial office. It is proper that they should make that appraisal known to the voters in a proper and dignified manner. A lawyer may with propriety endorse a candidate for judicial office and seek like endorsement from other lawyers. But the lawyer who endorses a judicial candidate or seeks that endorsement from other lawyers should be actuated by a sincere belief in the superior qualifications of the candidate for judicial service and not by personal or selfish motives; and a lawyer should not use or attempt to use the power or prestige of the judicial office to secure such endorsement. On the other hand, the lawyer whose endorsement is sought, if he believes the candidate lacks the essential qualifications for the office or believes the opposing candidate is better qualified, should have the courage and moral stamina to refuse the request for endorsement." *ABA Opinion* 189 (1938).

7. "[W]e are of the opinion that, whenever a candidate for judicial office merits the endorsement and support of lawyers, the lawyers may make financial contributions toward the campaign if its cost, when reasonably conducted, exceeds that which the candidate would be expected to bear personally." *ABA Opinion* 226 (1941).

8. See ABA Canon 1.

9. "Citizens have a right under our constitutional system to criticize governmental officials and agencies. Courts are not, and should not be, immune to such criticism." Konigsberg v. State Bar of California, 353 U.S. 252, 269 (1957).

10. "[E]very lawyer, worthy of respect, realizes that public confidence in our courts is the cornerstone of our governmental structure, and will refrain from unjustified attack on the character of the judges, while recognizing the duty to denounce and expose a corrupt or dishonest judge." Kentucky State Bar Ass'n v. Lewis, 282 S.W.2d 321, 326 (Ky.1955).

"We should be the last to deny that Mr. Meeker has the right to uphold the honor of the profession and to expose without fear or favor corrupt or dishonest conduct in the profession, whether the conduct be that of a judge or not.... However, this Canon [29] does not permit one to make charges which are false and untrue and unfounded in fact. When one's fancy leads him to make false charges, attacking the character and integrity of others, he does so at his peril. He should not do so without adequate proof of his charges and he is certainly not authorized to make careless, untruthful and vile charges against his professional brethren." In re Meeker, 76 N.M. 354, 364–65, 414 P.2d 862, 869 (1966), appeal dismissed, 385 U.S. 449, 17 L.Ed.2d 510, 87 S.Ct. 613 (1967).

seeably may be in conflict with his official duties.[11]

EC 8–9 The advancement of our legal system is of vital importance in maintaining the rule of law and in facilitating orderly changes; therefore, lawyers should encourage, and should aid in making, needed changes and improvements.

DISCIPLINARY RULES

DR 8–101 Action as a Public Official.

(A) **A lawyer who holds public office shall not:**

  (1) **Use his public position to obtain, or attempt to obtain, a special advantage in legislative matters for himself or for a client under circumstances where he knows or it is obvious that such action is not in the public interest.**

  (2) **Use his public position to influence, or attempt to influence, a tribunal to act in favor of himself or of a client.**

  (3) **Accept any thing of value from any person when the lawyer knows or it is obvious that the offer is for the pur-**

pose of influencing his action as a public official.

DR 8–102 Statements Concerning Judges and Other Adjudicatory Officers.[12]

(A) **A lawyer shall not knowingly make false statements of fact concerning the qualifications of a candidate for election or appointment to a judicial office.**

(B) **A lawyer shall not knowingly make false accusations against a judge or other adjudicatory officer.**

DR 8–103 Lawyer Candidate for Judicial Office.

(A) **A lawyer who is a candidate for judicial office shall comply with the applicable provisions of Canon 7 of the Code of Judicial Conduct.**

CANON 9

A Lawyer Should Avoid Even the Appearance of Professional Impropriety

ETHICAL CONSIDERATIONS

EC 9–1 Continuation of the American concept that we are to be governed by

---

11. "*Opinions 16, 30, 34, 77, 118* and *134* relate to *Canon 6,* and pass on questions concerning the propriety of the conduct of an attorney who is a public officer, in representing private interests adverse to those of the public body which he represents. The principle applied in those opinions is that an attorney holding public office should avoid all conduct which might lead the layman to conclude that the attorney is utilizing his public position to further his professional success or personal interests." *ABA Opinion* 192 (1939).

"The next question is whether a lawyer-member of a legislative body may appear as counsel or co-counsel at hearings before a zoning board of appeals, or similar tribunal, created by the legislative group of which he is a member. We are of the opinion that he may practice before fact-finding officers, hearing bodies and commissioners, since under our views he may appear as counsel in the courts where his municipality is a party. Decisions made at such hearings are usually subject to

administrative review by the courts upon the record there made. It would be inconsistent to say that a lawyer-member of a legislative body could not participate in a hearing at which the record is made, but could appear thereafter when the cause is heard by the courts on administrative review. This is subject to an important exception. He should not appear as counsel where the matter is subject to review by the legislative body of which he is a member.... We are of the opinion that where a lawyer does so appear there would be conflict of interests between his duty as an advocate for his client on the one hand and the obligation to his governmental unit on the other." In re Becker, 16 Ill.2d 488, 494–95, 158 N.E.2d 753, 756–57 (1959).

Cf. *ABA Opinions* 186 (1938), 136 (1935), 118 (1934), and 77 (1932).

12. Cf. ABA Canons 1 and 2.

rules of law requires that the people have faith that justice can be obtained through our legal system.[1] A lawyer should promote public confidence in our system and in the legal profession.[2]

EC 9–2 Public confidence in law and lawyers may be eroded by irresponsible or improper conduct of a lawyer. On occasion, ethical conduct of a lawyer may appear to laymen to be unethical. In order to avoid misunderstandings and hence to maintain confidence, a lawyer should fully and promptly inform his client of material developments in the matters being handled for the client. While a lawyer should guard against otherwise proper conduct that has a tendency to diminish public confidence in the legal system or in the legal profession, his duty to clients or to the public should never be subordinate merely because the full discharge of his obligation may be misunderstood or may tend to subject him or the legal profession to criticism. When explicit ethical guidance does not exist, a lawyer should determine his conduct by acting in a manner that promotes public confidence in the integrity and efficiency of the legal system and the legal profession.[3]

EC 9–3 After a lawyer leaves judicial office or other public employment, he should not accept employment in connection with any matter in which he had substantial responsibility prior to his leaving, since to accept employment would give the appearance of impropriety even if none exists.[4]

EC 9–4 Because the very essence of the legal system is to provide procedures by which matters can be presented in an impartial manner so that they may be decided solely upon the merits, any statement or suggestion by a lawyer that he can or would attempt to circumvent those procedures is detrimental to the legal system and tends to undermine public confidence in it.

EC 9–5 Separation of the funds of a client from those of his lawyer not only serves to protect the client but also avoids even the appearance of impropriety, and therefore commingling of such funds should be avoided.

EC 9–6 Every lawyer owes a solemn duty to uphold the integrity and honor of his profession; to encourage respect for the law and for the courts and the judges thereof; to observe the Code of Professional Responsibility; to act as a member of a learned profession, one dedicated to public service; to cooperate with his brother lawyers in supporting the organized bar through the devoting of his time, efforts, and financial support as his professional standing and ability reasonably permit; to conduct himself so as to reflect credit on the legal profession and to inspire the confidence, respect, and trust of his clients and of the public; and to strive to avoid not only professional impropriety but also the appearance of impropriety.[5]

1. "Integrity is the very breath of justice. Confidence in our law, our courts, and in the administration of justice is our supreme interest. No practice must be permitted to prevail which invites towards the administration of justice a doubt or distrust of its integrity." Erwin M. Jennings Co. v. DiGenova, 107 Conn. 491, 499, 141 A. 866, 868 (1928).

2. "A lawyer should never be reluctant or too proud to answer unjustified criticism of his profession, of himself, or of his brother lawyer. He should guard the reputation of his profession and of his brothers as zealously as he guards his own." Rochelle and Payne, *The Struggle for Public Understanding,* 25 Texas B.J. 109, 162 (1962).

3. See ABA Canon 29.

4. See ABA Canon 36.

5. "As said in Opinion 49 of the Committee on Professional Ethics and Grievances of the American Bar Association, page 134: 'An attorney should not only avoid impropriety but should avoid the appearance of impropriety.' " State ex rel. Nebraska State Bar Ass'n v. Richards, 165 Neb. 80, 93, 84 N.W.2d 136, 145 (1957).

"It would also be preferable that such contribution [to the campaign of a candidate for judicial office] be made to a campaign committee rather than to the candidate personally. In so doing, possible appearances of impropriety

EC 9-7 A lawyer has an obligation to the public to participate in collective efforts of the bar to reimburse persons who have lost money or property as a result of the misappropriation or defalcation of another lawyer, and contribution to a clients' security fund is an acceptable method of meeting this obligation.

DISCIPLINARY RULES

DR 9-101 Avoiding Even the Appearance of Impropriety.[6]

(A) A lawyer shall not accept private employment in a matter upon the merits of which he has acted in a judicial capacity.[7]

(B) A lawyer shall not accept private employment in a matter in which he had substantial responsibility while he was a public employee.[8]

(C) A lawyer shall not state or imply that he is able to influence improperly or upon irrelevant grounds any tribunal, legislative body,[9] or public official.

DR 9-102 Preserving Identity of Funds and Property of a

would be reduced to a minimum." *ABA Opinion* 226 (1941).

"The lawyer assumes high duties, and has imposed upon him grave responsibilities. He may be the means of much good or much mischief. Interests of vast magnitude are entrusted to him; confidence is reposed in him; life, liberty, character and property should be protected by him. He should guard, with jealous watchfulness, his own reputation, as well as that of his profession." People ex rel. Cutler v. Ford, 54 Ill. 520, 522 (1870), and also quoted in State Board of Law Examiners v. Sheldon, 43 Wyo. 522, 526, 7 P.2d 226, 227 (1932).

See *ABA Opinion* 150 (1936).

6. Cf. Code of Professional Responsibility, EC 5-6.

7. See *ABA* Canon 36.

"It is the duty of the judge to rule on questions of law and evidence in misdemeanor cases and examinations in felony cases. That duty calls for impartial and uninfluenced judgment, regardless of the effect on those immediately involved or others who may, directly or indirectly, be affected. Discharge of that duty might be greatly interfered with if the judge, in another capacity, were permitted to hold himself out to employment by those who are to be, or who may be, brought to trial in felony cases, even though he did not conduct the examination. His private interests as a lawyer in building up his clientele, his duty as such zealously to espouse the cause of his private clients and to defend against charges of crime brought by law-enforcement agencies of which he is a part, might prevent, or even destroy, that unbiased judicial judgment which is so essential in the administration of justice.

"In our opinion, acceptance of a judgeship with the duties of conducting misdemeanor trials, and examinations in felony cases to determine whether those accused should be bound over for trial in a higher court, ethically bars the judge from acting as attorney for the defendants upon such trial, whether they were examined by him or by some other judge. Such a practice would not only diminish public confidence in the administration of justice in both courts, but would produce serious conflict between the private interests of the judge as a lawyer, and of his clients, and his duties as a judge in adjudicating important phases of criminal processes in other cases. The public and private duties would be incompatible. The prestige of the judicial office would be diverted to private benefit, and the judicial office would be demeaned thereby." *ABA Opinion* 242 (1942).

"A lawyer, who has previously occupied a judicial position or acted in a judicial capacity, should refrain from accepting employment in any matter involving the same facts as were involved in any specific question which he acted upon in a judicial capacity and, for the same reasons, should also refrain from accepting any employment which might reasonably appear to involve the same facts." *ABA Opinion* 49 (1931).

See *ABA Opinion* 110 (1934).

8. See *ABA Opinions* 135 (1935) and 134 (1935); cf. ABA Canon 36 and *ABA Opinions* 39 (1931) and 26 (1930). But see *ABA Opinion* 37 (1931).

9. "[A statement by a governmental department or agency with regard to a lawyer resigning from its staff that includes a laudation of his legal ability] carries implications, probably not founded in fact, that the lawyer's acquaintance and previous relations with the personnel of the administrative agencies of the government place him in an advantageous position in practicing before such agencies. So to imply would not only represent what probably is untrue, but would be highly reprehensible." *ABA Opinion* 184 (1938).

Client.[10]

(A) **All funds of clients paid to a lawyer or law firm, other than advances for costs and expenses, shall be deposited in one or more identifiable bank accounts maintained in the state in which the law office is situated and no funds belonging to the lawyer or law firm shall be deposited therein except as follows:**

(1) **Funds reasonably sufficient to pay bank charges may be deposited therein.**

(2) **Funds belonging in part to a client and in part presently or potentially to the lawyer or law firm must be deposited therein, but the portion belonging to the lawyer or law firm may be withdrawn when due unless the right of the lawyer or law firm to receive it is disputed by the client, in which event the disputed portion shall not be withdrawn until the dispute is finally resolved.**

(B) **A lawyer shall:**

(1) **Promptly notify a client of the receipt of his funds, securities, or other properties.**

(2) **Identify and label securities and properties of a client promptly upon receipt and place them in a safe deposit box or other place of safekeeping as soon as practicable.**

(3) **Maintain complete records of all funds, securities, and other properties of a client coming into the possession of the lawyer and render appropriate accounts to his client regarding them.**

(4) **Promptly pay or deliver to the client as requested by a client the funds, securities, or other properties in the possession of the lawyer which the client is entitled to receive.**

DEFINITIONS *

As used in the Disciplinary Rules of the Code of Professional Responsibility:

(1) **"Differing interests" include every interest that will adversely affect either the judgment or the loyalty of a lawyer to a client, whether it be a conflicting, inconsistent, diverse, or other interest.**

10. See ABA Canon 11.

"Rule 9. ... A member of the State Bar shall not commingle the money or other property of a client with his own; and he shall promptly report to the client the receipt by him of all money and other property belonging to such client. Unless the client otherwise directs in writing, he shall promptly deposit his client's funds in a bank or trust company ... in a bank account separate from his own account and clearly designated as 'Clients' Funds Account' or 'Trust Funds Account' or words of similar import. Unless the client otherwise directs in writing, securities of a client in bearer form shall be kept by the attorney in a safe deposit box at a bank or trust company, ... which safe deposit box shall be clearly designated as 'Clients' Account' or 'Trust Account' or words of similar import, and be separate from the attorney's own safe deposit box." Cal.Business and Professions Code § 6076 (West 1962).

"[C]ommingling is committed when a client's money is intermingled with that of his attorney and its separate identity lost so that it may be used for the attorney's personal expenses or subjected to claims of his creditors.... The rule against commingling was adopted to provide against the probability in some cases, the possibility in many cases, and the danger in all cases that such commingling will result in the loss of clients' money." Black v. State Bar, 57 Cal.2d 219, 225–26, 368 P.2d 118, 122, 18 Cal.Rptr. 518, 522 (1962).

* "Confidence" and "secret" are defined in DR 4–101(A).

(2) "Law firm" includes a professional legal corporation.

(3) "Person" includes a corporation, an association, a trust, a partnership, and any other organization or legal entity.

(4) "Professional legal corporation" means a corporation, or an association treated as a corporation, authorized by law to practice law for profit.

(5) "State" includes the District of Columbia, Puerto Rico, and other federal territories and possessions.

(6) "Tribunal" includes all courts and all other adjudicatory bodies.

(7) "A Bar association" includes a bar association of specialists as referred to in DR 2–105(A)(1) or (3).

(8) "Qualified legal assistance organization" means an office or organization of one of the four types listed in DR 2–103(D)(1)–(4), inclusive that meets all the requirements thereof.

INDEX TO MODEL CODE

A

357

ABA CODE

Advertising,   EC 2–2, 2–6 to 2–15, DR 2–101, 2–102(A)—Continued
  Clients, regular, DR 2–101(B)(16)
  Commercial publicity, EC 2–8 to 2–10, DR 2–101, 2–102(A)
  Compensation for, EC 2–8, DR 2–101(B), (I), 2–103(B)
  Credit arrangements, EC 2–8, DR 2–101(B)(18)
  Deceptive, EC 2–9, DR 2–101(A)
  Display, DR 2–101(B)
  Fees, EC 2–8, DR 2–101(B)(18), (20), (25), (E), (F), (G)
    Consultation, DR 2–101(B)(20)
    Contingent, rates, DR 2–101(B)(22)
    Credit arrangements, DR 2–101(B)(18)
    Estimate, DR 2–101(B)(21), (23), (24), (25)
    Fixed, for specific services, DR 2–101(B)(25)
    Hourly rate, DR 2–101(B)(24)
    Schedule, DR 2–101(B)(23)
  Foreign language, fluency in, EC 2–8, DR 2–101(B)(14)
  Jurisdictional limitations of members of firm, required notice of, DR 2–102(D)
  Justification for, EC 2–2, 2–7, 2–8
  Law lists, EC 2–8
  Law office establishment, DR 2–102(A)(2)
  Law office, identification of, DR 2–102(A)(3)
  Legal directories, EC 2–8
  Legal documents, DR 2–101(H)(4)
  Legal notices, DR 2–101(B)(2)
  Legal publications, DR 2–101(B)(8), (H)(5)
  Letterheads,
    Of clients, DR 2–102(A)(4)
    Of law firm, DR 2–102(A)(4)
    Of lawyer, DR 2–102(A)(4), 2–102(B)
  Limited practice, EC 2–7, 2–8, 2–14, DR 2–101(B)(2), 2–105(A)(2)
  Magazine, EC 2–8, DR 2–101
  Memberships,
    Bar association, DR 2–101(B)(10)
    Legal fraternities and societies, DR 2–101(B)(11)
    Scientific, professional and technical associations, DR 2–101(B)(11)
  Military service, DR 2–101(B)(7)
  Name. See Name, use of
  Newspaper, EC 2–8, DR 2–101
  Office,
    Establishment, DR 2–102(A)(2)
    Identification of, DR 2–101(B)(1), 2–102(A)(3)
  Office address change, DR 2–102(A)(2)
  Office building directory, DR 2–102(A)(3)
  Office hours, EC 2–8, DR 2–101(B)(19)
  Office sign, DR 2–102(A)(3)
  Political, DR 2–101(H)(1)
  Prepaid or group service programs, participation in, DR 2–101(17)
  Public notices, DR 2–101(H)(2)
  Public office, DR 2–101(B)(6)
  Quality of service, representation concerning, EC 2–9
  Radio, EC 2–8, DR 2–101(B), (D), (I)
  References, bank, DR 2–101(B)(15)
  Regulation, reasons for, EC 2–2, 2–6 to 2–13
  Rules, change in, EC 2–10, DR 2–101(C)
  Schools and degrees, DR 2–101(B)(5)
  Self-laudation, EC 2–8, 2–101(A)
  Sign, DR 2–102(A)(3)
  Specialization, EC 2–8, 2–14, DR 2–101(B)(2), 2–105
  Teaching positions, DR 2–101(B)(9)
  Technical and professional licenses, DR 2–101(B)(12)
  Telephone directory, EC 2–8
  Television, EC 2–8, DR 2–101(B), (D), (I)

358

Bar applicant,—Continued
   Bar examiners, assisting, EC 1–2, 1–3, DR 1–101(B)

Bar associations,
   Advertising, DR 2–101(B)(10)
   Definitions, (7)
   Disciplinary authorities, assisting, EC 1–4, DR 1–103
   Educational activities, EC 6–2
   Lawyer referral service, DR 2–103(C)(1), (D)(3)
   Legal service programs, DR 2–103(D)(1)(d)
   Requesting lawyer's representation of individual, EC 2–29

Barratry. See Advice by lawyer to secure legal services; Recommendation of professional employment

Bequest by client to lawyer, EC 5–5

Best efforts. See Zeal

Bounds of law,
   Difficulty of ascertaining, EC 7–2 to 7–6
   Duty to observe, EC 7–1, DR 7–102

Bribes. See Gifts to tribunal officer or employee by lawyer

Building directory. See Advertising, building directory

Business card. See Advertising, cards, professional

Business relations with clients, EC 5–3 to 5–7, DR 5–104

C

Calling card. See Advertising, cards, professional

Candidate. See Political activity

Canons, purpose of, preliminary statement

Card. See Advertising, cards

Change of association. See Advertising, announcement of change of association

Change of firm name. See Advertising, announcement of change of firm name

Change of office address. See Advertising, announcement of change of office

Character requirements, Canon 1, EC 1–3

Circumvention of disciplinary rule, DR 1–102(A)(2)

Class action. See Advice by lawyer to secure legal services

Clients,
      See also Employment; Adverse effect on professional judgment; Fee for legal services; Indigents, representation of; Mental competence of client; Unpopular party, representation of
   Appearance as witness for, EC 5–9, 5–10, DR 5–101(B), 5–102
   Attorney-client privilege, EC 3–3, Canon 4
   Commingling of funds of, EC 9–5, DR 9–102
      Confidences of, Canon 4
      Counseling, EC 7–3, 7–5 to 7–9, 7–12, DR 7–102(A)(7), (B)(1), 7–106(A), 7–109(B)
      Decisions of, EC 5–12, 7–7, 7–8, 7–12
      Property, protection of, DR 9–102
      Secrets of, EC 3–3, Canon 4

Co-counsel,
      See also Association of counsel

D

PROFESSIONAL RESPONSIBILITY

Discipline of lawyer, grounds for,—Continued
    Communication with jurors, improper, DR 7–108
    Communication with tribunal, improper, DR 7–110(B)
    Compensation, accepting from third party, DR 5–107
    Confidences, improper use of, DR 4–101(B), (D)
    Confidential information, disclosure of, DR 4–101(B), (D)
    Conflict of interest with clients, disregard of duty to avoid, DR 5–101 to 5–107
    Conflicting interests, representation of, DR 5–105, 5–106, 5–107
    Crime of moral turpitude, DR 1–102(A)(3)
    Criminal conduct, DR 1–102, DR 7–102, 7–109(A)
    Criminal prosecution threatening, DR 7–105
    Differing interests, improper representation of, DR 5–105, 5–106
    Disregard of tribunal ruling, DR 7–106(A)
    Division of fee, improper, DR 2–107(A), 3–102
    Employees, failure to exercise reasonable care toward, DR 3–102, 4–101(D)
    Evidence,
        False or misleading, use of, DR 7–102(A)(4), (6)
        Suppression of, DR 7–103(B), 7–109(A)
    Extra-judicial statement, improper, DR 7–107
    Failure to act competently, DR 6–101
    Failure to act zealously, DR 7–101(A)
    Failure to disclose information concerning another lawyer or judge, DR 1–103
    Failure to disclose information to tribunal, DR 1–103, 7–102, 7–106(B)
    False accusations, DR 8–102(B)
    False statements concerning adjudicating officers, DR 8–102
    False statements in bar application, DR 1–101(A)
    Fees,
        Charging contingent fee in criminal case, DR 2–106(C)
        Charging illegal or clearly excessive, DR 2–106(A)
        Failure to return unearned, DR 2–110(A)(3)
    Fraud, dishonesty, deceit, misrepresentation, DR 1–102(A)(4)
    Further application of unqualified bar applicant, DR 1–101(B)
    Gift or loan to public official, DR 7–110(A)
    Guaranty of financial assistance, DR 5–103(B)
    Holding out as having limited practice, DR 2–105
    Holding out as a specialist, DR 2–105
    Illegal conduct, DR 1–102(A)(3), 7–102
    Improper argument before tribunal, DR 7–102(A), 7–106(C)(1), (3), (4)
    Institution of criminal charges, DR 7–103(A)
    Investigation of jurors, DR 7–108
    Limiting liability, DR 6–102
    Malpractice, DR 6–101, 6–102
    Moral turpitude, crime of, DR 1–102(A)(3)
    Negligence, DR 6–101
    Nonmeritorious claim, DR 2–109
    Nonmeritorious prosecution, DR 2–109
    Professional affiliation with nonlawyers, DR 3–103, 5–107(C)
    Public office, improper use of, DR 8–101
    Publicity, improper, DR 2–101, 2–102
    Recommendation of professional employment, prohibited, DR 2–103
    Restrictive covenant, entering prohibited, DR 2–108
    Secrets,
        Disclosure of, DR 4–101(B), (D)
        Improper use of, DR 4–101(B), (D)
    Solicitation of business, DR 2–103, 2–104
    Specialization, notice of, DR 2–105
    Suggestion of need of legal services, prohibited, DR 2–104
    Unauthorized practice of law, 3–101(B)
        Aiding laymen in, DR 3–101(A)
    Violation of disciplinary rule, DR 1–102(A)(1)
    Withdrawal,
        Failure to, DR 2–110(B)

Discipline of lawyer, grounds for,—Continued
Withdrawal—Continued
Improper, DR 2–110

Disclosure of improper conduct,
Of another lawyer, EC 1–4, DR 1–103
Of bar applicant, EC 1–2, 1–3, DR 1–101(B)
Of judge, DR 1–103(B)
Toward juror or venireman, EC 7–32, DR 7–108(G)

Discretion of government lawyer, exercise of,   EC 7–13, 7–14

Discussion of pending litigation with news media,   EC 7–33, DR 7–107

Disregarding court ruling,   DR 7–106(A)

Diverse interests. See Adverse effect on professional judgment

Division of legal fees,
Consent of client, when required for, EC 2–22, DR 2–107(A)(1)
Reasonableness of total fee, requirement of, EC 2–22, DR 2–107(A)(3)
With associated lawyer, EC 2–22, DR 2–107
With estate of deceased lawyer, EC 3–8, DR 3–102(A)(1), (2), (3)
With laymen, EC 3–8, DR 3–102

E

Education,
Continuing legal education programs, EC 6–2
Of laymen to recognize legal problems, EC 2–1 to 2–5, 8–1, 8–3, DR 2–104
Of laymen to select lawyers, EC 2–6 to 2–15, 18–1, DR 2–104(A)(2)
Requirement of education for bar applicant, EC 1–2

Elections,   DR 2–101(H)(1), 8–102(A)

Emotional instability. See Mental competence of lawyer

Employees of lawyer,
Delegation of tasks, EC 3–6
Duty of lawyer to control, EC 3–6, 4–2, 4–3, DR 4–101(D), 7–107(J)

Employment,
See also Advice by lawyer to secure legal services; Recommendation of professional
employment
Acceptance of,
Generally, EC 2–26 to 2–33
Indigent client, on behalf of, EC 2–25, 2–29
Instances when improper, EC 2–3, 2–4, 2–30, 4–6, 5–2, 5–3, 5–10, 5–14 to 5–16, 5–20, 5–24,
6–1, 6–3, 9–3, DR 2–103(E), 2–104, 2–109, 5–101, 5–105, 6–101(A)(1), 9–101(A), (B)
Multiple clients, on behalf of, EC 5–14 to 5–19, DR 5–105(A), (C)
Unpopular cause, on behalf of, EC 2–26 to 2–30
Unpopular client, on behalf of, EC 2–26 to 2–30
When able to render competent service, EC 2–30, 6–1, 6–3, DR 6–101
Arbitrator, in capacity as, EC 5–20
Contract,
Desirability of, EC 2–19
Restrictive covenant in, DR 2–108
Mediator, in capacity as, EC 5–20
Public, retirement from, EC 9–3, DR 9–101(A), (B)
Rejection of, EC 2–26 to 2–33, 4–5, 6–1, 6–3, 9–3, DR 2–103, 2–104, 2–109, 2–110, 6–101,
9–101(A), (B)
Withdrawal from,
Generally, EC 2–32, 5–3, 5–10, 5–14 to 5–16, 5–19, 7–8, DR 2–110, 5–102, 5–105,
7–101(A)(2)
Harm to client, avoidance of, EC 2–32, 4–6, 5–10, 5–15, DR 2–110(A)(2), 5–102(B), 5–105(B)

G

H

I

Improper influences,—Continued
    On judgment of lawyer. *See* Adverse effect on professional judgment

Improvement of legal system,   Canon 8

Incompetence,
    Mental. *See* Mental competence of bar applicant; Mental competence of client; Mental
        competence of lawyer
    Professional. *See* Competence, professional

Independent professional judgment, duty to preserve,   Canon 5

Indigents,
    Provision of legal services to, EC 2–16, 2–24, 2–25, 8–3, DR 2–103(D)(1)
    Representation of, EC 2–24, 2–25, 2–29

Integrity of legal profession, maintaining,   Canon 1, EC 1–1, 1–4, 8–7, 9–1, 9–2, 9–6, DR 1–101

Intent of client, as factor in giving advice,   EC 7–5, 7–6, DR 7–102(A)(7)

Interests of lawyer. See Adverse effect on professional judgment, interests of lawyer

Interests of other client. See Adverse effect on professional judgment, interests of other clients

Interests of third person. See Adverse effect on professional judgment, desires of third persons

Intermediary, prohibition against use of,   EC 5–21 to 5–24, DR 5–107

Interview,
    With opposing party, EC 7–18, DR 7–104
    With news media, EC 7–33, DR 7–107
    With witness, EC 7–27, 7–28, DR 7–109

Investigation expenses, advancing or guaranteeing payment,   EC 5–8, DR 5–103(B)

J

Judges,
    False statements concerning, DR 8–102
    Improper influences on,
        Gifts or loans to, EC 7–34, 7–110(A)
        Private communication with, EC 7–35, 7–39, DR 7–110(B)
    Misconduct toward,
        Criticisms of, EC 8–6, DR 8–102
        Disobedience of orders, EC 7–36, DR 7–106(A)
        False statement regarding, DR 8–102
    Name in partnership name, EC 2–12, DR 2–102(B)
    Retirement from bench, EC 9–3, DR 9–101
    Selection of, EC 8–6, DR 8–102, 8–103

Judgment of lawyer,   EC 3–2
    See also Adverse effect on professional judgment

Judicial rulings,   EC 7–22, DR 7–106(A)

Jury,
    Arguments before, EC 7–24, 7–25, 7–37, DR 7–102(A), 7–106(C)
    Communications with,
        After dismissal, EC 7–29, DR 7–108(D)
        Before trial, EC 7–29, 7–31, 7–33, DR 7–108(A), 7–108(C)
        During trial, EC 7–29, 7–31, 7–33, DR 7–108(B), 7–108(C)
    Improper influences on,
        Extra judicial statements, EC 7–29, 7–31, 7–33, DR 7–108
        Undue solicitude for, EC 7–36
    Investigation of members, EC 7–30, 7–31, DR 7–108(E), (F)
    Misconduct of, duty to reveal, EC 7–32, DR 7–108(G)

ABA CODE

Jury,—Continued
Misconduct toward, EC 7–30, 7–31, DR 7–108(E), (G)
Questioning members of after their dismissal, EC 7–29, DR 7–108(D)

K

Knowledge of intended crime, revealing,   DR 4–101(C)(3)

L

Law firm, definitions (2)

Law lists. See Advertising law lists

Law office. See Partnership

Law school, working with legal aid office or public defender office sponsored by, DR 2–103(D)(1)(a)

Lawyer-client privilege. See Attorney-client privilege

Lawyer referral services,   EC 2–15
Fee for listing, propriety of paying, DR 2–103(C)(1)
Listing of type referrals accepted, propriety of, DR 2–105(A)(2)
Request for referrals, propriety of, DR 2–103(C)(1), (D)
Working with, DR 2–103(C), (D)

Laypersons,
See also Unauthorized practice of law,
Need to legal services, EC 2–1 to 2–3, 2–6 to 2–8, 3–3, DR 2–104
Recognition of legal problems, need to improve, EC 2–1 to 2–3, 8–3
Selection of lawyer, need to facilitate, EC 2–7 to 2–10, 8–3

Legal aid offices, working with,   EC 2–25, DR 2–103(D)(1)

Legal corporation. See Professional legal corporation

Legal directory. See Advertising, law lists

Legal documents of clients, duty to safeguard,   EC 4–2, 4–3

Legal education programs. See Continuing legal education programs

Legal problems, recognition of by laymen,   EC 2–1 to 2–3, 8–3, DR 2–104

Legal system, duty to improve,   Canon 8

Legislature,
Improper influence upon, EC 9–2, 9–3, 9–4, DR 8–101(A)(1), 9–101(B), (C)
Representation of client before, EC 7–16, 7–17, 8–4, 8–5
Serving as member of, EC 8–8, DR 8–101

Letterhead. See Advertising, letterheads

Liability to client, limiting,   EC 6–6, DR 6–102

Licensing of lawyers,
As evidence of competence, EC 6–3
Control of, EC 3–1, 3–3 to 3–6, 3–9, DR 3–101
Modernization of, EC 3–5, 3–9, 8–3

Liens, attorneys',   EC 5–7, DR 5–103(A)(1)

Limited practice, holding out as having,   EC 2–8, 2–14, DR 2–101(B)(2), 2–105(A)(2)

Litigation,
Acquiring an interest in, EC 5–7, 5–8, DR 5–103
Expenses of, advancing or guaranteeing payment of, EC 5–7, 5–8, DR 5–103(B)

368

M

N

Name, use of,—Continued
  Proper for law firm, EC 2–11, DR 2–102(B)
  Proper for lawyer in law practice, EC 2–11, DR 2–102(B)
  Retired partner, EC 2–11, DR 2–102(A)(4), (B)
  Trade name, EC 2–11, DR 2–102(B)
  Withdrawn partner's, EC 2–11, 2–12, DR 2–102(B)

Need for legal services, suggestion of. See Advice by lawyer to secure legal services

Negligence of lawyer,   Canon 6

Negotiations with opposite party,   EC 7–18, 7–20, DR 7–104, 7–105

Neighborhood law offices, working with,   EC 2–6, 2–7, 2–25, DR 2–103(D)(1)(b)

Newspapers,
  Advertising in, EC 2–8 to 2–10, DR 2–101(A) to (C), (E), (F), (I)
  News releases in, during or pending trial, EC 7–33, DR 7–107
  News stories in, DR 2–101(I)

Non-meritorious position, duty to avoid,   EC 7–4, 7–5, 7–14, DR 2–109, 2–110(B)(1), 7–102(A)(1), (2), 7–103(A), 7–106(C)(1)

Non-profit organization, legal aid services of,   EC 2–24, 2–25, DR 2–103(D)(1), (4)(a), 2–104(A)(2), (3)

Notices. See Advertising

O

Objectives of client, duty to seek,   EC 7–1, 7–10, DR 7–101(A)(1), 7–102

"Of Counsel" designation,   DR 2–102(A)(4)

Offensive tactics by lawyer,   EC 7–4, 7–5, 7–10, DR 7–101, 7–102, 7–104, 7–105

Office building directory. See Advertising, building directory

Office sign,   DR 2–102(A)(3)

Opposing counsel,   EC 5–9, 7–20, 7–23, 7–35, 7–37, 7–38, DR 7–101(A)(1), 7–104(A)(1), 7–106(C)(5), 7–110(B)(2), (3)

Opposing party, communications with,   EC 7–18, DR 7–104

P

Partnership,
  Advertising. See Advertising
  Conflicts of interest, DR 5–105(D)
  Deceased member,
    Payments to estate of, EC 3–8, DR 3–102(A)(1), (2)
    Use of name, EC 2–11, DR 2–102(A)(4), (B)
  Dissolved, use of name of, EC 2–11 to 2–13, DR 2–102(A)(4), (B), (C)
  Holding out as, falsely, EC 2–13, DR 2–102(B), (C)
  Imputed disability of partner and associates, DR 5–105(D)
  Layperson, partnership with, EC 3–8, DR 3–103
  Members licensed in different jurisdictions, DR 2–102(D)
  Name, EC 2–11, 2–12, 2–13, DR 2–102(B)
  Nonexistent, holding out falsely, EC 2–13, DR 2–102(B), (C)

PROFESSIONAL RESPONSIBILITY

Q

Qualified legal assistance organization,   EC 2–33, DR 2–103(C)(2), (D), 2–104(A)(2), (3), definitions (8)

Quasi-judicial proceedings,   EC 7–15, 7–16, 8–4, DR 7–107(H)

R

Radio, broadcasting. See Advertising, radio

Reasonable fee. See Fee for legal services, amount of

Rebate, propriety of accepting,   EC 2–21, 2–22, 5–22, DR 2–107, 5–107

Recognition of legal problems, aiding laymen in,   EC 2–1 to 2–5, 8–3, DR 2–104

Recommendation of bar applicant, duty of lawyer to satisfy himself that applicant is qualified,   EC 1–3, DR 1–101(B)

Recommendation of professional employment,   EC 2–8, 2–15, DR 2–103

Records of funds, securities, and properties of clients,   EC 9–5, DR 9–102(B)(3)

Referral service. See Lawyer referral services

Refund of unearned fee when withdrawing, duty to give to client,   EC 2–32, DR 2–110(A)(3)

Regulation of legal profession,   EC 3–1, 3–3, 3–9, 8–3, 8–7, DR 3–101(B)

Rehabilitation of bar applicant or lawyer, recognition of,   EC 1–6

Representation of multiple clients. See Adverse effect on professional judgment, interests of other clients

Reputation of lawyer,   EC 2–6, 2–7

Requests for recommendation for employment,   EC 2–8, DR 2–103(C)

Requirements for bar admission,   EC 1–2, 1–6, DR 1–101(B)

Respect for law,   EC 1–5, 9–6

Restrictive covenant,   DR 2–108

Retention of employment. See Employment

Retirement,
> See also Name, use of, retired partner
From judicial office, EC 9–3, DR 9–101(A)
From public employment, EC 9–3, DR 9–101(B)
Plan for laymen employees', EC 3–8, DR 3–102(A)(3)

Revealing of confidences, Canon 4

Revealing of secrets, Canon 4

Revealing to tribunal,
Jury misconduct, EC 7–32, DR 7–108(G)
Representative capacity in which appearing, EC 7–15, 7–16, DR 7–106(B)(2)

Runner, prohibition against use of. See Recommendation of professional employment

S

T

Tribunal,—Continued
Representation of client before, Canon 7

Trustee, client naming lawyer as,   EC 5–6

U

Unauthorized practice of law,   Canon 3
See also Division of legal fees, with laymen; Partnership, laypersons with
Aiding a layman in the prohibited, EC 3–8, DR 3–101
Distinguished from delegation of tasks to subprofessionals, EC 3–5, 3–6, DR 3–102(A)(3)
Functional meaning of, EC 3–5, 3–9
Self-representation by layman not included in, EC 3–7

Undignified conduct, duty to avoid,   EC 7–36 to 7–38, DR 7–106(C)(6)

Unions, lawyers as members of,   EC 5–13

Unlawful conduct, aiding client in,   EC 7–5, 7–6, DR 7–102(A)(6), (7), (B)(1)

Unpopular party, representation of,   EC 2–27, 2–29 to 2–31

Unreasonable fees. See Fee for legal services, amount of, excessive

Unsolicited advice. See Advice by lawyer to secure legal services

V

Varying interests of clients. See Adverse effect on professional judgment, interests of other clients

Veniremen. See Communications with, venireman; Jury

Violation of disciplinary rule as cause for discipline,   DR 1–102(A)(1), (2)

Violation of law as cause for discipline,   EC 1–5, 7–6, DR 1–102(A)(3), (A)(4), 7–102(A)(3) to (A)(8)

Voluntary gifts by client to lawyer,   EC 5–5

Volunteered advice to secure legal services. See Advice by lawyer to secure legal services

W

Waiver of position of client,   DR 7–101(B)(1)

Will of client, gift to lawyer in,   EC 5–5

Withdrawal. See Employment, withdrawal from

Witness,
Communications with. *See* Communications with, witnesses
Expert, EC 7–28, DR 7–109(C)(3)
False testimony by, EC 7–26, 7–28, DR 7–102(A)(4), (B)(2)
Lawyer acting as, EC 5–9, 5–10, DR 5–101(B), 5–102
Member of lawyer's firm acting as, DR 5–101(B), 5–102
Payment to, EC 7–28, DR 7–109(C)
Questioning of, EC 7–25, DR 7–106(C)(2)
Secreting of, EC 7–27, DR 7–109(B)

Writing for lay publication, avoiding appearance of giving general solution,   EC 2–2, 2–5, DR 2–104(4)
Limitations upon, Canon 7

Z

Zeal,
    General duty of, EC 7–1, 7–8 to 7–10, DR 7–101(A)

RESTATEMENT OF LAW GOVERNING LAWYERS

In 1986 the American Law Institute ("ALI"), a prestigious group of practicing lawyers, judges, and academics, began drafting a *Restatement of the Law Governing Lawyers*. Unlike the ABA's Model Rules, the ALI has not proposed a code of regulations that it expects state courts to adopt as rules of court. Instead, it has drafted a series of principles, also called "black letter rules," followed by commentary and examples. Because the Restatement analyses and systematizes the law governing the practice of law, it goes beyond the ethics rules to cover other areas that affect the practice of law, such as tort doctrines relating to malpractice, vicarious liability, the work-product doctrine, the attorney-client evidentiary privilege, the agent-principal relationship, and related areas. The Restatement of the Law Governing Lawyers follows in the tradition of the other Restatements that the ALI has drafted over many years.

In 1998, the ALI completed this project and approved the Restatement, which it labeled "Restatement of the Law, Third," to signify that the American Law Institute is now working on a third major series of Restatements. The ALI published the final version of its Restatement in late 2000, which included various stylistic changes and a renumbering of some section numbers.

Following the Table of Contents is a *Conversion Table* of section numbers. This table lists the final and former section number for each section. The casebook refers to the former section numbers because the seventh edition was published before the Restatement assigned the final section numbers.

Table of Contents

Restatement of the Law (Third): The Law Governing Lawyers

CONVERSION TABLE – Tentative Drafts to Final Version
Numbers Shown are Section Numbers

Chapter I		Chapter III		Chapter V		Chapter VII	
Final	Former	Final	Former	Final	Former	Final	Former
1	1	34	46	68	118	105	165
2	2	35	47	69	119	106	166
3	3	36	48	70	120	107	167
4	4	37	49	71	121	108	168
5	5	38	50	72	122	109	169
6	6	39	51	73	123	110	170
7	7	40	52	74	124	111	171
8	8	41	53	75	125	112	172
9	10	42	54	76	126	113	173
10	11	43	55	77	127	114	174
11	12	44	56	78	128	115	175
12	13	45	57	79	129	116	176
13	14	46	58	80	130	117	177
		47	59	81	131	118	178

Chapter II

Final	Former
14	26
15	27
16	28
17	29
18	29A
19	30
20	31
21	32
22	33
23	34
24	35
25	37
26	38
27	39
28	40
29	41
30	42
31	43
32	44
33	45

Chapter IV

Final	Former
48	71
49	—
50	72
51	73
52	74
53	75
54	76
55	76A
56	77
57	78
58	79

Chapter V

Final	Former
59	111
60	112
61	113
62	114
63	115
64	116
65	117
66	117A
67	117B

Chapter V (cont.)		Chapter VII (cont.)	
Final	Former	Final	Former
82	132	119	179
83	133	120	180
84	134A		
85	134B		
86	135		
87	136		
88	137		
89	138		
90	139		
91	140		
92	141		
93	142		

Chapter VIII

Final	Former
121	201
122	202
123	203
124	204
125	206
126	207
127	208
128	209
129	210
130	211
131	212
132	213
133	214
134	215
135	216

Chapter VI

Final	Former
94	151
95	152
96	155
97	156
98	157
99	158
100	159
101	161
102	162
103	163
104	164

§ 1. Regulation of Lawyers—In General

Upon admission to the bar of any jurisdiction, a person becomes a lawyer and is subject to applicable law governing such matters as professional discipline, procedure and evidence, civil remedies, and criminal sanctions.

§ 2. Admission to Practice Law

In order to become a lawyer and qualify to practice law in a jurisdiction of admission, a prospective lawyer must comply with requirements of the jurisdiction relating to such matters as education, other demonstration of competence such as success in a bar examination, and character.

§ 3. Jurisdictional Scope of the Practice of Law by a Lawyer

A lawyer currently admitted to practice in a jurisdiction may provide legal services to a client:

(1) at any place within the admitting jurisdiction;

(2) before a tribunal or administrative agency of another jurisdiction or the federal government in compliance with requirements for temporary or regular admission to practice before that tribunal or agency; and

(3) at a place within a jurisdiction in which the lawyer is not admitted to the extent that the lawyer's activities arise out of or are otherwise reasonably related to the lawyer's practice under Subsection (1) or (2).

§ 4. Unauthorized Practice by a Nonlawyer

A person not admitted to practice as a lawyer (see § 2) may not engage in the unauthorized practice of law, and a lawyer may not assist a person to do so.

§ 5. Professional Discipline

(1) A lawyer is subject to professional discipline for violating any provision of an applicable lawyer code.

(2) A lawyer is also subject to professional discipline under Subsection (1) for attempting to commit a violation, knowingly assisting or inducing another to do so, or knowingly doing so through the acts of another.

(3) A lawyer who knows of another lawyer's violation of applicable rules of professional conduct raising a substantial question of the lawyer's honesty or trustworthiness or the lawyer's fitness as a lawyer in some other respect must report that information to appropriate disciplinary authorities.

§ 6. Judicial Remedies Available to a Client or Nonclient for Lawyer Wrongs

For a lawyer's breach of a duty owed to the lawyer's client or to a nonclient, judicial remedies may be available through judgment or order entered in accordance with the standards applicable to the remedy awarded, including standards concerning limitation of remedies. Judicial remedies include the following:

(1) awarding a sum of money as damages;

(2) providing injunctive relief, including requiring specific performance of a contract or enjoining its nonperformance;

(3) requiring restoration of a specific thing or awarding a sum of money to prevent unjust enrichment;

(4) ordering cancellation or reformation of a contract, deed, or similar instrument;

(5) declaring the rights of the parties, such as determining that an obligation claimed by the lawyer to be owed to the lawyer is not enforceable;

(6) punishing the lawyer for contempt;

(7) enforcing an arbitration award;

(8) disqualifying a lawyer from a representation;

(9) forfeiting a lawyer's fee (see § 37);

(10) denying the admission of evidence wrongfully obtained;

(11) dismissing the claim or defense of a litigant represented by the lawyer;

(12) granting a new trial; and

(13) entering a procedural or other sanction.

§ 7. Judicial Remedies Available to a Lawyer for Client Wrongs

A lawyer may obtain a remedy based on a present or former client's breach of a duty to the lawyer if the remedy:

(1) is appropriate under applicable law governing the remedy; and

(2) does not put the lawyer in a position prohibited by an applicable lawyer code.

§ 8. Lawyer Criminal Offenses

The traditional and appropriate activities of a lawyer in representing a client in accordance with the requirements of the applicable lawyer code are relevant factors for the tribunal in assessing the propriety of the lawyer's conduct under the criminal law. In other respects, a lawyer is guilty of an offense for an act committed in the course of representing a client to the same extent and on the same basis as would a nonlawyer acting similarly.

§ 9. Law–Practice Organizations—In General

(1) A lawyer may practice as a solo practitioner, as an employee of another lawyer or law firm, or as a member of a law firm constituted as a partnership, professional corporation, or similar entity.

(2) A lawyer employed by an entity described in Subsection (1) is subject to applicable law governing the creation, operation, management, and dissolution of the entity.

(3) Absent an agreement with the firm providing a more permissive rule, a lawyer leaving a law firm may solicit firm clients:

(a) prior to leaving the firm:

(i) only with respect to firm clients on whose matters the lawyer is actively and substantially working; and

(ii) only after the lawyer has adequately and timely informed the firm of the lawyer's intent to contact firm clients for that purpose; and

(b) after ceasing employment in the firm, to the same extent as any other nonfirm lawyer.

§ 10. Limitations on Nonlawyer Involvement in a Law Firm

(1) A nonlawyer may not own any interest in a law firm, and a nonlawyer may not be empowered to or actually direct or control the professional activities of a lawyer in the firm.

(2) A lawyer may not form a partnership or other business enterprise with a nonlawyer if any of the activities of the enterprise consist of the practice of law.

(3) A lawyer or law firm may not share legal fees with a person not admitted to practice as a lawyer, except that:

(a) an agreement by a lawyer with the lawyer's firm or another lawyer in the firm may provide for payment, over a reasonable period of time after the lawyer's death, to the lawyer's estate or to one or more specified persons;

(b) a lawyer who undertakes to complete unfinished legal business of a deceased lawyer may pay to the estate of the deceased lawyer a portion of the total compensation that fairly represents services rendered by the deceased lawyer; and

(c) a lawyer or law firm may include nonlawyer employees in a compensation or retirement plan, even though the plan is based in whole or in part on a profit-sharing arrangement.

§ 11. A Lawyer's Duty of Supervision

(1) A lawyer who is a partner in a law-firm partnership or a principal in a law firm organized as a corporation or similar entity is subject to professional discipline for failing to make reasonable efforts to ensure that the firm has in effect measures giving reasonable assurance that all lawyers in the firm conform to applicable lawyer-code requirements.

(2) A lawyer who has direct supervisory authority over another lawyer is subject to professional discipline for failing to make reasonable efforts to ensure that the other lawyer conforms to applicable lawyer-code requirements.

(3) A lawyer is subject to professional discipline for another lawyer's violation of the rules of professional conduct if:

(a) the lawyer orders or, with knowledge of the specific conduct, ratifies the conduct involved; or

(b) the lawyer is a partner or principal in the law firm, or has direct supervisory authority over the other lawyer, and knows of the conduct at a time when its consequences can be avoided or mitigated but fails to take reasonable remedial measures.

(4) With respect to a nonlawyer employee of a law firm, the lawyer is subject to professional discipline if either:

(a) the lawyer fails to make reasonable efforts to ensure:

(i) that the firm in which the lawyer practices has in effect measures giving reasonable assurance that the nonlawyer's conduct is compatible with the professional obligations of the lawyer; and

(ii) that conduct of a nonlawyer over whom the lawyer has direct supervisory authority is compatible with the professional obligations of the lawyer; or

(b) the nonlawyer's conduct would be a violation of the applicable lawyer code if engaged in by a lawyer, and

(i) the lawyer orders or, with knowledge of the specific conduct, ratifies the conduct; or

(ii) the lawyer is a partner or principal in the law firm, or has direct supervisory authority over the nonlawyer, and knows of the conduct at a time when its consequences can be avoided or mitigated but fails to take reasonable remedial measures.

§ 12. Duty of a Lawyer Subject to Supervision

(1) For purposes of professional discipline, a lawyer must conform to the requirements of an applicable lawyer code even if the lawyer acted at the direction of another lawyer or other person.

(2) For purposes of professional discipline, a lawyer under the direct supervisory authority of another lawyer does not violate an applicable lawyer code by acting in accordance with the supervisory lawyer's direction based on a reasonable resolution of an arguable question of professional duty.

§ 13. Restrictions on the Right to Practice Law

(1) A lawyer may not offer or enter into a law-firm agreement that restricts the right of the lawyer to practice law after terminating the relationship, except for a restriction incident to the lawyer's retirement from the practice of law.

(2) In settling a client claim, a lawyer may not offer or enter into an agreement that restricts the right of the lawyer to practice law, including the right to represent or take particular action on behalf of other clients.

§ 14. Formation of a Client–Lawyer Relationship

A relationship of client and lawyer arises when:

(1) a person manifests to a lawyer the person's intent that the lawyer provide legal services for the person; and either

(a) the lawyer manifests to the person consent to do so; or

(b) the lawyer fails to manifest lack of consent to do so, and the lawyer knows or reasonably should know that the person reasonably relies on the lawyer to provide the services; or

(2) a tribunal with power to do so appoints the lawyer to provide the services.

§ 15. A Lawyer's Duties to a Prospective Client

(1) When a person discusses with a lawyer the possibility of their forming a client-lawyer relationship for a matter and no such relationship ensues, the lawyer must:

(a) not subsequently use or disclose confidential information learned in the consultation, except to the extent permitted with respect to confidential information of a client or former client as stated in §§ 61–67;

(b) protect the person's property in the lawyer's custody as stated in §§ 44–46; and

(c) use reasonable care to the extent the lawyer provides the person legal services.

(2) A lawyer subject to Subsection (1) may not represent a client whose interests are materially adverse to those of a former prospective client in the same or a substantially related matter when the lawyer or another lawyer whose disqualification is imputed to the lawyer under §§ 123 and 124 has received from the prospective client confidential information that could be significantly harmful to the prospective client in the matter, except that such a representation is permissible if:

(a) (i) any personally prohibited lawyer takes reasonable steps to avoid exposure to confidential information other than information appropriate to determine whether to represent the prospective client, and (ii) such lawyer is screened as stated in § 124(2)(b) and (c); or

(b) both the affected client and the prospective client give informed consent to the representation under the limitations and conditions provided in § 122.

§ 16. A Lawyer's Duties to a Client—In General

To the extent consistent with the lawyer's other legal duties and subject to the other provisions of this Restatement, a lawyer must, in matters within the scope of the representation:

(1) proceed in a manner reasonably calculated to advance a client's lawful objectives, as defined by the client after consultation;

(2) act with reasonable competence and diligence;

(3) comply with obligations concerning the client's confidences and property, avoid impermissible conflicting interests, deal honestly with the client, and not employ advantages arising from the client-lawyer relationship in a manner adverse to the client; and

(4) fulfill valid contractual obligations to the client.

§ 17. A Client's Duties to a Lawyer

Subject to the other provisions of this Restatement, in matters covered by the representation a client must:

(1) compensate a lawyer for services and expenses as stated in Chapter 3;

(2) indemnify the lawyer for liability to which the client has exposed the lawyer without the lawyer's fault; and

(3) fulfill any valid contractual obligations to the lawyer.

§ 18. Client–Lawyer Contracts

(1) A contract between a lawyer and client concerning the client-lawyer relationship, including a contract modifying an existing contract, may be enforced by either party if the contract meets other applicable requirements, except that:

(a) if the contract or modification is made beyond a reasonable time after the lawyer has begun to represent the client in the matter (see § 38(1)), the client may avoid it unless the lawyer shows that the contract and the circumstances of its formation were fair and reasonable to the client; and

(b) if the contract is made after the lawyer has finished providing services, the client may avoid it if the client was not informed of facts needed to evaluate the appropriateness of the lawyer's compensation or other benefits conferred on the lawyer by the contract.

(2) A tribunal should construe a contract between client and lawyer as a reasonable person in the circumstances of the client would have construed it.

§ 19. Agreements Limiting Client or Lawyer Duties

(1) Subject to other requirements stated in this Restatement, a client and lawyer may agree to limit a duty that a lawyer would otherwise owe to the client if:

(a) the client is adequately informed and consents; and

(b) the terms of the limitation are reasonable in the circumstances.

(2) A lawyer may agree to waive a client's duty to pay or other duty owed to the lawyer.

§ 20. A Lawyer's Duty to Inform and Consult with a Client

(1) A lawyer must keep a client reasonably informed about the matter and must consult with a client to a reasonable extent concerning decisions to be made by the lawyer under §§ 21–23.

(2) A lawyer must promptly comply with a client's reasonable requests for information.

(3) A lawyer must notify a client of decisions to be made by the client under §§ 21–23 and must explain a matter to the extent reasonably necessary to permit the client to make informed decisions regarding the representation.

§ 21. Allocating the Authority to Decide Between a Client and a Lawyer

As between client and lawyer:

(1) A client and lawyer may agree which of them will make specified decisions, subject to the requirements stated in §§ 18, 19, 22, 23, and other provisions of this Restatement. The agreement may be superseded by another valid agreement.

(2) A client may instruct a lawyer during the representation, subject to the requirements stated in §§ 22, 23, and other provisions of this Restatement.

(3) Subject to Subsections (1) and (2) a lawyer may take any lawful measure within the scope of representation that is reasonably calculated to advance a client's objectives as defined by the client, consulting with the client as required by § 20.

(4) A client may ratify an act of a lawyer that was not previously authorized.

§ 22. Authority Reserved to a Client

(1) As between client and lawyer, subject to Subsection (2) and § 23, the following and comparable decisions are reserved to the client except when the client has validly authorized the lawyer to make the particular decision: whether and on what terms to settle a claim; how a criminal defendant should plead; whether a criminal defendant should waive jury trial; whether a criminal defendant should testify; and whether to appeal in a civil proceeding or criminal prosecution.

(2) A client may not validly authorize a lawyer to make the decisions described in Subsection (1) when other law (such as criminal-procedure rules governing pleas, jury-trial waiver, and defendant testimony) requires the client's personal participation or approval.

(3) Regardless of any contrary contract with a lawyer, a client may revoke a lawyer's authority to make the decisions described in Subsection (1).

§ 23. Authority Reserved to a Lawyer

As between client and lawyer, a lawyer retains authority that may not be overridden by a contract with or an instruction from the client:

(1) to refuse to perform, counsel, or assist future or ongoing acts in the representation that the lawyer reasonably believes to be unlawful;

(2) to make decisions or take actions in the representation that the lawyer reasonably believes to be required by law or an order of a tribunal.

§ 24. A Client with Diminished Capacity

(1) When a client's capacity to make adequately considered decisions in connection with the representation is diminished, whether because of minority, physical illness, mental disability, or other cause, the lawyer must, as far as reasonably possible, maintain a normal client-lawyer relationship with the client and act in the best interests of the client as stated in Subsection (2).

(2) A lawyer representing a client with diminished capacity as described in Subsection (1) and for whom no guardian or other representative is available to act, must, with respect to a matter within the scope of the representation, pursue the lawyer's reasonable view of the client's objectives or interests as the client would define them if able to make adequately considered decisions on the matter, even if the client expresses no wishes or gives contrary instructions.

(3) If a client with diminished capacity as described in Subsection (1) has a guardian or other person legally entitled to act for the client, the client's lawyer must treat that person as entitled to act with respect to the client's interests in the matter, unless:

(a) the lawyer represents the client in a matter against the interests of that person; or

(b) that person instructs the lawyer to act in a manner that the lawyer knows will violate the person's legal duties toward the client.

(4) A lawyer representing a client with diminished capacity as described in Subsection (1) may seek the appointment of a guardian or take other protective action within the scope of the representation when doing so is practical and will advance the client's objectives or interests, determined as stated in Subsection (2).

§ 25. Appearance Before a Tribunal

A lawyer who enters an appearance before a tribunal on behalf of a person is presumed to represent that person as a client. The presumption may be rebutted.

§ 26. A Lawyer's Actual Authority

A lawyer's act is considered to be that of a client in proceedings before a tribunal or in dealings with third persons when:

(1) the client has expressly or impliedly authorized the act;

(2) authority concerning the act is reserved to the lawyer as stated in § 23; or

(3) the client ratifies the act.

§ 27. A Lawyer's Apparent Authority

A lawyer's act is considered to be that of the client in proceedings before a tribunal or in dealings with a third person if the tribunal or third person reasonably assumes that the lawyer is authorized to do the act on the basis of the client's (and not the lawyer's) manifestations of such authorization.

§ 28. A Lawyer's Knowledge; Notification to a Lawyer; and Statements of a Lawyer

(1) Information imparted to a lawyer during and relating to the representation of a client is attributed to the client for the purpose of determining the client's rights and liabilities in matters in which the lawyer represents the client, unless those rights or liabilities require proof of the client's personal knowledge or intentions or the lawyer's legal duties preclude disclosure of the information to the client.

(2) Unless applicable law otherwise provides, a third person may give notification to a client, in a matter in which the client is represented by a lawyer, by giving notification to the client's lawyer, unless the third person knows of circumstances reasonably indicating that the lawyer's authority to receive notification has been abrogated.

(3) A lawyer's unprivileged statement is admissible in evidence against a client as if it were the client's statement if either:

(a) the client authorized the lawyer to make a statement concerning the subject; or

(b) the statement concerns a matter within the scope of the representation and was made by the lawyer during it.

§ 29. A Lawyer's Act or Advice as Mitigating or Avoiding a Client's Responsibility

(1) When a client's intent or mental state is in issue, a tribunal may consider otherwise admissible evidence of a lawyer's advice to the client.

(2) In deciding whether to impose a sanction on a person or to relieve a person from a criminal or civil ruling, default, or judgment, a tribunal may consider otherwise admissible evidence to prove or disprove that the lawyer who represented the person did so inadequately or contrary to the client's instructions.

§ 30. A Lawyer's Liability to a Third Person for Conduct on Behalf of a Client

(1) For improper conduct while representing a client, a lawyer is subject to professional discipline as stated in § 5, to civil liability as stated in Chapter 4, and to prosecution as provided in the criminal law (see § 7).

(2) Unless at the time of contracting the lawyer or third person disclaimed such liability, a lawyer is subject to liability to third persons on contracts the lawyer entered into on behalf of a client if:

(a) the client's existence or identity was not disclosed to the third person; or

(b) the contract is between the lawyer and a third person who provides goods or services used by lawyers and who, as the lawyer knows or reasonably should know, relies on the lawyer's credit.

(3) A lawyer is subject to liability to a third person for damages for loss proximately caused by the lawyer's acting without authority from a client under § 26 if:

(a) the lawyer tortiously misrepresents to the third person that the lawyer has authority to make a contract, conveyance, or affirmation on behalf of the client and the third person reasonably relies on the misrepresentation; or

(b) the lawyer purports to make a contract, conveyance, or affirmation on behalf of the client, unless the lawyer manifests that the lawyer does not warrant that the lawyer is authorized to act or the other party knows that the lawyer is not authorized to act.

§ 31. Termination of a Lawyer's Authority

(1) A lawyer must comply with applicable law requiring notice to or permission of a tribunal when terminating a representation and with an order of a tribunal requiring the representation to continue.

(2) Subject to Subsection (1) and § 33, a lawyer's actual authority to represent a client ends when:

(a) the client discharges the lawyer;

(b) the client dies or, in the case of a corporation or similar organization, loses its capacity to function as such;

(c) the lawyer withdraws;

(d) the lawyer dies or becomes physically or mentally incapable of providing representation, is disbarred or suspended from practicing law, or is ordered by a tribunal to cease representing a client; or

(e) the representation ends as provided by contract or because the lawyer has completed the contemplated services.

(3) A lawyer's apparent authority to act for a client with respect to another person ends when the other person knows or should know of facts

from which it can be reasonably inferred that the lawyer lacks actual authority, including knowledge of any event described in Subsection (2).

§ 32. Discharge by a Client and Withdrawal by a Lawyer

(1) Subject to Subsection (5), a client may discharge a lawyer at any time.

(2) Subject to Subsection (5), a lawyer may not represent a client or, where representation has commenced, must withdraw from the representation of a client if:

(a) the representation will result in the lawyer's violating rules of professional conduct or other law;

(b) the lawyer's physical or mental condition materially impairs the lawyer's ability to represent the client; or

(c) the client discharges the lawyer.

(3) Subject to Subsections (4) and (5), a lawyer may withdraw from representing a client if:

(a) withdrawal can be accomplished without material adverse effect on the interests of the client;

(b) the lawyer reasonably believes withdrawal is required in circumstances stated in Subsection (2);

(c) the client gives informed consent;

(d) the client persists in a course of action involving the lawyer's services that the lawyer reasonably believes is criminal, fraudulent, or in breach of the client's fiduciary duty;

(e) the lawyer reasonably believes the client has used or threatens to use the lawyer's services to perpetrate a crime or fraud;

(f) the client insists on taking action that the lawyer considers repugnant or imprudent;

(g) the client fails to fulfill a substantial financial or other obligation to the lawyer regarding the lawyer's services and the lawyer has given the client reasonable warning that the lawyer will withdraw unless the client fulfills the obligation;

(h) the representation has been rendered unreasonably difficult by the client or by the irreparable breakdown of the client-lawyer relationship; or

(i) other good cause for withdrawal exists.

(4) In the case of permissive withdrawal under Subsections (3)(f)-(i), a lawyer may not withdraw if the harm that withdrawal would cause significantly exceeds the harm to the lawyer or others in not withdrawing.

(5) Notwithstanding Subsections (1)–(4), a lawyer must comply with applicable law requiring notice to or permission of a tribunal when terminat-

ing a representation and with a valid order of a tribunal requiring the representation to continue.

§ 33. A Lawyer's Duties When a Representation Terminates

(1) In terminating a representation, a lawyer must take steps to the extent reasonably practicable to protect the client's interests, such as giving notice to the client of the termination, allowing time for employment of other counsel, surrendering papers and property to which the client is entitled, and refunding any advance payment of fee the lawyer has not earned.

(2) Following termination of a representation, a lawyer must:

(a) observe obligations to a former client such as those dealing with client confidences (see Chapter 5), conflicts of interest (see Chapter 8), client property and documents (see §§ 44–46), and fee collection (see § 41);

(b) take no action on behalf of a former client without new authorization and give reasonable notice, to those who might otherwise be misled, that the lawyer lacks authority to act for the client;

(c) take reasonable steps to convey to the former client any material communication the lawyer receives relating to the matter involved in the representation; and

(d) take no unfair advantage of a former client by abusing knowledge or trust acquired by means of the representation.

§ 34. Reasonable and Lawful Fees

A lawyer may not charge a fee larger than is reasonable in the circumstances or that is prohibited by law.

§ 35. Contingent–Fee Arrangements

(1) A lawyer may contract with a client for a fee the size or payment of which is contingent on the outcome of a matter, unless the contract violates § 34 or another provision of this Restatement or the size or payment of the fee is:

(a) contingent on success in prosecuting or defending a criminal proceeding; or

(b) contingent on a specified result in a divorce proceeding or a proceeding concerning custody of a child.

(2) Unless the contract construed in the circumstances indicates otherwise, when a lawyer has contracted for a contingent fee, the lawyer is entitled to receive the specified fee only when and to the extent the client receives payment.

§ 36. Forbidden Client–Lawyer Financial Arrangements

(1) A lawyer may not acquire a proprietary interest in the cause of action or subject matter of litigation that the lawyer is conducting for a client, except that the lawyer may:

   (a) acquire a lien as provided by § 43 to secure the lawyer's fee or expenses; and

   (b) contract with a client for a contingent fee in a civil case except when prohibited as stated in § 35.

(2) A lawyer may not make or guarantee a loan to a client in connection with pending or contemplated litigation that the lawyer is conducting for the client, except that the lawyer may make or guarantee a loan covering court costs and expenses of litigation, the repayment of which to the lawyer may be contingent on the outcome of the matter.

(3) A lawyer may not, before the lawyer ceases to represent a client, make an agreement giving the lawyer literary or media rights to a portrayal or account based in substantial part on information relating to the representation.

§ 37. Partial or Complete Forfeiture of a Lawyer's Compensation

A lawyer engaging in clear and serious violation of duty to a client may be required to forfeit some or all of the lawyer's compensation for the matter. Considerations relevant to the question of forfeiture include the gravity and timing of the violation, its willfulness, its effect on the value of the lawyer's work for the client, any other threatened or actual harm to the client, and the adequacy of other remedies.

§ 38. Client–Lawyer Fee Contracts

(1) Before or within a reasonable time after beginning to represent a client in a matter, a lawyer must communicate to the client, in writing when applicable rules so provide, the basis or rate of the fee, unless the communication is unnecessary for the client because the lawyer has previously represented that client on the same basis or at the same rate.

(2) The validity and construction of a contract between a client and a lawyer concerning the lawyer's fees are governed by § 18.

(3) Unless a contract construed in the circumstances indicates otherwise:

   (a) a lawyer may not charge separately for the lawyer's general office and overhead expenses;

   (b) payments that the law requires an opposing party or that party's lawyer to pay as attorney-fee awards or sanctions are credited to the client, not the client's lawyer, absent a contrary statute or court order; and

(c) when a lawyer requests and receives a fee payment that is not for services already rendered, that payment is to be credited against whatever fee the lawyer is entitled to collect.

§ 39. A Lawyer's Fee in the Absence of a Contract

If a client and lawyer have not made a valid contract providing for another measure of compensation, a client owes a lawyer who has performed legal services for the client the fair value of the lawyer's services.

§ 40. Fees on Termination

If a client-lawyer relationship ends before the lawyer has completed the services due for a matter and the lawyer's fee has not been forfeited under § 37:

(1) a lawyer who has been discharged or withdraws may recover the lesser of the fair value of the lawyer's services as determined under § 39 and the ratable proportion of the compensation provided by any otherwise enforceable contract between lawyer and client for the services performed; except that

(2) the tribunal may allow such a lawyer to recover the ratable proportion of the compensation provided by such a contract if:

(a) the discharge or withdrawal is not attributable to misconduct of the lawyer;

(b) the lawyer has performed severable services; and

(c) allowing contractual compensation would not burden the client's choice of counsel or the client's ability to replace counsel.

§ 41. Fee–Collection Methods

In seeking compensation claimed from a client or former client, a lawyer may not employ collection methods forbidden by law, use confidential information (as defined in Chapter 5) when not permitted under § 65, or harass the client.

§ 42. Remedies and the Burden of Persuasion

(1) A fee dispute between a lawyer and a client may be adjudicated in any appropriate proceeding, including a suit by the lawyer to recover an unpaid fee, a suit for a refund by a client, an arbitration to which both parties consent unless applicable law renders the lawyer's consent unnecessary, or in the court's discretion a proceeding ancillary to a pending suit in which the lawyer performed the services in question.

(2) In any such proceeding the lawyer has the burden of persuading the trier of fact, when relevant, of the existence and terms of any fee contract, the making of any disclosures to the client required to render a contract enforceable, and the extent and value of the lawyer's services.

§ 43. Lawyer Liens

(1) Except as provided in Subsection (2) or by statute or rule, a lawyer does not acquire a lien entitling the lawyer to retain the client's property in the lawyer's possession in order to secure payment of the lawyer's fees and disbursements. A lawyer may decline to deliver to a client or former client an original or copy of any document prepared by the lawyer or at the lawyer's expense if the client or former client has not paid all fees and disbursements due for the lawyer's work in preparing the document and nondelivery would not unreasonably harm the client or former client.

(2) Unless otherwise provided by statute or rule, client and lawyer may agree that the lawyer shall have a security interest in property of the client recovered for the client through the lawyer's efforts, as follows:

(a) the lawyer may contract in writing with the client for a lien on the proceeds of the representation to secure payment for the lawyer's services and disbursements in that matter;

(b) the lien becomes binding on a third party when the party has notice of the lien;

(c) the lien applies only to the amount of fees and disbursements claimed reasonably and in good faith for the lawyer's services performed in the representation; and

(d) the lawyer may not unreasonably impede the speedy and inexpensive resolution of any dispute concerning those fees and disbursements or the lien.

(3) A tribunal where an action is pending may in its discretion adjudicate any fee or other dispute concerning a lien asserted by a lawyer on property of a party to the action, provide for custody of the property, release all or part of the property to the client or lawyer, and grant such other relief as justice may require.

(4) With respect to property neither in the lawyer's possession nor recovered by the client through the lawyer's efforts, the lawyer may obtain a security interest on property of a client only as provided by other law and consistent with §§ 18 and 126. Acquisition of such a security interest is a business or financial transaction with a client within the meaning of § 126.

§ 44. Safeguarding and Segregating Property

(1) A lawyer holding funds or other property of a client in connection with a representation, or such funds or other property in which a client claims an interest, must take reasonable steps to safeguard the funds or property. A similar obligation may be imposed by law on funds or other property so held and owned or claimed by a third person. In particular, the lawyer must hold such property separate from the lawyer's property, keep records of it, deposit funds in an account separate from the lawyer's own funds, identify tangible objects, and comply with related requirements imposed by regulatory authorities.

(2) Upon receiving funds or other property in a professional capacity and in which a client or third person owns or claims an interest, a lawyer must promptly notify the client or third person. The lawyer must promptly render a full accounting regarding such property upon request by the client or third person.

§ 45. Surrendering Possession of Property

(1) Except as provided in Subsection (2), a lawyer must promptly deliver, to the client or nonclient so entitled, funds or other property in the lawyer's possession belonging to a client or nonclient.

(2) A lawyer may retain possession of funds or other property of a client or nonclient if:

(a) the client or nonclient consents;

(b) the lawyer's client is entitled to the property, the lawyer appropriately possesses the property for purposes of the representation, and the client has not asked for delivery of the property;

(c) the lawyer has a valid lien on the property (see § 43);

(d) there are substantial grounds for dispute as to the person entitled to the property; or

(e) delivering the property to the client or nonclient would violate a court order or other legal obligation of the lawyer.

§ 46. Documents Relating to a Representation

(1) A lawyer must take reasonable steps to safeguard documents in the lawyer's possession relating to the representation of a client or former client.

(2) On request, a lawyer must allow a client or former client to inspect and copy any document possessed by the lawyer relating to the representation, unless substantial grounds exist to refuse.

(3) Unless a client or former client consents to nondelivery or substantial grounds exist for refusing to make delivery, a lawyer must deliver to the client or former client, at an appropriate time and in any event promptly after the representation ends, such originals and copies of other documents possessed by the lawyer relating to the representation as the client or former client reasonably needs.

(4) Notwithstanding Subsections (2) and (3), a lawyer may decline to deliver to a client or former client an original or copy of any document under circumstances permitted by § 43(1).

§ 47. Fee–Splitting Between Lawyers Not in the Same Firm

A division of fees between lawyers who are not in the same firm may be made only if:

(1) (a) the division is in proportion to the services performed by each lawyer or (b) by agreement with the client, the lawyers assume joint responsibility for the representation;

(2) the client is informed of and does not object to the fact of division, the terms of the division, and the participation of the lawyers involved; and

(3) the total fee is reasonable (see § 34).

§ 48. Professional Negligence—Elements and Defenses Generally

In addition to the other possible bases of civil liability described in §§ 49, 55, and 56, a lawyer is civilly liable for professional negligence to a person to whom the lawyer owes a duty of care within the meaning of § 50 or § 51, if the lawyer fails to exercise care within the meaning of § 52 and if that failure is a legal cause of injury within the meaning of § 53, unless the lawyer has a defense within the meaning of § 54.

§ 49. Breach of Fiduciary Duty—Generally

In addition to the other possible bases of civil liability described in §§ 48, 55, and 56, a lawyer is civilly liable to a client if the lawyer breaches a fiduciary duty to the client set forth in § 16(3) and if that failure is a legal cause of injury within the meaning of § 53, unless the lawyer has a defense within the meaning of § 54.

§ 50. Duty of Care to a Client

For purposes of liability under § 48, a lawyer owes a client the duty to exercise care within the meaning of § 52 in pursuing the client's lawful objectives in matters covered by the representation.

§ 51. Duty of Care to Certain Nonclients

For purposes of liability under § 48, a lawyer owes a duty to use care within the meaning of § 52 in each of the following circumstances:

(1) to a prospective client, as stated in § 15;

(2) to a nonclient when and to the extent that:

(a) the lawyer or (with the lawyer's acquiescence) the lawyer's client invites the nonclient to rely on the lawyer's opinion or provision of other legal services, and the nonclient so relies; and

(b) the nonclient is not, under applicable tort law, too remote from the lawyer to be entitled to protection;

(3) to a nonclient when and to the extent that:

(a) the lawyer knows that a client intends as one of the primary objectives of the representation that the lawyer's services benefit the nonclient;

(b) such a duty would not significantly impair the lawyer's performance of obligations to the client; and

(c) the absence of such a duty would make enforcement of those obligations to the client unlikely; and

(4) to a nonclient when and to the extent that:

(a) the lawyer's client is a trustee, guardian, executor, or fiduciary acting primarily to perform similar functions for the nonclient;

(b) the lawyer knows that appropriate action by the lawyer is necessary with respect to a matter within the scope of the representation to prevent or rectify the breach of a fiduciary duty owed by the client to the nonclient, where (i) the breach is a crime or fraud or (ii) the lawyer has assisted or is assisting the breach;

(c) the nonclient is not reasonably able to protect its rights; and

(d) such a duty would not significantly impair the performance of the lawyer's obligations to the client.

§ 52. The Standard of Care

(1) For purposes of liability under §§ 48 and 49, a lawyer who owes a duty of care must exercise the competence and diligence normally exercised by lawyers in similar circumstances.

(2) Proof of a violation of a rule or statute regulating the conduct of lawyers:

(a) does not give rise to an implied cause of action for professional negligence or breach of fiduciary duty;

(b) does not preclude other proof concerning the duty of care in Subsection (1) or the fiduciary duty; and

(c) may be considered by a trier of fact as an aid in understanding and applying the standard of Subsection (1) or § 49 to the extent that (i) the rule or statute was designed for the protection of persons in the position of the claimant and (ii) proof of the content and construction of such a rule or statute is relevant to the claimant's claim.

§ 53. Causation and Damages

A lawyer is liable under § 48 or § 49 only if the lawyer's breach of a duty of care or breach of fiduciary duty was a legal cause of injury, as determined under generally applicable principles of causation and damages.

§ 54. Defenses; Prospective Liability Waiver; Settlement with a Client

(1) Except as otherwise provided in this Section, liability under §§ 48 and 49 is subject to the defenses available under generally applicable principles of law governing respectively actions for professional negligence and breach of fiduciary duty. A lawyer is not liable under § 48 or § 49 for any action or

inaction the lawyer reasonably believed to be required by law, including a professional rule.

(2) An agreement prospectively limiting a lawyer's liability to a client for malpractice is unenforceable.

(3) The client or former client may rescind an agreement settling a claim by the client or former client against the person's lawyer if:

(a) the client or former client was subjected to improper pressure by the lawyer in reaching the settlement; or

(b) (i) the client or former client was not independently represented in negotiating the settlement, and (ii) the settlement was not fair and reasonable to the client or former client.

(4) For purposes of professional discipline, a lawyer may not:

(a) make an agreement prospectively limiting the lawyer's liability to a client for malpractice; or

(b) settle a claim for such liability with an unrepresented client or former client without first advising that person in writing that independent representation is appropriate in connection therewith.

§ 55. Civil Remedies of a Client Other Than for Malpractice

(1) A lawyer is subject to liability to a client for injury caused by breach of contract in the circumstances and to the extent provided by contract law.

(2) A client is entitled to restitutionary, injunctive, or declaratory remedies against a lawyer in the circumstances and to the extent provided by generally applicable law governing such remedies.

§ 56. Liability to a Client or Nonclient Under General Law

Except as provided in § 57 and in addition to liability under §§ 48–55, a lawyer is subject to liability to a client or nonclient when a nonlawyer would be in similar circumstances.

§ 57. Nonclient Claims—Certain Defenses and Exceptions to Liability

(1) In addition to other absolute or conditional privileges, a lawyer is absolutely privileged to publish matter concerning a nonclient if:

(a) the publication occurs in communications preliminary to a reasonably anticipated proceeding before a tribunal or in the institution or during the course and as a part of such a proceeding;

(b) the lawyer participates as counsel in that proceeding; and

(c) the matter is published to a person who may be involved in the proceeding, and the publication has some relation to the proceeding.

(2) A lawyer representing a client in a civil proceeding or procuring the institution of criminal proceedings by a client is not liable to a nonclient for

wrongful use of civil proceedings or for malicious prosecution if the lawyer has probable cause for acting, or if the lawyer acts primarily to help the client obtain a proper adjudication of the client's claim in that proceeding.

(3) A lawyer who advises or assists a client to make or break a contract, to enter or dissolve a legal relationship, or to enter or not enter a contractual relation, is not liable to a nonclient for interference with contract or with prospective contractual relations or with a legal relationship, if the lawyer acts to advance the client's objectives without using wrongful means.

§ 58. Vicarious Liability

(1) A law firm is subject to civil liability for injury legally caused to a person by any wrongful act or omission of any principal or employee of the firm who was acting in the ordinary course of the firm's business or with actual or apparent authority.

(2) Each of the principals of a law firm organized as a general partnership without limited liability is liable jointly and severally with the firm.

(3) A principal of a law firm organized other than as a general partnership without limited liability as authorized by law is vicariously liable for the acts of another principal or employee of the firm to the extent provided by law.

§ 59. Definition of "Confidential Client Information"

Confidential client information consists of information relating to representation of a client, other than information that is generally known.

§ 60. A Lawyer's Duty to Safeguard Confidential Client Information

(1) Except as provided in §§ 61–67, during and after representation of a client:

(a) the lawyer may not use or disclose confidential client information as defined in § 59 if there is a reasonable prospect that doing so will adversely affect a material interest of the client or if the client has instructed the lawyer not to use or disclose such information;

(b) the lawyer must take steps reasonable in the circumstances to protect confidential client information against impermissible use or disclosure by the lawyer's associates or agents that may adversely affect a material interest of the client or otherwise than as instructed by the client.

(2) Except as stated in § 62, a lawyer who uses confidential information of a client for the lawyer's pecuniary gain other than in the practice of law must account to the client for any profits made.

§ 61. Using or Disclosing Information to Advance Client Interests

A lawyer may use or disclose confidential client information when the lawyer reasonably believes that doing so will advance the interests of the client in the representation.

§ 62. Using or Disclosing Information with Client Consent

A lawyer may use or disclose confidential client information when the client consents after being adequately informed concerning the use or disclosure.

§ 63. Using or Disclosing Information When Required by Law

A lawyer may use or disclose confidential client information when required by law, after the lawyer takes reasonably appropriate steps to assert that the information is privileged or otherwise protected against disclosure.

§ 64. Using or Disclosing Information in a Lawyer's Self–Defense

A lawyer may use or disclose confidential client information when and to the extent that the lawyer reasonably believes necessary to defend the lawyer or the lawyer's associate or agent against a charge or threatened charge by any person that the lawyer or such associate or agent acted wrongfully in the course of representing a client.

§ 65. Using or Disclosing Information in a Compensation Dispute

A lawyer may use or disclose confidential client information when and to the extent that the lawyer reasonably believes necessary to permit the lawyer to resolve a dispute with the client concerning compensation or reimbursement that the lawyer reasonably claims the client owes the lawyer.

§ 66. Using or Disclosing Information to Prevent Death or Serious Bodily Harm

(1) A lawyer may use or disclose confidential client information when the lawyer reasonably believes that its use or disclosure is necessary to prevent reasonably certain death or serious bodily harm to a person.

(2) Before using or disclosing information under this Section, the lawyer must, if feasible, make a good-faith effort to persuade the client not to act. If the client or another person has already acted, the lawyer must, if feasible, advise the client to warn the victim or to take other action to prevent the harm and advise the client of the lawyer's ability to use or disclose information as provided in this Section and the consequences thereof.

(3) A lawyer who takes action or decides not to take action permitted under this Section is not, solely by reason of such action or inaction, subject to professional discipline, liable for damages to the lawyer's client or any third person, or barred from recovery against a client or third person.

§ 67. Using or Disclosing Information to Prevent, Rectify, or Mitigate Substantial Financial Loss

(1) A lawyer may use or disclose confidential client information when the lawyer reasonably believes that its use or disclosure is necessary to prevent a crime or fraud, and:

(a) the crime or fraud threatens substantial financial loss;

(b) the loss has not yet occurred;

(c) the lawyer's client intends to commit the crime or fraud either personally or through a third person; and

(d) the client has employed or is employing the lawyer's services in the matter in which the crime or fraud is committed.

(2) If a crime or fraud described in Subsection (1) has already occurred, a lawyer may use or disclose confidential client information when the lawyer reasonably believes its use or disclosure is necessary to prevent, rectify, or mitigate the loss.

(3) Before using or disclosing information under this Section, the lawyer must, if feasible, make a good-faith effort to persuade the client not to act. If the client or another person has already acted, the lawyer must, if feasible, advise the client to warn the victim or to take other action to prevent, rectify, or mitigate the loss. The lawyer must, if feasible, also advise the client of the lawyer's ability to use or disclose information as provided in this Section and the consequences thereof.

(4) A lawyer who takes action or decides not to take action permitted under this Section is not, solely by reason of such action or inaction, subject to professional discipline, liable for damages to the lawyer's client or any third person, or barred from recovery against a client or third person.

§ 68. Attorney–Client Privilege

Except as otherwise provided in this Restatement, the attorney-client privilege may be invoked as provided in § 86 with respect to:

(1) a communication

(2) made between privileged persons

(3) in confidence

(4) for the purpose of obtaining or providing legal assistance for the client.

§ 69. Attorney–Client Privilege—"Communication"

A communication within the meaning of § 68 is any expression through which a privileged person, as defined in § 70, undertakes to convey information to another privileged person and any document or other record revealing such an expression.

§ 70. Attorney–Client Privilege—"Privileged Persons"

Privileged persons within the meaning of § 68 are the client (including a prospective client), the client's lawyer, agents of either who facilitate communications between them, and agents of the lawyer who facilitate the representation.

§ 71. Attorney–Client Privilege—"In Confidence"

A communication is in confidence within the meaning of § 68 if, at the time and in the circumstances of the communication, the communicating person reasonably believes that no one will learn the contents of the communication except a privileged person as defined in § 70 or another person with whom communications are protected under a similar privilege.

§ 72. Attorney–Client Privilege—Legal Assistance as the Object of a Privileged Communication

A communication is made for the purpose of obtaining or providing legal assistance within the meaning of § 68 if it is made to or to assist a person:

(1) who is a lawyer or who the client or prospective client reasonably believes to be a lawyer; and

(2) whom the client or prospective client consults for the purpose of obtaining legal assistance.

§ 73. The Privilege for an Organizational Client

When a client is a corporation, unincorporated association, partnership, trust, estate, sole proprietorship, or other for-profit or not-for-profit organization, the attorney-client privilege extends to a communication that:

(1) otherwise qualifies as privileged under §§ 68–72;

(2) is between an agent of the organization and a privileged person as defined in § 70;

(3) concerns a legal matter of interest to the organization; and

(4) is disclosed only to:

(a) privileged persons as defined in § 70; and

(b) other agents of the organization who reasonably need to know of the communication in order to act for the organization.

§ 74. The Privilege for a Governmental Client

Unless applicable law otherwise provides, the attorney-client privilege extends to a communication of a governmental organization as stated in § 73 and of an individual employee or other agent of a governmental organization as a client with respect to his or her personal interest as stated in §§ 68–72.

§ 75. The Privilege of Co–Clients

(1) If two or more persons are jointly represented by the same lawyer in a matter, a communication of either co-client that otherwise qualifies as privileged under §§ 68–72 and relates to matters of common interest is privileged as against third persons, and any co-client may invoke the privilege, unless it has been waived by the client who made the communication.

(2) Unless the co-clients have agreed otherwise, a communication described in Subsection (1) is not privileged as between the co-clients in a subsequent adverse proceeding between them.

§ 76. The Privilege in Common–Interest Arrangements

(1) If two or more clients with a common interest in a litigated or nonlitigated matter are represented by separate lawyers and they agree to exchange information concerning the matter, a communication of any such client that otherwise qualifies as privileged under §§ 68–72 that relates to the matter is privileged as against third persons. Any such client may invoke the privilege, unless it has been waived by the client who made the communication.

(2) Unless the clients have agreed otherwise, a communication described in Subsection (1) is not privileged as between clients described in Subsection (1) in a subsequent adverse proceeding between them.

§ 77. Duration of the Privilege

Unless waived (see §§ 78–80) or subject to exception (see §§ 81–85), the attorney-client privilege may be invoked as provided in § 86 at any time during or after termination of the relationship between client or prospective client and lawyer.

§ 78. Agreement, Disclaimer, or Failure to Object

The attorney-client privilege is waived if the client, the client's lawyer, or another authorized agent of the client:

    (1) agrees to waive the privilege;

    (2) disclaims protection of the privilege and

        (a) another person reasonably relies on the disclaimer to that person's detriment; or

        (b) reasons of judicial administration require that the client not be permitted to revoke the disclaimer; or

    (3) in a proceeding before a tribunal, fails to object properly to an attempt by another person to give or exact testimony or other evidence of a privileged communication.

§ 79. Subsequent Disclosure

The attorney-client privilege is waived if the client, the client's lawyer, or another authorized agent of the client voluntarily discloses the communication in a nonprivileged communication.

§ 80. Putting Assistance or a Communication in Issue

(1) The attorney-client privilege is waived for any relevant communication if the client asserts as to a material issue in a proceeding that:

    (a) the client acted upon the advice of a lawyer or that the advice was otherwise relevant to the legal significance of the client's conduct; or

    (b) a lawyer's assistance was ineffective, negligent, or otherwise wrongful.

(2) The attorney-client privilege is waived for a recorded communication if a witness:

    (a) employs the communication to aid the witness while testifying; or

    (b) employed the communication in preparing to testify, and the tribunal finds that disclosure is required in the interests of justice.

§ 81. A Dispute Concerning a Decedent's Disposition of Property

The attorney-client privilege does not apply to a communication from or to a decedent relevant to an issue between parties who claim an interest through the same deceased client, either by testate or intestate succession or by an inter vivos transaction.

§ 82. Client Crime or Fraud

The attorney-client privilege does not apply to a communication occurring when a client:

    (a) consults a lawyer for the purpose, later accomplished, of obtaining assistance to engage in a crime or fraud or aiding a third person to do so, or

    (b) regardless of the client's purpose at the time of consultation, uses the lawyer's advice or other services to engage in or assist a crime or fraud.

§ 83. Lawyer Self–Protection

The attorney-client privilege does not apply to a communication that is relevant and reasonably necessary for a lawyer to employ in a proceeding:

    (1) to resolve a dispute with a client concerning compensation or reimbursement that the lawyer reasonably claims the client owes the lawyer; or

(2) to defend the lawyer or the lawyer's associate or agent against a charge by any person that the lawyer, associate, or agent acted wrongfully during the course of representing a client.

§ 84. Fiduciary–Lawyer Communications

In a proceeding in which a trustee of an express trust or similar fiduciary is charged with breach of fiduciary duties by a beneficiary, a communication otherwise within § 68 is nonetheless not privileged if the communication:

(a) is relevant to the claimed breach; and

(b) was between the trustee and a lawyer (or other privileged person within the meaning of § 70) who was retained to advise the trustee concerning the administration of the trust.

§ 85. Communications Involving a Fiduciary Within an Organization

In a proceeding involving a dispute between an organizational client and shareholders, members, or other constituents of the organization toward whom the directors, officers, or similar persons managing the organization bear fiduciary responsibilities, the attorney-client privilege of the organization may be withheld from a communication otherwise within § 68 if the tribunal finds that:

(a) those managing the organization are charged with breach of their obligations toward the shareholders, members, or other constituents or toward the organization itself;

(b) the communication occurred prior to the assertion of the charges and relates directly to those charges; and

(c) the need of the requesting party to discover or introduce the communication is sufficiently compelling and the threat to confidentiality sufficiently confined to justify setting the privilege aside.

§ 86. Invoking the Privilege and Its Exceptions

(1) When an attempt is made to introduce in evidence or obtain discovery of a communication privileged under § 68:

(a) A client, a personal representative of an incompetent or deceased client, or a person succeeding to the interest of a client may invoke or waive the privilege, either personally or through counsel or another authorized agent.

(b) A lawyer, an agent of the lawyer, or an agent of a client from whom a privileged communication is sought must invoke the privilege when doing so appears reasonably appropriate, unless the client:

(i) has waived the privilege; or

(ii) has authorized the lawyer or agent to waive it.

(c) Notwithstanding failure to invoke the privilege as specified in Subsections (1)(a) and (1)(b), the tribunal has discretion to invoke the privilege.

(2) A person invoking the privilege must ordinarily object contemporaneously to an attempt to disclose the communication and, if the objection is contested, demonstrate each element of the privilege under § 68.

(3) A person invoking a waiver of or exception to the privilege (§§ 78–85) must assert it and, if the assertion is contested, demonstrate each element of the waiver or exception.

§ 87. Lawyer Work–Product Immunity

(1) Work product consists of tangible material or its intangible equivalent in unwritten or oral form, other than underlying facts, prepared by a lawyer for litigation then in progress or in reasonable anticipation of future litigation.

(2) Opinion work product consists of the opinions or mental impressions of a lawyer; all other work product is ordinary work product.

(3) Except for material which by applicable law is not so protected, work product is immune from discovery or other compelled disclosure to the extent stated in §§ 88 (ordinary work product) and 89 (opinion work product) when the immunity is invoked as described in § 90.

§ 88. Ordinary Work Product

When work product protection is invoked as described in § 90, ordinary work product (§ 87(2)) is immune from discovery or other compelled disclosure unless either an exception recognized in §§ 91–93 applies or the inquiring party:

(1) has a substantial need for the material in order to prepare for trial; and

(2) is unable without undue hardship to obtain the substantial equivalent of the material by other means.

§ 89. Opinion Work Product

When work product protection is invoked as described in § 90, opinion work product (§ 87(2)) is immune from discovery or other compelled disclosure unless either the immunity is waived or an exception applies (§§ 91–93) or extraordinary circumstances justify disclosure.

§ 90. Invoking the Lawyer Work–Product Immunity and Its Exceptions

(1) Work-product immunity may be invoked by or for a person on whose behalf the work product was prepared.

(2) The person invoking work-product immunity must object and, if the objection is contested, demonstrate each element of the immunity.

(3) Once a claim of work product has been adequately supported, a person entitled to invoke a waiver or exception must assert it and, if the assertion is contested, demonstrate each element of the waiver or exception.

§ 91. Voluntary Acts

Work-product immunity is waived if the client, the client's lawyer, or another authorized agent of the client:

(1) agrees to waive the immunity;

(2) disclaims protection of the immunity and:

(a) another person reasonably relies on the disclaimer to that person's detriment; or

(b) reasons of judicial administration require that the client not be permitted to revoke the disclaimer; or

(3) in a proceeding before a tribunal, fails to object properly to an attempt by another person to give or exact testimony or other evidence of work product; or

(4) discloses the material to third persons in circumstances in which there is a significant likelihood that an adversary or potential adversary in anticipated litigation will obtain it.

§ 92. Use of Lawyer Work Product in Litigation

(1) Work-product immunity is waived for any relevant material if the client asserts as to a material issue in a proceeding that:

(a) the client acted upon the advice of a lawyer or that the advice was otherwise relevant to the legal significance of the client's conduct; or

(b) a lawyer's assistance was ineffective, negligent, or otherwise wrongful.

(2) The work-product immunity is waived for recorded material if a witness

(a) employs the material to aid the witness while testifying, or

(b) employed the material in preparing to testify, and the tribunal finds that disclosure is required in the interests of justice.

§ 93. Client Crime or Fraud

Work-product immunity does not apply to materials prepared when a client consults a lawyer for the purpose, later accomplished, of obtaining assistance to engage in a crime or fraud or to aid a third person to do so or uses the materials for such a purpose.

§ 94. Advising and Assisting a Client—In General

(1) A lawyer who counsels or assists a client to engage in conduct that violates the rights of a third person is subject to liability:

    (a) to the third person to the extent stated in §§ 51 and 56–57; and

    (b) to the client to the extent stated in §§ 50, 55, and 56.

(2) For purposes of professional discipline, a lawyer may not counsel or assist a client in conduct that the lawyer knows to be criminal or fraudulent or in violation of a court order with the intent of facilitating or encouraging the conduct, but the lawyer may counsel or assist a client in conduct when the lawyer reasonably believes:

    (a) that the client's conduct constitutes a good-faith effort to determine the validity, scope, meaning, or application of a law or court order; or

    (b) that the client can assert a nonfrivolous argument that the client's conduct will not constitute a crime or fraud or violate a court order.

(3) In counseling a client, a lawyer may address nonlegal aspects of a proposed course of conduct, including moral, reputational, economic, social, political, and business aspects.

§ 95. An Evaluation Undertaken for a Third Person

(1) In furtherance of the objectives of a client in a representation, a lawyer may provide to a nonclient the results of the lawyer's investigation and analysis of facts or the lawyer's professional evaluation or opinion on the matter.

(2) When providing the information, evaluation, or opinion under Subsection (1) is reasonably likely to affect the client's interests materially and adversely, the lawyer must first obtain the client's consent after the client is adequately informed concerning important possible effects on the client's interests.

(3) In providing the information, evaluation, or opinion under Subsection (1), the lawyer must exercise care with respect to the nonclient to the extent stated in § 51(2) and not make false statements prohibited under § 98.

§ 96. Representing an Organization as Client

(1) When a lawyer is employed or retained to represent an organization:

    (a) the lawyer represents the interests of the organization as defined by its responsible agents acting pursuant to the organization's decision-making procedures; and

    (b) subject to Subsection (2), the lawyer must follow instructions in the representation, as stated in § 21(2), given by persons authorized so to act on behalf of the organization.

(2) If a lawyer representing an organization knows of circumstances indicating that a constituent of the organization has engaged in action or intends to act in a way that violates a legal obligation to the organization that will likely cause substantial injury to it, or that reasonably can be foreseen to be imputable to the organization and likely to result in substantial injury to it, the lawyer must proceed in what the lawyer reasonably believes to be the best interests of the organization.

(3) In the circumstances described in Subsection (2), the lawyer may, in circumstances warranting such steps, ask the constituent to reconsider the matter, recommend that a second legal opinion be sought, and seek review by appropriate supervisory authority within the organization, including referring the matter to the highest authority that can act in behalf of the organization.

§ 97. Representing a Governmental Client

A lawyer representing a governmental client must proceed in the representation as stated in § 96, except that the lawyer:

(1) possesses such rights and responsibilities as may be defined by law to make decisions on behalf of the governmental client that are within the authority of a client under §§ 22 and 21(2);

(2) except as otherwise provided by law, must proceed as stated in §§ 96(2) and 96(3) with respect to an act of a constituent of the governmental client that violates a legal obligation that will likely cause substantial public or private injury or that reasonably can be foreseen to be imputable to and thus likely result in substantial injury to the client;

(3) if a prosecutor or similar lawyer determining whether to file criminal proceedings or take other steps in such proceedings, must do so only when based on probable cause and the lawyer's belief, formed after due investigation, that there are good factual and legal grounds to support the step taken; and

(4) must observe other applicable restrictions imposed by law on those similarly functioning for the governmental client.

§ 98. Statements to a Nonclient

A lawyer communicating on behalf of a client with a nonclient may not:

(1) knowingly make a false statement of material fact or law to the nonclient,

(2) make other statements prohibited by law; or

(3) fail to make a disclosure of information required by law.

§ 99. A Represented Nonclient—The General Anti–Contact Rule

(1) A lawyer representing a client in a matter may not communicate about the subject of the representation with a nonclient whom the lawyer knows to be represented in the matter by another lawyer or with a represen-

tative of an organizational nonclient so represented as defined in § 100, unless:

    (a) the communication is with a public officer or agency to the extent stated in § 101;

    (b) the lawyer is a party and represents no other client in the matter;

    (c) the communication is authorized by law;

    (d) the communication reasonably responds to an emergency; or

    (e) the other lawyer consents.

(2) Subsection (1) does not prohibit the lawyer from assisting the client in otherwise proper communication by the lawyer's client with a represented nonclient.

§ 100. Definition of a Represented Nonclient

Within the meaning of § 99, a represented nonclient includes:

    (1) a natural person represented by a lawyer; and:

    (2) a current employee or other agent of an organization represented by a lawyer:

        (a) if the employee or other agent supervises, directs, or regularly consults with the lawyer concerning the matter or if the agent has power to compromise or settle the matter;

        (b) if the acts or omissions of the employee or other agent may be imputed to the organization for purposes of civil or criminal liability in the matter; or

        (c) if a statement of the employee or other agent, under applicable rules of evidence, would have the effect of binding the organization with respect to proof of the matter.

§ 101. A Represented Governmental Agency or Officer

(1) Unless otherwise provided by law (see § 99(1)(c)) and except as provided in Subsection (2), the prohibition stated in § 99 against contact with a represented nonclient does not apply to communications with employees of a represented governmental agency or with a governmental officer being represented in the officer's official capacity.

(2) In negotiation or litigation by a lawyer of a specific claim of a client against a governmental agency or against a governmental officer in the officer's official capacity, the prohibition stated in § 99 applies, except that the lawyer may contact any officer of the government if permitted by the agency or with respect to an issue of general policy.

§ 102. Information of a Nonclient Known to be Legally Protected

A lawyer communicating with a nonclient in a situation permitted under § 99 may not seek to obtain information that the lawyer reasonably should know the nonclient may not reveal without violating a duty of confidentiality to another imposed by law.

§ 103. Dealings with an Unrepresented Nonclient

In the course of representing a client and dealing with a nonclient who is not represented by a lawyer:

> (1) the lawyer may not mislead the nonclient, to the prejudice of the nonclient, concerning the identity and interests of the person the lawyer represents; and

> (2) when the lawyer knows or reasonably should know that the unrepresented nonclient misunderstands the lawyer's role in the matter, the lawyer must make reasonable efforts to correct the misunderstanding when failure to do so would materially prejudice the nonclient.

§ 104. Representing a Client in Legislative and Administrative Matters

A lawyer representing a client before a legislature or administrative agency:

> (1) must disclose that the appearance is in a representative capacity and not misrepresent the capacity in which the lawyer appears;

> (2) must comply with applicable law and regulations governing such representations; and

> (3) except as applicable law otherwise provides:

>> (a) in an adjudicative proceeding before a government agency or involving such an agency as a participant, has the legal rights and responsibilities of an advocate in a proceeding before a judicial tribunal; and

>> (b) in other types of proceedings and matters, has the legal rights and responsibilities applicable in the lawyer's dealings with a private person.

§ 105. Complying with Law and Tribunal Rulings

In representing a client in a matter before a tribunal, a lawyer must comply with applicable law, including rules of procedure and evidence and specific tribunal rulings.

§ 106. Dealing with Other Participants in Proceedings

In representing a client in a matter before a tribunal, a lawyer may not use means that have no substantial purpose other than to embarrass, delay, or burden a third person or use methods of obtaining evidence that are prohibited by law.

§ 107. **Prohibited Forensic Tactics**

In representing a client in a matter before a tribunal, a lawyer may not, in the presence of the trier of fact:

(1) state a personal opinion about the justness of a cause, the credibility of a witness, the culpability of a civil litigant, or the guilt or innocence of an accused, but the lawyer may argue any position or conclusion adequately supported by the lawyer's analysis of the evidence; or

(2) allude to any matter that the lawyer does not reasonably believe is relevant or that will not be supported by admissible evidence.

§ 108. **An Advocate as a Witness**

(1) Except as provided in Subsection (2), a lawyer may not represent a client in a contested hearing or trial of a matter in which:

(a) the lawyer is expected to testify for the lawyer's client; or

(b) the lawyer does not intend to testify but (i) the lawyer's testimony would be material to establishing a claim or defense of the client, and (ii) the client has not consented as stated in § 122 to the lawyer's intention not to testify.

(2) A lawyer may represent a client when the lawyer will testify as stated in Subsection (1)(a) if:

(a) the lawyer's testimony relates to an issue that the lawyer reasonably believes will not be contested or to the nature and value of legal services rendered in the proceeding;

(b) deprivation of the lawyer's services as advocate would work a substantial hardship on the client; or

(c) consent has been given by (i) opposing parties who would be adversely affected by the lawyer's testimony and, (ii) if relevant, the lawyer's client, as stated in § 122 with respect to any conflict of interest between lawyer and client (see § 125) that the lawyer's testimony would create.

(3) A lawyer may not represent a client in a litigated matter pending before a tribunal when the lawyer or a lawyer in the lawyer's firm will give testimony materially adverse to the position of the lawyer's client or materially adverse to a former client of any such lawyer with respect to a matter substantially related to the earlier representation, unless the affected client has consented as stated in § 122 with respect to any conflict of interest between lawyer and client (see § 125) that the testimony would create.

(4) A tribunal should not permit a lawyer to call opposing trial counsel as a witness unless there is a compelling need for the lawyer's testimony.

§ 109. An Advocate's Public Comment on Pending Litigation

(1) In representing a client in a matter before a tribunal, a lawyer may not make a statement outside the proceeding that a reasonable person would expect to be disseminated by means of public communication when the lawyer knows or reasonably should know that the statement will have a substantial likelihood of materially prejudicing a juror or influencing or intimidating a prospective witness in the proceeding. However, a lawyer may in any event make a statement that is reasonably necessary to mitigate the impact on the lawyer's client of substantial, undue, and prejudicial publicity recently initiated by one other than the lawyer or the lawyer's client.

(2) A prosecutor must, except for statements necessary to inform the public of the nature and extent of the prosecutor's action and that serve a legitimate law-enforcement purpose, refrain from making extrajudicial comments that have a substantial likelihood of heightening public condemnation of the accused.

§ 110. Frivolous Advocacy

(1) A lawyer may not bring or defend a proceeding or assert or controvert an issue therein, unless there is a basis for doing so that is not frivolous, which includes a good-faith argument for an extension, modification, or reversal of existing law.

(2) Notwithstanding Subsection (1), a lawyer for the defendant in a criminal proceeding or the respondent in a proceeding that could result in incarceration may so defend the proceeding as to require that the prosecutor establish every necessary element.

(3) A lawyer may not make a frivolous discovery request, fail to make a reasonably diligent effort to comply with a proper discovery request of another party, or intentionally fail otherwise to comply with applicable procedural requirements concerning discovery.

§ 111. Disclosure of Legal Authority

In representing a client in a matter before a tribunal, a lawyer may not knowingly:

>   (1) make a false statement of a material proposition of law to the tribunal; or

>   (2) fail to disclose to the tribunal legal authority in the controlling jurisdiction known to the lawyer to be directly adverse to the position asserted by the client and not disclosed by opposing counsel.

§ 112. Advocacy in Ex Parte and Other Proceedings

In representing a client in a matter before a tribunal, a lawyer applying for ex parte relief or appearing in another proceeding in which similar special requirements of candor apply must comply with the requirements of § 110 and §§ 118–120 and further:

(1) must not present evidence the lawyer reasonably believes is false;

(2) must disclose all material and relevant facts known to the lawyer that will enable the tribunal to reach an informed decision; and

(3) must comply with any other applicable special requirements of candor imposed by law.

§ 113. Improperly Influencing a Judicial Officer

(1) A lawyer may not knowingly communicate ex parte with a judicial officer before whom a proceeding is pending concerning the matter, except as authorized by law.

(2) A lawyer may not make a gift or loan prohibited by law to a judicial officer, attempt to influence the officer otherwise than by legally proper procedures, or state or imply an ability so to influence a judicial officer.

§ 114. A Lawyer's Statements Concerning a Judicial Officer

A lawyer may not knowingly or recklessly make publicly a false statement of fact concerning the qualifications or integrity of an incumbent of a judicial office or a candidate for election to such an office.

§ 115. Lawyer Contact with a Juror

A lawyer may not:

(1) except as allowed by law, communicate with or seek to influence a person known by the lawyer to be a member of a jury pool from which the jury will be drawn;

(2) except as allowed by law, communicate with or seek to influence a member of a jury; or

(3) communicate with a juror who has been excused from further service:

(a) when that would harass the juror or constitute an attempt to influence the juror's actions as a juror in future cases; or

(b) when otherwise prohibited by law.

§ 116. Interviewing and Preparing a Prospective Witness

(1) A lawyer may interview a witness for the purpose of preparing the witness to testify.

(2) A lawyer may not unlawfully obstruct another party's access to a witness.

(3) A lawyer may not unlawfully induce or assist a prospective witness to evade or ignore process obliging the witness to appear to testify.

(4) A lawyer may not request a person to refrain from voluntarily giving relevant testimony or information to another party, unless:

(a) the person is the lawyer's client in the matter; or

415

(b) (i) the person is not the lawyer's client but is a relative or employee or other agent of the lawyer or the lawyer's client, and (ii) the lawyer reasonably believes compliance will not materially and adversely affect the person's interests.

§ 117. Compensating a Witness

A lawyer may not offer or pay to a witness any consideration:

(1) in excess of the reasonable expenses of the witness incurred and the reasonable value of the witness's time spent in providing evidence, except that an expert witness may be offered and paid a noncontingent fee;

(2) contingent on the content of the witness's testimony or the outcome of the litigation; or

(3) otherwise prohibited by law.

§ 118. Falsifying or Destroying Evidence

(1) A lawyer may not falsify documentary or other evidence.

(2) A lawyer may not destroy or obstruct another party's access to documentary or other evidence when doing so would violate a court order or other legal requirements, or counsel or assist a client to do so.

§ 119. Physical Evidence of a Client Crime

With respect to physical evidence of a client crime, a lawyer:

(1) may, when reasonably necessary for purposes of the representation, take possession of the evidence and retain it for the time reasonably necessary to examine it and subject it to tests that do not alter or destroy material characteristics of the evidence; but

(2) following possession under Subsection (1), the lawyer must notify prosecuting authorities of the lawyer's possession of the evidence or turn the evidence over to them.

§ 120. False Testimony or Evidence

(1) A lawyer may not:

(a) knowingly counsel or assist a witness to testify falsely or otherwise to offer false evidence;

(b) knowingly make a false statement of fact to the tribunal;

(c) offer testimony or other evidence as to an issue of fact known by the lawyer to be false.

(2) If a lawyer has offered testimony or other evidence as to a material issue of fact and comes to know of its falsity, the lawyer must take reasonable remedial measures and may disclose confidential client information when necessary to take such a measure.

(3) A lawyer may refuse to offer testimony or other evidence that the lawyer reasonably believes is false, even if the lawyer does not know it to be false.

§ 121. The Basic Prohibition of Conflicts of Interest

Unless all affected clients and other necessary persons consent to the representation under the limitations and conditions provided in § 122, a lawyer may not represent a client if the representation would involve a conflict of interest. A conflict of interest is involved if there is a substantial risk that the lawyer's representation of the client would be materially and adversely affected by the lawyer's own interests or by the lawyer's duties to another current client, a former client, or a third person.

§ 122. Client Consent to a Conflict of Interest

(1) A lawyer may represent a client notwithstanding a conflict of interest prohibited by § 121 if each affected client or former client gives informed consent to the lawyer's representation. Informed consent requires that the client or former client have reasonably adequate information about the material risks of such representation to that client or former client.

(2) Notwithstanding the informed consent of each affected client or former client, a lawyer may not represent a client if:

(a) the representation is prohibited by law;

(b) one client will assert a claim against the other in the same litigation; or

(c) in the circumstances, it is not reasonably likely that the lawyer will be able to provide adequate representation to one or more of the clients.

§ 123. Imputation of a Conflict of Interest to an Affiliated Lawyer

Unless all affected clients consent to the representation under the limitations and conditions provided in § 122 or unless imputation hereunder is removed as provided in § 124, the restrictions upon a lawyer imposed by §§ 125–135 also restrict other affiliated lawyers who:

(1) are associated with that lawyer in rendering legal services to others through a law partnership, professional corporation, sole proprietorship, or similar association;

(2) are employed with that lawyer by an organization to render legal services either to that organization or to others to advance the interests or objectives of the organization; or

(3) share office facilities without reasonably adequate measures to protect confidential client information so that it will not be available to other lawyers in the shared office.

417

§ 124.   Removing Imputation

(1) Imputation specified in § 123 does not restrict an affiliated lawyer when the affiliation between the affiliated lawyer and the personally prohibited lawyer that required the imputation has been terminated, and no material confidential information of the client, relevant to the matter, has been communicated by the personally prohibited lawyer to the affiliated lawyer or that lawyer's firm.

(2) Imputation specified in § 123 does not restrict an affiliated lawyer with respect to a former-client conflict under § 132, when there is no substantial risk that confidential information of the former client will be used with material adverse effect on the former client because:

(a) any confidential client information communicated to the personally prohibited lawyer is unlikely to be significant in the subsequent matter;

(b) the personally prohibited lawyer is subject to screening measures adequate to eliminate participation by that lawyer in the representation; and

(c) timely and adequate notice of the screening has been provided to all affected clients.

(3) Imputation specified in § 123 does not restrict a lawyer affiliated with a former government lawyer with respect to a conflict under § 133 if:

(a) the personally prohibited lawyer is subject to screening measures adequate to eliminate involvement by that lawyer in the representation; and

(b) timely and adequate notice of the screening has been provided to the appropriate government agency and to affected clients.

§ 125.   A Lawyer's Personal Interest Affecting the Representation of a Client

Unless the affected client consents to the representation under the limitations and conditions provided in § 122, a lawyer may not represent a client if there is a substantial risk that the lawyer's representation of the client would be materially and adversely affected by the lawyer's financial or other personal interests.

§ 126.   Business Transactions Between a Lawyer and a Client

A lawyer may not participate in a business or financial transaction with a client, except a standard commercial transaction in which the lawyer does not render legal services, unless:

(1) the client has adequate information about the terms of the transaction and the risks presented by the lawyer's involvement in it;

(2) the terms and circumstances of the transaction are fair and reasonable to the client; and

(3) the client consents to the lawyer's role in the transaction under the limitations and conditions provided in § 122 after being encouraged, and given a reasonable opportunity, to seek independent legal advice concerning the transaction.

§ 127. A Client Gift to a Lawyer

(1) A lawyer may not prepare any instrument effecting any gift from a client to the lawyer, including a testamentary gift, unless the lawyer is a relative or other natural object of the client's generosity and the gift is not significantly disproportionate to those given other donees similarly related to the donor.

(2) A lawyer may not accept a gift from a client, including a testamentary gift, unless:

(a) the lawyer is a relative or other natural object of the client's generosity;

(b) the value conferred by the client and the benefit to the lawyer are insubstantial in amount; or

(c) the client, before making the gift, has received independent advice or has been encouraged, and given a reasonable opportunity, to seek such advice.

§ 128. Representing Clients with Conflicting Interests in Civil Litigation

Unless all affected clients consent to the representation under the limitations and conditions provided in § 122, a lawyer in civil litigation may not:

(1) represent two or more clients in a matter if there is a substantial risk that the lawyer's representation of one client would be materially and adversely affected by the lawyer's duties to another client in the matter; or

(2) represent one client to assert or defend a claim against or brought by another client currently represented by the lawyer, even if the matters are not related.

§ 129. Conflicts of Interest in Criminal Litigation

Unless all affected clients consent to the representation under the limitations and conditions provided in § 122, a lawyer in a criminal matter may not represent:

(1) two or more defendants or potential defendants in the same matter; or

(2) a single defendant, if the representation would involve a conflict of interest as defined in § 121.

§ 130. Multiple Representation in a Nonlitigated Matter

Unless all affected clients consent to the representation under the limitations and conditions provided in § 122, a lawyer may not represent two or more clients in a matter not involving litigation if there is a substantial risk that the lawyer's representation of one or more of the clients would be materially and adversely affected by the lawyer's duties to one or more of the other clients.

§ 131. Conflicts of Interest in Representing an Organization

Unless all affected clients consent to the representation under the limitations and conditions provided in § 122, a lawyer may not represent both an organization and a director, officer, employee, shareholder, owner, partner, member, or other individual or organization associated with the organization if there is a substantial risk that the lawyer's representation of either would be materially and adversely affected by the lawyer's duties to the other.

§ 132. A Representation Adverse to the Interests of a Former Client

Unless both the affected present and former clients consent to the representation under the limitations and conditions provided in § 122, a lawyer who has represented a client in a matter may not thereafter represent another client in the same or a substantially related matter in which the interests of the former client are materially adverse. The current matter is substantially related to the earlier matter if:

(1) the current matter involves the work the lawyer performed for the former client; or

(2) there is a substantial risk that representation of the present client will involve the use of information acquired in the course of representing the former client, unless that information has become generally known.

§ 133. A Former Government Lawyer or Officer

(1) A lawyer may not act on behalf of a client with respect to a matter in which the lawyer participated personally and substantially while acting as a government lawyer or officer unless both the government and the client consent to the representation under the limitations and conditions provided in § 122.

(2) A lawyer who acquires confidential information while acting as a government lawyer or officer may not:

(a) if the information concerns a person, represent a client whose interests are materially adverse to that person in a matter in which the information could be used to the material disadvantage of that person; or

(b) if the information concerns the governmental client or employer, represent another public or private client in circumstances described in § 132(2).

§ 134. Compensation or Direction of a Lawyer by a Third Person

(1) A lawyer may not represent a client if someone other than the client will wholly or partly compensate the lawyer for the representation, unless the client consents under the limitations and conditions provided in § 122 and knows of the circumstances and conditions of the payment.

(2) A lawyer's professional conduct on behalf of a client may be directed by someone other than the client if:

(a) the direction does not interfere with the lawyer's independence of professional judgment;

(b) the direction is reasonable in scope and character, such as by reflecting obligations borne by the person directing the lawyer; and

(c) the client consents to the direction under the limitations and conditions provided in § 122.

§ 135. A Lawyer with a Fiduciary or Other Legal Obligation to a Nonclient

Unless the affected client consents to the representation under the limitations and conditions provided in § 122, a lawyer may not represent a client in any matter with respect to which the lawyer has a fiduciary or other legal obligation to another if there is a substantial risk that the lawyer's representation of the client would be materially and adversely affected by the lawyer's obligation.

RULES OF PROFESSIONAL CONDUCT OF THE STATE BAR OF CALIFORNIA

(Adopted by the Board of Governors, Effective May 27, 1989.
Including Amendments Received Through Sept. 1, 2002)

Table of Rules

CHAPTER 1. PROFESSIONAL INTEGRITY IN GENERAL

RULE 1–100. Rules of Professional Conduct, in General

(A) Purpose and Function. The following rules are intended to regulate professional conduct of members of the State Bar through discipline. They have been adopted by the Board of Governors of the State Bar of California and approved by the Supreme Court of California pursuant to Business and Professions Code sections 6076 and 6077 to protect the public and to promote respect and confidence in the legal profession. These rules together with any standards adopted by the Board of Governors pursuant to these rules shall be binding upon all members of the State Bar.

For a willful breach of any of these rules, the Board of Governors has the power to discipline members as provided by law.

The prohibition of certain conduct in these rules is not exclusive. Members are also bound by applicable law including the State Bar Act (Bus. & Prof.Code, § 6000 et seq.) and opinions of California courts. Although not binding, opinions of ethics committees in California should be consulted by members for guidance on proper professional conduct. Ethics opinions and rules and standards promulgated by other jurisdictions and bar associations may also be considered.

These rules are not intended to create new civil causes of action. Nothing in these rules shall be deemed to create, augment, diminish, or eliminate any substantive legal duty of lawyers or the non-disciplinary consequences of violating such a duty.

(B) Definitions.

(1) "Law Firm" means:

(a) two or more lawyers whose activities constitute the practice of law, and who share its profits, expenses, and liabilities; or

(b) a law corporation which employs more than one lawyer; or

(c) a division, department, office, or group within a business entity, which includes more than one lawyer who performs legal services for the business entity; or

(d) a publicly funded entity which employs more than one lawyer to perform legal services.

(2) "Member" means a member of the State Bar of California.

(3) "Lawyer" means a member of the State Bar of California or a person who is admitted in good standing of and eligible to practice before the bar of any United States court or the highest court of the District of Columbia or any state, territory, or insular possession of the United States, or is licensed to practice law in, or is admitted in good standing and eligible to practice before the bar of the highest court of a foreign country or any political subdivision thereof.

(4) "Associate" means an employee or fellow employee who is employed as a lawyer.

(5) "Shareholder" means a shareholder in a professional corporation pursuant to Business and Professions Code section 6160 et seq.

(C) Purpose of Discussions. Because it is a practical impossibility to convey in black letter form all of the nuances of these disciplinary rules, the comments contained in the Discussions of the rules, while they do not add independent basis for imposing discipline, are intended to provide guidance for interpreting the rules and practicing in compliance with them.

(D) Geographic Scope of Rules.

(1) *As to members:* These rules shall govern the activities of members in and outside this state, except as members lawfully practicing outside this state may be specifically required by a jurisdiction in which they are practicing to follow rules of professional conduct different from these rules.

(2) *As to lawyers from other jurisdictions who are not members:* These rules shall also govern the activities of lawyers while engaged in the performance of lawyer functions in this state; but nothing contained in these rules shall be deemed to authorize the performance of such functions by such persons in this state except as otherwise permitted by law.

(E) These rules may be cited and referred to as "Rules of Professional Conduct of the State Bar of California."

Discussion

The Rules of Professional Conduct are intended to establish the standards for members for purposes of discipline. (See *Ames v. State Bar* (1973) 8 Cal.3d 910 [106 Cal.Rptr. 489].) The fact that a member has engaged in conduct that may be contrary to these rules does not automatically give rise to a civil cause of action. (See *Noble v. Sears, Roebuck & Co.* (1973) 33 Cal.App.3d 654 [109 Cal.Rptr. 269]; *Wilhelm v. Pray, Price, Williams & Russell* (1986) 186 Cal.App.3d 1324 [231

Cal.Rptr. 355].) These rules are not intended to supercede existing law relating to members in non-disciplinary contexts. (See, e.g., *Klemm v. Superior Court* (1977) 75 Cal.App.3d 893 [142 Cal.Rptr. 509] (motion for disqualification of counsel due to a conflict of interest); *Academy of California Optometrists, Inc. v. Superior Court* (1975) 51 Cal.App.3d 999 [124 Cal.Rptr. 668] (duty to return client files); *Chronometrics, Inc. v. Sysgen, Inc.* (1980) 110 Cal.App.3d 597 [168 Cal.Rptr. 196] (disqualification of member appropriate remedy for improper communication with adverse party).)

Law firm, as defined by subparagraph (B)(1), is not intended to include an association of lawyers who do not share profits, expenses, and liabilities. The subparagraph is not intended to imply that a law firm may include a person who is not a member in violation of the law governing the unauthorized practice of law.

RULE 1–110. Disciplinary Authority of the State Bar

A member shall comply with conditions attached to public or private reprovals or other discipline administered by the State Bar pursuant to Business and Professions Code sections 6077 and 6078 and rule 956, California Rules of Court.

RULE 1–120. Assisting, Soliciting, or Inducing Violations

A member shall not knowingly assist in, solicit, or induce any violation of these rules or the State Bar Act.

RULE 1–200. False Statement Regarding Admission to the State Bar

(A) A member shall not knowingly make a false statement regarding a material fact or knowingly fail to disclose a material fact in connection with an application for admission to the State Bar.

(B) A member shall not further an application for admission to the State Bar of a person whom the member knows to be unqualified in respect to character, education, or other relevant attributes.

(C) This rule shall not prevent a member from serving as counsel of record for an applicant for admission to practice in proceedings related to such admission.

Discussion

For purposes of rule 1–200 "admission" includes readmission.

RULE 1–300. Unauthorized Practice of Law

(A) A member shall not aid any person or entity in the unauthorized practice of law.

(B) A member shall not practice law in a jurisdiction where to do so would be in violation of regulations of the profession in that jurisdiction.

RULE 1–310. Forming a Partnership With a Non-lawyer

A member shall not form a partnership with a person who is not a lawyer if any of the activities of that partnership consist of the practice of law.

Discussion

Rule 1–310 is not intended to govern members' activities which cannot be considered to constitute the practice of law. It is intended solely to preclude a member from being involved in the practice of law with a person who is not a lawyer.

RULE 1–311. Employment of Disbarred, Suspended, Resigned, or Involuntarily Inactive Member

(A) For purposes of this rule:

(1) "Employ" means to engage the services of another, including employees, agents, independent contractors and consultants, regardless of whether any compensation is paid;

(2) "Involuntarily inactive member" means a member who is ineligible to practice law as a result of action taken pursuant to Business and Professions Code sections 6007, 6203(c), or California Rule of Court 958(d); and

(3) "Resigned member" means a member who has resigned from the State Bar while disciplinary charges are pending.

(B) A member shall not employ, associate professionally with, or aid a person the member knows or reasonably should know is a disbarred, suspended, resigned, or involuntarily inactive member to perform the following on behalf of the member's client:

(1) Render legal consultation or advice to the client;

(2) Appear on behalf of a client in any hearing or proceeding or before any judicial officer, arbitrator, mediator, court, public agency, referee, magistrate, commissioner, or hearing officer;

(3) Appear as a representative of the client at a deposition or other discovery matter;

(4) Negotiate or transact any matter for or on behalf of the client with third parties;

(5) Receive, disburse or otherwise handle the client's funds; or

(6) Engage in activities which constitute the practice of law.

(C) A member may employ, associate professionally with, or aid a disbarred, suspended, resigned, or involuntarily inactive member to perform research, drafting or clerical activities, including but not limited to:

(1) Legal work of a preparatory nature, such as legal research, the assemblage of data and other necessary information, drafting of pleadings, briefs, and other similar documents;

(2) Direct communication with the client or third parties regarding matters such as scheduling, billing, updates, confirmation of receipt or sending of correspondence and messages; or

(3) Accompanying an active member in attending a deposition or other discovery matter for the limited purpose of providing clerical assistance to the active member who will appear as the representative of the client.

(D) Prior to or at the time of employing a person the member knows or reasonably should know is a disbarred, suspended, resigned, or involuntarily inactive member, the member shall serve upon the State Bar written notice of the employment, including a full description of such person's current bar status. The written notice shall also list the activities prohibited in paragraph (B) and state that the disbarred, suspended, resigned, or involuntarily inactive member will not perform such activities. The member shall serve similar written notice upon each client on whose specific matter such person will work, prior to or at the time of employing such person to work on the client's specific matter. The member shall obtain proof of service of the client's written notice and shall retain such proof and a true and correct copy of the client's written notice for two years following termination of the member's employment with the client.

(E) A member may, without client or State Bar notification, employ a disbarred, suspended, resigned or involuntarily inactive member whose sole function is to perform office physical plant or equipment maintenance, courier or delivery services, catering, reception, typing or transcription, or other similar support activities.

(F) Upon termination of the disbarred, suspended, resigned, or involuntarily inactive member, the member shall promptly serve upon the State Bar written notice of the termination.

Discussion

For discussion of the activities that constitute the practice of law, see Farnham v. State Bar (1976) 17 Cal.3d 605 [131 Cal.Rptr. 611]; Bluestein v. State Bar (1974) 13 Cal.3d 162 [118 Cal.Rptr. 175]; Baron v. City of Los Angeles (1970) 2 Cal.3d 535 [86 Cal.Rptr. 673]; Crawford v. State Bar (1960) 54 Cal.2d 659 [7 Cal.Rptr. 746]; People v. Merchants Protective Corporation (1922) 189 Cal. 531 [209 P. 363]; People v. Landlords Professional Services (1989) 215 Cal.App.3d 1599 [264 Cal.Rptr. 548]; and People v. Sipper (1943) 61 Cal.App.2d Supp. 844 [142 P.2d 960].

Paragraph (D) is not intended to prevent or discourage a member from fully discussing with the client the activities that will be performed by the disbarred, suspended, resigned, or involuntarily inactive member on the client's matter. If a member's client is an organization, then the written notice required by paragraph (D) shall be served upon the highest authorized officer, employee, or constituent overseeing the particular engagement. (See rule 3–600.)

Nothing in rule 1–311 shall be deemed to limit or preclude any activity engaged in pursuant to rules 983, 983.1, 983.2, 988 of the California Rules of

Court, or any local rule of a federal district court concerning admission pro hac vice.

RULE 1–320. Financial Arrangements With Non-lawyers

(A) Neither a member nor a law firm shall directly or indirectly share legal fees with a person who is not a lawyer except that:

(1) An agreement between a member and a law firm, partner, or associate may provide for the payment of money after the member's death to the member's estate or to one or more specified persons over a reasonable period of time; or

(2) A member or law firm undertaking to complete unfinished legal business of a deceased member may pay to the estate of the deceased member or other person legally entitled thereto that proportion of the total compensation which fairly represents the services rendered by the deceased member;

(3) A member or law firm may include non-member employees in a compensation, profit-sharing, or retirement plan even though the plan is based in whole or in part on a profit-sharing arrangement, if such plan does not circumvent these rules or Business and Professions Code section 6000 et seq.; or

(4) A member may pay a prescribed registration, referral, or participation fee to a lawyer referral service established, sponsored, and operated in accordance with the State Bar of California's Minimum Standards for a Lawyer Referral Service in California.

(B) A member shall not compensate, give, or promise anything of value to any person or entity for the purpose of recommending or securing employment of the member or the member's law firm by a client, or as a reward for having made a recommendation resulting in employment of the member or the member's law firm by a client. A member's offering of or giving a gift or gratuity to any person or entity having made a recommendation resulting in the employment of the member or the member's law firm shall not of itself violate this rule, provided that the gift or gratuity was not offered or given in consideration of any promise, agreement, or understanding that such a gift or gratuity would be forthcoming or that referrals would be made or encouraged in the future.

(C) A member shall not compensate, give, or promise anything of value to any representative of the press, radio, television, or other communication medium in anticipation of or in return for publicity of the member, the law firm, or any other member as such in a news item, but the incidental provision of food or beverage shall not of itself violate this rule.

Discussion

Rule 1–320(C) is not intended to preclude compensation to the communications media in exchange for advertising the member's or law firm's availability for professional employment.

RULE 1–400. Advertising and Solicitation

(A) For purposes of this rule, "communication" means any message or offer made by or on behalf of a member concerning the availability for professional employment of a member or a law firm directed to any former, present, or prospective client, including but not limited to the following:

(1) Any use of firm name, trade name, fictitious name, or other professional designation of such member or law firm; or

(2) Any stationery, letterhead, business card, sign, brochure, or other comparable written material describing such member, law firm, or lawyers; or

(3) Any advertisement (regardless of medium) of such member or law firm directed to the general public or any substantial portion thereof; or

(4) Any unsolicited correspondence from a member or law firm directed to any person or entity.

(B) For purposes of this rule, a "solicitation" means any communication:

(1) Concerning the availability for professional employment of a member or a law firm in which a significant motive is pecuniary gain; and

(2) Which is;

(a) delivered in person or by telephone, or

(b) directed by any means to a person known to the sender to be represented by counsel in a matter which is a subject of the communication.

(C) A solicitation shall not be made by or on behalf of a member or law firm to a prospective client with whom the member or law firm has no family or prior professional relationship, unless the solicitation is protected from abridgment by the Constitution of the United States or by the Constitution of the State of California. A solicitation to a former or present client in the discharge of a member's or law firm's professional duties is not prohibited.

(D) A communication or a solicitation (as defined herein) shall not:

(1) Contain any untrue statement; or

(2) Contain any matter, or present or arrange any matter in a manner or format which is false, deceptive, or which tends to confuse, deceive, or mislead the public; or

(3) Omit to state any fact necessary to make the statements made, in the light of circumstances under which they are made, not misleading to the public; or

(4) Fail to indicate clearly, expressly, or by context, that it is a communication or solicitation, as the case may be; or

(5) Be transmitted in any manner which involves intrusion, coercion, duress, compulsion, intimidation, threats, or vexatious or harassing conduct.

(6) State that a member is a "certified specialist" unless the member holds a current certificate as a specialist issued by the Board of Legal Specialization, or any other entity accredited by the State Bar to designate specialists pursuant to standards adopted by the Board of Governors, and states the complete name of the entity which granted certification.

(E) The Board of Governors of the State Bar shall formulate and adopt standards as to communications which will be presumed to violate this rule 1–400. The standards shall only be used as presumptions affecting the burden of proof in disciplinary proceedings involving alleged violations of these rules. "Presumption affecting the burden of proof" means that presumption defined in Evidence Code sections 605 and 606. Such standards formulated and adopted by the Board, as from time to time amended, shall be effective and binding on all members.

(F) A member shall retain for two years a true and correct copy or recording of any communication made by written or electronic media. Upon written request, the member shall make any such copy or recording available to the State Bar, and, if requested, shall provide to the State Bar evidence to support any factual or objective claim contained in the communication.

Standards:

Pursuant to rule 1–400(E) the Board of Governors of the State Bar has adopted the following standards, effective May 27, 1989 as forms of "communication" defined in rule 1–400(A) which are presumed to be in violation of rule 1–400:

(1) A "communication" which contains guarantees, warranties, or predictions regarding the result of the representation.

(2) A "communication" which contains testimonials about or endorsements of a member unless such communication also contains an express disclaimer such as "this testimonial or endorsement does not constitute a guarantee, warranty, or prediction regarding the outcome of your legal matter."

(3) A "communication" which is delivered to a potential client whom the member knows or should reasonably have known is in such a physical, emotional, or mental state that he or she would not be expected to exercise reasonable judgment as to the retention of counsel.

(4) A "communication" which is transmitted at the scene of an accident or at or en route to a hospital, emergency care center, or other health care facility.

(5) A "communication," except professional announcements, seeking professional employment for pecuniary gain, which is transmitted by mail or equivalent means which does not bear the word "Advertisement,"

"Newsletter" or words of similar import in 12 point print on the first page. If such communication, including firm brochures, newsletters, recent legal developments advisories and similar materials, is transmitted in an envelope, the envelope shall bear the word "Advertisement," "Newsletter" or words of similar import on the outside thereof.

(6) A "communication" in the form of a firm name, trade name, fictitious name, or other professional designation which states or implies a relationship between any member in private practice and a government agency or instrumentality or a public or non-profit legal services organization.

(7) A "communication" in the form of a firm name, trade name, fictitious name, or other professional designation which states or implies that a member has a relationship to any other member or a law firm as a partner or associate, or officer or shareholder pursuant to Business and Professions Code sections 6160–6172 unless such relationship in fact exists.

(8) A "communication" which states or implies that a member or law firm is "of counsel" to another member or a law firm unless the former has a relationship with the latter (other than as a partner or associate, or officer or shareholder pursuant to Business and Professions Code sections 6160–6172) which is close, personal, continuous, and regular.

(9) A "communication" in the form of a firm name, trade name, fictitious name, or other professional designation used by a member or law firm in private practice which differs materially from any other such designation used by such member or law firm at the same time in the same community.

(10) A "communication" which implies that the member or member's law firm is participating in a lawyer referral service which has been certified by the State Bar of California or as having satisfied the Minimum Standards for Lawyer Referral Services in California, when that is not the case.

(11) [Repealed, effective June 1, 1997.]

(12) A "communication," except professional announcements, in the form of an advertisement primarily directed to seeking professional employment primarily for pecuniary gain transmitted to the general public or any substantial portion thereof by mail or equivalent means or by means of television, radio, newspaper, magazine or other form of commercial mass media which does not state the name of the member responsible for the communication. When the communication is made on behalf of a law firm, the communication shall state the name of at least one member responsible for it.

(13) A "communication" which contains a dramatization unless such communication contains a disclaimer which states "this is a dramatization" or words of similar import.

(14) A "communication" which states or implies "no fee without recovery" unless such communication also expressly discloses whether or not the client will be liable for costs.

(15) A "communication" which states or implies that a member is able to provide legal services in a language other than English unless the member can actually provide legal services in such language or the communication also states in the language of the communication (a) the employment title of the person who speaks such language and (b) that the person is not a member of the State Bar of California, if that is the case.

(16) An unsolicited "communication" transmitted to the general public or any substantial portion thereof primarily directed to seeking professional employment primarily for pecuniary gain which sets forth a specific fee or range of fees for a particular service where, in fact, the member charges a greater fee than advertised in such communication within a period of 90 days following dissemination of such communication, unless such communication expressly specifies a shorter period of time regarding the advertised fee. Where the communication is published in the classified or "yellow pages" section of telephone, business or legal directories or in other media not published more frequently than once a year, the member shall conform to the advertised fee for a period of one year from initial publication, unless such communication expressly specifies a shorter period of time regarding the advertised fee.

RULE 1–500. Agreements Restricting a Member's Practice

(A) A member shall not be a party to or participate in offering or making an agreement, whether in connection with the settlement of a lawsuit or otherwise, if the agreement restricts the right of a member to practice law, except that this rule shall not prohibit such an agreement which:

(1) Is a part of an employment, shareholders', or partnership agreement among members provided the restrictive agreement does not survive the termination of the employment, shareholder, or partnership relationship; or

(2) Requires payments to a member upon the member's retirement from the practice of law; or

(3) Is authorized by Business and Professions Code sections 6092.5, subdivision (i) or 6093.

(B) A member shall not be a party to or participate in offering or making an agreement which precludes the reporting of a violation of these rules.

Discussion

Paragraph (A) makes it clear that the practice, in connection with settlement agreements, of proposing that a member refrain from representing other clients in similar litigation, is prohibited. Neither counsel may demand or suggest such provisions nor may opposing counsel accede or agree to such provisions.

Paragraph (A) permits a restrictive covenant in a law corporation, partnership, or employment agreement. The law corporation shareholder, partner, or associate may agree not to have a separate practice during the existence of the relationship; however, upon termination of the relationship (whether voluntary or involuntary), the member is free to practice law without any contractual restriction except in the case of retirement from the active practice of law.

RULE 1–600. Legal Service Programs

(A) A member shall not participate in a nongovernmental program, activity, or organization furnishing, recommending, or paying for legal services, which allows any third person or organization to interfere with the member's independence of professional judgment, or with the client-lawyer relationship, or allows unlicensed persons to practice law, or allows any third person or organization to receive directly or indirectly any part of the consideration paid to the member except as permitted by these rules, or otherwise violates the State Bar Act or these rules.

(B) The Board of Governors of the State Bar shall formulate and adopt Minimum Standards for Lawyer Referral Services, which, as from time to time amended, shall be binding on members.

Discussion

The participation of a member in a lawyer referral service established, sponsored, supervised, and operated in conformity with the Minimum Standards for a Lawyer Referral Service in California is encouraged and is not, of itself, a violation of these rules.

Rule 1–600 is not intended to override any contractual agreement or relationship between insurers and insureds regarding the provision of legal services.

Rule 1–600 is not intended to apply to the activities of a public agency responsible for providing legal services to a government or to the public.

For purposes of paragraph (A), "a nongovernmental program, activity, or organization" includes, but is not limited to group, prepaid, and voluntary legal service programs, activities, or organizations.

RULE 1–700. Member as Candidate for Judicial Office

(A) A member who is a candidate for judicial office in California shall comply with Canon 5 of the Code of Judicial Ethics.

(B) For purposes of this rule "candidate for judicial office" means a member seeking judicial office by election. The determination of when a member is a candidate for judicial office is defined in the terminology section of the California Code of Judicial Ethics. A member's duty to comply with paragraph (A) shall end when the member announces withdrawal of the member's candidacy or when the results of the election are final, whichever occurs first.

Discussion

Nothing in rule 1–700 shall be deemed to limit the applicability of any other rule or law.

RULE 1–710. Member as Temporary Judge, Referee, or Court-Appointed Arbitrator

A member who is serving as a temporary judge, referee, or court-appointed arbitrator, and is subject under the Code of Judicial Ethics to Canon 6D, shall comply with the terms of that canon.

Discussion

This rule is intended to permit the State Bar to discipline members who violate applicable portions of the Code of Judicial Ethics while acting in a judicial capacity pursuant to an order or appointment by a court.

Nothing in rule 1–710 shall be deemed to limit the applicability of any other rule or law.

CHAPTER 2.   RELATIONSHIP AMONG MEMBERS

RULE 2–100.   Communication With a Represented Party

(A) While representing a client, a member shall not communicate directly or indirectly about the subject of the representation with a party the member knows to be represented by another lawyer in the matter, unless the member has the consent of the other lawyer.

(B) For purposes of this rule, a "party" includes:

(1) An officer, director, or managing agent of a corporation or association, and a partner or managing agent of a partnership; or

(2) An association member or an employee of an association, corporation, or partnership, if the subject of the communication is any act or omission of such person in connection with the matter which may be binding upon or imputed to the organization for purposes of civil or criminal liability or whose statement may constitute an admission on the part of the organization.

(C) This rule shall not prohibit:

(1) Communications with a public officer, board, committee, or body;

(2) Communications initiated by a party seeking advice or representation from an independent lawyer of the party's choice; or

(3) Communications otherwise authorized by law.

Discussion

Rule 2–100 is intended to control communications between a member and persons the member knows to be represented by counsel unless a statutory scheme or case law will override the rule. There are a number of express statutory schemes which authorize communications between a member and person who would otherwise be subject to this rule. These statutes protect a variety of other rights such as the right of employees to organize and to engage in collective bargaining, employee health and safety, or equal employment opportunity. Other applicable law also includes the authority of government prosecutors and investigators to conduct criminal investigations, as limited by the relevant decisional law.

Rule 2–100 is not intended to prevent the parties themselves from communicating with respect to the subject matter of the representation, and nothing in the rule prevents a member from advising the client that such communication can be made. Moreover, the rule does not prohibit a member who is also a party to a legal matter from directly or indirectly communicating on his or her own behalf with a represented party. Such a member has independent rights as a party which should not be abrogated because of his or her professional status. To prevent any possible abuse in such situations, the counsel for the opposing party may advise that party (1) about the risks and benefits of communications with a lawyer-party, and (2) not to accept or engage in communications with the lawyer-party.

Rule 2–100 also addresses the situation in which member A is contacted by an opposing party who is represented and, because of dissatisfaction with that party's counsel, seeks A's independent advice. Since A is employed by the opposition, the member cannot give independent advice.

As used in paragraph (A), "the subject of the representation," "matter," and "party" are not limited to a litigation context.

Paragraph (B) is intended to apply only to persons employed at the time of the communication. (See *Triple A Machine Shop, Inc. v. State of California* (1989) 213 Cal.App.3d 131 [261 Cal.Rptr. 493].)

Subparagraph (C)(2) is intended to permit a member to communicate with a party seeking to hire new counsel or to obtain a second opinion. A member contacted by such a party continues to be bound by other Rules of Professional Conduct. (See, e.g., rules 1–400 and 3–310.)

RULE 2–200. Financial Arrangements Among Lawyers

(A) A member shall not divide a fee for legal services with a lawyer who is not a partner of, associate of, or shareholder with the member unless:

(1) The client has consented in writing thereto after a full disclosure has been made in writing that a division of fees will be made and the terms of such division; and

(2) The total fee charged by all lawyers is not increased solely by reason of the provision for division of fees and is not unconscionable as that term is defined in rule 4–200.

(B) Except as permitted in paragraph (A) of this rule or rule 2–300, a member shall not compensate, give, or promise anything of value to any lawyer for the purpose of recommending or securing employment of the member or the member's law firm by a client, or as a reward for having made a recommendation resulting in employment of the member or the member's law firm by a client. A member's offering of or giving a gift or gratuity to any lawyer who has made a recommendation resulting in the employment of the member or the member's law firm shall not of itself violate this rule, provided that the gift or gratuity was not offered in consideration of any promise, agreement, or understanding that such a gift or gratuity would be forthcoming or that referrals would be made or encouraged in the future.

RULE 2–300. Sale or Purchase of a Law Practice of a Member, Living or Deceased

All or substantially all of the law practice of a member, living or deceased, including goodwill, may be sold to another member or law firm subject to all the following conditions:

(A) Fees charged to clients shall not be increased solely by reason of such sale.

(B) If the sale contemplates the transfer of responsibility for work not yet completed or responsibility for client files or information protected by Business and Professions Code section 6068, subdivision (e), then:

(1) if the seller is deceased or has a conservator or other person acting in a representative capacity, and no member has been appointed to act for the seller pursuant to Business and Professions Code section 6180.5, then prior to the transfer;

(a) the purchaser shall cause a written notice to be given to the client stating that the interest in the law practice is being transferred to the purchaser; that the client has the right to retain other counsel; that the client may take possession of any client papers and property, as required by rule 3–700(D); and that if no response is received to the notification within 90 days of the sending of such notice, or in the event the client's rights would be prejudiced by a failure to act during that time, the purchaser may act on behalf of the client until otherwise notified by the client. Such notice shall comply with the requirements as set forth in rule 1–400(D) and any provisions relating to attorney-client fee arrangements, and

(b) the purchaser shall obtain the written consent of the client provided that such consent shall be presumed until otherwise notified by the client if no response is received to the notification specified in subparagraph (a) within 90 days of the date of the sending of such notification to the client's last address as shown on the records of the seller, or the client's rights would be prejudiced by a failure to act during such 90-day period.

(2) in all other circumstances, not less than 90 days prior to the transfer;

(a) the seller, or the member appointed to act for the seller pursuant to Business and Professions Code Section 6180.5, shall cause a written notice to be given to the client stating that the interest in the law practice is being transferred to the purchaser; that the client has the right to retain other counsel; that the client may take possession of any client papers and property, as required by rule 3–700(D); and that if no response is received to the notification within 90 days of the sending of such notice, the purchaser may act on behalf of the client until otherwise notified by the client. Such notice shall comply with the requirements as set forth in rule 1–400(D) and any provisions relating to attorney-client fee arrangements, and

(b) the seller, or the member appointed to act for the seller pursuant to Business and Professions Code section 6180.5, shall obtain the written consent of the client prior to the transfer provided that such consent shall be presumed until otherwise notified by the client if no response is received to the notification specified in subparagraph (a) within 90 days of the date of the sending of such notification to the client's last address as shown on the records of the seller.

(C) If substitution is required by the rules of a tribunal in which a matter is pending, all steps necessary to substitute a member shall be taken.

(D) All activity of a purchaser or potential purchaser under this rule shall be subject to compliance with rules 3–300 and 3–310 where applicable.

(E) Confidential information shall not be disclosed to a non-member in connection with a sale under this rule.

(F) Admission to or retirement from a law partnership or law corporation, retirement plans and similar arrangements, or sale of tangible assets of a law practice shall not be deemed a sale or purchase under this rule.

Discussion

Paragraph (A) is intended to prohibit the purchaser from charging the former clients of the seller a higher fee than the purchaser is charging his or her existing clients.

"All or substantially all of the law practice of a member" means, for purposes of rule 2–300 that, for example, a member may retain one or two clients who have such a longstanding personal and professional relationship with the member that transfer of those clients' files is not feasible. Conversely, rule 2–300 is not intended to authorize the sale of a law practice in a piecemeal fashion except as may be required by subparagraph (B)(1)(a) or paragraph (D).

Transfer of individual client matters, where permitted, is governed by rule 2–200. Payment of a fee to a non-lawyer broker for arranging the sale or purchase of a law practice is governed by rule 1–320.

RULE 2–400. Prohibited Discriminatory Conduct in a Law Practice

(A) For purposes of this rule:

(1) "law practice" includes sole practices, law partnerships, law corporations, corporate and governmental legal departments, and other entities which employ members to practice law;

(2) "knowingly permit" means a failure to advocate corrective action where the member knows of a discriminatory policy or practice which results in the unlawful discrimination prohibited in paragraph (B); and

(3) "unlawfully" and "unlawful" shall be determined by reference to applicable state or federal statutes or decisions making unlawful discrimination in employment and in offering goods and services to the public.

(B) In the management or operation of a law practice, a member shall not unlawfully discriminate or knowingly permit unlawful discrimination on the basis of race, national origin, sex, sexual orientation, religion, age or disability in:

(1) hiring, promoting, discharging or otherwise determining the conditions of employment of any person; or

(2) accepting or terminating representation of any client.

(C) No disciplinary investigation or proceeding may be initiated by the State Bar against a member under this rule unless and until a tribunal of competent jurisdiction, other than a disciplinary tribunal, shall have first adjudicated a complaint of alleged discrimination and found that unlawful conduct occurred. Upon such adjudication, the tribunal finding or verdict shall then be admissible evidence of the occurrence or non-occurrence of the alleged discrimination in any disciplinary proceeding initiated under this rule. In order for discipline to be imposed under this rule, however, the finding of unlawfulness must be upheld and final after appeal, the time for filing an appeal must have expired, or the appeal must have been dismissed.

Discussion

In order for discriminatory conduct to be actionable under this rule, it must first be found to be unlawful by an appropriate civil administrative or judicial tribunal under applicable state or federal law. Until there is a finding of civil unlawfulness, there is no basis for disciplinary action under this rule.

A complaint of misconduct based on this rule may be filed with the State Bar following a finding of unlawfulness in the first instance even though that finding is thereafter appealed.

A disciplinary investigation or proceeding for conduct coming within this rule may be initiated and maintained, however, if such conduct warrants discipline under California Business and Professions Code sections 6106 and 6068, the California Supreme Court's inherent authority to impose discipline, or other disciplinary standard.

CHAPTER 3. PROFESSIONAL RELATIONSHIP WITH CLIENTS

RULE 3–110. Failing to Act Competently

(A) A member shall not intentionally, recklessly, or repeatedly fail to perform legal services with competence.

(B) For purposes of this rule, "competence" in any legal service shall mean to apply the 1) diligence, 2) learning and skill, and 3) mental, emotional, and physical ability reasonably necessary for the performance of such service.

(C) If a member does not have sufficient learning and skill when the legal service is undertaken the member may nonetheless perform such services competently by 1) associating with or where appropriate, professionally consulting another lawyer reasonably believed to be competent, or 2) by acquiring sufficient learning and skill before performance is required.

Discussion

The duties set forth in rule 3–110 include the duty to supervise the work of subordinate attorney and non-attorney employees or agents. (See, e.g., *Waysman v. State Bar* (1986) 41 Cal.3d 452; *Trousil v. State Bar* (1985) 38 Cal.3d 337, 342 [211 Cal.Rptr. 525]; *Palomo v. State Bar* (1984) 36 Cal.3d 785 [205 Cal.Rptr. 834]; *Crane v. State Bar* (1981) 30 Cal.3d 117, 122; *Black v. State Bar* (1972) 7 Cal.3d 676, 692 [103 Cal.Rptr. 288; 499 P.2d 968]; *Vaughn v. State Bar* (1972) 6 Cal.3d 847, 857–858 [100 Cal.Rptr. 713; 494 P.2d 1257]; *Moore v. State Bar* (1964) 62 Cal.2d 74, 81 [41 Cal.Rptr. 161; 396 P.2d 577].)

In an emergency a lawyer may give advice or assistance in a matter in which the lawyer does not have the skill ordinarily required where referral to or consultation with another lawyer would be impractical. Even in an emergency, however, assistance should be limited to that reasonably necessary in the circumstances.

RULE 3–120.   Sexual Relations With Client

(A) For purposes of this rule, "sexual relations" means sexual intercourse or the touching of an intimate part of another person for the purpose of sexual arousal, gratification, or abuse.

(B) A member shall not:

(1) Require or demand sexual relations with a client incident to or as a condition of any professional representation; or

(2) Employ coercion, intimidation, or undue influence in entering into sexual relations with a client; or

(3) Continue representation of a client with whom the member has sexual relations if such sexual relations cause the member to perform legal services incompetently in violation of rule 3–110.

(C) Paragraph (B) shall not apply to sexual relations between members and their spouses or to ongoing consensual sexual relationships which predate the initiation of the lawyer-client relationship.

(D) Where a lawyer in a firm has sexual relations with a client but does not participate in the representation of that client, the lawyers in the firm shall not be subject to discipline under this rule solely because of the occurrence of such sexual relations.

439

Discussion

Rule 3–120 is intended to prohibit sexual exploitation by a lawyer in the course of a professional representation. Often, based upon the nature of the underlying representation, a client exhibits great emotional vulnerability and dependence upon the advice and guidance of counsel. Attorneys owe the utmost duty of good faith and fidelity to clients. (See, e.g., *Greenbaum v. State Bar* (1976) 15 Cal.3d 893, 903 [126 Cal.Rptr. 785]; *Alkow v. State Bar* (1971) 3 Cal.3d 924, 935 [92 Cal.Rptr. 278]; *Cutler v. State Bar* (1969) 71 Cal.2d 241, 251 [78 Cal.Rptr. 172]; *Clancy v. State Bar* (1969) 71 Cal.2d 140, 146 [77 Cal.Rptr. 657].) The relationship between an attorney and client is a fiduciary relationship of the very highest character and all dealings between an attorney and client that are beneficial to the attorney will be closely scrutinized with the utmost strictness for unfairness. (See, e.g., *Giovanazzi v. State Bar* (1980) 28 Cal.3d 465, 472 [169 Cal.Rptr. 581]; *Benson v. State Bar* (1975) 13 Cal.3d 581, 586 [119 Cal.Rptr. 297]; *Lee v. State Bar* (1970) 2 Cal.3d 927, 939 [88 Cal.Rptr. 361]; *Clancy v. State Bar* (1969) 71 Cal.2d 140, 146 [77 Cal.Rptr. 657].) Where attorneys exercise undue influence over clients or take unfair advantage of clients, discipline is appropriate. (See, e.g., *Magee v. State Bar* (1962) 58 Cal.2d 423 [24 Cal.Rptr. 839]; *Lantz v. State Bar* (1931) 212 Cal. 213 [298 P. 497].) In all client matters, a member is advised to keep clients' interests paramount in the course of the member's representation.

For purposes of this rule, if the client is an organization, any individual overseeing the representation shall be deemed to be the client. (See rule 3–600.)

Although paragraph (C) excludes representation of certain clients from the scope of rule 3–120, such exclusion is not intended to preclude the applicability of other Rules of Professional Conduct, including rule 3–110.

RULE 3–200. Prohibited Objectives of Employment

A member shall not seek, accept, or continue employment if the member knows or should know that the objective of such employment is:

(A) To bring an action, conduct a defense, assert a position in litigation, or take an appeal, without probable cause and for the purpose of harassing or maliciously injuring any person; or

(B) To present a claim or defense in litigation that is not warranted under existing law, unless it can be supported by a good faith argument for an extension, modification, or reversal of such existing law.

RULE 3–210. Advising the Violation of Law

A member shall not advise the violation of any law, rule, or ruling of a tribunal unless the member believes in good faith that such law, rule, or ruling is invalid. A member may take appropriate steps in good faith to test the validity of any law, rule, or ruling of a tribunal.

Discussion

Rule 3–210 is intended to apply not only to the prospective conduct of a client but also to the interaction between the member and client and to the specific legal service sought by the client from the member. An example of the former is the handling of physical evidence of a crime in the possession of the client and offered to the member. (See *People v. Meredith* (1981) 29 Cal.3d 682 [175 Cal.Rptr. 612].) An example of the latter is a request that the member negotiate the return of stolen property in exchange for the owner's agreement not to report the theft to the police or prosecutorial authorities. (See *People v. Pic'l* (1982) 31 Cal.3d 731 [183 Cal.Rptr. 685].)

RULE 3–300. Avoiding Interests Adverse to a Client

A member shall not enter into a business transaction with a client; or knowingly acquire an ownership, possessory, security, or other pecuniary interest adverse to a client, unless each of the following requirements has been satisfied:

(A) The transaction or acquisition and its terms are fair and reasonable to the client and are fully disclosed and transmitted in writing to the client in a manner which should reasonably have been understood by the client; and

(B) The client is advised in writing that the client may seek the advice of an independent lawyer of the client's choice and is given a reasonable opportunity to seek that advice; and

(C) The client thereafter consents in writing to the terms of the transaction or the terms of the acquisition.

Discussion

Rule 3–300 is not intended to apply to the agreement by which the member is retained by the client, unless the agreement confers on the member an ownership, possessory, security, or other pecuniary interest adverse to the client. Such an agreement is governed, in part, by rule 4–200.

Rule 3–300 is not intended to apply where the member and client each make an investment on terms offered to the general public or a significant portion thereof. For example, rule 3–300 is not intended to apply where A, a member, invests in a limited partnership syndicated by a third party. B, A's client, makes the same investment. Although A and B are each investing in the same business, A did not enter into the transaction "with" B for the purposes of the rule.

Rule 3–300 is intended to apply where the member wishes to obtain an interest in client's property in order to secure the amount of the member's past due or future fees.

RULE 3–310. Avoiding the Representation of Adverse Interests

(A) For purposes of this rule:

(1) "Disclosure" means informing the client or former client of the relevant circumstances and of the actual and reasonably foreseeable adverse consequences to the client or former client;

(2) "Informed written consent" means the client's or former client's written agreement to the representation following written disclosure;

(3) "Written" means any writing as defined in Evidence Code section 250.

441

(B) A member shall not accept or continue representation of a client without providing written disclosure to the client where:

    (1) The member has a legal, business, financial, professional, or personal relationship with a party or witness in the same matter; or

    (2) The member knows or reasonably should know that:

        (a) the member previously had a legal, business, financial, professional, or personal relationship with a party or witness in the same matter; and

        (b) the previous relationship would substantially affect the member's representation; or

    (3) The member has or had a legal, business, financial, professional, or personal relationship with another person or entity the member knows or reasonably should know would be affected substantially by resolution of the matter or

    (4) The member has or had a legal, business, financial, or professional interest in the subject matter of the representation.

(C) A member shall not, without the informed written consent of each client:

    (1) Accept representation of more than one client in a matter in which the interests of the clients potentially conflict; or

    (2) Accept or continue representation of more than one client in a matter in which the interests of the clients actually conflict; or

    (3) Represent a client in a matter and at the same time in a separate matter accept as a client a person or entity whose interest in the first matter is adverse to the client in the first matter.

(D) A member who represents two or more clients shall not enter into an aggregate settlement of the claims of or against the clients without the informed written consent of each client.

(E) A member shall not, without the informed written consent of the client or former client, accept employment adverse to the client or former client where, by reason of the representation of the client or former client, the member has obtained confidential information material to the employment.

(F) A member shall not accept compensation for representing a client from one other than the client unless:

    (1) There is no interference with the member's independence of professional judgment or with the client-lawyer relationship; and

    (2) Information relating to representation of the client is protected as required by Business and Professions Code section 6068, subdivision (e); and

    (3) The member obtains the client's informed written consent, provided that no disclosure or consent is required if;

(a) such nondisclosure is otherwise authorized by law, or

(b) the member is rendering legal services on behalf of any public agency which provides legal services to other public agencies or the public.

Discussion

Rule 3–310 is not intended to prohibit a member from representing parties having antagonistic positions on the same legal question that has arisen in different cases, unless representation of either client would be adversely affected.

Other rules and laws may preclude making adequate disclosure under this rule. If such disclosure is precluded, informed written consent is likewise precluded. (See, e.g., Business and Professions Code section 6068, subsection (e).)

Paragraph (B) is not intended to apply to the relationship of a member to another party's lawyer. Such relationships are governed by rule 3–320.

Paragraph (B) is not intended to require either the disclosure of the new engagement to a former client or the consent of the former client to the new engagement. However, such disclosure or consent is required if paragraph (E) applies.

While paragraph (B) deals with the issues of adequate disclosure to the present client or clients of the member's present or past relationships to other parties or witnesses or present interest in the subject matter of the representation, paragraph (E) is intended to protect the confidences of another present or former client. These two paragraphs are to apply as complementary provisions.

Paragraph (B) is intended to apply only to a member's own relationships or interests, unless the member knows that a partner or associate in the same firm as the member has or had a relationship with another party or witness or has or had an interest in the subject matter of the representation.

Subparagraphs (C)(1) and (C)(2) are intended to apply to all types of legal employment, including the concurrent representation of multiple parties in litigation or in a single transaction or in some other common enterprise or legal relationship. Examples of the latter include the formation of a partnership for several partners or a corporation for several shareholders, the preparation of an ante-nuptial agreement, or joint or reciprocal wills for a husband and wife, or the resolution of an "uncontested" marital dissolution. In such situations, for the sake of convenience or economy, the parties may well prefer to employ a single counsel, but a member must disclose the potential adverse aspects of such multiple representation (e.g., Evid.Code, § 962) and must obtain the informed written consent of the clients thereto pursuant to subparagraph (C)(1). Moreover, if the potential adversity should become actual, the member must obtain the further informed written consent of the clients pursuant to paragraph (C)(2).

Subparagraph (C)(3) is intended to apply to representations of clients in both litigation and transactional matters.

There are some matters in which the conflicts are such that written consent may not suffice for non-disciplinary purposes. (See *Woods v. Superior Court* (1983) 149 Cal.App.3d 931 [197 Cal.Rptr. 185]; *Klemm v. Superior Court* (1977) 75 Cal.App.3d 893 [142 Cal.Rptr. 509]; *Ishmael v. Millington* (1966) 241 Cal. App.2d 520 [50 Cal.Rptr. 592].)

Paragraph (D) is not intended to apply to class action settlements subject to court approval.

Paragraph (F) is not intended to abrogate existing relationships between insurers and insureds whereby the insurer has the contractual right to unilaterally select counsel for the insured, where there is no conflict of interest. (See *San Diego Navy Federal Credit Union v. Cumis Insurance Society* (1984) 162 Cal. App.3d 358 [208 Cal.Rptr. 494].)

RULE 3–320. Relationship With Other Party's Lawyer

A member shall not represent a client in a matter in which another party's lawyer is a spouse, parent, child, or sibling of the member, lives with the member, is a client of the member, or has an intimate personal relationship with the member, unless the member informs the client in writing of the relationship.

Discussion

Rule 3–320 is not intended to apply to circumstances in which a member fails to advise the client of a relationship with another lawyer who is merely a partner or associate in the same law firm as the adverse party's counsel, and who has no direct involvement in the matter.

RULE 3–400. Limiting Liability to Client

A member shall not:

(A) Contract with a client prospectively limiting the member's liability to the client for the member's professional malpractice; or

(B) Settle a claim or potential claim for the member's liability to the client for the member's professional malpractice, unless the client is informed in writing that the client may seek the advice of an independent lawyer of the client's choice regarding the settlement and is given a reasonable opportunity to seek that advice.

Discussion

Rule 3–400 is not intended to apply to customary qualifications and limitations in legal opinions and memoranda, nor is it intended to prevent a member from reasonably limiting the scope of the member's employment or representation.

RULE 3–500. Communication

A member shall keep a client reasonably informed about significant developments relating to the employment or representation, including promptly complying with reasonable requests for information and copies of significant documents when necessary to keep the client so informed.

Comment

Rule 3–500 is not intended to change a member's duties to his or her clients. It is intended to make clear that, while a client must be informed of significant developments in the matter, a member will not be disciplined for failing to communicate insignificant or irrelevant information. (See Bus. & Prof.Code, § 6068, subd. (m).)

A member may contract with the client in their employment agreement that the client assumes responsibility for the cost of copying significant documents. This rule is not intended to prohibit a claim for the recovery of the member's expense in any subsequent legal proceeding.

Rule 3–500 is not intended to create, augment, diminish, or eliminate any application of the work product rule. The obligation of the member to provide work product to the client shall be governed by relevant statutory and decisional law. Additionally, this rule is not intended to apply to any document or correspondence that is subject to a protective order or non-disclosure agreement, or to override applicable statutory or decisional law requiring that certain information not be provided to criminal defendants who are clients of the member.

RULE 3–510. Communication of Settlement Offer

(A) A member shall promptly communicate to the member's client:

(1) All terms and conditions of any offer made to the client in a criminal matter; and

(2) All amounts, terms, and conditions of any written offer of settlement made to the client in all other matters.

(B) As used in this rule, "client" includes a person who possesses the authority to accept an offer of settlement or plea, or, in a class action, all the named representatives of the class.

Discussion

Rule 3–510 is intended to require that counsel in a criminal matter convey all offers, whether written or oral, to the client, as give and take negotiations are less common in criminal matters, and, even were they to occur, such negotiations should require the participation of the accused.

Any oral offers of settlement made to the client in a civil matter should also be communicated if they are "significant" for the purposes of rule 3–500.

RULE 3–600. Organization as Client

(A) In representing an organization, a member shall conform his or her representation to the concept that the client is the organization itself, acting through its highest authorized officer, employee, body, or constituent overseeing the particular engagement.

(B) If a member acting on behalf of an organization knows that an actual or apparent agent of the organization acts or intends or refuses to act in a manner that is or may be a violation of law reasonably imputable to the organization, or in a manner which is likely to result in substantial injury to the organization, the member shall not violate his or her duty of protecting all confidential information as provided in Business and Professions Code section 6068, subdivision (e). Subject to Business and Professions Code section 6068, subdivision (e), the member may take such actions as appear to the member to be in the best lawful interest of the organization. Such actions may include among others:

(1) Urging reconsideration of the matter while explaining its likely consequences to the organization; or

(2) Referring the matter to the next higher authority in the organization, including, if warranted by the seriousness of the matter, referral to the highest internal authority that can act on behalf of the organization.

(C) If, despite the member's actions in accordance with paragraph (B), the highest authority that can act on behalf of the organization insists upon action or a refusal to act that is a violation of law and is likely to result in substantial injury to the organization, the member's response is limited to the member's right, and, where appropriate, duty to resign in accordance with rule 3–700.

(D) In dealing with an organization's directors, officers, employees, members, shareholders, or other constituents, a member shall explain the identity of the client for whom the member acts, whenever it is or becomes apparent that the organization's interests are or may become adverse to those of the constituent(s) with whom the member is dealing. The member shall not mislead such a constituent into believing that the constituent may communicate confidential information to the member in a way that will not be used in the organization's interest if that is or becomes adverse to the constituent.

(E) A member representing an organization may also represent any of its directors, officers, employees, members, shareholders, or other constituents, subject to the provisions of rule 3–310. If the organization's consent to the dual representation is required by rule 3–310, the consent shall be given by an appropriate constituent of the organization other than the individual or constituent who is to be represented, or by the shareholder(s) or organization members.

Discussion

Rule 3–600 is not intended to enmesh members in the intricacies of the entity and aggregate theories of partnership.

Rule 3–600 is not intended to prohibit members from representing both an organization and other parties connected with it, as for instance (as simply one example) in establishing employee benefit packages for closely held corporations or professional partnerships.

Rule 3–600 is not intended to create or to validate artificial distinctions between entities and their officers, employees, or members, nor is it the purpose of the rule to deny the existence or importance of such formal distinctions. In dealing with a close corporation or small association, members commonly perform professional engagements for both the organization and its major constituents. When a change in control occurs or is threatened, members are faced with complex decisions involving personal and institutional relationships and loyalties and have frequently had difficulty in perceiving their correct duty. (See *People ex rel. Deukmejian v. Brown* (1981) 29 Cal.3d 150 [172 Cal.Rptr. 478]; *Goldstein v. Lees*

(1975) 46 Cal.App.3d 614 [120 Cal.Rptr. 253]; *Woods v. Superior Court* (1983) 149 Cal.App.3d 931 [197 Cal.Rptr. 185]; *In re Banks* (1978) 283 Or. 459 [584 P.2d 284]; 1 A.L.R. 4th 1105.)   In resolving such multiple relationships, members must rely on case law.

RULE 3–700. Termination of Employment

(A) In General.

(1) If permission for termination of employment is required by the rules of a tribunal, a member shall not withdraw from employment in a proceeding before that tribunal without its permission.

(2) A member shall not withdraw from employment until the member has taken reasonable steps to avoid reasonably foreseeable prejudice to the rights of the client, including giving due notice to the client, allowing time for employment of other counsel, complying with rule 3–700(D), and complying with applicable laws and rules.

(B) Mandatory Withdrawal. A member representing a client before a tribunal shall withdraw from employment with the permission of the tribunal, if required by its rules, and a member representing a client in other matters shall withdraw from employment, if:

(1) The member knows or should know that the client is bringing an action, conducting a defense, asserting a position in litigation, or taking an appeal, without probable cause and for the purpose of harassing or maliciously injuring any person; or

(2) The member knows or should know that continued employment will result in violation of these rules or of the State Bar Act; or

(3) The member's mental or physical condition renders it unreasonably difficult to carry out the employment effectively.

(C) Permissive Withdrawal. If rule 3–700(B) is not applicable, a member may not request permission to withdraw in matters pending before a tribunal, and may not withdraw in other matters, unless such request or such withdrawal is because:

(1) The client

(a) insists upon presenting a claim or defense that is not warranted under existing law and cannot be supported by good faith argument for an extension, modification, or reversal of existing law, or

(b) seeks to pursue an illegal course of conduct, or

(c) insists that the member pursue a course of conduct that is illegal or that is prohibited under these rules or the State Bar Act, or

(d) by other conduct renders it unreasonably difficult for the member to carry out the employment effectively, or

(e) insists, in a matter not pending before a tribunal, that the member engage in conduct that is contrary to the judgment and

447

advice of the member but not prohibited under these rules or the State Bar Act, or

(f) breaches an agreement or obligation to the member as to expenses or fees.

(2) The continued employment is likely to result in a violation of these rules or of the State Bar Act; or

(3) The inability to work with co-counsel indicates that the best interests of the client likely will be served by withdrawal; or

(4) The member's mental or physical condition renders it difficult for the member to carry out the employment effectively; or

(5) The client knowingly and freely assents to termination of the employment; or

(6) The member believes in good faith, in a proceeding pending before a tribunal, that the tribunal will find the existence of other good cause for withdrawal.

(D) Papers, Property, and Fees. A member whose employment has terminated shall:

(1) Subject to any protective order or non-disclosure agreement, promptly release to the client, at the request of the client, all the client papers and property. "Client papers and property" includes correspondence, pleadings, deposition transcripts, exhibits, physical evidence, expert's reports, and other items reasonably necessary to the client's representation, whether the client has paid for them or not; and

(2) Promptly refund any part of a fee paid in advance that has not been earned. This provision is not applicable to a true retainer fee which is paid solely for the purpose of ensuring the availability of the member for the matter.

Discussion

Subparagraph (A)(2) provides that "a member shall not withdraw from employment until the member has taken reasonable steps to avoid reasonably foreseeable prejudice to the rights of the clients." What such steps would include, of course, will vary according to the circumstances. Absent special circumstances, "reasonable steps" do not include providing additional services to the client once the successor counsel has been employed and rule 3-700(D) has been satisfied.

Paragraph (D) makes clear the member's duties in the recurring situation in which new counsel seeks to obtain client files from a member discharged by the client. It codifies existing case law. (See *Academy of California Optometrists v. Superior Court* (1975) 51 Cal.App.3d 999 [124 Cal.Rptr. 668]; *Weiss v. Marcus* (1975) 51 Cal.App.3d 590 [124 Cal.Rptr. 297].) Paragraph (D) also requires that the member "promptly" return unearned fees paid in advance. If a client disputes the amount to be returned, the member shall comply with rule 4-100(A)(2).

Paragraph (D) is not intended to prohibit a member from making, at the member's own expense, and retaining copies of papers released to the client, nor to prohibit a claim for the recovery of the member's expense in any subsequent legal proceeding.

CHAPTER 4. FINANCIAL RELATIONSHIP WITH CLIENTS

RULE 4–100. Preserving Identity of Funds and Property of a Client

(A) All funds received or held for the benefit of clients by a member or law firm, including advances for costs and expenses, shall be deposited in one or more identifiable bank accounts labelled "Trust Account," "Client's Funds Account" or words of similar import, maintained in the State of California, or, with written consent of the client, in any other jurisdiction where there is a substantial relationship between the client or the client's business and the other jurisdiction. No funds belonging to the member or the law firm shall be deposited therein or otherwise commingled therewith except as follows:

(1) Funds reasonably sufficient to pay bank charges.

(2) In the case of funds belonging in part to a client and in part presently or potentially to the member or the law firm, the portion belonging to the member or law firm must be withdrawn at the earliest reasonable time after the member's interest in that portion becomes fixed. However, when the right of the member or law firm to receive a portion of trust funds is disputed by the client, the disputed portion shall not be withdrawn until the dispute is finally resolved.

(B) A member shall:

(1) Promptly notify a client of the receipt of the client's funds, securities, or other properties.

(2) Identify and label securities and properties of a client promptly upon receipt and place them in a safe deposit box or other place of safekeeping as soon as practicable.

(3) Maintain complete records of all funds, securities, and other properties of a client coming into the possession of the member or law firm and render appropriate accounts to the client regarding them; preserve such records for a period of no less than five years after final appropriate distribution of such funds or properties; and comply with any order for an audit of such records issued pursuant to the Rules of Procedure of the State Bar.

(4) Promptly pay or deliver, as requested by the client, any funds, securities, or other properties in the possession of the member which the client is entitled to receive.

(C) The Board of Governors of the State Bar shall have the authority to formulate and adopt standards as to what "records" shall be maintained by members and law firms in accordance with subparagraph (B)(3). The standards formulated and adopted by the Board, as from time to time amended, shall be effective and binding on all members.

Standards:

Pursuant to rule 4–100(C) the Board of Governors of the State Bar has adopted the following standards, effective January 1, 1993, as to what "records" shall be maintained by members and law firms in accordance with subparagraph (B)(3).

(1) A member shall, from the date of receipt of client funds through the period ending five years from the date of appropriate disbursement of such funds, maintain:

(a) a written ledger for each client on whose behalf funds are held that sets forth:

(i) the name of such client,

(ii) the date, amount and source of all funds received on behalf of such client,

(iii) the date, amount, payee and purpose of each disbursement made on behalf of such client, and

(iv) the current balance for such client;

(b) a written journal for each bank account that sets forth:

(i) the name of such account,

(ii) the date, amount and client affected by each debit and credit, and

(iii) the current balance in such account;

(c) all bank statements and cancelled checks for each bank account; and

(d) each monthly reconciliation (balancing) of (a), (b), and (c).

(2) A member shall, from the date of receipt of all securities and other properties held for the benefit of client through the period ending five years from the date of appropriate disbursement of such securities and other properties, maintain a written journal that specifies:

(a) each item of security and property held;

(b) the person on whose behalf the security or property is held;

(c) the date of receipt of the security or property;

(d) the date of distribution of the security or property; and

(e) person to whom the security or property was distributed.

RULE 4–200.   Fees for Legal Services

(A) A member shall not enter into an agreement for, charge, or collect an illegal or unconscionable fee.

(B) Unconscionability of a fee shall be determined on the basis of all the facts and circumstances existing at the time the agreement is entered into except where the parties contemplate that the fee will be affected by later events. Among the factors to be considered, where appropriate, in determining the conscionability of a fee are the following:

(1) The amount of the fee in proportion to the value of the services performed.

(2) The relative sophistication of the member and the client.

(3) The novelty and difficulty of the questions involved and the skill requisite to perform the legal service properly.

(4) The likelihood, if apparent to the client, that the acceptance of the particular employment will preclude other employment by the member.

(5) The amount involved and the results obtained.

(6) The time limitations imposed by the client or by the circumstances.

(7) The nature and length of the professional relationship with the client.

(8) The experience, reputation, and ability of the member or members performing the services.

(9) Whether the fee is fixed or contingent.

(10) The time and labor required.

(11) The informed consent of the client to the fee.

RULE 4–210. Payment of Personal or Business Expenses Incurred by or for a Client

(A) A member shall not directly or indirectly pay or agree to pay, guarantee, represent, or sanction a representation that the member or member's law firm will pay the personal or business expenses of a prospective or existing client, except that this rule shall not prohibit a member:

(1) With the consent of the client, from paying or agreeing to pay such expenses to third persons from funds collected or to be collected for the client as a result of the representation; or

(2) After employment, from lending money to the client upon the client's promise in writing to repay such loan; or

(3) From advancing the costs of prosecuting or defending a claim or action or otherwise protecting or promoting the client's interests, the repayment of which may be contingent on the outcome of the matter. Such costs within the meaning of this subparagraph (3) shall be limited to all reasonable expenses of litigation or reasonable expenses in preparation for litigation or in providing any legal services to the client.

(B) Nothing in rule 4–210 shall be deemed to limit rules 3–300, 3–310, and 4–300.

RULE 4–300. Purchasing Property at a Foreclosure or a Sale Subject to Judicial Review

(A) A member shall not directly or indirectly purchase property at a probate, foreclosure, receiver's, trustee's, or judicial sale in an action or proceeding in which such member or any lawyer affiliated by reason of personal, business, or professional relationship with that member or with that member's law firm is acting as a lawyer for a party or as executor, receiver, trustee, administrator, guardian, or conservator.

(B) A member shall not represent the seller at a probate, foreclosure, receiver, trustee, or judicial sale in an action or proceeding in which the purchaser is a spouse or relative of the member or of another lawyer in the member's law firm or is an employee of the member or the member's law firm.

RULE 4–400. Gifts From Client

A member shall not induce a client to make a substantial gift, including a testamentary gift, to the member or to the member's parent, child, sibling, or spouse, except where the client is related to the member.

Discussion

A member may accept a gift from a member's client, subject to general standards of fairness and absence of undue influence. The member who participates in the preparation of an instrument memorializing a gift which is otherwise permissible ought not to be subject to professional discipline. On the other hand, where impermissible influence occurred, discipline is appropriate. (See *Magee v. State Bar* (1962) 58 Cal.2d 423 [24 Cal.Rptr. 839].)

CHAPTER 5. ADVOCACY AND REPRESENTATION

RULE 5–100. Threatening Criminal, Administrative, or Disciplinary Charges

(A) A member shall not threaten to present criminal, administrative, or disciplinary charges to obtain an advantage in a civil dispute.

(B) As used in paragraph (A) of this rule, the term "administrative charges" means the filing or lodging of a complaint with a federal, state, or local governmental entity which may order or recommend the loss or suspension of a license, or may impose or recommend the imposition of a fine, pecuniary sanction, or other sanction of a quasi-criminal nature but does not include filing charges with an administrative entity required by law as a condition precedent to maintaining a civil action.

(C) As used in paragraph (A) of this rule, the term "civil dispute" means a controversy or potential controversy over the rights and duties of two or more parties under civil law, whether or not an action has been commenced, and includes an administrative proceeding of a quasi-civil nature pending before a federal, state, or local governmental entity.

Discussion

Rule 5–100 is not intended to apply to a member's threatening to initiate contempt proceedings against a party for a failure to comply with a court order.

Paragraph (B) is intended to exempt the threat of filing an administrative charge which is a prerequisite to filing a civil complaint on the same transaction or occurrence.

For purposes of paragraph (C), the definition of "civil dispute" makes clear that the rule is applicable prior to the formal filing of a civil action.

RULE 5–110. Performing the Duty of Member in Government Service

A member in government service shall not institute or cause to be instituted criminal charges when the member knows or should know that the charges are not supported by probable cause. If, after the institution of criminal charges, the member in government service having responsibility for prosecuting the charges becomes aware that those charges are not supported by probable cause, the member shall promptly so advise the court in which the criminal matter is pending.

RULE 5–120. Trial Publicity

(A) A member who is participating or has participated in the investigation or litigation of a matter shall not make an extrajudicial statement that a reasonable person would expect to be disseminated by means of public communication if the member knows or reasonably should know that it will have a substantial likelihood of materially prejudicing an adjudicative proceeding in the matter.

(B) Notwithstanding paragraph (A), a member may state:

(1) the claim, offense or defense involved and, except when prohibited by law, the identity of the persons involved;

(2) the information contained in a public record;

(3) that an investigation of the matter is in progress;

(4) the scheduling or result of any step in litigation;

(5) a request for assistance in obtaining evidence and information necessary thereto;

(6) a warning of danger concerning the behavior of a person involved, when there is reason to believe that there exists the likelihood of substantial harm to an individual or the public interest; and

(7) in a criminal case, in addition to subparagraphs (1) through (6):

(a) the identity, residence, occupation, and family status of the accused;

(b) if the accused has not been apprehended, information necessary to aid in apprehension of that person;

(c) the fact, time, and place of arrest; and

(d) the identity of investigating and arresting officers or agencies and the length of the investigation.

(C) Notwithstanding paragraph (A), a member may make a statement that a reasonable member would believe is required to protect a client from the substantial undue prejudicial effect of recent publicity not initiated by the member or the member's client. A statement made pursuant to this paragraph shall be limited to such information as is necessary to mitigate the recent adverse publicity.

Discussion

Rule 5–120 is intended to apply equally to prosecutors and criminal defense counsel. Whether an extrajudicial statement violates rule 5–120 depends on many factors, including:

(1) whether the extrajudicial statement presents information clearly inadmissible as evidence in the matter for the purpose of proving or disproving a material fact in issue;

(2) whether the extrajudicial statement presents information the member knows is false, deceptive, or the use of which would violate Business and Professions Code section 6068(d);

(3) whether the extrajudicial statement violates a lawful "gag" order, or protective order, statute, rule of court, or special rule of confidentiality (for example, in juvenile, domestic, mental disability, and certain criminal proceedings); and

(4) the timing of the statement.

Paragraph (A) is intended to apply to statements made by or on behalf of the member. Subparagraph (B)(6) is not intended to create, augment, diminish, or eliminate any application of the lawyer-client privilege or of Business and Professions Code section 6068(e) regarding the member's duty to maintain client confidence and secrets.

RULE 5–200. Trial Conduct

In presenting a matter to a tribunal, a member:

(A) Shall employ, for the purpose of maintaining the causes confided to the member such means only as are consistent with truth;

(B) Shall not seek to mislead the judge, judicial officer, or jury by an artifice or false statement of fact or law;

(C) Shall not intentionally misquote to a tribunal the language of a book, statute, or decision;

(D) Shall not, knowing its invalidity, cite as authority a decision that has been overruled or a statute that has been repealed or declared unconstitutional; and

(E) Shall not assert personal knowledge of the facts at issue, except when testifying as a witness.

RULE 5–210. Member as Witness

A member shall not act as an advocate before a jury which will hear testimony from the member unless:

(A) The testimony relates to an uncontested matter; or

(B) The testimony relates to the nature and value of legal services rendered in the case; or

(C) The member has the informed, written consent of the client. If the member represents the People or a governmental entity, the consent shall be obtained from the head of the office or a designee of the head of the office by which the member is employed and shall be consistent with principles of recusal.

Discussion

Rule 5–210 is intended to apply to situations in which the member knows or should know that he or she ought to be called as a witness in litigation in which there is a jury. This rule is not intended to encompass situations in which the member is representing the client in an adversarial proceeding and is testifying before a judge. In non-adversarial proceedings, as where the member testifies on behalf of the client in a hearing before a legislative body, rule 5–210 is not applicable.

Rule 5–210 is not intended to apply to circumstances in which a lawyer in an advocate's firm will be a witness.

RULE 5–220. Suppression of Evidence

A member shall not suppress any evidence that the member or the member's client has a legal obligation to reveal or to produce.

RULE 5–300. Contact With Officials

(A) A member shall not directly or indirectly give or lend anything of value to a judge, official, or employee of a tribunal unless the personal or family relationship between the member and the judge, official, or employee is such that gifts are customarily given and exchanged. Nothing contained in this rule shall prohibit a member from contributing to the campaign fund of a judge running for election or confirmation pursuant to applicable law pertaining to such contributions.

(B) A member shall not directly or indirectly communicate with or argue to a judge or judicial officer upon the merits of a contested matter pending before such judge or judicial officer, except:

(1) In open court; or

(2) With the consent of all other counsel in such matter; or

(3) In the presence of all other counsel in such matter; or

(4) In writing with a copy thereof furnished to such other counsel; or

(5) In ex parte matters.

(C) As used in this rule, "judge" and "judicial officer" shall include law clerks, research attorneys, or other court personnel who participate in the decision-making process.

RULE 5–310. Prohibited Contact With Witnesses

A member shall not:

(A) Advise or directly or indirectly cause a person to secrete himself or herself or to leave the jurisdiction of a tribunal for the purpose of making that person unavailable as a witness therein.

(B) Directly or indirectly pay, offer to pay, or acquiesce in the payment of compensation to a witness contingent upon the content of the witness's testimony or the outcome of the case. Except where prohibited by law, a member may advance, guarantee, or acquiesce in the payment of:

(1) Expenses reasonably incurred by a witness in attending or testifying.

(2) Reasonable compensation to a witness for loss of time in attending or testifying.

(3) A reasonable fee for the professional services of an expert witness.

RULE 5–320. Contact With Jurors

(A) A member connected with a case shall not communicate directly or indirectly with anyone the member knows to be a member of the venire from which the jury will be selected for trial of that case.

(B) During trial a member connected with the case shall not communicate directly or indirectly with any juror.

(C) During trial a member who is not connected with the case shall not communicate directly or indirectly concerning the case with anyone the member knows is a juror in the case.

(D) After discharge of the jury from further consideration of a case a member shall not ask questions of or make comments to a member of that jury that are intended to harass or embarrass the juror or to influence the juror's actions in future jury service.

(E) A member shall not directly or indirectly conduct an out of court investigation of a person who is either a member of the venire or a juror in a manner likely to influence the state of mind of such person in connection with present or future jury service.

(F) All restrictions imposed by this rule also apply to communications with or investigations of members of the family of a person who is either a member of the venire or a juror.

(G) A member shall reveal promptly to the court improper conduct by a person who is either a member of the venire or a juror, or by another toward a person who is either a member of the venire or a juror or a member of his or her family, of which the member has knowledge.

(H) This Rule does not prohibit a member from communicating with persons who are members of a venire or jurors as a part of the official proceedings.

(I) For purpose of this rule "juror" means any empaneled, discharged, or excused juror.

SELECTED PROVISIONS FROM THE CALIFORNIA BUSINESS AND PROFESSIONS CODE

Table of Sections

458

ARTICLE 4. ADMISSION TO THE PRACTICE OF LAW

§ 6067. Oath

Every person on his admission shall take an oath to support the Constitution of the United States and the Constitution of the State of California, and faithfully to discharge the duties of any attorney at law to the best of his knowledge and ability. A certificate of the oath shall be indorsed upon his license.

§ 6068. Duties of Attorney

It is the duty of an attorney to do all of the following:

(a) To support the Constitution and laws of the United States and of this state.

(b) To maintain the respect due to the courts of justice and judicial officers.

(c) To counsel or maintain those actions, proceedings, or defenses only as appear to him or her legal or just, except the defense of a person charged with a public offense.

(d) To employ, for the purpose of maintaining the causes confided to him or her, those means only as are consistent with truth, and never to seek to mislead the judge or any judicial officer by an artifice or false statement of fact or law.

(e) To maintain inviolate the confidence, and at every peril to himself or herself to preserve the secrets, of his or her client.

(f) To abstain from all offensive personality, and to advance no fact prejudicial to the honor or reputation of a party or witness, unless required by the justice of the cause with which he or she is charged.

(g) Not to encourage either the commencement or the continuance of an action or proceeding from any corrupt motive of passion or interest.

(h) Never to reject, for any consideration personal to himself or herself, the cause of the defenseless or the oppressed.

(i) To cooperate and participate in any disciplinary investigation or other regulatory or disciplinary proceeding pending against the attorney. However, this subdivision shall not be construed to deprive an attorney of any privilege guaranteed by the Fifth Amendment to the Constitution of the United States or any other constitutional or statutory privileges. This subdivision shall not be construed to require an attorney to cooperate with a request that requires the attorney to waive any constitutional or statutory privilege or to comply with a request for information or other matters within an unreasonable period of time in light of the time constraints of the attorney's practice. Any exercise by an attorney of any constitutional or statutory privilege shall not be used against the attorney in a regulatory or disciplinary proceeding against him or her.

(j) To comply with the requirements of Section 6002.1.

(k) To comply with all conditions attached to any disciplinary probation, including a probation imposed with the concurrence of the attorney.

(*l*) To keep all agreements made in lieu of disciplinary prosecution with the agency charged with attorney discipline.

(m) To respond promptly to reasonable status inquiries of clients and to keep clients reasonably informed of significant developments in matters with regard to which the attorney has agreed to provide legal services.

(n) To provide copies to the client of certain documents under time limits and as is prescribed in a rule of professional conduct which the board shall adopt.

(o) To report to the agency charged with attorney discipline, in writing, within 30 days of the time the attorney has knowledge of any of the following:

(1) The filing of three or more lawsuits in a 12-month period against the attorney for malpractice or other wrongful conduct committed in a professional capacity.

(2) The entry of judgment against the attorney in any civil action for fraud, misrepresentation, breach of fiduciary duty, or gross negligence committed in a professional capacity.

(3) The imposition of any judicial sanctions against the attorney, except for sanctions for failure to make discovery or monetary sanctions of less than one thousand dollars ($1,000).

(4) The bringing of an indictment or information charging a felony against the attorney.

(5) The conviction of the attorney, including any verdict of guilty, or plea of guilty or no contest, of any felony, or any misdemeanor committed in the course of the practice of law, or in any manner such that a client of the attorney was the victim, or a necessary element of which, as determined by the statutory or common law definition of the misdemeanor, involves improper conduct of an attorney, including dishonesty or other moral turpitude, or an attempt or a conspiracy or solicitation of another to commit a felony or any misdemeanor of that type.

(6) The imposition of discipline against the attorney by any professional or occupational disciplinary agency or licensing board, whether in California or elsewhere.

(7) Reversal of judgment in a proceeding based in whole or in part upon misconduct, grossly incompetent representation, or wilful misrepresentation by an attorney.

(8) As used in this subdivision, "against the attorney" includes claims and proceedings against any firm of attorneys for the practice of law in which

461

the attorney was a partner at the time of the conduct complained of and any law corporation in which the attorney was a shareholder at the time of the conduct complained of unless the matter has to the attorney's knowledge already been reported by the law firm or corporation.

(9) The State Bar may develop a prescribed form for the making of reports required by this section, usage of which it may require by rule or regulation.

(10) This subdivision is only intended to provide that the failure to report as required herein may serve as a basis of discipline.

ARTICLE 6. DISCIPLINARY AUTHORITY OF THE COURTS

§ 6100. Disbarment or Suspension

For any of the causes provided in this article, arising after an attorney's admission to practice, he or she may be disbarred or suspended by the Supreme Court. Nothing in this article limits the inherent power of the Supreme Court to discipline, including to summarily disbar, any attorney.

§ 6101. Conviction of Crime; Notice of Pendency of Action; Record of Conviction; Proceedings

(a) Conviction of a felony or misdemeanor, involving moral turpitude, constitutes a cause for disbarment or suspension.

In any proceeding, whether under this article or otherwise, to disbar or suspend an attorney on account of that conviction, the record of conviction shall be conclusive evidence of guilt of the crime of which he or she has been convicted.

(b) The district attorney, city attorney, or other prosecuting agency shall notify the Office of the State Bar of California of the pendency of an action against an attorney charging a felony or misdemeanor immediately upon obtaining information that the defendant is an attorney. The notice shall identify the attorney and describe the crimes charged and the alleged facts. The prosecuting agency shall also notify the clerk of the court in which the action is pending that the defendant is an attorney, and the clerk shall record prominently in the file that the defendant is an attorney.

(c) The clerk of the court in which an attorney is convicted of a crime shall, within 48 hours after the conviction, transmit a certified copy of the record of conviction to the Office of the State Bar. Within five days of receipt, the Office of the State Bar shall transmit the record of any conviction which involves or may involve moral turpitude to the Supreme Court with such other records and information as may be appropriate to establish the Supreme Court's jurisdiction. The State Bar of California may procure and transmit the record of conviction to the Supreme Court when the clerk has not done so or when the conviction was had in a court other than a court of this state.

(d) The proceedings to disbar or suspend an attorney on account of such a conviction shall be undertaken by the Supreme Court pursuant to the procedure provided in this section and Section 6102, upon the receipt of the certified copy of the record of conviction.

(e) A plea or verdict of guilty, an acceptance of a nolo contendre plea, or a conviction after a plea of nolo contendere is deemed to be a conviction within the meaning of those sections.

§ 6102. Immediate Suspension and Subsequent Disbarment Upon Conviction of Crime; Crimes Involving Moral Turpitude or Felonies; Procedure

(a) Upon the receipt of the certified copy of the record of conviction, if it appears therefrom that the crime of which the attorney was convicted involved or that there is probable cause to believe that it involved moral turpitude or is a felony under the laws of California, the United States, or any state or territory thereof, the Supreme Court shall suspend the attorney until the time for appeal has elapsed, if no appeal has been taken, or until the judgment of conviction has been affirmed on appeal, or has otherwise become final, and until the further order of the court. Upon its own motion or upon good cause shown the court may decline to impose, or may set aside, the suspension when it appears to be in the interest of justice to do so, with due regard being given to maintaining the integrity of and confidence in the profession.

(b) For the purposes of this section, a crime is a felony under the law of California if it is declared to be so specifically or by subdivision (a) of Section 17 of the Penal Code, unless it is charged as a misdemeanor pursuant to paragraph (4) or (5) of subdivision (b) of Section 17 of the Penal Code, irrespective of whether in a particular case the crime may be considered a misdemeanor as a result of postconviction proceedings, including proceedings resulting in punishment or probation set forth in paragraph (1) or (3) of subdivision (b) of Section 17 of the Penal Code.

(c) After the judgment of conviction of an offense specified in subdivision (a) has become final or, irrespective of any subsequent order under Section 1203.4 of the Penal Code or similar statutory provision, an order granting probation has been made suspending the imposition of sentence, the Supreme Court shall summarily disbar the attorney if the offense is a felony under the laws of California, the United States, or any state or territory thereof, and an element of the offense is the specific intent to deceive, defraud, steal, or make or suborn a false statement, or involved moral turpitude.

(d) For purposes of this section, a conviction under the laws of another state or territory of the United States shall be deemed a felony if:

(1) The judgment or conviction was entered as a felony irrespective of any subsequent order suspending sentence or granting probation and irrespective of whether the crime may be considered a misdemeanor as a result of postconviction proceedings.

(2) The elements of the offense for which the member was convicted would constitute a felony under the laws of the State of California at the time the offense was committed.

(e) Except as provided in subdivision (c), if after adequate notice and opportunity to be heard (which hearing shall not be had until the judgment of conviction has become final or, irrespective of any subsequent order under Section 1203.4 of the Penal Code, an order granting probation has been made suspending the imposition of sentence), the court finds that the crime of which the attorney was convicted, or the circumstances of its commission, involved moral turpitude, it shall enter an order disbarring the attorney or suspending him or her from practice for a limited time, according to the gravity of the crime and the circumstances of the case; otherwise it shall dismiss the proceedings. In determining the extent of the discipline to be imposed in a proceeding pursuant to this article, any prior discipline imposed upon the attorney may be considered.

(f) The court may refer the proceedings or any part thereof or issue therein, including the nature or extent of discipline, to the State Bar for hearing, report, and recommendation.

(g) The record of the proceedings resulting in the conviction, including a transcript of the testimony therein, may be received in evidence.

(h) The Supreme Court shall prescribe rules for the practice and procedure in proceedings conducted pursuant to this section and Section 6101.

(i) The other provisions of this article providing a procedure for the disbarment or suspension of an attorney do not apply to proceedings pursuant to this section and Section 6101, unless expressly made applicable.

§ 6103. Disobedience of Court Order; Violation of Oath or Attorney's Duties

A wilful disobedience or violation of an order of the court requiring him to do or forbear an act connected with or in the course of his profession, which he ought in good faith to do or forbear, and any violation of the oath taken by him, or of his duties as such attorney, constitute causes for disbarment or suspension.

§ 6103.5 Written Offers of Settlement; Required Communication to Client; Discovery

(a) A member of the State Bar shall promptly communicate to the member's client all amounts, terms, and conditions of any written offer of settlement made by or on behalf of an opposing party. As used in this section, "client" includes any person employing the member of the State Bar who possesses the authority to accept an offer of settlement, or in a class action, who is a representative of the class.

(b) Any written offer of settlement or any required communication of a settlement offer, as described in subdivision (a), shall be discoverable by either party in any action in which the existence or communication of the offer of settlement is an issue before the trier of fact.

§ 6103.6 Compensation for Trustee Services; Donative Transfers; Violations Constituting Grounds for Discipline

Violation of Section 15687 of the Probate Code, or of Part 3.5 (commencing with Section 21350) of Division 11 of the Probate Code, shall be grounds for discipline, if the attorney knew or should have known of the facts leading to the violation. This section shall only apply to violations that occur on or after January 1, 1994.

§ 6104. Unauthorized Appearance

Corruptly or wilfully and without authority appearing as attorney for a party to an action or proceeding constitutes a cause for disbarment or suspension.

§ 6105. Permitting Misuse of Name

Lending his name to be used as attorney by another person who is not an attorney constitutes a cause for disbarment or suspension.

§ 6106. Moral Turpitude, Dishonesty or Corruption Irrespective of Criminal Conviction

The commission of any act involving moral turpitude, dishonesty or corruption, whether the act is committed in the course of his relations as an attorney or otherwise, and whether the act is a felony or misdemeanor or not, constitutes a cause for disbarment or suspension.

If the act constitutes a felony or misdemeanor, conviction thereof in a criminal proceeding is not a condition precedent to disbarment or suspension from practice therefor.

§ 6106.1 Advocacy of Overthrow of Government

Advocating the overthrow of the Government of the United States or of this State by force, violence, or other unconstitutional means, constitutes a cause for disbarment or suspension.

§ 6106.5 Insurance Claims; Fraud

It shall constitute cause for disbarment or suspension for an attorney to engage in any conduct prohibited under Section 1871.1 or 1871.4 of the Insurance Code.

§ 6106.7 Miller–Ayala Athlete Agents Act; Violation of Requirements

It shall constitute cause for the imposition of discipline of an attorney within the meaning of this chapter for an attorney to violate any provision of the Miller–Ayala Athlete Agents Act (Chapter 2.5 (commencing with Section 18895) of Division 8), or to violate any provision of Chapter 1 (commencing with Section 1500) of Part 6 of Division 2 of the Labor Code, prior to January 1, 1997, or to violate any provision of the law of any other state regulating athlete agents.

§ 6106.8 Sexual Involvement Between Lawyers and Clients; Rule of Professional Conduct

(a) The Legislature hereby finds and declares that there is no rule that governs propriety of sexual relationships between lawyers and clients. The Legislature further finds and declares that it is difficult to separate sound judgment from emotion or bias which may result from sexual involvement between a lawyer and his or her client during the period that an attorney-client relationship exists, and that emotional detachment is essential to the lawyer's ability to render competent legal services. Therefore, in order to ensure that a lawyer acts in the best interest of his or her client, a rule of professional conduct governing sexual relations between attorneys and their clients shall be adopted.

(b) With the approval of the Supreme Court, the State Bar shall adopt a rule of professional conduct governing sexual relations between attorneys and their clients in cases involving, but not limited to, probate matters and domestic relations, including dissolution proceedings, child custody cases, and settlement proceedings.

(c) The State Bar shall submit the proposed rule to the Supreme Court for approval no later than January 1, 1991.

(d) Intentional violation of this rule shall constitute a cause for suspension or disbarment.

[Editors' Note: See California Rules of Professional Conduct, Rule 3–120, reprinted supra.]

§ 6106.9 Sexual Relations Between Attorney and Client; Cause for Discipline; Complaints to State Bar

(a) It shall constitute cause for the imposition of discipline of an attorney within the meaning of this chapter for an attorney to do any of the following:

(1) Expressly or impliedly condition the performance of legal services for a current or prospective client upon the client's willingness to engage in sexual relations with the attorney.

(2) Employ coercion, intimidation, or undue influence in entering into sexual relations with a client.

(3) Continue representation of a client with whom the attorney has sexual relations if the sexual relations cause the attorney to perform legal services incompetently in violation of Rule 3–110 of the Rules of Professional Conduct of the State Bar of California, or if the sexual relations would, or would be likely to, damage or prejudice the client's case.

(b) Subdivision (a) shall not apply to sexual relations between attorneys and their spouses or persons in an equivalent domestic relationship or to ongoing consensual sexual relationships that predate the initiation of the attorney-client relationship.

(c) Where an attorney in a firm has sexual relations with a client but does not participate in the representation of that client, the attorneys in the firm shall not be subject to discipline under this section solely because of the occurrence of those sexual relations.

(d) For the purposes of this section, "sexual relations" means sexual intercourse or the touching of an intimate part of another person for the purpose of sexual arousal, gratification, or abuse.

(e) Any complaint made to the State Bar alleging a violation of subdivision (a) shall be verified under oath by the person making the complaint.

[Editors' Note: The Governor of California signed the bill that enacted § 6106.9 on September 16th, 1992. The second section of that bill also provided that—

"SEC. 2. Commencing January 1, 1993, the State Bar shall maintain statistical data regarding the number of complaints presented and the disposition or discipline imposed pursuant to Section 6106.9 of the Business and Professions Code. The State Bar shall submit a report to the Legislature regarding the statistical compilation on or before January 1, 1996.

"The State Bar shall also develop and implement uniform standards for the implementation of Section 6106.9 of the Business and Professions Code and policies and procedures to ensure that complaints will be handled in a responsive and sensitive manner. The State Bar shall also provide appropriate training to staff on the standards, policies, and practices."

ARTICLE 7.   UNLAWFUL PRACTICE OF LAW

§ 6128.   Deceit, Collusion, Delay of Suit and Improper Receipt of Money as Misdemeanor

Every attorney is guilty of a misdemeanor who either:

(a) Is guilty of any deceit or collusion, or consents to any deceit or collusion, with intent to deceive the court or any party.

(b) Willfully delays his client's suit with a view to his own gain.

(c) Willfully receives any money or allowance for or on account of any money which he has not laid out or become answerable for.

Any violation of the provisions of this section is punishable by imprisonment in the county jail not exceeding six months, or by a fine not exceeding two thousand five hundred dollars ($2,500), or by both.

§ 6129.   Buying Claim as Misdemeanor

Every attorney who, either directly or indirectly, buys or is interested in buying any evidence of debt or thing in action, with intent to bring suit thereon, is guilty of a misdemeanor.

Any violation of the provisions of this section is punishable by imprisonment in the county jail not exceeding six months, or by a fine not exceeding two thousand five hundred dollars ($2,500), or by both.

§ 6130. Disbarred or Suspended Attorney Suing as Assignee

No person, who has been an attorney, shall while a judgment of disbarment or suspension is in force appear on his own behalf as plaintiff in the prosecution of any action where the subject of the action has been assigned to him subsequent to the entry of the judgment of disbarment or suspension and solely for purpose of collection.

§ 6131. Aiding Defense Where Partner or Self Has Acted as Public Prosecutor; Misdemeanor and Disbarment

Every attorney is guilty of a misdemeanor and, in addition to the punishment prescribed therefor, shall be disbarred:

(a) Who directly or indirectly advises in relation to, or aids, or promotes the defense of any action or proceeding in any court the prosecution of which is carried on, aided or promoted by any person as district attorney or other public prosecutor with whom such person is directly or indirectly connected as a partner.

(b) Who, having himself prosecuted or in any manner aided or promoted any action or proceeding in any court as district attorney or other public prosecutor, afterwards, directly or indirectly, advises in relation to or takes any part in the defense thereof, as attorney or otherwise, or who takes or receives any valuable consideration from or on behalf of any defendant in any such action upon any understanding or agreement whatever having relation to the defense thereof.

This section does not prohibit an attorney from defending himself in person, as attorney or counsel, when prosecuted, either civilly or criminally.

ARTICLE 8.5   FEE AGREEMENTS

§ 6146. Limitations; Periodic Payments

(a) An attorney shall not contract for or collect a contingency fee for representing any person seeking damages in connection with an action for injury or damage against a health care provider based upon such person's alleged professional negligence in excess of the following limits:

(1) Forty percent of the first fifty thousand dollars ($50,000) recovered.

(2) Thirty-three and one-third percent of the next fifty thousand dollars ($50,000) recovered.

(3) Twenty-five percent of the next five hundred thousand dollars ($500,-000) recovered.

(4) Fifteen percent of any amount on which the recovery exceeds six hundred thousand dollars ($600,000).

The limitations shall apply regardless of whether the recovery is by settlement, arbitration, or judgment, or whether the person for whom the recovery is made is a responsible adult, an infant, or a person of unsound mind.

(b) If periodic payments are awarded to the plaintiff pursuant to Section 667.7 of the Code of Civil Procedure, the court shall place a total value on these payments based upon the projected life expectancy of the plaintiff and include this amount in computing the total award from which attorney's fees are calculated under this section.

(c) For purposes of this section:

(1) "Recovered" means the net sum recovered after deducting any disbursements or costs incurred in connection with prosecution or settlement of the claim. Costs of medical care incurred by the plaintiff and the attorney's office-overhead costs or charges are not deductible disbursements or costs for such purpose.

(2) "Health care provider" means any person licensed or certified pursuant to Division 2 (commencing with Section 500), or licensed pursuant to the Osteopathic Initiative Act, or the Chiropractic Initiative Act, or licensed pursuant to Chapter 2.5 (commencing with Section 1440) of Division 2 of the Health and Safety Code; and any clinic, health dispensary, or health facility, licensed pursuant to Division 2 (commencing with Section 1200) of the Health and Safety Code. "Health care provider" includes the legal representatives of a health care provider.

(3) "Professional negligence" is a negligent act or omission to act by a health care provider in the rendering of professional services, which act or omission is the proximate cause of a personal injury or wrongful death, provided that the services are within the scope of services for which the provider is licensed and which are not within any restriction imposed by the licensing agency or licensed hospital.

§ 6147. Contingency Fee Contracts; Duplicate Copy; Contents; Effect of Noncompliance; Recovery of Workers' Compensation Benefits

(a) An attorney who contracts to represent a client on a contingency fee basis shall, at the time the contract is entered into, provide a duplicate copy of the contract, signed by both the attorney and the client, or the client's guardian or representative, to the plaintiff, or to the plaintiff's guardian or representative. The contract shall be in writing and shall include, but is not limited to, all of the following:

(1) A statement of the contingency fee rate which the client and attorney have agreed upon.

(2) A statement as to how disbursements and costs incurred in connection with the prosecution or settlement of the claim will affect the contingency fee and the client's recovery.

469

(3) A statement as to what extent, if any, the client could be required to pay any compensation to the attorney for related matters that arise out of their relationship not covered by their contingency fee contract. This may include any amounts collected for the plaintiff by the attorney.

(4) Unless the claim is subject to the provisions of Section 6146, a statement that the fee is not set by law but is negotiable between attorney and client.

(5) If the claim is subject to the provisions of Section 6146, a statement that the rates set forth in that section are the maximum limits for the contingency fee agreement, and that the attorney and client may negotiate a lower rate.

(b) Failure to comply with any provision of this section renders the agreement voidable at the option of the plaintiff, and the attorney shall thereupon be entitled to collect a reasonable fee.

(c) This section shall not apply to contingency fee contracts for the recovery of workers' compensation benefits.

(d) This section shall become operative on January 1, 2000.

§ 6147.5 Contingency Fee Contracts; Recovery of Claims Between Merchants

(a) Sections 6147 and 6148 shall not apply to contingency fee contracts for the recovery of claims between merchants as defined in Section 2104 of the Commercial Code, arising from the sale or lease of goods or services rendered, or money loaned for use, in the conduct of a business or profession if the merchant contracting for legal services employs 10 or more individuals.

(b)(1) In the instances in which no written contract for legal services exists as permitted by subdivision (a), an attorney shall not contract for or collect a contingency fee in excess of the following limits:

(A) Twenty percent of the first three hundred dollars ($300) collected.

(B) Eighteen percent of the next one thousand seven hundred dollars ($1,700) collected.

(C) Thirteen percent of sums collected in excess of two thousand dollars ($2,000).

(2) However, the following minimum charges may be charged and collected:

(A) Twenty-five dollars ($25) in collections of seventy-five dollars ($75) to one hundred twenty-five dollars ($125).

(B) Thirty-three and one-third percent of collections less than seventy-five dollars ($75).

§ 6148. Contracts for Services in Cases Not Coming Within § 6147; Bills Rendered by Attorney; Contents; Failure to Comply

(a) In any case not coming within Section 6147 in which it is reasonably foreseeable that total expense to a client, including attorney fees will exceed one thousand dollars ($1,000), the contract for services in the case shall be in writing. At the time the contract is entered into, the attorney shall provide a duplicate copy of the contract signed by both the attorney and the client or the client's guardian or representative, to the client or to the client's guardian or representative. The written contract shall contain all of the following:

(1) Any basis of compensation including, but not limited to, hourly rates, statutory fees or flat fees, and other standard rates, fees, and charges applicable to the case.

(2) The general nature of the legal services to be provided to the client.

(3) The respective responsibilities of the attorney and the client as to the performance of the contract.

(b) All bills rendered by an attorney to a client shall clearly state the basis thereof. Bills for the fee portion of the bill shall include the amount, rate, basis for calculation, or other method of determination of the attorney's fees and costs. Bills for the cost and expense portion of the bill shall clearly identify the costs and expenses incurred and the amount of the costs and expenses. Upon request by the client, the attorney shall provide a bill to the client no later than 10 days following the request unless the attorney has provided a bill to the client within 31 days prior to the request, in which case the attorney may provide a bill to the client no later than 31 days following the date the most recent bill was provided. The client is entitled to make similar requests at intervals of no less than 30 days following the initial request. In providing responses to client requests for billing information, the attorney may use billing data that is currently effective on the date of the request, or, if any fees or costs to that date cannot be accurately determined, they shall be described and estimated.

(c) Failure to comply with any provision of this section renders the agreement voidable at the option of the client, and the attorney shall, upon the agreement being voided, be entitled to collect a reasonable fee.

(d) This section shall not apply to any of the following:

(1) Services rendered in an emergency to avoid foreseeable prejudice to the rights or interests of the client or where a writing is otherwise impractical.

(2) An arrangement as to the fee implied by the fact that the attorney's services are of the same general kind as previously rendered to and paid for by the client.

(3) If the client knowingly states in writing, after full disclosure of this section, that a writing concerning fees is not required.

(4) If the client is a corporation.

(e) This section applies prospectively only to fee agreements following its operative date.

(f) This section shall become operative on January 1, 2000.

§ 6149. Written Fee Contract: Confidential Communication

A written fee contract shall be deemed to be a confidential communication within the meaning of subdivision (e) of Section 6068 and of Section 952 of the Evidence Code.

§ 6149.5 Third–Party Liability Claim; Settlement by Insurer; Notice to Claimant; Effect on Action or Defense

(a) Upon the payment of one hundred dollars ($100) or more in settlement of any third-party liability claim the insurer shall provide written notice to the claimant if both of the following apply:

(1) The claimant is a natural person.

(2) The payment is delivered to the claimant's lawyer or other representative by draft, check, or otherwise.

(b) For purposes of this section, "written notice" includes providing to the claimant a copy of the cover letter sent to the claimant's attorney or other representative that accompanied the settlement payment.

(c) This section shall not create any cause of action for any person against the insurer based upon the insurer's failure to provide the notice to a claimant required by this section. This section shall not create a defense for any party to any cause of action based upon the insurer's failure to provide this notice.

ARTICLE 9.   UNLAWFUL SOLICITATION

§ 6151. Definitions

As used in this article:

(a) A runner or capper is any person, firm, association or corporation acting for consideration in any manner or in any capacity as an agent for an attorney at law or law firm, whether the attorney or any member of the law firm is admitted in California or any other jurisdiction, in the solicitation or procurement of business for the attorney at law or law firm as provided in this article.

(b) An agent is one who represents another in dealings with one or more third persons.

§ 6152. Prohibition of Solicitation

(a) It is unlawful for:

(1) Any person, in an individual capacity or in his capacity as a public or private employee, or for any firm, corporation, partnership or association to act as a runner or capper for any attorneys or to solicit any business for any such attorneys in and about the state prisons, county jails, city jails, city prisons, or other places of detention of persons, city receiving hospitals, city and county receiving hospitals, county hospitals, municipal courts, superior courts, or in any public institution or in any public place or upon any public street or highway or in and about private hospitals, sanitariums or in and about any private institution or upon private property of any character whatsoever.

(2) Any person to solicit another person to commit or join in the commission of a violation of subdivision (a).

(b) A general release from a liability claim obtained from any person during the period of the first physical confinement, whether as an inpatient or outpatient, in a clinic or health facility as defined in Sections 1203 and 1250 of the Health and Safety Code, as a result of the injury alleged to have given rise to the claim and primarily for treatment of the injury, is presumed fraudulent if the release is executed within 15 days after the commencement of confinement or prior to release from confinement, whichever occurs first.

(c) Nothing in this section shall be construed to prevent the recommendation of professional employment where that recommendation is not prohibited by the Rules of Professional Conduct of the State Bar of California.

(d) Nothing in this section shall be construed to mean that a public defender or assigned counsel may not make known his or her services as a criminal defense attorney to persons unable to afford legal counsel whether such persons are in custody or otherwise.

§ 6153. Violations; Penalty

Any person, firm, partnership, association, or corporation violating subdivision (a) of Section 6152 is punishable, upon a first conviction by imprisonment in a county jail for not more than one year. Upon a second or subsequent conviction, a person, firm, partnership, association, or corporation is punishable by imprisonment in a county jail for not more than one year, or by imprisonment in the state prison for 16 months or 2 or 3 years, or by a fine of up to ten thousand dollars ($10,000), or by both that imprisonment and fine.

Any person employed either as an officer, director, trustee, clerk, servant or agent of this state or of any county or other municipal corporation or subdivision thereof, who is found guilty of violating any of the provisions of this article, shall forfeit the right to his office and employment in addition to any other penalty provided in this article.

§ 6154. Runner or Capper Used to Procure Business; Void Contract; Divesting of Fees and Other Compensation; Fees Recovered From Workers' Compensation Actions

(a) Any contract for professional services secured by any attorney at law or law firm in this state through the services of a runner or capper is void. In any action against any attorney or law firm under the Unfair Practices Act, Chapter 4 (commencing with Section 17000) of Division 7, or Chapter 5 (commencing with Section 17200) of Division 7, any judgment shall include an order divesting the attorney or law firm of any fees and other compensation received pursuant to any such void contract. Those fees and compensation shall be recoverable as additional civil penalties under Chapter 4 (commencing with Section 17000) or Chapter 5 (commencing with Section 17200) of Division 7.

(b) Notwithstanding section 17206 or any other provision of law, any fees recovered pursuant to subdivision (a) in an action involving professional services related to the provision of workers' compensation shall be allocated as follows: if the action is brought by the Attorney General, one-half of the penalty collected shall be paid to the State General Fund, and one-half of the penalty collected shall be paid to the Workers' Compensation Fraud Account in the Insurance Fund; if the action is brought by a district attorney, one-half of the penalty collected shall be paid to the treasurer of the county in which the judgment was entered, and one-half of the penalty collected shall be paid to the Workers' Compensation Fraud Account in the Insurance Fund; if the action is brought by a city attorney or city prosecutor, one-half of the penalty collected shall be paid to the treasurer of the city in which the judgment was entered, and one-half of the penalty collected shall be paid to the Workers' Compensation Fraud Account in the Insurance Fund. Moneys deposited into the Workers' Compensation Fraud Account pursuant to this subdivision shall be used in the investigation and prosecution of Workers' Compensation Fraud, as appropriated by the Legislature.

ARTICLE 13. ARBITRATION OF ATTORNEYS' FEES

§ 6200. Establishment of System and Procedure; Arbitration and Mediation; Application of Article; Voluntary or Mandatory Nature; Rules; Immunity of Arbitrator and Mediator; Powers of Arbitrator; Confidentiality of Mediation

(a) The board of governors shall, by rule, establish, maintain, and administer a system and procedure for the arbitration, and may establish, maintain, and administer a system and procedure for mediation of disputes concerning fees, costs, or both, charged for professional services by members of the State Bar or by members of the bar of other jurisdictions. The rules may include provision for a filing fee in such amount as the board may, from time to time, determine.

(b) This article shall not apply to any of the following:

(1) Disputes where a member of the State Bar of California is also admitted to practice in another jurisdiction or where an attorney is only admitted to practice in another jurisdiction, and he or she maintains no office in the State of California, and no material portion of the services were rendered in the State of California.

(2) Claims for affirmative relief against the attorney for damages or otherwise based upon alleged malpractice or professional misconduct, except as provided in subdivision (a) of Section 6203.

(3) Disputes where the fee or cost to be paid by the client or on his or her behalf has been determined pursuant to statute or court order.

(c) Unless the client has agreed in writing to arbitration under this article of all disputes concerning fees, costs, or both, arbitration under this article shall be voluntary for a client and shall be mandatory for an attorney if commenced by a client. Mediation under this article shall be voluntary for an attorney and a client.

(d) The board of governors shall adopt rules to allow arbitration and mediation of attorney fee and cost disputes under this article to proceed under arbitration and mediation systems sponsored by local bar associations in this state. Rules of procedure promulgated by local bar associations are subject to review by the board to insure that they provide for a fair, impartial, and speedy hearing and award.

(e) In adopting or reviewing rules of arbitration under this section the board shall provide that the panel shall include one attorney member whose area of practice is either, at the option of the client, civil law, if the attorney's representation involved civil law, or criminal law, if the attorney's representation involved criminal law, as follows:

(1) If the panel is composed of three members the panel shall include one attorney member whose area of practice is either, at the option of the client, civil or criminal law, and shall include one lay member.

(2) If the panel is composed of one member, that member shall be an attorney whose area of practice is either, at the option of the client, civil or criminal law.

(f) In any arbitration or mediation conducted pursuant to this article by the State Bar or by a local bar association, pursuant to rules of procedure approved by the board of governors, an arbitrator or mediator, as well as the arbitrating association and its directors, officers, and employees, shall have the same immunity which attaches in judicial proceedings.

(g) In the conduct of arbitrations under this article the arbitrator or arbitrators may do all of the following:

(1) Take and hear evidence pertaining to the proceeding.

(2) Administer oaths and affirmations.

(3) Compel, by subpoena, the attendance of witnesses and the production of books, papers, and documents pertaining to the proceeding.

(h) Participation in mediation is a voluntary consensual process, based on direct negotiations between the attorney and his or her client, and is an extension of the negotiated settlement process. All discussions and offers of settlement are confidential and may not be disclosed in any subsequent arbitration or other proceedings.

ARTICLE 14. FUNDS FOR THE PROVISION OF LEGAL SERVICES TO INDIGENT PERSONS

§ 6210. Legislative Findings; Purpose

The Legislature finds that, due to insufficient funding, existing programs providing free legal services in civil matters to indigent persons, especially underserved client groups, such as the elderly, the disabled, juveniles, and non-English-speaking persons, do not adequately meet the needs of these persons. It is the purpose of this article to expand the availability and improve the quality of existing free legal services in civil matters to indigent persons, and to initiate new programs that will provide services to them. The Legislature finds that the use of funds collected by the State Bar pursuant to this article for these purposes is in the public interest, is a proper use of the funds, and is consistent with essential public and governmental purposes in the judicial branch of government. The Legislature further finds that the expansion, improvement, and initiation of legal services to indigent persons will aid in the advancement of the science of jurisprudence and the improvement of the administration of justice.

§ 6211. Establishment by Attorney of Demand Trust Account; Interest Earned to Be Paid to State Bar; Other Accounts Not Prohibited; Rules of Professional Conduct, Authority of Supreme Court or State Bar Not Affected

(a) An attorney or law firm, which in the course of the practice of law receives or disburses trust funds, shall establish and maintain an interest bearing demand trust account and shall deposit therein all client deposits that are nominal in amount or are on deposit for a short period of time. All such client funds may be deposited in a single unsegregated account. The interest earned on all such accounts shall be paid to the State Bar of California to be used for the purposes set forth in this article.

(b) Nothing in this article shall be construed to prohibit an attorney or law firm from establishing one or more interest bearing bank accounts or other trust investments as may be permitted by the Supreme Court, with the interest or dividends earned on the accounts payable to clients for trust funds not deposited in accordance with subdivision (a).

(c) With the approval of the Supreme Court, the State Bar may formulate and enforce rules of professional conduct pertaining to the use by attorneys or law firms of interest bearing trust accounts for unsegregated client funds pursuant to this article.

(d) Nothing in this article shall be construed as affecting or impairing the disciplinary powers and authority of the Supreme Court or of the State Bar or as modifying the statutes and rules governing the conduct of members of the State Bar.

§ 6212. Establishment by Attorney of Demand Trust Account; Amount of Interest; Remittance to State Bar; Statements and Reports

An attorney who, or a law firm which, establishes an interest bearing demand trust account pursuant to subdivision (a) of Section 6211 shall comply with all of the following provisions:

(a) The interest bearing trust account shall be established with a bank or such other financial institutions as are authorized by the Supreme Court.

(b) The rate of interest payable on any interest bearing demand trust account shall not be less than the rate paid by the depository institution to regular, nonattorney depositors. Higher rates offered by the institution to customers whose deposits exceed certain time or quantity qualifications, such as those offered in the form of certificates of deposit, may be obtained by an attorney or law firm so long as there is no impairment of the right to withdraw or transfer principal immediately (except as accounts generally may be subject to statutory notification requirements), even though interest may be sacrificed thereby.

(c) The depository institution shall be directed to do all of the following:

(1) To remit interest on the average daily balance in the account, less reasonable service charges, to the State Bar, at least quarterly.

(2) To transmit to the State Bar with each remittance a statement showing the name of the attorney or law firm for whom the remittance is sent, the rate of interest applied, and the amount of service charges deducted, if any.

(3) To transmit to the depositing attorney or law firm at the same time a report showing the amount paid to the State Bar for that period, the rate of interest applied, the amount of service charges deducted, if any, and the average daily account balance for each month of the period for which the report is made.

§ 6213. Definitions

As used in this article:

(a) "Qualified legal services project" means either of the following:

(1) A nonprofit project incorporated and operated exclusively in California which provides as its primary purpose and function legal services without charge to indigent persons and which has quality control procedures approved by the State Bar of California.

(2) A program operated exclusively in California by a nonprofit law school accredited by the State Bar of California which meets the requirements of subparagraphs (A) and (B).

(A) The program shall have operated for at least two years at a cost of at least twenty thousand dollars ($20,000) per year as an identifiable law school unit with a primary purpose and function of providing legal services without charge to indigent persons.

(B) The program shall have quality control procedures approved by the State Bar of California.

(b) "Qualified support center" means an incorporated nonprofit legal services center, which has as its primary purpose and function the provision of legal training, legal technical assistance, or advocacy support without charge and which actually provides through an office in California a significant level of legal training, legal technical assistance, or advocacy support without charge to qualified legal services projects on a statewide basis in California.

(c) "Recipient" means a qualified legal services project or support center receiving financial assistance under this article.

(d) "Indigent person" means a person whose income is (1) 125 percent or less of the current poverty threshold established by the United States Office of Management and Budget, or (2) who is eligible for Supplemental Security Income or free services under the Older Americans Act or Developmentally Disabled Assistance Act. With regard to a project which provides free services of attorneys in private practice without compensation, "indigent person" also means a person whose income is 75 percent or less of the maximum levels of income for lower income households as defined in Section 50079.5 of the Health and Safety Code. For the purpose of this subdivision, the income of a person who is disabled shall be determined after deducting the costs of medical and other disability-related special expenses.

(e) "Fee generating case" means any case or matter which, if undertaken on behalf of an indigent person by an attorney in private practice, reasonably may be expected to result in payment of a fee for legal services from an award to a client, from public funds, or from the opposing party. A case shall not be considered fee generating if adequate representation is unavailable and any of the following circumstances exist:

(1) The recipient has determined that free referral is not possible because of any of the following reasons:

(A) The case has been rejected by the local lawyer referral service, or if there is no such service, by two attorneys in private practice who have experience in the subject matter of the case.

(B) Neither the referral service nor any attorney will consider the case without payment of a consultation fee.

(C) The case is of the type that attorneys in private practice in the area ordinarily do not accept, or do not accept without prepayment of a fee.

(D) Emergency circumstances compel immediate action before referral can be made, but the client is advised that, if appropriate and consistent with professional responsibility, referral will be attempted at a later time.

(2) Recovery of damages is not the principal object of the case and a request for damages is merely ancillary to an action for equitable or other nonpecuniary relief, or inclusion of a counterclaim requesting damages is necessary for effective defense or because of applicable rules governing joinder of counterclaims.

(3) A court has appointed a recipient or an employee of a recipient pursuant to a statute or a court rule or practice of equal applicability to all attorneys in the jurisdiction.

(4) The case involves the rights of a claimant under a publicly supported benefit program for which entitlement to benefit is based on need.

(f) "Legal Services Corporation" means the Legal Services Corporation established under the Legal Services Corporation Act of 1974 (Public Law 93–355; 42 U.S.C. Sec. 2996 et seq.).

(g) "Older Americans Act" means the Older Americans Act of 1965, as amended (Public Law 89–73; 42 U.S.C. Sec. 3001 et seq.).

(h) "Developmentally Disabled Assistance Act" means the Developmentally Disabled Assistance and Bill of Rights Act of 1975, as amended (Public Law 94–103; 42 U.S.C. Sec. 6001 et seq.).

(i) "Supplemental security income recipient" means an individual receiving or eligible to receive payments under Title XVI of the federal Social Security Act, or payments under Chapter 3 (commencing with Section 12000) of Part 3 of Division 9 of the Welfare and Institutions Code.

§ 6214. Qualified Legal Service Projects

(a) Projects meeting the requirements of subdivision (a) of Section 6213 which are funded either in whole or part by the Legal Services Corporation or with Older American Act funds shall be presumed qualified legal services projects for the purpose of this article.

(b) Projects meeting the requirements of subdivision (a) of Section 6213 but not qualifying under the presumption specified in subdivision (a) shall qualify for funds under this article if they meet all of the following additional criteria:

(1) They receive cash funds from other sources in the amount of at least twenty thousand dollars ($20,000) per year to support free legal representation to indigent persons.

(2) They have demonstrated community support for the operation of a viable ongoing program.

(3) They provide one or both of the following special services:

(A) The coordination of the recruitment of substantial numbers of attorneys in private practice to provide free legal representation to indigent persons or to qualified legal services projects in California.

(B) The provision of legal representation, training, or technical assistance on matters concerning special client groups, including the elderly, the disabled, juveniles, and non-English-speaking groups, or on matters of specialized substantive law important to the special client groups.

§ 6214.5   Qualified Legal Services Projects;   Eligibility for Distributions of Funds

A law school program that meets the definition of a "qualified legal services project" as defined in paragraph (2) of subdivision (a) of Section 6213, and that applied to the State Bar for funding under this article not later than February 17, 1984, shall be deemed eligible for all distributions of funds made under Section 6216.

§ 6215.   Qualified Support Centers

(a) Support centers satisfying the qualifications specified in subdivision (b) of Section 6213 which were operating an office and providing services in California on December 31, 1980, shall be presumed to be qualified support centers for the purposes of this article.

(b) Support centers not qualifying under the presumption specified in subdivision (a) may qualify as a support center by meeting both of the following additional criteria:

(1) Meeting quality control standards established by the State Bar.

(2) Being deemed to be of special need by a majority of the qualified legal services projects.

§ 6216.   Distribution of Funds

The State Bar shall distribute all moneys received under the program established by this article for the provision of civil legal services to indigent persons. The funds first shall be distributed 18 months from the effective date of this article, or upon such a date, as shall be determined by the State Bar, that adequate funds are available to initiate the program. Thereafter, the funds shall be distributed on an annual basis. All distributions of funds shall be made in the following order and in the following manner:

(a) To pay the actual administrative costs of the program, including any costs incurred after the adoption of this article and a reasonable reserve therefor.

(b) Eighty-five percent of the funds remaining after payment of administrative costs allocated pursuant to this article shall be distributed to qualified legal services projects. Distribution shall be by a pro rata county-by-county formula based upon the number of persons whose income is 125 percent or less of the current poverty threshold per county. For the purposes of this section, the source of data identifying the number of persons per county shall be the latest available figures from the United States Department of Commerce, Bureau of the Census. Projects from more than one county may pool their funds to operate a joint, multicounty legal services project serving each of their respective counties.

(1)(A) In any county which is served by more than one qualified legal services project, the State Bar shall distribute funds for the county to those projects which apply on a pro rata basis, based upon the amount of their total budget expended in the prior year for legal services in that county as compared to the total expended in the prior year for legal services by all qualified legal services projects applying therefor in the county. In determining the amount of funds to be allocated to a qualified legal services project specified in paragraph (2) of subdivision (a) of Section 6213, the State Bar shall recognize only expenditures attributable to the representation of indigent persons as constituting the budget of the program.

(B) The State Bar shall reserve 10 percent of the funds allocated to the county for distribution to programs meeting the standards of subparagraph (A) of paragraph (3) and paragraphs (1) and (2) of subdivision (b) of Section 6214 and which perform the services described in subparagraph (A) of paragraph (3) of Section 6214 as their principal means of delivering legal services. The State Bar shall distribute the funds for that county to those programs which apply on a pro rata basis, based upon the amount of their total budget expended for free legal services in that county as compared to the total expended for free legal services by all programs meeting the standards of subparagraph (A) of paragraph (3) and paragraphs (1) and (2) of subdivision (b) of Section 6214 in that county. The State Bar shall distribute any funds for which no program has qualified pursuant hereto, in accordance with the provisions of subparagraph (A) of paragraph (1) of this subdivision.

(2) In any county in which there is no qualified legal services project providing services, the State Bar shall reserve for the remainder of the fiscal year for distribution the pro rata share of funds as provided for by this article. Upon application of a qualified legal services project proposing to provide legal services to the indigent of the county, the State Bar shall distribute the funds to the project. Any funds not so distributed shall be added to the funds to be distributed the following year.

(c) Fifteen percent of the funds remaining after payment of administrative costs allocated for the purposes of this article shall be distributed equally by the State Bar to qualified support centers which apply for the funds. The funds provided to support centers shall be used only for the provision of legal services within California. Qualified support centers that receive funds to provide services to qualified legal services projects from sources other than this article, shall submit and shall have approved by the State Bar a plan assuring that the services funded under this article are in addition to those already funded for qualified legal services projects by other sources.

§ 6217. Maintenance of Quality Services, Professional Standards, Attorney-Client Privilege; Funds to Be Expended in Accordance With Article; Interference With Attorney Prohibited

With respect to the provision of legal assistance under this article, each recipient shall ensure all of the following:

(a) The maintenance of quality service and professional standards.

(b) The expenditure of funds received in accordance with the provisions of this article.

(c) The preservation of the attorney-client privilege in any case, and the protection of the integrity of the adversary process from any impairment in furnishing legal assistance to indigent persons.

(d) That no one shall interfere with any attorney funded in whole or in part by this article in carrying out his or her professional responsibility to his or her client as established by the rules of professional responsibility and this chapter.

§ 6218. Eligibility for Services; Establishment of Guidelines; Funds to Be Expended in Accordance With Article

All legal services projects and support centers receiving funds pursuant to this article shall adopt financial eligibility guidelines for indigent persons.

(a) Qualified legal services programs shall ensure that funds appropriated pursuant to this article shall be used solely to defray the costs of providing legal services to indigent persons or for such other purposes as set forth in this article.

(b) Funds received pursuant to this article by support centers shall only be used to provide services to qualified legal services projects as defined in subdivision (a) of Section 6213 which are used pursuant to a plan as required by subdivision (c) of Section 6216, or as permitted by Section 6219.

§ 6219. Provision of Work Opportunities and Scholarships for Disadvantaged Law Students

Qualified legal services projects and support centers may use funds provided under this article to provide work opportunities with pay, and where feasible, scholarships for disadvantaged law students to help defray their law school expenses.

§ 6220. Private Attorneys Providing Legal Services Without Charge; Support Center Services

Attorneys in private practice who are providing legal services without charge to indigent persons shall not be disqualified from receiving the services of the qualified support centers.

§ 6221. Services for Indigent Members of Disadvantaged and Underserved Groups

Qualified legal services projects shall make significant efforts to utilize 20 percent of the funds allocated under this article for increasing the availability of services to the elderly, the disabled, juveniles, or other indigent persons who are members of disadvantaged and underserved groups within their service area.

§ 6222. Financial Statements; Submission to State Bar; State Bar Report

A recipient of funds allocated pursuant to this article annually shall submit a financial statement to the State Bar, including an audit of the funds by a certified public accountant or a fiscal review approved by the State Bar, a report demonstrating the programs on which they were expended, a report on the recipient's compliance with the requirements of Section 6217, and progress in meeting the service expansion requirements of Section 6221.

The Board of Governors of the State Bar shall include a report of receipts of funds under this article, expenditures for administrative costs, and disbursements of the funds, on a county-by-county basis, in the annual report of State Bar receipts and expenditures required pursuant to Section 6145.

§ 6223. Expenditure of Funds; Prohibitions

No funds allocated by the State Bar pursuant to this article shall be used for any of the following purposes:

(a) The provision of legal assistance with respect to any fee generating case, except in accordance with guidelines which shall be promulgated by the State Bar.

(b) The provision of legal assistance with respect to any criminal proceeding.

(c) The provision of legal assistance, except to indigent persons or except to provide support services to qualified legal services projects as defined by this article.

§ 6224. State Bar; Powers; Determination of Qualifications to Receive Funds; Denial of Funds; Termination; Procedures

The State Bar shall have the power to determine that an applicant for funding is not qualified to receive funding, to deny future funding, or to terminate existing funding because the recipient is not operating in compliance with the requirements or restrictions of this article.

A denial of an application for funding or for future funding or an action by the State Bar to terminate an existing grant of funds under this article shall not become final until the applicant or recipient has been afforded reasonable notice and an opportunity for a timely and fair hearing. Pending final determination of any hearing held with reference to termination of funding, financial assistance shall be continued at its existing level on a month-to-month basis. Hearings for denial shall be conducted by an impartial hearing officer whose decision shall be final. The hearing officer shall render a decision no later than 30 days after the conclusion of the hearing. Specific procedures governing the conduct of the hearings of this section shall be determined by the State Bar pursuant to Section 6225.

§ 6225. Implementation of Article; Adoption of Rules and Regulations; Procedures

The Board of Governors of the State Bar shall adopt the regulations and procedures necessary to implement this article and to ensure that the funds allocated herein are utilized to provide civil legal services to indigent persons, especially underserved client groups such as but not limited to the elderly, the disabled, juveniles, and non-English-speaking persons.

In adopting the regulations the Board of Governors shall comply with the following procedures:

(a) The board shall publish a preliminary draft of the regulations and procedures, which shall be distributed, together with notice of the hearings required by subdivision (b), to commercial banking institutions, to members of the State Bar, and to potential recipients of funds.

(b) The board shall hold at least two public hearings, one in southern California and one in northern California where affected and interested parties shall be afforded an opportunity to present oral and written testimony regarding the proposed regulations and procedures.

§ 6226. Implementation of Article; Resolution

The program authorized by this article shall become operative only upon the adoption of a resolution by the Board of Governors of the State Bar stating that regulations have been adopted pursuant to Section 6225 which conform the program to all applicable tax and banking statutes, regulations, and rulings.

§ 6227. Credit of State Not Pledged

Nothing in this article shall create an obligation or pledge of the credit of the State of California or of the State Bar of California. Claims arising by reason of acts done pursuant to this article shall be limited to the moneys generated hereunder.

§ 6228. Severability

If any provision of this article or the application thereof to any group or circumstances is held invalid, such invalidity shall not affect the other provisions or applications of this article which can be given effect without the invalid provision or application, and to this end the provisions of this article are severable.

NOTE, SOME IMPORTANT STATUTES FOR LAWYERS IN CALIFORNIA GOVERNMENT

The State has a large number of statutes dealing with professional responsibilities of governmental officials, particularly if they are lawyers. West's California Government Code, provides in part:

§ 8920. Prohibited Acts

(a) No Member of the Legislature, state elective or appointive officer, or judge or justice shall, while serving as such, have any interest, financial or otherwise, direct or indirect, or engage in any business or transaction or professional activity, or incur any obligation of any nature, which is in substantial conflict with the proper discharge of his duties in the public interest and of his responsibilities as prescribed in the laws of this state.

(b) No Member of the Legislature shall do any of the following:

(1) Accept other employment which he has reason to believe will either impair his independence of judgment as to his official duties or require him, or induce him, to disclose confidential information acquired by him in the course of and by reason of his official duties.

(2) Willfully and knowingly disclose, for pecuniary gain, to any other person, confidential information acquired by him in the course of and by reason of his official duties or use any such information for the purpose of pecuniary gain.

(3) Accept or agree to accept, or be in partnership with any person who accepts or agrees to accept, any employment, fee, or other thing of monetary value, or portion thereof, in consideration of his appearing, agreeing to appear, or taking any other action on behalf of another person before any state board or agency.

This subdivision shall not be construed to prohibit a member who is an attorney at law from practicing in that capacity before any court or before the Workers' Compensation Appeals Board and receiving compensation therefor. This subdivision shall not act to prohibit a member from acting as an advocate without compensation or making inquiry for information on behalf of a constituent before a state board or agency, or from engaging in activities on behalf of another which require purely ministerial acts by the board or agency and which in no way require the board or agency to exercise any discretion, or from engaging in activities involving a board or agency which are strictly on his or her own behalf. The prohibition contained in this subdivision shall not apply to a partnership or firm of which the Member of the Legislature is a member if the Member of the Legislature does not share directly or indirectly in the fee, less any expenses attributable to that fee, resulting from the transaction. The prohibition contained in this subdivision as it read immediately prior to January 1, 1983, shall not apply in connection with any matter pending before any state board or agency on or before January 2, 1967, if the affected member of the Legislature was an attorney of record or representative in the matter prior to January 2, 1967. The prohibition contained in this subdivision, as amended and operative on January 1, 1983, shall not apply to any activity of any Member in connection with a matter pending before any state board or agency on January 1, 1983, which was not prohibited by this section prior to that date, if the affected Member of the Legislature was an attorney of record or representative in the matter prior to January 1, 1983.

(4) Receive or agree to receive, directly or indirectly, any compensation, reward, or gift from any source except the State of California for any service, advice, assistance or other matter related to the legislative process, except fees for speeches or published works on legislative subjects and except, in connection therewith, reimbursement of expenses for actual expenditures for travel and reasonable subsistence for which no payment or reimbursement is made by the State of California;

(5) Participate, by voting or any other action, on the floor of either house, or in committee or elsewhere, in the passage or defeat of legislation in which he has a personal interest, except as follows:

(i) If, on the vote for final passage by the house of which he is a member, of the legislation in which he has a personal interest, he first files a statement (which shall be entered verbatim on the journal) stating in substance that he has a personal interest in the legislation to be voted on and notwithstanding that interest, he is able to cast a fair and objective vote on that legislation, he may cast his vote without violating any provision of this article;

(ii) If the member believes that, because of his personal interest, he should abstain from participating in the vote on the legislation, he shall so advise the presiding officer prior to the commencement of the vote and shall be excused from voting on the legislation without any entry on the journal of the fact of his personal interest. In the event a rule of the house, requiring that each member who is present vote aye or nay is invoked, the presiding officer shall order the member excused from compliance and shall order entered on the journal a simple statement that the member was excused from voting on the legislation pursuant to law.

The provisions of this section do not apply to persons who are members of the state civil service as defined in Article VII of the California Constitution.

§ 8921. Interest in Substantial Conflict With Proper Discharge of Duties

A person subject to this article has an interest which is in substantial conflict with the proper discharge of his duties in the public interest and of his responsibilities as prescribed in the laws of this state or a personal interest, arising from any situation, within the scope of this article, if he has reason to believe or expect that he will derive a direct monetary gain or suffer a direct monetary loss, as the case may be, by reason of his official activity. He does not have an interest which is in substantial conflict with the proper discharge of his duties in the public interest and of his responsibilities as prescribed in the laws of this state or a personal interest, arising from any situation, within the scope of this article, if any benefit or detriment accrues to him as a member of a business, profession, occupation, or group to no greater extent than any other member of such business, profession, occupation, or group.

See also: West California Government Code, Section 24004—restrictions on practice of law by sheriff, clerk, constable, or any of their deputies.

Id. Section 31000.6—employment of legal counsel by board of supervisors to assist county assessor where county counsel or district attorney have a conflict of interest; in the event of a dispute as to whether a conflict exists, the presiding judge of superior court decides.

Id. Section 41805—representation of defendants in criminal matters by city attorney (or his partner or associate) if the defendant is not accused of violation of such city's ordinances, the city expressly relieves the city attorney of all prosecutorial functions on his behalf, and the defendant is "informed of and expressly waives any rights created as a result of any potential conflict *** ."

NEW YORK CODE OF PROFESSIONAL RESPONSIBILITY

DISCIPLINARY RULES OF THE CODE OF PROFESSIONAL RESPONSIBILITY

The Disciplinary Rules of the Code of Professional Responsibility, promulgated as joint rules of the Appellate Divisions of the Supreme Court effective January 1, 2002, are now Part 1200 of Title 22 of New York Codes, Rules and Regulations (NYCRR).

§ 1200.1 DEFINITIONS *

1. "Differing interests" include every interest that will adversely affect either the judgment or the loyalty of a lawyer to a client, whether it be a conflicting, inconsistent, diverse, or other interest.

2. "Law firm" includes, but is not limited to, a professional legal corporation, a limited liability company or partnership engaged in the practice of law, the legal department of a corporation or other organization and a qualified legal assistance organization.

3. "Person" includes a corporation, an association, a trust, a partnership, and any other organization or legal entity.

4. "Professional legal corporation" means a corporation, or an association treated as a corporation, authorized by law to practice law for profit.

5. "State" includes the District of Columbia, Puerto Rico, and other federal territories and possessions.

6. "Tribunal" includes all courts, arbitrators and other adjudicatory bodies.

7. (Repealed).

8. "Qualified legal assistance organization" means an office or organization of one of the four types listed in DR 2–103(D)(1) through (4), inclusive, that meets all the requirements thereof.

9. "Fraud" does not include conduct, although characterized as fraudulent by statute or administrative rule, which lacks an element of scienter, deceit, intent to

---

* "Confidence" and "Secret" are defined in section 1200.19(a) of this Part. "Sexual relations" is defined in section 1200.29(a) of this Part. "Copy" is defined in section 1200.46(d)(10) of this Part.

mislead, or knowing failure to correct misrepresentations which can be reasonably expected to induce detrimental reliance by another.

10. "Domestic relations matters" means representation of a client in a claim, action or proceeding, or preliminary to the filing of a claim, action or proceeding, in either Supreme Court or Family Court, or in any court of appellate jurisdiction, for divorce, separation, annulment, custody, visitation, maintenance, child support, or alimony, or to enforce or modify a judgment or order in connection with any such claims, actions, or proceedings.

§ 1200.2 [DR 1–101.] Maintaining Integrity and Competence of the Legal Profession

(a) A lawyer is subject to discipline if the lawyer has made a materially false statement in, or has deliberately failed to disclose a material fact requested in connection with, the lawyer's application for admission to the bar.

(b) A lawyer shall not further the application for admission to the bar of another person that the lawyer knows to be unqualified in respect to character, education, or other relevant attribute.

§ 1200.3 [DR 1–102.] Misconduct

(a)[1] A lawyer or law firm shall not:

(1) Violate a Disciplinary Rule.

(2) Circumvent a Disciplinary Rule through actions of another.

(3) Engage in illegal conduct that adversely reflects on the lawyer's honesty, trustworthiness or fitness as a lawyer.

(4) Engage in conduct involving dishonesty, fraud, deceit, or misrepresentation.

(5) Engage in conduct that is prejudicial to the administration of justice.

(6) Unlawfully discriminate in the practice of law, including in hiring, promoting or otherwise determining conditions of employment, on the basis of age, race, creed, color, national origin, sex, disability, marital status, or sexual orientation. Where there is a tribunal with jurisdiction to hear a complaint, if timely brought, other than a Departmental Disciplinary Committee, a complaint based on unlawful discrimination shall be brought before such tribunal in the first instance. A certified copy of a determination by such a tribunal, which has become final and enforceable, and as to which the right to judicial or appellate review has been exhausted, finding that the lawyer has engaged in an unlawful discriminatory practice shall constitute *prima facie* evidence of professional misconduct in a disciplinary proceeding.

(7) Engage in any other conduct that adversely reflects on the lawyer's fitness as a lawyer.

§ 1200.4 [DR 1–103.] Disclosure of Information to Authorities

(a) A lawyer possessing knowledge, (1) not protected as a confidence or secret, of a violation, or (2) not gained in the lawyer's capacity as a member of a bona fide lawyer assistance or similar program or committee, of a violation of Section 1200.3 of this Part [DR 1–102] that raises a substantial question as to another lawyer's honesty,

1. So in original. No par. b has been enacted.

trustworthiness or fitness as a lawyer shall report such knowledge to a tribunal or other authority empowered to investigate or act upon such violation.

(b) A lawyer possessing knowledge or evidence, not protected as a confidence or secret, concerning another lawyer or a judge shall reveal fully such knowledge or evidence upon proper request of a tribunal or other authority empowered to investigate or act upon the conduct of lawyers or judges.

§ 1200.5 [DR 1–104.] Responsibilities of a Partner or Supervisory Lawyer and Subordinate Lawyers

(a) A law firm shall make reasonable efforts to ensure that all lawyers in the firm conform to the disciplinary rules.

(b) A lawyer with management responsibility in the law firm or direct supervisory authority over another lawyer shall make reasonable efforts to ensure that the other lawyer conforms to the disciplinary rules.

(c) A law firm shall adequately supervise, as appropriate, the work of partners, associates and nonlawyers who work at the firm. The degree of supervision required is that which is reasonable under the circumstances, taking into account factors such as the experience of the person whose work is being supervised, the amount of work involved in a particular matter, and the likelihood that ethical problems might arise in the course of working on the matter.

(d) A lawyer shall be responsible for a violation of the disciplinary rules by another lawyer or for the conduct of a nonlawyer employed or retained by or associated with the lawyer that would be a violation of the disciplinary rules if engaged in by a lawyer if:

(1) The lawyer orders, or directs the specific conduct, or, with knowledge of the specific conduct, ratifies it; or

(2) The lawyer is a partner in the law firm in which the other lawyer practices or the nonlawyer is employed, or has supervisory authority over the other lawyer or the nonlawyer, and knows of such conduct, or in the exercise or reasonable management or supervisory authority should have known of the conduct so that reasonable remedial action could be or could have been taken at a time when its consequences could be or could have been avoided or mitigated.

(e) A lawyer shall comply with these Disciplinary Rules notwithstanding that the lawyer acted at the direction of another person.

(f) A subordinate lawyer does not violate these Disciplinary Rules if that lawyer acts in accordance with a supervisory lawyer's reasonable resolution of an arguable question of professional duty.

§ 1200.5a [DR 1–105.] Disciplinary Authority and Choice of Law

(a) A lawyer admitted to practice in this state is subject to the disciplinary authority of this state, regardless of where the lawyer's conduct occurs. A lawyer may be subject to the disciplinary authority of both this state and another jurisdiction where the lawyer is admitted for the same conduct.

(b) In any exercise of the disciplinary authority of this state, the rules of professional conduct to be applied shall be as follows:

(1) For conduct in connection with a proceeding in a court before which a lawyer has been admitted to practice (either generally or for purposes of that proceeding), the rules to be applied shall be the rules of the jurisdiction in which the court sits, unless the rules of the court provide otherwise; and

(2) For any other conduct:

(i) If the lawyer is licensed to practice only in this state, the rules to be applied shall be the rules to be applied shall be the rules of this state, and

(ii) If the lawyer is licensed to practice in this state and another jurisdiction, the rules to be applied shall be the rules of the admitting jurisdiction in which the lawyer principally practices; provided, however, that if particular conduct clearly has its predominant effect in another jurisdiction in which the lawyer is licensed to practice, the rules of that jurisdiction shall be applied to that conduct.

§ 1200.5b [DR 1-106.]   Responsibilities Regarding Nonlegal Services

(a) With respect to lawyers or law firms providing nonlegal services to clients or other persons:

(1) A lawyer or law firm that provides nonlegal services to a person that are not distinct from legal services being provided to that person by the lawyer or law firm is subject to these Disciplinary Rules with respect to the provision of both legal and nonlegal services.

(2) A lawyer or law firm that provides nonlegal services to a person that are distinct from legal services being provided to that person by the lawyer or law firm is subject to these Disciplinary Rules with respect to the nonlegal services if the person receiving the services could reasonably believe that the nonlegal services are the subject of an attorney-client relationship.

(3) A lawyer or law firm that is an owner, controlling party or agent of, or that is otherwise affiliated with, an entity that the lawyer or law firm knows to be providing nonlegal services to a person is subject to these Disciplinary Rules with respect to the nonlegal services if the person receiving the services could reasonably believe that the nonlegal services are the subject of an attorney-client relationship.

(4) For purposes of DR 1-106 [1200.5b] (a)(2) and (a)(3), it will be presumed that the person receiving nonlegal services believes the services to be the subject of an attorney-client relationship unless the lawyer or law firm has advised the person receiving the services in writing that the services are not legal services and that the protection of an attorney-client relationship does not exist with respect to the nonlegal services, or if the interest of the lawyer or law firm in the entity providing nonlegal services is de minimis.

(b) Notwithstanding the provisions of DR 1-106 [1200.5b] (a), a lawyer or law firm that is an owner, controlling party, agent, or is otherwise affiliated with an entity that the lawyer or law firm knows is providing nonlegal services to a person shall not permit any nonlawyer providing such services or affiliated with that entity to direct or regulate the professional judgment of the lawyer or law firm in rendering legal services to any person, or to cause the lawyer or law firm to compromise its duty under DR 4-101 [1200.19] (b) and (d) with respect to the confidences and secrets of a client receiving legal services.

(c) For purposes of this Disciplinary Rule, "nonlegal services" shall mean those services that lawyers may lawfully provide and that are not prohibited as an unauthorized practice of law when provided by a nonlawyer.

§ 1200.5c [DR 1–107.] Contractual Relationship Between Lawyers and Nonlegal Professionals

(a) The practice of law has an essential tradition of complete independence and uncompromised loyalty to those it serves. Recognizing this tradition, clients of lawyers practicing in New York State are guaranteed "independent professional judgment and undivided loyalty uncompromised by conflicts of interest". Indeed, these guarantees represent the very foundation of the profession and allow and foster its continued role as a protector of the system of law. Therefore, a lawyer must remain completely responsible for his or her own independent professional judgment, maintain the confidences and secrets of clients, preserve funds of clients and third parties in his or her control, and otherwise comply with the legal and ethical principles governing lawyers in New York State. Multi-disciplinary practice between lawyers and nonlawyers is incompatible with the core values of the legal profession and therefore, a strict division between services provided by lawyers and those provided by nonlawyers is essential to protect those values. However, a lawyer or law firm may enter into and maintain a contractual relationship with a nonlegal professional or nonlegal professional service firm for the purpose of offering to the public, on a systematic and continuing basis, legal services performed by the lawyer or law firm, as well as other nonlegal professional services, notwithstanding the provisions of DR 5–101 [1200.20] (a), provided that:

(1) The profession of the nonlegal professional or nonlegal professional service firm is included in a list jointly established and maintained by the Appellate Divisions pursuant to Section 1205.3 of the Joint Appellate Division rules.

(2) The lawyer or law firm neither grants to the nonlegal professional or nonlegal professional service firm, nor permits such person or firm to obtain, hold or exercise, directly or indirectly, any ownership or investment interest in, or managerial or supervisory right, power or position in connection with the practice of law by the lawyer or law firm, nor, as provided in DR 2–103 [1200.8] (b)(1), shares legal fees with a nonlawyer or receives or gives any monetary or other tangible benefit for giving or receiving a referral; and

(3) The fact that the contractual relationship exists is disclosed by the lawyer or law firm to any client of the lawyer or law firm before the client is referred to the nonlegal professional service firm, or to any client of the nonlegal professional service firm before that client receives legal services from the lawyer or law firm; and the client has given informed written consent and has been provided with a copy of the "Statement of Client's Rights In Cooperative Business Arrangements" pursuant to section 1205.4 of the Joint Appellate Divisions rules.

(b) For purposes of DR 1–107 [1200–5c] (a):

(1) Each profession on the list maintained pursuant to a joint rule of the Appellate Divisions shall have been designated sua sponte, or approved by the Appellate Divisions upon application of a member of a nonlegal profession or nonlegal professional service firm, upon a determination that the profession is composed of individuals who, with respect to their profession:

493

(A) have been awarded a Bachelor's Degree or its equivalent from an accredited college or university;

(B) are licensed to practice the profession by an agency of the State of New York or the United States Government; and

(C) are required under penalty of suspension or revocation of license to adhere to a code of ethical conduct that is reasonably comparable to that of the legal profession.

(2) The term "ownership or investment interest" shall mean any such interest in any form of debt or equity, and shall include any interest commonly considered to be an interest accruing to or enjoyed by an owner or investor.

(c) DR 1–107 [1200.5c] (a)(1) shall not apply to relationships consisting solely of reciprocal referral agreements or understandings between a lawyer or law firm and a nonlegal professional or nonlegal professional service firm.

(d) Notwithstanding DR 3–102 [1200.17] (a), a lawyer or law firm may allocate costs and expenses with a nonlegal professional or nonlegal professional service firm pursuant to a contractual relationship permitted by DR 1–107 [1200.5c] (a), provided the allocation reasonably reflects only the costs and expenses incurred or expected to be incurred by each.

§ 1200.6 [DR 2–101.]   Publicity and Advertising

(a) A lawyer on behalf of himself or herself or partners or associates, shall not use or disseminate or participate in the preparation or dissemination of any public communication or communication to a prospective client containing statements or claims that are false, deceptive or misleading.

(b) (Repealed).

(c) It is proper to include information, provided its dissemination does not violate the provisions of section 1200.6(a) and (b), as to:

(1) legal and nonlegal education, degrees and other scholastic distinctions, dates of admission to any bar; areas of the law in which the lawyer or law firm practices, as authorized by the Code of Professional Responsibility; public offices and teaching positions held; memberships in bar associations or other professional societies or organizations, including offices and committee assignments therein; foreign language fluency;

(2) names of clients regularly represented, provided that the client has given prior written consent;

(3) bank references; credit arrangements accepted; prepaid or group legal services programs in which the attorney or firm participates; nonlegal services provided by the lawyer or by an entity owned and controlled by the lawyer; the existence of contractual relationships between the lawyer or law firm and a nonlegal professional or nonlegal professional service firm, to the extent permitted by section 1200.5c [DR 1–107], and the nature and extent of services available through those contractual relationships; and

(4) fees for initial consultation; contingent fee rates in civil matters when accompanied by a statement disclosing the information required by section 1200.6(*l*); range of fees for legal and non legal services, provided that there be available to the public free of charge a written statement clearly describing the scope of each advertised service; hourly rates; and fixed fees for specified legal and nonlegal services.

(d) Advertising and publicity shall be designed to educate the public to an awareness of legal needs and to provide information relevant to the selection of the most appropriate counsel. Information other than that specifically authorized in section 1200.6(c) that is consistent with these purposes may be disseminated providing that it does not violate any other provisions of this Rule.

(e) A lawyer or law firm advertising any fixed fee for specified legal services shall, at the time of fee publication, have available to the public a written statement clearly describing the scope of each advertised service, which statement shall be delivered to the client at the time of retainer for any such service. Such legal services shall include all those services which are recognized as reasonable and necessary under local custom in the area of practice in the community where the services are performed.

(f) If the advertisement is broadcast, it shall be prerecorded or taped and approved for broadcast by the lawyer, and a recording or videotape of the actual transmission shall be retained by the lawyer for a period of not less than one year following such transmission. All advertisements of legal services that are mailed, or are distributed other than by radio, television, directory, newspaper, magazine or other periodical, by a lawyer or law firm that practices law in this state, shall also be subject to the following provisions:

(1) A copy of each advertisement shall at the time of its initial mailing or distribution be filed with the Departmental Disciplinary Committee of the appropriate judicial department.

(2) Such advertisement shall contain no reference to the fact of filing.

(3) If such advertisement is directed to a predetermined address, a list, containing the names and addresses of all persons to whom the advertisement is being or will thereafter be mailed or distributed, shall be retained by the lawyer or law firm for a period of not less than one year following the last date of mailing or distribution.

(4) The advertisements filed pursuant to this subdivision shall be open to public inspection.

(5) The requirements of this subdivision shall not apply to such professional cards or other announcements the distribution of which is authorized by section 1200.7 of this Part [DR 2–102(A)].

(g) If a lawyer or law firm advertises a range of fees or an hourly rate for services, the lawyer or law firm may not charge more than the fee advertised for such services. If a lawyer or law firm advertises a fixed fee for specified legal services, or performs services described in a fee schedule, the lawyer or law firm may not charge more than the fixed fee for such stated legal service as set forth in the advertisement or fee schedule, unless the client agrees in writing that the services performed or to be performed were not legal services referred to or implied in the advertisement or in the fee schedule and, further, that a different fee arrangement shall apply to the transaction.

(h) Unless otherwise specified in the advertisement, if a lawyer publishes any fee information authorized under this Disciplinary Rule in a publication which is published more frequently than once per month, the lawyer shall be bound by any representation made therein for a period of not less than 30 days after such publication. If a lawyer publishes any fee information authorized under this Rule in a publication which is published once per month or less frequently, the lawyer shall be bound by any representation made therein until the publication of the succeeding issue. If a lawyer publishes any fee information authorized under this Rule in a publication which has no fixed date for publication of a succeeding issue, the lawyer shall be bound by any representation made therein for a reasonable period of time after publication, but in no event less than 90 days.

(i) Unless otherwise specified, if a lawyer broadcasts any fee information authorized under this Rule, the lawyer shall be bound by any representation made therein for a period of not less than 30 days after such broadcast.

(j) A lawyer shall not compensate or give any thing of value to representatives of the press, radio, television or other communication medium in anticipation of or in return for professional publicity in a news item.

(k) All advertisements of legal services shall include the name, office address and telephone number of the attorney or law firm whose services are being offered.

(l) A lawyer or law firm advertising any contingent fee rates shall, at the time of the fee publication, disclose:

(1) Whether percentages are computed before or after deduction of costs, disbursements and other expenses of litigation;

(2) That, in the event there is no recovery, the client shall remain liable for the expenses of litigation, including court costs and disbursements.

§ 1200.7 [DR 2–102.] Professional Notices, Letterheads, and Signs

(a) A lawyer or law firm may use professional cards, professional announcement cards, office signs, letterheads or similar professional notices or devices, provided the same do not violate any statute or court rule, and are in accordance with section 1200.6 of this Part [DR 2–101], including the following:

(1) A professional card of a lawyer identifying the lawyer by name and as a lawyer, and giving addresses, telephone numbers, the name of the law firm, and any information permitted under section 1200.6(c), (d)[DR 2–101] or section 1200.10 of this Part [DR 2–105]. A professional card of a law firm may also give the names of members and associates.

(2) A professional announcement card stating new or changed associations or addresses, change of firm name, or similar matters pertaining to the professional offices of a lawyer or law firm or of any nonlegal business conducted by the lawyer or law firm pursuant to section 1200.5b [DR 1–106]. It may state biographical data, the names of members of the firm and associates and the names and dates of predecessor firms in a continuing line of succession. It may state the nature of the legal practice if permitted under section 1200.10 of this Part [DR 2–105].

(3) A sign in or near the office and in the building directory identifying the law office and any nonlegal business conducted by the lawyer or law firm pursuant to section 1200.5b [DR 1–106]. The sign may state the nature of the practice if permitted under section 1200.10 of this Part [DR 2–105].

(4) A letterhead identifying the lawyer by name and as a lawyer, and giving addresses, telephone numbers, the name of the law firm, associates and any information permitted under section 1200.6(c), (d)[DR 2–101] or section 1200.10 of this Part [DR 2–105]. A letterhead of a law firm may also give the names of members and associates, and names and dates relating to deceased and retired members. A lawyer or law firm may be designated "Of Counsel" on a letterhead if there is a continuing relationship with a lawyer or law firm, other than as a partner or associate. A lawyer or law firm may be designated as "General Counsel" or by similar professional

reference on stationery of a client if the lawyer or the firm devotes a substantial amount of professional time in the representation of that client. The letterhead of a law firm may give the names and dates of predecessor firms in a continuing line of succession.

(b) A lawyer in private practice shall not practice under a trade name, a name that is misleading as to the identity of the lawyer or lawyers practicing under such name, or a firm name containing names other than those of one or more of the lawyers in the firm, except that the name of a professional corporation shall contain "P.C." or such symbols permitted by law, the name of a limited liability company or partnership shall contain "L.L.C.," "L.L.P." or such symbols permitted by law, and, if otherwise lawful, a firm may use as, or continue to include in its name the name or names of one or more deceased or retired members of the firm or of a predecessor firm in a continuing line of succession. Such terms as "legal clinic", "legal aid", "legal service office", "legal assistance office", "defender office" and the like, may be used only by qualified legal assistance organizations, except that the term "legal clinic" may be used by any lawyer or law firm provided the name of a participating lawyer or firm is incorporated therein. A lawyer or law firm may not include the name of a nonlawyer in its firm name, nor may a lawyer or law firm that has a contractual relationship with a nonlegal professional or professional service firm pursuant to section 1200.5c [DR 1–107] to provide legal and other professional services on a systematic and continuing basis include in its firm name the name of a nonlegal professional service firm or any individual nonlegal professional affiliated therewith. A lawyer who assumes a judicial, legislative or public executive or administrative post or office shall not permit his or her name to remain in the name of a law firm or to be used in professional notices of the firm during any significant period in which the lawyer is not actively and regularly practicing law as a member of the firm and, during such period, other members of the firm shall not use the lawyer's name in the firm name or in professional notices of the firm.

(c) A lawyer shall not hold himself or herself out as having a partnership with one or more other lawyers unless they are in fact partners.

(d) A partnership shall not be formed or continued between or among lawyers licensed in different jurisdictions unless all enumerations of the members and associates of the firm on its letterhead and in other permissible listings make clear the jurisdictional limitations on those members and associates of the firm not licensed to practice in all listed jurisdictions; however, the same firm name may be used in each jurisdiction.

§ 1200.8 [DR 2–103.] Solicitation and Recommendation of Professional Employment

(a) A lawyer shall not solicit professional employment from a prospective client:

(1) By in-person or telephone contact, except that a lawyer may solicit professional employment from a close friend, relative, former client or current client;

(2) By written or recorded communication if;

(i) The communication or contact violates section 1200.6(a) [DR 2–101];

(ii) The prospective client has made known to the lawyer a desire not to be solicited by the lawyer;

(iii) The solicitation involves coercion, duress or harassment;

(iv) The lawyer knows or reasonably should know that the age or the physical, emotional or mental state of the recipient make it unlikely that the recipient will be able to exercise reasonable judgment in retaining an attorney; or

(v) The lawyer intends or expects, but does not disclose, that the legal services necessary to handle the matter competently will be performed primarily by another lawyer who is not affiliated with the soliciting lawyer as a partner, associate or of counsel.

(b) A lawyer shall not compensate or give anything of value to a person or organization to recommend or obtain employment by a client, or as a reward for having made a recommendation resulting in employment by a client, except that:

(1) A lawyer or law firm may refer clients to a nonlegal professional or non-legal professional service firm pursuant to a contractual relationship with such nonlegal professional or nonlegal professional service firm to provide legal and other professional services on a systematic and continuing basis as permitted by section 1200.5c [DR 1–107], provided however that such referral shall not otherwise include any monetary or other tangible consideration or reward for such, or the sharing of legal fees; or

(2) A lawyer may pay the usual and reasonable fees or dues charged by a qualified legal assistance organization or referral fees to another lawyer as permitted by section 1200.12 of this Part [DR 2–107].

(c) No written solicitation shall be sent by a method that requires the recipient to travel to a location other than that at which the recipient ordinarily receives business or personal mail.

(d) A lawyer or the lawyer's partner or associate or any other affiliated lawyer may be recommended, employed or paid by, or may cooperate with one of the following offices or organizations which promote the use of the lawyer's services or those of a partner or associate or any other affiliated lawyer, or request one of the following offices or organizations to recommend or promote the use of the lawyer's services or those of the lawyer's partner or associate, or any other affiliated lawyer as a private practitioner, if there is no interference with the exercise of independent professional judgment on behalf of the client:

(1) A legal aid office or public defender office:

(i) Operated or sponsored by a duly accredited law school;

(ii) Operated or sponsored by a bona fide, non-profit community organization;

(iii) Operated or sponsored by a governmental agency; or

(iv) Operated, sponsored, or approved by a bar association;

(2) A military legal assistance office;

(3) A lawyer referral service operated, sponsored or approved by a bar association or authorized by law or court rule;

(4) Any bona fide organization which recommends, furnishes or pays for legal services to its members or beneficiaries provided the following conditions are satisfied:

(i) Neither the lawyer, nor the lawyer's partner, nor associate, nor any other affiliated lawyer nor any non-lawyer, shall have initiated or promoted such organization for the primary purpose of providing financial or other benefit to such lawyer, partner, associate or affiliated lawyer.

(ii) Such organization is not operated for the purpose of procuring legal work or financial benefit for any lawyer as a private practitioner outside of the legal services program of the organization.

(iii) The member or beneficiary to whom the legal services are furnished, and not such organization, is recognized as the client of the lawyer in the matter.

(iv) The legal service plan of such organization provides appropriate relief for any member or beneficiary who asserts a claim that representation by counsel furnished, selected or approved by the organization for the particular matter involved would be unethical, improper or inadequate under the circumstances of the matter involved; and the plan provides an appropriate procedure for seeking such relief.

(v) The lawyer does not know or have cause to know that such organization is in violation of applicable laws, rules of court or other legal requirements that govern its legal service operations.

(vi) Such organization has filed with the appropriate disciplinary authority, to the extent required by such authority, at least annually a report with respect to its legal service plan, if any, showing its terms, its schedule of benefits, its subscription charges, agreements with counsel and financial results of its legal service activities or, if it has failed to do so, the lawyer does not know or have cause to know of such failure.

(e) A lawyer shall not accept employment when the lawyer knows or it is obvious that the person who seeks services does so as a result of conduct prohibited under this Disciplinary Rule.

(f) Advertising not proscribed under section 1200.6 of this Part [DR 2–101] shall not be deemed in violation of any provision of this Disciplinary Rule.

§ 1200.9 [DR 2–104.]   Suggestion of Need of Legal Services

(a) (Repealed).

(b) (Repealed).

(c) A lawyer may accept employment which results from participation in activities designed to educate the public to recognize legal problems, to make intelligent selection of counsel or to utilize available legal services.

(d) A lawyer who is recommended, furnished or paid by a qualified legal assistance organization may represent a member or beneficiary thereof, to the extent and under the conditions prescribed therein.

(e) Without affecting the right to accept employment, a lawyer may speak publicly or write for publication on legal topics so long as the lawyer does not undertake to give individual advice.

(f) If success in asserting rights or defenses of a client in litigation in the nature of a class action is dependent upon the joinder of others, a lawyer may accept employment from those contacted for the purpose of obtaining their joinder, provided such acceptance does not violate any statute or court rule in the judicial department in which the lawyer practices.

§ 1200.10 [DR 2–105.]   Identification of Practice and Specialty

(a) A lawyer or law firm may publicly identify one or more areas of law in which the lawyer or the law firm practices, or may state that the practice of the lawyer or law firm is limited to one or more areas of law, provided that the lawyer or law firm shall not state that the lawyer or law firm is a specialist or specializes in a particular field of law, except as provided in section 1200.10(b), or (c) [DR 2–105].

(b) A lawyer admitted to engage in patent practice before the United States Patent and Trademark Office may use the designation "Patent Attorney" or a substantially similar designation.

(c) A lawyer may state that the lawyer has been recognized or certified as a specialist only as follows:

(1) A lawyer who is certified as a specialist in a particular area of law or law practice by a private organization approved for that purpose by the American Bar Association may state the fact of certification if, in conjunction therewith, the certifying organization is identified and the following statement is prominently made: "The [name of the private certifying organization] is not affiliated with any governmental authority. Certification is not a requirement for the practice of law in the State of New York and does not necessarily indicate greater competence than other attorneys experienced in this field of law."

(2) A lawyer who is certified as a specialist in a particular area of law or law practice by the authority having jurisdiction over specialization under the laws of another state or territory may state the fact of certification if, in conjunction therewith, the certifying state of territory is identified and the following statement is prominently made: "Certification granted by the [identify the state or territory] is not recognized by any governmental authority within the State of New York. Certification is not a requirement for the practice of law in the State of New York and does not necessarily indicate greater competence than other attorneys experienced in this field of law."

§ 1200.11 [DR 2–106.]   Fee for Legal Services

(a) A lawyer shall not enter into an agreement for, charge or collect an illegal or excessive fee.

(b) A fee is excessive when, after a review of the facts, a lawyer of ordinary prudence would be left with a definite and firm conviction that the fee is in excess of a reasonable fee. Factors to be considered as guides in determining the reasonableness of a fee may include the following:

(1) The time and labor required, the novelty and difficulty of the questions involved and the skill requisite to perform the legal service properly.

(2) The likelihood, if apparent or made known to the client, that the acceptance of the particular employment will preclude other employment by the lawyer.

(3) The fee customarily charged in the locality for similar legal services.

(4) The amount involved and the results obtained.

(5) The time limitations imposed by the client or by circumstances.

(6) The nature and length of the professional relationship with the client.

(7) The experience, reputation and ability of the lawyer or lawyers performing the services.

(8) Whether the fee is fixed or contingent.

(c) A lawyer shall not enter into an arrangement for, charge, or collect:

(1) A contingent fee for representing a defendant in a criminal case.

(2) Any fee in a domestic relations matter:

(i) The payment or amount of which is contingent upon the securing of a divorce or in any way determined by reference to the amount of maintenance, support, equitable distribution, or property settlement;

(ii) Unless a written retainer agreement is signed by the lawyer and client setting forth in plain language the nature of the relationship and the details of the fee arrangement. A lawyer shall not include in the written retainer agreement a nonrefundable fee clause; or

(iii) Based upon a security interest, confession of judgment or other lien, without prior notice to the client in a signed retainer agreement and approval from a tribunal after notice to the adversary. A lawyer shall not foreclose on a mortgage placed on the marital residence while the spouse who consents to the mortgage remains the titleholder and the residence remains the spouse's primary residence.

(3) A fee proscribed by law or rule of court.

(d) Promptly after a lawyer has been employed in a contingent fee matter, the lawyer shall provide the client with a writing stating the method by which the fee is to be determined, including the percentage or percentages that shall accrue to the lawyer in the event of settlement, trial or appeal, litigation and other expenses to be deducted from the recovery and whether such expenses are to be deducted before or, if not prohibited by statute or court rule, after the contingent fee is calculated. Upon conclusion of a contingent fee matter, the lawyer shall provide the client with a written statement stating the outcome of the matter, and if there is a recovery, showing the remittance to the client and the method of its determination.

(e) Where representation is in a civil matter, a lawyer shall resolve fee disputes by arbitration at the election of the client pursuant to a fee arbitration program established by the Chief Administrator of the Courts and approved by the justices of the Appellate Divisions.

(f) In domestic relations matters, a lawyer shall provide a prospective client with a statement of client's rights and responsibilities at the initial conference and prior to the signing of a written retainer agreement.

§ 1200.12 [DR 2–107.] Division of Fees Among Lawyers

(a) A lawyer shall not divide a fee for legal services with another lawyer who is not a partner in or associate of the lawyer's law firm, unless:

(1) The client consents to employment of the other lawyer after a full disclosure that a division of fees will be made.

(2) The division is in proportion to the services performed by each lawyer or, by a writing given to the client, each lawyer assumes joint responsibility for the representation.

(3) The total fee of the lawyers does not exceed reasonable compensation for all legal services they rendered the client.

(b) This Disciplinary Rule does not prohibit payment to a former partner or associate pursuant to a separation or retirement agreement.

§ 1200.13 [DR 2–108.]   Agreements Restricting the Practice of a Lawyer

(a) A lawyer shall not be a party to or participate in a partnership or employment agreement with another lawyer that restricts the right of a lawyer to practice law after the termination of a relationship created by the agreement, except as a condition to payment of retirement benefits.

(b) In connection with the settlement of a controversy or suit, a lawyer shall not enter into an agreement that restricts the right of a lawyer to practice law.

§ 1200.14 [DR 2–109.]   Obligation to Decline Employment

(a) [1] A lawyer shall not accept employment on behalf of a person if the lawyer knows or it is obvious that such person wishes to:

(1) Bring a legal action, conduct a defense, or assert a position in litigation, or otherwise have steps taken for such person, merely for the purpose of harassing or maliciously injuring any person.

(2) Present a claim or defense in litigation that is not warranted under existing law, unless it can be supported by a good faith argument for an extension, modification, or reversal of existing law.

§ 1200.15 [DR 2–110.]   Withdrawal From Employment

(a) In general.

(1) If permission for withdrawal from employment is required by the rules of a tribunal, a lawyer shall not withdraw from employment in a proceeding before that tribunal without its permission.

(2) Even when withdrawal is otherwise permitted or required under subdivision (a)(1), (b) or (c) of this section, a lawyer shall not withdraw from employment until the lawyer has taken steps to the extent reasonably practicable to avoid foreseeable prejudice to the rights of the client, including giving due notice to the client, allowing time for employment of other counsel, delivering to the client all papers and property to which the client is entitled and complying with applicable laws and rules.

(3) A lawyer who withdraws from employment shall refund promptly any part of a fee paid in advance that has not been earned.

(b) Mandatory withdrawal.
A lawyer representing a client before a tribunal, with its permission if required by its rules, shall withdraw from employment, and a lawyer representing a client in other matters shall withdraw from employment, if:

(1) The lawyer knows or it is obvious that the client is bringing the legal action, conducting the defense, or asserting a position in the litigation, or is otherwise having steps taken, merely for the purpose of harassing or maliciously injuring any person.

(2) The lawyer knows or it is obvious that continued employment will result in violation of a Disciplinary Rule.

(3) The lawyer's mental or physical condition renders it unreasonably difficult to carry out the employment effectively.

(4) The lawyer is discharged by his or her client.

1. So in original. No par. b has been enacted.

(c) Permissive withdrawal. Except as stated in subdivision (a) of this section, a lawyer may withdraw from representing a client if withdrawal can be accomplished without material adverse effect on the interests of the client, or if:

(1) The client:

(i) Insists upon presenting a claim or defense that is not warranted under existing law and cannot be supported by good faith argument for an extension, modification, or reversal of existing law.

(ii) Persists in a course of action involving the lawyer's services that the lawyer reasonably believes is criminal or fraudulent.

(iii) Insists that the lawyer pursue a course of conduct which is illegal or prohibited under the Disciplinary Rules.

(iv) By other conduct renders it unreasonably difficult for the lawyer to carry out employment effectively.

(v) Insists, in a matter not pending before a tribunal, that the lawyer engage in conduct which is contrary to the judgment and advice of the lawyer but not prohibited under the Disciplinary Rules.

(vi) Deliberately disregards an agreement or obligation to the lawyer as to expenses or fees.

(vii) Has used the lawyer's services to perpetrate a crime or fraud.

(2) The lawyer's continued employment is likely to result in a violation of a Disciplinary Rule.

(3) The lawyer's inability to work with co-counsel indicates that the best interests of the client likely will be served by withdrawal.

(4) The lawyer's mental or physical condition renders it difficult for the lawyer to carry out the employment effectively.

(5) The lawyer's client knowingly and freely assents to termination of the employment.

(6) The lawyer believes in good faith, in a proceeding pending before a tribunal, that the tribunal will find the existence of other good cause for withdrawal.

§ 1200.15–a [DR 2–111.]   Sale of Law Practice

(a) A lawyer retiring from a private practice of law, a law firm one or more members of which are retiring from the private practice of law with the firm, or the personal representative of a deceased, disabled or missing lawyer, may sell a law practice, including good will, to one or more lawyers or law firms, who may purchase the practice. The seller and the buyer may agree on reasonable restrictions on the seller's private practice of law, notwithstanding any other provision of this Code. Retirement shall include the cessation of the private practice of law in the geographic area, that is, the county and city and any county or city contiguous thereto, in which the practice to be sold has been conducted.

(b) Confidences and Secrets.

(1) With respect to each matter subject to the contemplated sale, the seller may provide prospective buyers with any information not protected as a confidence or secret under section 1200.19 of this Part [DR 4–101].

(2) Notwithstanding section 1200.19 [DR 4–101], the seller may provide the prospective buyer with information as to individual clients:

(i) concerning the identity of the client, except as provided in section 1200.15a(b)(6) of this Part [DR 2–111];

(ii) concerning the status and general nature of the matter;

(iii) available in public court files; and,

(iv) concerning the financial terms of the attorney-client relationship and the payment status of the client's account.

(3) Prior to making any disclosure of confidences or secrets that may be permitted under section 1200.15a(b)(2) of this Part [DR 2–111], the seller shall provide the prospective buyer with information regarding the matters involved in the proposed sale sufficient to enable the prospective buyer to determine whether any conflicts of interest exist. Where sufficient information cannot be disclosed without revealing client confidences or secrets, the seller may make the disclosures necessary for the prospective buyer to determine whether any conflict of interest exists, subject to section 1200.15a(b)(6) of this Part [DR 2–111]. If the prospective buyer determines that conflicts of interest exist prior to reviewing the information, or determines during the course of review that a conflict of interest exists, the prospective buyer shall not review or continue to review the information unless seller shall have obtained the consent of the client in accordance with section 1200.19(c)(1) of this Part [DR 4–101].

(4) Prospective buyers shall maintain the confidentiality of and shall not use any client information received in connection with the proposed sale in the same manner and to the same extent as if the prospective buyers represented the client.

(5) Absent the consent of the client after full disclosure, a seller shall not provide a prospective buyer with information if doing so would cause a violation of the attorney-client privilege.

(6) If the seller has reason to believe that the identity of the client or the fact of the representation itself constitutes a confidence or secret in the circumstances, the seller may not provide such information to a prospective buyer without first advising the client of the identity of the prospective buyer and obtaining the client's consent to the proposed disclosure.

(c) Written notice of the sale shall be given jointly by the seller and the buyer to each of the seller's clients and shall include information regarding;

(1) The client's right to retain other counsel or to take possession of the file;

(2) That fact that the client's consent to the transfer of the client's file or matter to the buyer will be presumed if the client does not take any action or otherwise object within 90 days of the sending of the notice, subject to any court rule or statute requiring express approval by the client or a court;

(3) The fact that agreements between the seller and the seller's clients as to fees will be honored by the buyer;

(4) Proposed fee increases, if any, permitted under section 1200.15a(e) of this Part [DR 2–111]; and

(5) The identity and background of the buyer or buyers, including principal office address, bar admissions, number of years in practice in the state, whether the buyer has ever been disciplined for professional misconduct or convicted of a crime, and whether the buyer currently intends to re-sell the practice.

(d) When the buyer's representation of a client of the seller would give rise to a waivable conflict of interest, the buyer shall not undertake such representation unless the necessary waiver or waivers have been obtained in writing.

(e) The fee charged a client by the buyer shall not be increased by reason of the sale, unless permitted by a retainer agreement with the client or otherwise specifically agreed to by the client.

§ 1200.16 [DR 3–101.] Aiding Unauthorized Practice of Law

(a) A lawyer shall not aid a non-lawyer in the unauthorized practice of law.

(b) A lawyer shall not practice law in a jurisdiction where to do so would be in violation of regulations of the profession in that jurisdiction.

§ 1200.17 [DR 3–102.] Dividing Legal Fees With a Non-lawyer

(a)[1] A lawyer or law firm shall not share legal fees with a non-lawyer, except that:

(1) An agreement by a lawyer with his or her firm, partner, or associate may provide for the payment of money, over a reasonable period of time after the lawyer's death, to the lawyer's estate or to one or more specified persons.

(2) A lawyer who undertakes to complete unfinished legal business of a deceased lawyer may pay to the estate of the deceased lawyer that proportion of the total compensation which fairly represents the services rendered by the deceased lawyer.

(3) A lawyer or law firm may compensate a non-lawyer employee, or include a non-lawyer employee in a retirement plan, based in whole or in part on a profit-sharing arrangement.

§ 1200.18 [DR 3–103.] Forming a Partnership With a Non-lawyer

(a)[1] A lawyer shall not form a partnership with a non-lawyer if any of the activities of the partnership consist of the practice of law.

§ 1200.19 [DR 4–101.] Preservation of Confidences and Secrets of a Client

(a) "Confidence" refers to information protected by the attorney-client privilege under applicable law, and "secret" refers to other information gained in the professional relationship that the client has requested be held inviolate or the disclosure of which would be embarrassing or would be likely to be detrimental to the client.

(b) Except when permitted under subdivision (c) of this section, a lawyer shall not knowingly:

(1) Reveal a confidence or secret of a client.

(2) Use a confidence or secret of a client to the disadvantage of the client.

(3) Use a confidence or secret of a client for the advantage of the lawyer or of a third person, unless the client consents after full disclosure.

(c) A lawyer may reveal:

(1) Confidences or secrets with the consent of the client or clients affected, but only after a full disclosure to them.

1. So in original. No par. b has been enacted.

1. So in original. No par. b has been enacted.

(2) Confidences or secrets when permitted under Disciplinary Rules or required by law or court order.

(3) The intention of a client to commit a crime and the information necessary to prevent the crime.

(4) Confidences or secrets necessary to establish or collect the lawyer's fee or to defend the lawyer or his or her employees or associates against an accusation of wrongful conduct.

(5) Confidences or secrets to the extent implicit in withdrawing a written or oral opinion or representation previously given by the lawyer and believed by the lawyer still to be relied upon by a third person where the lawyer has discovered that the opinion or representation was based on materially inaccurate information or is being used to further a crime or fraud.

(d) A lawyer shall exercise reasonable care to prevent his or her employees, associates, and others whose services are utilized by the lawyer from disclosing or using confidences or secrets of a client, except that a lawyer may reveal the information allowed by subdivision (c) of this section through an employee.

§ 1200.20 [DR 5–101.]   Conflicts of Interest–Lawyer's Own Interests

(a) A lawyer shall not accept or continue employment if the exercise of professional judgment on behalf of the client will be or reasonably may be affected by the lawyer's own financial, business, property, or personal interests, unless a disinterested lawyer would believe that the representation of the client will not be adversely affected thereby and the client consents to the representation after full disclosure of the implications of the lawyer's interest.

§ 1200.21 [DR 5–102.]   Lawyers as Witness

(a) A lawyer shall not act, or accept employment that contemplates the lawyer's acting, as an advocate on issues of fact before any tribunal if the lawyer knows or it is obvious that the lawyer ought to be called as a witness on a significant issue on behalf of the client, except that the lawyer may act as an advocate and also testify:

(1) If the testimony will relate solely to an uncontested issue.

(2) If the testimony will relate solely to a matter of formality and there is no reason to believe that substantial evidence will be offered in opposition to the testimony.

(3) If the testimony will relate solely to the nature and value of legal services rendered in the case by the lawyer or the lawyer's firm to the client.

(4) As to any matter, if disqualification as an advocate would work a substantial hardship on the client because of the distinctive value of the lawyer as counsel in the particular case.

(b) Neither a lawyer nor the lawyer's firm shall accept employment in contemplated or pending litigation if the lawyer knows or it is obvious that the lawyer or another lawyer in the lawyer's firm may be called as a witness on a significant issue other than on behalf of the client, and it is apparent that the testimony would or might be prejudicial to the client.

(c) If, after undertaking employment in contemplated or pending litigation, a lawyer learns or it is obvious that the lawyer ought to be called as a witness on a significant issue on behalf of the client, the lawyer shall not serve as an advocate on issues of fact before the tribunal, except that the lawyer may continue as an advocate on issues of fact and may testify in the circumstances enumerated in 1200.21(b)(1) through (4) of this Part [DR 5–102].

(d) If, after undertaking employment in contemplated or pending litigation, a lawyer learns or it is obvious that the lawyer or a lawyer in his or her firm may be called as a witness on a significant issue other than on behalf of the client, the lawyer may continue the representation until it is apparent that the testimony is or may be prejudicial to the client at which point the lawyer and the firm must withdraw from acting as an advocate before the tribunal.

§ 1200.22 [DR 5–103.] Avoiding Acquisition of Interest in Litigation

(a) A lawyer shall not acquire a proprietary interest in the cause of action or subject matter of litigation he or she is conducting for a client, except that the lawyer may:

(1) Acquire a lien granted by law to secure the lawyer's fee or expenses.

(2) Except as provided in section 1200.11(c)(2) or (3) of this Part [DR 2–106], contract with a client for a reasonable contingent fee in a civil case.

(b) While representing a client in connection with contemplated or pending litigation, a lawyer shall not advance or guarantee financial assistance to the client, except that:

(1) A lawyer may advance or guarantee the expenses of litigation, including court costs, expenses of investigation, expenses of medical examination, and costs of obtaining and presenting evidence, provided the client remains ultimately liable for such expenses.

(2) Unless prohibited by law or rule of court, a lawyer representing an indigent client on a pro bono basis may pay court costs and reasonable expenses of litigation on behalf of the client.

§ 1200.23 [DR 5–104.] Transactions Between Lawyer and Client

(a) A lawyer shall not enter into a business transaction with a client if they have differing interests therein and if the client expects the lawyer to exercise professional judgment therein for the protection of the client, unless:

(1) The transaction and terms on which the lawyer acquires the interest are fair and reasonable to the client and are fully disclosed and transmitted in writing to the client in a manner that can be reasonably understood by the client;

(2) The lawyer advises the client to seek the advice of independent counsel in the transaction; and

(3) The client consents in writing, after full disclosure, to the terms of the transaction and to the lawyer's inherent conflict of interest in the transaction.

(b) Prior to conclusion of all aspects of the matter giving rise to employment, a lawyer shall not negotiate or enter into any arrangement or understanding:

(1) With a client or a prospective client by which the lawyer acquires an interest in literary or media rights with respect to the subject matter of the employment or proposed employment.

507

(2) With any person by which the lawyer transfers or assigns any interest in literary or media rights with respect to the subject matter of employment by a client or prospective client.

§ 1200.24 [DR 5–105.] Conflict of Interest: Simultaneous Representation

(a) A lawyer shall decline proffered employment if the exercise of independent professional judgment in behalf of a client will be or is likely to be adversely affected by the acceptance of the proffered employment, or if it would be likely to involve the lawyer in representing differing interests, except to the extent permitted under subdivision (c) of this section.

(b) A lawyer shall not continue multiple employment if the exercise of independent professional judgment in behalf of a client will be or is likely to be adversely affected by the lawyer's representation of another client, or if it would be likely to involve the lawyer in representing differing interests, except to the extent permitted under subdivision (c) of this section.

(c) In the situations covered by subdivisions (a) and (b) of this section, a lawyer may represent multiple clients if a disinterested lawyer would believe that the lawyer can competently represent the interest of each and if each consents to the representation after full disclosure of the implications of the simultaneous representation and the advantages and risks involved.

(d) While lawyers are associated in a law firm, none of them shall knowingly accept or continue employment when any one of them practicing alone would be prohibited from doing so under sections 1200.20(a) [DR 5–101], 1200.24(a) or (b) [DR 5–105], 1200.27(a) or (b) [DR 5–108], or 1200.45(b) [DR 9-101] of this Part, except as otherwise provided therein.

(e) A law firm shall keep records of prior engagements, which records shall be made at or near the time of such engagements and shall have a policy implementing a system by which proposed engagements are checked against current and previous engagements, so as to render effective assistance to lawyers within the firm in complying with section 1200.24(d) [DR 5–105] of this Part. Failure to keep records or to have a policy which complies with this subdivision, whether or not a violation of section 1200.24(d) [DR 5–105] of this Part occurs, shall be a violation by the firm. In cases where a violation of this subdivision by the firm is a substantial factor in causing a violation of section 1200.24(d) [DR 5–105] of this Part by a lawyer, the firm, as well as the individual lawyer, shall also be responsible for the violation of section 1200.24(d) [DR 5–105] of this Part.

§ 1200.25 [DR 5–106.] Settling Similar Claims of Clients

(a) [1] A lawyer who represents two or more clients shall not make or participate in the making of an aggregate settlement of the claims of or against the clients, unless each client has consented after full disclosure of the implications of the aggregate settlement and the advantages and risks involved, including the existence and nature of all the claims involved and the participation of each person in the settlement.

§ 1200.26 [DR 5–107.] Avoiding Influence by Others Than the Client

(a) Except with the consent of the client after full disclosure a lawyer shall not:

1. So in original. No par. b has been enacted.

(1) Accept compensation for legal services from one other than the client.

(2) Accept from one other than the client any thing of value related to his or her representation of or employment by the client.

(b) Unless authorized by law, a lawyer shall not permit a person who recommends, employs, or pays the lawyer to render legal service for another to direct or regulate his or her professional judgment in rendering such legal services, or to cause the lawyer to compromise the lawyer's duty to maintain the confidences and secrets of the client under section 1200.19(b) of this Part [DR 9–101].

(c) A lawyer shall not practice with or in the form of a limited liability company, limited liability partnership or professional corporation authorized to practice law for a profit, if:

(1) A non-lawyer owns any interest therein, except that a fiduciary representative of the estate of a lawyer may hold the stock or interest of the lawyer for a reasonable time during administration;

(2) A non-lawyer is a member, corporate director or officer thereof; or

(3) A non-lawyer has the right to direct or control the professional judgment of a lawyer.

§ 1200.27 [DR 5–108.]   Conflict of Interest—Former Client

(a) Except as provided in section 1200.45(b) [DR 9–101] with respect to current or former government lawyers, a lawyer who has represented a client in a matter shall not, without the consent of the former client after full disclosure:

(1) Thereafter represent another person in the same or a substantially related matter in which that person's interests are materially adverse to the interests of the former client.

(2) Use any confidences or secrets of the former client except as permitted by section 1200.19(c) [DR 4–101] or when the confidence or secret has become generally known.

(b) Except with the consent of the affected client after full disclosure, a lawyer shall not knowingly represent a person in the same or a substantially related matter in which a firm with which the lawyer formerly was associated had previously represented a client:

(1) Whose interests are materially adverse to that person; and

(2) About whom the lawyer had acquired information protected by section 1200.19(b) of this Part [DR 4–101] that is material to the matter.

(c) Notwithstanding the provisions of section 1200.24(d) [DR 5–105] of this Part, when a lawyer has terminated an association with a firm, the firm is prohibited from thereafter representing a person with interests that are materially adverse to those of a client represented by the formerly associated lawyer and not currently represented by the firm only if the law firm or any lawyer remaining in the firm has information protected by section 1200.19(b) [DR 4–101] of the Part that is material to the matter, unless the affected client consents after full disclosure.

§ 1200.28 [DR 5–109.]   Organization as Client

(a) When a lawyer employed or retained by an organization is dealing with the organization's directors, officers, employees, members, shareholders or other constituents, and it appears that the organization's interests may differ from those of the constituents with whom the lawyer is dealing, the lawyer shall explain that the lawyer is the lawyer for the organization and not for any of the constituents.

(b) If a lawyer for an organization knows that an officer, employee or other person associated with the organization is engaged in action, intends to act or refuses to act in a matter related to the representation that is a violation of a legal obligation to the organization, or a violation of law that reasonably might be imputed to the organization, and is likely to result in substantial injury to the organization, the lawyer shall proceed as is reasonably necessary in the best interest of the organization. In determining how to proceed, the lawyer shall give due consideration to the seriousness of the violation and its consequences, the scope and nature of the lawyer's representation, the responsibility in the organization and the apparent motivation of the person involved, the policies of the organization concerning such matters and any other relevant considerations. Any measures taken shall be designed to minimize disruption of the organization and the risk of revealing information relating to the representation to persons outside the organization, such measures may include, among others:

(1) Asking reconsideration of the matter;

(2) Advising that a separate legal opinion on the matter be sought for presentation to appropriate authority in the organization; and

(3) Referring the matter to higher authority in the organization, including, if warranted by the seriousness of the matter, referral to the highest authority that can act in behalf of the organization as determined by applicable law.

(c) If, despite the lawyer's efforts in accordance with section 1200.28(b) of this Part [DR 5–109], the highest authority that can act on behalf of the organization insists upon action, or a refusal to act, that is clearly a violation of law and is likely to result in a substantial injury to the organization, the lawyer may resign in accordance with section 1200.15 of this Part [DR 2–110].

§ 1200.29 [DR 5–110.] Membership in Legal Services Organization

(a) [1] A lawyer may serve as a director, officer or member of a not-for-profit legal services organization, apart from the law firm in which the lawyer practices, notwithstanding that the organization serves persons having interests that differ from those of a client of the lawyer or the lawyer's firm, provided that the lawyer shall not knowingly participate in a decision or action of the organization:

(1) If participating in the decision or action would be incompatible with the lawyer's duty of loyalty to a client under section 1200.20 through 1200.29 of this Part [DR 5–101 through DR 5–111]; or

(2) Where the decision or action could have a material adverse effect on the representation of a client of the organization whose interests differ from those of a client of the lawyer or the lawyer's firm.

§ 1200.29-a [DR 5–111.] Sexual Relations With Clients

(a) "Sexual relations" means sexual intercourse or the touching of an intimate part of another person for the purpose of sexual arousal, sexual gratification, or sexual abuse.

(b) A lawyer shall not:

(1) Require or demand sexual relations with a client or third party incident to or as a condition of any professional representation.

(2) Employ coercion, intimidation, or undue influence in entering into sexual relations with a client.

(3) In domestic relations matters, enter into sexual relations with a client during the course of the lawyer's representation of the client.

(c) Section 1200.29a(b) [DR 5–111] shall not apply to sexual relations between lawyers and their spouses or to ongoing consensual sexual relationships that predate the initiation of the lawyer-client relationship.

(d) Where a lawyer in a firm has sexual relations with a client but does not participate in the representation of that client, the lawyers in the firm shall not be subject to discipline under this rule solely because of the occurrence of such sexual relations.

§ 1200.30 [DR 6–101.]   Failing to Act Competently

(a) [1] A lawyer shall not:

(1) Handle a legal matter which the lawyer knows or should know that he or she is not competent to handle, without associating with a lawyer who is competent to handle it.

(2) Handle a legal matter without preparation adequate in the circumstances.

(3) Neglect a legal matter entrusted to the lawyer.

§ 1200.31 [DR 6–102.]   Limiting Liability to Client

(a) [1] A lawyer shall not seek, by contract or other means, to limit prospectively the lawyer's individual liability to a client for malpractice, or, without first advising that person that independent representation is appropriate in connection therewith, to settle a claim for such liability with an unrepresented client or former client.

§ 1200.32 [DR 7–101.]   Representing a Client Zealously

(a) A lawyer shall not intentionally:

(1) Fail to seek the lawful objectives of the client through reasonably available means permitted by law and the Disciplinary Rules, except as provided by subdivision (b) of this section. A lawyer does not violate this Disciplinary Rule, however, by acceding to reasonable requests of opposing counsel which do not prejudice the rights of the client, by being punctual in fulfilling all professional commitments, by avoiding offensive tactics, or by treating with courtesy and consideration all persons involved in the legal process.

(2) Fail to carry out a contract of employment entered into with a client for professional services, but the lawyer may withdraw as permitted under sections 1200.15 [DR 2–110], 1200.21 [DR 5–102] and 1200.24 [DR 5–105] of this Part.

(3) Prejudice or damage the client during the course of the professional relationship, except as required under section 1200.33(b) [DR 7–102] or as authorized by section 1200.15 [DR 2–110] of this Part.

(b) In the representation of a client, a lawyer may:

1. So in original. No par. b has been enacted.

1. So in original. No par. b has been enacted.

(1) Where permissible, exercise professional judgment to waive or fail to assert a right or position of the client.

(2) Refuse to aid or participate in conduct that the lawyer believes to be unlawful, even though there is some support for an argument that the conduct is legal.

§ 1200.33 [DR 7–102.] Representing a Client Within the Bounds of the Law

(a) In the representation of a client, a lawyer shall not:

(1) File a suit, assert a position, conduct a defense, delay a trial, or take other action on behalf of the client when the lawyer knows or when it is obvious that such action would serve merely to harass or maliciously injure another.

(2) Knowingly advance a claim or defense that is unwarranted under existing law, except that the lawyer may advance such claim or defense if it can be supported by good faith argument for an extension, modification, or reversal of existing law.

(3) Conceal or knowingly fail to disclose that which the lawyer is required by law to reveal.

(4) Knowingly use perjured testimony or false evidence.

(5) Knowingly make a false statement of law or fact.

(6) Participate in the creation or preservation of evidence when the lawyer knows or it is obvious that the evidence is false.

(7) Counsel or assist the client in conduct that the lawyer knows to be illegal or fraudulent.

(8) Knowingly engage in other illegal conduct or conduct contrary to a Disciplinary Rule.

(b) A lawyer who receives information clearly establishing that:

(1) The client has, in the course of the representation, perpetrated a fraud upon a person or tribunal shall promptly call upon the client to rectify the same, and if the client refuses or is unable to do so, the lawyer shall reveal the fraud to the affected person or tribunal, except when the information is protected as a confidence or secret.

(2) A person other than the client has perpetrated a fraud upon a tribunal shall promptly reveal the fraud to the tribunal.

§ 1200.34 [DR 7–103.] Performing the Duty of Public Prosecutor or Other Government Lawyer

(a) A public prosecutor or other government lawyer shall not institute or cause to be instituted criminal charges when he or she knows or it is obvious that the charges are not supported by probable cause.

(b) A public prosecutor or other government lawyer in criminal litigation shall make timely disclosure to counsel for the defendant, or to a defendant who has no counsel, of the existence of evidence, known to the prosecutor or other government lawyer, that tends to negate the guilt of the accused, mitigate the degree of the offense or reduce the punishment.

§ 1200.35 [DR 7–104.] Communicating With Represented and Unrepresented Parties

(a) During the course of the representation of a client a lawyer shall not:

(1) Communicate or cause another to communicate on the subject of the representation with a party the lawyer knows to be represented by a lawyer in that matter unless the lawyer has the prior consent of the lawyer representing such other party or is authorized by law to do so.

(2) Give advice to a party who is not represented by a lawyer, other than the advice to secure counsel, if the interests of such party are or have a reasonable possibility of being in conflict with the interests of the lawyer's client.

(b) Notwithstanding the prohibitions of section 1200.35(a) of this Part [DR 7–104], and unless prohibited by law, a lawyer may cause a client to communicate with a represented party, if that party is legally competent, and counsel the client with respect to those communications, provided the lawyer gives reasonable advance notice to the represented person's counsel that such communications will be taking place.

§ 1200.36 [DR 7–105.] Threatening Criminal Prosecution

(a) [1] A lawyer shall not present, participate in presenting, or threaten to present criminal charges solely to obtain an advantage in a civil matter.

§ 1200.37 [DR 7–106.] Trial Conduct

(a) A lawyer shall not disregard or advise the client to disregard a standing rule of a tribunal or a ruling of a tribunal made in the course of a proceeding, but the lawyer may take appropriate steps in good faith to test the validity of such rule or ruling.

(b) In presenting a matter to a tribunal, a lawyer shall disclose:

(1) Controlling legal authority known to the lawyer to be directly adverse to the position of the client and which is not disclosed by opposing counsel.

(2) Unless privileged or irrelevant, the identities of the clients the lawyer represents and of the persons who employed the lawyer.

(c) In appearing as a lawyer before a tribunal, a lawyer shall not:

(1) State or allude to any matter that he or she has no reasonable basis to believe is relevant to the case or that will not be supported by admissible evidence.

(2) Ask any question that he or she has no reasonable basis to believe is relevant to the case and that is intended to degrade a witness or other person.

(3) Assert personal knowledge of the facts in issue, except when testifying as a witness.

(4) Assert a personal opinion as to the justness of a cause, as to the credibility of a witness, as to the culpability of a civil litigant, or as to the guilt or innocence of an accused; but the lawyer may argue, upon analysis of the evidence, for any position or conclusion with respect to the matters stated herein.

(5) Fail to comply with known local customs of courtesy or practice of the bar or a particular tribunal without giving to opposing counsel timely notice of the intent not to comply.

1. So in original. No par. b has been enacted.

(6) Engage in undignified or discourteous conduct which is degrading to a tribunal.

(7) Intentionally or habitually violate any established rule of procedure or of evidence.

§ 1200.38 [DR 7–107.]   Trial Publicity

(a) A lawyer participating in or associated with a criminal or civil matter, or associated in a law firm or government agency with a lawyer participating in or associated with a criminal or civil matter, shall not make an extrajudicial statement that a reasonable person would expect to be disseminated by means of public communication if the lawyer knows or reasonably should know that it will have a substantial likelihood of materially prejudicing an adjudicative proceeding in that matter. Notwithstanding the foregoing, a lawyer may make a statement that a reasonable lawyer would believe is required to protect a client from the substantial prejudicial effect of recent publicity not initiated by the lawyer or the lawyer's client. A statement so made shall be limited to such information as is necessary to mitigate the recent adverse publicity.

(b) A statement ordinarily is likely to prejudice materially an adjudicative proceeding when it refers to a civil matter triable to a jury, a criminal matter, or any other proceeding that could result in incarceration, and the statement relates to:

(1) The character, credibility, reputation or criminal record of a party, suspect in a criminal investigation or witness, or the identity of a witness, or the expected testimony of a party or witness.

(2) In a criminal case or proceeding that could result in incarceration, the possibility of a plea of guilty to the offense or the existence or contents of any confession, admission, or statement given by a defendant or suspect or that person's refusal or failure to make a statement.

(3) The performance or results of any examination or test or the refusal or failure of a person to submit to an examination or test, or the identity or nature of physical evidence expected to be presented.

(4) Any opinion as to the guilt or innocence of a defendant or suspect in a criminal case or proceeding that could result in incarceration.

(5) Information the lawyer knows or reasonably should know is likely to be inadmissible as evidence in a trial and would if disclosed create a substantial risk of prejudicing an impartial trial.

(6) The fact that a defendant has been charged with a crime, unless there is included therein a statement explaining that the charge is merely an accusation and that the defendant is presumed innocent until and unless proven guilty.

(c) Provided that the statement complies with section 1200.39(a) [DR 7–107] of this Part, a lawyer involved with the investigation or litigation of a matter may state the following without elaboration:

(1) The general nature of the claim or defense.

(2) The information contained in a public record.

(3) That an investigation of the matter is in progress.

(4) The scheduling or result of any step in litigation.

(5) A request for assistance in obtaining evidence and information necessary thereto.

(6) A warning of danger concerning the behavior of a person involved, when there is reason to believe that there exists the likelihood of substantial harm to an individual or to the public interest.

(7) In a criminal case:

(i) The identity, age, residence, occupation and family status of the accused.

(ii) If the accused has not been apprehended, information necessary to aid in apprehension of that person.

(iii) The fact, time and place of arrest, resistance, pursuit, use of weapons, and a description of physical evidence seized, other than as contained only in a confession, admission, or statement.

(iv) The identity of investigating and arresting officers or agencies and the length of the investigation.

§ 1200.39 [DR 7–108.] Communication With or Investigation of Jurors

(a) Before the trial of a case a lawyer connected therewith shall not communicate with or cause another to communicate with anyone the lawyer knows to be a member of the venire from which the jury will be selected for the trial of the case.

(b) During the trial of a case:

(1) A lawyer connected therewith shall not communicate with or cause another to communicate with any member of the jury.

(2) A lawyer who is not connected therewith shall not communicate with or cause another to communicate with a juror concerning the case.

(c) Subdivisions (a) and (b) of this section do not prohibit a lawyer from communicating with members of the venire or jurors in the course of official proceedings.

(d) After discharge of the jury from further consideration of a case with which the lawyer was connected, the lawyer shall not ask questions of or make comments to a member of that jury that are calculated merely to harass or embarrass the juror or to influence the juror's actions in future jury service.

(e) A lawyer shall not conduct or cause, by financial support or otherwise, another to conduct a vexatious or harassing investigation of either a member of the venire or a juror.

(f) All restrictions imposed by this section upon a lawyer also apply to communications with or investigations of members of a family of a member of the venire or a juror.

(g) A lawyer shall reveal promptly to the court improper conduct by a member of the venire or a juror, or by another toward a member of the venire or a juror or a member of his or her family of which the lawyer has knowledge.

§ 1200.40 [DR 7–109.] Contact With Witnesses

(a) A lawyer shall not suppress any evidence that the lawyer or the client has a legal obligation to reveal or produce.

(b) A lawyer shall not advise or cause a person to hide or to leave the jurisdiction of a tribunal for the purpose of making the person unavailable as a witness therein.

(c) A lawyer shall not pay, offer to pay, or acquiesce in the payment of compensation to a witness contingent upon the content of his or her testimony or the outcome of the case. But a lawyer may advance, guarantee, or acquiesce in the payment of:

(1) Expenses reasonably incurred by a witness in attending or testifying.

(2) Reasonable compensation to a witness for the loss of time in attending, testifying, preparing to testify or otherwise assisting counsel.

(3) A reasonable fee for the professional services of an expert witness.

§ 1200.41 [DR 7–110.]   Contact With Officials

(a) A lawyer shall not give or lend anything of value to a judge, official, or employee of a tribunal except as permitted by the Code of Judicial Conduct, but a lawyer may make a contribution to the campaign fund of a candidate for judicial office in conformity with the Code of Judicial Conduct.

(b) In an adversary proceeding, a lawyer shall not communicate, or cause another to communicate, as to the merits of the cause with a judge or an official before whom the proceeding is pending, except:

(1) In the course of official proceedings in the cause.

(2) In writing if the lawyer promptly delivers a copy of the writing to opposing counsel or to an adverse party who is not represented by a lawyer.

(3) Orally upon adequate notice to opposing counsel or to an adverse party who is not represented by a lawyer.

(4) As otherwise authorized by law, or by the Code of Judicial Conduct.

§ 1200.42 [DR 8–101.]   Action as a Public Official

(a) [1] A lawyer who holds public office shall not:

(1) Use the public position to obtain, or attempt to obtain, a special advantage in legislative matters for the lawyer or for a client under circumstances where the lawyer knows or it is obvious that such action is not in the public interest.

(2) Use the public position to influence, or attempt to influence, a tribunal to act in favor of the lawyer or of a client.

(3) Accept anything of value from any person when the lawyer knows or it is obvious that the offer is for the purpose of influencing the lawyer's action as a public official.

§ 1200.43 [DR 8–102.]   Statements Concerning Judges and Other Adjudicatory Officers

(a) A lawyer shall not knowingly make false statements of fact concerning the qualifications of a candidate for election or appointment to a judicial office.

(b) A lawyer shall not knowingly make false accusations against a judge or other adjudicatory officer.

§ 1200.44 [DR 8–103.]   Lawyer Candidate for Judicial Office

(a) [1] A lawyer who is a candidate for judicial office shall comply with section 100.5 of the Chief Administrator's Rules Governing Judicial Conduct (22 NYCRR) and Canon 5 of the Code of Judicial Conduct.

1. So in original. No par. b has been enacted.

§ 1200.45 [DR 9–101.] Avoiding Even the Appearance of Impropriety

(a) A lawyer shall not accept private employment in a matter upon the merits of which the lawyer has acted in a judicial capacity.

(b) Except as law may otherwise expressly permit:

(1) A lawyer shall not represent a private client in connection with a matter in which the lawyer participated personally and substantially as a public officer or employee, and no lawyer in a firm with which that lawyer is associated may knowingly undertake or continue representation in such a matter unless:

(i) The disqualified lawyer is effectively screened from any participation, direct or indirect, including discussion, in the matter and is apportioned no part of the fee therefrom; and

(ii) There are no other circumstances in the particular representation that create an appearance of impropriety.

(2) A lawyer having information that the lawyer knows is confidential government information about a person, acquired when the lawyer was a public officer or employee, may not represent a private client whose interests are adverse to that person in a matter in which the information could be used to the material disadvantage of that person. A firm with which that lawyer is associated may knowingly undertake or continue representation in the matter only if the disqualified lawyer is effectively screened from any participation, direct or indirect, including discussion, in the matter and is apportioned no part of the fee therefrom.

(3) A lawyer serving as a public officer or employee shall not:

(i) Participate in a matter in which the lawyer participated personally and substantially while in private practice or nongovernmental employment, unless under applicable law no one is, or by lawful delegation may be, authorized to act in the lawyer's stead in the matter; or

(ii) Negotiate for private employment with any person who is involved as a party or as attorney for a party in a matter in which the lawyer is participating personally and substantially.

(c) A lawyer shall not state or imply that the lawyer is able to influence improperly or upon irrelevant grounds any tribunal, legislative body, or public official.

(d) A lawyer related to another lawyer as parent, child, sibling or spouse shall not represent in any matter a client whose interests differ from those of another party to the matter who the lawyer knows is represented by the other lawyer unless the client consents to the representation after full disclosure and the lawyer concludes that the lawyer can adequately represent the interests of the client.

§ 1200.46 [DR 9–102.] Preserving Identity of Funds and Property of Others; Fiduciary Responsibility; Commingling and Misappropriation of Client Funds or Property; Maintenance of Bank Accounts; Recordkeeping; Examination of Records

(a) **Prohibition Against Commingling and Misappropriation of Client Funds or Property.** A lawyer in possession of any funds or other property belonging to another person, where such possession is ~~incident~~ to his or her ~~practice of law,~~ is a fiduciary, and must not misappropriate such funds ~~or~~ property ~~or commingle~~ such funds or property with ~~his or~~ her own.

(b) Separate Accounts.

(1) A lawyer who is in possession of funds belonging to another person incident to the lawyer's practice of law, shall maintain such funds in a banking institution within the State of New York which agrees to provide dishonored check reports in accordance with the provisions of Part 1300 of the joint rules of the Appellate Division. "Banking institution" means a state or national bank, trust company, savings bank, savings and loan association or credit union. Such funds shall be maintained, in the lawyer's own name, or in the name of a firm of lawyers of which he or she is a member, or in the name of the lawyer or firm of lawyers by whom he or she is employed, in a special account or accounts, separate from any business or personal accounts of the lawyer or lawyer's firm, and separate from any accounts which the lawyer may maintain as executor, guardian, trustee or receiver, or in any other fiduciary capacity, into which special account or accounts all funds held in escrow or otherwise entrusted to the lawyer or firm shall be deposited; provided, however, that such funds may be maintained in a banking institution located outside the State of New York if such banking institution complies with such Part 1300 of this Title, and the lawyer has obtained the prior written approval of the person to whom such funds belong which specifies the name and address of the office or branch of the banking institution where such funds are to be maintained.

(2) A lawyer or the lawyer's firm shall identify the special bank account or accounts required by section 1200.46(b)(1) of this Part [DR 9–102] as an "Attorney Special Account", or "Attorney Trust Account", or "Attorney Escrow Account", and shall obtain checks and deposit slips that bear such title. Such title may be accompanied by such other descriptive language as the lawyer may deem appropriate, provided that such additional language distinguishes such special account or accounts from other bank accounts that are maintained by the lawyer or lawyer's firm.

(3) Funds reasonably sufficient to maintain the account or to pay account charges may be deposited therein.

(4) Funds belonging in part to a client or third person and in part presently or potentially to the lawyer or law firm shall be kept in such special account or accounts, but the portion belonging to the lawyer or law firm may be withdrawn when due unless the right of the lawyer or law firm to receive it is disputed by the client or third person, in which event the disputed portion shall not be withdrawn until the dispute is finally resolved.

(c) Notification of Receipt of Property; Safekeeping; Rendering Accounts; Payment or Delivery of Property. A lawyer shall:

(1) Promptly notify a client or third person of the receipt of funds, securities, or other properties in which the client or third person has an interest.

(2) Identify and label securities and properties of a client or third person promptly upon receipt and place them in a safe deposit box or other place of safekeeping as soon as practicable.

(3) Maintain complete records of all funds, securities, and other properties of a client or third person coming into the possession of the lawyer and render appropriate accounts to the client or third person regarding them.

(4) Promptly pay or deliver to the client or third person as requested by the client or third person the funds, securities, or other properties in the possession of the lawyer which the client or third person is entitled to receive.

(d) Required Bookkeeping Records. A lawyer shall maintain for seven years after the events which they record:

(1) The records of all deposits in and withdrawals from the special accounts specified in section 1200.46(b) of this Part [DR 9–102] and of any other bank account which records the operations of the lawyer's practice of law. These records shall specifically identify the date, source and description of each item deposited, as well as the date, payee and purpose of each withdrawal or disbursement.

(2) A record for special accounts, showing the source of all funds deposited in such accounts, the names of all persons for whom the funds are or were held, the amount of such funds, the description and amounts, and the names of all persons to whom such funds were disbursed.

(3) Copies of all retainer and compensation agreements with clients.

(4) Copies of all statements to clients or other persons showing the disbursement of funds to them or on their behalf.

(5) Copies of all bills rendered to clients.

(6) Copies of all records showing payments to lawyers, investigators or other persons, not in the lawyer's regular employ, for services rendered or performed.

(7) Copies of all retainer and closing statements filed with the Office of Court Administration.

(8) All checkbooks and check stubs, bank statements, prenumbered canceled checks and duplicate deposit slips.

(9) Lawyers shall make accurate entries of all financial transactions in their records of receipts and disbursements, in their special accounts, in their ledger books or similar records, and in any other books of account kept by them in the regular course of their practice, which entries shall be made at or near the time of the act, condition or event recorded.

(10) For Purposes of section 1200.46(d) of this Part [DR 9–102], a lawyer may satisfy the requirements of maintaining "copies" by maintaining any of the following items; original records, photocopies, microfilm, optical imaging, and any other medium that preserves an image of the document that cannot be altered without detection.

(e) Authorized Signatories. All special account withdrawals shall be made only to a named payee and not to cash. Such withdrawals shall be made by check or, with the prior written approval of the party entitled to the proceeds, by bank transfer. Only an attorney admitted to practice law in New York State shall be an authorized signatory of a special account.

(f) Missing Clients. Whenever any sum of money is payable to a client and the lawyer is unable to locate the client, the lawyer shall apply to the court in which the action was brought if in the unified court system, or, if no action was commenced in the unified court system, to the Supreme Court in the county in which the lawyer maintains an office for the practice of law, for an order directing payment to the lawyer of any fees and disbursements that are owed by the client and the balance, if any, to the Lawyers' Fund for Client Protection for safeguarding and disbursement to persons who are entitled thereto.

(g) Designation of Successor Signatories.

(1) Upon the death of a lawyer who was the sole signatory on an attorney trust, escrow or special account, an application may be made to the Supreme Court for an order designating a successor signatory for such trust, escrow or special account who shall be a member of the bar in good standing and admitted to the practice of law in New York State.

(2) An application to designate a successor signatory shall be made to the Supreme Court in the judicial district in which the deceased lawyer maintained an office for the practice of law. The application may be made by the legal representative of the deceased lawyer's estate; a lawyer who was affiliated with the deceased lawyer in the practice of law; any person who has a beneficial interest in such trust, escrow or special account; an officer of a city or county bar association; or counsel for an attorney disciplinary committee. No lawyer may charge a legal fee for assisting with an application to designate a successor signatory pursuant to this rule.

(3) The Supreme Court may designate a successor signatory and may direct the safeguarding of funds from such trust, escrow or special account, and the disbursement of such funds to persons who are entitled thereto, and may order that funds in such account be deposited with the Lawyers' Fund for Client Protection for safeguarding and disbursement to persons who are entitled thereto.

(h) Dissolution of a Firm. Upon the dissolution of any firm of lawyers, the former partners or members shall make appropriate arrangements for the maintenance by one of them or by a successor firm of the records specified in section 1200.46(d) of this Part [DR 9-102].

(i) Availability of Bookkeeping Records; Records Subject to Production in Disciplinary Investigations and Proceedings. The financial records required by this Disciplinary Rule shall be located, or made available, at the principal New York State office of the lawyers subject hereto and any such records shall be produced in response to a notice or subpoena duces tecum issued in connection with a complaint before or any investigation by the appropriate grievance or departmental disciplinary committee, or shall be produced at the direction of the appropriate Appellate Division before any person designated by it. All books and records produced pursuant to this subdivision shall be kept confidential, except for the purpose of the particular proceeding, and their contents shall not be disclosed by anyone in violation of the lawyer-client privilege.

(j) Disciplinary Action. A lawyer who does not maintain and keep the accounts and records as specified and required by this disciplinary rule, or who does not produce any such records pursuant to this Rule, shall be deemed in violation of these rules and shall be subject to disciplinary proceedings.

§ 1210.1   Statement of Client's Rights: Posting

Every attorney with an office located in the State of New York shall insure that there is posted in that office, in a manner visible to clients of the attorney, a statement of client's rights in the form set forth below. Attorneys in offices that provide legal services without fee may delete from the statement those provisions dealing with fees. The statement shall contain the following:

STATEMENT OF CLIENT'S RIGHTS

1. You are entitled to be treated with courtesy and consideration at all times by your lawyer and the other lawyers and personnel in your lawyers office.

2. You are entitled to an attorney capable of handling your legal matter competently and diligently, in accordance with the highest standards of the profession. If you are not satisfied with how your matter is being handled, you have the right to withdraw from the attorney-client relationship at any time (court approval may be required in some matters and your attorney may have a claim against you for the value of services rendered to you up to the point of discharge).

3. You are entitled to your lawyer's independent professional judgment and undivided loyalty uncompromised by conflicts of interest.

4. You are entitled to be charged a reasonable fee and to have your lawyer explain at the outset how the fee will be computed and the manner and frequency of billing. You are entitled to request and receive a written itemized bill from your attorney at reasonable intervals. You may refuse to enter into any fee arrangement that you find unsatisfactory. In the event of a fee dispute, you may have the right to seek arbitration; your attorney will provide you with the necessary information regarding arbitration in the event of a fee dispute, or upon your request.

5. You are entitled to have your questions and concerns addressed in a prompt manner and to have your telephone calls returned promptly.

6. You are entitled to be kept informed as to the status of your matter and to request and receive copies of papers. You are entitled to sufficient information to allow you to participate meaning fully in the development of your matter.

7. You are entitled to have your legitimate objectives respected by your attorney, including whether or not to settle your matter (court approval of a settlement is required in some matters).

8. You have the right to privacy in your dealings with your lawyer and to have your secrets and confidences preserved to the extent permitted by law.

9. You are entitled to have your attorney conduct himself or herself ethically in accordance with the Code of Professional Responsibility.

10. You may not be refused representation on the basis of race, creed, color, religion, sex, sexual orientation, age, national origin or disability.

AMERICAN BAR ASSOCIATION STANDARDS RELATING TO THE ADMINISTRATION OF CRIMINAL JUSTICE

THIRD EDITION *

Approved February 3, 1992

CHAPTER 3.   THE PROSECUTION FUNCTION

Table of Contents

* A.B.A. Standards for Criminal Justice (3d ed. 1992). Copyright © 1993, American Bar Association. Reprinted with permission. On February 3, 1992, the A.B.A. House of Delegates approved new black letter standards concerning the Prosecution Function.

522

PART I.   GENERAL STANDARDS

Standard 3–1.1   The Function of the Standards

These standards are intended to be used as a guide to professional conduct and performance. They are not intended to be used as criteria for the judicial evaluation of alleged misconduct of the prosecutor to determine the validity of a conviction. They may or may not be relevant in such judicial evaluation, depending upon all the circumstances.

Standard 3–1.2   The Function of the Prosecutor

(a) The office of prosecutor is charged with responsibility for prosecutions in its jurisdiction.

(b) The prosecutor is an administrator of justice, an advocate, and an officer of the court; the prosecutor must exercise sound discretion in the performance of his or her functions.

(c) The duty of the prosecutor is to seek justice, not merely to convict.

(d) It is an important function of the prosecutor to seek to reform and improve the administration of criminal justice. When inadequacies or injustices in the substantive or procedural law come to the prosecutor's attention, he or she should stimulate efforts for remedial action.

(e) It is the duty of the prosecutor to know and be guided by the standards of professional conduct as defined by applicable professional traditions, ethical codes, and law in the prosecutor's jurisdiction. The prosecutor should make use of the guidance afforded by an advisory council of the kind described in standard 4–1.5.

Standard 3–1.3   Conflicts of Interest

(a) A prosecutor should avoid a conflict of interest with respect to his or her official duties.

(b) A prosecutor should not represent a defendant in criminal proceedings in a jurisdiction where he or she is also employed as a prosecutor.

(c) A prosecutor should not, except as law may otherwise expressly permit, participate in a matter in which he or she participated personally and substantially while in private practice or non-governmental employment unless under applicable law no one is, or by lawful delegation may be, authorized to act in the prosecutor's stead in the matter.

(d) A prosecutor who has formerly represented a client in a matter in private practice should not thereafter use information obtained from that representation to the disadvantage of the former client unless the rules of attorney-client confidentiality do not apply or the information has become generally known.

(e) A prosecutor should not, except as law may otherwise expressly permit, negotiate for private employment with any person who is involved as an accused or as an attorney or agent for an accused in a matter in which the prosecutor is participating personally and substantially.

(f) A prosecutor should not permit his or her professional judgment or obligations to be affected by his or her own political, financial, business, property, or personal interests.

(g) A prosecutor who is related to another lawyer as parent, child, sibling or spouse should not participate in the prosecution of a person who the prosecutor knows is represented by the other lawyer. Nor should a prosecutor who has a significant personal or financial relationship with another lawyer participate in the prosecution of a person who the prosecutor knows is represented by the other lawyer, unless the prosecutor's supervisor, if any, is informed and approves or unless there is no other prosecutor authorized to act in the prosecutor's stead.

(h) A prosecutor should not recommend the services of particular defense counsel to accused persons or witnesses unless requested by the accused person or witness to make such a recommendation, and should not make a referral that is likely to create a conflict of interest. Nor should a prosecutor comment upon the reputation or abilities of defense counsel to an accused person or witness who is seeking or may seek such counsel's services unless requested by such person.

Standard 3–1.4   Public Statements

(a) A prosecutor should not make or authorize the making of an extrajudicial statement that a reasonable person would expect to be disseminated by means of public communication if the prosecutor knows or reasonably should know that it will have a substantial likelihood of prejudicing a criminal proceeding.

(b) A prosecutor should exercise reasonable care to prevent investigators, law enforcement personnel, employees or other persons assisting or associated with the prosecutor from making an extrajudicial statement that the prosecutor would be prohibited from making under this standard.

Standard 3–1.5   Duty to Respond to Misconduct

(a) Where a prosecutor knows that another person associated with the prosecutor's office is engaged in action, intends to act or refuses to act in a manner that is a violation of a legal obligation to the prosecutor's office or a violation of law, the prosecutor should follow the policies of the prosecutor's office concerning such matters. If such policies are unavailing or do not exist, the prosecutor should ask the person to reconsider the action or inaction which is at issue if such a request is aptly timed to prevent such misconduct and is otherwise feasible. If such a request for reconsideration is unavailing, inapt or otherwise not feasible or if the seriousness of the matter so requires, the prosecutor should refer the matter to higher authority in the prosecutor's office, including, if warranted by the seriousness of the matter, referral to the chief prosecutor.

(b) If, despite the prosecutor's efforts in accordance with section (a), the chief prosecutor insists upon action, or a refusal to act, that is clearly a violation of law, the prosecutor may take further remedial action, including revealing the information necessary to remedy this violation to other appropriate governmental officials not in the prosecutor's office.

PART II.   ORGANIZATION OF THE PROSECUTION FUNCTION

Standard 3–2.1   Prosecution Authority to Be Vested in a Public Official

The prosecution function should be performed by a public prosecutor who is a lawyer subject to the standards of professional conduct and discipline.

Standard 3–2.2   Interrelationship of Prosecution Offices Within a State

(a) Local authority and responsibility for prosecution is properly vested in a district, county, or city attorney. Wherever possible, a unit of prosecution should be designed on the basis of population, caseload, and other relevant factors sufficient to warrant at least one fulltime prosecutor and the supporting staff necessary to effective prosecution.

(b) In some states, conditions such as geographical area and population may make it appropriate to create a statewide system of prosecution in which the state attorney general is the chief prosecutor and the local prosecutors are deputies.

(c) In all states, there should be coordination of the prosecution policies of local prosecution offices to improve the administration of justice and assure the maximum practicable uniformity in the enforcement of the criminal law throughout the state. A state association of prosecutors should be established in each state.

(d) To the extent needed, a central pool of supporting resources and personnel, including laboratories, investigators, accountants, special counsel, and other experts, should be maintained by the state government and should be available to assist all local prosecutors.

Standard 3–2.3   Assuring High Standards of Professional Skill

(a) The function of public prosecution requires highly developed professional skills. This objective can best be achieved by promoting continuity of service and broad experience in all phases of the prosecution function.

(b) Wherever feasible, the offices of chief prosecutor and staff should be full-time occupations.

(c) Professional competence should be the basis for selection for prosecutorial office. Prosecutors should select their personnel without regard to partisan political influence.

(d) Special efforts should be made to recruit qualified women and members of minority groups for prosecutorial office.

(e) In order to achieve the objective of professionalism and to encourage competent lawyers to accept such offices, compensation for prosecutors and their staffs should be commensurate with the high responsibilities of the office and comparable to the compensation of their peers in the private sector.

Standard 3–2.4   Special Assistants, Investigative Resources, Experts

(a) Funds should be provided to enable a prosecutor to appoint special assistants from among the trial bar experienced in criminal cases, as needed for the prosecution of a particular case or to assist generally.

(b) Funds should be provided to the prosecutor for the employment of a regular staff of professional investigative personnel and other necessary supporting personnel, under the prosecutor's direct control, to the extent warranted by the responsibilities and scope of the office; the prosecutor should also be provided with funds for the employment of qualified experts as needed for particular cases.

Standard 3–2.5   Prosecutor's Handbook; Policy Guidelines and Procedures

(a) Each prosecutor's office should develop a statement of (i) general policies to guide the exercise of prosecutorial discretion and (ii) procedures of the office. The objectives of these policies as to discretion and procedures should be to achieve a fair, efficient, and effective enforcement of the criminal law.

(b) In the interest of continuity and clarity, such statement of policies and procedures should be maintained in an office handbook. This handbook should be available to the public, except for subject matters declared "confidential," when it is reasonably believed that public access to their contents would adversely affect the prosecution function.

Standard 3–2.6   Training Programs

Training programs should be established within the prosecutor's office for new personnel and for continuing education of the staff. Continuing education programs for prosecutors should be substantially expanded and public funds should be provided to enable prosecutors to attend such programs.

Standard 3–2.7   Relations With Police

(a) The prosecutor should provide legal advice to the police concerning police functions and duties in criminal matters.

(b) The prosecutor should cooperate with police in providing the services of the prosecutor's staff to aid in training police in the performance of their function in accordance with law.

Standard 3–2.8   Relations With the Courts and Bar

(a) A prosecutor should not intentionally misrepresent matters of fact or law to the court.

(b) A prosecutor's duties necessarily involve frequent and regular official contacts with the judge or judges of the prosecutor's jurisdiction. In such contacts the prosecutor should carefully strive to preserve the appearance as well as the reality of the correct relationship which professional traditions, ethical codes, and applicable law require between advocates and judges.

(c) A prosecutor should not engage in unauthorized ex parte discussions with or submission of material to a judge relating to a particular case which is or may come before the judge.

(d) A prosecutor should not fail to disclose to the tribunal legal authority in the controlling jurisdiction known to the prosecutor to be directly adverse to the prosecutor's position and not disclosed by defense counsel.

(e) A prosecutor should strive to develop good working relationships with defense counsel in order to facilitate the resolution of ethical problems. In particular, a prosecutor should assure defense counsel that if counsel finds it necessary to deliver physical items which may be relevant to a pending case or investigation to the prosecutor, the prosecutor will not offer the fact of such delivery by defense counsel as evidence before a jury for purposes of establishing defense counsel's client's culpability. However, nothing in this Standard shall prevent a prosecutor from offering evidence of the fact of such delivery in a subsequent proceeding for the purpose of proving a crime or fraud in the delivery of the evidence.

Standard 3–2.9   Prompt Disposition of Criminal Charges

(a) A prosecutor should avoid unnecessary delay in the disposition of cases. A prosecutor should not fail to act with reasonable diligence and promptness in prosecuting an accused.

(b) A prosecutor should not intentionally use procedural devices for delay for which there is no legitimate basis.

(c) The prosecution function should be so organized and supported with staff and facilities as to enable it to dispose of all criminal charges promptly. The prosecutor should be punctual in attendance in court and in the submission of all motions, briefs, and other papers. The prosecutor should emphasize to all witnesses the importance of punctuality in attendance in court.

(d) A prosecutor should not intentionally misrepresent facts or otherwise mislead the court in order to obtain a continuance.

(e) A prosecutor, without attempting to get more funding for additional staff, should not carry a workload that, by reason of its excessive size, interferes with the rendering of quality representation, endangers the interests of justice in the speedy disposition of charges, or may lead to the breach of professional obligations.

Standard 3–2.10   Supercession and Substitution of Prosecutor

(a) Procedures should be established by appropriate legislation to the end that the governor or other elected state official is empowered by law to suspend and supersede a local prosecutor upon making a public finding, after reasonable notice and hearing, that the prosecutor is incapable of fulfilling the duties of office.

(b) The governor or other elected official should be empowered by law to substitute special counsel in the place of the local prosecutor in a particular case, or category of cases, upon making a public finding that this is required for the protection of the public interest.

Standard 3–2.11   Literary or Media Agreements

A prosecutor, prior to conclusion of all aspects of a matter, should not enter into any agreement or understanding by which the prosecutor acquires an interest in literary or media rights to a portrayal or account based in substantial part on information relating to that matter.

PART III.   INVESTIGATION FOR PROSECUTION DECISION

Standard 3–3.1   Investigative Function of Prosecutor

(a) A prosecutor ordinarily relies on police and other investigative agencies for investigation of alleged criminal acts, but the prosecutor has an affirmative responsibility to investigate suspected illegal activity when it is not adequately dealt with by other agencies.

(b) A prosecutor should not invidiously discriminate against or in favor of any person on the basis of race, religion, sex, sexual preference, or ethnicity in exercising discretion to investigate or to prosecute. A prosecutor should not use other improper considerations in exercising such discretion.

(c) A prosecutor should not knowingly use illegal means to obtain evidence or to employ or instruct or encourage others to use such means.

(d) A prosecutor should not discourage or obstruct communication between prospective witnesses and defense counsel. A prosecutor should not advise any person or cause any person to be advised to decline to give to the defense information which such person has the right to give.

(e) A prosecutor should not secure the attendance of persons for interviews by use of any communication which has the appearance or color of a subpoena or similar judicial process unless the prosecutor is authorized by law to do so.

(f) A prosecutor should not promise not to prosecute for prospective criminal activity, except where such activity is part of an officially supervised investigative and enforcement program.

(g) Unless a prosecutor is prepared to forego impeachment of a witness by the prosecutor's own testimony as to what the witness stated in an interview or to seek leave to withdraw from the case in order to present the impeaching testimony, a prosecutor should avoid interviewing a prospective witness except in the presence of a third person.

Standard 3–3.2   Relations With Victims and Prospective Witnesses

(a) A prosecutor should not compensate a witness, other than an expert, for giving testimony, but it is not improper to reimburse an ordinary witness for the reasonable expenses of attendance upon court, attendance for depositions pursuant to statute or court rule, or attendance for pretrial interviews. Payments to a witness may be for transportation and loss of income, provided there is no attempt to conceal the fact of reimbursement.

(b) A prosecutor should advise a witness who is to be interviewed of his or her rights against self-incrimination and the right to counsel whenever the law so requires. It is also proper for a prosecutor to so advise a witness whenever the prosecutor knows or has reason to believe that the witness may be the subject of a criminal prosecution. However, a prosecutor should not so advise a witness for the purpose of influencing the witness in favor of or against testifying.

(c) The prosecutor should readily provide victims and witnesses who request it information about the status of cases in which they are interested.

(d) The prosecutor should seek to insure that victims and witnesses who may need protections against intimidation are advised of and afforded such protections where feasible.

(e) The prosecutor should insure that victims and witnesses are given notice as soon as practicable of scheduling changes which will affect the victims' or witnesses' required attendance at judicial proceedings.

(f) The prosecutor should not require victims and witnesses to attend judicial proceedings unless their testimony is essential to the prosecution or is required by law. When their attendance is required, the prosecutor should seek to reduce to a minimum the time they must spend at the proceedings.

(g) The prosecutor should seek to insure that victims of serious crimes or their representatives are given timely notice of: (i) judicial proceedings relating to the victims' case; (ii) disposition of the case, including plea bargains, trial and sentencing; and (iii) any decision or action in the case which results in the accused's provisional or final release from custody.

(h) Where practical, the prosecutor should seek to insure that victims of serious crimes or their representatives are given an opportunity to consult with and to provide information to the prosecutor prior to the decision whether or not to prosecute, to pursue a disposition by plea, or to dismiss the charges.

Standard 3–3.3   Relations With Expert Witnesses

(a) A prosecutor who engages an expert for an opinion should respect the independence of the expert and should not seek to dictate the formation of the expert's opinion on the subject. To the extent necessary, the prosecutor should explain to the expert his or her role in the trial as an impartial expert called to aid the fact finders and the manner in which the examination of witnesses is conducted.

(b) A prosecutor should not pay an excessive fee for the purpose of influencing the expert's testimony or to fix the amount of the fee contingent upon the testimony the expert will give or the result in the case.

Standard 3–3.4   Decision to Charge

(a) The decision to institute criminal proceedings should be initially and primarily the responsibility of the prosecutor.

(b) Prosecutors should take reasonable care to ensure that investigators working at their direction or under their authority are adequately trained in the standards governing the issuance of arrest and search warrants and should inform investigators that they should seek the approval of a prosecutor in close or difficult cases.

(c) The prosecutor should establish standards and procedures for evaluating complaints to determine whether criminal proceedings should be instituted.

(d) Where the law permits a citizen to complain directly to a judicial officer or the grand jury, the citizen complainant should be required to present the complaint for prior approval to the prosecutor, and the prosecutor's action or recommendation thereon should be communicated to the judicial officer or grand jury.

Standard 3–3.5   Relations With Grand Jury

(a) Where the prosecutor is authorized to act as legal adviser to the grand jury, the prosecutor may appropriately explain the law and express an opinion on the legal significance of the evidence but should give due deference to its status as an independent legal body.

(b) The prosecutor should not make statements or arguments in an effort to influence grand jury action in a manner which would be impermissible at trial before a petit jury.

(c) The prosecutor's communications and presentations to the grand jury should be on the record.

Standard 3–3.6   Quality and Scope of Evidence Before Grand Jury

(a) A prosecutor should only make statements or arguments to the grand jury and only present evidence to the grand jury which the prosecutor believes is appropriate or authorized under law for presentation to the grand jury. In appropriate cases, the prosecutor may present witnesses to summarize admissible evidence available to the prosecutor which the prosecutor believes he or she will be able to present at trial. The prosecutor should also inform the grand jurors that they have the right to hear any available witnesses, including eyewitnesses.

(b) No prosecutor should knowingly fail to disclose to the grand jury evidence which tends to negate guilt or mitigate the offense.

(c) A prosecutor should recommend that the grand jury not indict if he or she believes the evidence presented does not warrant an indictment under governing law.

(d) If the prosecutor believes that a witness is a potential defendant, the prosecutor should not seek to compel the witness's testimony before the grand jury without informing the witness that he or she may be charged and that the witness should seek independent legal advice concerning his or her rights.

(e) The prosecutor should not compel the appearance of a witness before the grand jury whose activities are the subject of the inquiry if the witness states in advance that if called he or she will exercise the constitutional privilege not to testify, unless the prosecutor intends to judicially challenge the exercise of the privilege or to seek a grant of immunity according to the law.

(f) A prosecutor in presenting a case to a grand jury should not intentionally interfere with the independence of the grand jury, preempt a function of the grand jury, or abuse the processes of the grand jury.

(g) Unless the law of the jurisdiction so permits, a prosecutor should not use the grand jury in order to obtain tangible, documentary or testimonial evidence to assist the prosecutor in preparation for trial of a defendant who has already been charged by indictment or information.

(h) Unless the law of the jurisdiction so permits, a prosecutor should not use the grand jury for the purpose of aiding or assisting in any administrative inquiry.

Standard 3–3.7   Quality and Scope of Evidence for Information

Where the prosecutor is empowered to charge by information, the prosecutor's decisions should be governed by the principles embodied in standards 3–3.6 and 3–3.9, where applicable.

Standard 3–3.8   Discretion as to Noncriminal Disposition

(a) The prosecutor should consider in appropriate cases the availability of noncriminal disposition, formal or informal, in deciding whether to press criminal charges which would otherwise be supported by probable cause; especially in the case of a first offender, the nature of the offense may warrant noncriminal disposition.

(b) Prosecutors should be familiar with the resources of social agencies which can assist in the evaluation of cases for diversion from the criminal process.

Standard 3–3.9   Discretion in the Charging Decision

(a) A prosecutor should not institute, or cause to be instituted, or permit the continued pendency of criminal charges when the prosecutor knows that the charges are not supported by probable cause. A prosecutor should not institute, cause to be instituted, or permit the continued pendency of criminal charges in the absence of sufficient admissible evidence to support a conviction.

(b) The prosecutor is not obliged to present all charges which the evidence might support. The prosecutor may in some circumstances and for good cause consistent with the public interest decline to prosecute, notwithstanding that sufficient evidence may exist which would support a conviction. Illustrative of the factors which the prosecutor may properly consider in exercising his or her discretion are:

    (i) the prosecutor's reasonable doubt that the accused is in fact guilty;

    (ii) the extent of the harm caused by the offense;

    (iii) the disproportion of the authorized punishment in relation to the particular offense or the offender;

    (iv) possible improper motives of a complainant;

    (v) reluctance of the victim to testify;

    (vi) cooperation of the accused in the apprehension or conviction of others; and

    (vii) availability and likelihood of prosecution by another jurisdiction.

(c) A prosecutor should not be compelled by his or her supervisor to prosecute a case in which he or she has a reasonable doubt about the guilt of the accused.

(d) In making the decision to prosecute, the prosecutor should give no weight to the personal or political advantages or disadvantages which might be involved or to a desire to enhance his or her record of convictions.

(e) In cases which involve a serious threat to the community, the prosecutor should not be deterred from prosecution by the fact that in the jurisdiction juries have tended to acquit persons accused of the particular kind of criminal act in question.

(f) The prosecutor should not bring or seek charges greater in number or degree than can reasonably be supported with evidence at trial or than are necessary to fairly reflect the gravity of the offense.

(g) The prosecutor should not condition a dismissal of charges, nolle prosequi, or similar action on the accused's relinquishment of the right to seek civil redress unless the accused has agreed to the action knowingly and intelligently, freely and voluntarily, and where such waiver is approved by the court.

Standard 3-3.10   Role in First Appearance and Preliminary Hearing

(a) A prosecutor who is present at the first appearance (however denominated) of the accused before a judicial officer should not communicate with the accused unless a waiver of counsel has been entered, except for the purpose of aiding in obtaining counsel or in arranging for the pretrial release of the accused. A prosecutor should not fail to make reasonable efforts to assure that the accused has been advised of the right to, and the procedure for obtaining, counsel and has been given reasonable opportunity to obtain counsel.

(b) The prosecutor should cooperate in good faith in arrangements for release under the prevailing system for pretrial release.

(c) The prosecutor should not seek to obtain from an unrepresented accused a waiver of important pretrial rights, such as the right to a preliminary hearing.

(d) The prosecutor should not seek a continuance solely for the purpose of mooting the preliminary hearing by securing an indictment.

(e) Except for good cause, the prosecutor should not seek delay in the preliminary hearing after an arrest has been made if the accused is in custody.

(f) The prosecutor should ordinarily be present at a preliminary hearing where such hearing is required by law.

533

Standard 3-3.11   Disclosure of Evidence by the Prosecutor

(a) A prosecutor should not intentionally fail to make timely disclosure to the defense, at the earliest feasible opportunity, of the existence of all evidence or information which tends to negate the guilt of the accused or mitigate the offense charged or which would tend to reduce the punishment of the accused.

(b) A prosecutor should not fail to make a reasonably diligent effort to comply with a legally proper discovery request.

(c) A prosecutor should not intentionally avoid pursuit of evidence because he or she believes it will damage the prosecution's case or aid the accused.

PART IV.   PLEA DISCUSSIONS

Standard 3-4.1   Availability for Plea Discussions

(a) The prosecutor should have and make known a general policy or willingness to consult with defense counsel concerning disposition of charges by plea.

(b) A prosecutor should not engage in plea discussions directly with an accused who is represented by defense counsel, except with defense counsel's approval. Where the defendant has properly waived counsel, the prosecuting attorney may engage in plea discussions with the defendant, although, where feasible, a record of such discussions should be made and preserved.

(c) A prosecutor should not knowingly make false statements or representations as to fact or law in the course of plea discussions with defense counsel or the accused.

Standard 3-4.2   Fulfillment of Plea Discussions

(a) A prosecutor should not make any promise or commitment assuring a defendant or defense counsel that a court will imposed a specific sentence or a suspension of sentence; a prosecutor may properly advise the defense what position will be taken concerning disposition.

(b) A prosecutor should not imply a greater power to influence the disposition of a case than is actually possessed.

(c) A prosecutor should not fail to comply with a plea agreement, unless a defendant fails to comply with a plea agreement or other extenuating circumstances are present.

Standard 3-4.3   Record of Reasons for Nolle Prosequi Disposition

Whenever felony criminal charges are dismissed by way of nolle prosequi (or its equivalent), the prosecutor should make a record of the reasons for the action.

PART V. THE TRIAL

Standard 3–5.1   Calendar Control

Control over the trial calendar should be vested in the court. The prosecuting attorney should advise the court of facts relevant in determining the order of the cases on the court's calendar.

Standard 3–5.2   Courtroom Professionalism

(a) As an officer of the court, the prosecutor should support the authority of the court and the dignity of the trial courtroom by strict adherence to codes of professionalism and by manifesting a professional attitude toward the judge, opposing counsel, witnesses, defendants, jurors, and others in the courtroom.

(b) When court is in session, the prosecutor should address the court, not opposing counsel, on all matters relating to the case.

(c) A prosecutor should comply promptly with all orders and directives of the court, but the prosecutor has a duty to have the record reflect adverse rulings or judicial conduct which the prosecutor considers prejudicial. The prosecutor has a right to make respectful requests for reconsideration of adverse rulings.

(d) Prosecutors should cooperate with courts and the organized bar in developing codes of professionalism for each jurisdiction.

Standard 3–5.3   Selection of Jurors

(a) The prosecutor should prepare himself or herself prior to trial to discharge effectively the prosecution function in the selection of the jury and the exercise of challenges for cause and peremptory challenges.

(b) In those cases where it appears necessary to conduct a pretrial investigation of the background of jurors, investigatory methods of the prosecutor should neither harass nor unduly embarrass potential jurors or invade their privacy and, whenever possible, should be restricted to an investigation of records and sources of information already in existence.

(c) The opportunity to question jurors personally should be used solely to obtain information for the intelligent exercise of challenges. A prosecutor should not intentionally use the voir dire to present factual matter which the prosecutor knows will not be admissible at trial or to argue the prosecution's case to the jury.

Standard 3–5.4   Relations With Jury

(a) A prosecutor should not intentionally communicate privately with persons summoned for jury duty or impaneled as jurors prior to or during trial. The prosecutor should avoid the reality or appearance of any such communications.

(b) The prosecutor should treat jurors with deference and respect, avoiding the reality or appearance of currying favor by a show of undue solicitude for their comfort or convenience.

(c) After discharge of the jury from further consideration of a case, a prosecutor should not intentionally make comments to or ask questions of a juror for the purpose of harassing or embarrassing the juror in any way which will tend to influence judgment in future jury service. If the prosecutor believes that the verdict may be subject to legal challenge, he or she may properly, if no statute or rule prohibits such course, communicate with jurors to determine whether such challenge may be available.

Standard 3–5.5 Opening Statement

The prosecutor's opening statement should be confined to a statement of the issues in the case and the evidence the prosecutor intends to offer which the prosecutor believes in good faith will be available and admissible. A prosecutor should not allude to any evidence unless there is a good faith and reasonable basis for believing that such evidence will be tendered and admitted in evidence.

Standard 3–5.6 Presentation of Evidence

(a) A prosecutor should not knowingly offer false evidence, whether by documents, tangible evidence, or the testimony of witnesses, or fail to seek withdrawal thereof upon discovery of its falsity.

(b) A prosecutor should not knowingly and for the purpose of bringing inadmissible matter to the attention of the judge or jury offer inadmissible evidence, ask legally objectionable questions, or make other impermissible comments or arguments in the presence of the judge or jury.

(c) A prosecutor should not permit any tangible evidence to be displayed in the view of the judge or jury which would tend to prejudice fair consideration by the judge or jury until such time as a good faith tender of such evidence is made.

(d) A prosecutor should not tender tangible evidence in the view of the judge or jury if it would tend to prejudice fair consideration by the judge or jury unless there is a reasonable basis for its admission in evidence. When there is any substantial doubt about the admissibility of such evidence, it should be tendered by an offer of proof and a ruling obtained.

Standard 3–5.7 Examination of Witnesses

(a) The interrogation of all witnesses should be conducted fairly, objectively, and with due regard for the dignity and legitimate privacy of the witness, and without seeking to intimidate or humiliate the witness unnecessarily.

(b) The prosecutor's belief that the witness is telling the truth does not preclude cross-examination, but may affect the method and scope of cross-examination. A prosecutor should not use the power of cross-examination to discredit or undermine a witness if the prosecutor knows the witness is testifying truthfully.

(c) A prosecutor should not call a witness in the presence of the jury who the prosecutor knows will claim a valid privilege not to testify.

(d) A prosecutor should not ask a question which implies the existence of a factual predicate for which a good faith belief is lacking.

Standard 3–5.8   Argument to the Jury

(a) In closing argument to the jury, the prosecutor may argue all reasonable inferences from evidence in the record. The prosecutor should not intentionally misstate the evidence or mislead the jury as to the inferences it may draw.

(b) The prosecutor should not express his or her personal belief or opinion as to the truth or falsity of any testimony or evidence or the guilt of the defendant.

(c) The prosecutor should not make arguments calculated to appeal to the prejudices of the jury.

(d) The prosecutor should refrain from argument which would divert the jury from its duty to decide the case on the evidence.

Standard 3–5.9   Facts Outside the Record

The prosecutor should not intentionally refer to or argue on the basis of facts outside the record whether at trial or on appeal, unless such facts are matters of common public knowledge based on ordinary human experience or matters of which the court may take judicial notice.

Standard 3–5.10   Comments by Prosecutor After Verdict

The prosecutor should not make public comments critical of a verdict, whether rendered by judge or jury.

PART VI.   SENTENCING

Standard 3–6.1   Role in Sentencing

(a) The prosecutor should not make the severity of sentences the index of his or her effectiveness. To the extent that the prosecutor becomes involved in the sentencing process, he or she should seek to assure that a fair and informed judgment is made on the sentence and to avoid unfair sentence disparities.

(b) Where sentence is fixed by the court without jury participation, the prosecutor should be afforded the opportunity to address the court at sentencing and to offer a sentencing recommendation.

(c) Where sentence is fixed by the jury, the prosecutor should present evidence on the issue within the limits permitted in the jurisdiction, but the prosecutor should avoid introducing evidence bearing on sentence which will prejudice the jury's determination of the issue of guilt.

Standard 3–6.2   Information Relevant to Sentencing

(a) The prosecutor should assist the court in basing its sentence on complete and accurate information for use in the presentence report. The prosecutor should disclose to the court any information in the prosecutor's files relevant to the sentence. If incompleteness or inaccurateness in the presentence report comes to the prosecutor's attention, the prosecutor should take steps to present the complete and correct information to the court and to defense counsel.

(b) The prosecutor should disclose to the defense and to the court at or prior to the sentencing proceeding all unprivileged mitigating information known to the prosecutor, except when the prosecutor is relieved of this responsibility by a protective order of the tribunal.

CHAPTER 4.   THE DEFENSE FUNCTION *

Table of Contents

* A.B.A. Standards for Criminal Justice (3d ed. 1991). Copyright © 1993, American Bar Association. Reprinted with permission. On February 11, 1991, the A.B.A. House of Delegates approved new black letter standards concerning the Defense Function.

PART I.   GENERAL STANDARDS

Standard 4–1.1   The Function of the Standards

These standards are intended to be used as a guide to professional conduct and performance.   They are not intended to be used as criteria for the judicial evaluation of alleged misconduct of defense counsel to determine the validity of a conviction.   They may or may not be relevant in such judicial evaluation, depending upon all the circumstances.

Standard 4–1.2   The Function of Defense Counsel

(a) Counsel for the accused is an essential component of the administration of criminal justice.   A court properly constituted to hear a criminal case must be viewed as a tripartite entity consisting of the judge (and jury, where appropriate), counsel for the prosecution, and counsel for the accused.

(b) The basic duty defense counsel owes to the administration of justice and as an officer of the court is to serve as the accused's counselor and advocate with courage and devotion and to render effective, quality representation.

(c) Since the death penalty differs from other criminal penalties in its finality, defense counsel in a capital case should respond to this difference by

539

making extraordinary efforts on behalf of the accused. Defense counsel should comply with the ABA Guidelines for the Appointment and Performance of Counsel in Death Penalty Cases.

(d) Defense counsel should seek to reform and improve the administration of criminal justice. When inadequacies or injustices in the substantive or procedural law come to defense counsel's attention, he or she should stimulate efforts for remedial action.

(e) Defense counsel, in common with all members of the bar, is subject to standards of conduct stated in statutes, rules, decisions of courts, and codes, canons, or other standards of professional conduct. Defense counsel has no duty to execute any directive of the accused which does not comport with law or such standards. Defense counsel is the professional representative of the accused, not the accused's alter ego.

(f) Defense counsel should not intentionally misrepresent matters of fact or law to the court.

(g) Defense counsel should disclose to the tribunal legal authority in the controlling jurisdiction known to defense counsel to be directly adverse to the position of the accused and not disclosed by the prosecutor.

(h) It is the duty of defense counsel to know and be guided by the standards of professional conduct as defined in codes and canons of the legal profession applicable in defense counsel's jurisdiction. Once representation has been undertaken, the functions and duties of defense counsel are the same whether defense counsel is assigned, privately retained, or serving in a legal aid or defender program.

Standard 4–1.3   Delays; Punctuality; Workload

(a) Defense counsel should act with reasonable diligence and promptness in representing a client.

(b) Defense counsel should avoid unnecessary delay in the disposition of cases. Defense counsel should be punctual in attendance upon court and in the submission of all motions, briefs, and other papers. Defense counsel should emphasize to the client and all witnesses the importance of punctuality in attendance in court.

(c) Defense counsel should not intentionally misrepresent facts or otherwise mislead the court in order to obtain a continuance.

(d) Defense counsel should not intentionally use procedural devices for delay for which there is no legitimate basis.

(e) Defense counsel should not carry a workload that, by reason of its excessive size, interferes with the rendering of quality representation, endangers the client's interest in the speedy disposition of charges, or may lead to the breach of professional obligations. Defense counsel should not accept employment for the purpose of delaying trial.

Standard 4–1.4   Public Statements

Defense counsel should not make or authorize the making of an extrajudicial statement that a reasonable person would expect to be disseminated by means of public communication if defense counsel knows or reasonably should know that it will have a substantial likelihood of prejudicing a criminal proceeding.

Standard 4–1.5   Advisory Councils on Professional Conduct

(a) In every jurisdiction, an advisory body of lawyers selected for their experience, integrity, and standing at the trial bar should be established as an advisory council on problems of professional conduct in criminal cases. This council should provide prompt and confidential guidance and advice to lawyers seeking assistance in the application of standards of professional conduct in criminal cases.

(b) Communications between an inquiring lawyer and an advisory council member have the same attorney-client privilege for protection of the client's confidences as ordinarily exists between any other lawyer and client. The council member should be bound by statute or rule of court in the same manner as a lawyer is ordinarily bound in that jurisdiction not to reveal any disclosure of the client. Confidences may also be revealed, however, to the extent necessary:

> (i) if the inquiring lawyer's client challenges the effectiveness of the lawyer's conduct of the case and the lawyer relies on the guidance received from the council member, or

> (ii) if the inquiring lawyer's conduct is called into question in an authoritative disciplinary inquiry or proceeding.

Standard 4–1.6   Trial Lawyer's Duty to Administration of Justice

(a) The bar should encourage through every available means the widest possible participation in the defense of criminal cases by lawyers. Lawyers should be encouraged to qualify themselves for participation in criminal cases both by formal training and through experience as associate counsel.

(b) All such qualified lawyers should stand ready to undertake the defense of an accused regardless of public hostility toward the accused or personal distaste for the offense charged or the person of the defendant.

(c) Such qualified lawyers should not assert or announce a general unwillingness to appear in criminal cases. Law firms should encourage partners and associates to become qualified and to appear in criminal cases.

(d) Such qualified lawyers should not seek to avoid appointment by a tribunal to represent an accused except for good cause, such as: representing the accused is likely to result in violation of applicable ethical codes or other law, representing the accused is likely to result in an unreasonable financial burden on the lawyer, or the client or crime is so repugnant to the lawyer as to be likely to impair the client-lawyer relationship or the lawyer's ability to represent the client.

PART II.   ACCESS TO COUNSEL

Standard 4–2.1   Communication

Every jurisdiction should guarantee by statute or rule of court the right of an accused person to prompt and effective communication with a lawyer and should require that reasonable access to a telephone or other facilities be provided for that purpose.

Standard 4–2.2   Referral Service for Criminal Cases

(a) To assist persons who wish to retain defense counsel privately and who do not know a lawyer or how to engage one, every jurisdiction should have a referral service for criminal cases. The referral service should maintain a list of defense counsel willing and qualified to undertake the defense of a criminal case; it should be so organized that it can provide prompt service at all times.

(b) The availability of the referral service should be publicized. In addition, notices containing the essential information about the referral service and how to contact it should be posted conspicuously in police stations, jails, and wherever else it is likely to give effective notice.

Standard 4–2.3   Prohibited Referrals

(a) Defense counsel should not give anything of value to a person for recommending the lawyer's services.

(b) Defense counsel should not accept a referral from any source, including prosecutors, law enforcement personnel, victims, bondsmen, or court personnel where the acceptance of such a referral is likely to create a conflict of interest.

PART III.   LAWYER–CLIENT RELATIONSHIP

Standard 4–3.1   Establishment of Relationship

(a) Defense counsel should seek to establish a relationship of trust and confidence with the accused and should discuss the objectives of the representation and whether defense counsel will continue to represent the accused if there is an appeal. Defense counsel should explain the necessity of full disclosure of all facts known to the client for an effective defense, and defense counsel should explain the extent to which counsel's obligation of confidentiality makes privileged the accused's disclosures.

(b) To ensure the privacy essential for confidential communication between defense counsel and client, adequate facilities should be available for private discussions between counsel and accused in jails, prisons, courthouses, and other places where accused persons must confer with counsel.

(c) Personnel of jails, prisons, and custodial institutions should be prohibited by law or administrative regulations from examining or otherwise interfering with any communication or correspondence between client and defense counsel relating to legal action arising out of charges or incarceration.

Standard 4–3.2   Interviewing the Client

(a) As soon as practicable, defense counsel should seek to determine all relevant facts known to the accused.   In so doing, defense counsel should probe for all legally relevant information without seeking to influence the direction of the client's responses.

(b) Defense counsel should not instruct the client or intimate to the client in any way that the client should not be candid in revealing facts so as to afford defense counsel free rein to take action which would be precluded by counsel's knowing of such facts.

Standard 4–3.3   Fees

(a) Defense counsel should not enter into an agreement for, charge, or collect an illegal or unreasonable fee.

(b) In determining the amount of the fee in a criminal case, it is proper to consider the time and effort required, the responsibility assumed by counsel, the novelty and difficulty of the questions involved, the skill requisite to proper representation, the likelihood that other employment will be precluded, the fee customarily charged in the locality for similar services, the gravity of the charge, the experience, reputation, and ability of defense counsel, and the capacity of the client to pay the fee.

(c) Defense counsel should not imply that his or her compensation is for anything other than professional services rendered by defense counsel or by others for defense counsel.

(d) Defense counsel should not divide a fee with a nonlawyer, except as permitted by applicable ethical codes of conduct.

(e) Defense counsel not in the same firm should not divide fees unless the division is in proportion to the services performed by each counsel or, by written agreement with the client, each counsel assumes joint responsibility for the representation, the client is advised of and does not object to the participation of all counsel involved, and the total fee is reasonable.

(f) Defense counsel should not enter into an arrangement for, charge, or collect a contingent fee for representing a defendant in a criminal case.

(g) When defense counsel has not regularly represented the client, defense counsel should communicate the basis or rate of the fee to the client, preferably in writing, before or within a reasonable time after commencing the representation.

543

Standard 4–3.4 Obtaining Literary or Media Rights From the Accused

Defense counsel, prior to conclusion of all aspects of the matter giving rise to his or her employment, should not enter into any agreement or understanding with a client or a prospective client by which defense counsel acquires an interest in literary or media rights to a portrayal or account based in substantial part on information relating to the employment or proposed employment.

Standard 4–3.5 Conflicts of Interest

(a) Defense counsel should not permit his or her professional judgment or obligations to be affected by his or her own political, financial, business, property, or personal interests.

(b) Defense counsel should disclose to the defendant at the earliest feasible opportunity any interest in or connection with the case or any other matter that might be relevant to the defendant's selection of counsel to represent him or her or counsel's continuing representation. Such disclosure should include communication of information reasonably sufficient to permit the client to appreciate the significance of any conflict or potential conflict of interest.

(c) Except for preliminary matters such as initial hearings or applications for bail, defense counsel who are associated in practice should not undertake to defend more than one defendant in the same criminal case if the duty to one of the defendants may conflict with the duty to another. The potential for conflict of interest in representing multiple defendants is so grave that ordinarily defense counsel should decline to act for more than one of several codefendants except in unusual situations when, after careful investigation, it is clear either that no conflict is likely to develop at trial, sentencing, or at any other time in the proceeding or that common representation will be advantageous to each of the codefendants represented and, in either case, that:

(i) the several defendants give an informed consent to such multiple representation; and

(ii) the consent of the defendants is made a matter of judicial record. In determining the presence of consent by the defendants, the trial judge should make appropriate inquiries respecting actual or potential conflicts of interest of counsel and whether the defendants fully comprehend the difficulties that defense counsel sometimes encounters in defending multiple clients.

(d) Defense counsel who has formerly represented a defendant should not thereafter use information related to the former representation to the disadvantage of the former client unless the information has become generally known or the ethical obligation of confidentiality otherwise does not apply.

(e) In accepting payment of fees by one person for the defense of another, defense counsel should be careful to determine that he or she will not be confronted with a conflict of loyalty since defense counsel's entire loyalty is due the accused. Defense counsel should not accept such compensation unless:

(i) the accused consents after disclosure;

(ii) there is no interference with defense counsel's independence of professional judgment or with the client-lawyer relationship; and

(iii) information relating to the representation of the accused is protected from disclosure as required by defense counsel's ethical obligation of confidentiality.

Defense counsel should not permit a person who recommends, employs, or pays defense counsel to render legal services for another to direct or regulate counsel's professional judgment in rendering such legal services.

(f) Defense counsel should not defend a criminal case in which counsel's partner or other professional associate is or has been the prosecutor in the same case.

(g) Defense counsel should not represent a criminal defendant in a jurisdiction in which he or she is also a prosecutor.

(h) Defense counsel who formerly participated personally and substantially in the prosecution of a defendant should not thereafter represent any person in the same or a substantially related matter. Defense counsel who was formerly a prosecutor should not use confidential information about a person acquired when defense counsel was a prosecutor in the representation of a client whose interests are adverse to that person in a matter.

(i) Defense counsel who is related to a prosecutor as parent, child, sibling or spouse should not represent a client in a criminal matter where defense counsel knows the government is represented in the matter by such prosecutor. Nor should defense counsel who has a significant personal or financial relationship with a prosecutor represent a client in a criminal matter where defense counsel knows the government is represented in the matter by such prosecutor, except upon consent by the client after consultation regarding the relationship.

(j) Defense counsel should not act as surety on a bond either for the accused represented by counsel or for any other accused in the same or a related case.

(k) Except as law may otherwise expressly permit, defense counsel should not negotiate to employ any person who is significantly involved as an attorney or employee of the government in a matter in which defense counsel is participating personally and substantially.

Standard 4–3.6 Prompt Action to Protect the Accused

Many important rights of the accused can be protected and preserved only by prompt legal action. Defense counsel should inform the accused of his or her rights at the earliest opportunity and take all necessary action to vindicate such rights. Defense counsel should consider all procedural steps which in good faith may be taken, including, for example, motions seeking pretrial release of the accused, obtaining psychiatric examination of the accused when a need appears, moving for change of venue or continuance, moving to suppress illegally obtained evidence, moving for severance from jointly charged defendants, and seeking dismissal of the charges.

Standard 4–3.7   Advice and Service on Anticipated Unlawful Conduct

(a) It is defense counsel's duty to advise a client to comply with the law, but counsel may advise concerning the meaning, scope, and validity of a law.

(b) Defense counsel should not counsel a client in or knowingly assist a client to engage in conduct which defense counsel knows to be illegal or fraudulent but defense counsel may discuss the legal consequences of any proposed course of conduct with a client.

(c) Defense counsel should not agree in advance of the commission of a crime that he or she will serve as counsel for the defendant, except as part of a bona fide effort to determine the validity, scope, meaning, or application of the law, or where the defense is incident to a general retainer for legal services to a person or enterprise engaged in legitimate activity.

(d) Defense counsel should not reveal information relating to representation of a client unless the client consents after consultation, except for disclosures that are impliedly authorized in order to carry out the representation and except that defense counsel may reveal such information to the extent he or she reasonably believes necessary to prevent the client from committing a criminal act that defense counsel believes is likely to result in imminent death or substantial bodily harm.

Standard 4–3.8   Duty to Keep Client Informed

(a) Defense counsel should keep the client informed of the developments in the case and the progress of preparing the defense and should promptly comply with reasonable requests for information.

(b) Defense counsel should explain developments in the case to the extent reasonably necessary to permit the client to make informed decisions regarding the representation.

Standard 4–3.9   Obligations of Hybrid and Standby Counsel

(a) Defense counsel whose duty is to actively assist a pro se accused should permit the accused to make the final decisions on all matters, including strategic and tactical matters relating to the conduct of the case.

(b) Defense counsel whose duty is to assist a pro se accused only when the accused requests assistance may bring to the attention of the accused matters beneficial to him or her, but should not actively participate in the conduct of the defense unless requested by the accused or insofar as directed to do so by the court.

PART IV.   INVESTIGATION AND PREPARATION

Standard 4–4.1   Duty to Investigate

(a) Defense counsel should conduct a prompt investigation of the circumstances of the case and to explore all avenues leading to facts relevant to the merits of the case and the penalty in the event of conviction.   The investigation should include efforts to secure information in the possession of the prosecution and law enforcement authorities.   The duty to investigate exists regardless of the accused's admissions or statements to defense counsel of facts constituting guilt or the accused's stated desire to plead guilty.

(b) Defense counsel should not seek to acquire possession of physical evidence personally or through use of an investigator where defense counsel's sole purpose is to obstruct access to such evidence.

Standard 4–4.2   Illegal Investigation

Defense counsel should not knowingly use illegal means to obtain evidence or information or to employ, instruct, or encourage others to do so.

Standard 4–4.3   Relations With Prospective Witnesses

(a) Defense counsel, in representing an accused, should not use means that have no substantial purpose other than to embarrass, delay, or burden a third person, or use methods of obtaining evidence that violate the legal rights of such a person.

(b) Defense counsel should not compensate a witness, other than an expert, for giving testimony, but it is not improper to reimburse a witness for the reasonable expenses of attendance upon court, including transportation and loss of income, attendance for depositions pursuant to statute or court rule, or attendance for pretrial interviews, provided there is no attempt to conceal the fact of reimbursement.

(c) It is not necessary for defense counsel or defense counsel's investigator, in interviewing a prospective witness, to caution the witness concerning possible self-incrimination and the need for counsel.

(d) Defense counsel should not discourage or obstruct communication between prospective witnesses and the prosecutor.   It is unprofessional conduct to advise any person other than a client, or cause such person to be advised to decline to give to the prosecutor or defense counsel for codefendants information which such person has a right to give.

(e) Unless defense counsel is prepared to forego impeachment of a witness by counsel's own testimony as to what the witness stated in an interview or to seek leave to withdraw from the case in order to present such impeaching testimony, defense counsel should avoid interviewing a prospective witness except in the presence of a third person.

Standard 4–4.4   Relations With Expert Witnesses

(a) Defense counsel who engages an expert for an opinion should respect the independence of the expert and should not seek to dictate the formation of the expert's opinion on the subject. To the extent necessary, defense counsel should explain to the expert his or her role in the trial as an impartial witness called to aid the fact finders and the manner in which the examination of witnesses is conducted.

(b) Defense counsel should not pay an excessive fee for the purpose of influencing an expert's testimony or fix the amount of the fee contingent upon the testimony an expert will give or the result in the case.

Standard 4–4.5   Compliance With Discovery Procedure

Defense counsel should make a reasonably diligent effort to comply with a legally proper discovery request.

Standard 4–4.6   Physical Evidence

(a) Defense counsel who receives a physical item under circumstances implicating a client in criminal conduct should disclose the location of or should deliver that item to law enforcement authorities only: (1) if required by law or court order, or (2) as provided in paragraph (d).

(b) Unless required to disclose, defense counsel should return the item to the source from whom defense counsel received it, except as provided in paragraphs (c) and (d). In returning the item to the source, defense counsel should advise the source of the legal consequences pertaining to possession or destruction of the item. Defense counsel should also prepare a written record of these events for his or her file, but should not give the source a copy of such record.

(c) Defense counsel may receive the item for a reasonable period of time during which defense counsel: (1) intends to return it to the owner; (2) reasonably fears that return of the item to the source will result in destruction of the item; (3) reasonably fears that return of the item to the source will result in physical harm to anyone; (4) intends to test, examine, inspect, or use the item in any way as part of defense counsel's representation of the client; or (5) cannot return it to the source. If defense counsel tests or examines the item, he or she should thereafter return it to the source unless there is reason to believe that the evidence might be altered or destroyed or used to harm another or return is otherwise impossible. If defense counsel retains the item, he or she should retain it in his or her law office in a manner that does not impede the lawful ability of law enforcement authorities to obtain the item.

(d) If the item received is contraband, i.e. an item, possession of which is in and of itself a crime, such as narcotics, defense counsel may suggest that the client destroy it where there is no pending case or investigation relating to this evidence and where such destruction is clearly not in violation of any criminal statute. If such destruction is not permitted by law or if in defense counsel's judgment he or she cannot retain the item, whether or not it is contraband, in a way that does not pose an unreasonable risk of physical harm to anyone, defense counsel should disclose the location of or should deliver the item to law enforcement authorities.

(e) If defense counsel discloses the location of or delivers the item to law enforcement authorities under paragraphs (a) or (d), or to a third party under paragraph (c)(1), he or she should do so in the way best designed to protect the client's interests.

PART V. CONTROL AND DIRECTION OF LITIGATION

Standard 4–5.1 Advising the Accused

(a) After informing himself or herself fully on the facts and the law, defense counsel should advise the accused with complete candor concerning all aspects of the case, including a candid estimate of the probable outcome.

(b) Defense counsel should not intentionally understate or overstate the risks, hazards, or prospects of the case to exert undue influence on the accused's decision as to his or her plea.

(c) Defense counsel should caution the client to avoid communication about the case with witnesses, except with the approval of counsel, to avoid any contact with jurors or prospective jurors, and to avoid either the reality or the appearance of any other improper activity.

Standard 4–5.2 Control and Direction of the Case

(a) Certain decisions relating to the conduct of the case are ultimately for the accused and others are ultimately for defense counsel. The decisions which are to be made by the accused after full consultation with counsel include:

(i) what pleas to enter;

(ii) whether to accept a plea agreement;

(iii) whether to waive jury trial;

(iv) whether to testify in his or her own behalf; and

(v) whether to appeal.

(b) Strategic and tactical decisions should be made by defense counsel after consultation with the client where feasible and appropriate. Such decisions include what witnesses to call, whether and how to conduct cross-examination, what jurors to accept or strike, what trial motions should be made, and what evidence should be introduced.

(c) If a disagreement on significant matters of tactics or strategy arises between defense counsel and the client, defense counsel should make a record of the circumstances, counsel's advice and reasons, and the conclusion reached. The record should be made in a manner which protects the confidentiality of the lawyer-client relationship.

PART VI. DISPOSITION WITHOUT TRIAL

Standard 4–6.1   Duty to Explore Disposition Without Trial

(a) Whenever the law, nature, and circumstances of the case permit, defense counsel should explore the possibility of an early diversion of the case from the criminal process through the use of other community agencies.

(b) Defense counsel may engage in plea discussions with the prosecutor. Under no circumstances should defense counsel recommend to a defendant acceptance of a plea unless appropriate investigation and study of the case has been completed, including an analysis of controlling law and the evidence likely to be introduced at trial.

Standard 4–6.2   Plea Discussions

(a) Defense counsel should keep the accused advised of developments arising out of plea discussions conducted with the prosecutor.

(b) Defense counsel should promptly communicate and explain to the accused all significant plea proposals made by the prosecutor.

(c) Defense counsel should not knowingly make false statements concerning the evidence in the course of plea discussions with the prosecutor.

(d) Defense counsel should not seek concessions favorable to one client by any agreement which is detrimental to the legitimate interests of a client in another case.

(e) Defense counsel representing two or more clients in the same or related cases should not participate in making an aggregated agreement as to guilty or nolo contendere pleas, unless each client consents after consultation, including disclosure of the existence and nature of all the claims or pleas involved.

PART VII. TRIAL

Standard 4–7.1   Courtroom Professionalism

(a) As an officer of the court, defense counsel should support the authority of the court and the dignity of the trial courtroom by strict adherence to codes of professionalism and by manifesting a professional attitude toward the judge, opposing counsel, witnesses, jurors, and others in the courtroom.

(b) Defense counsel should not engage in unauthorized ex parte discussions with or submission of material to a judge relating to a particular case which is or may come before the judge.

(c) When court is in session, defense counsel should address the court and should not address the prosecutor directly on all matters relating to the case.

(d) Defense counsel should comply promptly with all orders and directives of the court, but defense counsel has a duty to have the record reflect adverse rulings or judicial conduct which counsel considers prejudicial to his or her client's legitimate interests. Defense counsel has a right to make respectful requests for reconsiderations of adverse rulings.

(e) Defense counsel should cooperate with courts and the organized bar in developing codes of professionalism for each jurisdiction.

Standard 4–7.2   Selection of Jurors

(a) Defense counsel should prepare himself or herself prior to trial to discharge effectively his or her function in the selection of the jury, including the raising of any appropriate issues concerning the method by which the jury panel was selected and the exercise of both challenges for cause and peremptory challenges.

(b) In those cases where it appears necessary to conduct a pretrial investigation of the background of jurors, investigatory methods of defense counsel should neither harass nor unduly embarrass potential jurors or invade their privacy and, whenever possible, should be restricted to an investigation of records and sources of information already in existence.

(c) The opportunity to question jurors personally should be used solely to obtain information for the intelligent exercise of challenges. Defense counsel should not intentionally use the voir dire to present factual matter which defense counsel knows will not be admissible at trial or to argue counsel's case to the jury.

Standard 4–7.3   Relations With Jury

(a) Defense counsel should not intentionally communicate privately with persons summoned for jury duty or impaneled as jurors prior to or during the trial. Defense counsel should avoid the reality or appearance of any such communications.

(b) Defense counsel should treat jurors with deference and respect, avoiding the reality or appearance of currying favor by a show of undue solicitude for their comfort or convenience.

(c) After discharge of the jury from further consideration of a case, defense counsel should not intentionally make comments to or ask questions of a juror for the purpose of harassing or embarrassing the juror in any way which will tend to influence judgment in future jury service. If defense counsel believes that the verdict may be subject to legal challenge, he or she may properly, if no statute or rule prohibits such course, communicate with jurors to determine whether such challenge may be available.

Standard 4–7.4   Opening Statement

Defense counsel's opening statement should be confined to a statement of the issues in the case and the evidence defense counsel believes in good faith will be available and admissible. Defense counsel should not allude to any evidence unless there is a good faith and reasonable basis for believing such evidence will be tendered and admitted in evidence.

Standard 4–7.5   Presentation of Evidence

(a) Defense counsel should not knowingly offer false evidence, whether by documents, tangible evidence, or the testimony of witnesses, or fail to take reasonable remedial measures upon discovery of its falsity.

(b) Defense counsel should not knowingly and for the purpose of bringing inadmissible matter to the attention of the judge or jury to offer inadmissible evidence, ask legally objectionable questions, or make other impermissible comments or arguments in the presence of the judge or jury.

(c) Defense counsel should not permit any tangible evidence to be displayed in the view of the judge or jury which would tend to prejudice fair consideration of the case by the judge or jury until such time as a good faith tender of such evidence is made.

(d) Defense counsel should not tender tangible evidence in the presence of the judge or jury if it would tend to prejudice fair consideration of the case unless there is a reasonable basis for its admission in evidence. When there is any substantial doubt about the admissibility of such evidence, it should be tendered by an offer of proof and a ruling obtained.*

Standard 4–7.6   Examination of Witnesses

(a) The interrogation of all witnesses should be conducted fairly, objectively, and with due regard for the dignity and legitimate privacy of the

---

* EDITORS' NOTE. The Commentary to this Standard reads, in part, as follows:

Use of False Evidence

When evidence that a lawyer knows to be false is provided by a person who is not the client, the lawyer must refuse to offer it regardless of the client's wishes. When false evidence is offered by the client, however, a conflict may arise between the lawyer's duty to keep the client's revelations confidential and the duty of candor to the court. Upon ascertaining that material evidence is false, the lawyer should seek to persuade the client that the evidence should not be offered or, if it has been offered, that its false character should immediately be disclosed. If the persuasion is ineffective, the lawyer must take reasonable remedial measures. The advocate's proper course with respect to reasonable remedial measures, ordinarily, is to remonstrate with the client confidentially. If that fails, the advocate should seek to withdraw if that will remedy the situation. If withdrawal will not remedy the situation or is impossible, the advocate should make

disclosure to the court. It is for the court then to determine what should be done—making a statement about the matter to the trier of fact, ordering a mistrial, or perhaps nothing.[1] Counsel's duty to rectify the presentation of false evidence continues only until the conclusion of the proceeding at which the evidence was offered.[2]

1. A separate standard relating to defense counsel's obligations when his or her client proposes to testify or testifies perjuriously was considered for inclusion in these Standards but was not adopted for lack of consensus as to the appropriate approach. Counsel should pay close attention to the ethics code rules adopted on this subject in his or her jurisdiction. See also ABA Model Rule of Professional Conduct 3.3; ABA Model Code of Professional Responsibility DR 7–102(A)(4); Nix v. Whiteside, 475 U.S. 157 (1986); ABA Standing Committee on Ethics and Professional Responsibility, Formal Opinion 87–353 (1987).

2. See ABA Model Rule of Professional Conduct 3.3(b).

witness, and without seeking to intimidate or humiliate the witness unnecessarily.

(b) Defense counsel's belief or knowledge that the witness is telling the truth does not preclude cross-examination.

(c) Defense counsel should not call a witness in the presence of the jury who the lawyer knows will claim a valid privilege not to testify.

(d) Defense counsel should not ask a question which implies the existence of a factual predicate for which a good faith belief is lacking.

Standard 4–7.7 Argument to the Jury

(a) In closing argument to the jury, defense counsel may argue all reasonable inferences from the evidence in the record. Defense counsel should not intentionally misstate the evidence or mislead the jury as to the inferences it may draw.

(b) Defense counsel should not express a personal belief or opinion in his or her client's innocence or personal belief or opinion in the truth or falsity of any testimony or evidence.

(c) Defense counsel should not make arguments calculated to appeal to the prejudices of the jury.

(d) Defense counsel should refrain from argument which would divert the jury from its duty to decide the case on the evidence.

Standard 4–7.8 Facts Outside the Record

Defense counsel should not intentionally refer to or argue on the basis of facts outside the record whether at trial or on appeal, unless such facts are matters of common public knowledge based on ordinary human experience or matters of which the court can take judicial notice.

Standard 4–7.9 Posttrial Motions

Defense counsel's responsibility includes presenting appropriate posttrial motions to protect the defendant's rights.

PART VIII. AFTER CONVICTION

Standard 4–8.1 Sentencing

(a) Defense counsel should, at the earliest possible time, be or become familiar with all of the sentencing alternatives available to the court and with community and other facilities which may be of assistance in a plan for meeting the accused's needs. Defense counsel's preparation should also include familiarization with the court's practices in exercising sentencing discretion, the practical consequences of different sentences, and the normal pattern of sentences for the offense involved, including any guidelines applicable at either the sentencing or parole stages. The consequences of the various

553

dispositions available should be explained fully by defense counsel to the accused.

(b) Defense counsel should present to the court any ground which will assist in reaching a proper disposition favorable to the accused. If a presentence report or summary is made available to defense counsel, he or she should seek to verify the information contained in it and should be prepared to supplement or challenge it if necessary. If there is no presentence report or if it is not disclosed, defense counsel should submit to the court and the prosecutor all favorable information relevant to sentencing and in an appropriate case, with the consent of the accused, be prepared to suggest a program of rehabilitation based on defense counsel's exploration of employment, educational, and other opportunities made available by community services.

(c) Defense counsel should also insure that the accused understands the nature of the presentence investigation process, and in particular the significance of statements made by the accused to probation officers and related personnel. Where appropriate, defense counsel should attend the probation officer's interview with the accused.

(d) Defense counsel should alert the accused to the right of allocution, if any, and to the possible dangers of making a statement that might tend to prejudice an appeal.

Standard 4-8.2   Appeal

(a) After conviction, defense counsel should explain to the defendant the meaning and consequences of the court's judgment and defendant's right of appeal. Defense counsel should give the defendant his or her professional judgment as to whether there are meritorious grounds for appeal and as to the probable results of an appeal. Defense counsel should also explain to the defendant the advantages and disadvantages of an appeal. The decision whether to appeal must be the defendant's own choice.

(b) Defense counsel should take whatever steps are necessary to protect the defendant's rights of appeal.

Standard 4-8.3   Counsel on Appeal

(a) Appellate counsel should not seek to withdraw from a case solely on the basis of his or her own determination that the appeal lacks merit.

(b) Appellate counsel should give a client his or her best professional evaluation of the questions that might be presented on appeal. Counsel, when inquiring into the case, should consider all issues that might affect the validity of the judgment of conviction and sentence, including any that might require initial presentation in a postconviction proceeding. Counsel should advise on the probable outcome of a challenge to the conviction or sentence. Counsel should endeavor to persuade the client to abandon a wholly frivolous appeal or to eliminate contentions lacking in substance.

(c) If the client chooses to proceed with an appeal against the advice of counsel, counsel should present the case, so long as such advocacy does not involve deception of the court. When counsel cannot continue without misleading the court, counsel may request permission to withdraw.

(d) Appellate counsel has the ultimate authority to decide which arguments to make on appeal. When appellate counsel decides not to argue all of the issues that his or her client desires to be argued, appellate counsel should inform the client of his or her pro se briefing rights.

(e) In a jurisdiction with an intermediate appellate court, counsel for a defendant-appellant or a defendant-appellee should continue to represent the client if the prosecution seeks review in the highest court, unless new counsel is substituted or unless the court permits counsel to withdraw. Similarly, in any jurisdiction, such appellate counsel should continue to represent the client if the prosecution seeks review in the Supreme Court of the United States.

Standard 4–8.4 Conduct of Appeal

(a) Appellate counsel should be diligent in perfecting appeals and expediting their prompt submission to appellate courts.

(b) Appellate counsel should be accurate in referring to the record and the authorities upon which counsel relies in the presentation to the court of briefs and oral argument.

(c) Appellate counsel should not intentionally refer to or argue on the basis of facts outside the record on appeal, unless such facts are matters of common public knowledge based on ordinary human experience or matters of which the court may take judicial notice.

Standard 4–8.5 Post–Conviction Remedies

After a conviction is affirmed on appeal, appellate counsel should determine whether there is any ground for relief under other post-conviction remedies. If there is a reasonable prospect of a favorable result, counsel should explain to the defendant the advantages and disadvantages of taking such action. Appellate counsel is not obligated to represent the defendant in a post-conviction proceeding unless counsel has agreed to do so. In other respects, the responsibility of a lawyer in a post-conviction proceeding should be guided generally by the standards governing the conduct of lawyers in criminal cases.

Standard 4–8.6 Challenges to the Effectiveness of Counsel

(a) If defense counsel, after investigation, is satisfied that another defense counsel who served in an earlier phase of the case did not provide effective assistance, he or she should not hesitate to seek relief for the defendant on that ground.

(b) If defense counsel, after investigation, is satisfied that another defense counsel who served in an earlier phase of the case provided effective assistance, he or she should so advise the client and may decline to proceed further.

(c) If defense counsel concludes that he or she did not provide effective assistance in an earlier phase of the case, defense counsel should explain this conclusion to the defendant and seek to withdraw from representation with an explanation to the court of the reason therefor.

(d) Defense counsel whose conduct of a criminal case is drawn into question is entitled to testify concerning the matters charged and is not precluded from disclosing the truth concerning the accusation to the extent defense counsel reasonably believes necessary, even though this involves revealing matters which were given in confidence.

SELECTED FEDERAL STATUTES AND RULES

1. BRIBERY, GRAFT, AND CONFLICTS OF INTEREST, 18 U.S.C.A. §§ 202–09—Excerpts

§ 202. Definitions

(a) For the purpose of sections 203, 205, 207, 208, and 209 of this title the term "special Government employee" shall mean an officer or employee of the executive or legislative branch of the United States Government, of any independent agency of the United States or of the District of Columbia, who is retained, designated, appointed, or employed to perform, with or without compensation, for not to exceed one hundred and thirty days during any period of three hundred and sixty-five consecutive days, temporary duties either on a full-time or intermittent basis, a part-time United States commissioner, or a part-time United States magistrate judge, or, regardless of the number of days of appointment, an independent counsel appointed under chapter 40 of title 28 and any person appointed by that independent counsel under section 594(c) of title 28. Notwithstanding the next preceding sentence, every person serving as a part-time local representative of a Member of Congress in the Member's home district or State shall be classified as a special Government employee. Notwithstanding section 29(c) and (d) of the Act of August 10, 1956 (70A Stat. 632; 5 U.S.C. 30r(c) and (d)), a Reserve officer of the Armed Forces, or an officer of the National Guard of the United States, unless otherwise an officer or employee of the United States, shall be classified as a special Government employee while on active duty solely for training. A Reserve officer of the Armed Forces or an officer of the National Guard of the United States who is voluntarily serving a period of extended active duty in excess of one hundred and thirty days shall be classified as an officer of the United States within the meaning of section 203 and sections 205 through 209 and 218. A Reserve officer of the Armed Forces or an officer of the National Guard of the United States who is serving involuntarily shall be classified as a special Government employee. The terms "officer or employee" and "special Government employee" as used in sections 203, 205, 207 through 209, and 218, shall not include enlisted members of the Armed Forces.

(b) For the purposes of sections 205 and 207 of this title, the term "official responsibility" means the direct administrative or operating authority, whether intermediate or final, and either exercisable alone or with others, and either personally or through subordinates, to approve, disapprove, or otherwise direct Government action.

(c) Except as otherwise provided in such sections, the terms "officer" and "employee" in sections 203, 205, 207 through 209, and 218 of this title shall not include the President, the Vice President, a Member of Congress, or a Federal judge.

(d) The term "Member of Congress" in sections 204 and 207 means—

(1) a United States Senator; and

(2) a Representative in, or a Delegate or Resident Commissioner to, the House of Representatives.

(e) As used in this chapter [18 U.S.C.A. §§ 201 et seq.], the term—

(1) "executive branch" includes each executive agency as defined in title 5, and any other entity or administrative unit in the executive branch;

(2) "judicial branch" means the Supreme Court of the United States; the United States courts of appeals; the United States district courts; the Court of International Trade; the United States bankruptcy courts; any court created pursuant to article I of the United States Constitution, including the Court of Appeals for the Armed Forces, the United States Court of Federal Claims, and the United States Tax Court, but not including a court of a territory or possession of the United States; the Federal Judicial Center; and any other agency, office, or entity in the judicial branch; and

(3) "legislative branch" means—

(A) the Congress; and

(B) the Office of the Architect of the Capitol, the United States Botanic Garden, the General Accounting Office, the Government Printing Office, the Library of Congress, the Office of Technology Assessment, the Congressional Budget Office, the United States Capitol Police, and any other agency, entity, office, or commission established in the legislative branch.

§ 203. Compensation to Members of Congress, officers, and others in matters affecting the Government

(a) Whoever, otherwise than as provided by law for the proper discharge of official duties, directly or indirectly—

(1) demands, seeks, receives, accepts, or agrees to receive or accept any compensation for any representational services, as agent or attorney or otherwise, rendered or to be rendered either personally or by another—

(A) at a time when such person is a Member of Congress, Member of Congress Elect, Delegate, Delegate Elect, Resident Commissioner, or Resident Commissioner Elect; or

(B) at a time when such person is an officer or employee or Federal judge of the United States in the executive, legislative, or judicial branch of the Government, or in any agency of the United States, in relation to any proceeding, application, request for a ruling or other determination, contract, claim, controversy, charge, accusation, arrest, or other particular matter in which the United States is a party or has a direct and substantial interest, before any department, agency, court, court-martial, officer, or any civil, military, or naval commission; or

(2) knowingly gives, promises, or offers any compensation for any such representational services rendered or to be rendered at a time when the person to whom the compensation is given, promised, or offered, is or was such a Member, Member Elect, Delegate, Delegate Elect, Commissioner, Commission Elect, Federal judge, officer, or employee;

shall be subject to the penalties set forth in section 216 of this title.

(b) Whoever, otherwise than as provided by law for the proper discharge of official duties, directly or indirectly—

(1) demands, seeks, receives, accepts, or agrees to receive or accept any compensation for any representational services, as agent or attorney or otherwise, rendered or to be rendered either personally or by another, at a time when such person is an officer or employee of the District of Columbia, in relation to any proceeding, application, request for a ruling or other determination, contract, claim, controversy, charge, accusation, arrest, or other particular matter in which the District of Columbia is a party or has a direct and substantial interest, before any department, agency, court, officer, or commission; or

(2) knowingly gives, promises, or offers any compensation for any such representational services rendered or to be rendered at a time when the person to whom the compensation is given, promised, or offered, is or was an officer or employee of the District of Columbia;

shall be subject to the penalties set forth in section 216 of this title.

(c) A special Government employee shall be subject to subsections (a) and (b) only in relation to a particular matter involving a specific party or parties—

(1) in which such employee has at any time participated personally and substantially as a Government employee or as a special Government employee through decision, approval, disapproval, recommendation, the rendering of advice, investigation or otherwise; or

(2) which is pending in the department or agency of the Government in which such employee is serving except that paragraph (2) of this subsection shall not apply in the case of a special Government employee who has served in such department or agency no more than sixty days during the immediately preceding period of three hundred and sixty-five consecutive days.

(d) Nothing in this section prevents an officer or employee, including a special Government employee, from acting, with or without compensation, as agent or attorney for or otherwise representing his parents, spouse, child, or any person for whom, or for any estate for which, he is serving as guardian, executor, administrator, trustee, or other personal fiduciary except—

(1) in those matters in which he has participated personally and substantially as a Government employee or as a special Government employee through decision, approval, disapproval, recommendation, the rendering of advice, investigation, or otherwise; or

(2) in those matters that are the subject of his official responsibility, subject to approval by the Government official responsible for appointment to his position.

(e) Nothing in this section prevents a special Government employee from acting as agent or attorney for another person in the performance of work under a grant by, or a contract with or for the benefit of, the United States if the head of the department or agency concerned with the grant or contract certifies in writing that the national interest so requires and publishes such certification in the Federal Register.

(f) Nothing in this section prevents an individual from giving testimony under oath or from making statements required to be made under penalty of perjury.

§ 204. Practice in United States Court of Federal Claims or the United States Court of Appeals for the Federal Circuit by Members of Congress

Whoever, being a Member of Congress or Member of Congress Elect, practices in the United States Court of Federal Claims or the United States Court of Appeals for the Federal Circuit shall be subject to the penalties set forth in section 216 of this title.

§ 205. Activities of officers and employees in claims against and other matters affecting the Government

(a) Whoever, being an officer or employee of the United States in the executive, legislative, or judicial branch of the Government or in any agency of the United States, other than in the proper discharge of his official duties—

(1) acts as agent or attorney for prosecuting any claim against the United States, or receives any gratuity, or any share of or interest in any such claim, in consideration of assistance in the prosecution of such claim; or

(2) acts as agent or attorney for anyone before any department, agency, court, court-martial, officer, or civil, military, or naval commission in connection with any covered matter in which the United States is a party or has a direct and substantial interest;

shall be subject to the penalties set forth in section 216 of this title.

(b) Whoever, being an officer or employee of the District of Columbia or an officer or employee of the Office of the United States Attorney for the

District of Columbia, otherwise than in the proper discharge of official duties—

(1) acts as agent or attorney for prosecuting any claim against the District of Columbia, or receives any gratuity, or any share of or interest in any such claim in consideration of assistance in the prosecution of such claim; or

(2) acts as agent or attorney for anyone before any department, agency, court, officer, or commission in connection with any covered matter in which the District of Columbia is a party or has a direct and substantial interest;

shall be subject to the penalties set forth in section 216 of this title.

(c) A special Government employee shall be subject to subsections (a) and (b) only in relation to a covered matter involving a specific party or parties—

(1) in which he has at any time participated personally and substantially as a Government employee or special Government employee through decision, approval, disapproval, recommendation, the rendering of advice, investigation, or otherwise; or

(2) which is pending in the department or agency of the Government in which he is serving.

Paragraph (2) shall not apply in the case of a special Government employee who has served in such department or agency no more than sixty days during the immediately preceding period of three hundred and sixty-five consecutive days.

(d)(1) Nothing in subsection (a) or (b) prevents an officer or employee, if not inconsistent with the faithful performance of that officer's or employee's duties, from acting without compensation as agent or attorney for, or otherwise representing—

(A) any person who is the subject of disciplinary, loyalty, or other personnel administration proceedings in connection with those proceedings; or

(B) except as provided in paragraph (2), any cooperative, voluntary, professional, recreational, or similar organization or group not established or operated for profit, if a majority of the organization's or group's members are current officers or employees of the United States or of the District of Columbia, or their spouses or dependent children.

(2) Paragraph (1)(B) does not apply with respect to a covered matter that—

(A) is a claim under subsection (a)(1) or (b)(1);

(B) is a judicial or administrative proceeding where the organization or group is a party; or

(C) involves a grant, contract, or other agreement (including a request for any such grant, contract, or agreement) providing for the disbursement of Federal funds to the organization or group.

(e) Nothing in subsection (a) or (b) prevents an officer or employee, including a special Government employee, from acting, with or without compensation, as agent or attorney for, or otherwise representing, his parents, spouse, child, or any person for whom, or for any estate for which, he is serving as guardian, executor, administrator, trustee, or other personal fiduciary except—

(1) in those matters in which he has participated personally and substantially as a Government employee or special Government employee through decision, approval, disapproval, recommendation, the rendering of advice, investigation, or otherwise, or

(2) in those matters which are the subject of his official responsibility,

subject to approval by the Government official responsible for appointment to his position.

(f) Nothing in subsection (a) or (b) prevents a special Government employee from acting as agent or attorney for another person in the performance of work under a grant by, or a contract with or for the benefit of, the United States if the head of the department or agency concerned with the grant or contract certifies in writing that the national interest so requires and publishes such certification in the Federal Register.

(g) Nothing in this section prevents an officer or employee from giving testimony under oath or from making statements required to be made under penalty for perjury or contempt.

(h) For the purpose of this section, the term "covered matter" means any judicial or other proceeding, application, request for a ruling or other determination, contract, claim, controversy, investigation, charge, accusation, arrest, or other particular matter.

(i) Nothing in this section prevents an employee from acting pursuant to—

(1) chapter 71 of title 5;

(2) section 1004 or chapter 12 of title 39;

(3) section 3 of the Tennessee Valley Authority Act of 1933 (16 U.S.C. 831b);

(4) chapter 10 of title I of the Foreign Service Act of 1980 (22 U.S.C. 4104 et seq.); or

(5) any provision of any other Federal or District of Columbia law that authorizes labor-management relations between an agency or instrumentality of the United States or the District of Columbia and any labor organization that represents its employees.

§ 207. Restrictions on former officers, employees, and elected officials of the executive and legislative branches

(a) Restrictions on all officers and employees of the executive branch and certain other agencies.—

(1) Permanent restrictions on representation on particular matters.—Any person who is an officer or employee (including any special Government employee) of the executive branch of the United States (including any independent agency of the United States), or of the District of Columbia, and who, after the termination of his or her service or employment with the United States or the District of Columbia, knowingly makes, with the intent to influence, any communication to or appearance before any officer or employee of any department, agency, court, or court-martial of the United States or the District of Columbia, on behalf of any other person (except the United States or the District of Columbia) in connection with a particular matter—

    (A) in which the United States or the District of Columbia is a party or has a direct and substantial interest,

    (B) in which the person participated personally and substantially as such officer or employee, and

    (C) which involved a specific party or specific parties at the time of such participation,

shall be punished as provided in section 216 of this title.

(2) Two-year restrictions concerning particular matters under official responsibility.—Any person subject to the restrictions contained in paragraph (1) who, within 2 years after the termination of his or her service or employment with the United States or the District of Columbia, knowingly makes, with the intent to influence, any communication to or appearance before any officer or employee of any department, agency, court, or court-martial of the United States or the District of Columbia, on behalf of any other person (except the United States or the District of Columbia), in connection with a particular matter—

    (A) in which the United States or the District of Columbia is a party or has a direct and substantial interest,

    (B) which such person knows or reasonably should know was actually pending under his or her official responsibility as such officer or employee within a period of 1 year before the termination of his or her service or employment with the United States or the District of Columbia, and

    (C) which involved a specific party or specific parties at the time it was so pending,

shall be punished as provided in section 216 of this title.

(3) Clarification of restrictions.—The restrictions contained in paragraphs (1) and (2) shall apply—

(A) in the case of an officer or employee of the executive branch of the United States (including any independent agency), only with respect to communications to or appearances before any officer or employee of any department, agency, court, or court-martial of the United States on behalf of any other person (except the United States), and only with respect to a matter in which the United States is a party or has a direct and substantial interest; and

(B) in the case of an officer or employee of the District of Columbia, only with respect to communications to or appearances before any officer or employee of any department, agency, or court of the District of Columbia on behalf of any other person (except the District of Columbia), and only with respect to a matter in which the District of Columbia is a party or has a direct and substantial interest.

(b) One-year restrictions on aiding or advising.—

(1) In general.—Any person who is a former officer or employee of the executive branch of the United States (including any independent agency) and is subject to the restrictions contained in subsection (a)(1), or any person who is a former officer or employee of the legislative branch or a former Member of Congress, who personally and substantially participated in any ongoing trade or treaty negotiation on behalf of the United States within the 1-year period preceding the date on which his or her service or employment with the United States terminated, and who had access to information concerning such trade or treaty negotiation which is exempt from disclosure under section 552 of title 5, which is so designated by the appropriate department or agency, and which the person knew or should have known was so designated, shall not, on the basis of that information, knowingly represent, aid, or advise any other person (except the United States) concerning such ongoing trade or treaty negotiation for a period of 1 year after his or her service or employment with the United States terminates. Any person who violates this subsection shall be punished as provided in section 216 of this title.

(2) Definition.—For purposes of this paragraph—

(A) the term "trade negotiation" means negotiations which the President determines to undertake to enter into a trade agreement pursuant to section 1102 of the Omnibus Trade and Competitiveness Act of 1988, and does not include any action taken before that determination is made; and

(B) the term "treaty" means an international agreement made by the President that requires the advice and consent of the Senate.

(c) One-year restrictions on certain senior personnel of the executive branch and independent agencies.—

(1) Restrictions.—In addition to the restrictions set forth in subsections (a) and (b), any person who is an officer or employee (including any special Government employee) of the executive branch of the United States (including an independent agency), who is referred to in paragraph (2), and who, within 1 year after the termination of his or her service or employment as such officer or employee, knowingly makes, with the intent to influence, any communication to or appearance before any officer or employee of the department or agency in which such person served within 1 year before such termination, on behalf of any other person (except the United States), in connection with any matter on which such person seeks official action by any officer or employee of such department or agency, shall be punished as provided in section 216 of this title.

(2) **Persons to whom restrictions apply.**—(A) Paragraph (1) shall apply to a person (other than a person subject to the restrictions of subsection (d))—

(i) employed at a rate of pay specified in or fixed according to subchapter II of chapter 53 of title 5,

(ii) employed in a position which is not referred to in clause (i) and for which the basic rate of pay, exclusive of any locality-based pay adjustment under section 5302 of title 5 (or any comparable adjustment pursuant to interim authority of the President), is equal to or greater than the rate of basic pay payable for level 5 of the Senior Executive Service;

(iii) appointed by the President to a position under section 105(a)(2)(B) of title 3 or by the Vice President to a position under section 106(a)(1)(B) of title 3, or

(iv) employed in a position which is held by an active duty commissioned officer of the uniformed services who is serving in a grade or rank for which the pay grade (as specified in section 201 of title 37) is pay grade O–7 or above.

(B) Paragraph (1) shall not apply to a special Government employee who serves less than 60 days in the 1-year period before his or her service or employment as such employee terminates.

(C) At the request of a department or agency, the Director of the Office of Government Ethics may waive the restrictions contained in paragraph (1) with respect to any position, or category of positions, referred to in clause (ii) or (iv) of subparagraph (A), in such department or agency if the Director determines that—

(i) the imposition of the restrictions with respect to such position or positions would create an undue hardship on the department or agency in obtaining qualified personnel to fill such position or positions, and

(ii) granting the waiver would not create the potential for use of undue influence or unfair advantage.

(d) Restrictions on very senior personnel of the executive branch and independent agencies.—

(1) **Restrictions.**—In addition to the restrictions set forth in subsections (a) and (b), any person who—

(A) serves in the position of Vice President of the United States,

(B) is employed in a position in the executive branch of the United States (including any independent agency) at a rate of pay payable for level I of the Executive Schedule or employed in a position in the Executive Office of the President at a rate of pay payable for level II of the Executive Schedule, or

(C) is appointed by the President to a position under section 105(a)(2)(A) of title 3 or by the Vice President to a position under section 106(a)(1)(A) of title 3,

and who, within 1 year after the termination of that person's service in that position, knowingly makes, with the intent to influence, any communication to or appearance before any person described in paragraph (2), on behalf of any other person (except the United States), in connection with any matter on which such person seeks official action by any officer or employee of the executive branch of the United States, shall be punished as provided in section 216 of this title.

(2) **Persons who may not be contacted.**—The persons referred to in paragraph (1) with respect to appearances or communications by a person in a position described in subparagraph (A), (B), or (C) of paragraph (1) are—

(A) any officer or employee of any department or agency in which such person served in such position within a period of 1 year before such person's service or employment with the United States Government terminated, and

(B) any person appointed to a position in the executive branch which is listed in sections 5312, 5313, 5314, 5315, or 5316 of title 5.

(e) Restrictions on Members of Congress and officers and employees of the legislative branch.—

(1) **Members of Congress and elected officers.**—(A) Any person who is a Member of Congress or an elected officer of either House of Congress and who, within 1 year after that person leaves office, knowingly makes, with the intent to influence, any communication to or appearance before any of the persons described in subparagraph (B) or (C), on behalf of any other person (except the United States) in connection with any matter on which such former Member of Congress or elected officer seeks action by a Member, officer, or employee of either House of Congress, in his or her official capacity, shall be punished as provided in section 216 of this title.

(B) The persons referred to in subparagraph (A) with respect to appearances or communications by a former Member of Congress are any Member, officer, or employee of either House of Congress, and any employee of any other legislative office of the Congress.

(C) The persons referred to in subparagraph (A) with respect to appearances or communications by a former elected officer are any Member, officer, or employee of the House of Congress in which the elected officer served.

(2) Personal staff.—(A) Any person who is an employee of a Senator or an employee of a Member of the House of Representatives and who, within 1 year after the termination of that employment, knowingly makes, with the intent to influence, any communication to or appearance before any of the persons described in subparagraph (B), on behalf of any other person (except the United States) in connection with any matter on which such former employee seeks action by a Member, officer, or employee of either House of Congress, in his or her official capacity, shall be punished as provided in section 216 of this title.

(B) The persons referred to in subparagraph (A) with respect to appearances or communications by a person who is a former employee are the following:

(i) the Senator or Member of the House of Representatives for whom that person was an employee; and

(ii) any employee of that Senator or Member of the House of Representatives.

(3) Committee staff.—Any person who is an employee of a committee of Congress and who, within 1 year after the termination of that person's employment on such committee, knowingly makes, with the intent to influence, any communication to or appearance before any person who is a Member or an employee of that committee or who was a Member of the committee in the year immediately prior to the termination of such person's employment by the committee, on behalf of any other person (except the United States) in connection with any matter on which such former employee seeks action by a Member, officer, or employee of either House of Congress, in his or her official capacity, shall be punished as provided in section 216 of this title.

(4) Leadership staff.—(A) Any person who is an employee on the leadership staff of the House of Representatives or an employee on the leadership staff of the Senate and who, within 1 year after the termination of that person's employment on such staff, knowingly makes, with the intent to influence, any communication to or appearance before any of the persons described in subparagraph (B), on behalf of any other person (except the United States) in connection with any matter on which such former employee seeks action by a Member, officer, or employee of either House of Congress, in his or her official capacity, shall be punished as provided in section 216 of this title.

(B) The persons referred to in subparagraph (A) with respect to appearances or communications by a former employee are the following:

(i) in the case of a former employee on the leadership staff of the House of Representatives, those persons are any Member of the leadership of the House of Representatives and any employee on the leadership staff of the House of Representatives; and

(ii) in the case of a former employee on the leadership staff of the Senate, those persons are any Member of the leadership of the Senate and any employee on the leadership staff of the Senate.

(5) Other legislative offices.—(A) Any person who is an employee of any other legislative office of the Congress and who, within 1 year after the termination of that person's employment in such office, knowingly makes, with the intent to influence, any communication to or appearance before any of the persons described in subparagraph (B), on behalf of any other person (except the United States) in connection with any matter on which such former employee seeks action by any officer or employee of such office, in his or her official capacity, shall be punished as provided in section 216 of this title.

(B) The persons referred to in subparagraph (A) with respect to appearances or communications by a former employee are the employees and officers of the former legislative office of the Congress of the former employee.

(6) Limitation on restrictions.—(A) The restrictions contained in paragraphs (2), (3), and (4) apply only to acts by a former employee who, for at least 60 days, in the aggregate, during the 1-year period before that former employee's service as such employee terminated, was paid a rate of basic pay equal to or greater than an amount which is 75 percent of the basic rate of pay payable for a Member of the House of Congress in which such employee was employed.

(B) The restrictions contained in paragraph (5) apply only to acts by a former employee who, for at least 60 days, in the aggregate, during the 1-year period before that former employee's service as such employee terminated, was employed in a position for which the rate of basic pay, exclusive of any locality-based pay adjustment under section 5302 of title 5 (or any comparable adjustment pursuant to interim authority of the President), is equal to or greater than the basic rate of pay payable for level 5 of the Senior Executive Service.

(7) Definitions.—As used in this subsection—

(A) the term "committee of Congress" includes standing committees, joint committees, and select committees;

(B) a person is an employee of a House of Congress if that person is an employee of the Senate or an employee of the House of Representatives;

(C) the term "employee of the House of Representatives" means an employee of a Member of the House of Representatives, an employee of a committee of the House of Representatives, an employee of a joint committee of the Congress whose pay is disbursed by the Clerk of the House of Representatives, and an employee on the leadership staff of the House of Representatives;

(D) the term "employee of the Senate" means an employee of a Senator, an employee of a committee of the Senate, an employee of a joint committee of the Congress whose pay is disbursed by the Secretary of the Senate, and an employee on the leadership staff of the Senate;

(E) a person is an employee of a Member of the House of Representatives if that person is an employee of a Member of the House of Representatives under the clerk hire allowance;

(F) a person is an employee of a Senator if that person is an employee in a position in the office of a Senator;

(G) the term "employee of any other legislative office of the Congress" means an officer or employee of the Architect of the Capitol, the United States Botanic Garden, the General Accounting Office, the Government Printing Office, the Library of Congress, the Office of Technology Assessment, the Congressional Budget Office, the Copyright Royalty Tribunal, the United States Capitol Police, and any other agency, entity, or office in the legislative branch not covered by paragraph (1), (2), (3), or (4) of this subsection;

(H) the term "employee on the leadership staff of the House of Representatives" means an employee of the office of a Member of the leadership of the House of Representatives described in subparagraph (L), and any elected minority employee of the House of Representatives;

(I) the term "employee on the leadership staff of the Senate" means an employee of the office of a Member of the leadership of the Senate described in subparagraph (M);

(J) the term "Member of Congress" means a Senator or a Member of the House of Representatives;

(K) the term "Member of the House of Representatives" means a Representative in, or a Delegate or Resident Commissioner to, the Congress;

(L) the term "Member of the leadership of the House of Representatives" means the Speaker, majority leader, minority leader, majority whip, minority whip, chief deputy majority whip, chief deputy minority whip, chairman of the Democratic Steering Committee, chairman and vice chairman of the Democratic Caucus, chairman, vice chairman, and secretary of the Republican Conference, chairman of the Republican Research Committee, and chairman of the Republican Policy Committee, of the House of Representatives (or any similar position created on or after the effective date set forth in section 102(a) of the Ethics Reform Act of 1989);

(M) the term "Member of the leadership of the Senate" means the Vice President, and the President pro tempore, Deputy President pro tempore, majority leader, minority leader, majority whip, minority whip, chairman and secretary of the Conference of the Majority, chairman and secretary of the Conference of the Minority, chairman and co-chairman of the Majority Policy Committee, and chairman of the Minority Policy Committee, of the Senate (or any similar position created on or after the effective date set forth in section 102(a) of the Ethics Reform Act of 1989).

(f) Restrictions relating to foreign entities.—

(1) Restrictions.—Any person who is subject to the restrictions contained in subsection (c), (d), or (e) and who knowingly, within 1 year after leaving the position, office, or employment referred to in such subsection—

(A) represents a foreign entity before any officer or employee of any department or agency of the United States with the intent to influence a decision of such officer or employee in carrying out his or her official duties, or

(B) aids or advises a foreign entity with the intent to influence a decision of any officer or employee of any department or agency of the United States, in carrying out his or her official duties,

shall be punished as provided in section 216 of this title.

(2) Special rule for Trade Representative.—With respect to a person who is the United States Trade Representative or Deputy United States Trade Representative, the restrictions described in paragraph (1) shall apply to representing, aiding, or advising foreign entities at any time after the termination of that person's service as the United States Trade Representative.

(3) Definition.—For purposes of this subsection, the term "foreign entity" means the government of a foreign country as defined in section 1(e) of the Foreign Agents Registration Act of 1938, as amended, or a foreign political party as defined in section 1(f) of that Act.

(g) Special rules for detailees.—For purposes of this section, a person who is detailed from one department, agency, or other entity to another department, agency, or other entity shall, during the period such person is detailed, be deemed to be an officer or employee of both departments, agencies, or such entities.

(h) Designations of separate statutory agencies and bureaus.—

(1) Designations.—For purposes of subsection (c) and except as provided in paragraph (2), whenever the Director of the Office of Government Ethics determines that an agency or bureau within a department or agency in the executive branch exercises functions which are distinct and separate from the remaining functions of the department or agency and that there exists no potential for use of undue influence or unfair advantage based on past Government service, the Director shall by rule designate such agency or bureau as a separate department or agency. On an annual basis the Director of the Office of Government Ethics shall review the designations and determinations made under this subparagraph and, in consultation with the department or agency concerned, make such additions and deletions as are necessary. Departments and agencies shall cooperate to the fullest extent with the Director of the Office of Government Ethics in the exercise of his or her responsibilities under this paragraph.

(2) Inapplicability of designations.—No agency or bureau within the Executive Office of the President may be designated under paragraph (1) as a separate department or agency. No designation under paragraph (1) shall apply to persons referred to in subsection (c)(2)(A)(i) or (iii).

(i) Definitions.—For purposes of this section—

(1) the term "officer or employee", when used to describe the person to whom a communication is made or before whom an appearance is made, with the intent to influence, shall include—

    (A) in subsections (a), (c), and (d), the President and the Vice President; and

    (B) in subsection (f), the President, the Vice President, and Members of Congress;

(2) the term "participated" means an action taken as an officer or employee through decision, approval, disapproval, recommendation, the rendering of advice, investigation, or other such action; and

(3) the term "particular matter" includes any investigation, application, request for a ruling or determination, rulemaking, contract, controversy, claim, charge, accusation, arrest, or judicial or other proceeding.

(j) Exceptions.—

(1) Official government duties.—The restrictions contained in this section shall not apply to acts done in carrying out official duties on behalf of the United States or the District of Columbia or as an elected official of a State or local government.

(2) State and local governments and institutions, hospitals, and organizations.—The restrictions contained in subsections (c), (d), and (e) shall not apply to acts done in carrying out official duties as an employee of—

    (A) an agency or instrumentality of a State or local government if the appearance, communication, or representation is on behalf of such government, or

(B) an accredited, degree-granting institution of higher education, as defined in section 101 of the Higher Education Act of 1965, or a hospital or medical research organization, exempted and defined under section 501(c)(3) of the Internal Revenue Code of 1986, if the appearance, communication, or representation is on behalf of such institution, hospital, or organization.

(3) International organizations.—The restrictions contained in this section shall not apply to an appearance or communication on behalf of, or advice or aid to, an international organization in which the United States participates, if the Secretary of State certifies in advance that such activity is in the interests of the United States.

(4) Special knowledge.—The restrictions contained in subsections (c), (d), and (e) shall not prevent an individual from making or providing a statement, which is based on the individual's own special knowledge in the particular area that is the subject of the statement, if no compensation is thereby received.

(5) Exception for scientific or technological information.—The restrictions contained in subsections (a), (c), and (d) shall not apply with respect to the making of communications solely for the purpose of furnishing scientific or technological information, if such communications are made under procedures acceptable to the department or agency concerned or if the head of the department or agency concerned with the particular matter, in consultation with the Director of the Office of Government Ethics, makes a certification, published in the Federal Register, that the former officer or employee has outstanding qualifications in a scientific, technological, or other technical discipline, and is acting with respect to a particular matter which requires such qualifications, and that the national interest would be served by the participation of the former officer or employee. For purposes of this paragraph, the term "officer or employee" includes the Vice President.

(6) Exception for testimony.—Nothing in this section shall prevent an individual from giving testimony under oath, or from making statements required to be made under penalty of perjury. Notwithstanding the preceding sentence—

(A) a former officer or employee of the executive branch of the United States (including any independent agency) who is subject to the restrictions contained in subsection (a)(1) with respect to a particular matter may not, except pursuant to court order, serve as an expert witness for any other person (except the United States) in that matter; and

(B) a former officer or employee of the District of Columbia who is subject to the restrictions contained in subsection (a)(1) with respect to a particular matter may not, except pursuant to court order, serve as an expert witness for any other person (except the District of Columbia) in that matter.

(7) Political parties and campaign committees.—(A) Except as provided in subparagraph (B), the restrictions contained in subsections (c), (d), and (e) shall not apply to a communication or appearance made solely on behalf of a candidate in his or her capacity as a candidate, an authorized committee, a national committee, a national Federal campaign committee, a State committee, or a political party.

(B) Subparagraph (A) shall not apply to—

(i) any communication to, or appearance before, the Federal Election Commission by a former officer or employee of the Federal Election Commission; or

(ii) a communication or appearance made by a person who is subject to the restrictions contained in subsections (c), (d), or (e) if, at the time of the communication or appearance, the person is employed by a person or entity other than—

(I) a candidate, an authorized committee, a national committee, a national Federal campaign committee, a State committee, or a political party; or

(II) a person or entity who represents, aids, or advises only persons or entities described in subclause (I).

(C) For purposes of this paragraph—

(i) the term "candidate" means any person who seeks nomination for election, or election, to Federal or State office or who has authorized others to explore on his or her behalf the possibility of seeking nomination for election, or election, to Federal or State office;

(ii) the term "authorized committee" means any political committee designated in writing by a candidate as authorized to receive contributions or make expenditures to promote the nomination for election, or the election, of such candidate, or to explore the possibility of seeking nomination for election, or the election, of such candidate, except that a political committee that receives contributions or makes expenditures to promote more than 1 candidate may not be designated as an authorized committee for purposes of subparagraph (A);

(iii) the term "national committee" means the organization which, by virtue of the bylaws of a political party, is responsible for the day-to-day operation of such political party at the national level;

(iv) the term "national Federal campaign committee" means an organization that, by virtue of the bylaws of a political party, is established primarily for the purpose of providing assistance, at the national level, to candidates nominated by that party for election to the office of Senator or Representative in, or Delegate or Resident Commissioner to, the Congress;

(v) the term "State committee" means the organization which, by virtue of the bylaws of a political party, is responsible for the day-to-day operation of such political party at the State level;

(vi) the term "political party" means an association, committee, or organization that nominates a candidate for election to any Federal or State elected office whose name appears on the election ballot as the candidate of such association, committee, or organization; and

(vii) the term "State" means a State of the United States, the District of Columbia, the Commonwealth of Puerto Rico, and any territory or possession of the United States.

(k)(1)(A) The President may grant a waiver of a restriction imposed by this section to any officer or employee described in paragraph (2) if the President determines and certifies in writing that it is in the public interest to grant the waiver and that the services of the officer or employee are critically needed for the benefit of the Federal Government. Not more than 25 officers and employees currently employed by the Federal Government at any one time may have been granted waivers under this paragraph.

(B)(i) A waiver granted under this paragraph to any person shall apply only with respect to activities engaged in by that person after that person's Federal Government employment is terminated and only to that person's employment at a Government-owned, contractor operated entity with which the person served as an officer or employee immediately before the person's Federal Government employment began.

(ii) Notwithstanding clause (i), a waiver granted under this paragraph to any person who was an officer or employee of Lawrence Livermore National Laboratory, Los Alamos National Laboratory, or Sandia National Laboratory immediately before the person's Federal Government employment began shall apply to that person's employment by any such national laboratory after the person's employment by the Federal Government is terminated.

(2) Waivers under paragraph (1) may be granted only to civilian officers and employees of the executive branch, other than officers and employees in the Executive Office of the President.

(3) A certification under paragraph (1) shall take effect upon its publication in the Federal Register and shall identify—

(A) the officer or employee covered by the waiver by name and by position, and

(B) the reasons for granting the waiver.

A copy of the certification shall also be provided to the Director of the Office of Government Ethics.

(4) The President may not delegate the authority provided by this subsection.

(5)(A) Each person granted a waiver under this subsection shall prepare reports, in accordance with subparagraph (B), stating whether the person has engaged in activities otherwise prohibited by this section for each six-month period described in subparagraph (B), and if so, what those activities were.

(B) A report under subparagraph (A) shall cover each six-month period beginning on the date of the termination of the person's Federal Government employment (with respect to which the waiver under this subsection was granted) and ending two years after that date. Such report shall be filed with the President and the Director of the Office of Government Ethics not later than 60 days after the end of the six-month period covered by the report. All reports filed with the Director under this paragraph shall be made available for public inspection and copying.

(C) If a person fails to file any report in accordance with subparagraphs (A) and (B), the President shall revoke the waiver and shall notify the person of the revocation. The revocation shall take effect upon the person's receipt of the notification and shall remain in effect until the report is filed.

(D) Any person who is granted a waiver under this subsection shall be ineligible for appointment in the civil service unless all reports required of such person by subparagraphs (A) and (B) have been filed.

(E) As used in this subsection, the term "civil service" has the meaning given that term in section 2101 of title 5.

§ 208. Acts affecting a personal financial interest

(a) Except as permitted by subsection (b) hereof, whoever, being an officer or employee of the executive branch of the United States Government, or of any independent agency of the United States, a Federal Reserve bank director, officer, or employee, or an officer or employee of the District of Columbia, including a special Government employee, participates personally and substantially as a Government officer or employee, through decision, approval, disapproval, recommendation, the rendering of advice, investigation, or otherwise, in a judicial or other proceeding, application, request for a ruling or other determination, contract, claim, controversy, charge, accusation, arrest, or other particular matter in which, to his knowledge, he, his spouse, minor child, general partner, organization in which he is serving as officer, director, trustee, general partner or employee, or any person or organization with whom he is negotiating or has any arrangement concerning prospective employment, has a financial interest—

Shall be subject to the penalties set forth in section 216 of this title.

(b) Subsection (a) shall not apply—

(1) if the officer or employee first advises the Government official responsible for appointment to his or her position of the nature and circumstances of the judicial or other proceeding, application, request for a ruling or other determination, contract, claim, controversy, charge, accusation, arrest, or other particular matter and makes full disclosure of

the financial interest and receives in advance a written determination made by such official that the interest is not so substantial as to be deemed likely to affect the integrity of the services which the Government may expect from such officer or employee;

(2) if, by regulation issued by the Director of the Office of Government Ethics, applicable to all or a portion of all officers and employees covered by this section, and published in the Federal Register, the financial interest has been exempted from the requirements of subsection (a) as being too remote or too inconsequential to affect the integrity of the services of the Government officers or employees to which such regulation applies;

(3) in the case of a special Government employee serving on an advisory committee within the meaning of the Federal Advisory Committee Act (including an individual being considered for an appointment to such a position), the official responsible for the employee's appointment, after review of the financial disclosure report filed by the individual pursuant to the Ethics in Government Act of 1978, certifies in writing that the need for the individual's services outweighs the potential for a conflict of interest created by the financial interest involved; or

(4) if the financial interest that would be affected by the particular matter involved is that resulting solely from the interest of the officer or employee, or his or her spouse or minor child, in birthrights—

(A) in an Indian tribe, band, nation, or other organized group or community, including any Alaska Native village corporation as defined in or established pursuant to the Alaska Native Claims Settlement Act, which is recognized as eligible for the special programs and services provided by the United States to Indians because of their status as Indians,

(B) in an Indian allotment the title to which is held in trust by the United States or which is inalienable by the allottee without the consent of the United States, or

(C) in an Indian claims fund held in trust or administered by the United States,

if the particular matter does not involve the Indian allotment or claims fund or the Indian tribe, band, nation, organized group or community, or Alaska Native village corporation as a specific party or parties.

(c)(1) For the purpose of paragraph (1) of subsection (b), in the case of class A and B directors of Federal Reserve banks, the Board of Governors of the Federal Reserve System shall be deemed to be the Government official responsible for appointment.

(2) The potential availability of an exemption under any particular paragraph of subsection (b) does not preclude an exemption being granted pursuant to another paragraph of subsection (b).

(d)(1) Upon request, a copy of any determination granting an exemption under subsection (b)(1) or (b)(3) shall be made available to the public by the agency granting the exemption pursuant to the procedures set forth in section 105 of the Ethics in Government Act of 1978. In making such determination available, the agency may withhold from disclosure any information contained in the determination that would be exempt from disclosure under section 552 of title 5. For purposes of determinations under subsection (b)(3), the information describing each financial interest shall be no more extensive than that required of the individual in his or her financial disclosure report under the Ethics in Government Act of 1978.

(2) The Office of Government Ethics, after consultation with the Attorney General, shall issue uniform regulations for the issuance of waivers and exemptions under subsection (b) which shall—

(A) list and describe exemptions; and

(B) provide guidance with respect to the types of interests that are not so substantial as to be deemed likely to affect the integrity of the services the Government may expect from the employee.

§ 209. Salary of Government officials and employees payable only by United States

(a) Whoever receives any salary, or any contribution to or supplementation of salary, as compensation for his services as an officer or employee of the executive branch of the United States Government, of any independent agency of the United States, or of the District of Columbia, from any source other than the Government of the United States, except as may be contributed out of the treasury of any State, county, or municipality; or

Whoever, whether an individual, partnership, association, corporation, or other organization pays, or makes any contribution to, or in any way supplements the salary of, any such officer or employee under circumstances which would make its receipt a violation of this subsection—

Shall be subject to the penalties set forth in section 216 of this title.

(b) Nothing herein prevents an officer or employee of the executive branch of the United States Government, or of any independent agency of the United States, or of the District of Columbia, from continuing to participate in a bona fide pension, retirement, group life, health or accident insurance, profit-sharing, stock bonus, or other employee welfare or benefit plan maintained by a former employer.

(c) This section does not apply to a special Government employee or to an officer or employee of the Government serving without compensation, whether or not he is a special Government employee, or to any person paying, contributing to, or supplementing his salary as such.

(d) This section does not prohibit payment or acceptance of contributions, awards, or other expenses under the terms of Chapter 41 of title 5.

(e) This section does not prohibit the payment of actual relocation expenses incident to participation, or the acceptance of same by a participant in an executive exchange or fellowship program in an executive agency: *Provided,* That such program has been established by statute or Executive order of the President, offers appointments not to exceed three hundred and sixty-five days, and permits no extensions in excess of ninety additional days or, in the case of participants in overseas assignments, in excess of three hundred and sixty-five days.

(f) This section does not prohibit acceptance or receipt, by any officer or employee injured during the commission of an offense described in section 351 or 1751 of this title, of contributions or payments from an organization which is described in section 501(c)(3) of the Internal Revenue Code of 1986 and which is exempt from taxation under section 501(a) of such Code.

2.   18 U.S.C.A. § 1905

§ 1905.   Disclosure of confidential information generally

Whoever, being an officer or employee of the United States or of any department or agency thereof, any person acting on behalf of the Office of Federal Housing Enterprise Oversight, or agent of the Department of Justice as defined in the Antitrust Civil Process Act (15 U.S.C. 1311–1314), publishes, divulges, discloses, or makes known in any manner or to any extent not authorized by law any information coming to him in the course of his employment or official duties or by reason of any examination or investigation made by, or return, report or record made to or filled with, such department or agency or officer or employee thereof, which information concerns or relates to the trade secrets, processes, operations, style of work, or apparatus, or to the identity, confidential statistical data, amount or source of any income, profits, losses, or expenditures of any person, firm, partnership, corporation, or association; or permits any income return or copy thereof or any book containing any abstract or particulars thereof to be seen or examined by any person except as provided by law; shall be fined under this title, or imprisoned not more than one year, or both; and shall be removed from office or employment.

3.   28 U.S.C.A. §§ 47, 144, 372, 454–55

§ 47.   Disqualification of trial judge to hear appeal

No judge shall hear or determine an appeal from the decision of a case or issue tried by him.

§ 144.   Bias or prejudice of judge

Whenever a party to any proceeding in a district court makes and files a timely and sufficient affidavit that the judge before whom the matter is pending has a personal bias or prejudice either against him or in favor of any adverse party, such judge shall proceed no further therein, but another judge shall be assigned to hear such proceeding.

The affidavit shall state the facts and the reasons for the belief that bias or prejudice exists, and shall be filed not less than ten days before the beginning of the term at which the proceeding is to be heard, or good cause shall be shown for failure to file it within such time. A party may file only one such affidavit in any case. It shall be accompanied by a certificate of counsel of record stating that it is made in good faith.

§ 372. Retirement for disability; substitute judge on failure to Retire; judicial discipline

(a) ***

(b) ***

(c)(1) Any person alleging that a circuit, district, or bankruptcy judge, or a magistrate judge, has engaged in conduct prejudicial to the effective and expeditious administration of the business of the courts, or alleging that such a judge or magistrate judge is unable to discharge all the duties of office by reason of mental or physical disability, may file with the clerk of the court of appeals for the circuit a written complaint containing a brief statement of the facts constituting such conduct. ***

(2) Upon receipt of a complaint filed under paragraph (1) of this subsection, the clerk shall promptly transmit such complaint to the chief judge of the circuit, or, if the conduct complained of is that of the chief judge, to that circuit judge in regular active service next senior in date of commission (hereafter, for purposes of this subsection only, included in the term "chief judge"). The clerk shall simultaneously transmit a copy of the complaint to the judge or magistrate judge whose conduct is the subject of the complaint.

(3) After expeditiously reviewing a complaint, the chief judge, by written order stating his reasons, may—

(A) dismiss the complaint, if he finds it to be (i) not in conformity with paragraph (1) of this subsection, (ii) directly related to the merits of a decision or procedural ruling, or (iii) frivolous; or

(B) conclude the proceeding if he finds that appropriate corrective action has been taken or that action on the complaint is no longer necessary because of intervening events.

The chief judge shall transmit copies of his written order to the complainant and to the judge or magistrate judge whose conduct is the subject of the complaint.

(4) If the chief judge does not enter an order under paragraph (3) of this subsection, such judge shall promptly—

(A) appoint himself and equal numbers of circuit and district judges of the circuit to a special committee to investigate the facts and allegations contained in the complaint;

(B) certify the complaint and any other documents pertaining thereto to each member of such committee; and

(C) provide written notice to the complainant and the judge or magistrate judge whose conduct is the subject of the complaint of the action taken under this paragraph.

A judge appointed to a special committee under this paragraph may continue to serve on that committee after becoming a senior judge or, in the case of the chief judge of the circuit, after his or her term as chief judge terminates under subsection (a)(3) or (c) of section 45 of this title. If a judge appointed to a committee under this paragraph dies, or retires from office under section 371(a) of this title, while serving on the committee, the chief judge of the circuit may appoint another circuit or district judge, as the case may be, to the committee.

(5) Each committee appointed under paragraph (4) of this subsection shall conduct an investigation as extensive as it considers necessary, and shall expeditiously file a comprehensive written report thereon with the judicial council of the circuit. Such report shall present both the findings of the investigation and the committee's recommendations for necessary and appropriate action by the judicial council of the circuit.

(6) Upon receipt of a report filed under paragraph (5) of this subsection, the judicial council—

(A) may conduct any additional investigation which it considers to be necessary;

(B) shall take such action as is appropriate to assure the effective and expeditious administration of the business of the courts within the circuit, including, but not limited to, any of the following actions:

(i) directing the chief judge of the district of the magistrate judge whose conduct is the subject of the complaint to take such action as the judicial council considers appropriate;

(ii) certifying disability of a judge appointed to hold office during good behavior whose conduct is the subject of the complaint, pursuant to the procedures and standards provided under subsection (b) of this section;

(iii) requesting that any such judge appointed to hold office during good behavior voluntarily retire, with the provision that the length of service requirements under section 371 * of this title shall not apply;

* Editors' Note: Section 371 refers to age and service requirements for purposes of a retirement annuity.

(iv) ordering that, on a temporary basis for a time certain, no further cases be assigned to any judge or magistrate judge whose conduct is the subject of a complaint;

(v) censuring or reprimanding such judge or magistrate judge by means of private communication;

(vi) censuring or reprimanding such judge or magistrate judge by means of public announcement; or

(vii) ordering such other action as it considers appropriate under the circumstances, except that (I) in no circumstances may the council order removal from office of any judge appointed to hold office during good behavior, and (II) any removal of a magistrate judge shall be in accordance with section 631 of this title and any removal of a bankruptcy judge shall be in accordance with section 152 of this title;

(C) may dismiss the complaint; and

(D) shall immediately provide written notice to the complainant and to such judge or magistrate judge of the action taken under this paragraph.

(7)(A) In addition to the authority granted under paragraph (6) of this subsection, the judicial council may, in its discretion, refer any complaint under this subsection, together with the record of any associated proceedings and its recommendations for appropriate action, to the Judicial Conference of the United States.

(B) In any case in which the judicial council determines, on the basis of a complaint and an investigation under this subsection, or on the basis of information otherwise available to the council, that a judge appointed to hold office during good behavior may have engaged in conduct—

(i) which might constitute one or more grounds for impeachment under article II of the Constitution; or

(ii) which, in the interest of justice, is not amenable to resolution by the judicial council,

the judicial council shall promptly certify such determination, together with any complaint and a record of any associated proceedings, to the Judicial Conference of the United States.

(C) A judicial council acting under authority of this paragraph shall, unless contrary to the interests of justice, immediately submit written notice to the complainant and to the judge or magistrate judge whose conduct is the subject of the action taken under this paragraph.

(8)(A) Upon referral or certification of any matter under paragraph (7) of this subsection, the Judicial Conference, after consideration of the prior proceedings and such additional investigation as it considers appropriate, shall by majority vote take such action, as described in paragraph (6)(B) of this subsection, as it considers appropriate. If the Judicial Conference concurs in the determination of the council, or makes its own determination, that consideration of impeachment may be warranted, it shall so certify and transmit the determination and the record of proceedings to the House of Representatives for whatever action the House of Representatives considers to be necessary. Upon receipt of the determination and record of proceedings in the House of Representatives, the Clerk of the House of Representatives shall make available to the public the determination and any reasons for the determination.

(B) If a judge or magistrate judge has been convicted of a felony and has exhausted all means of obtaining direct review of the conviction, or the time for seeking further direct review of the conviction has passed and no such review has been sought, the Judicial Conference may, by majority vote and without referral or certification under paragraph (7), transmit to the House of Representatives a determination that consideration of impeachment may be warranted, together with appropriate court records, for whatever action the House of Representatives considers to be necessary.

(9)(A) In conducting any investigation under this subsection, the judicial council, or a special committee appointed under paragraph (4) of this subsection, shall have full subpoena powers as provided in section 332(d) of this title.

(B) In conducting any investigation under this subsection, the Judicial Conference, or a standing committee appointed by the Chief Justice under section 331 of this title, shall have full subpoena powers as provided in that section.

(10) A complainant, judge, or magistrate judge aggrieved by a final order of the chief judge under paragraph (3) of this subsection may petition the judicial council for review thereof. A complainant, judge, or magistrate judge aggrieved by an action of the judicial council under paragraph (6) of this subsection may petition the Judicial Conference of the United States for review thereof. The Judicial Conference, or the standing committee established under section 331 of this title, may grant a petition filed by a complainant, judge, or magistrate judge under this paragraph. Except as expressly provided in this paragraph, all orders and determinations, including denials of petitions for review, shall be final and conclusive and shall not be judicially reviewable on appeal or otherwise.

(11) Each judicial council and the Judicial Conference may prescribe such rules for the conduct of proceedings under this subsection, including the processing of petitions for review, as each considers to be appropriate. Such rules shall contain provisions requiring that—

(A) adequate prior notice of any investigation be given in writing to the judge or magistrate judge whose conduct is the subject of the complaint;

(B) the judge or magistrate judge whose conduct is the subject of the complaint be afforded an opportunity to appear (in person or by counsel) at proceedings conducted by the investigating panel, to present oral and documentary evidence, to compel the attendance of witnesses or the production of documents, to cross-examine witnesses, and to present argument orally or in writing; and

(C) the complainant be afforded an opportunity to appear at proceedings conducted by the investigating panel, if the panel concludes that the complainant could offer substantial information.

Any such rule shall be made or amended only after giving appropriate public notice and an opportunity for comment. Any rule promulgated under this subsection shall be a matter of public record, and any such rule promulgated by a judicial council may be modified by the Judicial Conference. No rule promulgated under this subsection may limit the period of time within which a person may file a complaint under this subsection.

(12) No judge or magistrate judge whose conduct is the subject of an investigation under this subsection shall serve upon a special committee appointed under paragraph (4) of this subsection, upon a judicial council, upon the Judicial Conference, or upon the standing committee established under section 331 of this title, until all related proceedings under this subsection have been finally terminated.

(13) No person shall be granted the right to intervene or to appear as amicus curiae in any proceeding before a judicial council or the Judicial Conference under this subsection.

(14) Except as provided in paragraph (8), all papers, documents, and records of proceedings related to investigations conducted under this subsection shall be confidential and shall not be disclosed by any person in any proceeding except to the extent that—

(A) the judicial council of the circuit in its discretion releases a copy of a report of a special investigative committee under paragraph (5) to the complainant whose complaint initiated the investigation by that special committee and to the judge or magistrate judge whose conduct is the subject of the complaint;

(B) the judicial council of the circuit, the Judicial Conference of the United States, or the Senate or the House of Representatives by resolution, releases any such material which is believed necessary to an impeachment investigation or trial of a judge under article I of the Constitution; or

(C) such disclosure is authorized in writing by the judge or magistrate judge who is the subject of the complaint and by the chief judge of the circuit, the Chief Justice, or the chairman of the standing committee established under section 331 of this title.

(15) Each written order to implement any action under paragraph (6)(B) of this subsection, which is issued by a judicial council, the Judicial Conference, or the standing committee established under section 331 of this title, shall be made available to the public through the appropriate clerk's office of the court of appeals for the circuit. Unless contrary to the interests of justice, each such order issued under this paragraph shall be accompanied by written reasons therefor.

(16) Upon the request of a judge or magistrate judge whose conduct is the subject of a complaint under this subsection, the judicial council may, if the complaint has been finally dismissed under paragraph (6)(C), recommend that the Director of the Administrative Office of the United States Courts award reimbursement, from funds appropriated to the Federal judiciary, for those reasonable expenses, including attorneys' fees, incurred by that judge or magistrate judge during the investigation which would not have been incurred but for the requirements of this subsection.

(17) Except as expressly provided in this subsection, nothing in this subsection shall be construed to affect any other provision of this title, the Federal Rules of Civil Procedure, the Federal Rules of Criminal Procedure, the Federal Rules of Appellate Procedure, or the Federal Rules of Evidence.

(18) The United States Court of Federal Claims, the Court of International Trade, and the Court of Appeals for the Federal Circuit shall each prescribe rules, consistent with the foregoing provisions of this subsection, establishing procedures for the filing of complaints with respect to the conduct of any judge of such court and for the investigation and resolution of such complaints. In investigating and taking action with respect to any such complaint, each such court shall have the powers granted to a judicial council under this subsection.

§ 454. Practice of law by justices and judges

Any justice or judge appointed under the authority of the United States who engages in the practice of law is guilty of a high misdemeanor.

§ 455. Disqualification of justice, judge, or magistrate judge

(a) Any justice, judge, or magistrate judge of the United States shall disqualify himself in any proceeding in which his impartiality might reasonably be questioned.

(b) He shall also disqualify himself in the following circumstances:

(1) Where he has a personal bias or prejudice concerning a party, or personal knowledge of disputed evidentiary facts concerning the proceeding;

(2) Where in private practice he served as lawyer in the matter in controversy, or a lawyer with whom he previously practiced law served during such association as a lawyer concerning the matter, or the judge or such lawyer has been a material witness concerning it;

(3) Where he has served in governmental employment and in such capacity participated as counsel, adviser or material witness concerning the proceeding or expressed an opinion concerning the merits of the particular case in controversy;

(4) He knows that he, individually or as a fiduciary, or his spouse or minor child residing in his household, has a financial interest in the subject matter in controversy or in a party to the proceeding, or any other interest that could be substantially affected by the outcome of the proceeding;

(5) He or his spouse, or a person within the third degree of relationship to either of them, or the spouse of such a person:

(i) Is a party to the proceeding, or an officer, director, or trustee of a party;

(ii) Is acting as a lawyer in the proceeding;

(iii) Is known by the judge to have an interest that could be substantially affected by the outcome of the proceeding;

(iv) Is to the judge's knowledge likely to be a material witness in the proceeding.

(c) A judge should inform himself about his personal and fiduciary financial interests, and make a reasonable effort to inform himself about the personal financial interests of his spouse and minor children residing in his household.

(d) For the purposes of this section the following words or phrases shall have the meaning indicated:

(1) "proceeding" includes pretrial, trial, appellate review, or other stages of litigation;

(2) the degree of relationship is calculated according to the civil law system;

(3) "fiduciary" includes such relationships as executor, administrator, trustee, and guardian;

(4) "financial interest" means ownership of a legal or equitable interest, however small, or a relationship as director, adviser, or other active participant in the affairs of a party, except that:

(i) Ownership in a mutual or common investment fund that holds securities is not a "financial interest" in such securities unless the judge participates in the management of the fund;

(ii) An office in an educational, religious, charitable, fraternal, or civic organization is not a "financial interest" in securities held by the organization;

(iii) The proprietary interest of a policyholder in a mutual insurance company, of a depositor in a mutual savings association, or a similar proprietary interest, is a "financial interest" in the organization only if the outcome of the proceeding could substantially affect the value of the interest;

(iv) Ownership of government securities is a "financial interest" in the issuer only if the outcome of the proceeding could substantially affect the value of the securities.

(e) No justice, judge, or magistrate judge shall accept from the parties to the proceeding a waiver of any ground for disqualification enumerated in subsection (b). Where the ground for disqualification arises only under subsection (a), waiver may be accepted provided it is preceded by a full disclosure on the record of the basis for disqualification.

(f) Notwithstanding the preceding provisions of this section, if any justice, judge, magistrate judge or bankruptcy judge to whom a matter has been assigned would be disqualified, after substantial judicial time has been devoted to the matter, because of the appearance or discovery, after the matter was assigned to him or her, that he or she individually or as a fiduciary, or his or her spouse or minor child residing in his or her household, has a financial interest in a party (other than an interest that could be substantially affected by the outcome), disqualification is not required if the justice, judge, magistrate judge, bankruptcy judge, spouse or minor child, as the case may be, divests himself or herself of the interest that provides the grounds for the disqualification.

4. 5 U.S.C.A. APPENDIX 4, §§ 101–111

FINANCIAL DISCLOSURE REQUIREMENTS OF FEDERAL PERSONNEL

§ 101. Persons required to file

(a) Within thirty days of assuming the position of an officer or employee described in subsection (f), an individual shall file a report containing the information described in section 102(b) unless the individual has left another position described in subsection (f) within thirty days prior to assuming such new position or has already filed a report under this title with respect to nomination for the new position or as a candidate for the position.

(b)(1) Within five days of the transmittal by the President to the Senate of the nomination of an individual (other than an individual nominated for appointment to a position as a Foreign Service Officer or a grade or rank in the uniformed services for which the pay grade prescribed by section 201 of title 37, United States Code, is O–6 or below) to a position, appointment to which requires the advice and consent of the Senate, such individual shall file a report containing the information described in section 102(b). Such individual shall, not later than the date of the first hearing to consider the nomination of such individual, make current the report filed pursuant to this paragraph by filing the information required by section 102(a)(1)(A) with respect to income and honoraria received as of the date which occurs five days before the date of such hearing. Nothing in this Act shall prevent any Congressional committee from requesting, as a condition of confirmation, any additional financial information from any Presidential nominee whose nomination has been referred to that committee.

(2) An individual whom the President or the President-elect has publicly announced he intends to nominate to a position may file the report required by paragraph (1) at any time after that public announcement, but not later than is required under the first sentence of such paragraph.

(c) Within thirty days of becoming a candidate as defined in section 301 of the Federal Campaign Act of 1971, in a calendar year for nomination or election to the office of President, Vice President, or Member of Congress, or on or before May 15 of that calendar year, whichever is later, but in no event later than 30 days before the election, and on or before May 15 of each successive year an individual continues to be a candidate, an individual other than an incumbent President, Vice President, or Member of Congress shall file a report containing the information described in section 102(b). Notwithstanding the preceding sentence, in any calendar year in which an individual continues to be a candidate for any office but all elections for such office relating to such candidacy were held in prior calendar years, such individual need not file a report unless he becomes a candidate for another vacancy in that office or another office during that year.

(d) Any individual who is an officer or employee described in subsection (f) during any calendar year and performs the duties of his position or office for a period in excess of sixty days in that calendar year shall file on or before May 15 of the succeeding year a report containing the information described in section 102(a).

(e) Any individual who occupies a position described in subsection (f) shall, on or before the thirtieth day after termination of employment in such position, file a report containing the information described in section 102(a) covering the preceding calendar year if the report required by subsection (d) has not been filed and covering the portion of the calendar year in which such termination occurs up to the date the individual left such office or position, unless such individual has accepted employment in another position described in subsection (f).

(f) The officers and employees referred to in subsections (a), (d), and (e) are—

(1) the President;

(2) the Vice President;

(3) each officer or employee in the executive branch, including a special Government employee as defined in section 202 of title 18, United States Code, who occupies a position classified above GS–15 of the General Schedule or, in the case of positions not under the General Schedule, for which the rate of basic pay is equal to or greater than 120 percent of the minimum rate of basic pay payable for GS–15 of the General Schedule; each member of a uniformed service whose pay grade is at or in excess of O–7 under section 201 of title 37, United States Code; and each officer or employee in any other position determined by the Director of the Office of Government Ethics to be of equal classification;

(4) each employee appointed pursuant to section 3105 of title 5, United States Code;

(5) any employee not described in paragraph (3) who is in a position in the executive branch which is excepted from the competitive service by reason of being of a confidential or policymaking character, except that the Director of the Office of Government Ethics may, by regulation, exclude from the application of this paragraph any individual, or group of individuals, who are in such positions, but only in cases in which the Director determines such exclusion would not affect adversely the integrity of the Government or the public's confidence in the integrity of the Government;

(6) the Postmaster General, the Deputy Postmaster General, each Governor of the Board of Governors of the United States Postal Service and each officer or employee of the United States Postal Service or Postal Rate Commission who occupies a position for which the rate of basic pay is equal to or greater than 120 percent of the minimum rate of basic pay payable for GS–15 of the General Schedule;

(7) the Director of the Office of Government Ethics and each designated agency ethics official;

(8) any civilian employee not described in paragraph (3), employed in the Executive Office of the President (other than a special government employee) who holds a commission of appointment from the President;

(9) a Member of Congress as defined under section 109(12);

(10) an officer or employee of the Congress as defined under section 109(13);

(11) a judicial officer as defined under section 109(10); and

(12) a judicial employee as defined under section 109(8).

(g)(1) Reasonable extensions of time for filing any report may be granted under procedures prescribed by the supervising ethics office for each branch, but the total of such extensions shall not exceed ninety days.

(2)(A) In the case of an individual who is serving in the Armed Forces, or serving in support of the Armed Forces, in an area while that area is designated by the President by Executive order as a combat zone for purposes of section 112 of the Internal Revenue Code of 1986 [26 U.S.C.A. § 112], the date for the filing of any report shall be extended so that the date is 180 days after the later of—

(i) the last day of the individual's service in such area during such designated period; or

(ii) the last day of the individual's hospitalization as a result of injury received or disease contracted while serving in such area.

(B) The Office of Government Ethics, in consultation with the Secretary of Defense, may prescribe procedures under this paragraph.

(h) The provisions of subsections (a), (b), and (e) shall not apply to an individual who, as determined by the designated agency ethics official or Secretary concerned (or in the case of a Presidential appointee under subsection (b), the Director of the Office of Government Ethics), the congressional ethics committees, or the Judicial Conference, is not reasonably expected to perform the duties of his office or position for more than sixty days in a calendar year, except that if such individual performs the duties of his office or position for more than sixty days in a calendar year—

(1) the report required by subsections (a) and (b) shall be filed within fifteen days of the sixtieth day, and

(2) the report required by subsection (e) shall be filed as provided in such subsection.

(i) The supervising ethics office for each branch may grant a publicly available request for a waiver of any reporting requirement under this section for an individual who is expected to perform or has performed the duties of his office or position less than one hundred and thirty days in a calendar year, but only if the supervising ethics office determines that—

(1) such individual is not a full-time employee of the Government,

(2) such individual is able to provide services specially needed by the Government,

(3) it is unlikely that the individual's outside employment or financial interests will create a conflict of interest, and

(4) public financial disclosure by such individual is not necessary in the circumstances.

§ 102. Contents of reports

(a) Each report filed pursuant to section 101(d) and (e) shall include a full and complete statement with respect to the following:

(1)(A) The source, type, and amount or value of income (other than income referred to in subparagraph (B)) from any source (other than from current employment by the United States Government), and the source, date, and amount of honoraria from any source, received during the preceding calendar year, aggregating $200 or more in value and, effective January 1, 1991, the source, date, and amount of payments made to charitable organizations in lieu of honoraria, and the reporting individual shall simultaneously file with the applicable supervising ethics office, on a confidential basis, a corresponding list of recipients of all such payments, together with the dates and amounts of such payments.

(B) The source and type of income which consists of dividends, rents, interest, and capital gains, received during the preceding calendar year which exceeds $200 in amount or value, and an indication of which of the following categories the amount or value of such item of income is within:

    (i) not more than $1,000,

    (ii) greater than $1,000 but not more than $2,500,

    (iii) greater than $2,500 but not more than $5,000,

    (iv) greater than $5,000 but not more than $15,000,

    (v) greater than $15,000 but not more than $50,000,

    (vi) greater than $50,000 but not more than $100,000,

    (vii) greater than $100,000 but not more than $1,000,000,

    (viii) greater than $1,000,000 but not more than $5,000,000, or

    (ix) greater than $5,000,000.

(2)(A) The identity of the source, a brief description, and the value of all gifts aggregating more than the minimal value as established by section 7342(a)(5) of title 5, United States Code, or $250, whichever is greater, received from any source other than a relative of the reporting individual during the preceding calendar year, except that any food, lodging, or entertainment received as personal hospitality of an individual need not be reported, and any gift with a fair market value of $100 or less, as adjusted at the same time and by the same percentage as the minimal value is adjusted, need not be aggregated for purposes of this subparagraph.

(B) The identity of the source and a brief description (including a travel itinerary, dates, and nature of expenses provided) of reimbursements received from any source aggregating more than the minimal value as established by section 7342(a)(5) of title 5, United States Code, or $250, whichever is greater and received during the preceding calendar year.

(C) In an unusual case, a gift need not be aggregated under subparagraph (A) if a publicly available request for a waiver is granted.

(3) The identity and category of value of any interest in property held during the preceding calendar year in a trade or business, or for investment or the production of income, which has a fair market value which exceeds $1,000 as of the close of the preceding calendar year, excluding any personal liability owned to the reporting individual by a spouse, or by a parent, brother, sister, or child of the reporting individual or of the reporting individual's spouse, or any deposits aggregating $5,000 or less in a personal savings account. For purposes of this paragraph, a personal savings account shall include any certificate of deposit or any other form of deposit in a bank, savings and loan association, credit union, or similar financial institution.

(4) The identity and category of value of the total liabilities owed to any creditor other than a spouse, or a parent, brother, sister, or child of the reporting individual or of the reporting individual's spouse which exceed $10,000 at any time during the preceding calendar year, excluding—

(A) any mortgage secured by real property which is a personal residence of the reporting individual or his spouse; and

(B) any loan secured by a personal motor vehicle, household furniture, or appliances, which loan does not exceed the purchase price of the item which secures it.

With respect to revolving charge accounts, only those with an outstanding liability which exceeds $10,000 as of the close of the preceding calendar year need be reported under this paragraph.

(5) Except as provided in this paragraph, a brief description, the date, and category of value of any purchase, sale or exchange during the preceding calendar year which exceeds $1,000—

(A) in real property, other than property used solely as a personal residence of the reporting individual or his spouse; or

(B) in stocks, bonds, commodities futures, and other forms of securities.

Reporting is not required under this paragraph of any transaction solely by and between the reporting individual, his spouse, or dependent children.

(6)(A) The identity of all positions held on or before the date of filing during the current calendar year (and, for the first report filed by an individual, during the two-year period preceding such calendar year) as an officer, director, trustee, partner, proprietor, representative, employee, or consultant of any corporation, company, firm, partnership, or other business enterprise, any nonprofit organization, any labor organization, or any educational or other institution other than the United States. This subparagraph shall not require the reporting of positions held in any religious, social, fraternal, or political entity and positions solely of an honorary nature.

(B) If any person, other than the United States Government, paid a nonelected reporting individual compensation in excess of $5,000 in any of the two calendar years prior to the calendar year during which the individual files his first report under this title, the individual shall include in the report—

(i) the identity of each source of such compensation; and

(ii) a brief description of the nature of the duties performed or services rendered by the reporting individual for each such source.

The preceding sentence shall not require any individual to include in such report any information which is considered confidential as a result of a privileged relationship, established by law, between such individual and any person nor shall it require an individual to report any information with respect to any person for whom services were provided by any firm or association of which such individual was a member, partner, or employee unless such individual was directly involved in the provision of such services.

(7) A description of the date, parties to, and terms of any agreement or arrangement with respect to (A) future employment; (B) a leave of absence during the period of the reporting individual's Government service; (C) continuation of payments by a former employer other than the United States Government; and (D) continuing participation in an employee welfare or benefit plan maintained by a former employer.

(8) The category of the total cash value of any interest of the reporting individual in a qualified blind trust, unless the trust instrument was executed prior to July 24, 1995 and precludes the beneficiary from receiving information on the total cash value of any interest in the qualified blind trust.

(b)(1) Each report filed pursuant to subsections (a), (b), and (c) of section 101 shall include a full and complete statement with respect to the information required by—

(A) paragraph (1) of subsection (a) for the year of filing and the preceding calendar year,

(B) paragraphs (3) and (4) of subsection (a) as of the date specified in the report but which is less than thirty-one days before the filing date, and

(C) paragraphs (6) and (7) of subsection (a) as of the filing date but for periods described in such paragraphs.

(2)(A) In lieu of filling out one or more schedules of a financial disclosure form, an individual may supply the required information in an alternative format, pursuant to either rules adopted by the supervising ethics office for the branch in which such individual serves or pursuant to a specific written determination by such office for a reporting individual.

(B) In lieu of indicating the category of amount or value of any item contained in any report filed under this title, a reporting individual may indicate the exact dollar amount of such item.

(c) In the case of any individual described in section 101(e), any reference to the preceding calendar year shall be considered also to include that part of the calendar year of filing up to the date of the termination of employment.

(d)(1) The categories for reporting the amount or value of the items covered in paragraphs (3), (4), (5), and (8) of subsection (a) are as follows:

    (A) not more than $15,000;

    (B) greater than $15,000 but not more than $50,000;

    (C) greater than $50,000 but not more than $100,000;

    (D) greater than $100,000 but not more than $250,000;

    (E) greater than $250,000 but not more than $500,000;

    (F) greater than $500,000 but not more than $1,000,000;

    (G) greater than $1,000,000 but not more than $5,000,000;

    (H) greater than $5,000,000 but not more than $25,000,000;

    (I) greater than $25,000,000 but not more than $50,000,000; and

    (J) greater than $50,000,000.

(2) For the purposes of paragraph (3) of subsection (a) if the current value of an interest in real property (or an interest in a real estate partnership) is not ascertainable without an appraisal, an individual may list (A) the date of purchase and the purchase price of the interest in the real property, or (B) the assessed value of the real property for tax purposes, adjusted to reflect the market value of the property used for the assessment if the assessed value is computed at less than 100 percent of such market value, but such individual shall include in his report a full and complete description of the method used to determine such assessed value, instead of specifying a category of value pursuant to paragraph (1) of this subsection. If the current value of any other item required to be reported under paragraph (3) of subsection (a) is not ascertainable without an appraisal, such individual may list the book value of a corporation whose stock is not publicly traded, the net worth of a business partnership, the equity value of an individually owned business, or with respect to other holdings, any recognized indication of value, but such individual shall include in his report a full and complete description of the method used in determining such value. In lieu of any value referred to in the preceding sentence, an individual may list the assessed value of the item for tax purposes, adjusted to reflect the market value of the item used for the assessment if the assessed value is computed at less than 100 percent of such market value, but a full and complete description of the method used in determining such assessed value shall be included in the report.

(e)(1) Except as provided in the last sentence of this paragraph, each report required by section 101 shall also contain information listed in paragraphs (1) through (5) of subsection (a) of this section respecting the spouse or dependent child of the reporting individual as follows:

    (A) The source of items of earned income earned by a spouse from any person which exceed $1,000 and the source and amount of any honoraria received by a spouse, except that, with respect to earned income (other than honoraria), if the spouse is self-employed in business or a profession, only the nature of such business or profession need be reported.

(B) All information required to be reported in subsection (a)(1)(B) with respect to income derived by a spouse or dependent child from any asset held by the spouse or dependent child and reported pursuant to subsection (a)(3).

(C) In the case of any gifts received by a spouse or dependent child which are not received totally independent of the relationship of the spouse or dependent child to the reporting individual, the identity of the source and a brief description of gifts of transportation, lodging, food, or entertainment and a brief description and the value of other gifts.

(D) In the case of any reimbursements received by a spouse or dependent child which are not received totally independent of the relationship of the spouse or dependent child to the reporting individual, the identity of the source and a brief description of each such reimbursement.

(E) In the case of items described in paragraphs (3) through (5) of subsection (a), all information required to be reported under these paragraphs other than items (i) which the reporting individual certifies represent the spouse's or dependent child's sole financial interest or responsibility and which the reporting individual has no knowledge of, (ii) which are not in any way, past or present, derived from the income, assets, or activities of the reporting individual, and (iii) from which the reporting individual neither derives, nor expects to derive, any financial or economic benefit.

(F) For purposes of this section, categories with amounts or values greater than $1,000,000 set forth in sections 102(a)(1)(B) and 102(d)(1) shall apply to the income, assets, or liabilities of spouses and dependent children only if the income, assets, or liabilities are held jointly with the reporting individual. All other income, assets, or liabilities of the spouse or dependent children required to be reported under this section in an amount or value greater than $1,000,000 shall be categorized only as an amount or value greater than $1,000,000.

Reports required by subsections (a), (b), and (c) of section 101 shall, with respect to the spouse and dependent child of the reporting individual, only contain information listed in paragraphs (1), (3), and (4) of subsection (a), as specified in this paragraph.

(2) No report shall be required with respect to a spouse living separate and apart from the reporting individual with the intention of terminating the marriage or providing for permanent separation; or with respect to any income or obligations of an individual arising from the dissolution of his marriage or the permanent separation from his spouse.

(f)(1) Except as provided in paragraph (2), each reporting individual shall report the information required to be reported pursuant to subsections (a), (b), and (c) of this section with respect to the holdings of and the income from a trust or other financial arrangement from which income is received by, or with respect to which a beneficial interest in principal or income is held by, such individual, his spouse, or any dependent child.

(2) A reporting individual need not report the holdings of or the source of income from any of the holdings of—

(A) any qualified blind trust (as defined in paragraph (3));

(B) a trust—

(i) which was not created directly by such individual, his spouse, or any dependent child, and

(ii) the holdings or sources of income of which such individual, his spouse, and any dependent child have no knowledge of; or

(C) an entity described under the provisions of paragraph (8),

but such individual shall report the category of the amount of income received by him, his spouse, or any dependent child from the trust or other entity under subsection (a)(1)(B) of this section.

(3) For purposes of this subsection, the term "qualified blind trust" includes any trust in which a reporting individual, his spouse, or any minor or dependent child has a beneficial interest in the principal or income, and which meets the following requirements:

(A)(i) The trustee of the trust and any other entity designated in the trust instrument to perform fiduciary duties is a financial institution, an attorney, a certified public accountant, a broker, or an investment advisor who—

(I) is independent of and not associated with any interested party so that the trustee or other person cannot be controlled or influenced in the administration of the trust by any interested party; and

(II) is not and has not been an employee of or affiliated with any interested party and is not a partner of, or involved in any joint venture or other investment with, any interested party; and

(III) is not a relative of any interested party.

(ii) Any officer or employee of a trustee or other entity who is involved in the management or control of the trust—

(I) is independent of and not associated with any interested party so that such officer or employee cannot be controlled or influenced in the administration of the trust by any interested party;

(II) is not a partner of, or involved in any joint venture or other investment with, any interested party; and

(III) is not a relative of any interested party.

(B) Any asset transferred to the trust by an interested party is free of any restriction with respect to its transfer or sale unless such restriction is expressly approved by the supervising ethics office of the reporting individual.

(C) The trust instrument which establishes the trust provides that—

(i) except to the extent provided in subparagraph (B) of this paragraph, the trustee in the exercise of his authority and discretion to manage and control the assets of the trust shall not consult or notify any interested party;

(ii) the trust shall not contain any asset the holding of which by an interested party is prohibited by any law or regulation;

(iii) the trustee shall promptly notify the reporting individual and his supervising ethics office when the holdings of any particular asset transferred to the trust by any interested party are disposed of or when the value of such holding is less than $1,000;

(iv) the trust tax return shall be prepared by the trustee or his designee, and such return and any information relating thereto (other than the trust income summarized in appropriate categories necessary to complete an interested party's tax return), shall not be disclosed to any interested party;

(v) an interested party shall not receive any report on the holdings and sources of income of the trust, except a report at the end of each calendar quarter with respect to the total cash value of the interest of the interested party in the trust or the net income or loss of the trust or any reports necessary to enable the interested party to complete an individual tax return required by law or to provide the information required by subsection (a)(1) of this section, but such report shall not identify any asset or holding;

(vi) except for communications which solely consist of requests for distributions of cash or other unspecified assets of the trust, there shall be no direct or indirect communication between the trustee and an interested party with respect to the trust unless such communication is in writing and unless it relates only (I) to the general financial interest and needs of the interested party (including, but not limited to, an interest in maximizing income or long-term capital gain), (II) to the notification of the trustee of a law or regulation subsequently applicable to the reporting individual which prohibits the interested party from holding an asset, which notification directs that the asset not be held by the trust, or (III) to directions to the trustee to sell all of an asset initially placed in the trust by an interested party which in the determination of the reporting individual creates a conflict of interest or the appearance thereof due to the subsequent assumption of duties by the reporting individual (but nothing herein shall require any such direction); and

(vii) the interested parties shall make no effort to obtain information with respect to the holdings of the trust, including obtaining a copy of any trust tax return filed or any information relating thereto except as otherwise provided in this subsection.

(D) The proposed trust instrument and the proposed trustee is approved by the reporting individual's supervising ethics office.

(E) For purposes of this subsection, "interested party" means a reporting individual, his spouse, and any minor or dependent child; "broker" has the meaning set forth in section 3(a)(4) of the Securities and Exchange Act of 1934 (15 U.S.C. 78c(a)(4)); and "investment adviser" includes any investment adviser who, as determined under regulations prescribed by the supervising ethics office, is generally involved in his role as such an adviser in the management or control of trusts.

(F) Any trust qualified by a supervising ethics office before the effective date of title II of the Ethics Reform Act of 1989 shall continue to be governed by the law and regulations in effect immediately before such effective date.

(4)(A) An asset placed in a trust by an interested party shall be considered a financial interest of the reporting individual, for the purposes of any applicable conflict of interest statutes, regulations, or rules of the Federal Government (including section 208 of title 18, United States Code), until such time as the reporting individual is notified by the trustee that such asset has been disposed of, or has a value of less than $1,000.

(B)(i) The provisions of subparagraph (A) shall not apply with respect to a trust created for the benefit of a reporting individual, or the spouse, dependent child, or minor child of such a person, if the supervising ethics office for such reporting individual finds that—

(I) the assets placed in the trust consist of a well-diversified portfolio of readily marketable securities;

(II) none of the assets consist of securities of entities having substantial activities in the area of the reporting individual's primary area of responsibility;

(III) the trust instrument prohibits the trustee, notwithstanding the provisions of paragraphs (3)(C)(iii) and (iv) of this subsection, from making public or informing any interested party of the sale of any securities;

(IV) the trustee is given power of attorney, notwithstanding the provisions of paragraph (3)(C)(v) of this subsection, to prepare on behalf of any interested party the personal income tax returns and similar returns which may contain information relating to the trust; and

(V) except as otherwise provided in this paragraph, the trust instrument provides (or in the case of a trust established prior to the effective date of this Act which by its terms does not permit amendment, the trustee, the reporting individual, and any any other interested party agree in writing) that the trust shall be administered in accordance with the requirements of this subsection and the trustee of such trust meets the requirements of paragraph (3)(A).

(ii) In any instance covered by subparagraph (B) in which the reporting individual is an individual whose nomination is being considered by a congressional committee, the reporting individual shall inform the congressional committee considering his nomination before or during the period of such individual's confirmation hearing of his intention to comply with this paragraph.

(5)(A) The reporting individual shall, within thirty days after a qualified blind trust is approved by his supervising ethics office, file with such office a copy of—

(i) the executed trust instrument of such trust (other than those provisions which relate to the testamentary disposition of the trust assets), and

(ii) a list of the assets which were transferred to such trust, including the category of value of each asset as determined under subsection (d) of this section.

This subparagraph shall not apply with respect to a trust meeting the requirements for being considered a qualified blind trust under paragraph (7) of this subsection.

(B) The reporting individual shall, within thirty days of transferring an asset (other than cash) to a previously established qualified blind trust, notify his supervising ethics office of the identity of each such asset and the category of value of each asset as determined under subsection (d) of this section.

(C) Within thirty days of the dissolution of a qualified blind trust, a reporting individual shall—

(i) notify his supervising ethics office of such dissolution, and

(ii) file with such office a copy of a list of the assets of the trust at the time of such dissolution and the category of value under subsection (d) of this section of each such asset.

(D) Documents filed under subparagraphs (A), (B), and (C) of this paragraph and the lists provided by the trustee of assets placed in the trust by an interested party which have been sold shall be made available to the public in the same manner as a report is made available under section 105 and the provisions of that section shall apply with respect to such documents and lists.

(E) A copy of each written communication with respect to the trust under paragraph (3)(C)(vi) shall be filed by the person initiating the communication with the reporting individual's supervising ethics office within five days of the date of the communication.

(6)(A) A trustee of a qualified blind trust shall not knowingly and willfully, or negligently, (i) disclose any information to an interested party with respect to such trust that may not be disclosed under paragraph (3) of this subsection; (ii) acquire any holding the ownership of which is prohibited by the trust instrument; (iii) solicit advice from any interested party with respect to such trust, which solicitation is prohibited by paragraph (3) of this subsection or the trust agreement; or (iv) fail to file any document required by this subsection.

(B) A reporting individual shall not knowingly and willfully, or negligently, (i) solicit or receive any information with respect to a qualified blind trust of which he is an interested party that may not be disclosed under paragraph (3)(C) of this subsection or (ii) fail to file any document required by this subsection.

(C)(i) The Attorney General may bring a civil action in any appropriate United States district court against any individual who knowingly and willfully violates the provisions of subparagraph (A) or (B) of this paragraph. The court in which such action is brought may assess against such individual a civil penalty in any amount not to exceed $10,000.

(ii) The Attorney General may bring a civil action in any appropriate United States district court against any individual who negligently violates the provisions of subparagraph (A) or (B) of this paragraph. The court in which such action is brought may assess against such individual a civil penalty in any amount not to exceed $5,000.

(7) Any trust may be considered to be a qualified blind trust if—

(A) the trust instrument is amended to comply with the requirements of paragraph (3) or, in the case of a trust instrument which does not by its terms permit amendment, the trustee, the reporting individual, and any other interested party agree in writing that the trust shall be administered in accordance with the requirements of this subsection and the trustee of such trust meets the requirements of paragraph (3)(A); except that in the case of any interested party who is a dependent child, a parent or guardian of such child may execute the agreement referred to in this subparagraph;

(B) a copy of the trust instrument (except testamentary provisions) and a copy of the agreement referred to in subparagraph (A), and a list of the assets held by the trust at the time of approval by the supervising ethics office, including the category of value of each asset as determined under subsection (d) of this section, are filed with such office and made available to the public as provided under paragraph (5)(D) of this subsection; and

(C) the supervising ethics office determines that approval of the trust arrangement as a qualified blind trust is in the particular case appropriate to assure compliance with applicable laws and regulations.

(8) A reporting individual shall not be required to report the financial interests held by a widely held investment fund (whether such fund is a mutual fund, regulated investment company, pension or deferred compensation plan, or other investment fund), if—

(A)(i) the fund is publicly traded; or

(ii) the assets of the fund are widely diversified; and

(B) the reporting individual neither exercises control over nor has the ability to exercise control over the financial interests held by the fund.

(g) Political campaign funds, including campaign receipts and expenditures, need not be included in any report filed pursuant to this title.

(h) A report filed pursuant to subsection (a), (d), or (e) of section 101 need not contain the information described in subparagraphs (A), (B), and (C) of subsection (a)(2) with respect to gifts and reimbursements received in a period when the reporting individual was not an officer or employee of the Federal Government.

(i) A reporting individual shall not be required under this title to report—

(1) financial interests in or income derived from—

(A) any retirement system under title 5, United States Code (including the Thrift Savings Plan under subchapter III of chapter 84 of such title); or

(B) any other retirement system maintained by the United States for officers or employees of the United States, including the President, or for members of the uniformed services; or

(2) benefits received under the Social Security Act.

§ 103. Filing of reports

(a) Except as otherwise provided in this section, the reports required under this title shall be filed by the reporting individual with the designated agency ethics official at the agency by which he is employed (or in the case of an individual described in section 101(e), was employed) or in which he will serve. The date any report is received (and the date of receipt of any supplemental report) shall be noted on such report by such official.

(b) The President, the Vice President, and independent counsel and persons appointed by independent counsel under chapter 40 of title 28, United States Code, shall file reports required under this title with the Director of the Office of Government Ethics.

(c) Copies of the reports required to be filed under this title by the Postmaster General, the Deputy Postmaster General, the Governors of the Board of Governors of the United States Postal Service, designated agency ethics officials, employees described in section 105(a)(2)(A) or (B), 106(a)(1)(A) or (B), or 107(a)(1)(A) or (b)(1)(A)(i), of title 3, United States Code, candidates for the office of President or Vice President and officers and employees in (and nominees to) offices or positions which require confirmation by the Senate or by both Houses of Congress other than individuals nominated to be judicial officers and those referred to in subsection (f) shall be transmitted to the Director of the Office of Government Ethics. The Director shall forward a copy of the report of each nominee to the congressional committee considering the nomination.

(d) Reports required to be filed under this title by the Director of the Office of Government Ethics shall be filed in the Office of Government Ethics and, immediately after being filed, shall be made available to the public in accordance with this title.

(e) Each individual identified in section 101(c) who is a candidate for nomination or election to the Office of President or Vice President shall file the reports required by this title with the Federal Election Commission.

(f) Reports required of members of the uniformed services shall be filed with the Secretary concerned.

(g) Each supervising ethics office shall develop and make available forms for reporting the information required by this title.

(h)(1) The reports required under this title shall be filed by a reporting individual with—

(A)(i)(I) the Clerk of the House of Representatives, in the case of a Representative in Congress, a Delegate to Congress, the Resident Commissioner from Puerto Rico, an officer or employee of the Congress whose compensation is disbursed by the Chief Administrative Officer of the House of Representatives, an officer or employee of the Architect of the Capitol, the United States Botanic Garden, the Congressional Budget Office, the Government Printing Office, the Library of Congress, or the Copyright Royalty Tribunal (including any individual terminating service, under section 101(e), in any office or position referred to in this subclause), or an individual described in section 101(c) who is a candidate for nomination or election as a Representative in Congress, a Delegate to Congress, or the Resident Commissioner from Puerto Rico; and

(II) the Secretary of the Senate, in the case of a Senator, an officer or employee of the Congress whose compensation is disbursed by the Secretary of the Senate, an officer or employee of the General Accounting Office, the Office of Technology Assessment, or the Office of the Attending Physician (including any individual terminating service, under section 101(e), in any office or position referred to in this subclause), or an individual described in section 101(c) who is a candidate for nomination or election as a Senator; and

(ii) in the case of an officer or employee of the Congress as described under section 101(f)(10) who is employed by an agency or commission established in the legislative branch after the date of the enactment of the Ethics Reform Act of 1989—

(I) the Secretary of the Senate or the Clerk of the House of Representatives, as the case may be, as designated in the statute establishing such agency or commission; or

(II) if such statute does not designate such committee, the Secretary of the Senate for agencies and commissions established in even numbered calendar years, and the Clerk of the House of Representatives for agencies and commissions established in odd numbered calendar years; and

(B) the Judicial Conference with regard to a judicial officer or employee described under paragraphs (11) and (12) of section 101(f) (including individuals terminating service in such office or position under section 101(e) or immediately preceding service in such office or position).

(2) The date any report is received (and the date of receipt of any supplemental report) shall be noted on such report by such committee.

(i) A copy of each report filed under this title by a Member or an individual who is a candidate for the office of Member shall be sent by the Clerk of the House of Representatives or Secretary of the Senate, as the case may be, to the appropriate State officer designated under section 316(a) of the Federal Election Campaign Act of 1971 of the State represented by the Member or in which the individual is a candidate, as the case may be, within the 30–day period beginning on the day the report is filed with the Clerk or Secretary.

(j)(1) A copy of each report filed under this title with the Clerk of the House of Representatives shall be sent by the Clerk to the Committee on Standards of Official Conduct of the House of Representatives within the 7–day period beginning on the day the report is filed.

(2) A copy of each report filed under this title with the Secretary of the Senate shall be sent by the Secretary to the Select Committee on Ethics of the Senate within the 7–day period beginning on the day the report is filed.

(k) In carrying out their responsibilities under this title with respect to candidates for office, the Clerk of the House of Representatives and the Secretary of the Senate shall avail themselves of the assistance of the Federal Election Commission. The Commission shall make available to the Clerk and the Secretary on a regular basis a complete list of names and addresses of all candidates registered with the Commission, and shall cooperate and coordinate its candidate information and notification program with the Clerk and the Secretary to the greatest extent possible.

§ 104. Failure to file or filing false reports

(a) The Attorney General may bring a civil action in any appropriate United States district court against any individual who knowingly and willfully falsifies or who knowingly and willfully fails to file or report any information that such individual is required to report pursuant to section 102. The court in which such action is brought may assess against such individual a civil penalty in any amount, not to exceed $10,000.

(b) The head of each agency, each Secretary concerned, the Director of the Office of Government Ethics, each congressional ethics committee, or the Judicial Conference, as the case may be, shall refer to the Attorney General the name of any individual which such official or committee has reasonable cause to believe has willfully failed to file a report or has willfully falsified or willfully failed to file information required to be reported. Whenever the Judicial Conference refers a name to the Attorney General under this subsection, the Judicial Conference also shall notify the judicial council of the circuit in which the named individual serves of the referral.

(**c**) The President, the Vice President, the Secretary concerned, the head of each agency, the Office of Personnel Management, a congressional ethics committee, and the Judicial Conference, may take any appropriate personnel or other action in accordance with applicable law or regulation against any individual failing to file a report or falsifying or failing to report information required to be reported.

(**d**)(**1**) Any individual who files a report required to be filed under this title more than 30 days after the later of—

(**A**) the date such report is required to be filed pursuant to the provisions of this title and the rules and regulations promulgated thereunder; or

(**B**) if a filing extension is granted to such individual under section 101(g), the last day of the filing extension period,

shall *** pay a filing fee of $200. All such fees shall be deposited in the miscellaneous receipts of the Treasury. The authority under this paragraph to direct the payment of a filing fee may be delegated by the supervising ethics office in the executive branch to other agencies in the executive branch.

(**2**) The supervising ethics office may waive the filing fee under this subsection in extraordinary circumstances.

§ 105. Custody of and public access to reports

(**a**) Each agency, each supervising ethics office in the executive or judicial branch, the Clerk of the House of Representatives, and the Secretary of the Senate shall make available to the public, in accordance with subsection (b), each report filed under this title with such agency or office or with the Clerk or the Secretary of the Senate, except that—

(**1**) this section does not require public availability of a report filed by any individual in the Central Intelligence Agency, the Defense Intelligence Agency, National Imagery and Mapping Agency, or the National Security Agency, or any individual engaged in intelligence activities in any agency of the United States, if the President finds or has found that, due to the nature of the office or position occupied by such individual, public disclosure of such report would, be[1] revealing the identity of the individual or other sensitive information, compromise the national interest of the United States; and such individuals may be authorized, notwithstanding section 104(a), to file such additional reports as are necessary to protect their identity from public disclosure if the President

---

1. So in original. Probably should be "by".

first finds or has found that such filing is necessary in the national interest; and

(2) any report filed by an independent counsel whose identity has not been disclosed by the division of the court under chapter 40 of title 28, United States Code, and any report filed by any person appointed by that independent counsel under such chapter, shall not be made available to the public under this title.

(b)(1) Except as provided in the second sentence of this subsection, each agency, each supervising ethics office in the executive or judicial branch, the Clerk of the House of Representatives, and the Secretary of the Senate shall, within thirty days after any report is received under this title by such agency or office or by the Clerk or the Secretary of the Senate, as the case may be, permit inspection of such report by or furnish a copy of such report to any person requesting such inspection or copy. With respect to any report required to be filed by May 15 of any year, such report shall be made available for public inspection within 30 calendar days after May 15 of such year or within 30 days of the date of filing of such a report for which an extension is granted pursuant to section 101(g). The agency, office, Clerk, or Secretary of the Senate, as the case may be may require a reasonable fee to be paid in any amount which is found necessary to recover the cost of reproduction or mailing of such report excluding any salary of any employee involved in such reproduction or mailing. A copy of such report may be furnished without charge or at a reduced charge if it is determined that waiver or reduction of the fee is in the public interest.

(2) Notwithstanding paragraph (1), a report may not be made available under this section to any person nor may any copy thereof be provided under this section to any person except upon a written application by such person stating—

(A) that person's name, occupation and address;

(B) the name and address of any other person or organization on whose behalf the inspection or copy is requested; and

(C) that such person is aware of the prohibitions on the obtaining or use of the report.

Any such application shall be made available to the public throughout the period during which the report is made available to the public.

(3)(A) This section does not require the immediate and unconditional availability of reports filed by an individual described in section 109(8) or 109(10) of this Act [sections 109(8) or 109(10) or Appendix 4 of this title] if a finding is made by the Judicial Conference, in consultation with United States Marshall Service, that revealing personal and sensitive information could endanger that individual.

(B) A report may be redacted pursuant to this paragraph only—

(i) to the extent necessary to protect the individual who filed the report; and

(ii) for as long as the danger to such individual exists.

(C) The Administrative Office of the United States Courts shall submit to the Committees on the Judiciary of the House of Representatives and of the Senate an annual report with respect to the operation of this paragraph including—

(i) the total number of reports redacted pursuant to this paragraph;

(ii) the total number of individuals whose reports have been redacted pursuant to this paragraph; and

(iii) the types of threats against individuals whose reports are redacted, if appropriate.

(D) The Judicial Conference, in consultation with the Department of Justice, shall issue regulations setting forth the circumstances under which redaction is appropriate under this paragraph and the procedures for redaction.

(E) This paragraph shall expire on December 31, 2005, and apply to filings through calendar year 2005.

(c)(1) It shall be unlawful for any person to obtain or use a report—

(A) for any unlawful purpose;

(B) for any commercial purpose, other than by news and communications media for dissemination to the general public;

(C) for determining or establishing the credit rating of any individual; or

(D) for use, directly or indirectly, in the solicitation of money for any political, charitable, or other purpose.

(2) The Attorney General may bring a civil action against any person who obtains or uses a report for any purpose prohibited in paragraph (1) of this subsection. The court in which such action is brought may assess against such person a penalty in any amount not to exceed $10,000. Such remedy shall be in addition to any other remedy available under statutory or common law.

(d) Any report filed with or transmitted to an agency or supervising ethics office or to the Clerk of the House of Representatives or the Secretary of the Senate pursuant to this title shall be retained by such agency or office or by the Clerk or the Secretary of the Senate, as the case may be. Such report shall be made available to the public for a period of six years after receipt of the report. After such six-year period the report shall be destroyed unless needed in an ongoing investigation, except that in the case of an individual who filed the report pursuant to section 101(b) and was not subsequently confirmed by the Senate, or who filed the report pursuant to section 101(c) and was not subsequently elected, such reports shall be destroyed one year after the individual either is no longer under consideration by the Senate or is no longer a candidate for nomination or election to the

Office of President, Vice President, or as a Member of Congress, unless needed in an ongoing investigation.

§ 106. Review of reports

(a)(1) Each designated agency ethics official or Secretary concerned shall make provisions to ensure that each report filed with him under this title is reviewed within sixty days after the date of such filing, except that the Director of the Office of Government Ethics shall review only those reports required to be transmitted to him under this title within sixty days after the date of transmittal.

(2) Each congressional ethics committee and the Judicial Conference shall make provisions to ensure that each report filed under this title is reviewed within sixty days after the date of such filing.

(b)(1) If after reviewing any report under subsection (a), the Director of the Office of Government Ethics, the Secretary concerned, the designated agency ethics official, a person designated by the congressional ethics committee, or a person designated by the Judicial Conference, as the case may be, is of the opinion that on the basis of information contained in such report the individual submitting such report is in compliance with applicable laws and regulations, he shall state such opinion on the report, and shall sign such report.

(2) If the Director of the Office of Government Ethics, the Secretary concerned, the designated agency ethics official, a person designated by the congressional ethics committee, or a person designated by the Judicial Conference, after reviewing any report under subsection (a)—

(A) believes additional information is required to be submitted, he shall notify the individual submitting such report what additional information is required and the time by which it must be submitted, or

(B) is of the opinion, on the basis of information submitted, that the individual is not in compliance with applicable laws and regulations, he shall notify the individual, afford a reasonable opportunity for a written or oral response, and after consideration of such response, reach an opinion as to whether or not, on the basis of information submitted, the individual is in compliance with such laws and regulations.

(3) If the Director of the Office of Government Ethics, the Secretary concerned, the designated agency ethics official, a person designated by a congressional ethics committee, or a person designated by the Judicial Conference, reaches an opinion under paragraph (2)(B) that an individual is not in compliance with applicable laws and regulations, the official or committee shall notify the individual of that opinion and, after an opportunity for personal consultation (if practicable), determine and notify the individual of which steps, if any, would in the opinion of such official or committee be appropriate for assuring compliance with such laws and regulations and the date by which such steps should be taken. Such steps may include, as appropriate—

(A) divestiture,

(B) restitution,

(C) the establishment of a blind trust,

(D) request for an exemption under section 208(b) of title 18, United States Code, or

(E) voluntary request for transfer, reassignment, limitation of duties, or resignation.

The use of any such steps shall be in accordance with such rules or regulations as the supervising ethics office may prescribe.

(4) If steps for assuring compliance with applicable laws and regulations are not taken by the date set under paragraph (3) by an individual in a position in the executive branch (other than in the Foreign Service or the uniformed services), appointment to which requires the advice and consent of the Senate, the matter shall be referred to the President for appropriate action.

(5) If steps for assuring compliance with applicable laws and regulations are not taken by the date set under paragraph (3) by a member of the Foreign Service or the uniformed services, the Secretary concerned shall take appropriate action.

(6) If steps for assuring compliance with applicable laws and regulations are not taken by the date set under paragraph (3) by any other officer or employee, the matter shall be referred to the head of the appropriate agency, the congressional ethics committee, or the Judicial Conference, for appropriate action; except that in the case of the Postmaster General or Deputy Postmaster General, the Director of the Office of Government Ethics shall recommend to the Governors of the Board of Governors of the United States Postal Service the action to be taken.

(7) Each supervising ethics office may render advisory opinions interpreting this title within its respective jurisdiction. Notwithstanding any other provision of law, the individual to whom a public advisory opinion is rendered in accordance with this paragraph, and any other individual covered by this title who is involved in a fact situation which is indistinguishable in all material aspects, and who acts in good faith in accordance with the provisions and findings of such advisory opinion shall not, as a result of such act, be subject to any penalty or sanction provided by this title.

§ 107. Confidential reports and other additional requirements

(a)(1) Each supervising ethics office may require officers and employees under its jurisdiction (including special Government employees as defined in section 202 of title 18, United States Code) to file confidential financial disclosure reports, in such form as the supervising ethics office may prescribe. The information required to be reported under this subsection by the officers and employees of any department or agency shall be set forth in rules or regulations prescribed by the supervising ethics office, any may be less extensive than otherwise required by this title, or more extensive when determined by the supervising ethics office to be necessary and appropriate in light of sections 202 through 209 of title 18, United States Code, regulations promulgated thereunder, or the authorized activities of such officers or employees. Any individual required to file a report pursuant to section 101 shall not be required to file a confidential report pursuant to this subsection, except with respect to information which is more extensive than information otherwise required by this title. Subsections (a), (b), and (d) of section 105 shall not apply with respect to any such report.

(2) Any information required to be provided by an individual under this subsection shall be confidential and shall not be disclosed to the public.

(3) Nothing in this subsection exempts any individual otherwise covered by the requirement to file a public financial disclosure report under this title from such requirement.

(b) The provisions of this title requiring the reporting of information shall supersede any general requirement under any other provision of law or regulation with respect to the reporting of information required for purposes of preventing conflicts of interest or apparent conflicts of interest. Such provisions of this title shall not supersede the requirements of section 7342 of title 5, United States Code.

(c) Nothing in this Act requiring reporting of information shall be deemed to authorize the receipt of income, gifts, or reimbursements; the holding of assets, liabilities, or positions; or the participation in transactions that are prohibited by law, Executive order, rule, or regulation.

§ 108. Authority of Comptroller General

(a) The Comptroller General shall have access to financial disclosure reports filed under this title for the purposes of carrying out his statutory responsibilities.

(b) No later than December 31, 1992, and regularly thereafter, the Comptroller General shall conduct a study to determine whether the provisions of this title are being carried out effectively.

§ 109. Definitions

For the purposes of this title, the term—

(1) "congressional ethics committees" means the Select Committee on Ethics of the Senate and the Committee on Standards of Official Conduct of the House of Representatives;

(2) "dependent child" means, when used with respect to any reporting individual, any individual who is a son, daughter, stepson, or stepdaughter and who—

(A) is unmarried and under age 21 and is living in the household of such reporting individual; or

(B) is a dependent of such reporting individual within the meaning of section 152 of the Internal Revenue Code of 1986;

(3) "designated agency ethics official" means an officer or employee who is designated to administer the provisions of this title within an agency;

(4) "executive branch" includes each Executive agency (as defined in section 105 of title 5, United States Code), other than the General Accounting Office, and any other entity or administrative unit in the executive branch;

(5) "gift" means a payment, advance, forbearance, rendering, or deposit of money, or any thing of value, unless consideration of equal or greater value is received by the donor, but does not include—

(A) bequest and other forms of inheritance;

(B) suitable mementos of a function honoring the reporting individual;

(C) food, lodging, transportation, and entertainment provided by a foreign government within a foreign country or by the United States Government, the District of Columbia, or a State or local government or political subdivision thereof;

(D) food and beverages which are not consumed in connection with a gift of overnight lodging;

(E) communications to the offices of a reporting individual, including subscriptions to newspapers and periodicals; or

(F) consumable products provided by home-State businesses to the offices of a reporting individual who is an elected official, if those products are intended for consumption by persons other than such reporting individual;

(6) "honoraria" has the meaning given such term in section 505 of this Act;

(7) "income" means all income from whatever source derived, including but not limited to the following items: compensation for services, including fees, commissions, and similar items; gross income derived from business (and net income if the individual elects to include it); gains derived from dealings in property; interest; rents; royalties; dividends; annuities; income from life insurance and endowment contracts; pensions; income from discharge of indebtedness; distributive share of partnership income; and income from an interest in an estate or trust;

(8) "judicial employee" means any employee of the judicial branch of the Government, of the United States Sentencing Commission, of the Tax Court, of the Court of Federal Claims, of the Court of Appeals for Veterans Claims, or of the United States Court of Appeals for the Armed Forces, who is not a judicial officer and who is authorized to perform adjudicatory functions with respect to proceedings in the judicial branch, or who occupies a position for which the rate of basic pay is equal to or greater than 120 percent of the minimum rate of basic pay payable for GS–15 of the General Schedule;

(9) "Judicial Conference" means the Judicial Conference of the United States;

(10) "judicial officer" means the Chief Justice of the United States, the Associate Justices of the Supreme Court, and the judges of the United States courts of appeals, United States district courts, including the district courts in Guam, the Northern Mariana Islands, and the Virgin Islands, Court of Appeals for the Federal Circuit, Court of International Trade, Tax Court, Court of Federal Claims, Court of Appeals for Veterans Claims, United States Court of Appeals for the Armed Forces, and any court created by Act of Congress, the judges of which are entitled to hold office during good behavior;

(11) "legislative branch" includes—

    (A) the Architect of the Capitol;

    (B) the Botanic Gardens;

    (C) the Congressional Budget Office;

    (D) the General Accounting Office;

    (E) the Government Printing Office;

    (F) the Library of Congress;

    (G) the United States Capitol Police;

    (H) the Office of Technology Assessment; and

    (I) any other agency, entity, office, or commission established in the legislative branch;

(12) "Member of Congress" means a United States Senator, a Representative in Congress, a Delegate to Congress, or the Resident Commissioner from Puerto Rico;

(13) "officer or employee of the Congress" means—

    (A) any individual described under subparagraph (B), other than a Member of Congress or the Vice President, whose compensation is disbursed by the Secretary of the Senate or the Chief Administrative Officer of the House of Representatives;

    (B)(i) each officer or employee of the legislative branch who, for at least 60 days, occupies a position for which the rate of basic pay is equal to or greater than 120 percent of the minimum rate of basic pay payable for GS–15 of the General Schedule; and

    (ii) at least one principal assistant designated for purposes of this paragraph by each Member who does not have an employee who occupies a position for which the rate of basic pay is equal to or greater than 120 percent of the minimum rate of basic pay payable for GS–15 of the General Schedule;

(14) "personal hospitality of any individual" means hospitality extended for a nonbusiness purpose by an individual, not a corporation or organization, at the personal residence of that individual or his family or on property or facilities owned by that individual or his family;

(15) "reimbursement" means any payment or other thing of value received by the reporting individual, other than gifts, to cover travel-related expenses of such individual other than those which are—

(A) provided by the United States Government, the District of Columbia, or a State or local government or political subdivision thereof;

(B) required to be reported by the reporting individual under section 7342 of title 5, United States Code; or

(C) required to be reported under section 304 of the Federal Election Campaign Act of 1971 (2 U.S.C. 434);

(16) "relative" means an individual who is related to the reporting individual, as father, mother, son, daughter, brother, sister, uncle, aunt, great aunt, great uncle, first cousin, nephew, niece, husband, wife, grandfather, grandmother, grandson, granddaughter, father-in-law, mother-in-law, son-in-law, daughter-in-law, brother-in-law, sister-in-law, stepfather, stepmother, stepson, stepdaughter, stepbrother, stepsister, half brother, half sister, or who is the grandfather or grandmother of the spouse of the reporting individual, and shall be deemed to include the fiance or fiancee of the reporting individual;

(17) "Secretary concerned" has the meaning set forth in section 101(a)(9) of title 10, United States Code, and, in addition, means—

(A) the Secretary of Commerce, with respect to matters concerning the National Oceanic and Atmospheric Administration;

(B) the Secretary of Health and Human Services, with respect to matters concerning the Public Health Service; and

(C) the Secretary of State, with respect to matters concerning the Foreign Service;

(18) "supervising ethics office" means—

(A) the Select Committee on Ethics of the Senate, for Senators, officers and employees of the Senate, and other officers or employees of the legislative branch required to file financial disclosure reports with the Secretary of the Senate pursuant to section 103(h) of this title;

(B) the Committee on Standards of Official Conduct of the House of Representatives, for Members, officers and employees of the House of Representatives and other officers or employees of the legislative branch required to file financial disclosure reports with the Clerk of the House of Representatives pursuant to section 103(h) of this title;

(C) the Judicial Conference for judicial officers and judicial employees; and

(D) the Office of Government Ethics for all executive branch officers and employees; and

(19) "value" means a good faith estimate of the dollar value if the exact value is neither known nor easily obtainable by the reporting individual.

§ 110. Notice of actions taken to comply with ethics agreements

(a) In any case in which an individual agrees with that individual's designated agency ethics official, the Office of Government Ethics, a Senate confirmation committee, a congressional ethics committee, or the Judicial Conference, to take any action to comply with this Act or any other law or regulation governing conflicts of interest of, or establishing standards of conduct applicable with respect to, officers or employees of the Government, that individual shall notify in writing the designated agency ethics official, the Office of Government Ethics, the appropriate committee of the Senate, the congressional ethics committee, or the Judicial Conference, as the case may be, of any action taken by the individual pursuant to that agreement. Such notification shall be made not later than the date specified in the agreement by which action by the individual must be taken, or not later than three months after the date of the agreement, if no date for action is so specified.

(b) If an agreement described in subsection (a) requires that the individual recuse himself or herself from particular categories of agency or other official action, the individual shall reduce to writing those subjects regarding which the recusal agreement will apply and the process by which it will be determined whether the individual must recuse himself or herself in a specific instance. An individual shall be considered to have complied with the requirements of subsection (a) with respect to such recusal agreement if such individual files a copy of the document setting forth the information described in the preceding sentence with such individual's designated agency ethics official or the appropriate supervising ethics office within the time prescribed in the last sentence of subsection (a).

§ 111. Administration of provisions

The provisions of this title shall be administered by—

(1) the Director of the Office of Government Ethics, the designated agency ethics official, or the Secretary concerned, as appropriate, with regard to officers and employees described in paragraphs (1) through (8) of section 101(f);

(2) the Select Committee on Ethics of the Senate and the Committee on Standards of Official Conduct of the House of Representatives, as appropriate, with regard to officers and employees described in paragraphs (9) and (10) of section 101(f); and

(3) the Judicial Conference in the case of an officer or employee described in paragraphs (11) and (12) of section 101(f).

The Judicial Conference may delegate any authority it has under this title to an ethics committee established by the Judicial Conference.

5. SAMPLE FEDERAL DISTRICT COURT RULES

UNITED STATES DISTRICT COURTS FOR THE SOUTHERN AND EASTERN DISTRICTS OF NEW YORK

Local Civil Rule 1.3. Admission to the Bar

(a) A member in good standing of the bar of the state of New York, or a member in good standing of the bar of the United States District Court in New Jersey, Connecticut or Vermont and of the bar of the State in which such district court is located, provided such district court by its rule extends a corresponding privilege to members of the bar of this court, may be admitted to practice in this court on compliance with the following provisions:

Each applicant for admission shall file with the clerk, at least ten (10) days prior to hearing (unless, for good cause shown, the judge shall shorten the time), a verified written petition for admission on a form supplied by the clerk stating: (1) applicant's residence and office address; (2) the time when, and courts where, admitted; (3) applicant's legal training and experience; (4) whether applicant has ever been held in contempt of court, and, if so, the nature of the contempt and the final disposition thereof; (5) whether applicant has ever been censured, suspended or disbarred by any court, and, if so, the facts and circumstances connected therewith; (6) that applicant has read and is familiar with (a) the provisions of the Judicial Code (Title 28, U.S.C.) which pertain to the jurisdiction of, and practice in, the United States District Courts; (b) the Federal Rules of Civil Procedure; (c) the Federal Rules of Criminal Procedure; (d) the Federal Rules of Evidence; (e) the Local Rules of the United States District Court for the Southern and Eastern Districts of New York; and (f) the New York State Lawyer's Code of Professional Responsibility as adopted from time to time by the Appellate Divisions of the State of New York; and (7) that applicant will faithfully adhere to all rules applicable to applicant's conduct in connection with any activities in this court.

The petition shall be accompanied by a certificate of the clerk of the court for each of the states in which the applicant is a member of the bar, which has been issued within thirty (30) days and states that the applicant is a member in good standing of the bar of that state court. The petition shall also be accompanied by an affidavit of an attorney of this court who has known the applicant for at least one year, stating when the affiant was admitted to practice in this court, how long and under what circumstances the attorney has known the applicant, and what the attorney knows of the applicant's character and experience at the bar. Such petition shall be placed at the head of the calendar and, on the call thereof, the attorney whose affidavit accompanied the petition shall personally move the admission of the applicant. If the petition is granted, the applicant shall take the oath of office and sign the roll of attorneys.

(b) A member in good standing of the bar of either the Southern or Eastern District of New York may be admitted to the bar of the other district without formal application (1) upon filing in that district a certificate of the Clerk of the United States District Court for the district in which the applicant is a member of the bar, which has been issued within thirty (30) days and states that the applicant is a member in good standing of the bar of that court and (2) upon taking the oath of office, signing the roll of attorneys of that district, and paying the fee required in that district.

(c) A member in good standing of the bar of any state or of any United States District Court may be permitted to argue or try a particular case in whole or in part as counsel or advocate, upon motion and upon filing with the Clerk of the District Court a certificate of the court for each of the states in which the applicant is a member of the bar, which has been issued within thirty (30) days and states that the applicant is a member in good standing of the bar of that state court. Only an attorney who has been so admitted or who is a member of the bar of this court may enter appearances for parties, sign stipulations or receive payments upon judgments, decrees or orders.

(d) If an attorney who is a member of the bar of this court, or who has been authorized to appear in a case in this court, changes his or her residence or office address, the attorney shall immediately notify the clerk of the court, in addition to serving and filing a notice of change of address in each pending case in which the attorney has appeared.

6. FEDERAL RULES OF APPELLATE PROCEDURE

RULE 45. Clerk's Duties

(a) General Provisions. *** Neither the clerk nor any deputy clerk may practice as an attorney or counselor in any court while in office. ***

RULE 46. Attorneys

(a) Admission to the Bar.

(1) Eligibility. An attorney is eligible for admission to the bar of a court of appeals if that attorney is of good moral and professional character and is admitted to practice before the Supreme Court of the United States, the highest court of a state, another United States court of appeals, or a United States district court (including the district courts for Guam, the Northern Mariana Islands, and the Virgin Islands).

(2) Application. An applicant must file an application for admission, on a form approved by the court that contains the applicant's personal statement showing eligibility for membership. The applicant must subscribe to the following oath or affirmation:

"I, _____, do solemnly swear [or affirm] that I will conduct myself as an attorney and counselor of this court, uprightly and according to law; and that I will support the Constitution of the United States."

(3) Admission Procedures. On written or oral motion of a member of the court's bar, the court will act on the application. An applicant may be admitted by oral motion in open court. But, unless the court orders otherwise, an applicant need not appear before the court to be admitted. Upon admission, an applicant must pay the clerk the fee prescribed by local rule or court order.

(b) Suspension or Disbarment.

(1) Standard. A member of the court's bar is subject to suspension or disbarment by the court if the member:

(A) has been suspended or disbarred from practice in any other court; or

(B) is guilty of conduct unbecoming a member of the court's bar.

(2) Procedure. The member must be given an opportunity to show good cause, within the time prescribed by the court, why the member should not be suspended or disbarred.

(3) Order. The court must enter an appropriate order after the member responds and a hearing is held, if requested, or after the time prescribed for a response expires, if no response is made.

(c) Discipline. A court of appeals may discipline an attorney who practices before it for conduct unbecoming a member of the bar or for failure to comply with any court rule. First, however, the court must afford the attorney reasonable notice, an opportunity to show cause to the contrary, and, if requested, a hearing.

7. U.S. SUPREME COURT RULES

RULE 7. Prohibition Against Practice

No employee of this Court shall practice as an attorney or counselor in any court or before any agency of government while employed by the Court; nor shall any person after leaving such employment participate in any professional capacity in any case pending before this Court or in any case being considered for filing in this Court, until two years have elapsed after separation; nor shall a former employee ever participate in any professional capacity in any case that was pending in this Court during the employee's tenure.

RULE 8. Disbarment and Disciplinary Action

1. Whenever a member of the Bar of this Court has been disbarred or suspended from practice in any court of record, or has engaged in conduct

unbecoming a member of the Bar of this Court, the Court will enter an order suspending that member from practice before this Court and affording the member an opportunity to show cause, within 40 days, why a disbarment order should not be entered. Upon response, or if no response is timely filed, the Court will enter an appropriate order.

2. After reasonable notice and an opportunity to show cause why disciplinary action should not be taken, and after a hearing if material facts are in dispute, the Court may take any appropriate disciplinary action against any attorney who is admitted to practice before it for conduct unbecoming a member of the Bar or for failure to comply with these Rules or any Rule or order of the Court.

8.   CITIZENS PROTECTION ACT OF 1998 (the McDade Act)

28 U.S.C.A. § 530B

§ 530B.   Ethical standards for attorneys for the Government

(a) An attorney for the Government shall be subject to State laws and rules, and local Federal court rules, governing attorneys in each State where such attorney engages in that attorney's duties, to the same extent and in the same manner as other attorneys in that State.

(b) The Attorney General shall make and amend rules of the Department of Justice to assure compliance with this section.

(c) As used in this section, the term "attorney for the Government" includes any attorney described in section 77.2(a) of part 77 of title 28 of the Code of Federal Regulations and also includes any independent counsel, or employee of such a counsel, appointed under chapter 40.

9.   FEDERAL RULES OF CIVIL PROCEDURE, RULES 11 & 23

Rule 11.   Signing of Pleadings, Motions, and Other Papers; Representations to Court; Sanctions

(a) **Signature.** Every pleading, written motion, and other paper shall be signed by at least one attorney of record in the attorney's individual name, or, if the party is not represented by an attorney, shall be signed by the party. Each paper shall state the signer's address and telephone number, if any. Except when otherwise specifically provided by rule or statute, pleadings need not be verified or accompanied by affidavit. An unsigned paper shall be stricken unless omission of the signature is corrected promptly after being called to the attention of the attorney or party.

(b) **Representations to Court.** By presenting to the court (whether by signing, filing, submitting, or later advocating) a pleading, written motion, or other paper, an attorney or unrepresented party is certifying that to the best of the person's knowledge, information, and belief, formed after an inquiry reasonable under the circumstances,—

(1) it is not being presented for any improper purpose, such as to harass or to cause unnecessary delay or needless increase in the cost of litigation;

(2) the claims, defenses, and other legal contentions therein are warranted by existing law or by a nonfrivolous argument for the extension, modification, or reversal of existing law or the establishment of new law;

(3) the allegations and other factual contentions have evidentiary support or, if specifically so identified, are likely to have evidentiary support after a reasonable opportunity for further investigation or discovery; and

(4) the denials of factual contentions are warranted on the evidence or, if specifically so identified, are reasonably based on a lack of information or belief.

(c) Sanctions. If, after notice and a reasonable opportunity to respond, the court determines that subdivision (b) has been violated, the court may, subject to the conditions stated below, impose an appropriate sanction upon the attorneys, law firms, or parties that have violated subdivision (b) or are responsible for the violation.

(1) How Initiated.

(A) By Motion. A motion for sanctions under this rule shall be made separately from other motions or requests and shall describe the specific conduct alleged to violate subdivision (b). It shall be served as provided in Rule 5, but shall not be filed with or presented to the court unless, within 21 days after service of the motion (or such other period as the court may prescribe), the challenged paper, claim, defense, contention, allegation, or denial is not withdrawn or appropriately corrected. If warranted, the court may award to the party prevailing on the motion the reasonable expenses and attorney's fees incurred in presenting or opposing the motion. Absent exceptional circumstances, a law firm shall be held jointly responsible for violations committed by its partners, associates, and employees.

(B) On Court's Initiative. On its own initiative, the court may enter an order describing the specific conduct that appears to violate subdivision (b) and directing an attorney, law firm, or party to show cause why it has not violated subdivision (b) with respect thereto.

(2) Nature of Sanction; Limitations. A sanction imposed for violation of this rule shall be limited to what is sufficient to deter repetition of such conduct or comparable conduct by others similarly situated. Subject to the limitations in subparagraphs (A) and (B), the sanction may consist of, or include, directives of a nonmonetary nature, an order to pay a penalty into court, or, if imposed on motion and warranted for effective deterrence, an order directing payment to the movant of some or all of the reasonable attorneys' fees and other expenses incurred as a direct result of the violation.

(A) Monetary sanctions may not be awarded against a represented party for a violation of subdivision (b)(2).

(B) Monetary sanctions may not be awarded on the court's initiative unless the court issues its order to show cause before a voluntary dismissal or settlement of the claims made by or against the party which is, or whose attorneys are, to be sanctioned.

(3) Order. When imposing sanctions, the court shall describe the conduct determined to constitute a violation of this rule and explain the basis for the sanction imposed.

(d) Inapplicability to Discovery. Subdivisions (a) through (c) of this rule do not apply to disclosures and discovery requests, responses, objections, and motions that are subject to the provisions of Rules 26 through 37.

Rule 23. Class Actions

(a) Prerequisites to a Class Action. One or more members of a class may sue or be sued as representative parties on behalf of all only if (1) the class is so numerous that joinder of all members is impracticable, (2) there are questions of law or fact common to the class, (3) the claims or defenses of the representative parties are typical of the claims or defenses of the class, and (4) the representative parties will fairly and adequately protect the interests of the class.

(b) Class Actions Maintainable. An action may be maintained as a class action if the prerequisites of subdivision (a) are satisfied, and in addition:

(1) the prosecution of separate actions by or against individual members of the class would create a risk of

(A) inconsistent or varying adjudications with respect to individual members of the class which would establish incompatible standards of conduct for the party opposing the class, or

(B) adjudications with respect to individual members of the class which would as a practical matter be dispositive of the interests of the other members not parties to the adjudications or substantially impair or impede their ability to protect their interests; or

(2) the party opposing the class has acted or refused to act on grounds generally applicable to the class, thereby making appropriate final injunctive relief or corresponding declaratory relief with respect to the class as a whole; or

(3) the court finds that the questions of law or fact common to the members of the class predominate over any questions affecting only individual members, and that a class action is superior to other available methods for the fair and efficient adjudication of the controversy. The matters pertinent to the findings include: (A) the interest of members of the class in individually controlling the prosecution or defense of separate actions; (B) the extent and nature of any litigation concerning the controversy already commenced by or against members of the class; (C) the desirability or undesirability of concentrating the litigation of the claims in the particular forum; (D) the difficulties likely to be encountered in the management of a class action.

(c) Determination by Order Whether Class Action to be Maintained; Notice; Judgment; Actions Conducted Partially as Class Actions.

(1) As soon as practicable after the commencement of an action brought as a class action, the court shall determine by order whether it is to be so maintained. An order under this subdivision may be conditional, and may be altered or amended before the decision on the merits.

(2) In any class action maintained under subdivision (b)(3), the court shall direct to the members of the class the best notice practicable under the circumstances, including individual notice to all members who can be identified through reasonable effort. The notice shall advise each member that (A) the court will exclude the member from the class if the member so requests by a specified date; (B) the judgment, whether favorable or not, will include all members who do not request exclusion; and (C) any member who does not request exclusion may, if the member desires, enter an appearance through counsel.

(3) The judgment in an action maintained as a class action under subdivision (b)(1) or (b)(2), whether or not favorable to the class, shall include and describe those whom the court finds to be members of the class. The judgment in an action maintained as a class action under subdivision (b)(3), whether or not favorable to the class, shall include and specify or describe those to whom the notice provided in subdivision (c)(2) was directed, and who have not requested exclusion, and whom the court finds to be members of the class.

(4) When appropriate (A) an action may be brought or maintained as a class action with respect to particular issues, or (B) a class may be divided into subclasses and each subclass treated as a class, and the provisions of this rule shall then be construed and applied accordingly.

(d) Orders in Conduct of Actions. In the conduct of actions to which this rule applies, the court may make appropriate orders: (1) determining the course of proceedings or prescribing measures to prevent undue repetition or complication in the presentation of evidence or argument; (2) requiring, for the protection of the members of the class or otherwise for the fair conduct of the action, that notice be given in such manner as the court may direct to some or all of the members of any step in the action, or of the proposed extent of the judgment, or of the opportunity of members to signify whether they consider the representation fair and adequate, to intervene and present claims or defenses, or otherwise to come into the action; (3) imposing conditions on the representative parties or on intervenors; (4) requiring that the pleadings be amended to eliminate therefrom allegations as to representation of absent persons, and that the action proceed accordingly; (5) dealing with similar procedural matters. The orders may be combined with an order under Rule 16, and may be altered or amended as may be desirable from time to time.

(e) Dismissal or Compromise. A class action shall not be dismissed or compromised without the approval of the court, and notice of the proposed dismissal or compromise shall be given to all members of the class in such manner as the court directs.

(f) Appeals. A court of appeals may in its discretion permit an appeal from an order of a district court granting or denying class action certification under this rule if application is made to it within ten days after entry of the order. An appeal does not stay proceedings in the district court unless the district judge or the court of appeals so orders.

10.   15 U.S.C.A. § 7245 (Sarbanes–Oxley Act of 2002, § 307)*

15 U.S.C.A. § 7245.   Rules of professional responsibility for attorneys

Not later than 180 days after July 30, 2002, the [Securities and Exchange] Commission shall issue rules, in the public interest and for the protection of investors, setting forth minimum standards of professional conduct for attorneys appearing and practicing before the Commission in any way in the representation of issuers, including a rule—

(1) requiring an attorney to report evidence of a material violation of securities law or breach of fiduciary duty or similar violation by the company or any agent thereof, to the chief legal counsel or the chief executive officer of the company (or the equivalent thereof); and

(2) if the counsel or officer does not appropriately respond to the evidence (adopting, as necessary, appropriate remedial measures or sanctions with respect to the violation), requiring the attorney to report the evidence to the audit committee of the board of directors of the issuer or to another committee of the board of directors comprised solely of directors not employed directly or indirectly by the issuer, or to the board of directors.

Sarbanes–Oxley Act of 2002, Pub.L. 107–204, Title III, § 307, July 30, 2002, 116 Stat. 784.

* Editors' Note: This statutory section is part of a much longer statute passed in July 2002, in the wake of the collapse of Enron and other corporate bankruptcies. This section requires the SEC to prepare regulations that it has not yet issued at the time this Standards Supplement went to press.

ABA MODEL CODE OF JUDICIAL CONDUCT (1990)

[The Model Code of Judicial Conduct was adopted by the House of Delegates of the American Bar Association in August 1990. It is designed to replace the previous code, which had been adopted in 1972 and last amended in 1999. The Model Code of Judicial Conduct is copyrighted by the American Bar Association, and reprinted here with permission. Portions of the previous (1972) Judicial Code are quoted in the margin.]

PREAMBLE

[1] Our legal system is based on the principle that an independent, fair and competent judiciary will interpret and apply the laws that govern us. The role of the judiciary is central to American concepts of justice and the rule of law. Intrinsic to all sections of this Code are the precepts that judges, individually and collectively, must respect and honor the judicial office as a public trust and strive to enhance and maintain confidence in our legal system. The judge is an arbiter of facts and law for the resolution of disputes and a highly visible symbol of government under the rule of law.

[2] The Code of Judicial Conduct is intended to establish standards for ethical conduct of judges. It consists of broad statements called Canons, specific rules set forth in Sections under each Canon, a Terminology Section, an Application Section and Commentary. The text of the Canons and the Sections, including the Terminology and Application Sections, is authoritative. The Commentary, by explanation and example, provides guidance with respect to the purpose and meaning of the Canons and Sections. The Commentary is not intended as a statement of additional rules. When the text uses "shall" or "shall not," it is intended to impose binding obligations the violation of which can result in disciplinary action. When "should" or "should not" is used, the text is intended as hortatory and as a statement of what is or is not appropriate conduct but not as a binding rule under which a judge may be disciplined. When "may" is used, it denotes permissible discretion or, depending on the context, it refers to action that is not covered by specific proscriptions.

[3] The Canons and Sections are rules of reason. They should be applied consistent with constitutional requirements, statutes, other court rules and decisional law and in the context of all relevant circumstances. The Code is to be construed so as not to impinge on the essential independence of judges in making judicial decisions.

[4] The Code is designed to provide guidance to judges and candidates for judicial office and to provide a structure for regulating conduct through disciplinary agencies. It is not designed or intended as a basis for civil liability or criminal prosecution. Furthermore, the purpose of the Code would be subverted if the Code were invoked by lawyers for mere tactical advantage in a proceeding.

[5] The text of the Canons and Sections is intended to govern conduct of judges and to be binding upon them. It is not intended, however, that every transgression will result in disciplinary action. Whether disciplinary action is appropriate, and the degree of discipline to be imposed, should be determined through a reasonable and reasoned application of the text and should depend on such factors as the seriousness

of the transgression, whether there is a pattern of improper activity and the effect of the improper activity on others or on the judicial system. See ABA Standards Relating to Judicial Discipline and Disability Retirement.[1]

[6] The Code of Judicial Conduct is not intended as an exhaustive guide for the conduct of judges. They should also be governed in their judicial and personal conduct by general ethical standards. The Code is intended, however, to state basic standards which should govern the conduct of all judges and to provide guidance to assist judges in establishing and maintaining high standards of judicial and personal conduct.

TERMINOLOGY

Terms explained below are noted with an asterisk (*) in the Sections where they appear. In addition, the Sections where terms appear are referred to after the explanation of each term below.

[1] "**Aggregate**" in relation to contributions for a candidate under Sections 3E(1)(e) and 5C(3) and (4) denotes not only contributions in cash or in kind made directly to a candidate's committee or treasurer, but also, except in retention elections, all contributions made indirectly with the understanding that they will be used to support the election of the candidate or to oppose the election of the candidate's opponent. See Sections 3E(1)(e), 5C(3) and 5C(4).

[2] "**Appropriate authority**" denotes the authority with responsibility for initiation of disciplinary process with respect to the violation to be reported. See Sections 3D(1) and 3D(2).

[3] "**Candidate**." A candidate is a person seeking selection for or retention in judicial office by election or appointment. A person becomes a candidate for judicial office as soon as he or she makes a public announcement of candidacy, declares or files as a candidate with the election or appointment authority, or authorizes solicitation or acceptance of contributions or support. The term "candidate" has the same meaning when applied to a judge seeking election or appointment to nonjudicial office. See Preamble and Sections 5A, 5B, 5C and 5E.

[4] "**Continuing part-time judge**." A continuing part-time judge is a judge who serves repeatedly on a part-time basis by election or under a continuing appointment, including a retired judge subject to recall who is permitted to practice law. See Application Section C.

[5] "**Court personnel**" does not include the lawyers in a proceeding before a judge. See Sections 3B(7)(c) and 3B(9).

[6] "**De minimis**" [†] denotes an insignificant interest that could not raise reasonable question as to a judge's impartiality. See Sections 3E(1)(c) and 3E(1)(d).

---

1. Judicial disciplinary procedures adopted in the jurisdictions should comport with the requirements of due process. The ABA Standards Relating to Judicial Discipline and Disability Retirement are cited as an example of how these due process requirements may be satisfied.

† **Editors' note:** In contrast, Canon 3C(3)(c) of the ABA Model Code of Judicial Conduct (1972, as amended) defined "financial interest" very differently; there was no such thing as a "de minimis" legal or equitable interest. It provided:

(c) "financial interest" means ownership of a legal or equitable interest, however small, or a relationship as director, advisor, or other active participant in the affairs of a party, except that:

(i) ownership in a mutual or common investment fund that holds securities is not a "financial interest" in such securities unless the judge participates in the management of the fund;

(ii) an office in an educational, religious, charitable, fraternal, or civic organization

[7] **"Economic interest"** † denotes ownership of a more than de minimis legal or equitable interest, or a relationship as officer, director, advisor or other active participant in the affairs of a party, except that:

(i) ownership of an interest in a mutual or common investment fund that holds securities is not an economic interest in such securities unless the judge participates in the management of the fund or a proceeding pending or impending before the judge could substantially affect the value of the interest;

(ii) service by a judge as an officer, director, advisor or other active participant in an educational, religious, charitable, fraternal or civic organization, or service by a judge's spouse, parent or child as an officer, director, advisor or other active participant in any organization does not create an economic interest in securities held by that organization;

(iii) a deposit in a financial institution, the proprietary interest of a policy holder in a mutual insurance company, of a depositor in a mutual savings association or of a member in a credit union, or a similar proprietary interest, is not an economic interest in the organization unless a proceeding pending or impending before the judge could substantially affect the value of the interest;

(iv) ownership of government securities is not an economic interest in the issuer unless a proceeding pending or impending before the judge could substantially affect the value of the securities. See Sections 3E(1)(c) and 3E(2).

[8] **"Fiduciary"** includes such relationships as executor, administrator, trustee, and guardian. See Sections 3E(2) and 4E.

[9] **"Knowingly,"** "knowledge," "known" or "knows" denotes actual knowledge of the fact in question. A person's knowledge may be inferred from circumstances. See Sections 3D, 3E(1), and 5A(3).

[10] **"Law"** denotes court rules as well as statutes, constitutional provisions and decisional law. See Sections 2A, 3A, 3B(2), 3B(6), 4B, 4C, 4D(5), 4F, 4I, 5A(2), 5A(3), 5B(2), 5C(1), 5C(3) and 5D.

[11] **"Member of the candidate's family"** denotes a spouse, child, grandchild, parent, grandparent or other relative or person with whom the candidate maintains a close familial relationship. See Section 5A(3)(a).

[12] **"Member of the judge's family"** denotes a spouse, child, grandchild, parent, grandparent, or other relative or person with whom the judge maintains a close familial relationship. See Sections 4D(3), 4E and 4G.

[13] **"Member of the judge's family residing in the judge's household"** denotes any relative of a judge by blood or marriage, or a person treated by a judge as a member of the judge's family, who resides in the judge's household. See Sections 3E(1) and 4D(5).

is not a "financial interest" in securities held by the organization;

(iii) the proprietary interest of a policy holder in a mutual insurance company, of a depositor in a mutual savings association, or a similar proprietary interest, is a "financial interest" in the organization only if the outcome of the proceeding could substantially affect the value of the interest;

(iv) ownership of government securities is a "financial interest" in the issuer only if the outcome of the proceeding could substantially affect the value of the securities.

† See note on previous page.

[14] **"Nonpublic information"** denotes information that, by law, is not available to the public. Nonpublic information may include but is not limited to: information that is sealed by statute or court order, impounded or communicated in camera; and information offered in grand jury proceedings, presentencing reports, dependency cases or psychiatric reports. See Section 3B(11).

[15] **"Periodic part-time judge."** A periodic part-time judge is a judge who serves or expects to serve repeatedly on a part-time basis but under a separate appointment for each limited period of service or for each matter. See Application Section D.

[16] **"Political organization"** denotes a political party or other group, the principal purpose of which is to further the election or appointment of candidates to political office. See Sections 5A(1), 5B(2) and 5C(1).

[17] **"Pro tempore part-time judge."** A pro tempore part-time judge is a judge who serves or expects to serve once or only sporadically on a part-time basis under a separate appointment for each period of service or for each case heard. See Application Section E.

[18] **"Public election."** This term includes primary and general elections; it includes partisan elections, nonpartisan elections and retention elections. See Section 5C.

[19] **"Require."** The rules prescribing that a judge "require" certain conduct of others are, like all of the rules in this Code, rules of reason. The use of the term "require" in that context means a judge is to exercise reasonable direction and control over the conduct of those persons subject to the judge's direction and control. See Sections 3B(3), 3B(4), 3B(5), 3B(6), 3B(9) and 3C(2).

[20] **"Third degree of relationship."** The following persons are relatives within the third degree of relationship: great-grandparent, grandparent, parent, uncle, aunt, brother, sister, child, grandchild, great-grandchild, nephew or niece. See Section 3E(1)(d).

CANON 1

A Judge Shall Uphold the Integrity and Independence of the Judiciary

A. An independent and honorable judiciary is indispensable to justice in our society. A judge should participate in establishing, maintaining and enforcing high standards of conduct, and shall personally observe those standards so that the integrity and independence of the judiciary will be preserved. The provisions of this Code are to be construed and applied to further that objective.

Commentary:

[1] Deference to the judgments and rulings of courts depends upon public confidence in the integrity and independence of judges. The integrity and independence of judges depends in turn upon their acting without fear or favor. Although judges should be independent, they must comply with the law, including the provisions of this Code. Public confidence in the impartiality of the judiciary is maintained by the adherence of each judge to this responsibility. Conversely, violation of this Code

diminishes public confidence in the judiciary and thereby does injury to the system of government under law.

CANON 2

A Judge Shall Avoid Impropriety and the Appearance of Impropriety in All of the Judge's Activities

A. A judge shall respect and comply with the law* and shall act at all times in a manner that promotes public confidence in the integrity and impartiality of the judiciary.

Commentary:

[1] Public confidence in the judiciary is eroded by irresponsible or improper conduct by judges. A judge must avoid all impropriety and appearance of impropriety. A judge must expect to be the subject of constant public scrutiny. A judge must therefore accept restrictions on the judge's conduct that might be viewed as burdensome by the ordinary citizen and should do so freely and willingly.

[2] The prohibition against behaving with impropriety or the appearance of impropriety applies to both the professional and personal conduct of a judge. Because it is not practicable to list all prohibited acts, the proscription is necessarily cast in general terms that extend to conduct by judges that is harmful although not specifically mentioned in the Code. Actual improprieties under this standard include violations of law, court rules or other specific provisions of this Code. The test for appearance of impropriety is whether the conduct would create in reasonable minds a perception that the judge's ability to carry out judicial responsibilities with integrity, impartiality and competence is impaired.

[3] See also Commentary under Section 2C.

B. A judge shall not allow family, social, political or other relationships to influence the judge's judicial conduct or judgment. A judge shall not lend the prestige of judicial office to advance the private interests of the judge or others; nor shall a judge convey or permit others to convey the impression that they are in a special position to influence the judge. A judge shall not testify voluntarily as a character witness.

Commentary:

[1] Maintaining the prestige of judicial office is essential to a system of government in which the judiciary functions independently of the executive and legislative branches. Respect for the judicial office facilitates the orderly conduct of legitimate judicial functions. Judges should distinguish between proper and improper use of the prestige of office in all of their activities. For example, it would be improper for a judge to allude to his or her judgeship to gain a personal advantage such as deferential treatment when stopped by a police officer for a traffic offense. Similarly, judicial letterhead must not be used for conducting a judge's personal business.

[2] A judge must avoid lending the prestige of judicial office for the advancement of the private interests of others. For example, a judge must not use the judge's judicial position to gain advantage in a civil suit involving a member of the judge's family. In contracts for publication of a judge's writings, a judge should retain control

* See, Terminology.

over the advertising to avoid exploitation of the judge's office. As to the acceptance of awards, see Section 4D(5)(a) and Commentary.

[3]   Although a judge should be sensitive to possible abuse of the prestige of office, a judge may, based on the judge's personal knowledge, serve as a reference or provide a letter of recommendation. However, a judge must not initiate the communication of information to a sentencing judge or a probation or corrections officer but may provide to such persons information for the record in response to a formal request.

[4]   Judges may participate in the process of judicial selection by cooperating with appointing authorities and screening committees seeking names for consideration, and by responding to official inquiries concerning a person being considered for a judgeship. See also Canon 5 regarding use of a judge's name in political activities.

[5]   A judge must not testify voluntarily as a character witness because to do so may lend the prestige of the judicial office in support of the party for whom the judge testifies. Moreover, when a judge testifies as a witness, a lawyer who regularly appears before the judge may be placed in the awkward position of cross-examining the judge. A judge may, however, testify when properly summoned. Except in unusual circumstances where the demands of justice require, a judge should discourage a party from requiring the judge to testify as a character witness.

C.   A judge shall not hold membership in any organization that practices invidious discrimination on the basis of race, sex, religion or national origin.

Commentary:

[1]   Membership of a judge in an organization that practices invidious discrimination gives rise to perceptions that the judge's impartiality is impaired. Section 2C refers to the current practices of the organization. Whether an organization practices invidious discrimination is often a complex question to which judges should be sensitive. The answer cannot be determined from a mere examination of an organization's current membership rolls but rather depends on how the organization selects members and other relevant factors, such as that the organization is dedicated to the preservation of religious, ethnic or cultural values of legitimate common interest to its members, or that it is in fact and effect an intimate, purely private organization whose membership limitations could not be constitutionally prohibited. Absent such factors, an organization is generally said to discriminate invidiously if it arbitrarily excludes from membership on the basis of race, religion, sex or national origin persons who would otherwise be admitted to membership. *See New York State Club Ass'n. Inc. v. City of New York,* 108 S.Ct. 2225, 101 L.Ed.2d 1 (1988); *Board of Directors of Rotary International v. Rotary Club of Duarte,* 481 U.S. 537, 107 S.Ct. 1940 (1987), 95 L.Ed.2d 474; *Roberts v. United States Jaycees,* 468 U.S. 609, 104 S.Ct. 3244, 82 L.Ed.2d 462 (1984).

[2]   Although Section 2C relates only to membership in organizations that invidiously discriminate on the basis of race, sex, religion or national origin, a judge's membership in an organization that engages in any discriminatory membership practices prohibited by the law of the jurisdiction also violates Canon 2 and Section 2A and gives the appearance of impropriety. In addition, it would be a violation of Canon 2 and Section 2A for a judge to arrange a meeting at a club that the judge knows practices invidious discrimination on the basis of race, sex, religion or national origin in its membership or other policies, or for the judge to regularly use such a club. Moreover, public manifestation by a judge of the judge's knowing approval of invidious

discrimination on any basis gives the appearance of impropriety under Canon 2 and diminishes public confidence in the integrity and impartiality of the judiciary, in violation of Section 2A.

[3]   When a person who is a judge on the date this Code becomes effective [in the jurisdiction in which the person is a judge]² learns that an organization to which the judge belongs engages in invidious discrimination that would preclude membership under Section 2C or under Canon 2 and Section 2A, the judge is permitted, in lieu of resigning, to make immediate efforts to have the organization discontinue its invidiously discriminatory practices, but is required to suspend participation in any other activities of the organization.   If the organization fails to discontinue its invidiously discriminatory practices as promptly as possible (and in all events within a year of the judge's first learning of the practices), the judge is required to resign immediately from the organization.

CANON 3

A Judge Shall Perform the Duties of Judicial Office Impartially and Diligently

A.   JUDICIAL DUTIES IN GENERAL.   The judicial duties of a judge take precedence over all the judge's other activities.   The judge's judicial duties include all the duties of the judge's office prescribed by law *.   In the performance of these duties, the following standards apply.

B.   ADJUDICATIVE RESPONSIBILITIES.

(1) A judge shall hear and decide matters assigned to the judge except those in which disqualification is required.

(2) A judge shall be faithful to the law * and maintain professional competence in it.   A judge shall not be swayed by partisan interests, public clamor or fear of criticism.

(3) A judge shall require * order and decorum in proceedings before the judge.

(4) A judge shall be patient, dignified and courteous to litigants, jurors, witnesses, lawyers and others with whom the judge deals in an official capacity, and shall require * similar conduct of lawyers, and of staff, court officials and others subject to the judge's direction and control.

Commentary:

[1]   The duty to hear all proceedings fairly and with patience is not inconsistent with the duty to dispose promptly of the business of the court. Judges can be efficient and businesslike while being patient and deliberate.

(5) A judge shall perform judicial duties without bias or prejudice.   A judge shall not, in the performance of judicial duties, by words or conduct manifest bias or prejudice, including but not limited to bias or prejudice based upon race, sex, religion, national origin, disability, age,

---

2.   The language within the brackets should be deleted when the jurisdiction adopts this provision.

* See, Terminology.

sexual orientation or socioeconomic status, and shall not permit staff, court officials and others subject to the judge's direction and control to do so.

Commentary:

[1]   A judge must refrain from speech, gestures or other conduct that could reasonably be perceived as sexual harassment and must require the same standard of conduct of others subject to the judge's direction and control.

[2]   A judge must perform judicial duties impartially and fairly. A judge who manifests bias on any basis in a proceeding impairs the fairness of the proceeding and brings the judiciary into disrepute. Facial expression and body language, in addition to oral communication, can give to parties or lawyers in the proceeding, jurors, the media and others an appearance of judicial bias. A judge must be alert to avoid behavior that may be perceived as prejudicial.

   (6) A judge shall require * lawyers in proceedings before the judge to refrain from manifesting, by words or conduct, bias or prejudice based upon race, sex, religion, national origin, disability, age, sexual orientation or socioeconomic status, against parties, witnesses, counsel or others.   This Section 3B(6) does not preclude legitimate advocacy when race, sex, religion, national origin, disability, age, sexual orientation or socioeconomic status, or other similar factors, are issues in the proceeding.

   (7) A judge shall accord to every person who has a legal interest in a proceeding, or that person's lawyer, the right to be heard according to law*. A judge shall not initiate, permit, or consider ex parte communications, or consider other communications made to the judge outside the presence of the parties concerning a pending or impending proceeding except that:

   (a) Where circumstances require, ex parte communications for scheduling, administrative purposes or emergencies that do not deal with substantive matters or issues on the merits are authorized; provided:

      (i) the judge reasonably believes that no party will gain a procedural or tactical advantage as a result of the ex parte communication, and

      (ii) the judge makes provision promptly to notify all other parties of the substance of the ex parte communication and allows an opportunity to respond.

   (b) A judge may obtain the advice of a disinterested expert on the law * applicable to a proceeding before the judge if the judge gives notice to the parties of the person consulted and the substance of the advice, and affords the parties reasonable opportunity to respond.

   (c) A judge may consult with court personnel * whose function is to aid the judge in carrying out the judge's adjudicative responsibilities or with other judges.

* See, Terminology.

(d) A judge may, with the consent of the parties, confer separately with the parties and their lawyers in an effort to mediate or settle matters pending before the judge.

(e) A judge may initiate or consider any ex parte communications when expressly authorized by law * to do so.

Commentary:

[1] The proscription against communications concerning a proceeding includes communications from lawyers, law teachers, and other persons who are not participants in the proceeding, except to the limited extent permitted.

[2] To the extent reasonably possible, all parties or their lawyers shall be included in communications with a judge.

[3] Whenever presence of a party or notice to a party is required by Section 3B(7), it is the party's lawyer, or if the party is unrepresented the party, who is to be present or to whom notice is to be given.

[4] An appropriate and often desirable procedure for a court to obtain the advice of a disinterested expert on legal issues is to invite the expert to file a brief *amicus curiae.*

[5] Certain ex parte communication is approved by Section 3B(7) to facilitate scheduling and other administrative purposes and to accommodate emergencies. In general, however, a judge must discourage ex parte communication and allow it only if all the criteria stated in Section 3B(7) are clearly met. A judge must disclose to all parties all ex parte communications described in Sections 3B(7)(a) and 3B(7)(b) regarding a proceeding pending or impending before the judge.

[6] A judge must not independently investigate facts in a case and must consider only the evidence presented.

[7] A judge may request a party to submit proposed findings of fact and conclusions of law, so long as the other parties are apprised of the request and are given an opportunity to respond to the proposed findings and conclusions.

[8] A judge must make reasonable efforts, including the provision of appropriate supervision, to ensure that Section 3B(7) is not violated through law clerks or other personnel on the judge's staff.

[9] If communication between the trial judge and the appellate court with respect to a proceeding is permitted, a copy of any written communication or the substance of any oral communication should be provided to all parties.

(8) A judge shall dispose of all judicial matters promptly, efficiently and fairly.

Commentary:

[1] In disposing of matters promptly, efficiently and fairly, a judge must demonstrate due regard for the rights of the parties to be heard and to have issues resolved without unnecessary cost or delay. Containing costs while preserving fundamental rights of parties also protects the interests of witnesses and the general public. A judge should monitor and supervise cases so as to reduce or eliminate dilatory practices, avoidable delays and unnecessary costs. A judge should encourage and seek

* See, Terminology.

to facilitate settlement, but parties should not feel coerced into surrendering the right to have their controversy resolved by the courts.

[2]   Prompt disposition of the court's business requires a judge to devote adequate time to judicial duties, to be punctual in attending court and expeditious in determining matters under submission, and to insist that court officials, litigants and their lawyers cooperate with the judge to that end.

(9) A judge shall not, while a proceeding is pending or impending in any court, make any public comment that might reasonably be expected to affect its outcome or impair its fairness or make any nonpublic comment that might substantially interfere with a fair trial or hearing. The judge shall require * similar abstention on the part of court personnel * subject to the judge's direction and control. This Section does not prohibit judges from making public statements in the course of their official duties or from explaining for public information the procedures of the court. This Section does not apply to proceedings in which the judge is a litigant in a personal capacity.

Commentary:

[1]   The requirement that judges abstain from public comment regarding a pending or impending proceeding continues during any appellate process and until final disposition. This Section does not prohibit a judge from commenting on proceedings in which the judge is a litigant in a personal capacity, but in cases such as a writ of mandamus where the judge is a litigant in an official capacity, the judge must not comment publicly. The conduct of lawyers relating to trial publicity is governed by [Rule 3.6 of the ABA Model Rules of Professional Conduct]. (Each jurisdiction should substitute an appropriate reference to its rule.)

(10) A judge shall not commend or criticize jurors for their verdict other than in a court order or opinion in a proceeding, but may express appreciation to jurors for their service to the judicial system and the community.

Commentary:

[1]   Commending or criticizing jurors for their verdict may imply a judicial expectation in future cases and may impair a juror's ability to be fair and impartial in a subsequent case.

(11) A judge shall not disclose or use, for any purpose unrelated to judicial duties, nonpublic information * acquired in a judicial capacity.

C. ADMINISTRATIVE RESPONSIBILITIES.

(1) A judge shall diligently discharge the judge's administrative responsibilities without bias or prejudice and maintain professional competence in judicial administration, and should cooperate with other judges and court officials in the administration of court business.

(2) A judge shall require * staff, court officials and others subject to the judge's direction and control to observe the standards of fidelity and diligence that apply to the judge and to refrain from manifesting bias or prejudice in the performance of their official duties.

* See, Terminology.

(3) A judge with supervisory authority for the judicial performance of other judges shall take reasonable measures to assure the prompt disposition of matters before them and the proper performance of their other judicial responsibilities.

(4) A judge shall not make unnecessary appointments. A judge shall exercise the power of appointment impartially and on the basis of merit. A judge shall avoid nepotism and favoritism. A judge shall not approve compensation of appointees beyond the fair value of services rendered.

Commentary:

[1] Appointees of a judge include assigned counsel, officials such as referees, commissioners, special masters, receivers and guardians and personnel such as clerks, secretaries and bailiffs. Consent by the parties to an appointment or an award of compensation does not relieve the judge of the obligation prescribed by Section 3C(4).

(5) A judge shall not appoint a lawyer to a position if the judge either knows that the lawyer has contributed more than [\$] within the prior [   ] years to the judge's election campaign,[3] or learns of such a contribution by means of a timely motion by a party or other person properly interested in the matter, unless

(a) the position is substantially uncompensated;

(b) the lawyer has been selected in rotation from a list of qualified and available lawyers compiled without regard to their having made political contributions; or

(c) the judge or another presiding or administrative judge affirmatively finds that no other lawyer is willing, competent and able to accept the position.

D. DISCIPLINARY RESPONSIBILITIES.

(1) A judge who receives information indicating a substantial likelihood that another judge has committed a violation of this Code should take appropriate action. A judge having knowledge * that another judge has committed a violation of this Code that raises a substantial question as to the other judge's fitness for office shall inform the appropriate authority *.

(2) A judge who receives information indicating a substantial likelihood that a lawyer has committed a violation of the Rules of Professional Conduct [substitute correct title if the applicable rules of lawyer conduct have a different title] should take appropriate action. A judge having knowledge * that a lawyer has committed a violation of the Rules of Professional Conduct [substitute correct title if the applicable rules of lawyer conduct have a different title] that raises a substantial question as to the lawyer's honesty, trustworthiness or fitness as a lawyer in other respects shall inform the appropriate authority *.

(3) Acts of a judge, in the discharge of disciplinary responsibilities, required or permitted by Sections 3D(1) and 3D(2) are part of a judge's

---

3. This provision is meant to be applicable wherever judges are subject to public election; specific amount and time limitations, to be determined based on circumstances within the jurisdiction, should be inserted in the brackets.

* See, Terminology.

judicial duties and shall be absolutely privileged, and no civil action predicated thereon may be instituted against the judge.

Commentary:

[1]   Appropriate action may include direct communication with the judge or lawyer who has committed the violation, other direct action if available, and reporting the violation to the appropriate authority or other agency or body.

E.   DISQUALIFICATION.

(1) A judge shall disqualify himself or herself in a proceeding in which the judge's impartiality might reasonably be questioned, including but not limited to instances where:

Commentary:

[1]   Under this rule, a judge is disqualified whenever the judge's impartiality might reasonably be questioned, regardless whether any of the specific rules in Section 3E(1) apply.   For example, if a judge were in the process of negotiating for employment with a law firm, the judge would be disqualified from any matters in which that law firm appeared, unless the disqualification was waived by the parties after disclosure by the judge.

[2]   A judge should disclose on the record information that the judge believes the parties or their lawyers might consider relevant to the question of disqualification, even if the judge believes there is no real basis for disqualification.

[3]   By decisional law, the rule of necessity may override the rule of disqualification.   For example, a judge might be required to participate in judicial review of a judicial salary statute, or might be the only judge available in a matter requiring immediate judicial action, such as a hearing on probable cause or a temporary restraining order.   In the latter case, the judge must disclose on the record the basis for possible disqualification and use reasonable efforts to transfer the matter to another judge as soon as practicable.

(a)   the judge has a personal bias or prejudice concerning a party or a party's lawyer, or personal knowledge * of disputed evidentiary facts concerning the proceeding;

(b)   the judge served as a lawyer in the matter in controversy, or a lawyer with whom the judge previously practiced law served during such association as a lawyer concerning the matter, or the judge has been a material witness concerning it;

Commentary:

[1]   A lawyer in a government agency does not ordinarily have an association with other lawyers employed by that agency within the meaning of Section 3E(1)(b); a judge formerly employed by a government agency, however, should disqualify himself or herself in a proceeding if the judge's impartiality might reasonably be questioned because of such association.

(c)   the judge knows * that he or she, individually or as a fiduciary, or the judge's spouse, parent or child wherever residing, or any other member of the judge's family residing in the judge's household *, has an

* See, Terminology.

economic interest * in the subject matter in controversy or in a party to the proceeding or has any other more than de minimis * interest that could be substantially affected by the proceeding;

(d) the judge or the judge's spouse, or a person within the third degree of relationship * to either of them, or the spouse of such a person:

(i) is a party to the proceeding, or an officer, director or trustee of a party;

(ii) is acting as a lawyer in the proceeding;

(iii) is known * by the judge to have a more than de minimis * interest that could be substantially affected by the proceeding;

(iv) is to the judge's knowledge * likely to be a material witness in the proceeding.

(e) the judge knows or learns by means of a timely motion that a party or a party's lawyer has within the previous [   ] year[s] made aggregate* contributions to the judge's campaign in an amount that is greater than [[[$] for an individual or [$] for an entity]] [[is reasonable and appropriate for an individual or an entity]].[4]

Commentary:

The fact that a lawyer in a proceeding is affiliated with a law firm with which a relative of the judge is affiliated does not of itself disqualify the judge. Under appropriate circumstances, the fact that "the judge's impartiality might reasonably be questioned" under Section 3E(1), or that the relative is known by the judge to have an interest in the law firm that could be "substantially affected by the outcome of the proceeding" under Section 3E(1)(d)(iii) may require the judge's disqualification.

(2) A judge shall keep informed about the judge's personal and fiduciary * economic interests *, and make a reasonable effort to keep informed about the personal economic interests of the judge's spouse and minor children residing in the judge's household.

F. REMITTAL OF DISQUALIFICATION. A judge disqualified by the terms of Section 3E may disclose on the record the basis of the judge's disqualification and may ask the parties and their lawyers to consider, out of the presence of the judge, whether to waive disqualification. If following disclosure of any basis for disqualification other than personal bias or prejudice concerning a party, the parties and lawyers, without participation by the judge, all agree that the judge should not be disqualified, and the judge is then willing to participate, the judge may participate in the proceeding. The agreement shall be incorporated in the record of the proceeding.

Commentary:

A remittal procedure provides the parties an opportunity to proceed without delay if they wish to waive the disqualification. To assure that consideration of the question

---

4. This provision is meant to be applicable wherever judges are subject to public election. Jurisdictions that adopt specific dollar limits on contributions in section 5(C)(3) should adopt the same limits in section 3(E)(1)(e). Where specific dollar amounts determined by local circumstances are not used, the "reasonable and appropriate" language should be used.

* See, Terminology.

of remittal is made independently of the judge, a judge must not solicit, seek or hear comment on possible remittal or waiver of the disqualification unless the lawyers jointly propose remittal after consultation as provided in the rule. A party may act through counsel if counsel represents on the record that the party has been consulted and consents. As a practical matter, a judge may wish to have all parties and their lawyers sign the remittal agreement.

CANON 4

A Judge Shall So Conduct the Judge's Extra–Judicial Activities as to Minimize the Risk of Conflict With Judicial Obligations

A. EXTRA–JUDICIAL ACTIVITIES IN GENERAL. A judge shall conduct all of the judge's extra-judicial activities so that they do not:

(1) cast reasonable doubt on the judge's capacity to act impartially as a judge;

(2) demean the judicial office; or

(3) interfere with the proper performance of judicial duties.

Commentary:

[1] Complete separation of a judge from extra-judicial activities is neither possible nor wise; a judge should not become isolated from the community in which the judge lives.

[2] Expressions of bias or prejudice by a judge, even outside the judge's judicial activities, may cast reasonable doubt on the judge's capacity to act impartially as a judge. Expressions which may do so include jokes or other remarks demeaning individuals on the basis of their race, sex, religion, national origin, disability, age, sexual orientation or socioeconomic status. See Section 2C and accompanying Commentary.

B. AVOCATIONAL ACTIVITIES. A judge may speak, write, lecture, teach and participate in other extra-judicial activities concerning the law*, the legal system, the administration of justice and non-legal subjects, subject to the requirements of this Code.

Commentary:

[1] As a judicial officer and person specially learned in the law, a judge is in a unique position to contribute to the improvement of the law, the legal system, and the administration of justice, including revision of substantive and procedural law and improvement of criminal and juvenile justice. To the extent that time permits, a judge is encouraged to do so, either independently or through a bar association, judicial conference or other organization dedicated to the improvement of the law. Judges may participate in efforts to promote the fair administration of justice, the independence of the judiciary and the integrity of the legal profession and may express opposition to the persecution of lawyers and judges in other countries because of their professional activities.

[2] In this and other Sections of Canon 4, the phrase "subject to the requirements of this Code" is used, notably in connection with a judge's governmental, civic

* See, Terminology.

or charitable activities. This phrase is included to remind judges that the use of permissive language in various Sections of the Code does not relieve a judge from the other requirements of the Code that apply to the specific conduct.

C. GOVERNMENTAL, CIVIC OR CHARITABLE ACTIVITIES.

(1) A judge shall not appear at a public hearing before, or otherwise consult with, an executive or legislative body or official except on matters concerning the law*, the legal system or the administration of justice or except when acting pro se in a matter involving the judge or the judge's interests.

Commentary:

See Section 2B regarding the obligation to avoid improper influence.

(2) A judge shall not accept appointment to a governmental committee or commission or other governmental position that is concerned with issues of fact or policy on matters other than the improvement of the law*, the legal system or the administration of justice. A judge may, however, represent a country, state or locality on ceremonial occasions or in connection with historical, educational or cultural activities.

Commentary:

[1] Section 4C(2) prohibits a judge from accepting any governmental position except one relating to the law, legal system or administration of justice as authorized by Section 4C(3). The appropriateness of accepting extra-judicial assignments must be assessed in light of the demands on judicial resources created by crowded dockets and the need to protect the courts from involvement in extra-judicial matters that may prove to be controversial. Judges should not accept governmental appointments that are likely to interfere with the effectiveness and independence of the judiciary.

[2] Section 4C(2) does not govern a judge's service in a nongovernmental position. See Section 4C(3) permitting service by a judge with organizations devoted to the improvement of the law, the legal system or the administration of justice and with educational, religious, charitable, fraternal or civic organizations not conducted for profit. For example, service on the board of a public educational institution, unless it were a law school, would be prohibited under Section 4C(2), but service on the board of a public law school or any private educational institution would generally be permitted under Section 4C(3).

(3) A judge may serve as an officer, director, trustee or non-legal advisor of an organization or governmental agency devoted to the improvement of the law *, the legal system or the administration of justice or of an educational, religious, charitable, fraternal or civic organization not conducted for profit, subject to the following limitations and the other requirements of this Code.

Commentary:

[1] Section 4C(3) does not apply to a judge's service in a governmental position unconnected with the improvement of the law, the legal system or the administration of justice; see Section 4C(2).

* See, Terminology.

[2]   See Commentary to Section 4B regarding use of the phrase "subject to the following limitations and the other requirements of this Code." As an example of the meaning of the phrase, a judge permitted by Section 4C(3) to serve on the board of a fraternal institution may be prohibited from such service by Sections 2C or 4A if the institution practices invidious discrimination or if service on the board otherwise casts reasonable doubt on the judge's capacity to act impartially as a judge.

[3]   Service by a judge on behalf of a civic or charitable organization may be governed by other provisions of Canon 4 in addition to Section 4C. For example, a judge is prohibited by Section 4G from serving as a legal advisor to a civic or charitable organization.

(a) A judge shall not serve as an officer, director, trustee or non-legal advisor if it is likely that the organization

(i) will be engaged in proceedings that would ordinarily come before the judge, or

(ii) will be engaged frequently in adversary proceedings in the court of which the judge is a member or in any court subject to the appellate jurisdiction of the court of which the judge is a member.

Commentary:

[1]   The changing nature of some organizations and of their relationship to the law makes it necessary for a judge regularly to reexamine the activities of each organization with which the judge is affiliated to determine if it is proper for the judge to continue the affiliation. For example, in many jurisdictions charitable hospitals are now more frequently in court than in the past. Similarly, the boards of some legal aid organizations now make policy decisions that may have political significance or imply commitment to causes that may come before the courts for adjudication.

(b) A judge as an officer, director, trustee or non-legal advisor, or as a member or otherwise:

(i) may assist such an organization in planning fund-raising and may participate in the management and investment of the organization's funds, but shall not personally participate in the solicitation of funds or other fund-raising activities, except that a judge may solicit funds from other judges over whom the judge does not exercise supervisory or appellate authority;

(ii) may make recommendations to public and private fund-granting organizations on projects and programs concerning the law *, the legal system or the administration of justice;

(iii) shall not personally participate in membership solicitation if the solicitation might reasonably be perceived as coercive or, except as permitted in Section 4C(3)(b)(i), if the membership solicitation is essentially a fund-raising mechanism;

(iv) shall not use or permit the use of the prestige of judicial office for fund-raising or membership solicitation.

* See, Terminology.

Commentary:

[1]   A judge may solicit membership or endorse or encourage membership efforts for an organization devoted to the improvement of the law, the legal system or the administration of justice or a nonprofit educational, religious, charitable, fraternal or civic organization as long as the solicitation cannot reasonably be perceived as coercive and is not essentially a fund-raising mechanism.   Solicitation of funds for an organization and solicitation of memberships similarly involve the danger that the person solicited will feel obligated to respond favorably to the solicitor if the solicitor is in a position of influence or control.   A judge must not engage in direct, individual solicitation of funds or memberships in person, in writing or by telephone except in the following cases: 1) a judge may solicit for funds or memberships other judges over whom the judge does not exercise supervisory or appellate authority, 2) a judge may solicit other persons for membership in the organizations described above if neither those persons nor persons with whom they are affiliated are likely ever to appear before the court on which the judge serves and 3) a judge who is an officer of such an organization may send a general membership solicitation mailing over the judge's signature.

[2]   Use of an organization letterhead for fund-raising or membership solicitation does not violate Section 4C(3)(b) provided the letterhead lists only the judge's name and office or other position in the organization, and, if comparable designations are listed for other persons, the judge's judicial designation.   In addition, a judge must also make reasonable efforts to ensure that the judge's staff, court officials and others subject to the judge's direction and control do not solicit funds on the judge's behalf for any purpose, charitable or otherwise.

[3]   A judge must not be a speaker or guest of honor at an organization's fund-raising event, but mere attendance at such an event is permissible if otherwise consistent with this Code.

D.   FINANCIAL ACTIVITIES.

(1)   **A judge shall not engage in financial and business dealings that:**

(a)   **may reasonably be perceived to exploit the judge's judicial position, or**

(b)   **involve the judge in frequent transactions or continuing business relationships with those lawyers or other persons likely to come before the court on which the judge serves.**

Commentary:

[1]   The Time for Compliance provision of this Code (Application, Section F) postpones the time for compliance with certain provisions of this Section in some cases.

[2]   When a judge acquires in a judicial capacity information, such as material contained in filings with the court, that is not yet generally known, the judge must not use the information for private gain.   See Section 2B; see also Section 3B(11).

[3]   A judge must avoid financial and business dealings that involve the judge in frequent transactions or continuing business relationships with persons likely to come either before the judge personally or before other judges on the judge's court.   In addition, a judge should discourage members of the judge's family from engaging in dealings that would reasonably appear to exploit the judge's judicial position.   This rule is necessary to avoid creating an appearance of exploitation of office or favoritism

and to minimize the potential for disqualification. With respect to affiliation of relatives of judge with law firms appearing before the judge, see Commentary to Section 3E(1) relating to disqualification.

[4] Participation by a judge in financial and business dealings is subject to the general prohibitions in Section 4A against activities that tend to reflect adversely on impartiality, demean the judicial office, or interfere with the proper performance of judicial duties. Such participation is also subject to the general prohibition in Canon 2 against activities involving impropriety or the appearance of impropriety and the prohibition in Section 2B against the misuse of the prestige of judicial office. In addition, a judge must maintain high standards of conduct in all of the judge's activities, as set forth in Canon 1. See Commentary for Section 4B regarding use of the phrase "subject to the requirements of this Code."

(2) A judge may, subject to the requirements of this Code, hold and manage investments of the judge and members of the judge's family *, including real estate, and engage in other remunerative activity.

Commentary:

[1] This Section provides that, subject to the requirements of this Code, a judge may hold and manage investments owned solely by the judge, investments owned solely by a member or members of the judge's family, and investments owned jointly by the judge and members of the judge's family.

(3) A judge shall not serve as an officer, director, manager, general partner, advisor or employee of any business entity except that a judge may, subject to the requirements of this Code, manage and participate in:

(a) a business closely held by the judge or members of the judge's family *, or

(b) a business entity primarily engaged in investment of the financial resources of the judge or members of the judge's family.

Commentary:

[1] Subject to the requirements of this Code, a judge may participate in a business that is closely held either by the judge alone, by members of the judge's family, or by the judge and members of the judge's family.

[2] Although participation by a judge in a closely-held family business might otherwise be permitted by Section 4D(3), a judge may be prohibited from participation by other provisions of this Code when, for example, the business entity frequently appears before the judge's court or the participation requires significant time away from judicial duties. Similarly, a judge must avoid participating in a closely-held family business if the judge's participation would involve misuse of the prestige of judicial office.

(4) A judge shall manage the judge's investments and other financial interests to minimize the number of cases in which the judge is disqualified. As soon as the judge can do so without serious financial detriment, the judge shall divest himself or herself of investments and other financial interests that might require frequent disqualification.

* See, Terminology.

638

(5) A judge shall not accept, and shall urge members of the judge's family residing in the judge's household* not to accept, a gift, bequest, favor or loan from anyone except for:

Commentary:

[1] Section 4D(5) does not apply to contributions to a judge's campaign for judicial office, a matter governed by Canon 5.

[2] Because a gift, bequest, favor or loan to a member of the judge's family residing in the judge's household might be viewed as intended to influence the judge, a judge must inform those family members of the relevant ethical constraints upon the judge in this regard and discourage those family members from violating them. A judge cannot, however, reasonably be expected to know or control all of the financial or business activities of all family members residing in the judge's household.

(a) a gift incident to a public testimonial, books, tapes and other resource materials supplied by publishers on a complimentary basis for official use, or an invitation to the judge and the judge's spouse or guest to attend a bar-related function or an activity devoted to the improvement of the law*, the legal system or the administration of justice;

Commentary:

[1] Acceptance of an invitation to a law-related function is governed by Section 4D(5)(a); acceptance of an invitation paid for by an individual lawyer or group of lawyers is governed by Section 4D(5)(h).

[2] A judge may accept a public testimonial or a gift incident thereto only if the donor organization is not an organization whose members comprise or frequently represent the same side in litigation, and the testimonial and gift are otherwise in compliance with other provisions of this Code. See Sections 4A(1) and 2B.

(b) a gift, award or benefit incident to the business, profession or other separate activity of a spouse or other family member of a judge residing in the judge's household, including gifts, awards and benefits for the use of both the spouse or other family member and the judge (as spouse or family member), provided the gift, award or benefit could not reasonably be perceived as intended to influence the judge in the performance of judicial duties;

(c) ordinary social hospitality;

(d) a gift from a relative or friend, for a special occasion, such as a wedding, anniversary or birthday, if the gift is fairly commensurate with the occasion and the relationship;

Commentary:

[1] A gift to a judge, or to a member of the judge's family living in the judge's household, that is excessive in value raises questions about the judge's impartiality and the integrity of the judicial office and might require disqualification of the judge where disqualification would not otherwise be required. See, however, Section 4D(5)(e).

* See, Terminology.

(e) a gift, bequest, favor or loan from a relative or close personal friend whose appearance or interest in a case would in any event require disqualification under Section 3E;

(f) a loan from a lending institution in its regular course of business on the same terms generally available to persons who are not judges;

(g) a scholarship or fellowship awarded on the same terms and based on the same criteria applied to other applicants; or

(h) any other gift, bequest, favor or loan, only if: the donor is not a party or other person who has come or is likely to come or whose interests have come or are likely to come before the judge; and, if its value exceeds $150.00, the judge reports it in the same manner as the judge reports compensation in Section 4H.

Commentary:

[1] Section 4D(5)(h) prohibits judges from accepting gifts, favors, bequests or loans from lawyers or their firms if they have come or are likely to come before the judge; it also prohibits gifts, favors, bequests or loans from clients of lawyers or their firms when the clients' interests have come or are likely to come before the judge.

E. FIDUCIARY ACTIVITIES.

(1) A judge shall not serve as executor, administrator or other personal representative, trustee, guardian, attorney in fact or other fiduciary *, except for the estate, trust or person of a member of the judge's family *, and then only if such service will not interfere with the proper performance of judicial duties.

(2) A judge shall not serve as a fiduciary * if it is likely that the judge as a fiduciary will be engaged in proceedings that would ordinarily come before the judge, or if the estate, trust or ward becomes involved in adversary proceedings in the court on which the judge serves or one under its appellate jurisdiction.

(3) The same restrictions on financial activities that apply to a judge personally also apply to the judge while acting in a fiduciary* capacity.

Commentary:

[1] The Time for Compliance provision of this Code (Application, Section F) postpones the time for compliance with certain provisions of this Section in some cases.

[2] The restrictions imposed by this Canon may conflict with the judge's obligation as a fiduciary. For example, a judge should resign as trustee if detriment to the trust would result from divestiture of holdings the retention of which would place the judge in violation of Section 4D(4).

F. SERVICE AS ARBITRATOR OR MEDIATOR. A judge shall not act as an arbitrator or mediator or otherwise perform judicial functions in a private capacity unless expressly authorized by law *.

* See, Terminology.

Commentary:

Section 4F does not prohibit a judge from participating in arbitration, mediation or settlement conferences performed as part of judicial duties.

G. PRACTICE OF LAW. A judge shall not practice law. Notwithstanding this prohibition, a judge may act pro se and may, without compensation, give legal advice to and draft or review documents for a member of the judge's family *.

Commentary:

[1] This prohibition refers to the practice of law in a representative capacity and not in a pro se capacity. A judge may act for himself or herself in all legal matters, including matters involving litigation and matters involving appearances before or other dealings with legislative and other governmental bodies. However, in so doing, a judge must not abuse the prestige of office to advance the interests of the judge or the judge's family. See Section 2(B).

[2] The Code allows a judge to give legal advice to and draft legal documents for members of the judge's family, so long as the judge receives no compensation. A judge must not, however, act as an advocate or negotiator for a member of the judge's family in a legal matter.

Canon 6, new in the 1972 Code, reflected concerns about conflicts of interest and appearances of impropriety arising from compensation for off-the-bench activities. Since 1972, however, reporting requirements that are much more comprehensive with respect to what must be reported and with whom reports must be filed have been adopted by many jurisdictions. The Committee believes that although reports of compensation for extra-judicial activities should be required, reporting requirements preferably should be developed to suit the respective jurisdictions, not simply adopted as set forth in a national model code of judicial conduct. Because of the Committee's concern that deletion of this Canon might lead to the misconception that reporting compensation for extra-judicial activities is no longer important, the substance of Canon 6 is carried forward as Section 4H in this Code for adoption in those jurisdictions that do not have other reporting requirements. In jurisdictions that have separately established reporting requirements, Section 4H(2) (Public Reporting) may be deleted and the caption for Section 4H modified appropriately.

* * *

H. COMPENSATION, REIMBURSEMENT AND REPORTING.

(1) COMPENSATION AND REIMBURSEMENT. A judge may receive compensation and reimbursement of expenses for the extra-judicial activities permitted by this Code, if the source of such payments does not give the appearance of influencing the judge's performance of judicial duties or otherwise give the appearance of impropriety.

(a) Compensation shall not exceed a reasonable amount nor shall it exceed what a person who is not a judge would receive for the same activity.

* See, Terminology.

(b) **Expense reimbursement shall be limited to the actual cost of travel, food and lodging reasonably incurred by the judge and, where appropriate to the occasion, by the judge's spouse or guest. Any payment in excess of such an amount is compensation.**

(2) **PUBLIC REPORTS. A judge shall report the date, place and nature of any activity for which the judge received compensation, and the name of the payor and the amount of compensation so received. Compensation or income of a spouse attributed to the judge by operation of a community property law is not extra-judicial compensation to the judge. The judge's report shall be made at least annually and shall be filed as a public document in the office of the clerk of the court on which the judge serves or other office designated by law *.**

Commentary:

[1]   See Section 4D(5) regarding reporting of gifts, bequests and loans.

[2]   The Code does not prohibit a judge from accepting honoraria or speaking fees provided that the compensation is reasonable and commensurate with the task performed. A judge should ensure, however, that no conflicts are created by the arrangement. A judge must not appear to trade on the judicial position for personal advantage. Nor should a judge spend significant time away from court duties to meet speaking or writing commitments for compensation. In addition, the source of the payment must not raise any question of undue influence or the judge's ability or willingness to be impartial.

I.   Disclosure of a judge's income, debts, investments or other assets is required only to the extent provided in this Canon and in Sections 3E and 3F, or as otherwise required by law *.

Commentary:

[1]   Section 3E requires a judge to disqualify himself or herself in any proceeding in which the judge has an economic interest. See "economic interest" as explained in the Terminology Section. Section 4D requires a judge to refrain from engaging in business and from financial activities that might interfere with the impartial performance of judicial duties; Section 4H requires a judge to report all compensation the judge received for activities outside judicial office. A judge has the rights of any other citizen, including the right to privacy of the judge's financial affairs, except to the extent that limitations established by law are required to safeguard the proper performance of the judge's duties.

CANON 5 [5]

A Judge or Judicial Candidate Shall Refrain From Inappropriate Political Activity

A.   ALL JUDGES AND CANDIDATES.

(1) **Except as authorized in Sections 5B(2), 5C(1) and 5C(3), a judge or a candidate * for election or appointment to judicial office shall not:**

---

* See, Terminology.

5.   Introductory Note to Canon 5: There is wide variation in the methods of judicial selection used, both among jurisdictions and within the jurisdictions themselves. In a given state, judges may be selected by one method initially, retained by a different method, and selected by still another method to fill interim vacancies.

According to figures compiled in 1987 by the National Center for State Courts, 32 states and

(a) act as a leader or hold an office in a political organization *;

(b) publicly endorse or publicly oppose another candidate for public office;

(c) make speeches on behalf of a political organization;

(d) attend political gatherings; or

(e) solicit funds for, pay an assessment to or make a contribution to a political organization or candidate, or purchase tickets for political party dinners or other functions.

Commentary:

[1]   A judge or candidate for judicial office retains the right to participate in the political process as a voter.

[2]   Where false information concerning a judicial candidate is made public, a judge or another judicial candidate having knowledge of the facts is not prohibited by Section 5A(1) from making the facts public.

[3]   Section 5A(1)(a) does not prohibit a candidate for elective judicial office from retaining during candidacy a public office such as county prosecutor, which is not "an office in a political organization."

[4]   Section 5A(1)(b) does not prohibit a judge or judicial candidate from privately expressing his or her views on judicial candidates or other candidates for public office.

[5]   A candidate does not publicly endorse another candidate for public office by having that candidate's name on the same ticket.

(2) A judge shall resign from judicial office upon becoming a candidate * for a non-judicial office either in a primary or in a general election, except that the judge may continue to hold judicial office while being a candidate for election to or serving as a delegate in a state constitutional convention if the judge is otherwise permitted by law* to do so.

(3) A candidate * for a judicial office:

(a) shall maintain the dignity appropriate to judicial office and act in a manner consistent with the integrity and independence of

the District of Columbia use a merit selection method (in which an executive such as a governor appoints a judge from a group of nominees selected by a judicial nominating commission) to select judges in the state either initially or to fill an interim vacancy. Of those 33 jurisdictions, a merit selection method is used in 18 jurisdictions to choose judges of courts of last resort, in 13 jurisdictions to choose judges of intermediate appellate courts, in 12 jurisdictions to choose judges of general jurisdiction courts and in 5 jurisdictions to choose judges of limited jurisdiction courts.

Methods of judicial selection other than merit selection include nonpartisan election (10 states use it for initial selection at all court levels, another 10 states use it for initial selection for at least one court level) and partisan election (8 states use it for initial selection at all court levels, another 7 states use it for initial selection for at least one level). In a small minority of the states, judicial selection methods include executive or legislative appointment (without nomination of a group of potential appointees by a judicial nominating commission) and court selection. In addition, the federal judicial system utilizes an executive appointment method. See State Court Organization 1987 (National Center for State Courts, 1988).

* See, Terminology.

the judiciary, and shall encourage members of the candidate's family
* to adhere to the same standards of political conduct in support of
the candidate as apply to the candidate;

Commentary:

[1]   Although a judicial candidate must encourage members of his or her family to adhere to the same standards of political conduct in support of the candidate that apply to the candidate, family members are free to participate in other political activity.

(b) shall prohibit employees and officials who serve at the pleasure of the candidate *, and shall discourage other employees and officials subject to the candidate's direction and control from doing on the candidate's behalf what the candidate is prohibited from doing under the Sections of this Canon;

(c) except to the extent permitted by Section 5C(2), shall not authorize or knowingly * permit any other person to do for the candidate * what the candidate is prohibited from doing under the Sections of this Canon;

(d) shall not:

(i) make pledges or promises of conduct in office other than the faithful and impartial performance of the duties of the office;

(ii) make statements that commit or appear to commit the candidate with respect to cases, controversies or issues that are likely to come before the court; or

(iii) knowingly * misrepresent the identity, qualifications, present position or other fact concerning the candidate or an opponent;

Commentary:

[1]   Section 5A(3)(d) prohibits a candidate for judicial office from making statements that appear to commit the candidate regarding cases, controversies or issues likely to come before the court. As a corollary, a candidate should emphasize in any public statement the candidate's duty to uphold the law regardless of his or her personal views. See also Section 3B(9), the general rule on public comment by judges. Section 5A(3)(d) does not prohibit a candidate from making pledges or promises respecting improvements in court administration. Nor does this Section prohibit an incumbent judge from making private statements to other judges or court personnel in the performance of judicial duties. This Section applies to any statement made in the process of securing judicial office, such as statements to commissions charged with judicial selection and tenure and legislative bodies confirming appointment. See also Rule 8.2 of the ABA Model Rules of Professional Conduct.

(e) may respond to personal attacks or attacks on the candidate's record as long as the response does not violate Section 5A(3)(d).

B. CANDIDATES SEEKING APPOINTMENT TO JUDICIAL OR OTHER GOVERNMENTAL OFFICE.

(1) A candidate * for appointment to judicial office or a judge seeking other governmental office shall not solicit or accept funds, personally or through a committee or otherwise, to support his or her candidacy.

* See, Terminology.

(2) A candidate * for appointment to judicial office or a judge seeking other governmental office shall not engage in any political activity to secure the appointment except that:

(a) such persons may:

(i) communicate with the appointing authority, including any selection or nominating commission or other agency designated to screen candidates;

(ii) seek support or endorsement for the appointment from organizations that regularly make recommendations for reappointment or appointment to the office, and from individuals to the extent requested or required by those specified in Section 5B(2)(a); and

(iii) provide to those specified in Sections 5B(2)(a)(i) and 5B(2)(a)(ii) information as to his or her qualifications for the office;

(b) a non-judge candidate * for appointment to judicial office may, in addition, unless otherwise prohibited by law *:

(i) retain an office in a political organization *,

(ii) attend political gatherings, and

(iii) continue to pay ordinary assessments and ordinary contributions to a political organization or candidate and purchase tickets for political party dinners or other functions.

Commentary:

[1] Section 5B(2) provides a limited exception to the restrictions imposed by Sections 5A(1) and 5D. Under Section 5B(2), candidates seeking reappointment to the same judicial office or appointment to another judicial office or other governmental office may apply for the appointment and seek appropriate support.

[2] Although under Section 5B(2) nonjudge candidates seeking appointment to judicial office are permitted during candidacy to retain office in a political organization, attend political gatherings and pay ordinary dues and assessments, they remain subject to other provisions of this Code during candidacy. See Sections 5B(1), 5B(2)(a), 5E and Application Section.

C. **JUDGES AND CANDIDATES SUBJECT TO PUBLIC ELECTION.**

(1) A judge or a candidate * subject to public election * may, except as prohibited by law *:

(a) at any time

(i) purchase tickets for and attend political gatherings;

(ii) identify himself or herself as a member of a political party; and

(iii) contribute to a political organization *;

(b) when a candidate for election

(i) speak to gatherings on his or her own behalf;

* See, Terminology.

   (ii) appear in newspaper, television and other media advertisements supporting his or her candidacy;

   (iii) distribute pamphlets and other promotional campaign literature supporting his or her candidacy; and

   (iv) publicly endorse or publicly oppose other candidates for the same judicial office in a public election in which the judge or judicial candidate is running.

Commentary:

   [1]   Section 5C(1) permits judges subject to election at any time to be involved in limited political activity. Section 5D, applicable solely to incumbent judges, would otherwise bar this activity.

   (2) A candidate* shall not personally solicit or accept campaign contributions or personally solicit publicly stated support. A candidate may, however, establish committees of responsible persons to conduct campaigns for the candidate through media advertisements, brochures, mailings, candidate forums and other means not prohibited by law. Such committees may solicit and accept reasonable campaign contributions, manage the expenditure of funds for the candidate's campaign and obtain public statements of support for his or her candidacy. Such committees are not prohibited from soliciting and accepting reasonable campaign contributions and public support from lawyers. A candidate's committees may solicit contributions and public support for the candidate's campaign no earlier than [one year] before an election and no later than [90] days after the last election in which the candidate participates during the election year. A candidate shall not use or permit the use of campaign contributions for the private benefit of the candidate or others.

Commentary:

   [1]   There is legitimate concern about a judge's impartiality when parties whose interests may come before a judge, or the lawyer who represents such parties, are known to have made contributions to the election campaigns of judicial candidates. This is among the reasons that merit selection of judges is a preferable manner in which to select the judiciary. Notwithstanding that preference, Section 5(c)(2) recognizes that in many jurisdictions judicial candidates must raise funds to support their candidacies for election to judicial office. It therefore permits a candidate, other than a candidate for appointment, to establish campaign committees to solicit and accept public support and reasonable financial contributions. In order to guard against the possibility that conflicts of interest will arise, the candidate must instruct his or her campaign committees at the start of the campaign to solicit or accept only contributions that are reasonable and appropriate under the circumstances. Though not prohibited, campaign contributions of which a judge has knowledge, made by lawyers or others who appear before the judge, may, by virtue of their size or source, raise questions about a judge's impartiality and be cause for disqualification as provided under Section3E.

   [2]   Campaign committees established under Section 5C(2) should manage campaign finances responsibly, avoiding deficits that might necessitate post-election fundraising, to the extent possible.

   * See, Terminology.

[3]   Section 5C(2) does not prohibit a candidate from initiating an evaluation by a judicial selection commission or bar association, or, subject to the requirements of this Code, from responding to a request for information from any organization.

(3) A candidate shall instruct his or her campaign committee(s) at the start of the campaign not to accept campaign contributions for any election that exceed, in the aggregate*, [\$] from an individual or [\$] from an entity. This limitation is in addition to the limitations provided in Section 5C(2).[6]

(4) In addition to complying with all applicable statutory requirements for disclosure of campaign contributions, campaign committees established by a candidate shall file with [   ][7] a report stating the name, address, occupation and employer or each person who has made campaign contributions to the committee whose value in the aggregate* exceed [\$].[8] The report must be filed within [   ][9] days following the election.

(5) Except as prohibited by law *, a candidate * for judicial office in a public election * may permit the candidate's name: (a) to be listed on election materials along with the names of other candidates for elective public office, and (b) to appear in promotions of the ticket.

Commentary:

[1]   Section 5C(3) provides a limited exception to the restrictions imposed by Section 5A(1).

D. INCUMBENT JUDGES. A judge shall not engage in any political activity except (i) as authorized under any other Section of this Code, (ii) on behalf of measures to improve the law *, the legal system or the administration of justice, or (iii) as expressly authorized by law.

Commentary:

[1]   Neither Section 5D nor any other section of the Code prohibits a judge in the exercise of administrative functions from engaging in planning and other official activities with members of the executive and legislative branches of government. With respect to a judge's activity on behalf of measures to improve the law, the legal system and the administration of justice, see Commentary to Section 4B and Section 4C(1) and its Commentary.

E. APPLICABILITY. Canon 5 generally applies to all incumbent judges and judicial candidates *. A successful candidate, whether or not an incum-

* See, Terminology.

6. Jurisdictions wishing to adopt campaign contribution limits that are lower than generally applicable campaign finance regulations provide should adopt this provision, inserting appropriate dollar amounts where brackets appear.

7. Each jurisdiction should identify an appropriate depository for the information required under this provision, giving consideration to the public's need for convenient and timely access to the information. Electronic filing is to be preferred.

8. Jurisdictions wishing to adopt campaign contribution disclosure levels lower than those set in generally applicable campaign finance regulations should adopt this provision, inserting appropriate dollar amounts where brackets appear.

9. A time period chosen by the adopting jurisdiction should appear in the bracketed space.

* See, Terminology.

bent, is subject to judicial discipline for his or her campaign conduct; an unsuccessful candidate who is a lawyer is subject to lawyer discipline for his or her campaign conduct. A lawyer who is a candidate for judicial office is subject to [Rule 8.2(b) of the ABA Model Rules of Professional Conduct]. (An adopting jurisdiction should substitute a reference to its applicable rule.)

APPLICATION OF THE CODE OF JUDICIAL CONDUCT

A. Anyone, whether or not a lawyer, who is an officer of a judicial system [10] and who performs judicial functions, including an officer such as a magistrate, court commissioner, special master or referee, is a judge within the meaning of this Code. All judges shall comply with this Code except as provided below.

Commentary:

[1] The four categories of judicial service in other than a full-time capacity are necessarily defined in general terms because of the widely varying forms of judicial service. For the purposes of this Section, as long as a retired judge is subject to recall the judge is considered to "perform judicial functions." The determination of which category and, accordingly, which specific Code provisions apply to an individual judicial officer, depend upon the facts of the particular judicial service.

B. RETIRED JUDGE SUBJECT TO RECALL. A retired judge subject to recall who by law is not permitted to practice law is not required to comply:

(1) except while serving as a judge, with Section 4F; and

(2) at any time with Section 4E.

C. CONTINUING PART–TIME JUDGE. A continuing part-time judge *:

(1) is not required to comply

(a) except while serving as a judge, with Section 3B(9); and

(b) at any time with Sections 4C(2), 4D(3), 4E(1), 4F, 4G, 4H, 5A(1), 5B(2) and 5D.

(2) shall not practice law in the court on which the judge serves or in any court subject to the appellate jurisdiction of the court on which the judge serves, and shall not act as a lawyer in a proceeding in which the judge has served as a judge or in any other proceeding related thereto.

Commentary:

[1] When a person who has been a continuing part-time judge is no longer a continuing part-time judge, including a retired judge no longer subject to recall, that person may act as a lawyer in a proceeding in which he or she has served as a judge or in any other proceeding related thereto only with the express consent of all parties pursuant to [Rule 1.12(a) of the ABA Model Rules of Professional Conduct]. (An adopting jurisdiction should substitute a reference to its applicable rule).

10. Applicability of this Code to administrative law judges should be determined by each adopting jurisdiction. Administrative law judges generally are affiliated with the executive branch of government rather than the judicial branch and each adopting jurisdiction should consider the unique characteristics of particular administrative law judge positions in adopting and adapting the Code for administrative law judges. See, e.g., Model Code of Judicial Conduct for Federal Administrative Law Judges, endorsed by the National Conference of Administrative Law Judges in February 1989.

D. PERIODIC PART–TIME JUDGE. A periodic part-time judge *:

(1) **is not required to comply**

(a) **except while serving as a judge, with Section 3B(9);**

(b) **at any time, with Sections 4C(2), 4C(3)(a), 4D(1)(b), 4D(3), 4D(4), 4D(5), 4E, 4F, 4G, 4H, 5A(1), 5B(2) and 5D.**

(2) **shall not practice law in the court on which the judge serves or in any court subject to the appellate jurisdiction of the court on which the judge serves, and shall not act as a lawyer in a proceeding in which the judge has served as a judge or in any other proceeding related thereto.**

Commentary:

[1] When a person who has been a periodic part-time judge is no longer a periodic part-time judge (no longer accepts appointments), that person may act as a lawyer in a proceeding in which he or she has served as a judge or in any other proceeding related thereto only with the express consent of all parties pursuant to [Rule 1.12(a) of the ABA Model Rules of Professional Conduct]. (An adopting jurisdiction should substitute a reference to its applicable rule).

E. PRO TEMPORE PART–TIME JUDGE. A pro tempore part-time judge *:

(1) **is not required to comply**

(a) **except while serving as a judge, with Sections 2A, 2B, 3B(9) and 4C(1);**

(b) **at any time with Sections 2C, 4C(2), 4C(3)(a), 4C(3)(b), 4D(1)(b), 4D(3), 4D(4), 4D(5), 4E, 4F, 4G, 4H, 5A(1), 5A(2), 5B(2) and 5D.**

(2) **A person who has been a pro tempore part-time judge * shall not act as a lawyer in a proceeding in which the judge has served as a judge or in any other proceeding related thereto except as otherwise permitted by [Rule 1.12(a) of the ABA Model Rules of Professional Conduct]. (An adopting jurisdiction should substitute a reference to its applicable rule.)**

F. TIME FOR COMPLIANCE. A person to whom this Code becomes applicable shall comply immediately with all provisions of this Code except Sections 4D(2), 4D(3) and 4E and shall comply with these Sections as soon as reasonably possible and shall do so in any event within the period of one year.

Commentary:

[1] If serving as a fiduciary when selected as judge, a new judge may, notwithstanding the prohibitions in Section 4E, continue to serve as fiduciary but only for that period of time necessary to avoid serious adverse consequences to the beneficiary of the fiduciary relationship and in no event longer than one year. Similarly, if engaged at the time of judicial selection in a business activity, a new judge may, notwithstanding the prohibitions in Section 4D(3), continue in that activity for a reasonable period but in no event longer than one year.

---

* See, Terminology.

CALIFORNIA CODE OF JUDICIAL ETHICS

Amended by the Supreme Court of California effective December 13, 2000;
previously amended effective March 4, 1999

Preface
Preamble
Terminology

Canon 1.   A Judge Shall Uphold the Integrity and Independence of the Judiciary.
Canon 2.   A Judge Shall Avoid Impropriety and the Appearance of Impropriety in All of the Judge's Activities.
Canon 3.   A Judge Shall Perform the Duties of Judicial Office Impartially and Diligently.
Canon 4.   A Judge Shall So Conduct the Judge's Quasi-Judicial and Extrajudicial Activities as to Minimize the Risk of Conflict With Judicial Obligations.
Canon 5.   A Judge or Judicial Candidate Shall Refrain From Inappropriate Political Activity.
Canon 6.   Compliance With the Code of Judicial Ethics.

PREFACE

Formal standards of judicial conduct have existed for more than 50 years. The original Canons of Judicial Ethics promulgated by the American Bar Association were modified and adopted in 1949 for application in California by the Conference of California Judges (now the California Judges Association).

In 1969, the American Bar Association determined that current needs and problems warranted revision of the Canons. In the revision process, a special American Bar Association committee, headed by former California Chief Justice Roger Traynor, sought and considered the views of the bench and bar and other interested persons. The American Bar Association Code of Judicial Conduct was adopted by the House of Delegates of the American Bar Association August 16, 1972.

Effective January 5, 1975, the California Judges Association adopted a new California Code of Judicial Conduct adapted from the American Bar Association 1972 Model Code. The California code was recast in gender-neutral form in 1986.

In 1990, the American Bar Association Model Code was further revised after a lengthy study. The California Judges Association again reviewed the model code and adopted a revised California Code of Judicial Conduct on October 5, 1992.

Proposition 190 (amending Cal. Const., art. VI, § 18(m), effective March 1, 1995) created a new constitutional provision that states, "The Supreme Court shall make rules for the conduct of judges, both on and off the bench, and for judicial candidates[*] in the conduct of their campaigns. These rules shall be referred to as the Code of Judicial Ethics."

The Supreme Court formally adopted the 1992 Code of Judicial Conduct in March 1995, as a transitional measure pending further review.

The Supreme Court formally adopted the Code of Judicial Ethics effective January 15, 1996.

The Supreme Court formally adopted amendments to the Code of Judicial Ethics effective April 15, 1996. The *Advisory Committee Commentary* is published by the Supreme Court Advisory Committee on Judicial Ethics.

PREAMBLE

Our legal system is based on the principle that an independent, fair, and competent judiciary will interpret and apply the laws that govern us. The role of the judiciary is central to American concepts of justice and the rule of law. Intrinsic to this code are the precepts that judges, individually and collectively, must respect and honor the judicial office as a public trust and strive to enhance and maintain confidence in our legal system. The judge is an arbiter of facts and law for the resolution of disputes and a highly visible member of government under the rule of law.

The Code of Judicial Ethics ("Code") establishes standards for ethical conduct of judges on and off the bench and for candidates for judicial office. The Code consists of broad declarations called Canons, with subparts, and a Terminology section. Following each Canon is a Commentary section prepared by the Supreme Court Advisory Committee on Judicial Ethics. The Commentary, by explanation and example, provides guidance as to the purpose and meaning of the Canons. The Commentary does not constitute additional rules and should not be so construed. All members of the judiciary must comply with the Code. Compliance is required to preserve the integrity of the bench and to ensure the confidence of the public.

The Canons should be read together as a whole, and each provision should be construed in context and consistent with every other provision. They are to be applied in conformance with constitutional requirements, statutes, other court rules, and decisional law. Nothing in the Code shall either impair the essential independence of judges in making judicial decisions or provide a separate basis for civil liability or criminal prosecution.

The Code governs the conduct of judges and judicial candidates and is binding upon them. Whether disciplinary action is appropriate, and the degree of discipline to be imposed, requires a reasoned application of the text and consideration of such factors as the seriousness of the transgression, whether there is a pattern of improper activity, and the effect of the improper activity on others or on the judicial system.

TERMINOLOGY

Terms explained below are noted with an asterisk (*) in the Canons where they appear. In addition, the Canons in which terms appear are cited after the explanation of each term below.

* Terms with an asterisk (*) are defined in the Terminology section.

"Appropriate authority" denotes the authority with responsibility for initiation of the disciplinary process with respect to a violation to be reported. See Commentary to Canon 3D.

"Candidate." A candidate is a person seeking election for or retention of judicial office by election. A person becomes a candidate for judicial office as soon as he or she makes a public announcement of candidacy, declares or files as a candidate with the election authority, or authorizes solicitation or acceptance of contributions or support. The term "candidate" has the same meaning when applied to a judge seeking election to nonjudicial office, unless on leave of absence. See Preamble and Canons 2B(3), the preliminary paragraph of 5, 5A, 5B, 5C, and 6E.

"Court personnel" does not include the lawyers in a proceeding before a judge. See Canons 3B(4), 3B(7)(b), 3B(9), and 3C(2).

"Fiduciary" includes such relationships as executor, administrator, trustee, and guardian. See Canons 4E, 6B, and 6F (*Commentary*).

"Law" denotes court rules as well as statutes, constitutional provisions, and decisional law. See Canons 1 (*Commentary*), 2A, 2C (*Commentary*), 3A, 3B(2), 3B(7), 3E, 4B (*Commentary*), 4C, 4D(6)(a)–(b), 4F, 4H, and 5D.

"Member of the judge's family" denotes a spouse, child, grandchild, parent, grandparent, or other relative or person with whom the judge maintains a close familial relationship. See Canons 2B(2), 4D(1) (*Commentary*), 4D(2), 4E, 4G (*Commentary*), and 5A.

"Member of the judge's family residing in the judge's household" denotes a spouse and those persons who reside in the judge's household who are relatives of the judge including relatives by marriage, or persons with whom the judge maintains a close familial relationship. See Canons 4D(5) and 4D(6).

"Nonprofit youth organization" is any nonprofit corporation or association, not organized for the private gain of any person, whose purposes are irrevocably dedicated to benefiting and serving the interests of minors and which maintains its nonprofit status in accordance with applicable state and federal tax laws. See Canon 2C.

"Nonpublic information" denotes information that, by law, is not available to the public. Nonpublic information may include but is not limited to information that is sealed by statute or court order, impounded or communicated in camera; and information offered in grand jury proceedings, presentencing reports, dependency cases, or psychiatric reports. See Canon 3B(11).

"Political organization" denotes a political party, political action committee, or other group, the principal purpose of which is to further the election or appointment of candidates to nonjudicial office. See Canon 5A.

"Temporary Judge." A temporary judge is an active or inactive member of the bar who serves or expects to serve as a judge once, sporadically, or regularly on a part-time basis under a separate court appointment for each period of service or for each case heard. See Canons 4C(3)(d)(i), 6A, and 6D.

"Require." Any Canon prescribing that a judge "require" certain conduct of others means that a judge is to exercise reasonable direction and control over the conduct of those persons subject to the judge's direction and control. See Canons 3B(3), 3B(4), 3B(6), 3B(8) (*Commentary*), 3B(9), and 3C(2).

CANON 1

A Judge Shall Uphold the Integrity and Independence of the Judiciary

An independent and honorable judiciary is indispensable to justice in our society. A judge should participate in establishing, maintaining, and enforcing high standards of conduct, and shall personally observe those standards so that the integrity and independence of the judiciary will be preserved. The provisions of this Code are to be construed and applied to further that objective. A judicial decision or administrative act later determined to be incorrect legally is not itself a violation of this Code.

Advisory Committee Commentary

Deference to the judgments and rulings of courts depends upon public confidence in the integrity and independence of judges. The integrity and independence of judges depend in turn upon their acting without fear or favor. Although judges should be independent, they must comply with the law* and the provisions of this Code. Public confidence in the impartiality of the judiciary is maintained by the adherence of each judge to this responsibility. Conversely, violations of this Code diminish public confidence in the judiciary and thereby do injury to the system of government under law.

The basic function of an independent and honorable judiciary is to maintain the utmost integrity in decision making, and this Code should be read and interpreted with that function in mind.

CANON 2

A Judge Shall Avoid Impropriety and the Appearance of Impropriety in all of the Judge's Activities

A. Promoting Public Confidence. A judge shall respect and comply with the law* and shall act at all times in a manner that promotes public confidence in the integrity and impartiality of the judiciary.

Advisory Committee Commentary

Public confidence in the judiciary is eroded by irresponsible or improper conduct by judges. A judge must avoid all impropriety and appearance of impropriety. A judge must expect to be the subject of constant public scrutiny. A judge must therefore accept restrictions on the judge's conduct that might be viewed as burdensome by other members of the community and should do so freely and willingly.

The prohibition against behaving with impropriety or the appearance of impropriety applies to both the professional and personal conduct of a judge.

The test for the appearance of impropriety is whether a person aware of the facts might reasonably entertain a doubt that the judge would be able to act with integrity, impartiality, and competence.

See also Commentary under Canon 2C.

B. Use of the Prestige of Judicial Office

(1) A judge shall not allow family, social, political, or other relationships to influence the judge's judicial conduct or judgment, nor shall a judge convey

* [Pub. Note: This term is explained in the section titled "Terminology", supra.]

or permit others to convey the impression that any individual is in a special position to influence the judge.

(2) A judge shall not lend the prestige of judicial office to advance the pecuniary or personal interests of the judge or others; nor shall a judge testify voluntarily as a character witness. A judge shall not initiate communications with a sentencing judge or a probation or corrections officer, but may provide them with information for the record in response to an official request. A judge may initiate communications with a probation or corrections officer concerning a member of the judge's family,* provided the judge is not identified as a judge in the communication.

Advisory Committee Commentary

A strong judicial branch, based on the prestige which comes from effective and ethical performance, is essential to a system of government in which the judiciary functions independently of the executive and legislative branches. Judges should distinguish between proper and improper use of the prestige of office in all of their activities.

A judge must avoid lending the prestige of judicial office for the advancement of the private interests of the judge or others. For example, a judge must not use the judicial position to gain advantage in a civil suit involving a member of the judge's family;* or use his or her position to gain deferential treatment when stopped by a police officer for a traffic offense.

As to the use of a judge's title to identify a judge's role in the presentation and creation of legal education programs and materials, see Commentary to Canon 4B. In contracts for publication of a judge's writings, a judge should retain control over the advertising, to the extent feasible, to avoid exploitation of the judge's office. As to the acceptance of awards, see Canon 4D(6)(c) and Commentary.

A judge must not testify as a character witness without being subpoenaed because to do so may lend the prestige of the judicial office in support of the party for whom the judge testifies. A judge may provide information on behalf of a lawyer or a judge involved in disciplinary proceedings, and shall provide information to disciplinary bodies when officially requested to do so. This Canon does not afford judges a privilege against testifying in response to any official summons.

This Canon does not preclude internal discussions among judges regarding the application of substantive or procedural provisions of law to any pending criminal or civil case.

(3) A judge may respond to judicial selection inquiries, provide recommendations (including a general character reference, relating to the evaluation of persons being considered for a judgeship), and otherwise participate in the process of judicial selection.

(4) A judge shall not use the judicial title in any written communication intended to advance the personal or pecuniary interest of the judge. A judge may serve as a reference or provide a letter of recommendation only if based on the judge's personal knowledge of the individual. These written communications may include the judge's title and be written on stationery that uses the judicial title.

C. Membership in Organizations. A judge shall not hold membership in any organization that practices invidious discrimination on the basis of race, sex, religion, national origin, or sexual orientation.

This Canon does not apply to membership in a religious organization or an official military organization of the United States. So long as membership does not violate Canon 4A, this Canon does not bar membership in a nonprofit youth organization.*

Advisory Committee Commentary

Membership of a judge in an organization that practices invidious discrimination gives rise to a perception that the judge's impartiality is impaired. This Canon exempts membership in religious and military organizations and, subject to Canon 4A, does not bar membership in nonprofit youth organizations.* These exemptions are necessary because membership in United States military organizations is subject to current valid military regulations, and religious beliefs are constitutionally protected. Membership in nonprofit youth organizations* is not barred to accommodate individual rights of intimate association and free expression.

Canon 2C refers to the current practices of the organization. Whether an organization practices invidious discrimination is often a complex question to which judges should be sensitive. The answer cannot be determined from a mere examination of an organization's current membership rolls but rather depends on how the organization selects members and other relevant factors, such as whether the organization is dedicated to the preservation of religious, ethnic, or cultural values of legitimate common interest to its members, or whether it is in fact and effect an intimate, purely private organization whose membership limitations could not be constitutionally prohibited. Absent such factors, an organization is generally said to discriminate invidiously if it arbitrarily excludes from membership on the basis of race, religion, sex, national origin, or sexual orientation persons who would otherwise be admitted to membership.

Although Canon 2C relates only to membership in organizations that invidiously discriminate on the basis of race, sex, religion, national origin, or sexual orientation, a judge's membership in an organization that engages in any discriminatory membership practices prohibited by law* also violates Canon 2 and Canon 2A and gives the appearance of impropriety. In addition, it would be a violation of Canon 2 and Canon 2A for a judge to arrange a meeting at a club that the judge knows practices such invidious discrimination or for the judge to use such a club regularly. Moreover, public manifestation by a judge of the judge's knowing approval of invidious discrimination on any basis gives the appearance of impropriety under Canon 2 and diminishes public confidence in the integrity and impartiality of the judiciary in violation of Canon 2A.

CANON 3

A Judge Shall Perform the Duties of Judicial Office Impartially and Diligently

A. Judicial Duties in General. All of the judicial duties prescribed by law* shall take precedence over all other activities of every judge. In the performance of these duties, the following standards apply.

B. Adjudicative Responsibilities

(1) A judge shall hear and decide all matters assigned to the judge except those in which he or she is disqualified.

Advisory Committee Commentary

Canon 3B(1) is based upon the affirmative obligation contained in the Code of Civil Procedure.

(2) A judge shall be faithful to the law* regardless of partisan interests, public clamor, or fear of criticism, and shall maintain professional competence in the law.*

* [Pub. Note: This term is explained in the
section titled "Terminology", supra.]

(3) A judge shall require* order and decorum in proceedings before the judge.

(4) A judge shall be patient, dignified, and courteous to litigants, jurors, witnesses, lawyers, and others with whom the judge deals in an official capacity, and shall require* similar conduct of lawyers and of all court staff and personnel* under the judge's direction and control.

(5) A judge shall perform judicial duties without bias or prejudice. A judge shall not, in the performance of judicial duties, by words or conduct manifest bias or prejudice, including but not limited to bias or prejudice based upon race, sex, religion, national origin, disability, age, sexual orientation, or socioeconomic status.

Advisory Committee Commentary

A judge must refrain from speech, gestures, or other conduct that could reasonably be perceived as sexual harassment.

(6) A judge shall require* lawyers in proceedings before the judge to refrain from manifesting, by words or conduct, bias or prejudice based upon race, sex, religion, national origin, disability, age, sexual orientation, or socioeconomic status against parties, witnesses, counsel, or others. This Canon does not preclude legitimate advocacy when race, sex, religion, national origin, disability, age, sexual orientation, socioeconomic status or other similar factors are issues in the proceeding.

(7) A judge shall accord to every person who has a legal interest in a proceeding, or that person's lawyer, full right to be heard according to law.* A judge shall not initiate, permit, or consider ex parte communications, or consider other communications made to the judge outside the presence of the parties concerning a pending or impending proceeding, except as follows:

> (a) A judge may obtain the advice of a disinterested expert on the law* applicable to a proceeding before the judge if the judge gives notice to the parties of the person consulted and the substance of the advice, and affords the parties reasonable opportunity to respond.

> (b) A judge may consult with court personnel* whose function is to aid the judge in carrying out the judge's adjudicative responsibilities or with other judges.

> (c) A judge may, with the consent of the parties, confer separately with the parties and their lawyers in an effort to mediate or settle matters pending before the judge.

> (d) A judge may initiate ex parte communications, where circumstances require, for scheduling, administrative purposes, or emergencies that do not deal with substantive matters provided:

>> (i) the judge reasonably believes that no party will gain a procedural or tactical advantage as a result of the ex parte communication, and

* [Pub. Note: This term is explained in the section titled "Terminology", supra.]

(ii) the judge makes provision promptly to notify all other parties of the substance of the ex parte communication and allows an opportunity to respond.

(e) A judge may initiate or consider any ex parte communication when expressly authorized by law* to do so.

Advisory Committee Commentary

The proscription against communications concerning a proceeding includes communications from lawyers, law professors, and other persons who are not participants in the proceeding, except to the limited extent permitted by the exceptions noted in Canon 3B(7).

This Canon does not prohibit a judge from initiating or considering an ex parte communication when authorized to do so by stipulation of the parties.

This Canon does not prohibit court staff from communicating scheduling information or carrying out similar administrative functions.

An appropriate and often desirable procedure for a court to obtain the advice of a disinterested expert on legal issues is to invite the expert to file an amicus curiae brief.

A judge must not independently investigate facts in a case and must consider only the evidence presented, unless otherwise authorized by law.* For example, a judge is statutorily authorized to investigate and consult witnesses informally in small claims cases.

(8) A judge shall dispose of all judicial matters fairly, promptly, and efficiently.

Advisory Committee Commentary

The obligation of a judge to dispose of matters promptly and efficiently must not take precedence over the judge's obligation to dispose of the matters fairly and with patience. A judge should monitor and supervise cases so as to reduce or eliminate dilatory practices, avoidable delays, and unnecessary costs. A judge should encourage and seek to facilitate settlement, but parties should not feel coerced into surrendering the right to have their controversy resolved by the courts.

Prompt disposition of the court's business requires a judge to devote adequate time to judicial duties, to be punctual in attending court and expeditious in determining matters under submission, and to require* that court officials, litigants, and their lawyers cooperate with the judge to that end.

(9) A judge shall not make any public comment about a pending or impending proceeding in any court, and shall not make any nonpublic comment that might substantially interfere with a fair trial or hearing. The judge shall require* similar abstention on the part of court personnel* subject to the judge's direction and control. This Canon does not prohibit judges from making statements in the course of their official duties or from explaining for public information the procedures of the court, and does not apply to proceedings in which the judge is a litigant in a personal capacity. Other than cases in which the judge has personally participated, this Canon does not prohibit judges from discussing in legal education programs and materials, cases and issues pending in appellate courts. This educational exemption does not apply to cases over which the judge has presided or to comments or discussions that might interfere with a fair hearing of the case.

* [Pub. Note: This term is explained in the section titled "Terminology", supra.]

The requirement that judges abstain from public comment regarding a pending or impending proceeding continues during any appellate process and until final disposition. This Canon does not prohibit a judge from commenting on proceedings in which the judge is a litigant in a personal capacity, but in cases such as a writ of mandamus where the judge is a litigant in an official capacity, the judge must not comment publicly.

(10) A judge shall not commend or criticize jurors for their verdict other than in a court order or opinion in a proceeding, but may express appreciation to jurors for their service to the judicial system and the community.

Advisory Committee Commentary

Commending or criticizing jurors for their verdict may imply a judicial expectation in future cases and may impair a juror's ability to be fair and impartial in a subsequent case.

(11) A judge shall not disclose or use, for any purpose unrelated to judicial duties, nonpublic information* acquired in a judicial capacity.

Advisory Committee Commentary

This Canon makes it clear that judges cannot make use of information from affidavits, jury results, or court rulings, before they become public information, in order to gain a personal advantage.

C. Administrative Responsibilities

(1) A judge shall diligently discharge the judge's administrative responsibilities without bias or prejudice and maintain professional competence in judicial administration, and shall cooperate with other judges and court officials in the administration of court business.

(2) A judge shall require* staff and court personnel* under the judge's direction and control to observe appropriate standards of conduct and to refrain from manifesting bias or prejudice based upon race, sex, religion, national origin, disability, age, sexual orientation, or socioeconomic status in the performance of their official duties.

(3) A judge with supervisory authority for the judicial performance of other judges shall take reasonable measures to ensure the prompt disposition of matters before them and the proper performance of their other judicial responsibilities.

(4) A judge shall not make unnecessary court appointments. A judge shall exercise the power of appointment impartially and on the basis of merit. A judge shall avoid nepotism and favoritism. A judge shall not approve compensation of appointees above the reasonable value of services rendered.

Advisory Committee Commentary

Appointees of a judge include assigned counsel, officials such as referees, commissioners, special masters, receivers, and guardians, and personnel such as clerks, secretaries, court reporters, court interpreters, and bailiffs. Consent by the parties to an appointment or an award of compensation does not relieve the judge of the obligation prescribed by Canon 3C(4).

D. Disciplinary Responsibilities

(1) Whenever a judge has reliable information that another judge has violated any provision of the Code of Judicial Ethics, the judge shall take or

* [Pub. Note: This term is explained in the section titled "Terminology", supra.]

initiate appropriate corrective action, which may include reporting the violation to the appropriate authority.*

(2) Whenever a judge has personal knowledge that a lawyer has violated any provision of the Rules of Professional Conduct, the judge shall take appropriate corrective action.

(3) A judge who is charged by prosecutorial complaint, information, or indictment or convicted of a crime in the United States, other than one that would be considered a misdemeanor not involving moral turpitude or an infraction under California law, but including all misdemeanors involving violence (including assaults), the use or possession of controlled substances, the misuse of prescriptions, or the personal use or furnishing of alcohol, shall promptly and in writing report that fact to the Commission of Judicial Performance.

Advisory Committee Commentary

Appropriate corrective action could include direct communication with the judge or lawyer who has committed the violation, other direct action if available, or a report of the violation to the presiding judge, appropriate authority,* or other agency or body. Judges should note that in addition to the action required by Canon 3D(2), California law imposes additional reporting requirements regarding lawyers.

(Canon 3D(3) amended effective March 4, 1999; previously amended effective June 19, 1997; adopted effective January 15, 1996.)

E. Disqualification.

(1) A judge shall disqualify himself or herself in any proceeding in which disqualification is required by law.

(2) In all trial proceedings, a judge shall disclose on the record information that the judge believes the parties or their lawyers might consider relevant to the question of disqualification, even if the judge believes there is no actual basis for disqualification.

(3) An appellate justice shall disqualify himself or herself in any proceeding if for any reason: (i) the justice believes his or her recusal would further the interest of justice; or (ii) the justice substantially doubts his or her capacity to be impartial; or (iii) the circumstances are such that a reasonable person aware of the facts would doubt the justice's ability to be impartial. Disqualification is required in the following instances:

(a) The appellate justice has appeared or otherwise served as a lawyer in the pending matter, or has appeared or served as a lawyer in any other matter involving any of the same parties if that other matter related to the same contested issues of fact and law as the present matter.

(b) Within the last two years, (i) a party to the proceeding, or an officer, director or trustee thereof, either was a client of the justice when the justice was engaged in the private practice of law or was a client of a lawyer with whom the justice was associated in the private practice of

* [Pub. Note: This term is explained in the section titled "Terminology", supra.]

law; or (ii) a lawyer in the proceeding was associated with the justice in the private practice of law.

(c) The appellate justice represented a public officer or entity and personally advised or in any way represented such officer or entity concerning the factual or legal issues in the present proceeding in which the public officer or entity now appears.

(d) The appellate justice, or his or her spouse, or a minor child residing in the household, has a financial interest or is a fiduciary who has a financial interest in the proceeding, or is a director, advisor, or other active participant in the affairs of a party. A financial interest is defined as ownership of more than a 1 percent legal or equitable interest in a party, or a legal or equitable interest in a party of a fair market value exceeding one thousand five hundred dollars. Ownership in a mutual or common investment fund that holds securities does not itself constitute a financial interest; holding office in an educational, religious, charitable, fraternal or civic organization does not confer a financial interest in the organization's securities; and a proprietary interest of a policyholder in a mutual insurance company or mutual savings association or similar interest is not a financial interest unless the outcome of the proceeding could substantially affect the value of the interest. A justice shall make reasonable efforts to keep informed about his or her personal and fiduciary interests and those of his or her spouse and of minor children living in the household.

(e) The justice or his or her spouse, or a person within the third degree of relationship to either of them, or the spouse thereof, is a party or an officer, director or trustee of a party to the proceeding, or a lawyer or spouse of a lawyer in the proceeding is the spouse, former spouse, child, sibling, or parent of the justice or of the justice's spouse, or such a person is associated in the private practice of law with a lawyer in the proceeding.

(f) The justice (i) served as the judge before whom the proceeding was tried or heard in the lower court, (ii) has a personal knowledge of disputed evidentiary facts concerning the proceeding, or (iii) has a personal bias or prejudice concerning a party or a party's lawyer. The justice's spouse or a person within the third degree of relationship to the justice or his or her spouse, or the person's spouse, was a witness in the proceeding.

(g) A temporary or permanent physical impairment renders the judge unable properly to perceive the evidence or conduct the proceedings.

Advisory Committee Commentary

Canon 3(E)(1) sets forth the general duty to disqualify applicable to a judge of any court. Sources for determining when recusal or disqualification is appropriate may include the applicable provisions of the Code of Civil Procedure, other provisions of the Code of Judicial Ethics, the Code of Conduct for United States Judges, the American Bar Association's Model Code of Judicial Conduct, and related case law.

The introductory paragraph to Canon 3E(3) sets forth the general standards for recusal of an appellate justice. The term "appellate justice" includes justices of both the Courts of Appeal and the Supreme Court. Generally, the provisions concerning disqualification of an appellate justice are intended to assist justices in determining whether recusal is appropriate and to inform the public why recusal may occur.

However, the rule of necessity may override the rule of disqualification. For example, a judge might be required to participate in judicial review of a judicial salary statute, or might be the only judge available in a matter requiring judicial action, such as a hearing on probable cause or a temporary restraining order. In the latter case, the judge must promptly disclose on the record the basis for possible disqualification and use reasonable efforts to transfer the matter to another judge as soon as practicable.

Canon 3E amended effective December 13, 2000; previously amended effective June 19, 1997, and March 4, 1999.

CANON 4

A Judge Shall so Conduct the Judge's Quasi–Judicial and Extrajudicial Activities as to Minimize the Risk of Conflict With Judicial Obligations

A. Extrajudicial Activities in General A judge shall conduct all of the judge's extrajudicial activities so that they do not

(1) cast reasonable doubt on the judge's capacity to act impartially;

(2) demean the judicial office; or

(3) interfere with the proper performance of judicial duties.

Advisory Committee Commentary

Complete separation of a judge from extrajudicial activities is neither possible nor wise; a judge should not become isolated from the community in which the judge lives.

Expressions of bias or prejudice by a judge, even outside the judge's judicial activities, may cast reasonable doubt on the judge's capacity to act impartially as a judge. Expressions which may do so include jokes or other remarks demeaning individuals on the basis of a classification such as their race, sex, religion, sexual orientation, or national origin. See Canon 2C and accompanying Commentary.

B. Quasi-judicial and Avocational Activities A judge may speak, write, lecture, teach, and participate in activities concerning legal and nonlegal subject matters, subject to the requirements of this Code.

Advisory Committee Commentary

As a judicial officer and person specially learned in the law,* a judge is in a unique position to contribute to the improvement of the law,* the legal system, and the administration of justice, including revision of substantive and procedural law* and improvement of criminal and juvenile justice.   To the extent that time permits, a judge may do so, either independently or through a bar or judicial association or other group dedicated to the improvement of the law.*

It may be necessary to promote legal education programs and materials by identifying authors and speakers by judicial title.   This is permissible, provided such use of the judicial title does not contravene Canons 2A and 2B.

Judges are not precluded by their office from engaging in other social, community, and intellectual endeavors so long as they do not interfere with the obligations under Canons 2C and 4A.

* [Pub. Note: This term is explained in the section titled "Terminology", supra.]

C. Governmental, Civic, or Charitable Activities

(1) A judge shall not appear at a public hearing or officially consult with an executive or legislative body or public official except on matters concerning the law,* the legal system, or the administration of justice or in matters involving the judge's private economic or personal interests.

Advisory Committee Commentary

See Canon 2B regarding the obligation to avoid improper influence.

(2) A judge shall not accept appointment to a governmental committee or commission or other governmental position that is concerned with issues of fact or policy on matters other than the improvement of the law,* the legal system, or the administration of justice. A judge may, however, serve in the military reserve or represent a national, state, or local government on ceremonial occasions or in connection with historical, educational, or cultural activities.

Advisory Committee Commentary

Canon 4C(2) prohibits a judge from accepting any governmental position except one relating to the law, legal system, or administration of justice as authorized by Canon 4C(3). The appropriateness of accepting extrajudicial assignments must be assessed in light of the demands on judicial resources and the need to protect the courts from involvement in extrajudicial matters that may prove to be controversial. Judges shall not accept governmental appointments that are likely to interfere with the effectiveness and independence of the judiciary, or which constitute a public office within the meaning of the California Constitution, article VI, section 17.*

Canon 4C(2) does not govern a judge's service in a nongovernmental position. See Canon 4C(3) permitting service by a judge with organizations devoted to the improvement of the law, the legal system, or the administration of justice and with educational, religious, charitable, fraternal, or civic organizations not conducted for profit. For example, service on the board of a public educational institution, other than a law school, would be prohibited under Canon 4C(2), but service on the board of a public law school or any private educational institution would generally be permitted under Canon 4C(3).*

(3) Subject to the following limitations and the other requirements of this Code,

    (a) a judge may serve as an officer, director, trustee, or nonlegal advisor of an organization or governmental agency devoted to the improvement of the law,* the legal system, or the administration of justice provided that such position does not constitute a public office within the meaning of the California Constitution, article VI, section 17;

    (b) a judge may serve as an officer, director, trustee, or nonlegal advisor of an educational, religious, charitable, fraternal, or civic organization not conducted for profit;

Advisory Committee Commentary

Canon 4C(3) does not apply to a judge's service in a governmental position unconnected with the improvement of the law, the legal system, or the administration of justice. See Canon 4C(2).*

Canon 4C(3) uses the phrase, "Subject to the following limitations and the other requirements of this Code." As an example of the meaning of the phrase, a judge

* [Pub. Note: This term is explained in the
section titled "Terminology", supra.]

permitted by Canon 4C(3) to serve on the board of a fraternal institution may be prohibited from such service by Canon 2C or 4A if the institution practices invidious discrimination or if service on the board otherwise casts reasonable doubt on the judge's capacity to act impartially as a judge.

Service by a judge on behalf of a civic or charitable organization may be governed by other provisions of Canon 4 in addition to Canon 4C. For example, a judge is prohibited by Canon 4G from serving as a legal advisor to a civic or charitable organization.

Service on the board of a homeowners' association or a neighborhood protective group is proper if it is related to the protection of the judge's own economic interests. See Canons 4D(2) and 4D(4). See Canon 2B regarding the obligation to avoid improper use of the prestige of a judge's office.

(c) a judge shall not serve as an officer, director, trustee, or nonlegal advisor if it is likely that the organization

(i) will be engaged in judicial proceedings that would ordinarily come before the judge; or

(ii) will be engaged frequently in adversary proceedings in the court of which the judge is a member or in any court subject to the appellate jurisdiction of the court of which the judge is a member.

Advisory Committee Commentary

The changing nature of some organizations and of their relationship to the law* makes it necessary for the judge regularly to reexamine the activities of each organization with which the judge is affiliated to determine if it is proper for the judge to continue the affiliation. Some organizations regularly engage in litigation to achieve their goals or fulfill their purposes. Judges should avoid a leadership role in such organizations as it could compromise the appearance of impartiality.

(d) a judge as an officer, director, trustee, or nonlegal advisor, or as a member or otherwise

(i) may assist such an organization in planning fund raising and may participate in the management and investment of the organization's funds, but shall not personally participate in the solicitation of funds or other fund-raising activities, except that a judge may privately solicit funds for such an organization from other judges (excluding court commissioners, referees, retired judges, and temporary judges*);

(ii) may make recommendations to public and private fund-granting organizations on projects and programs concerning the law,* the legal system, or the administration of justice;

(iii) shall not personally participate in membership solicitation if the solicitation might reasonably be perceived as coercive or if the membership solicitation is essentially a fund-raising mechanism, except as permitted in Canon 4C(3)(d)(i);

(iv) shall not permit the use of the prestige of his or her judicial office for fund raising or membership solicitation but may be a speaker, guest of honor, or recipient of an award for public or charitable service provided the judge does not personally solicit funds and complies with Canon 4A(1), (2), and (3).

* [Pub. Note: This term is explained in the section titled "Terminology", supra.]

A judge may solicit membership or endorse or encourage membership efforts for an organization devoted to the improvement of the law,* the legal system, or the administration of justice, or a nonprofit educational, religious, charitable, fraternal, or civic organization as long as the solicitation cannot reasonably be perceived as coercive and is not essentially a fund-raising mechanism. Solicitation of funds for an organization and solicitation of memberships similarly involve the danger that the person solicited will feel obligated to respond favorably to the solicitor if the solicitor is in a position of influence or control. A judge must not engage in direct, individual solicitation of funds or memberships in person, in writing, or by telephone except in the following cases: (1) a judge may solicit other judges (excluding court commissioners, referees, retired judges, court-appointed arbitrators, and temporary judges*) for funds or memberships; (2) a judge may solicit other persons for membership in the organizations described above if neither those persons nor persons with whom they are affiliated are likely ever to appear before the court on which the judge serves; and (3) a judge who is an officer of such an organization may send a general membership solicitation mailing over the judge's signature.

Use of an organization letterhead for fund raising or membership solicitation does not violate Canon 4C(3)(d), provided the letterhead lists only the judge's name and office or other position in the organization, and designates the judge's judicial title only if other persons whose names appear on the letterhead have comparable designations. In addition, a judge must also make reasonable efforts to ensure that the judge's staff, court officials, and others subject to the judge's direction and control do not solicit funds on the judge's behalf for any purpose, charitable or otherwise.

D. Financial Activities

(1) A judge shall not engage in financial and business dealings that

(a) may reasonably be perceived to exploit the judge's judicial position, or

(b) involve the judge in frequent transactions or continuing business relationships with lawyers or other persons likely to appear before the court on which the judge serves.

The Time for Compliance provision of this Code (Canon 6F) postpones the time for compliance with certain provisions of this Canon in some cases.

A judge must avoid financial and business dealings that involve the judge in frequent transactions or continuing business relationships with persons likely to appear either before the judge personally or before other judges on the judge's court. A judge shall discourage members of the judge's family* from engaging in dealings that would reasonably appear to exploit the judge's judicial position or that involve family members in frequent transactions or continuing business relationships with persons likely to appear before the judge. This rule is necessary to avoid creating an appearance of exploitation of office or favoritism and to minimize the potential for disqualification.

Participation by a judge in financial and business dealings is subject to the general prohibitions in Canon 4A against activities that tend to reflect adversely on impartiality, demean the judicial office, or interfere with the proper performance of judicial duties. Such participation is also subject to the general prohibition in Canon 2 against activities involving impropriety or the appearance of impropriety and the prohibition in Canon 2B against the misuse of the prestige of judicial office.

In addition, a judge must maintain high standards of conduct in all of the judge's activities, as set forth in Canon 1.

(2) A judge may, subject to the requirements of this Code, hold and manage investments of the judge and members of the judge's family,* including real estate, and engage in other remunerative activities. A judge shall not

* [Pub. Note: This term is explained in the section titled "Terminology", supra.]

participate in, nor permit the judge's name to be used in connection with, any business venture or commercial advertising that indicates the judge's title or affiliation with the judiciary or otherwise lend the power or prestige of his or her office to promote a business or any commercial venture.

(3) A judge shall not serve as an officer, director, manager, or employee of a business affected with a public interest, including, without limitation, a financial institution, insurance company, or public utility.

Advisory Committee Commentary

Although participation by a judge in business activities might otherwise be permitted by Canon 4D, a judge may be prohibited from participation by other provisions of this Code when, for example, the business entity frequently appears before the judge's court or the participation requires significant time away from judicial duties. Similarly, a judge must avoid participating in any business activity if the judge's participation would involve misuse of the prestige of judicial office. See Canon 2B.

(4) A judge shall manage personal investments and financial activities so as to minimize the necessity for disqualification. As soon as reasonably possible, a judge shall divest himself or herself of investments and other financial interests that would require frequent disqualification.

(5) Under no circumstance shall a judge accept a gift, bequest or favor if the donor is a party whose interests have come or are reasonably likely to come before the judge. A judge shall discourage members of the judge's family residing in the judge's household* from accepting similar benefits from parties who have come or are reasonably likely to come before the judge.

Advisory Committee Commentary

In addition to the prohibitions set forth in Canon 4D(5) regarding gifts, other laws may be applicable to judges, including, for example, Code of Civil Procedure section 170.9 and the Political Reform Act of 1974 (Gov. Code, § 81000 et seq.).

Canon 4D(5) does not apply to contributions to a judge's campaign for judicial office, a matter governed by Canon 5.

Because a gift, bequest, or favor to a member of the judge's family residing in the judge's household* might be viewed as intended to influence the judge, a judge must inform those family members of the relevant ethical constraints upon the judge in this regard and discourage those family members from violating them. A judge cannot, however, reasonably be expected to know or control all of the financial or business activities of all family members residing in the judge's household.*

The application of Canon 4D(5) requires recognition that a judge cannot reasonably be expected to anticipate all persons or interests that may come before the court.

(6) A judge shall not accept and shall discourage members of the judge's family residing in the judge's household* from accepting a gift, bequest, favor, or loan from anyone except as hereinafter provided:

(a) any gift incidental to a public testimonial, books, tapes, and other resource materials supplied by publishers on a complimentary basis for official use, or an invitation to the judge and the judge's spouse or guest to attend a bar-related function or an activity devoted to the improvement of the law,* the legal system, or the administration of justice;

* [Pub. Note: This term is explained in the section titled "Terminology", supra.]

(b) advances or reimbursement for the reasonable cost of travel, transportation, lodging, and subsistence which is directly related to participation in any judicial, educational, civic, or governmental program, or bar-related function or activity, devoted to the improvement of the law,* the legal system, or the administration of justice;

Advisory Committee Commentary

Acceptance of an invitation to a law-related function is governed by Canon 4D(6)(a); acceptance of an invitation paid for by an individual lawyer or group of lawyers is governed by Canon 4D(6)(d).

(c) a gift, award, or benefit incident to the business, profession, or other separate activity of a spouse or other member of the judge's family residing in the judge's household,* including gifts, awards, and benefits for the use of both the spouse or other family member and the judge, provided the gift, award, or benefit could not reasonably be perceived as intended to influence the judge in the performance of judicial duties;

(d) ordinary social hospitality;

Advisory Committee Commentary

Although Canon 4D(6)(d) does not preclude ordinary social hospitality between members of the bench and bar, a judge should carefully weigh acceptance of such hospitality to avoid any appearance of bias. See Canon 2B.

(e) a gift for a special occasion from a relative or friend, if the gift is fairly commensurate with the occasion and the relationship;

Advisory Committee Commentary

A gift to a judge, or to a member of the judge's family residing in the judge's household, that is excessive in value raises questions about the judge's impartiality and the integrity of the judicial office and might require disqualification of the judge where disqualification would not otherwise be required. See, however, Canon 4D(6)(f).*

(f) a gift, bequest, favor, or loan from a relative or close personal friend whose appearance or interest in a case would in any event require disqualification under Canon 3E;

(g) a loan in the regular course of business on the same terms generally available to persons who are not judges;

(h) a scholarship or fellowship awarded on the same terms and based on the same criteria applied to other applicants.

E. Fiduciary Activities

(1) A judge shall not serve as executor, administrator, or other personal representative, trustee, guardian, attorney in fact, or other fiduciary,* except for the estate, trust, or person of a member of the judge's family,* and then only if such service will not interfere with the proper performance of judicial duties.

(2) A judge shall not serve as a fiduciary* if it is likely that the judge as a fiduciary* will be engaged in proceedings that would ordinarily come before

* [Pub. Note: This term is explained in the section titled "Terminology", supra.]

the judge, or if the estate, trust, or minor or conservatee becomes engaged in contested proceedings in the court on which the judge serves or one under its appellate jurisdiction.

(3) The same restrictions on financial activities that apply to a judge personally also apply to the judge while acting in a fiduciary* capacity.

Advisory Committee Commentary

The Time for Compliance provision of this Code (Canon 6F) postpones the time for compliance with certain provisions of this Canon in some cases.

The restrictions imposed by this Canon may conflict with the judge's obligation as a fiduciary.* For example, a judge shall resign as trustee if detriment to the trust would result from divestiture of trust holdings the retention of which would place the judge in violation of Canon 4D(4).

F. Service as Arbitrator or Mediator A judge shall not act as an arbitrator or mediator or otherwise perform judicial functions in a private capacity unless expressly authorized by law.*

Advisory Committee Commentary

Canon 4F does not prohibit a judge from participating in arbitration, mediation, or settlement conferences performed as part of his or her judicial duties.

G. Practice of Law A judge shall not practice law.

Advisory Committee Commentary

This prohibition refers to the practice of law in a representative capacity and not in a pro se capacity. A judge may act for himself or herself in all legal matters, including matters involving litigation and matters involving appearances before or other dealings with legislative and other governmental bodies. However, in so doing, a judge must not abuse the prestige of office to advance the interests of the judge or member of the judge's family.* See Canon 2B.

H. Compensation and Reimbursement A judge may receive compensation and reimbursement of expenses as provided by law* for the extrajudicial activities permitted by this Code, if the source of such payments does not give the appearance of influencing the judge's performance of judicial duties or otherwise give the appearance of impropriety.

(1) Compensation shall not exceed a reasonable amount nor shall it exceed what a person who is not a judge would receive for the same activity.

(2) Expense reimbursement shall be limited to the actual cost of travel, food, lodging, and other costs reasonably incurred by the judge and, where appropriate to the occasion, by the judge's spouse or guest. Any payment in excess of such an amount is compensation.

Advisory Committee Commentary

Judges should be aware of the statutory limitations on accepting gifts, including honoraria.

CANON 5

A Judge or Judicial Candidate* Shall Refrain From Inappropriate Political Activity

Judges are entitled to entertain their personal views on political questions. They are not required to surrender their rights or opinions as citizens. They shall, however, avoid political activity that may create the appearance of political bias or impropriety. Judicial independence and impartiality should dictate the conduct of judges and candidates* for judicial office.

A. Political Organizations Judges and candidates* for judicial office shall not

(1) act as leaders or hold any office in a political organization;*

(2) make speeches for a political organization* or candidate* for nonjudicial office or publicly endorse or publicly oppose a candidate for nonjudicial office;

(3) personally solicit funds for a political organization* or nonjudicial candidate;* or make contributions to a political party or political organization* or to a nonjudicial candidate in excess of five hundred dollars in any calendar year per political party or political organization* or candidate,* or in excess of an aggregate of one thousand dollars in any calendar year for all political parties or political organizations* or nonjudicial candidates.*

Advisory Committee Commentary

The term "political activity" should not be construed so narrowly as to prevent private comment.

This provision does not prohibit a judge from signing a petition to qualify a measure for the ballot without the use of the judge's official title.

In judicial elections, judges are neither required to shield themselves from campaign contributions nor are they prohibited from soliciting contributions from anyone including attorneys. Nevertheless, there are necessary limits on judges facing election if the appearance of impropriety is to be avoided. Although it is improper for a judge to receive a gift from an attorney subject to exceptions noted in Canon 4D(6), a judge's campaign may receive attorney contributions.

Although attendance at political gatherings is not prohibited, any such attendance should be restricted so that it would not constitute an express public endorsement of a nonjudicial candidate* or a measure not directly affecting the administration of justice otherwise prohibited by this Canon.

Subject to the monetary limitation herein to political contributions, a judge may purchase tickets for political dinners or other similar dinner functions. Any admission price to such a political dinner or function in excess of the actual cost of the meal shall be considered a political contribution. The prohibition in Canon 5A(3) does not preclude judges from contributing to a campaign fund for distribution among judges who are candidates for reelection or retention, nor does it apply to contributions to any judge or candidate* for judicial office.

Under this Canon, a judge may publicly endorse another judicial candidate.* Such endorsements are permitted because judicial officers have a special obligation to uphold

* [Pub. Note: This term is explained in the
section titled "Terminology", supra.]

668

the integrity and impartiality of the judiciary and are in a unique position to know the qualifications necessary to serve as a competent judicial officer.

Although members of the judge's family* are not subject to the provisions of this Code, a judge shall not avoid compliance with this Code by making contributions through a spouse or other family member.

B. Conduct During Judicial Campaigns A candidate* for election or appointment to judicial office shall not (1) make statements to the electorate or the appointing authority that commit or appear to commit the candidate* with respect to cases, controversies, or issues that could come before the courts, or (2) knowingly misrepresent the identity, qualifications, present position, or any other fact concerning the candidate* or his or her opponent.

C. Speaking at Political Gatherings Candidates* for judicial office may speak to political gatherings only on their own behalf or on behalf of another candidate for judicial office.

D. Measures to Improve the Law Except as otherwise permitted in this Code, judges shall not engage in any political activity, other than in relation to measures concerning the improvement of the law,* the legal system, or the administration of justice.

CANON 6

Compliance With the Code of Judicial Ethics

A. Judges Anyone who is an officer of the state judicial system and who performs judicial functions, including, but not limited to, a magistrate, court commissioner, referee, court-appointed arbitrator, judge of the State Bar Court, temporary judge,* or special master, is a judge within the meaning of this Code. All judges shall comply with this Code except as provided below.

Advisory Committee Commentary

For the purposes of this Canon, if a retired judge is serving in the assigned judges program, the judge is considered to "perform judicial functions." Because retired judges who are privately retained may perform judicial functions, their conduct while performing those functions should be guided by this Code.

B. Retired Judge Serving in the Assigned Judges Program A retired judge who has filed an application to serve on assignment, meets the eligibility requirements set by the Chief Justice for service, and has received an acknowledgment of participation in the assigned judges program shall comply with all provisions of this Code, except for the following:

4C(2)—Appointment to governmental positions
4D(2)—Participation in business entities and managing investments
4E— Fiduciary* activities

C. Retired Judge as Arbitrator or Mediator A retired judge serving in the assigned judges program is not required to comply with Canon 4F

* [Pub. Note: This term is explained in the section titled "Terminology", supra.]   * [Pub. Note: This term is explained in the section titled "Terminology", supra.]

of this Code relating to serving as an arbitrator or mediator, or performing judicial functions in a private capacity, except as otherwise provided in the *Standards and Guidelines for Judges Serving on Assignment* promulgated by the Chief Justice.

Advisory Committee Commentary

In California, article VI, section 6 of the California Constitution provides that a "retired judge who consents may be assigned to any court" by the Chief Justice. Retired judges who are serving in the Assigned Judges Program pursuant to the above provision are bound by Canon 6B, including the requirement of Canon 4G barring the practice of law. Other provisions of California law, and standards and guidelines for eligibility and service set by the Chief Justice, further define the limitations on who may serve on assignment.

D. Temporary Judge*, Referee, or Court-appointed Arbitrator[1]
A temporary judge, a person serving as a referee pursuant to Code of Civil Procedure section 638 or 639, or a court-appointed arbitrator shall comply only with the following code provisions:

(1) A temporary judge, referee or court-appointed arbitrator shall comply with Canons 1 [integrity and independence of the judiciary], 2A [promoting public confidence], 3B(3) [order and decorum] and (4) [patient, dignified, and courteous treatment], 3B(6) [require lawyers to refrain from manifestations of any form of bias or prejudice], 3D(1) [action regarding misconduct by another judge] and (2) [action regarding misconduct by a lawyer], when the temporary judge, referee or court-appointed arbitrator is actually presiding in a proceeding or communicating with the parties, counsel, or court personnel while serving in the capacity of a temporary judge, referee or court-appointed arbitrator in the case.

(2) A temporary judge, referee or court-appointed arbitrator shall, from the time of notice and acceptance of appointment until termination of the appointment:

(a) Comply with Canons 2B(1) [not allow family or other relationships to influence judicial conduct], 3B(1) [hear and decide all matters unless disqualified] and (2) [be faithful to and maintain competence in the law], 3B(5) [perform judicial duties without bias or prejudice], 3B(7) [accord full right to be heard to those entitled; avoid ex parte communications, except as specified] and (8) [dispose of matters fairly and promptly], 3C(1) [discharge administrative responsibilities without bias and with competence and cooperatively], (2) [require staff and personnel to observe standards of conduct and refrain from bias and prejudice] and (4) [make only fair, necessary, and appropriate appointments];

(b) Not lend the prestige of judicial office to advance his, her, or another person's pecuniary or personal interests and not use his or her judicial title in any written communication intended to advance his, her, or another person's

---

* [Pub. Note: This term is explained in the section titled "Terminology", supra.]

1. Reference should be made to relevant commentary to analogous or individual Canons cited or described in this Canon and appearing elsewhere in this Code.

pecuniary or personal interests, except to show his, her, or another person's qualifications;

(c) Not personally solicit memberships or donations for religious, fraternal, educational, civic, or charitable organizations from the parties and lawyers appearing before the temporary judge, referee, or court-appointed arbitrator;

(d) Under no circumstance accept a gift, bequest, or favor if the donor is a party, person, or entity whose interests are reasonably likely to come before the temporary judge, referee, or court-appointed arbitrator. A temporary judge, referee, or court-appointed arbitrator shall discourage members of the judge's family residing in the judge's household from accepting benefits from parties who are reasonably likely to come before the temporary judge, referee, or court-appointed arbitrator.

(e) Disqualify himself or herself in any proceeding in which disqualification is required by law;

(f) In all proceedings, disclose in writing or on the record information as required by law, or information that the temporary judge, referee or court-appointed arbitrator believes the parties or their lawyers might consider relevant to the question of disqualification, even where it is believed that there is no actual basis for disqualification; and

(g) In all proceedings, disclose in writing or on the record membership in any organization that practices invidious discrimination on the basis of race, sex, religion, national origin, or sexual orientation, except for membership in a religious or an official military organization of the United States and membership in a nonprofit youth organization so long as membership does not violate Canon 4A [conduct of extrajudicial activities].

(3) A temporary judge, referee, or court-appointed arbitrator, from the time of notice and acceptance of appointment until the case is no longer pending in any court, shall not make any public comment about a pending or impending proceeding in which the temporary judge, referee, or court-appointed arbitrator has been engaged, and shall not make any nonpublic comment that might substantially interfere with such proceeding. The temporary judge, referee or court-appointed arbitrator shall require similar abstention on the part of court personnel subject to his or her control. This Canon does not prohibit the following:

(a) Statements made in the course of the official duties of the temporary judge, referee or court-appointed arbitrator; and

(b) Explanations for public information about the procedures of the court.

(4) From the time of appointment and continuing for two years after the case is no longer pending in any court, a temporary judge, referee or court-appointed arbitrator shall under no circumstances accept a gift, bequest, or favor from a party, person, or entity whose interests have come before the temporary judge, referee or court-appointed arbitrator in the matter. The

temporary judge, referee or court-appointed arbitrator shall discourage family members residing in the household of the temporary judge, referee or court-appointed arbitrator from accepting any benefits from such parties, persons or entities during the time period stated in this subdivision. The demand for or receipt by a temporary judge, referee or court-appointed arbitrator of a fee for his or her services rendered or to be rendered shall not be a violation of this Canon.

(5) A temporary judge, referee or court-appointed arbitrator shall, from time of notice and acceptance of appointment and continuing indefinitely after the termination of the appointment:

(a) Comply with Canons 3(B)(11) [no disclosure of nonpublic information acquired in a judicial capacity] (except as required by law);

(b) Not commend or criticize jurors sitting in a proceeding before the temporary judge, referee or court-appointed arbitrator for their verdict other than in a court order or opinion in such proceeding, but may express appreciation to jurors for their service to the judicial system and the community.

(6) A temporary judge, referee or court-appointed arbitrator shall comply with Canon 6D(2) until the appointment has been terminated formally or until there is no reasonable probability that the temporary judge, referee or court-appointed arbitrator will further participate in the matter. A rebuttable presumption that the appointment has been formally terminated shall arise if, within one year from the appointment or from the date of the last hearing scheduled in the matter, which ever is later, neither the appointing court nor counsel for any party in the matter has informed the temporary judge, referee or court-appointed arbitrator that the appointment remains in effect.

(7) A lawyer who has been a temporary judge, referee, or court-appointed arbitrator in a matter shall not accept any representation relating to the matter without the informed written consent of all parties.

(8) When by reason of serving as a temporary judge, referee, or court-appointed arbitrator in a matter, he or she has received confidential information from a party, the person shall not, without the informed written consent of the party, accept employment in another matter in which the confidential information is material.

(Canon 6D amended effective March 4, 1999.)

Advisory Committee Commentary

Any exceptions to the Canons do not excuse a judicial officer's separate statutory duty to disclose information that may result in the judicial officer's recusal or disqualification.

E. Judicial Candidate

A candidate* for judicial office shall comply with the provisions of Canon 5.

F. Time for Compliance A person to whom this Code becomes applicable shall comply immediately with all provisions of this Code except

Canons 4D(2) and 4F and shall comply with these Canons as soon as reasonably possible and shall do so in any event within a period of one year.

Canon 6D amended effective March 4, 1999; previously amended effective April 15, 1996; adopted effective January 15, 1996.

Advisory Committee Commentary

If serving as a fiduciary* when selected as a judge, a new judge may, notwithstanding the prohibitions in Canon 4F, continue to serve as fiduciary* but only for that period of time necessary to avoid adverse consequences to the beneficiary of the fiduciary relationship and in no event longer than one year. Similarly, if engaged at the time of judicial selection in a business activity, a new judge may, notwithstanding the prohibitions in Canon 4D(2), continue in that activity for a reasonable period but in no event longer than one year.

* [Pub. Note: This term is explained in the section titled "Terminology", supra.]

CALIFORNIA RULE ON CONFIDENTIALITY OF PROCEEDINGS BEFORE THE COMMISSION ON JUDICIAL PERFORMANCE

RULE 102. Confidentiality and Disclosure

(a) (Scope of rule) Except as provided in this rule, all papers filed with and proceedings before the commission shall be confidential. Nothing in this rule prohibits the respondent judge or anyone other than a commission member or member of commission staff from making statements regarding the judge's conduct underlying a complaint or proceeding.

(b) (Disclosure after institution of formal proceedings) When the commission institutes formal proceedings, the following shall not be confidential:

(1) The notice of formal proceedings and all subsequent papers filed with the commission and the special masters, all stipulations entered, all findings of fact and conclusions of law made by the special masters and by the commission, and all determinations of removal, censure, and public admonishment made by the commission;

(2) The formal hearing before the special masters and the appearance before the commission.

(c) (Explanatory statements) The commission may issue explanatory statements under article VI, section 18(k) of the California Constitution.

(d) (Submission of proposed statement of clarification and correction regarding commission proceedings by judge) Notwithstanding rule 102(a), if public reports concerning a commission proceeding result in substantial unfairness to the judge involved in the proceeding, including unfairness resulting from reports which are false or materially misleading or inaccurate, the involved judge may submit a proposed statement of clarification and correction to the commission and request its issuance. The commission shall either issue the requested statement, advise the judge in writing that it declines to issue the requested statement, or issue a modified statement.

(e) (Disclosure to complainant) Upon completion of an investigation or proceeding, the commission shall disclose to the person complaining against the judge that the commission (1) has found no basis for action against the judge, (2) has taken an appropriate corrective action, the nature of which shall not be disclosed, or (3) has publicly admonished, censured, removed, or retired the judge, or has found the person unfit to serve as a subordinate judicial officer. The name of the judge shall not be used in any written communication to the complainant, unless formal proceedings have been instituted. Written communications to the complainant in which the judge's name is not used shall include the date of the complaint as a cross-reference.

(f) (Public safety) When the commission receives information concerning a threat to the safety of any person or persons, information concerning such a threat may be provided to the person threatened, to persons or organizations responsible for the safety of the person threatened, and to law enforcement and/or any appropriate prosecutorial agency.

(g) (Disclosure of information to prosecuting authorities) The commission may release to prosecuting authorities at any time information which reveals possible criminal conduct by the judge or former judge or by any other individual or entity.

(h) (Disclosure of records of disciplinary action to public entity upon request or consent of judge) If a judge or former judge requests or consents to release of commission records of disciplinary action to a public entity, the commission may release those records.

(i) (Disclosure of records of disciplinary action to appointing authorities) Pursuant to article VI, section 18.5 of the California Constitution, the commission shall, upon request, provide to the Governor of any State of the Union, the President of the United States, or the Commission on Judicial Appointments the text of any private admonishment or advisory letter issued after March 1, 1995 or any other disciplinary action together with any information that the commission deems necessary to a full understanding of the commission's action, with respect to any applicant under consideration for any judicial appointment, provided that:

(1) The request is in writing; and

(2) Any information released to the appointing authority is simultaneously provided to the applicant.

All information disclosed to appointing authorities under this subdivision remains privileged and confidential. Private admonishments and advisory letters issued before March 1, 1995 shall only be disclosed under this section with the judge's written consent.

(j) (Disclosure of information regarding pending proceedings to appointing authorities) The commission may, upon request, in the interest of justice or to maintain public confidence in the administration of justice, provide to the Governor of any State of the Union, the President of the United States, the Commission on Judicial Appointments, or any other state or federal authorities responsible for judicial appointments information concerning any pending investigation or proceeding with respect to any applicant under consideration for any judicial appointment, provided that:

(1) The request is in writing; and

(2) Any information released to the appointing authority is simultaneously provided to the applicant.

All information disclosed to appointing authorities under this subdivision remains privileged and confidential.

(k) (Disclosure of information to public entities upon retirement or resignation) If a judge retires or resigns from judicial office after a complaint is filed with the commission, at the time of closing the complaint, investigation or other proceeding, the commission may, in the interest of justice or to maintain public confidence in the administration of justice, release information concerning the complaint, investigation and proceedings to the State Bar, to prosecutorial agencies, to state or federal authorities responsible for judicial appointments, to regulatory agencies, or to the Chief Justice of the California Supreme Court, provided that the commission has completed a preliminary investigation.

(*l*) (Disclosure of information about subordinate judicial officers to presiding judges) The commission may release to a presiding judge or his or her designee information concerning a complaint or an investigation involving a subordinate judicial officer consistent with the commission's jurisdiction under article VI, section 18.1 of the California Constitution.

AMERICAN BAR ASSOCIATION CANONS OF PROFESSIONAL ETHICS *

Preamble.

In America, where the stability of Courts and of all departments of government rests upon the approval of the people, it is peculiarly essential that the system for establishing and dispensing Justice be developed to a high point of efficiency and so maintained that the public shall have absolute confidence in the integrity and impartiality of its administration. The future of the Republic, to a great extent, depends upon our maintenance of Justice pure and unsullied. It cannot be so maintained unless the conduct and the motives of the members of our profession are such as to merit the approval of all just men.

No code or set of rules can be framed, which will particularize all the duties of the lawyer in the varying phases of litigation or in all the relations of professional life. The following canons of ethics are adopted by the American Bar Association as a general guide, yet the enumeration of particular duties should not be construed as a denial of the existence of others equally imperative, though not specifically mentioned.

1. The Duty of the Lawyer to the Courts

It is the duty of the lawyer to maintain towards the Courts a respectful attitude, not for the sake of the temporary incumbent of the judicial office, but for the maintenance of its supreme importance. Judges, not being wholly free to defend themselves, are peculiarly entitled to receive the support of the Bar against unjust criticism and clamor. Whenever there is proper ground for serious complaint of a judicial officer, it is the right and duty of the lawyer to submit his grievances to the proper authorities. In such cases, but not otherwise, such charges should be encouraged and the person making them should be protected.

2. The Selection of Judges

It is the duty of the Bar to endeavor to prevent political considerations from outweighing judicial fitness in the selections of Judges. It should protest earnestly and actively against the appointment or election of those who are unsuitable for the Bench; and it should strive to have elevated thereto only those willing to forego other employments, whether of a business, political or other character, which may embarrass their free and fair consider-

* These Canons, to and including Canon 32 and the recommended oath, were adopted by the American Bar Association at Its Thirty-First Annual Meeting at Seattle, Washington, on August 27, 1908. The Canons were applied, as amended, until the adoption of the Code in 1970. Reprinted with permission. Copyright © American Bar Association.

ation of questions before them for decision. The aspiration of lawyers for judicial position should be governed by an impartial estimate of their ability to add honor to the office and not by a desire for the distinction the position may bring to themselves.

3. Attempts to Exert Personal Influence on the Court

Marked attention and unusual hospitality on the part of a lawyer to a Judge, uncalled for by the personal relations of the parties, subject both the Judge and the lawyer to misconstructions of motive and should be avoided. A lawyer should not communicate or argue privately with the Judge as to the merits of a pending cause, and he deserves rebuke and denunciation for any device or attempt to gain from a Judge special personal consideration or favor. A self-respecting independence in the discharge of professional duty, without denial or diminution of the courtesy and respect due the Judge's station, is the only proper foundation for cordial personal and official relations between Bench and Bar.

4. When Counsel for an Indigent Prisoner

A lawyer assigned as counsel for an indigent prisoner ought not to ask to be excused for any trivial reason, and should always exert his best efforts in his behalf.

5. The Defense or Prosecution of Those Accused of Crime

It is the right of the lawyer to undertake the defense of a person accused of crime, regardless of his personal opinion as to the guilt of the accused; otherwise innocent persons, victims only of suspicious circumstances, might be denied proper defense. Having undertaken such defense, the lawyer is bound, by all fair and honorable means, to present every defense that the law of the land permits, to the end that no person may be deprived of life or liberty, but by due process of law.

The primary duty of a lawyer engaged in public prosecution is not to convict, but to see that justice is done. The suppression of facts or the secreting of witnesses capable of establishing the innocence of the accused is highly reprehensible.

6. Adverse Influences and Conflicting Interests

It is the duty of a lawyer at the time of retainer to disclose to the client all the circumstances of his relations to the parties, and any interest in or connection with the controversy, which might influence the client in the selection of counsel.

It is unprofessional to represent conflicting interests, except by express consent of all concerned given after a full disclosure of the facts. Within the meaning of this canon, a lawyer represents conflicting interests when, in behalf of one client, it is his duty to contend for that which duty to another client requires him to oppose.

The obligation to represent the client with undivided fidelity and not to divulge his secrets or confidences forbids also the subsequent acceptance of retainers or employment from others in matters adversely affecting any interest of the client with respect to which confidence has been reposed.

7.   Professional Colleagues and Conflicts of Opinion

A client's proffer of assistance of additional counsel should not be regarded as evidence of want of confidence, but the matter should be left to the determination of the client.   A lawyer should decline association as colleague if it is objectionable to the original counsel, but if the lawyer first retained is relieved, another may come into the case.

When lawyers jointly associated in a cause cannot agree as to any matter vital to the interest of the client, the conflict of opinion should be frankly stated to him for his final determination.   His decision should be accepted unless the nature of the difference makes it impracticable for the lawyer whose judgment has been overruled to co-operate effectively.   In this event it is his duty to ask the client to relieve him.

Efforts, direct or indirect, in any way to encroach upon the professional employment of another lawyer, are unworthy of those who should be brethren at the Bar; but, nevertheless, it is the right of any lawyer, without fear or favor, to give proper advice to those seeking relief against unfaithful or neglectful counsel, generally after communication with the lawyer of whom the complaint is made.

8.   Advising Upon the Merits of a Client's Cause

A lawyer should endeavor to obtain full knowledge of his client's cause before advising thereon, and he is bound to give a candid opinion of the merits and probable result of pending or contemplated litigation.   The miscarriages to which justice is subject, by reason of surprises and disappointments in evidence and witnesses, and through mistakes of juries and errors of Courts, even though only occasional, admonish lawyers to beware of bold and confident assurances to clients, especially where the employment may depend upon such assurance.   Whenever the controversy will admit of fair adjustment, the client should be advised to avoid or to end the litigation.

9.   Negotiations With Opposite Party

A lawyer should not in any way communicate upon the subject of controversy with a party represented by counsel; much less should he undertake to negotiate or compromise the matter with him, but should deal only with his counsel.   It is incumbent upon the lawyer most particularly to avoid everything that may tend to mislead a party not represented by counsel, and he should not undertake to advise him as to the law.

10.   Acquiring Interest in Litigation

The lawyer should not purchase any interest in the subject matter of the litigation which he is conducting.

11. Dealing With Trust Property

The lawyer should refrain from any action whereby for his personal benefit or gain he abuses or takes advantage of the confidence reposed in him by his client.

Money of the client or collected for the client or other trust property coming into the possession of the lawyer should be reported and accounted for promptly, and should not under any circumstances be commingled with his own or be used by him.

12. Fixing the Amount of the Fee

In fixing fees, lawyers should avoid charges which overestimate their advice and services, as well as those which undervalue them. A client's ability to pay cannot justify a charge in excess of the value of the service, though his poverty may require a less charge, or even none at all. The reasonable requests of brother lawyers, and of their widows and orphans without ample means, should receive special and kindly consideration.

In determining the amount of the fee, it is proper to consider: (1) the time and labor required, the novelty and difficulty of the questions involved and the skill requisite properly to conduct the cause; (2) whether the acceptance of employment in the particular case will preclude the lawyer's appearance for others in cases likely to arise out of the transaction, and in which there is a reasonable expectation that otherwise he would be employed, or will involve the loss of other employment while employed in the particular case or antagonisms with other clients; (3) the customary charges of the Bar for similar services; (4) the amount involved in the controversy and the benefits resulting to the client from the services; (5) the contingency or the certainty of the compensation; and (6) the character of the employment, whether casual or for an established and constant client. No one of these considerations in itself is controlling. They are mere guides in ascertaining the real value of the service.

In determining the customary charges of the Bar for similar services, it is proper for a lawyer to consider a schedule of minimum fees adopted by a Bar Association, but no lawyer should permit himself to be controlled thereby or to follow it as his sole guide in determining the amount of his fee.

In fixing fees it should never be forgotten that the profession is a branch of the administration of justice and not a mere money-getting trade.

13. Contingent Fees

A contract for a contingent fee, where sanctioned by law, should be reasonable under all the circumstances of the case, including the risk and uncertainty of the compensation, but should always be subject to the supervision of a court, as to its reasonableness.

14. Suing a Client for a Fee

Controversies with clients concerning compensation are to be avoided by the lawyer so far as shall be compatible with his self-respect and with his right to receive reasonable recompense for his services; and lawsuits with clients should be resorted to only to prevent injustice, imposition or fraud.

15. How Far a Lawyer May Go in Supporting a Client's Cause

Nothing operates more certainly to create or to foster popular prejudice against lawyers as a class, and to deprive the profession of that full measure of public esteem and confidence which belongs to the proper discharge of its duties than does the false claim, often set up by the unscrupulous in defense of questionable transactions, that it is the duty of the lawyer to do whatever may enable him to succeed in winning his client's cause.

It is improper for a lawyer to assert in argument his personal belief in his client's innocence or in the justice of his cause.

The lawyer owes "entire devotion to the interest of the client, warm zeal in the maintenance and defense of his rights and the exertion of his utmost learning and ability," to the end that nothing be taken or be withheld from him, save by the rules of law, legally applied. No fear of judicial disfavor or public unpopularity should restrain him from the full discharge of his duty. In the judicial forum the client is entitled to the benefit of any and every remedy and defense that is authorized by the law of the land, and he may expect his lawyer to assert every such remedy or defense. But it is steadfastly to be borne in mind that the great trust of the lawyer is to be performed within and not without the bounds of the law. The office of attorney does not permit, much less does it demand of him for any client, violation of law or any manner of fraud or chicane. He must obey his own conscience and not that of his client.

16. Restraining Clients from Improprieties

A lawyer should use his best efforts to restrain and to prevent his clients from doing those things which the lawyer himself ought not to do, particularly with reference to their conduct towards Courts, judicial officers, jurors, witnesses and suitors. If a client persists in such wrongdoing the lawyer should terminate their relation.

17. Ill-Feeling and Personalities Between Advocates

Clients, not lawyers, are the litigants. Whatever may be the ill-feeling existing between clients, it should not be allowed to influence counsel in their conduct and demeanor toward each other or toward suitors in the case. All personalities between counsel should be scrupulously avoided. In the trial of a cause it is indecent to allude to the personal history or the personal peculiarities and idiosyncrasies of counsel on the other side. Personal colloquies between counsel which cause delay and promote unseemly wrangling should also be carefully avoided.

18. Treatment of Witnesses and Litigants

A lawyer should always treat adverse witnesses and suitors with fairness and due consideration, and he should never minister to the malevolence or prejudices of a client in the trial or conduct of a cause. The client cannot be made the keeper of the lawyer's conscience in professional matters. He has no right to demand that his counsel shall abuse the opposite party or indulge in offensive personalities. Improper speech is not excusable on the ground that it is what the client would say if speaking in his own behalf.

19. Appearance of Lawyer as Witness for His Client

When a lawyer is a witness for his client, except as to merely formal matters, such as the attestation or custody of an instrument and the like, he should leave the trial of the case to other counsel. Except when essential to the ends of justice, a lawyer should avoid testifying in court in behalf of his client.

20. Newspaper Discussion of Pending Litigation

Newspaper publications by a lawyer as to pending or anticipated litigation may interfere with a fair trial in the Courts and otherwise prejudice the due administration of justice. Generally they are to be condemned. If the extreme circumstances of a particular case justify a statement to the public, it is unprofessional to make it anonymously. An *ex parte* reference to the facts should not go beyond quotation from the records and papers on file in the court; but even in extreme cases it is better to avoid any *ex parte* statement.

21. Punctuality and Expedition

It is the duty of the lawyer not only to his client, but also to the Courts and to the public to be punctual in attendance, and to be concise and direct in the trial and disposition of causes.

22. Candor and Fairness

The conduct of the lawyer before the Court and with other lawyers should be characterized by candor and fairness.

It is not candid or fair for the lawyer knowingly to misquote the contents of a paper, the testimony of a witness, the language or the argument of opposing counsel, or the language of a decision or a textbook; or with knowledge of its invalidity, to cite as authority a decision that has been overruled, or a statute that has been repealed; or in argument to assert as a fact that which has not been proved, or in those jurisdictions where a side has the opening and closing arguments to mislead his opponent by concealing or withholding positions in his opening argument upon which his side then intends to rely.

It is unprofessional and dishonorable to deal other than candidly with the facts in taking the statements of witnesses, in drawing affidavits and other documents, and in the presentation of causes.

A lawyer should not offer evidence which he knows the Court should reject, in order to get the same before the jury by argument for its admissibility, nor should he address to the Judge arguments upon any point not properly calling for determination by him. Neither should he introduce into an argument, addressed to the court, remarks or statements intended to influence the jury or bystanders.

These and all kindred practices are unprofessional and unworthy of an officer of the law charged, as is the lawyer, with the duty of aiding in the administration of justice.

23. Attitude Toward Jury

All attempts to curry favor with juries by fawning, flattery or pretended solicitude for their personal comfort are unprofessional. Suggestions of counsel, looking to the comfort or convenience of jurors, and propositions to dispense with argument, should be made to the Court out of the jury's hearing. A lawyer must never converse privately with jurors about the case; and both before and during the trial he should avoid communicating with them, even as to matters foreign to the cause.

24. Right of Lawyer to Control the Incidents of the Trial

As to incidental matters pending the trial, not affecting the merits of the cause, or working substantial prejudice to the rights of the client, such as forcing the opposite lawyer to trial when he is under affliction or bereavement; forcing the trial on a particular day to the injury of the opposite lawyer when no harm will result from a trial at a different time; agreeing to an extension of time for signing a bill of exceptions, cross interrogatories and the like, the lawyer must be allowed to judge. In such matters no client has a right to demand that his counsel shall be illiberal, or that he do anything therein repugnant to his own sense of honor and propriety.

25. Taking Technical Advantage of Opposite Counsel; Agreements With Him

A lawyer should not ignore known customs or practice of the Bar or of a particular Court, even when the law permits, without giving timely notice to the opposing counsel. As far as possible, important agreements, affecting the rights of clients, should be reduced to writing; but it is dishonorable to avoid performance of an agreement fairly made because it is not reduced to writing, as required by rules of Court.

26. Professional Advocacy Other Than Before Courts

A lawyer openly, and in his true character may render professional services before legislative or other bodies, regarding proposed legislation and in advocacy of claims before departments of government, upon the same principles of ethics which justify his appearance before the Courts; but it is unprofessional for a lawyer so engaged to conceal his attorneyship, or to employ secret personal solicitations, or to use means other than those addressed to the reason and understanding, to influence action.

27. Advertising, Direct or Indirect

It is unprofessional to solicit professional employment by circulars, advertisements, through touters or by personal communications or interviews not warranted by personal relations. Indirect advertisements for professional employment such as furnishing or inspiring newspaper comments, or procuring his photograph to be published in connection with causes in which the lawyer has been or is engaged or concerning the manner of their conduct, the magnitude of the interest involved, the importance of the lawyer's position, and all other like self-laudation, offend the traditions and lower the tone of our profession and are reprehensible; but the customary use of simple professional cards is not improper.

Publication in reputable law lists in a manner consistent with the standards of conduct imposed by these canons of brief biographical and informative data is permissible. Such data must not be misleading and may include only a statement of the lawyer's name and the names of his professional associates; addresses, telephone numbers, cable addresses; branches of the profession practiced; date and place of birth and admission to the bar; schools attended; with dates of graduation, degrees and other educational distinctions; public or quasi-public offices; posts of honor; legal authorships; legal teaching positions; memberships and offices in bar associations and committees thereof, in legal and scientific societies and legal fraternities; foreign language ability; the fact of listings in other reputable law lists; the names and addresses of references; and, with their written consent, the names of clients regularly represented. A certificate of compliance with the Rules and Standards issued by the Standing Committee on Law Lists may be treated as evidence that such list is reputable.

It is not improper for a lawyer who is admitted to practice as a proctor in admiralty to use that designation on his letterhead or shingle or for a lawyer who has complied with the statutory requirements of admission to practice before the patent office, to so use the designation "patent attorney" or "patent lawyer" or "trademark attorney" or "trademark lawyer" or any combination of those terms.

28. Stirring Up Litigation, Directly or Through Agents

It is unprofessional for a lawyer to volunteer advice to bring a lawsuit, except in rare cases where ties of blood, relationship or trust make it his duty to do so. Stirring up strife and litigation is not only unprofessional, but it is indictable at common law. It is disreputable to hunt up defects in titles or other causes of action and inform thereof in order to be employed to bring suit or collect judgment, or to breed litigation by seeking out those with claims for personal injuries or those having any other grounds of action in order to secure them as clients, or to employ agents or runners for like purposes, or to pay or reward, directly or indirectly, those who bring or influence the bringing of such cases to his office, or to remunerate policemen, court or prison officials, physicians, hospital *attachés* or others who may succeed, under the guise of giving disinterested friendly advice, in influencing the criminal, the sick and the injured, the ignorant or others, to seek his professional services. A duty to the public and to the profession devolves upon every member of the Bar having knowledge of such practices upon the part of any practitioner immediately to inform thereof, to the end that the offender may be disbarred.

29. Upholding the Honor of the Profession

Lawyers should expose without fear or favor before the proper tribunals corrupt or dishonest conduct in the profession, and should accept without hesitation employment against a member of the Bar who has wronged his client. The counsel upon the trial of a cause in which perjury has been committed owe it to the profession and to the public to bring the matter to the knowledge of the prosecuting authorities. The lawyer should aid in guarding the Bar against the admission to the profession of candidates unfit or unqualified because deficient in either moral character or education. He should strive at all times to uphold the honor and to maintain the dignity of the profession and to improve not only the law but the administration of justice.

30. Justifiable and Unjustifiable Litigations

The lawyer must decline to conduct a civil cause or to make a defense when convinced that it is intended merely to harass or to injure the opposite party or to work oppression or wrong. But otherwise it is his right, and, having accepted retainer, it becomes his duty to insist upon the judgment of the Court as to the legal merits of his client's claim. His appearance in Court should be deemed equivalent to an assertion on his honor that in his opinion his client's case is one proper for judicial determination.

31. Responsibility for Litigation

No lawyer is obliged to act either as adviser or advocate for every person who may wish to become his client. He has the right to decline employment. Every lawyer upon his own responsibility must decide what employment he will accept as counsel, what causes he will bring into Court for plaintiffs, what cases he will contest in Court for defendants. The responsibility for advising as to questionable transactions, for bringing questionable suits, for urging questionable defenses, is the lawyer's responsibility. He cannot escape it by urging as an excuse that he is only following his client's instructions.

32. The Lawyer's Duty in Its Last Analysis

No client, corporate or individual, however powerful, nor any cause, civil or political, however important, is entitled to receive nor should any lawyer render any service or advice involving disloyalty to the law whose ministers we are, or disrespect of the judicial office, which we are bound to uphold, or corruption of any person or persons exercising a public office or private trust, or deception or betrayal of the public. When rendering any such improper service or advice, the lawyer invites and merits stern and just condemnation. Correspondingly, he advances the honor of his profession and the best interests of his client when he renders service or gives advice tending to impress upon the client and his undertaking exact compliance with the strictest principles of moral law. He must also observe and advise his client to observe the statute law, though until a statute shall have been construed and interpreted by competent adjudication, he is free and is entitled to advise as to its validity and as to what he conscientiously believes to be its just meaning and extent. But above all a lawyer will find his highest honor in a deserved reputation for fidelity to private trust and to public duty, as an honest man and as a patriotic and loyal citizen.

33. Partnerships—Names

Partnerships among lawyers for the practice of their profession are very common and are not to be condemned. In the formation of partnerships and the use of partnership names care should be taken not to violate any law, custom, or rule of court locally applicable. Where partnerships are formed between lawyers who are not all admitted to practice in the courts of the state, care should be taken to avoid any misleading name or representation which would create a false impression as to the professional position or privileges of the member not locally admitted. In the formation of partnerships for the practice of law, no person should be admitted or held out as a practitioner or member who is not a member of the legal profession duly authorized to practice, and amenable to professional discipline. In the selection and use of a firm name, no false, misleading, assumed or trade name should be used. The continued use of the name of a deceased or former partner, when permissible by local custom, is not unethical, but care should be taken that no imposition or deception is practiced through this use. When a member of the firm, on becoming a judge, is precluded from practicing law, his name should not be continued in the firm name.

Partnerships between lawyers and members of other professions or non-professional persons should not be formed or permitted where any part of the partnership's employment consists of the practice of law.

34. Division of Fees

No division of fees for legal services is proper, except with another lawyer, based upon a division of service or responsibility.

35. Intermediaries

The professional services of a lawyer should not be controlled or exploited by any lay agency, personal or corporate, which intervenes between client and lawyer. A lawyer's responsibilities and qualifications are individual. He should avoid all relations which direct the performance of his duties by or in the interest of such intermediary. A lawyer's relation to his client should be personal, and the responsibility should be direct to the client. Charitable societies rendering aid to the indigents are not deemed such intermediaries.

A lawyer may accept employment from any organization, such as an association, club or trade organization, to render legal services in any matter in which the organization, as an entity, is interested, but this employment should not include the rendering of legal services to the members of such an organization in respect to their individual affairs.

36. Retirement From Judicial Position or Public Employment

A lawyer should not accept employment as an advocate in any matter upon the merits of which he has previously acted in a judicial capacity.

A lawyer, having once held public office or having been in the public employ, should not after his retirement accept employment in connection with any matter which he has investigated or passed upon while in such office or employ.

37. Confidences of a Client

It is the duty of a lawyer to preserve his client's confidences. This duty outlasts the lawyer's employment, and extends as well to his employees; and neither of them should accept employment which involves or may involve the disclosure or use of these confidences, either for the private advantage of the lawyer or his employees or to the disadvantage of the client, without his knowledge and consent, and even though there are other available sources of such information. A lawyer should not continue employment when he discovers that this obligation prevents the performance of his full duty to his former or to his new client.

If a lawyer is accused by his client, he is not precluded from disclosing the truth in respect to the accusation. The announced intention of a client to commit a crime is not included within the confidences which he is bound to respect. He may properly make such disclosures as may be necessary to prevent the act or protect those against whom it is threatened.

38. Compensation, Commissions and Rebates

A lawyer should accept no compensation, commissions, rebates or other advantages from others without the knowledge and consent of his client after full disclosure.

39. Witnesses

A lawyer may properly interview any witness or prospective witness for the opposing side in any civil or criminal action without the consent of opposing counsel or party. In doing so, however, he should scrupulously avoid any suggestion calculated to induce the witness to suppress or deviate from the truth, or in any degree to affect his free and untrammeled conduct when appearing at the trial or on the witness stand.

40. Newspapers

A lawyer may with propriety write articles for publications in which he gives information upon the law; but he should not accept employment from such publications to advise inquirers in respect to their individual rights.

41. Discovery of Imposition and Deception

When a lawyer discovers that some fraud or deception has been practiced, which has unjustly imposed upon the court or a party, he should endeavor to rectify it; at first by advising his client, and if his client refuses to forego the advantage thus unjustly gained, he should promptly inform the injured person or his counsel, so that they may take appropriate steps.

42. Expenses of Litigation

A lawyer may not properly agree with a client that the lawyer shall pay or bear the expenses of litigation; he may in good faith advance expenses as a matter of convenience, but subject to reimbursement.

43. Approved Law Lists

It shall be improper for a lawyer to permit his name to be published in a law list the conduct, management or contents of which are calculated or likely to deceive or injure the public or the profession, or to lower the dignity or standing of the profession.

44. Withdrawal From Employment as Attorney or Counsel

The right of an attorney or counsel to withdraw from employment, once assumed, arises only from good cause. Even the desire or consent of the client is not always sufficient. The lawyer should not throw up the unfinished task to the detriment of his client except for reasons of honor or self-respect. If the client insists upon an unjust or immoral course in the conduct of his case, or if he persists over the attorney's remonstrance in presenting frivolous defenses, or if he deliberately disregards an agreement or obligation as to fees or expenses, the lawyer may be warranted in withdrawing on due notice to the client, allowing him time to employ another lawyer. So also when a lawyer discovers that his client has no case and the client is determined to continue it; or even if the lawyer finds himself incapable of conducting the case effectively. Sundry other instances may arise in which withdrawal is to be justified. Upon withdrawing from a case after a retainer has been paid, the attorney should refund such part of the retainer as has not been clearly earned.

45. Specialists

The canons of the American Bar Association apply to all branches of the legal profession; specialists in particular branches are not to be considered as exempt from the application of these principles.

46. Notice to Local Lawyers

A lawyer available to act as an associate of other lawyers in a particular branch of the law or legal service may send to local lawyers only and publish in his local legal journal, a brief and dignified announcement of his availability to serve other lawyers in connection therewith. The announcement should be in a form which does not constitute a statement or representation of special experience or expertness.

47. Aiding the Unauthorized Practice of Law

No lawyer shall permit his professional services, or his name, to be used in aid of, or to make possible, the unauthorized practice of law by any lay agency, personal or corporate.

AMERICAN BAR ASSOCIATION STANDING COMMITTEE ON ETHICS AND PROFESSIONAL RESPONSIBILITY

COMPOSITION AND JURISDICTION *

The Standing Committee on Ethics and Professional Responsibility, which consists of ten members, may:

(1) by the concurrence of a majority of its members, express its opinion on proper professional or judicial conduct, either on its own initiative or when requested to do so by a member of the bar or the judiciary;

(2) periodically publish its issued opinions to the profession in summary or complete form and, on request, provide copies of opinions to members of the bar, the judiciary, and the public;

(3) provide under its supervision informal responses to ethics inquiries the answers to which are substantially governed by applicable ethical codes and existing written opinions;

(4) on request, advise or otherwise assist professional organizations and courts in their activities relating to the development, modification and interpretation of statements of the ethical standards of the profession such as the Model Rules of Professional Conduct, the predecessor Model Code of Professional Responsibility and the Code of Judicial Conduct;

(5) recommend amendments to or clarifications of the Model Rules of Professional Conduct or the Code of Judicial Conduct; and

(6) adopt rules relating to the procedures to be used in issuing opinions, effective when approved by the Board of Governors.

RULES OF PROCEDURE

1. The Committee may express its opinion on questions of proper professional and judicial conduct. The Model Rules of Professional Conduct and the Code of Judicial Conduct, as they may be amended or superseded, contain the standards to be applied. For as long as a significant number of jurisdictions continue to base their professional standards on the predecessor Model Code of Professional Responsibility, the Committee will continue to refer also to the Model Code in its opinions.

2. The Committee may issue an opinion on its own initiative or upon a request from a member of the bar or the judiciary or from a professional organization or a court.

3. The Committee may issue opinions of two kinds: Formal Opinions and Informal Opinions. Formal Opinions are those upon subjects the Com-

---

* As defined by the By-Laws of the American Bar Association, Article 30.7, as revised. Formerly called the Standing Committee on Professional Ethics.

mittee determines to be of widespread interest or unusual importance. Other opinions are Informal Opinions. The Committee will assign to each opinion a non-duplicative identifying number, with distinction between Formal Opinions and Informal Opinions.

4. The Committee will not usually issue an opinion on a question that is known to be pending before a court in a proceeding in which the requestor is involved. The Committee's published opinions will not identify the person who was the requestor or whose conduct is the subject of the opinion. The Committee will not issue an opinion on a question of law.

5. The Committee may invite or accept written information relevant to a particular opinion from a person or persons interested in such an opinion before the Committee begins its work on an opinion. Ordinarily, the Committee will not invite anyone to make an oral presentation or argument in support of that position.

6. When a Committee or staff member receives an inquiry about the status of a draft opinion from anyone outside the Committee, the member may inform the inquirer that the Committee is considering the question. Draft opinions may, in appropriate circumstances, be shown to other interested ABA Committees and entities. Committee and staff members shall not, absent unusual circumstances, discuss the substance of pending opinions with the public, but may mention topics related to pending opinions in a general fashion.

7. Before issuing an opinion with respect to judicial conduct the Committee will submit the proposed opinion to the Judges' Advisory Committee and consider any objection or comment from the Judges' Advisory Committee and any member of it. The Committee may assume that the Judges' Advisory Committee and its members have no objection or comment if none is received by the Committee within 30 days after the submission.

8. If the Committee decides not to issue a requested opinion the requestor will be promptly notified.

9. The Committee will issue an opinion only with the concurrence of six members in a vote taken at a meeting or in a telephone conference call. When a Committee member votes against a position declaring a Committee policy, that vote may be recorded in the minutes, which may include the name of the dissenting Committee member. The minutes shall not reflect the names of Committee members voting for or against any non-Committee policy question except that a member's vote shall be recorded and identified at the member's request.

When drafting an opinion, policy statement or other document to be publicly disseminated, the Committee shall make every effort to reach a consensus. When, after a full examination of the issue and an exchange of views, the Committee cannot reach a consensus, a dissenting opinion may be appropriate to express the views of a Committee member or members. A member may place a statement of dissent in the Committee file or request that the dissent be published with the opinion.

10. The Chair may assign to one or more members the responsibility of preparing a proposed opinion for consideration by the Committee. The Committee will issue a requested opinion as promptly as feasible.

11. A Formal Opinion overrules an earlier Formal Opinion or Informal Opinion to the extent of conflict. An Informal Opinion overrules an earlier Informal Opinion to the extent of conflict but does not overrule an earlier Formal Opinion.

12. Opinions of the Committee issued before the effective dates of the Model Rules of Professional Conduct, the predecessor Model Code of Professional Responsibility and the Code of Judicial Conduct continue in effect to the extent not inconsistent with those standards and not overruled or limited by later opinions.

13. The Committee will make opinions and/or summaries of opinions available for publication in the *American Bar Association Journal*. The Committee will cause Formal Opinions and Informal Opinions to be published in loose-leaf form.

14. The Committee may through its staff arrange to provide informal responses to ethics inquiries the answers to which are substantially governed by applicable ethical codes and opinions of this Committee or other ethics committees. The staff will maintain a log of such inquiries that will periodically be reviewed by the Committee.

15. Information contained in Committee files relating to requests for opinions that would disclose the identity of the inquirer or the person whose conduct is the subject of the opinion will not voluntarily be disclosed by the Association without the consent of the affected persons.

LAWYER'S CREED OF PROFESSIONALISM*

The ABA House of Delegates, at its August 1988 meeting, adopted as ABA policy a recommendation that state and local bar associations "encourage their members to accept as a guide for their individual conduct, and to comply with, a lawyers' creed of professionalism." The ABA Torts and Insurance Practice Section, which had sought and won the ABA's approval of such a policy, also set forth an example of such a "Lawyer's Creed of Professionalism." This document is published below in full text. The House of Delegates made clear that "nothing in such a creed shall be deemed to supersede or in any way amend the Model Rules of Professional Conduct or other disciplinary codes, alter existing standards of conduct against which lawyer negligence might be judged or become a basis for the imposition of civil liability of any kind."

At the same meeting, the House of Delegates authorized the dissemination to the profession of a "Lawyer's Pledge of Professionalism," which the ABA Young Lawyer's Section had proposed. This document is also published below in full text, and reprinted with permission.

Preamble

As a lawyer I must strive to make our system of justice work fairly and efficiently. In order to carry out that responsibility, not only will I comply with the letter and spirit of the disciplinary standards applicable to all lawyers, but I will also conduct myself in accordance with the following Creed of Professionalism when dealing with my client, opposing parties, their counsel, the courts and the general public.

A. With respect to my client:

1. I will be loyal and committed to my client's cause, but I will not permit that loyalty and commitment to interfere with my ability to provide my client with objective and independent advice;

2. I will endeavor to achieve my client's lawful objectives in business transactions and in litigation as expeditiously and economically as possible;

3. In appropriate cases, I will counsel my client with respect to mediation, arbitration and other alternative methods of resolving disputes;

4. I will advise my client against pursuing litigation (or any other course of action) that is without merit and against insisting on tactics which are intended to delay resolution of the matter or to harass or drain the financial resources of the opposing party;

5. I will advise my client that civility and courtesy are not to be equated with weakness;

6. While I must abide by my client's decision concerning the objectives of the representation, I nevertheless will counsel my client that a willingness to initiate or engage in settlement discussions is consistent with zealous and effective representation.

---

* Not adopted by the ABA House of Delegates. Not American Bar Association Policy. Reprinted with permission. Copyrighted by the A.B.A.

B. With respect to opposing parties and their counsel:

1. I will endeavor to be courteous and civil, both in oral and in written communications;

2. I will not knowingly make statements of fact or of law that are untrue;

3. In litigation proceedings I will agree to reasonable requests for extensions of time or for waiver of procedural formalities when the legitimate interests of my client will not be adversely affected;

4. I will endeavor to consult with opposing counsel before scheduling depositions and meetings and before re-scheduling hearings, and I will cooperate with opposing counsel when scheduling changes are requested;

5. I will refrain from utilizing litigation or any other course of conduct to harass the opposing party;

6. I will refrain from engaging in excessive and abusive discovery, and I will comply with all reasonable discovery requests;

7. I will refrain from utilizing delaying tactics;

8. In depositions and other proceedings, and in negotiations, I will conduct myself with dignity, avoid making groundless objections and refrain from engaging in acts of rudeness or disrespect;

9. I will not serve motions and pleadings on the other party, or his counsel, at such a time or in such a manner as will unfairly limit the other party's opportunity to respond;

10. In business transactions I will not quarrel over matters of form or style, but will concentrate on matters of substance and content;

11. I will clearly identify, for other counsel or parties, all changes that I have made in documents submitted to me for review.

C. With respect to the courts and other tribunals:

1. I will be a vigorous and zealous advocate on behalf of my client, while recognizing, as an officer of the court, that excessive zeal may be detrimental to my client's interests as well as to the proper functioning of our system of justice;

2. Where consistent with my client's interests, I will communicate with opposing counsel in an effort to avoid litigation and to resolve litigation that has actually commenced;

3. I will voluntarily withdraw claims or defenses when it becomes apparent that they do not have merit or are superfluous;

4. I will refrain from filing frivolous motions;

5. I will make every effort to agree with other counsel, as early as possible, on a voluntary exchange of information and on a plan for discovery;

6. I will attempt to resolve, by agreement, my objections to matters contained in my opponent's pleadings and discovery requests;

7. When scheduling hearings or depositions have to be canceled, I will notify opposing counsel, and, if appropriate, the court (or other tribunal) as early as possible;

8. Before dates for hearings or trials are set—or if that is not feasible, immediately after such dates have been set—I will attempt to verify the availability of key participants and witnesses so that I can promptly notify the court (or other tribunal) and opposing counsel of any likely problem in that regard;

9. In civil matters, I will stipulate to facts as to which there is no genuine dispute;

10. I will endeavor to be punctual in attending court hearings, conferences and depositions;

11. I will at all times be candid with the court.

D. With respect to the public and to our system of justice:

1. I will remember that, in addition to commitment to my client's cause, my responsibilities as a lawyer include a devotion to the public good;

2. I will endeavor to keep myself current in the areas in which I practice and, when necessary, will associate with, or refer my client to, counsel knowledgeable in another field of practice;

3. I will be mindful of the fact that, as a member of a self-regulating profession, it is incumbent on me to report violations by fellow lawyers of any disciplinary rule;

4. I will be mindful of the need to protect the image of the legal profession in the eyes of the public and will be so guided when considering methods and content of advertising;

5. I will be mindful that the law is a learned profession and that among its desirable goals are devotion to public service, improvement of administration of justice, and the contribution of uncompensated time and civic influence on behalf of those persons who cannot afford adequate legal assistance.

CIVILITY CODES

PROPOSED STANDARDS FOR PROFESSIONAL CONDUCT WITHIN THE SEVENTH FEDERAL JUDICIAL CIRCUIT*

Preamble

A Lawyer's conduct should be characterized at all times by personal courtesy and professional integrity in the fullest sense of those terms. In fulfilling our duty to represent a client vigorously as lawyers, we will be mindful of our obligations to the administration of justice, which is a truth-seeking process designed to resolve human and societal problems in a rational, peaceful, and efficient manner.

A judge's conduct should be characterized at all times by courtesy and patience toward all participants. As judges we owe to all participants in a legal proceeding respect, diligence, punctuality, and protection against unjust and improper criticism or attack.

Conduct that may be characterized as uncivil, abrasive, abusive, hostile, or obstructive impedes the fundamental goal of resolving disputes rationally, peacefully, and efficiently. Such conduct tends to delay and often to deny justice.

The following standards are designed to encourage us, judges and lawyers, to meet our obligations to each other, to litigants and to the system of justice, and thereby achieve the twin goals of civility and professionalism, both of which are hallmarks of a learned profession dedicated to public service.

We expect judges and lawyers will make a mutual and firm commitment to these standards. Voluntary adherence is expected as part of a commitment by all participants to improve the administration of justice throughout the circuit.

These standards shall not be used as a basis for litigation or for sanctions or penalties. Nothing in these standards supersedes or detracts from existing disciplinary codes or alters existing standards of conduct against which lawyer negligence may be determined.

These standards should be reviewed and followed by all judges and lawyers participating in any proceeding in this Circuit. Copies may be made available to clients to reinforce our obligation to maintain and foster these standards.

Lawyers' Duties to Other Counsel

1. We will practice our profession with a continuing awareness that our role is to advance the legitimate interests of our clients. In our dealings with others we will not reflect the ill feelings of our clients. We will treat all

* Final Report of the Committee on Civility   F.R.D. 441, 448 (1992).
of the Seventh Federal Judicial Circuit, 143

other counsel, parties, and witnesses in a civil and courteous manner, not only in court, but also in all other written and oral communications.

2. We will not, even when called upon by a client to do so, abuse or indulge in offensive conduct directed to other counsel, parties, or witnesses. We will abstain from disparaging personal remarks or acrimony toward other counsel, parties, or witnesses. We will treat adverse witnesses and parties with fair consideration.

3. We will not encourage or knowingly authorize any person under our control to engage in conduct that would be improper if we were to engage in such conduct.

4. We will not, absent good cause, attribute bad motives or improper conduct to other counsel or bring the profession into disrepute by unfounded accusations of impropriety.

5. We will not seek court sanctions without first conducting a reasonable investigation and unless fully justified by the circumstances and necessary to protect our client's lawful interests.

6. We will adhere to all express promises and to agreements with other counsel, whether oral or in writing, and will adhere in good faith to all agreements implied by the circumstances or local customs.

7. When we reach an oral understanding on a proposed agreement or a stipulation and decide to commit it to writing, the drafter will endeavor in good faith to state the oral understanding accurately and completely. The drafter will provide the opportunity for review of the writing to other counsel. As drafts are exchanged between or among counsel, changes from prior drafts will be identified in the draft or otherwise explicitly brought to the attention of other counsel. We will not include in a draft matters to which there has been no agreement without explicitly advising other counsel in writing of the addition.

8. We will endeavor to confer early with other counsel to assess settlement possibilities. We will not falsely hold out the possibility of settlement as a means to adjourn discovery or to delay trial.

9. In civil actions, we will stipulate to relevant matters if they are undisputed and if no good faith advocacy basis exists for not stipulating.

10. We will not use any form of discovery or discovery scheduling as a means of harassment.

11. We will make good faith efforts to resolve by agreement our objections to matters contained in pleadings and discovery requests and objections.

12. We will not time the filing or service of motions or pleadings in any way that unfairly limits another party's opportunity to respond.

13. We will not request an extension of time solely for the purpose of unjustified delay or to obtain a tactical advantage.

14. We will consult other counsel regarding scheduling matters in a good faith effort to avoid scheduling conflicts.

15. We will endeavor to accommodate previously scheduled dates for hearings, depositions, meetings, conferences, vacations, seminars, or other functions that produce good faith calendar conflicts on the part of other counsel. If we have been given an accommodation because of a calendar conflict, we will notify those who have accommodated us as soon as the conflict has been removed.

16. We will notify other counsel and, if appropriate, the court or other persons, at the earliest possible time when hearings, depositions, meetings, or conferences are to be canceled or postponed. Early notice avoids unnecessary travel and expense of counsel and may enable the court to use the previously reserved time for other matters.

17. We will agree to reasonable requests for extensions of time and for waiver of procedural formalities, provided our clients' legitimate rights will not be materially or adversely affected.

18. We will not cause any default or dismissal to be entered without first notifying opposing counsel, when we know his or her identity.

19. We will take depositions only when actually needed to ascertain facts or information or to perpetuate testimony. We will not take depositions for the purposes of harassment or to increase litigation expenses.

20. We will not engage in any conduct during a deposition that would not be appropriate in the presence of a judge.

21. We will not obstruct questioning during a deposition or object to deposition questions unless necessary under the applicable rules to preserve an objection or privilege for resolution by the court.

22. During depositions we will ask only those questions we reasonably believe are necessary for the prosecution or defense of an action.

23. We will carefully craft document production requests so they are limited to those documents we reasonably believe are necessary for the prosecution or defense of an action. We will not design production requests to place an undue burden or expense on a party.

24. We will respond to document requests reasonably and not strain to interpret the request in an artificially restrictive manner to avoid disclosure of relevant and non-privileged documents. We will not produce documents in a manner designed to hide or obscure the existence of particular documents.

25. We will carefully craft interrogatories so they are limited to those matters we reasonably believe are necessary for the prosecution or defense of an action, and we will not design them to place an undue burden or expense on a party.

26. We will respond to interrogatories reasonably and will not strain to interpret them in an artificially restrictive manner to avoid disclosure of relevant and non-privileged information.

27. We will base our discovery objections on a good faith belief in their merit and will not object solely for the purpose of withholding or delaying the disclosure of relevant information.

28. When a draft order is to be prepared by counsel to reflect a court ruling, we will draft an order that accurately and completely reflects the court's ruling. We will promptly prepare and submit a proposed order to other counsel and attempt to reconcile any differences before the draft order is presented to the courts.

29. We will not ascribe a position to another counsel that counsel has not taken or otherwise seek to create an unjustified inference based on counsel's statements or conduct.

30. Unless specifically permitted or invited by the court, we will not send copies of correspondence between counsel to the court.

Lawyers' Duties to the Court

1. We will speak and write civilly and respectfully in all communications with the court.

2. We will be punctual and prepared for all court appearances so that all hearings, conferences, and trials may commence on time; if delayed, we will notify the court and counsel, if possible.

3. We will be considerate of the time constraints and pressures on the court and court staff inherent in their efforts to administer justice.

4. We will not engage in any conduct that brings disorder or disruption to the courtroom. We will advise our clients and witnesses appearing in court of the proper conduct expected and required there and, to the best of our ability, prevent our clients and witnesses from creating disorder or disruption.

5. We will not knowingly misrepresent, mischaracterize, misquote, or mis-cite facts or authorities in any oral or written communication to the court.

6. We will not write letters to the court in connection with a pending action, unless invited or permitted by the court.

7. Before dates for hearings or trials are set, or if that is not feasible, immediately after such date has been set, we will attempt to verify the availability of necessary participants and witnesses so we can promptly notify the court of any likely problems.

8. We will act and speak civilly to court marshals, clerks, court reporters, secretaries, and law clerks with an awareness that they, too, are an integral part of the judicial system.

THE NORTHAMPTON COUNTY BAR ASSOCIATION GUIDE TO CONDUCT AND ETIQUETTE AT THE BAR

These guiding principles comprise the considered opinion of the Bench and Bar of Northampton County concerning professional etiquette and are a result of suggestions made by the Bench at the request of the Bar.

1. Lawyers should dress in a fashion consistent with the respect they expect the public to have for their profession. Lawyers should not appear before the Court in overcoats or other wearing apparel designed for outdoor wear. Lawyers who are at the courthouse for reasons other than a Court appearance should nonetheless recognize the courthouse as the center and focus of their professional activity and dress accordingly. The same formality of dress that is appropriate for the courtroom is appropriate for an appearance before a Judge at the Judge's office or in the Judge's chambers.

2. Lawyers should ask permission to address the Court rather than just jumping up and starting to talk. The proper method of requesting such permission is to preface one's remark by the phrase: "May it please the Court ..."

3. Lawyers should request permission to approach the bench prior to doing so. While at sidebar, lawyers should not rest upon nor "drape themselves" over the bench.

4. Lawyers should first address the Court and opposing counsel before addressing the jury. The proper form of doing this is to first address the Court: "May it please the Court." The Court then acknowledges counsel. Counsel then addresses opposing counsel first: "Mr., Ms., Mrs., _____," and then "Ladies and Gentlemen of the Jury."

5. Lawyers should always stand when addressing the court. This should be done even at the call of the hearing list and the various trial lists.

6. Lawyers when making objections should stand and state a brief (one word if possible) reason for the objection, such as "Objection: Hearsay." If it is necessary to enlarge the record after an objection, lawyers should approach the bench and quietly, out of the hearing of the jury, state their reasons. They should not present their arguments to the jury but only to the Court.

7. In addressing a witness lawyers should stand behind their desk and if for any reason they want to approach the witness, they should only do so after obtaining the court's permission.

8. When marking exhibits for identification, it is suggested that the courteous way of doing this is to give the exhibit to the court reporter to have the exhibit marked, and to then exhibit it to the court and to opposing counsel. All of these actions should be performed before questions are again directed to the witness. The court reporter cannot possibly mark an exhibit and record testimony at the same time. Where there are a multitude of exhibits, they should be marked in advance by the court reporter or the lawyers. When possible and not too cumbersome, separate copies of exhibits should be provided for the Court. This permits the original to remain with the court reporter and avoids the problem of lawyers having to search for them on the bench or elsewhere.

9. Lawyers should always keep their voices up and remind their witnesses to do the same.

10. Lawyers should never directly address opposing counsel in Court. Lawyers should directly address only the Court, the jury, and the witnesses.

11. A lawyer should not call any witness, even his or her client, by the witness' first name.

12. Lawyers should limit voir dire questions to the proper purpose of voir dire and should not attempt to instruct the jury as to the law or to argue their case to the jury by means of voir dire questions.

13. As a tactical point, there is a great weight of authority to the effect that cases are won or lost on direct examination. Young lawyers uniformly have a tendency to overdo the cross-examination of witnesses.

14. Motion Court convenes at 9:00 A.M. every day except weekends and holidays. Except for rules to show cause, lawyers should supply to all opposing counsel a copy of the proposed motion and notice of the date the motion is to be presented at least three days prior to presenting the motion. A motion should not be presented to any Judge other than the Motion Judge, nor at any time other than during Motion Court, unless emergency relief is required.

15. Lawyers should be on time for all court appearances, including all calls of the list.

16. Lawyers who have cases on a miscellaneous hearing list should remain immediately available, so that when their case is called they are ready to begin promptly.

17. Lawyers should not initiate conversation with jurors who have served on a jury in a case they were trying.

18. If a lawyer has an uncontested motion or rule to show cause and cannot get to Motion Court, he or she may leave it with the Court Administrator who will present it to the Motion Judge and return it to the lawyer.

19. All lawyers, in accordance with the Court Rules and Rule 1.1 of the Rules of Professional Conduct, should be prepared at all times when they appear before the Court.

20. Lawyers should exhibit courtesy in the courtroom toward opposing counsel as well as to the court and to witnesses.

21. Lawyers should at all times deal with each other honestly and with respect. It is suggested that communication between counsel in the presence of clients and before the court shall be with respect and courtesy—"Treat others as you would have them treat you."

22. Lawyers should be cognizant of the effect of use of gender specific terms when addressing another lawyer. Such language tends to degrade the recipient in the eyes of clients and others.

23. By the very nature of our profession, heated exchanges occur. Threats of physical violence, however, cannot and should not be tolerated or condoned under any circumstances.

24. Whenever possible, trial counsel should include the authority relied upon in points for charge and refrain from unduly repetitious points.

25. Lawyers should wait until all of the assignments have been announced on a miscellaneous hearing or argument list before engaging others in conversation or gathering their briefcases, charts, and other paraphernalia and leaving the courtroom.

26. Lawyers should be available in their offices or at the Courthouse to respond to telephone civil status calls at least one-half hour prior to the designated time.

27. Trials or hearings may not be continued without Court approval. Discovery deadlines fixed by court order may not be extended without Court approval. The mere agreement of counsel to a continuance or to an extension is insufficient.

28. The Court's overall view is that it is pleased with the courtroom demeanor of the Northampton County Bar.

29. These guidelines should not be construed as being a criticism of the Bar in general, or of any lawyers in particular, but merely as suggestions to all members of the Bar who are perhaps not aware of these matters.

30. The Court has particularly expressed its satisfaction with the preparedness of counsel at pretrial conferences and will continue to insist that this level of preparedness be maintained.

Revised January 1994

†